white way of ~~k~~

spirits.

Praise for
Lucy Maud Montgomery

NATIONAL BESTSELLER

Shortlisted for the B.C. National Award
for Canadian Non-Fiction

"*Lucy Maud Montgomery: The Gift of Wings* soars with the energy of its title, but delves even deeper into Montgomery's dark side. . . . Rubio deftly paints the portrait of a multitasking modern woman with an amazing work ethic."
– *The Globe and Mail*

"Truly gifted biographers have the knack of making a reader feel as if he or she is walking around inside the subject's soul. Mary Henley Rubio is one of those, as she so aptly demonstrates with her absolutely gripping biography of Lucy Maud Montgomery. . . . Nothing short of brilliant, an un-put-downable read, and a wonderful examination of this troubled woman's tragic life." – *Ottawa Citizen*

"A poignant story about a real family . . . pure Canadian Gothic: a story of sexual repression, class conflict and family secrets."
– *The Gazette* (Montreal)

"Richly readable . . . Scholarly, meticulously researched and laced with warmth and insight, Rubio's book may offer the definitive slant on the life and work of the Prince Edward Island writer. . . . [Rubio] offers a well-nuanced, captivating and challenging account of Montgomery's remarkable life. . . . Well measured, endlessly interesting and superbly written, Rubio's account of Maud Montgomery's tragic, accomplished life is impossible to set aside." – *The London Free Press*

Co-editor,
The Selected Journals of L. M. Montgomery
(five volumes, 1985–2004)

Co-author, *Writing a Life: L. M. Montgomery*

Harvesting Thistles: The Textual Garden of L. M. Montgomery

Co-editor, *Anne of Green Gables*, Norton Critical Edition

MARY HENLEY RUBIO

Lucy Maud Montgomery

THE GIFT OF WINGS

ANCHOR CANADA

Anchor Canada is a registered trademark.

Library and Archives Canada Cataloguing in Publication has been applied for.

ISBN: 978-0-385-66760-9

Anne of Green Gables is a trademark of the
Anne of Green Gables Licensing Authority Inc.

Quotations from the unpublished journals of the L.M. Montgomery Collection, Archival
and Special Collections, University of Guelph Library.

Quotations from *The Selected Journals of L.M. Montgomery*, Vols. I to V copyright 1985,
1987, 1983, 1998, and 2004, University of Guelph, edited by Mary Rubio and Elizabeth
Waterston, and published by Oxford University Press Canada, are reproduced with the
permission of Mary Rubio, Elizabeth Waterston and the University of Guelph,
courtesy of the L.M. Montgomery Collection, Archival and Special Collections,
University of Guelph Library.

Cover and interior pictures/images courtesy of University of Guelph Library,
L.M. Montgomery Collections

Printed and bound in the USA

Published in Canada by
Anchor Canada, a division of
Random House of Canada Limited

Visit Random House of Canada Limited's website: www.randomhouse.ca

BVG   10   9   8   7   6   5   4   3   2   1

This book is dedicated to
Elizabeth Hillman Waterston,
an inspirational teacher to decades of students
and my colleague, collaborator, and valued friend for many years,
and to
my two beloved and supportive daughters,
Tracy and Jennie,
who have assisted my research and writing
in so many different ways.

CONTENTS

INTRODUCTION

In November 1907, Lucy Maud Montgomery wrote to a friend that biography is a *"screaming farce."* She added that the best biographies give only two-dimensional portraits, but every person has a half dozen "different sides."[1] In 2008, one hundred years after the publication of *Anne of Green Gables*, we know much more about the many sides of "Maud," as she liked to be called. And in fact many now feel that Maud's greatest literary creation was her own tortured self-portrait, now published in her private journals more than fifty years after her death. But the truth may be even more complicated than that.

Maud's life feels at times like a smoke-and-mirrors game. By 1920, when her name was famous all over the English-speaking world, Maud began preparing material for those who would later interpret her life. She compiled scrapbooks, account books, review-clipping books, and a multitude of other memorabilia. Although she was (in her son's words) a "packrat" by nature, this material was also intended as a cache of information for those who would later become her biographers. She carefully recopied her journals, starting in 1919, making an edited, permanent copy. *She* saw her journals as her greatest gift to future biographers: they presented her life as *she* wanted it remembered.

When Elizabeth Waterston and I began editing the L. M. Montgomery journals in the 1980s, we took them at face value. Later we came to question elements in these fascinating life-documents. They did not hold *the* truth, we felt, so much as *a* truth. These journals, frank in so many ways, and so rich as social history, began to seem to us a cache of concealments, displacements, contradictions, and omissions. Initially, they seemed such a boon, but eventually they became another layer to excavate through. This biography will track some of my own processes, as well as my conclusions. In the nearly three decades that she has been the object of my part-time research I have never grown bored with Maud. She is truly a biographer's dream subject: you never feel that you have found the master key that *fully* unlocks all the rooms in her house.

In 1908, Lucy Maud Montgomery burst onto the literary scene with her first novel, *Anne of Green Gables.* At age thirty-three, she had already published scores of short stories and poems, but this best-selling novel achieved instant acclaim, with seven impressions printed in its first year alone. It churned up so much attention that her home province, Prince Edward Island, soon had a flood of visitors, all wanting to see the landscapes she painted so vividly. Her publisher demanded sequels, and she obliged, eventually making her beloved Island a site for tourists from all over the world. Her books appeared to be "simple little tales" (to echo her own modest phrasing in a journal entry dated October 15, 1908), but that was misleading: the last quarter century of scholarly research has shown that her writing has been, in fact, a very powerful agent of social change.

Anne of Green Gables was not written as a novel for children. It was aimed at a general audience of adults and children, men and women, sophisticates and simple readers, as were many of her other books. It appealed to famous statesmen as much as to ordinary people. In 1908, the celebrated author Mark Twain wrote Maud to praise "Anne" as "the dearest and most moving and delightful child since the immortal Alice." In 1910, Earl Grey, one of Canada's most beloved Governors General and an esteemed writer himself, travelled to Prince Edward Island just to meet her. In 1923, she was the first Canadian woman to be elected as a member of the British Royal Society of Arts.

By 1925, translations into other languages were expanding her readership in Sweden, Holland, Poland, Denmark, Norway, Finland, Australia, and France. Two prime ministers of Great Britain expressed admiration for her books: Stanley Baldwin made a point of meeting her during his 1927 tour of Canada; his successor, Ramsay MacDonald, is reported to have said that he read all of her books that he could find—not just once, but several times.

At home in Ontario, where she moved in 1911 following her marriage to Presbyterian minister Ewan Macdonald, Maud was in constant demand as a storyteller and speaker. She was also active in organizations associated with the Canadian cultural scene, particularly the Canadian Authors Association. In

1928, a rapturous audience of two thousand gave her a standing ovation at the annual Canadian Book Week in Toronto, Ontario. In 1935, she was elected to the Literary and Artistic Institute of France for her contributions to literature. In the same year, she was made an Officer of the Order of the British Empire (OBE) in Canada. In 1937, the Montreal *Family Herald and Star* reported from a survey that she and Charles Dickens were the "most read" authors in Canada. Also in 1937, the Prince Edward Island National Park was established to preserve the landscapes her books had made so famous. Her status as an international celebrity seemed secure.

By the time of her death in 1942, she had published over twenty books, and more than five hundred short stories and five hundred poems, all while raising a family, living a busy life as the wife of a country minister, and completing ten volumes of secret journals. Her books were read all over the English-speaking world, and were translated into many more languages. No other Canadian writer had reached such a pinnacle of success on so many fronts: she was truly an international celebrity.

But a reversal of her literary reputation had been slowly occurring. For the first decade after *Anne of Green Gables* was published, critics praised Maud's books. However, as Modernism set in, with its grim focus on the breakdown of social norms, critics dimmed their view of her cheerful books, with their witty treatment of human behaviour and their celebration of the imagination and nature. Instead, the professional critics started faulting her novels for their splashes of purple prose and their "sentimentalism," ignoring the darker soundings that haunted her stories before the reader got to the "happy endings."

In the mid-1920s, the growing cadre of men who panned her books included influential newsmen, university professors, and writers in Canada, and they all knew each other. In 1926, one of Canada's powerful newspaper critics led the attack, labelling her books the nadir of Canadian fiction. A much respected professor of literature termed her books "naïve" with an "innocence" that suggested "ignorance of life." A grudging evaluation was made by another male novelist, who wrote: " . . . not that those books may not have their readers who profit from them: I have found that out. But how a woman who judges so accurately can stand *writing* that stuff . . ." In the face of such attacks, even the critics who had previously lauded her writing started being careful to temper their praise.

Nevertheless, all these men were impressed (and annoyed) by her sales success. While some allowed that her large readership *might* speak to some undefined cultural need, others felt that her popularity merely proved her "lowbrow" quality. These detractors spoke with such a powerful voice in Canada between the mid-1920s and her death in 1942 that her work fell into disfavour. Librarians heeded what the influential critics said, and some libraries even shunned her books. In 1967, the don of Canadian librarians, Sheila Egoff, wrote a groundbreaking study of Canadian children's literature that gave definition to the field. She repeated the view of the earlier critics, and attacked Maud for "sentimental dishonesty." By the 1970s the general wisdom was that Montgomery was a sentimental writer who appealed to the uncultured and masses of undiscriminating women and children, and still in the 1980s, expressing an admiration for Maud's books was rather risky. She was relegated strictly to the category of "children's writer," and was judged by her weakest books, not by her best.

My thinking for this biography began in summer 1974. At that time, I was a young academic attending an international children's literature conference in Toronto, which brought together librarians, academics, and writers from North America and the United Kingdom. I was surprised to hear several Canadians there refer to Maud's writing in terms that depicted it as a national embarrassment. That, I learned, was the legacy of the critics of the previous fifty years: their view was entrenched.

This puzzled me. I had come from the United States and a background in American literature. I taught Mark Twain's *Huckleberry Finn* at the University of Guelph. In my view, *Anne of Green Gables* held up very well in comparison. The main difference was that Huck, a boy, could challenge conventions, but Anne, a girl, had to conform to them. Otherwise, there were many interesting similarities between the two books. Each author had a wonderfully comic way with satire, and each book—though telling a simple, episodic story—had a great deal of depth.

I soon discovered that one of my senior colleagues, Elizabeth Waterston, believed that Maud was undervalued, too. In 1967—Canada's centennial year and the year Sheila Egoff's book was published—Elizabeth had written the first substantial scholarly article taking Maud's books seriously. Soon after, she had been quietly advised by a distinguished university colleague not to waste any more time writing about Maud if she wished to advance up the academic ladder. He meant the advice in a kindly way, fearing that her critical talents would be squandered on an unworthy subject—at least in the eyes of the English Department's Promotion and Tenure Committee.

By 1974, Elizabeth had moved on, and had become Chair of the Department of English at the University of Guelph. In 1975, a group of us in the department decided to start the journal *CCL: Canadian Children's Literature*. (We had already started a course in "Children's Literature," a new academic field then.) Maud became the focus of our third issue, with Elizabeth's 1967 piece reprinted as the lead article. We were scrabbling for material in a new field, and I set about writing a comparison of *Huckleberry Finn* and *Anne*. Writing this article intensified my interest in Maud. I didn't like the sequels as much as I liked *Anne of Green Gables*, but there was something magnetic about her writing.

This ultimately led to a long journey into literary archaeology. In the late 1970s I met Maud's son, Dr. E. Stuart Macdonald (who, as our friendship developed, I came to call "Stuart"), after sending him a complimentary copy of our special issue. By this time, I had formed an image of the personality I believed to be behind Maud's books: she had a wonderful sense of humour and she looked at humankind with a bemused, tolerant smile. I thought she must have been the ideal mother, and said so early in my first meeting with her son. That ill-advised remark clearly hit a nerve, and I will never forget Dr. Macdonald's slow, appraising look, first *at* me and then *into* me and finally *through* me. A succinct (and more measured) version of his response to me is found in a letter he once wrote to a Swedish woman:

> . . . although in her writings, [my mother] . . . gave the impression
> of broad tolerance of human weaknesses, she did not condone any
> such elasticity in herself or her family. . . . She was extremely sensi-
> tive, although an excellent dissembler, and though she experienced
> great peaks, she also fell to great depths emotionally, which does not
> make for tranquillity. This rigidity and sensitivity, prevented any
> easy camaraderie in the family, but she was capable of inspiring
> deep affection in us all.[2]

By the end of the interview, I was rather intimidated by Maud's son, a busy and respected medical doctor who knew how to speak his mind forcefully when journalists and academics intruded on his time. But my curiosity about his mother's personality was piqued to the extreme. Where did those funny, happy novels come from?

Dr. Macdonald died suddenly of an aneurysm in 1982, and Elizabeth Waterston and I began the long process of editing Maud's journals together. Maud had willed them to Dr. Macdonald with the instruction that he should publish them eventually. I expected them to answer my evolving fascination with Maud's hold on people—including me. A friend working on a Ph.D. told me her theory: "I reread Montgomery to wash the academic sludge out of my mind." Other's comments confirmed that reading Maud's books seemed to make people feel happy, refreshed, and part of a special community. I mused over the possibility of measuring happiness through people's neural responses while reading different writers, and I fancied the fun in matching Maud against a Faulkner or a Joyce.

As Elizabeth and I went through the journals together, editing them, we puzzled over the astonishing disjunction between the bright, happy novels and the dark, often painful life. How could one personality produce such different documents simultaneously—writing cheerful novels in the morning and tortured journals in the evening, so to speak? Maud was quite aware of her own bifurcated life. As a minister's wife with a very judgmental nature, she developed a carefully controlled public persona and revealed little of her inner thoughts. Her journals were clearly a safety valve for a highly volatile woman. What was this complex woman really like?

Once, when a journalist came to interview her, she wrote that she was keeping her inner life private and hidden: "Well, I'll give him the bare facts he wants. He will not know any more about the real me or my real life for it all. . . . The only key to *that* is found in this old journal."[3] But as Elizabeth and I worked closely with the journals, those "tell-all" documents, we discovered they did *not* reveal everything.

Dr. Macdonald had asked me to write a biography of his mother based on her journals shortly before he died. I argued that the proper order was to publish the journals first, and then write a biography, after more research. Elizabeth and I wrote a short biography called *Writing a Life: L. M. Montgomery* in 1995, and it is now available on the Internet (www.lmmrc.ca). Dr. Macdonald told me that if I did write his mother's biography, he wanted it to be as truthful as possible for several reasons: first, because she herself hated prettied-up biographies that made no attempt to get behind the real truths in lives; second, because her achievements would be more remarkable if people knew the conditions under which she wrote; and finally, because there would be things people could learn from her life that might prevent them from making the same mistakes. His mother had left him written instructions that he was to publish all of her journals intact, eventually, but there is much in this biography that is not in her journals and that he himself did not know.

This longer biography represents my attempt to answer more questions. By the time of Dr. Macdonald's death, I had seen the depth of his loyalty to his mother, alongside some unresolved feelings, including anger. What was the quality that made those who knew his mother so loyal to her memory, including all of the family's housemaids? (I had started locating them in the late 1970s, and talked to them and other acquaintances before people's memories were tainted by the publication of the journals.) How could one explain the contradictions in Maud's character? Where in this complicated woman did her books actually originate? What gave her books their staying power as bestsellers? (Their sales were not inflated by being required novels on courses.) And, most puzzling of all, what was the basis of their appeal to readers of diverse cultural backgrounds, in different generations, with varied experiences and temperaments and educational backgrounds, all over the world?

In 1984, I travelled to Denmark and Poland with Elizabeth Waterston and Ruth Macdonald, Dr. Stuart Macdonald's widow. We saw a command performance of a Polish musical based on *The Blue Castle* in Krakow, and a drama based on *Anne of Green Gables* in Warsaw. When the audiences found out that we were from Canada, and represented their beloved "L. M. Montgomery," we were mobbed in both theatres by autograph-seekers. The passion in Poland was astonishing. In 1992, my younger daughter and I retraced Maud's 1911 honeymoon path in Scotland and England. Staying in bed-and-breakfasts, we met only *one* hostess on the entire trip who did not know of Maud's books. As my contacts with other countries outside North America developed (Germany, Israel, China, Japan, Russia, Norway, Sweden, Spain, India) through the Internet, I was staggered by her worldwide appeal.

It particularly surprised me when people said that they reread their favourite Montgomery novel(s) every year. (After all, there are many *other* good books in the world, and our lives are finite!) As I dug deeper, and met other scholars, I began to see that Maud's books actually changed people's lives. Where did these books get *that* power?

Editing the journals helped reveal where her novels came from, at least in part. All the stories that Maud told were essentially variations on her own personal narrative—those of young girls and women trying to find a home and a life where there is love, approval, and respect. From the orphaned Anne (who wants to be adopted into a home where she will be loved and valued), through Emily of New Moon (an orphan who likewise wants love and acceptance but who also wants a writing career), to Valancy Stirling of *The Blue Castle* (who wants to escape a cruel mother and find love in marriage), Maud's heroines begin life without the comforting kindness of a protective mother. This might explain the interest of girls and women in her books, but it hardly explains their appeal to famous statesmen in England.

The more we worked with the journals, the more obvious became the shaping and pruning. We found almost no outright factual falsehoods in her journals, but there were evasions and omissions. It was as if Maud had become an actor in the drama of her own life, a movie that she was writing, directing, acting, editing, and reviewing. As we edited the last three volumes (published in 1992, 1998, and 2004) we recognized the extent to which Maud was constantly rereading, revisioning, and reshaping her own life document—no real surprise since she recopied all her journals, beginning in 1919.

More puzzles emerged. How far could one trust the journals, which were designed as a creative work on their own? What was the emerging narrative trajectory that shaped her life story as she wrote it over a period of fifty-five years? Did the narrative trajectory affect the way she interpreted her life—and, even more interesting, did that trajectory itself affect the choices that she made in her life? And what about the gaps? What segments of her "film" were cut and discarded?

After the publication of Maud's journals began in 1985, revealing, to almost everyone's surprise, that she was often a tormented woman in her private life, arbiters of literary taste started giving her a second look. Other developments fuelled this re-evaluation: the birth of feminism, new attention to popular culture and the oral tradition, new theories about language, subjectivity, and literary value. It was a turbulent period in the academy, producing an explosion of new scholarship that challenged the old, and Maud was one of its many beneficiaries—and not just in North America. Articles and doctoral theses about her from abroad began spilling into the critical void. Judging by the more recent Internet blogs and websites devoted to her, she has certainly regained her place in the literary firmament. She is now widely acknowledged to have been an extremely important cultural influence.

———

This biography, then, is not a mere retelling of Maud's own compelling account of her life. It is based on my own research and analysis conducted over several decades during a busy career in academia and raising a family. I have examined old newspapers, magazines, and archival records, trying to absorb the ambiance of her time. I have tried to verify the stories in her journals, given that she had always intended them for eventual publication. It is self-evident that anyone as concerned with her legacy as Maud was would present herself as she wanted to be remembered, only giving away intimate (or damaging) revelations when it suited her. Having her eye on the future reader certainly worked against full disclosure, and she herself admits there are certain things she cannot commit to her journals. Some of those blanks are filled in here.

My research took me into many areas ancillary to literature—the Scottish-Anglo heritage from which Maud emerged, the educational practice in Prince Edward Island, the publishing industry in the nineteenth and early-twentieth centuries, the history of religion and science, the development of the professions, major historical events such as World War I, the spread of communication networks, the legal profession (which touched her life in so many ways), the practice of medicine, psychiatry, and pharmacology in the first half of the past century, and the history of the book trade, including the influence of her books in other countries. I try to set her life in those contexts.

When I first began this project in the early 1980s, personal computers had not come into use, search engines were unheard of, and the potentials of the digital world were only a gleam in the eye of twenty-five-year-old Bill Gates and others. The development of e-mail has greatly increased my contact with scholars and readers in countries around the world. The L. M. Montgomery Collection at the University of Guelph has become its most consulted archival resource, attracting scholars from many foreign countries. Every contact has enriched my understanding of Maud's reach and impact, which truly circles the globe.

The story of Lucy Maud Montgomery's life begins—in its most elemental form—with the birth of a little girl, Lucy Maud, on Prince Edward Island in 1874. It moves through time until she becomes a best-selling author at age thirty-six, then marries, and lives the rest of her life in Ontario, as a committed author and public-spirited citizen. But her life is much more than her "lived" life.

Her "story" extends into the *impact* of her books. In a twentieth-century society still dominated by patriarchy, she was one of the many forces convincing young women that they could have careers in many different professional fields (such as medicine and law), opening new vistas for them.

In the same way, her influence extended to young women who aspired to become authors. They saw that it was possible for a woman writer to work with the community she knew, rather than tackling the sweep of great world events. After all, what goes on in the human heart rules both the domestic and the larger political world. These young writers saw that stories about plain people in small communities could catch a wide audience. It might also be said that Maud was an early pioneer in the technique of "branding" a named but imaginary fictional community. From Maud's "Avonlea" in Prince Edward Island, Margaret Laurence could move to "Manawaka" on the Canadian prairies, Alice Munro to "Jubilee" in south-western Ontario, and Margaret Atwood could depict new fictional neighbourhoods within Toronto. The creation of named fictional communities continued with Canadian male authors, with Stephen Leacock's "Mariposa" in *Sunshine Sketches of a Little Town* (1912), and with Robertson Davies in his "Deptford" novels in the 1970s. Around the world, many other women writers would claim Maud as their favourite childhood writer—and sometimes as their model, as in the case of Astrid Lindgren, Swedish author of the "Pippi Longstocking" tales. Maud's characters may have been ordinary people, but she moved into people's inner emotions and dealt in miniature with events occurring on a much larger scale in the world outside. Her magic chariot was "the story."

The tale of her impact continues. Her creativity has spread from the book realm to other media. *Anne of Green Gables* was first made into a silent film in 1919 and then into a "talkie" in 1934. *Anne of Windy Poplars* became a film in 1940, and there have been many other interpretations of the Anne story since: in musicals, plays, television, movies, videos, comics, and animated films. An immensely successful musical based on *Anne of Green Gables* was developed in 1965 and is performed each year in the Charlottetown Festival. Theatrical versions are regularly staged by schools across North America, and Anne's life has been extended into "prequels" in book and film. Her *Emily of New Moon* series—the books that budding writers love—have recently been made into an animated television series by a Japanese studio, following the earlier *Anne of Green Gables*. The economic impact of her books is beyond measure.

Maud's own personal story took on a completely new life with the publication of her secret journals long after her death. Covering the period between 1889 and 1942, *The Selected Journals of L. M. Montgomery* were published in five volumes between 1985 and 2004, establishing her as one of the most readable female diarists of the twentieth century. These journals reveal a woman much engaged in the intellectual world she found herself in, even when she was living in rural outposts before television and radio. Her reading was prodigious and omnivorous—not only fiction, but also history, biography, science, psychology, medicine, anything that might explain the evolving world to her. She had been catapulted from a bucolic, rural childhood into a turbulence heading towards two world wars. She wrote in November 1901 that the story of "human genius" was seen in "its colossal mechanical contrivances. Two or three thousand years ago men wrote immortal poems. Today they create marvellous inventions and bend the erstwhile undreamed of forces of nature to their will."

Maud's own life story carries us through the social and economic history of the twentieth-century world. We witness the new arsenal of medications developed to alleviate human disease and misery, the development of railroads, automobiles, airplanes, the telegraph, the telephone, the radio, silent and then talkie movies, electric refrigerators, washing machines, and many other marvels of science and technology, especially those pertaining to modern warfare. In February 1932, she calls this new warfare "a hideous revel of mechanical massacre."

In 1942, Maud exited from her own stage play (and life). About that sad event, we can only reflect that "the manner of a death is hardly the measure of a life." As the distinguished Canadian novelist Robertson Davies said at the time of her passing: "Nations grow in the eyes of the world less by the work of their statesmen than their artists. Thousands of people all over the globe are hazy about the exact nature of Canada's government and our relation to the British Empire, but they have clear recollections of *Anne of Green Gables*."[4] The impact of Maud's writing will continue in the twenty-first century—her heroines will continue to charm us, but as we come to know her better as a woman, her own story also will haunt our imaginations.

PART ONE

———

The PEI Years

1874–1911

CHAPTER 1

What's in a place?

The febrile intensity of Lucy Maud Montgomery's imagination was both stirred and soothed by her early home of Cavendish, Prince Edward Island, in the Canadian Maritimes. Located where the land and sea met, it was a landscape of extremes—extremes in weather, extremes in beliefs, extremes in human passions—all contained in one of the world's most beautiful settings. The land itself was the perfect correlative to extremes in Maud's personality. A passionate young woman poured into the container of strict Presbyterianism, she characterized herself:

> I have a very uncomfortable blend in my make-up—the passionate Montgomery blood and the Puritan Macneill conscience. Neither is strong enough wholly to control the other. The Puritan conscience can't prevent the hot-blood from having its way—in part at least—but it *can* poison all the pleasure and it does. Passion says, "Go on. Take what crumbs of happiness fall in your way." Conscience says, "Do so if you will. Feed your soul on those blood-red husks; but I'll scourge you well for it afterwards." (April 8, 1898)

The landscape of her childhood was capricious—subtle—and yet dramatic. On a clear summer day in Cavendish, the white beaches, sand dunes, red sandstone cliffs, and the sea itself stretched as far as the eye could see. At sunset, subtle shades of purples and mauves, of salmon pinks and saffron yellows, spread in glorious streaks across the sky, drawing the eye up from the darkening green fields, blue sky, and red soil. Sea mists rolled in, bringing an eerie feeling of a timeless world. Shapes softened, appearing reclusive and mysterious, even ghostly. But the grey, chill mists could suddenly dissipate, burned off by the morning sun, and the dazzling colours returned. Maud — whose moods were always responsive to the world around her — revelled in her love for the Island landscape:[1]

> . . . where red roads wound like gay satin ribbons in and out among green fields and woods, and where I gazed always on the splendid pageant of the sea — splendid with ever-changing beauty of dawn and noon and midnight, of storm and calm, wind and rain, starlight, moonlight, sunset. . . . I *loved* the trees around my old home with a personal love; I loved the little ferny nooks along the lanes of the woods; I loved the red roads climbing up amid the dark firs; I loved the farm fields, each individualized by some peculiarity of shape of fence or tree clump. To me they spoke with a thousand voices, each with a new and fascinating tale to tell.[2]

The orderly little rural village of Cavendish, founded in 1790 by Maud Montgomery's own Scottish Presbyterian ancestors, consisted of forty families. The farms, with neat frame houses and flower-filled gardens, were laid out along the winding roads running parallel to the sea. The fields were separated by rail and rock fences (dikes), but there was a strong sense of community that centred in the churches, the post office (in the Macneill kitchen), the one-room schoolhouse next to the carefully tended cemetery, and the public meeting hall. The sense of community grew from the bloodlines of kinship, the love of the land and sea, their shared religion, and the need to work together to survive.

Cavendish people were self-sufficient. In the summer they grew crops and orchard fruit, while animals grazed on the gently rolling farmland. Sawmills produced lumber for the frame houses and barns. The men cleared and tilled the land, maintained the dikes and the barns, and fished. Lobsters were so plentiful that only the poorest people ate them. Tradespeople of every variety lived in Cavendish (or nearby Rustico): tanners and shoemakers, sheep-shearers and butchers, blacksmiths, seamstresses. The Jack sisters sheared all the local sheep, while farm women "carded" it, spun it, and used it for clothing.

Women were essential. They processed foods for pantries and root cellars, such as wines, jams, and cheeses; they raised chickens and sold butter and eggs. They bore and raised large families, tended the sick, and prepared the dead for burial. Children were expected to be useful, picking apples, digging potatoes, tending animals and gardens, running lunches to men at work. Being a "good worker" was a high compliment, and Maud's Macneill relatives were hard workers. Her Grandfather Macneill had one of the best apple orchards on the Island, as well as a successful fishing business.

Life in Cavendish was governed by the seasons and the rhythms of nature. When storms blew in, the community battened down the hatches. Winter winds might sweep the glistening snow to the height of windows, but the inhabitants were cozy in their kitchens, sitting beside crackling wood stoves, reading or telling tales. Winter provisions had been stowed in cupboards and cellars. At night, lamps were snuffed and newspapers put away. Prayers or Bible-reading ended the day, and families retired to unheated bedrooms to sleep under feather or quilted comforters in beds pre-warmed by hot irons or rocks. Many farmhouses were protected from the sea gales by a sheltering windbreak of spruce trees.

Children lived mostly outdoors from April to December. Maud describes fishing in "the brooks, picking gum in the spruce copses, berrying in the stumps and gypsying to the shore." Following a summer storm, children explored the washed-up treasures on the shoreline. Over the years as the sea eroded the headland, the repetitive lapping of the waves, in spite of all its erosive force, was soothing and reassuring.

In the long winter afternoons and early evenings, Cavendish children sat with the adults in the warm kitchens. The more fanciful adults might launch into storytelling mode, telling of netherworld creatures that came from the sea or out of night mists, of fairies or tree-sprites that lived on the land, of Scottish heroes fighting against oppression, of clan rivalries and villainous treachery, or of lost loves and sea adventures. These legends told children who they were and what their clan valued. The tales were repeated over and over, with pleasure in the telling. A good storyteller, like Maud's Grandfather Macneill, could make the familiar stories spellbinding.

The closest railroad was eleven miles away, but items could be brought by sea, or overland by the Mayfield Road from Charlottetown, twenty miles south-east, the eleventh-largest city in the Dominion of Canada in the 1880s. The impetuous urgency of the outside world reached Charlottetown by telegraph and boat. Newspapers—most of them with heated political sympathies—were produced in Charlottetown and other smaller towns.

Farmwives subscribed to women's magazines from the Boston and New York areas, and kept up with current fashions. Peddlers (colporteurs) came around with their tin wares, patent medicines, housewares, books, and other items (including dyes that might turn a young girl's hair green, as happened to Anne of Green Gables).

The Island of Maud's birth was on the cusp of technological and cultural advancements. Since 1852, telegraph cables had connected PEI with the mainland. Charlottetown, incorporated in 1855, had in 1859 replaced gas with electric lights. In 1866, the first horseless carriage, a steam-powered motor-car, was brought from Philadelphia by Father Belcourt of Rustico, the "first Canadian motorist, the first to import [a car] . . . and the first Canadian to have a car accident."[3] In 1873, the year before Maud's birth, Prince Edward Island joined the Dominion of Canada, partly to fund the construction of Island railroads. Although time in Cavendish still moved to the diurnal and seasonal rhythms, new technologies were shrinking the world, and Cavendish citizens engaged with the intellectual debates of the times.

Speakers and performers came to give programs in the local community hall. In between such events, the articulate and intelligent farmers of Cavendish organized formal debates over issues of the day such as "Should there be Free Trade between Canada and the United States?" "Slavery," and "Imperial Federation." On March 19, 1886, the topic was "Should women be given the right to vote?" (The first speaker argued that women paid taxes, so they should be able to vote; a second speaker countered that since women did not bear arms, they should not. The belief that women were inferior to men, responded the next speaker, had been long discredited. But, he added, a man and his wife were one before God, so they should have only one vote.) Maud's Cavendish was a stimulating cultural and intellectual environment.[4]

The minds of these sturdy, industrious Scottish immigrants could roil like the sea. They were easily inflamed by events, real or imaginary. Sharp-tongued words occasionally replaced the ancient claymores of medieval clan warfare. The Scottish custom of "flyting," or mental fencing remained, with insults flung in fun, part of the oral tradition of the Celtic heritage.[5] Occasionally tempers flared, but the verbal tournaments usually ended with laughter. Most of Maud Montgomery's immediate kindred were feisty and literate Scots-Canadians, particularly gifted in wit and rapier-like wordplay. Theirs was a culture that lived by words: first God's, then man's. A stern religion, which demanded constant self-examination, kept this explosive mixture in order. When disputes broke out, ministers were the peacekeepers, calming tempers.

There were genuine theological schisms, however. The Presbyterian church was located in the centre of the community, on land provided by Maud's Macneill clan. The Presbyterian Church was organized democratically, with power resting at the local level: historically, in Scotland, it had been a hothouse of violent internal feuds. Indeed, in Cavendish, there was also a Baptist church—founded by disgruntled Presbyterians—at the other end of the village. Serious doctrinal differences divided the two churches. The Baptists believed in salvation from sin by the ritual of immersion and public confession. Presbyterians thought sinful man could not achieve salvation so easily: many still believed in "Predestination," the doctrine holding that man was inherently sinful, and only God determined who would be "saved." These "Elect" (the "chosen ones") were believed to be picked by an omnipotent God's arbitrary will and pleasure—not necessarily by their good deeds in life. Still, children were taught to behave themselves, as there was no point in taking chances. Bad behaviour suggested exclusion from the "Elect."

In the late nineteenth century, bitter religious schisms soured Cavendish tempers for many years. This phenomenon took place elsewhere, of course: people were deeply suspicious of different faiths and ethnicities. However, the young Presbyterians and Baptists could put aside disputes if there was an interesting speaker or a "social": church activities were the centre of village social life.

Virtually everyone in Cavendish was related to everyone else through almost a century of intermarriage: of the forty families, ten were named Macneill. The other founding families—the Simpsons and the Clarks—had intermarried with the Macneills. Marrying cousins was common, and was beginning to cause concern. Maud's grandfather was sensibly set against the practice. He observed both good and bad traits being intensified by intermarriage, sometimes producing a highly gifted person, but at other times resulting in mental instability. Sometimes, both came out in the same person.

As a child, Maud observed human nature in its most elemental form—in a tightly knit rural village where inhabitants were bound together through shared experiences and communal memory. Bickering among the clans and the branches of a family was carried to school with the children, intensified, and returned home. Tales spread from one house to the next. People's fear of being "talked about" was an effective means of social control. Along with other children, Maud was constantly reminded of the catchphrase *"What will people say?"* Continuous watchfulness made Cavendish an easily agitated hive of gossip—an immensely rich landscape for a future novelist.

What's in a name?

A Cavendish pedigree depended on three factors. First, how long had a given family lived on Prince Edward Island? Next, did they have "connections" in "the Old Country"? And finally, did they have material wealth, personal integrity, and political clout? On all three grids, Maud Montgomery was born to high position, and she grew up knowing this. She carried the Montgomery name, as well as the Macneill and Woolner heritage.

The Montgomerys had been among the earliest British settlers on Prince Edward Island, coming to Canada by choice in the early 1770s as well-to-do Scottish Lowlanders, they had received grants of land for military service. (The post-1800 Scottish immigrants, mostly from the Highlands, were of a lower economic class and left Scotland under duress, fleeing the "Highland clearances," the economic change brought by the arrival of sheep farming, forcing people out of Scotland as the feudal clan system broke up.) The Prince Edward Island Montgomerys spoke English, not Gaelic like the Highlanders. Established in Canada decades before the influx of the Highlanders, Maud's Montgomery ancestors claimed descent from a "cadet" in the house of the Earl of Eglinton, based in Ayrshire, Scotland, and felt in a much higher class.

In fact, the Scottish Montgomeries claimed to be among the oldest of the Scottish clans, arriving in the United Kingdom in the train of William the Conqueror in 1066. They traced their ancestry to a French knight called "Mundegumbri," who had settled in what is now Ayrshire in the twelfth century. The historical record shows that the Montgomerie clan prospered through the centuries, acquiring titles of nobility. In 1388, Sir John Montgomerie was immortalized in Scottish balladry for the capture of the legendary Harry Hotspur. It is worth noting that the Prince Edward Island Montgomerys had no written proof of these ancestral connections, but Maud nevertheless grew up with great pride in her paternal name.

In family legend, three Montgomery brothers sailed for Upper Canada. One stopped in Prince Edward Island at the insistence of his seasick wife, Mary McShannon Montgomery—she was said to have bribed the ship's captain with whisky to let her go ashore, and then refused to embark on the ship again. Later in her life, Maud heard the story of what happened to the other two brothers who sailed on to Upper Canada: one stayed, and is alleged to have given his name to Toronto's Eglinton Avenue; the other is believed to have returned to Scotland, never to be heard from again. (Maud told these legends in speeches and adapted them in her fiction, writing that Mary McShannon Montgomery's husband's revenge was to inscribe on his wife's eventual tombstone, "Here I Stay!")

But ship records do not fully support these legends. A recently discovered list from the brigantine the *Edinburgh*—which sailed in July 1771 from Campbelltown, Kintyre, Scotland, to Malpeque, Prince Edward Island— records only one Hugh Montgomery and his family, as well as another relative. The record indicates they paid their way only to PEI.[6] But another legend that Maud grew up hearing appears to be true—that Mary McShannon's family were professional "harpers" to the Scottish Montgomerie clan because of their talents in storytelling and playing musical instruments.[7]

The Canadian Montgomerys possibly romanticized their connections; however, records do show that the Scottish Montgomeries were exceptional as a colourful, dramatic clan, characterized as a "hard-living, hard-riding set" who did "not enjoy long lives."[8] Maud's grandfather, Donald Montgomery (born in 1808), told how he was once stopped in the street by a stranger who mistook him for the current head of the Scottish Montgomerie clan, Archibald William, the thirteenth Earl of Eglinton (1819–1861). In fact, Maud's grandfather and his Scottish contemporary did share a facial likeness, so there may have been truth in his story.[9]

The thirteenth Earl of Eglinton was notoriously dashing and romantic. He had a love of gaming as well as an excessive—and fatal—love for chivalry and romance. In 1839, at the age of twenty, he mounted the largest and last medieval tournament of the nineteenth century. Two years in preparation, this pseudo-tournament consumed most of his fortune, and, thanks to the unpredictable Scottish climate, was a complete disaster. Some hundred thousand spectators watched the debacle of pseudo-medieval knights on horses tilting and jousting in slippery mud, trying to hold anachronistic umbrellas over their heads to protect their elegantly embroidered clothes and armour from the rain.[10] One historian says that this tournament "marked a turning point" for Lord Eglinton, who "ceased to spend most of his time enjoying himself and became the epitome of the Victorian gentleman, an indefatigable public servant, a faithful husband, unfailingly considerate and courteous to everyone, genuinely loved by all classes, good at everything except money management. When he died, *Blackwood's Magazine* wrote, 'Of him it may emphatically be said that honour was his polar star'" (108, 110).[11]

Maud's grandfather, Senator Donald Montgomery, was a distinguished member of the Prince Edward Island legislature from 1832 to 1874. After the Island entered the Canadian Confederation in 1873, he served in the Senate of Canada for twenty years until his death, at age eighty-six, in 1893. In a society where property brought status, Senator Montgomery held 225 acres of prime land at Park Corner, some thirteen miles west of Cavendish. He had nine children with his first wife, Ann Murray; his second wife, Louisa Cundall Gall, a plain-faced woman, possessed an independent income and excellent social connections on the Island.

Among the Senator's sons, Hugh John (Maud's father, born in 1841) had many of the same traits as the fabled Montgomerie clan of Scottish history: they were charmers, full of personal style and love of romantic chivalry; they were energetic and extravagant, good at making money but poor at handling it; they shared physical traits like heavy-lidded eyes and exceptionally small hands and mouths. Maud inherited these same physical features. She apparently did not know that several Montgomerie ancestors had written poetry and published it privately.[12]

Maud's maternal great-great-grandfather, John Macneill (born circa 1750), had come to Charlottetown from the Kintyre peninsula of Argyllshire, Scotland, around 1772. Of the twelve children from his marriage to Margaret Simpson, nine sons were reputed to be "clever, high-spirited and domineering." (The records say nothing of the daughters.) Around 1790, John Macneill obtained farm property out on the North Shore of the Island and moved there with two other Scottish families, the Simpsons and the Clarks, to found the community of Cavendish.[13]

The Macneills also boasted a notable lineage. In the "Old Country," Hector Macneill (a cousin of the early John Macneill) had published books of poetry in Scotland steadily from 1795 until his death; he is mentioned in Lord Byron's *English Bards and Scotch Reviewers*. According to Maud, legend held that several of the ballads attributed to his Ayrshire friend, the famous Robert Burns, were written by him (including "Come under my Plaidie" and "I lo'e ne'er a laddie but ane"). Maud treasured her copy of the *Published Works of Hector Macneill Esquire* (1856), and she always spoke of the literary strain running through her Macneill clan as an important part of her sense of herself, as well as her potential. In fact, a notable literary and artistic strain was present in both clans.

In Canada, John Macneill's oldest son, William Simpson Macneill (1781–1870), apprenticed under the famous colonial lawyer and writer Thomas McCulloch of Nova Scotia. W. S. Macneill lived in Cavendish as a farmer, businessman, Commissioner of Public Works, and magistrate (this involved writing wills, performing marriages, and facilitating educational and other progress). For his bride, Eliza Townsend of Park Corner, he built the house in which his great-granddaughter Lucy Maud Montgomery would be raised. Only its foundations remain today, restored by Macneill's great-grandson, John Macneill (born in 1930), on the farm he inherited and maintains as a historic site with his wife, Jennie Moore Macneill, and their son. In the PEI House of Assembly from 1814 to 1838, William Simpson Macneill wore the mantle of Speaker so well that the name "Speaker Macneill" stuck. Over one hundred years later, his severe-looking portrait in the Charlottetown legislative chambers reputedly so discomfited another Speaker that he had it moved out of his view. Speaker Macneill had what Maud later described as the "good" Macneill traits: intellect, stability of purpose, and an excellent memory. She recounted that he also embodied the clan's faults: volatility of temper, tendency towards clan jealousy, and fierce pride. Speaker Macneill and his wife had eleven children. In his prime, he was said to have known the name of every man, woman, and child on the Island.[14]

Maud's grandfather, Alexander Marquis Macneill, was a man of local substance and stature. He inherited his father's property, was a justice of the peace, an elder in the Presbyterian Church, postmaster of Cavendish, and a good businessman. His apple orchards drew envy, and they, with his mackerel fishing business, provided him with a rare commodity in a nineteenth-century rural community: a steady supply of cash. That he had grown up in the shadow of an intimidating and powerful father, Speaker Macneill, without attaining either his father's political standing or that of his brother (William S. Macneill, an M.P.P. for North Rustico), may have contributed to his personal irascibility. Alexander Macneill, though often a difficult and temperamental man, was a solid and respected citizen. He was also known as a storyteller of great skill. The Macneills of his generation were intense, often brilliant, dedicated, hard-working, judgmental, and sharp-edged. As well, they prided themselves on their quick wit. They may not have had the easygoing charm of the

Montgomerys, but they were impressive and respected as leaders in the community.

Maud was also proud of her heritage on her grandmother's side. Her slender and stylish maternal grandmother also came from a remarkable family. Lucy Woolner Macneill (1824–1911) claimed a family connection with Sir Thomas Woolner, the English sculptor who reputedly told the story of "Enoch Arden" to his friend, English Poet Laureate Alfred Lord Tennyson. Her mother, Sarah Kemp Woolner, was possibly related to Sir Robert Kemp, a major landowner in the East Anglian community of Dunwich, England; Sarah Kemp had married Robert Woolner, a "working farmer" who rented the large Corporation Farm just outside Dunwich.[15] The communities on England's east coast were populated by tall, slender, and graceful East Anglians, claiming physical traits from eleventh- and twelfth-century Scandinavian traders and raiders, and the Woolners were generally handsome, talented, well-grounded, and sensible people.

Dunwich, England—Maud's grandmother's birthplace—is known for its ancient and distinguished history. It was a port city when the Romans invaded Britain in A.D. 43. In 631, its first bishop founded a school there, believed to be the fifth school established in England. By the time of the Domesday Survey in 1086, Dunwich had three thousand inhabitants. But it was a city built on eroding cliffs. By 1585, its sandy headland, seventeen churches, their graves and graveyards, and the bulk of the medieval town had washed into the ocean. It acquired the name of "City in the Sea."

By 1824, the year of Lucy Woolner's birth, the population of Dunwich had dwindled to some two hundred people. In local legend, submerged church bells rang under the sea, making an eerie, otherworldly sound. Following storms, old skulls from the graveyards were still occasionally washing up on the beach at the end of the twentieth century. Until the British Reform Bill of 1832 (which dispensed with "rotten boroughs"), Dunwich—the seat of the powerful Downing family of Britain, who gave their name to Downing Street in London—remained a town of wealth and tradition for political reasons.

But when Maud's ancestors left it, it was a city in fast decline. By the late nineteenth century, romantic and historic Dunwich remained a haunt for artists, poets, and writers. This "Old Country" background was a source of pride to colonial Canadians. Alexander Macneill had learned the town's history from his wife's father, and romanticized it through his own storytelling. While it was Lucy's place of birth, it was he who recreated it in narrative.

Maud had heard so much about the romance of Dunwich that she went to visit it on her honeymoon.

In 1836, Maud's great-grandparents, Robert and Sarah Woolner, established themselves in Rustico (near Cavendish) through extraordinarily precise and methodical planning. When Maud's grandmother Lucy was eleven, her father sent her oldest brother, Chester (age seventeen) to scout Prince Edward Island as a site for emigration. Chester purchased property, and prepared a home to receive the family the following year. In May 1836, Robert Woolner and his wife arrived with their younger children, horses, cattle, farm implements, and seeds, in time to put in spring crops. They came to a finished house—good planning, given that Sarah would deliver her eighth child a few weeks later. Chester then returned to work the farm to the end of its lease; profits from the English farm helped pay for the family's expensive move. That organizational precision was the Woolner style. Most immigrants came with few possessions, their way paid by emigration societies. The dignified, cultured Woolners were intelligent, good managers, and self-determining—likewise, resourceful people of remarkable ability.[16]

The Woolners' North Rustico farm abutted William S. Macneill's property through the back woods. At age nineteen, in 1843, Lucy Ann Woolner married Alexander Marquis Macneill, bringing with her a pride in her own family heritage. Lucy was Anglican, but she converted to her husband's Presbyterianism, as was conventional for wives in that time. She moved as a bride into the home owned by the forceful, aging Speaker Macneill and his wife, Eliza. By the time her in-laws died, in 1870 and 1869 respectively, Lucy Woolner Macneill and her husband had raised their entire family of six children to adulthood.

Alexander and Lucy Macneill set high standards for their children. The eldest son, Leander, took a degree from the University of Edinburgh in Scotland, one of the world's most prestigious universities, and became a very successful minister. The second son, John Franklin, purchased a large farm adjacent to that of his parents. The third son, Chester, followed a career in law, eventually moving to British Columbia. Daughter Annie married John Campbell of Park Corner, thirteen miles away, one of the good farms on the North Shore. The next daughter was Clara (born in 1853), who became Lucy Maud's mother after marrying the son of Senator Montgomery. The last Macneill daughter, Emily, a dark beauty, married John Malcolm Montgomery, one of the most prominent and well-liked men of Malpeque, farther west along the North Shore.

Although family events were much discussed in the Macneill household, one unhappy story was generally kept quiet: the tale of the sad, short marriage of Maud's parents, Clara and Hugh John Montgomery. The Macneills could not have been pleased to learn that their beautiful, talented daughter Clara intended to marry Hugh John Montgomery, despite his family's status. Their objections would have been political, theological, and personal.[17]

The Macneills were staunch Liberals, deeply scornful of the Conservatives, on an island where politics were taken very seriously. Senator Donald Montgomery (Hugh John's father and Maud's grandfather) was not just a Conservative, he was also said to be a drinking crony of Sir John A. Macdonald, Canada's first prime minister and a very skilful politician. Sir John A. Macdonald's detractors claimed that he ruled with one hand on the whisky bottle and the other in the pork barrel. The strict Presbyterian Macneills regarded the freewheeling Montgomerys as "little better than brands yet unplucked from the burning" (June 2, 1931).

And worse, Hugh John was a poor businessman. After several unproductive ventures before his marriage, he opened a store with his brother-in-law, Duncan McIntyre, a dissolute man who probably falsified the account books and cheated him. Scottish entrepreneurs were making fortunes all over North America, but Hugh John Montgomery could not even keep one small country store running successfully. Worse, he was unlikely to inherit much, in spite of being the oldest son: his father had selected a younger, more promising son to inherit the Park Corner property, and in his will left only one hundred dollars to Hugh John, the same token amount that he left to the daughters. (The Senator's youngest son, Cuthbert, who had been slated to take over his father's farm, died shortly before his father, so the farm eventually went to the middle son, James Townsend Montgomery.) Although charismatic and from a fine family, where notions of old-world class structure still permeated colonial thought, Hugh John showed doubtful promise as a provider.

Maud grew up feeling the tension between the different families in her heritage — the "passionate Montgomery blood" and the "Puritan Macneill conscience" were kept in precarious balance through the Woolner common sense, self-control, and grit.

CHAPTER 2

Maud's birth and early years

Hugh John Montgomery was thirty-three when he married twenty-one-year-old Clara Woolner Macneill on March 4, 1874. They moved into a small wooden frame house in the village of Clifton (now called New London) on the North Shore, where Hugh John's general store was located. Just under nine months later, on November 30, 1874, Clara gave birth to her first and only child, Lucy Maud Montgomery. (First children are often late, and Maud's early birth was undoubtedly noted.)

Clara died of "galloping consumption" (tuberculosis) on September 14, 1876, when her baby was only twenty-one months old. Hugh John's store had already failed, reinforcing his bad image in the Macneill eyes. He brought his sick wife back to be cared for, and die, at her parents' home in Cavendish. The baby "Lucy Maud" remained there, to be raised by her maternal grandparents, Alexander and Lucy Macneill, aged fifty-six and fifty-two respectively. Their own six children were grown, and only the youngest, Emily, was still at home. (Emily remained until her marriage in 1881, when Maud was seven.)

At age fifty, reflecting on how her childhood had been blighted by her young mother's death, Maud Montgomery would write that three simple words had fortified and sustained her throughout a troubled life. She remembered sleeping over with her cousin, Pensie Macneill, in a frigid farmhouse and hearing Pensie's mother, Mrs. Charles Macneill, creep into their bedroom to make sure the little girls were warm enough. Maud pretended to be asleep, but wasn't.

"Mrs. Charles" bent over us. *"Dear little children,"* she said gently and tenderly.

That was all. Mrs. Charles has been for many years in her grave. She was a very illiterate, simple-minded woman from whose lips no pearls of wisdom or jewels of inspiration ever dropped. But I have forgotten most of the wisdom and culture I have listened to; and I shall never forget those three simple words of love. I came from a household where affection was never expressed in words. Stern Grandfather, reserved Grandmother would never have said to me "dear little child" even had they felt it. And I loved such expression—I craved it. I have never forgotten it. (March 1, 1925)

Her grandparents' sternness was not unusual. The child-rearing advice that came from the Bible was "Spare the rod and spoil the child." Her grandparents seem to have been more progressive than many parents, however, in that they did not use corporal punishment on Maud. But for all the eloquent words in their culture, these two grandparents did not indulge in the special language of childish endearment that their sensitive little granddaughter longed and needed to hear.

The earliest picture we have of Maud was taken in 1880 when she was about six. Her distinctive features are apparent: the high forehead, the heavy eyelids, and the tiny "Montgomery mouth" and jaw.[18] Her abundant hair is brown, her eyes are blue, her body is small, fragile, and waiflike. She is brushed and shined, as befits a child from a prominent Island family. She sits stiffly, where she has been put, in a chair too big for her, her hands crossed in a good-little-girl position. She does not look comfortable, perched on an adult chair, with a photographer arranging her image, but she is obedient and re-markably poised. Because of the long exposure times required in nineteenth-century photography, photographic subjects had to remain motionless for several minutes. So her face registers no emotion—no apparent fear, pleasure, impatience, or excitement. The ability to face the world through a composed, inscrutable mask, while deciding how to respond to a situation, would become her trademark in later life.

Behind the composed face of the 1880 photograph was a complex per-sonality. Maud was a lovable child—clever, articulate, imaginative—but she was not easily managed. Given to extremes, she was excitable and impulsive, overreacting to each joy and sorrow.

Maud's later recollection of her two imaginary childhood playmates, "Katie Maurice" and "Lucy Gray," reveals her early imagination. These "friends" lived in a "fairy room" behind a bookcase in the Macneill sitting room. Looking through the two oval glass doors of the bookcase (which was used for storing good china), Maud saw her own reflection twice: the left-hand reflection was "Katie Maurice" and to the right was "Lucy Gray." She recalled that she would stand in front of Katie and "prattle to her for hours, giving and receiving confidences . . . at twilight when the fire had been lighted . . . , and the room and its reflections were a glamour of light and shadow" (March 26, 1905). Lucy Gray was a widow who was "always sad and always had dismal stories of her troubles to relate to me," wrote the adult Maud in her journals. (Maud claimed that she preferred Katie Maurice to Lucy Gray, but to be fair to both she gave them equal amounts of time.)

Maud was precocious and inquisitive. She told the story of attending church one Sunday with her Aunt Emily, and asking, in a whisper, where her dead mother was. Her aunt merely pointed upwards. Maud looked up and saw the trap door in the ceiling, and spent the rest of the sermon wondering why they didn't just get a ladder, climb up, and retrieve her mother. But she also recalled being scared to ask questions, fearing ridicule if they were too obvious. She learned as a child that it was safest to keep her mental musings to herself.

There were many playmates in the village: children of all ages played together, and Maud was related to most of her Cavendish friends. The happy, active, free outdoor life Maud led in her Cavendish surroundings was an ideal palliative for her overly sensitive and emotional nature. Maud recalled how children could "wade on the rock shore, and bathe on the sand shore; climb the cliffs and poke sea-swallows out of their nests; gather pebbles, dulse, sea-moss, kelp, 'snails' and mussels; run races on the sand, dig 'wells' in it, build mounds, climb the shining 'sand-hills' and slide down in a merry smother of sand, pile up drift wood, collect and unravel into twine the nets of wrecked lobster-traps, make 'shore pies,' peep through the spy-glass at the fishing boats."[19] When the children saw distant sailing vessels, they glimpsed the exciting world beyond.

As well as the seashore, Maud also loved the woods around the village. She later named her favourite walk—along a ferny path in a hollow—"Lovers' Lane." (Her books have made this location famous.) She walked alongside a bubbling brook in dappled shade, under the cover of tall trees, smelling wild-flowers, spicy ferns, and aromatic cedars and pines. Small fish darted in the pools of cool water. Towards the end of Lovers' Lane, white birches rustled, and the path led onto the property of David and Margaret Macneill, an eld-erly brother and sister related to "her Macneills" (this couple provided a par-tial model for Matthew and Marilla in *Anne of Green Gables*). She grew up feeling a part of this idyllic, safe, and cozy landscape.

There was another way home from David and Margaret Macneill's home, through the "Haunted Wood," a forest of dense pine trees. The lower horizon-tal branches of these trees had died for lack of sunlight as the treetops lofted to the sky, and these spiky branches threatened to catch and impale anyone fool-ish enough to enter the thick grove. It lay parallel to an open road, the "hill road," but Maud sometimes walked home through the Haunted Wood just to feel the frisson of fear. It was the stuff that fed her young imagination, and she could work herself into a delightful terror by imagining its storybook dangers. It was easy for her to transplant the fairy folk and fearsome ghosts from the Scottish oral tradition and balladry into the tamer woods of Prince Edward Island.

But while the surroundings of her childhood were idyllic, her home life was not always so. Grandfather Macneill could be a sharp and irascible man. His erratic behaviour (which ranged from general irritability through raging tempers to "arbitrary kindness") made her feel highly insecure, particularly given his tendency towards barbed sarcasm. But his difficult nature did teach her to be thoughtful, watchful, and analytic—it was necessary to constantly evaluate her grandfather's moods. For self-protection against his hurtful com-ments, she learned the skill of instantly "reading" people through facial ex-pressions, body language, and movements, and this fed her writing talent.

Yet, her grandfather was not an unkind man. He had merely grown up in a judgmental family, under the gaze of a powerful, articulate father whose se-vere words and looks controlled others. Alexander Macneill perpetuated these tactics. Later, Maud wrote:

> There were many fine things about Grandfather Macneill. He had
> a rich poetic mind, a keen intelligence and a refined perception.
> He was a good conversationalist and a lover of nature . . . He had
> no patience with anything that fell short of his ideals, and never
> seemed to have any conception how harsh and brutal were some
> of the things he said, especially to children. . . . (January 7, 1910).

When she was nine, Maud fell sick through the winter with a cough, con-stant colds, and night sweats. This was alarming given that a lung ailment—

consumption—had killed her mother. She recalled her Grandfather Macneill bending over her as she lay sick in bed and saying, "You will be in your grave before spring" (recounted in entry of May 3, 1908). She believed him, and cried inconsolably for many nights. Saying such a thing to a sick child was a measure of his insensitivity, but the comment probably came from genuine grief. Maud would later describe how hurt she was in her childhood by the fact that her grandfather praised her cousins to her, but criticized her.

> Consequently I believed for years that I was the only one of his grandchildren that he disliked. Later in life I discovered that he was just the same to them—saying harsh or sarcastic things to them and praising me. . . . If he had only reversed the process—at least to the extent of saying his kind things to our faces and holding his tongue to others about our faults . . . he would have exercised a much stronger influence for good over us. (January 7, 1910)

By the time he died, in 1898, when Maud was twenty-three, her grandfather had become crotchety and autocratic, feuding bitterly with his equally irascible son, John Franklin Macneill (who lived next door with his own growing family), and with anyone else who irritated him. Maud knew her grandfather as a force to be watched and feared.

One skill Maud did learn (or inherit) from Grandfather Macneill was the ability to tell stories. In the kitchen of their Cavendish house (where the post office was located) she saw him hold his audience spellbound, and she absorbed the structures and techniques of oral storytelling.

As she grew up, Maud showed more and more symptoms of a fragile nervous temperament. Hypersensitive as a child, she grew moody and brooding in puberty. Her grandmother, Lucy Woolner Macneill, was a steadfast and stable personality. As Maud grew older, this temperamental and precocious granddaughter grew increasingly difficult to handle, particularly when "Maudie" and her volatile grandfather "sparked."

Maud later complained in her journals that her grandmother was "emotionally narrow," incapable of understanding Maud's complex personality: grandmother's "method of dealing with my nature and temperament was the most unwise she could possibly have adopted" (January 2, 1905). Sensible,

self-contained Lucy was determined to teach her granddaughter to conduct
herself with discipline, self-control, and dignity, and to consider in advance
the consequences of her impulsive tendencies.

In a patriarchal society, men were allowed to be moody, but women had
to be more self-effacing. In fact, Lucy succeeded admirably at teaching young
Maud to manage her moods. But it was not without pain and resentment on
Maud's part. Maud recalled the death of a beloved kitten, which left her weeping and heartbroken. Her grandmother did not like cats (especially in the
house), and knowing the greater sorrow of losing a grown daughter,
Grandmother Macneill sniffed unsympathetically that someday Maud would
experience *real grief*, according to Maud's journals.[20]

In spite of the tensions in the Macneill household, Maud had some advantages. One rare benefit was having her own bedroom. This was unusual in
a time when large families were the norm, bedrooms were few, and houses
contained several generations. At times, her grandparents' own farmhouse had
held up to ten people: Alexander, Lucy, their six children, and Alexander's
aged parents. In the winter Maud slept downstairs near the kitchen, where it
was warmer, but in the summer she slept upstairs in her own beloved bedroom, overlooking the fields.

And there were other advantages. Most of the other children went bare-
foot in summer, and wore hand-me-down clothing. But Lucy Macneill had
good taste, and dressed Maud well, insisting that she wear proper-fitting
clothes and shoes. This engendered in Maud a growing sense of difference
from others, which predictably had both positive and negative effects, ones she
would later exploit in fiction. Maud's father did not contribute to her
upkeep—and Maud's grandfather often reminded her of this—but her grandmother had some money of her own that she used without grudge for Maud.

Lucy Macneill's home was known as the best place for teachers
to board—it was central, with the school just down a lane and across the
road. But, more important, Lucy, a skilful cook, kept an excellent table in
her tidy home. This was no small matter. Housewives dried, canned, smoked,
or salted meats and other foods to preserve them from spoiling; they made
cheeses, wines, preserves, and kept root vegetables in a deep cellar; they
kept chickens for eggs, and cows provided milk and butter. Meals were made
up daily for consumption in the home. Before refrigeration and an
understanding of how bacteria multiplied, careless food preparation
could make people very ill. Staples like bread could pick up foreign objects

when kneaded on a dirty, crowded workspace. Before hot running water and detergents, food was often served on greasy dishes. These hazards made a clean, efficient household like Lucy Macneill's particularly desirable, and it brought Maud extra attention from teachers. As well, Lucy used the money she earned from keeping boarders to benefit her granddaughter in other ways.

In the four years after his young wife's death, Hugh John remained on Prince Edward Island. His occasional visits both thrilled and disturbed Maud, who sensed her grandparents' reservations about her father. As a child she did not understand the reasons for their disapproval, but she did resent their attitude, and she denied her father's shortcomings in her own mind. Her physical resemblance to her father was a daily reminder to her grandparents: her facial features and her short, slight physique favoured him rather than the taller, handsome Macneill and Woolner clans.

As a young girl she loved visiting her Aunt Annie Macneill Campbell and her "merry Campbell cousins" in Park Corner. She preferred visiting the boisterous Campbell house to her well-to-do Grandfather Donald Montgomery's home, across the road, where there was a more formal lifestyle, with servants. In reality, the Montgomerys of Park Corner cared little about Hugh John's daughter "Maudie": she was a girl, not a boy.

When Maud's father, Hugh John, was thirty-nine, and she was six, he departed for the west to seek his ever-elusive fortune, settling in Saskatchewan. Maud wrote in her journals that her father sent her affectionate birthday cards. Curiously, none of these have survived in her scrapbooks, which hold every other significant piece of paper and memorabilia that crossed her lifelong path. The truth about Hugh John's merits as a parent does not matter, however: Maud excused him for all his delinquencies. But she also felt *herself* less worthy because he appeared tarnished in the Macneills' eyes. Her Grandfather Montgomery's lack of interest and her own father's neglect intensified her own sense of unworthiness. Had she been a boy, she knew they would have valued her more.

In some other respects, however, fate served Maud well when it dropped her off in her maternal grandparents' home. Her firm, steady grandmother inculcated traits of discipline in tempestuous Maud, helping her learn, as "Anne of Green Gables" does, to control her impulses and to work towards goals. In fact, Lucy Woolner Macneill had learned to manage everything—cranky old in-laws, six children, and a husband given to fluctuating moods. A volatile little grandchild was only one more challenge. Lucy had raised each of her own three girls to be a "proper lady." And likewise with Maud, the practical Lucy's objective was to divert the child's gifts into domestic channels so that she would eventually make a desirable, efficient wife. Although Maud had a sweet face as a child, she was not going to grow into a beauty like her mother, Clara, and she had to be made marriageable, with dignified womanly behaviour.[21]

Proper, high-minded Lucy Woolner Macneill conveyed ideas about women's place in society that would sadly trammel Maud throughout her life. Male dominance was inscribed in law and social practice. Women did not become "persons" in Canadian law until 1929. Church teaching also held that women must be subordinate to men. (In the Presbyterian Church, the elders, the members of the management session, and the ministers and moderators were, of course, all male.) The Bible taught women the virtue of submission to male authority. The saying that "A woman's place is in the home" was unassailable conventional wisdom everywhere, and Maud quoted it herself in her early interviews.

Maud's life spanned a time when patriarchal structures were arguably more damaging to women than at any other period in history in the western world. In urban areas, industrialization was undermining women's power in private spheres, without admitting them to public areas of power. "The Woman Question" was a hot topic in North America and Britain. A typical item from the Charlottetown paper on December 28, 1882, sneers at "women's rights," quoting King David in the Bible: "To everything there is a season," and this was "not the season or the time for a 'woman's rights' debate." Maud's well-intentioned grandmother, both by example and by edict, trained Maud in these near-universal cultural beliefs that women were biologically and mentally inferior to men. The ideal woman was an "angel in the house," always quiet, patient, and ladylike. It is interesting, however, that Lucy was also, to an extent, an independent thinker: it would be Lucy who supported Maud's wish for higher education, which her grandfather, Alexander Macneill, considered a waste of money.

Maud retained mixed feelings about her grandmother, describing her as rigid, narrow, and cold in her journals. But by all accounts, during Maud's lifetime she spoke of her grandmother with love and affection. In a 1912 interview, Maud described her as the "very pretty, and so young-looking" grandmother, the only mother she ever knew. To her friends and acquaintances later in her life, Maud frequently praised her grandmother's intelligence, her great fund of practical knowledge, her emotional stability, and her management skills.[22] Maud learned to appreciate her grandmother's steady ways. She knew that her grandparents, and her grandmother in particular, loved her, and that love inspired deep gratitude. There is no doubt much truth in Lucy Woolner Macneill's obituary, which praised her "spirit, industry, and unfailing kindness."[23]

Living on the shores of time: the impact of school and church

When Maud arrived in Cavendish as a baby, she was welcomed into a close-knit community, united by kinship, culture, and religion. Religion provided the conceptual framework for her formative years.

A child's week brought daily Bible-reading in the family and church-going. Children were depicted in sermons in ambiguous ways: sometimes as icons of innocence, but more often as beings conceived and born in a state of sin, needing God's special election to be saved. Children grew up in a complicated world, where the forces of Good and Evil were in constant competition for their souls.

The sermons Maud heard in the Presbyterian church depicted a dramatic Manichaean universe, full of visual symbols. Hell was a subterranean lake of fire, brimstone, and burning sulphur, presided over by a plotting, energetic Devil: every man, woman, and child was in danger of his corruption. Heaven was a place above the clouds with golden streets and winged angels sitting at God's feet, chanting songs of praise. Maud was ever alert to the imagery used in these sermons and songs. She suffered from spasms of fear about Hell in childhood. The sermons were delivered extemporaneously by Presbyterian ministers rigorously trained in rhetoric as well as in languages, history, and moral philosophy. Parishioners would discuss points from an interesting sermon throughout the week.

In Scotland, Presbyterianism had evolved as a branch of Christianity that fought (among other things) for the right to conceptualize a different relationship with God, based on individual conscience. Followers should communicate with God directly, independently of priests or bishops (preachers were mainly considered experts in the interpretation of the Bible, not conduits of God's word). The word of God was available in the Bible, teaching both through formal commandments and stories. As the Bible put it, "In the beginning was the Word, and the Word was with God, and the Word was God."

In practical terms, this meant that each Presbyterian—man or woman, boy or girl—must be taught to read. Only the literate could fully exercise their religion. (Towards this end, John Knox, the thunderous father of Presbyterianism in Scotland, had declared that there must be "a school in every parish.") As a result, the Scots developed both a rich oral culture and a deep respect for books and learning, which they carried worldwide when they emigrated.

The selection of ministers, as well as much church governance, was always handled at the local level by democratic process. This produced a different and more egalitarian society than that in England. In the Church of England governance came from above, and education of the lower classes was discouraged. The Scots had been taught to see public education of ordinary people as empowering.[24]

Wherever they emigrated abroad, the Scots set up impressive local systems of education. The colony of Prince Edward Island passed a Free Education Act in 1852, believed to be the first of its kind in the British dominions.[25] The Scottish settlers in Cavendish had established their own school in 1834; by 1872, two years before Maud's birth, it was lauded as "unquestionably one of the best schools in the county; accordingly students from distant localities frequently attended." By the time Maud was ready for school, there were between forty and fifty pupils.

Very early in her schooling, it was clear to her teachers (and others around her) that Maud had exceptional intelligence. She started school at age six, but had already taught herself to read from the school readers her aunts and uncles had used. Her Aunt Emily took her to school on her first day, and Maud later recalled humiliating herself by forgetting to remove her bonnet when she sat down at her seat. But she soon distinguished herself with her reading ability. In her journal entry of January 7, 1910, she remembered the praise from her teacher, Mr. James Kay Ross, on that first day of school. She was asked to read James Watt's eighteenth-century poem "How Doth the Little Busy Bee" in the advanced *Royal Reader*. Mr. Ross announced to the rest of the one-room school: "This little girl reads better than any of you, although she is younger and has never been to school before." Maud's journal entry recalls this as the first compliment she ever received. In those days parents rarely praised their children overtly. Praise might lead to "conceit," and that was akin to sinful pride. Maud was clearly eager to earn praise at school instead.

Schooling was intense in nineteenth-century Cavendish. There were four school terms a year, with quarterly vacations. School went year round, with no

summer break, and was held six days a week. On the seventh day, the Lord's
Day, there was Sunday school. At the end of the fourth term, students put on
a concert to display their learning. Oral performance and self-expression were
very important. Maud was an excellent public performer. She easily memorized long book passages and poems. Although she was naturally somewhat
shy, she loved recitation. Around her, adults memorized favourite poems for
personal pleasure and public performance. While still a child, Maud learned
"The Cottar's Saturday Night" for recitation. She also memorized the entire
text of Sir Walter Scott's "The Lady of the Lake" (its twenty-nine cantos run to
fifty pages of small print).

Mr. Ross, her first teacher, like those who followed him, had taken
teacher training at Prince of Wales College in Charlottetown, studying Latin,
Mathematics, Geography, Farming Principles, Literature, and Language
Skills. He was as well trained as the average college graduate today. The
school trustees examined each school at the end of the term, and a good showing was essential. A teacher whose students performed poorly brought public
disgrace on himself and his community.

After Mr. Ross left, the next teacher, James K. Fraser, who boarded with
the Macneills, instituted a new pedagogical approach: giving prizes out of his
own salary to reward students for good behaviour and performance. Through
his generosity, Cavendish children obtained valued books, and Maud remembered him with kindness all her life. Like many other young Island men,
he was teaching in order to make enough money to continue on to university
to take theological training. In the spring of 1883 Mr. Fraser departed. He was
replaced by a new teacher, a Mr. James McLeod, by all accounts a good
teacher, but less popular because he resorted to the standard disciplinary
method of whipping children.

One important legacy from Mr. Fraser was a book he lent Maud, *A Bad
Boy's Diry, by Little George* (1880), about a mischievous child in constant trouble. When she was about nine, Maud began keeping her own diary, using this
book as a model. She says that, "Although not very mischievous by nature,
being bookish and dreamy, nevertheless I schemed and planned many
naughty tricks for no other reason than that I might have them to write in my
'dere diry'" (May 12, 1902). She adopted the affected style of "little Georgie" in
her writing. Paper was not easily obtained, but she could purloin discarded
"letter bills," which came to the post office in their home. She also acquired
the small yellow notebooks sent by a well-known patent medicine firm,

"Dr. Pierce's of Buffalo." She tied together sheets of paper with thread, enclosed her scribblings in blood-red covers, and began recording her private thoughts and imaginative life. This little red book started a journalizing habit she maintained all her life.

Whatever their faults, Maud's forebears were proud of their literacy, their educational system, their religion, and their cultural heritage in general. They believed that education was empowering, providing individuals with personal agency and the ability to make society better. They were clannish, morally serious, and imbued with a strong work ethic. They took pride in their self-sufficiency and their accomplishments, and the schools they set up contributed to their success. Maud gained enormous self-confidence and learned discipline at her school.

Maud and her culture

Young Maud's mind was fed by the dramatic sermons she heard, along with the gentler Bible stories that were regular fare for children of her era. But it was stimulated also by a culture in which the ability to tell a story well brought people respect and power. Local events were turned into oral narratives. As one journalist later put it, "The Island is crammed with stories, stories of sailors and great storms, stories of ghosts and the Devil, stories of lovers and wooing and runaway matches, stories of queer people and witches, stories of the good little people themselves."[26]

The wreck of the *Marco Polo* near Cavendish on July 25, 1883, when she was nearly nine, had an important effect on Maud's imagination. The fabled clipper ship—once the fastest in the world—ran full-sail, in a savage storm, straight towards the Cavendish beach. When the ship broke in half, the sailors clung to the heaving remains all night.

During salvage operations, the *Marco Polo*'s captain stayed in Alexander Macneill's house. People came for their mail, and stayed to listen to the captain and Grandfather Macneill swap yarns. Maud and other children hovered. The salty old captain recounted stories about the *Marco Polo*'s unusual design, her dramatic launching years earlier, and her record-breaking round-the-world voyages. It was a storytelling feast. Grandfather responded with stories drawn from his Island life, flavoured with rich and poetic language from the Bible, his own extensive reading, and the oral tradition of

the Scots. That shipwreck was a bonanza for a gifted spinner of stories like
Alexander Macneill.[27]

The salvage operation ended and the captain paid off his "rough tars"
with a bag of gold sovereigns in front of wide-eyed Maud. She had never seen
anything like the sailors from this crew, some twenty men—Norwegians,
Swedes, Dutchmen, Germans, Irishmen, Scotchmen, Spaniards, and two
Tahitians, with "wooly heads, thick lips, and gold earrings." The sailors
painted the "quiet village a glowing scarlet" all summer. After they all departed, Maud listened to her grandfather as he turned the tale of the *Marco
Polo* into local legend, crafting it in his own style.

The *Marco Polo*'s wreck stretched Maud's emerging sense of narrative
possibilities, and it showed her the intense pleasure in story. It proved that
someone who could tell tales well could rivet the attention of others. It
demonstrated to her that the local events around her could be turned into a
story. She developed a new respect for her grandfather, who shaped his stories better than others; she listened, admired, enjoyed, and learned. She
tucked the story of the *Marco Polo* away in her repertoire, and later in adolescence she used it and some of her grandfather's other stories to help
launch her public career.

Maud had a very unusual memory, with excellent recall of anything she
had either read, heard, or felt. She also absorbed the techniques of oral storytelling. (Being able to remember great numbers of poems, stories, or local
tales—and to better others' stories in playful competition—is still part of the
Island culture.)

There were other good raconteurs in the Macneill family, too: Maud's eccentric Great-Uncle Jimmie Macneill (who would reappear as Cousin Jimmie
in the *Emily* trilogy) and her grandfather's older sister, Mary Macneill Lawson,
a widow who moved around, living with different relatives, drawing her narratives from family history and local happenings. Women's stories were told
whenever women did church work together, had quilting parties, or visited for
afternoon tea.

Maud wanted to be a storyteller, but she had few listeners at home. If her
grandfather was in the kitchen, he dominated, and she and her grandmother
remained silent. When her father visited in the fall of 1883, he listened to her
storytelling and to her writing. When she read him some of her poetry, he
laughed at her blank verse, calling it "very blank indeed." This, of course, was
very hurtful. She had to turn elsewhere for listeners.

Maud adopted the role of a "Story Girl" with her playmates at school and in the extended family. She had lots of friends, including many Macneill cousins. In her Uncle John F. Macneill's house, across the field, were six first cousins. The oldest girl, Lucy, three years younger than Maud, was a devoted playmate for many years. Down the shore road towards Rustico was a second cousin, Pensie Macneill, two years older than Maud. Maud's third cousin, Amanda Macneill, was her own age and her closest friend for a time. Maud held her own through her storytelling ability. And there were more cousins over at Park Corner. The effusive and irrepressible Campbells also lived in a storytelling family, and they competed vigorously in the telling of yarns and funny stories when she visited.[28] For several years, from when Maud was seven until she was eleven, her grandmother boarded two boys, Wellington and Dave Nelson. About her own age, the tractable and less-imaginative Nelson boys were an admiring and uncritical audience for her—a good reason for her to call them the best playmates she ever had.

Storytelling had many functions in Maud's culture besides entertainment. It was also a method of teaching children family values. And it provided a bulwark against the erasures of death and time. When people were buried, they did not leave the community, or pass out of mind. They merely became an absent presence, moving into "eternal" time. Maud and others repeated endless tales about the departed; walking through the graveyard was often a stimulus to these tales. The village graveyard was next to the Cavendish school, across the road from Maud's grandfather's property and the Presbyterian Church. Children could play in the graveyard, and the dead were never far away.

The concept of time in Maud's era was derived from religion. "Human time" was a mere bubble in "eternal time." Maud describes a baby's birth in one of her novels by saying it "made a safe landing on the shores of time." Towards the end of her own life, she would speak of "when time gets through with me." Eternal time was God's time, the infinity out of which humans were born. In human time, they strutted about for a period and then died. Every sermon reminded the people of Cavendish of eternal time, and the short duration of human lives in it. When time finished with them, they took their restful spots in the centrally located graveyard: the boundaries of time between the sleepers were then erased. They had merely slipped behind the "veil" into a spiritual realm.

Maud's young mother, who had died in 1876 at age twenty-three, lay in this graveyard. Close by was the tombstone of Maud's great-grandmother, who died in 1869, as well as her great-great-grandmother, who died in 1849. Little Maud grew up with a sense of the proximity of maternal lineage and the other graveyard inhabitants. They lived on through stories told about them. Her own comments, standing at her father's grave, recounted on October 14, 1930, reflect this: "There separated from me by a few feet of earth was what was left of father—of the outward man I knew. I might call to him but he would not answer. Yet I felt so tenderly, preciously, dreadfully near to him. As if, under that sod, his great tired beautiful blue eyes had opened and were looking at me."

When little Maud saw her mother's tombstone from the schoolyard, she felt some consolation in her mother's presence, but her mother represented less a helpful presence than a terrible loss. When Maud clashed with her grandparents, her mind turned to her mother, close by, but buried and mute, unable to help. It is no surprise, then, that this gifted and well-cared-for grand-daughter of prominent Cavendish citizens would eventually create classic fictions about little children orphaned in childhood.

The impulse to shape narratives about herself and her environment provided enormous comfort to this sensitive and needy child. It gave her a sense of having some control over her own environment and destiny.

Maud's reading during the golden age of print

The Industrial Revolution, the rise of public education and a self-improving middle class, inventions in printing and bookmaking, the inception of public libraries, and the development of rail and shipping systems of distribution—all these factors had created a hugely expanding reading public by the 1890s. In this golden age of print, writers scrambled to provide a range of material for weekly serials and monthly magazines, in addition to poems and short stories for use as "filler" in newspapers. Novels were also needed for the new lending libraries.

Young Maud was steadily absorbing from her reading the literary patterns that she would later blend with the oral traditions of her community. The *Royal Readers* were full of stories and poems, introducing children to a range of canonical English, Scottish, and American writers, as well as a few new Canadian ones. Maud had access to her grandmother's monthly *Godey's Lady's Book*, a potpourri of reading material ranging from quality fiction to discussions of household management and even to fashionable clothing patterns (the same patterns used by local dressmakers from Cavendish to British Columbia, and Boston to San Francisco). Maud recalled examining the fashion plates with dreamy fascination.

When her Uncle Leander, now a minister in Saint John, New Brunswick, came home, he brought current reading material with him, some of it fiction. The people in Cavendish also had access to the new and important books from Great Britain and the United States through their local public lending library, which had been established in the 1850s.

Other reading material available to Maud was more "child-friendly": *Little Katey and Jolly Jim*, Louisa May Alcott's *Little Women*, and the "Pansy" books by Isabella Macdonald Alden. The Nelson boys let her read their copy of Hans Christian Andersen's selected tales (which one of the boys had won as a prize while boarding at the Macneills). She also had occasional access to a children's magazine called *Wide Awake* that introduced major British, American, and Canadian writers.

The Macneills also possessed two weightier volumes, entitled "Histories of the World," which Maud read several times: these started with the story of the Garden of Eden, progressed through the "Glory that was Greece and the Grandeur that was Rome," and ended with Queen Victoria's reign, presented as the pinnacle of civilized life on the planet. Maud also loved a missionary book about the Pacific Islands, with its pictures of "cannibal chiefs with their extraordinary hair arrangements" (January 7, 1910). Books such as these were imbued with the belief that British colonization was the only way to civilize the world, and those who were not white Christians were primitive, inferior, and "heathen." Some of the better-resourced churches on Prince Edward Island sent missionaries out to foreign countries, and one of the few acceptable ways for a woman to find adventure and travel was to become a missionary, or the wife of one. (Two of Maud's Aunt Emily Montgomery's female relatives went into foreign missionary service.)

Other kinds of literature were found in the reasonably well-stocked Macneill library as well, including Scottish classics such as Robert Burns's poetry and Sir Walter Scott's novels—Maud read Scott's novels over and over as she was growing up, and there are many references to them in her own writing. Like her own family stories, these encouraged the romanticizing of her Scottish heritage.[29]

Another book of great interest to Maud was John Bunyan's *Pilgrim's*

Progress (1678), with its beautifully engraved nineteenth-century illustrations. She internalized its message that human life was a temporary sojourn in a sinful vale of tears. The first part of this allegory (the story was originally written for adults, but often read by children) followed the protagonist, Christian, as he bravely made his way through a landscape at once symbolic and dangerous, on his route to Heaven. The second part depicted his weak wife, Christiana, making the same journey. Maud had reservations: "I never liked Christiana's adventures half so well as Christian's . . . she had not half the fascination of that solitary intrepid figure who faced all alone the shadows of the dark valley and the encounter with [the monster] 'Apollyon.'" (January 7, 1910, appearing again in *Emily of New Moon*). The overt message in the contrast between the journeys of Christian and Christiana is that women can follow the lead of a strong man who has forged ahead, but females lack the courage, brainpower, and stamina to persevere on their own. These stories reinforced the patriarchal stories that Maud would have been familiar with from the Bible, teaching that women, weaker than men, should "obey" their husbands, and fixing the female place in life as subordinate.

There was other religious reading material as well, such as the best-selling sermons of the famous American preacher Dr. DeWitt Talmadge; Maud liked these for their "vivid word-painting and dramatic climaxes" (January 7, 1910). She also read *The Memoirs of Anzonetta Peters*, a book written by a minister that claimed to be the autobiography of a very devout dyig child. Anzonetta records her righteous sayings before being gathered to the bosom of God in a dramatic and sentimental death. When Maud became seriously ill with respiratory problems as a small child, she tried to imitate Anzonetta, and she wrote in her diary that she wished she were "in heaven now, with mother and George Whitefield and Anzonetta B. Peters." She comments later, "I did not really wish it . . . but I believed that I *ought* to wish it and so I tried to" (January 7, 1910). Maud's penchant for pathos and sentimentality may have had some origin in these popular religious texts.

One idea that Maud absorbed from her devotional reading and religious training was that pleasure and fun were inherently sinful. Later she recalled how, as an impressionable and precocious young child, she made herself drink from a cup she hated just because it seemed sinful to drink from one she liked. It is no surprise that what she called "spiritual struggles" began to preoccupy her.

Maud dared not raise religious questions with her grandparents, who would have been angered by childish scrutiny of standard doctrine. Sadly, they denied her the confidence that comes to a child who is listened to, no matter how puerile and quaint its questions (though Maud told herself that if her mother had been alive, *she* would have listened). Instead she was left to brood darkly, morbidly affected by the terrifying sermons she had heard and by her religious reading.

The sounds of battle

By age twelve, Maud was already beginning to manifest the kind of drive and complexity that made her into anything but an ordinary person. A photograph of Maud in 1886 shows her standing on the threshold of puberty. She's becoming as judgmental as her grandfather, and she knows from him how to put withering force behind a disdainful or appraising look. She's still young and lovable, but she is wired with energy and possibility. She knows she is the smartest girl in the school. This photograph shows Maud with the most genuine self-assurance she will ever know. Here she appears to feel her strength much more than her vulnerability. She looks confident that she is on the path to an exciting destiny.

When this picture was taken, Maud had not yet learned that being a female in the nineteenth century was to be harnessed to the agendas of others—as wife, mother, and housekeeper, and as caretaker of the elderly. When she grew up, Maud would add several additional obligations to this list: serving her publisher and public as a producer of books, her community as a minister's wife, and a large extended group of relatives and others as a financial resource or support. But in this photograph, she is still her own confident person.

The age of twelve is often seen as a watershed time for young girls. They are developmentally ahead of boys, but about to discover the handicap of their gender. As young girls grew up in Maud's time, they discovered that their "scope for imagination" receded. Women were expected to hitch their wagon to their husbands' stars and live their lives vicariously through husband and children. Those not able to find a husband would be pitied and despised. Girls in Prince Edward Island were lucky in that they were ensured a basic grade-eight education equal to a young man's, but their future, nevertheless, was marriage.

The late nineteenth century had seen much debate about the role of education in women's lives. If young women attended Prince of Wales College to become teachers, and many did, they were expected to resign their positions as soon as they married. Acadia and Dalhousie Universities in Nova Scotia, and Mount Allison in New Brunswick, had shown leadership in admitting and graduating women in Canada, and a very small number of gifted and determined women were entering professions. Nevertheless, a general conviction persisted in Prince Edward Island and elsewhere that women had less brain capacity than men, and that giving women too much education was bad for both their mental and physical health.

The belief that it was in a woman's interests to be denied higher education was founded on the best scientific knowledge of the era. In 1873, the year before Maud's birth, Dr. Edward H. Clarke's book *Sex in Education, or a Fair Chance for Girls* argued that women's bodies were a battleground in which two organs—the brain and the ovaries—struggled for dominance. Higher education, he said, would cause the ovaries to atrophy, with a potential result being the end of the human race. His book went through seventeen editions, and the magazines and newspapers of the era reflected these beliefs.

Advertisements and essays in Charlottetown papers, as well as books imported from cultural centres like Edinburgh, Boston, and London, constantly referred to women as the "weaker sex." Patent medications frequently advertised themselves for women who had weakened themselves through education and learning. Women were cautioned in the publications about the dangers of seeking to overdevelop their minds lest the strain damage them. "Let wives and mothers and sisters . . . discover the precise arts that charm most easily the masculine mind," insisted one typical article in the Charlottetown *Examiner*, "and practice them, let them make their homes bright and cheerful, their conversations enticing, and not too intellectual" (February 4, 1882).

Although Maud was growing up in a society that had low intellectual expectations of women, she had already gained the same local education as the young men around her. Bright and ambitious, she fumed when her male cousins patronized her because she was a girl. And her frustrations over the inequity would grow: if any of them wanted a university education and showed aptitude, it would be granted to them—but not to her. And yet she could also see that she had far more ability than most of her male cousins.

Her Uncle John F. Macneill's sons, Prescott and Frank, grew up hearing their autocratic father patronize his gentle wife, and learned disrespect for females as a result. They were younger than Maud, but felt superior to her. Little surprise that Maud did not like either of them: "Prescott was meanness and pettiness incarnate . . . Frank, the second son, was a good-looking, empty-headed, conceited youth" (January 12, 1912). Her Uncle Leander's sons, closer to her age, were only slightly better in her view. The summer of 1887 was one of many in which Uncle Leander's family came for a long vacation in the "old" home. Maud's grandmother, who adored Leander (her first-born son), expected Maud to wait on his family as willingly as she herself did. Her sons looked down on Maud as the "poor country cousin" who should tend to the extra work when they visited. Maud liked her cousin Fred fairly well, but she loathed Murray, his older brother, who was undeniably brilliant—and fully aware of his intellectual gifts. "Unless a girl bowed down and worshiped him he had no use for her," Maud wrote after she was famous (January 7, 1910). Gender relations soured what might otherwise have been a happy time for her.

When Maud clashed with her cousins, her uncles, or her grandparents, she thought of the parents who might have defended her. She was sure that they would have valued her intellectual gifts, even if she was a girl.

The winter that she turned twelve, her father sent the exciting news from the west that he was going to wed again. When he married a younger woman named Mary Ann McRae in 1887, Maud began to fantasize about going to live with her father and her "new" mother. Out came pen and paper, and loving letters flowed westward, with pressed flowers enclosed.

In 1887, a big change was afoot in Cavendish. School trustees hired the first female schoolteacher. Women teachers were paid less, and the local trustees opted for economy—and perhaps for adventure—in hiring a woman. The "lady-teacher," Miss Izzie Robinson, faced a daunting responsibility: running different levels of classes with some fifty pupils, ranging from little girls in pinafores to young men almost as old as she was, and much bigger.

Miss Robinson asked to board at Maud's grandparents' house, as other teachers before her had done. This time Lucy Macneill balked. Perhaps, like many older women, she was prejudiced against female teachers. Perhaps she simply wanted respite from the extra work created by boarders. More likely, she took the measure of Izzie's personality and saw that this female teacher's pushy manner would irritate her cranky husband. But Izzie argued her case strongly and moved into the Macneill household.

Once there, Izzie soon became the target of Alexander Macneill's sarcastic barbs (which he called "bars"). Maud was not yet thirteen, but the escalating friction between Grandfather and Izzie stayed with her for life. This was to be Maud's first opportunity to observe male prejudice against women escalating into a major clash. The throwing of barbs became cruel and aggressive, especially when used by a highly articulate and intelligent older man against an inexperienced young woman. Few young female teachers, feeling insecure in their first teaching position, would have been able to summon up humour when they were the toad under Alexander Macneill's well-sharpened verbal harrow.

At first Maud expected the praise from Izzie Robinson that she had become accustomed to receiving from other teachers. She recited her compositions to Miss Robinson and was disappointed by the tepid response. She entered the *Montreal Witness* school composition, where she won honourable mention for a story about Cape Le Force, one of her grandfather's favourite tales. Miss Robinson had not promoted this competition much in the school, and she may have resented Maud's success. When the feud with Maud's grandfather intensified, the nettled Miss Robinson resorted to the tactic of taking out her frustrations on vulnerable young Maud, humbling her in public and mocking her with a "venomous sneer" (January 7, 1910). Her grandfather's self-indulgent harassment of Miss Robinson cost Maud much of a year's schooling and resulted in her being wounded in subtle but deep ways.

When the relationship between Izzie and Maud grew too damaging, her grandparents withdrew her from school, arranging for her to stay with her Aunt Emily and Uncle John Montgomery in Malpeque. Maud adored her Uncle John, her father's cousin, probably seeing in him an alternate father-figure. He was a school trustee and member of Parliament, and he had the Montgomery jollity that could turn any gathering into a festive occasion. Aunt Emily, a busy mother and housewife, now expecting another baby, likely agreed to take Maud because she needed some help.

Over-sensitive Maud was already rubbed raw by her grandfather and Izzie Robinson. She had resented the way Leander's sons treated her as a servant, and she had no intention of becoming her Aunt Emily's drudge, either. Emily had been raised in Alexander Macneill's judgmental household where angry, snappish words were a form of control. Predictably, Maud clashed with yet another adult who used sarcasm as a putdown. Aunt Emily found Maud stubborn, balky, and moody—a volatile child with emotional needs she could not meet. In the end, Maud remained in Malpeque for only three months, March until May, 1888. The outcome of this unhappy visit was that Maud disliked her Aunt Emily for the rest of her life, and vice versa. Maud's extended family of intense and outspoken people would provide fertile ground for future fiction.[30]

When Maud arrived home from Malpeque, Miss Izzie Robinson was still the local teacher, but she was boarding elsewhere. Maud was not allowed to return to school. Her grandmother, desperate for things to occupy Maud, and obviously wanting her granddaughter to develop the skills of an accomplished young woman, arranged for her to take organ lessons. (Home organs were the rage: newspaper ads promoted them as something every cultured woman should learn to play.) Lucy Macneill somehow nudged Hugh John, who finally had a well-paying patronage job out west, to pay a portion of the cost of the organ and help with the cost of music lessons for his daughter. As gifted as Maud was, music was not among her artistic talents, but for the summer and fall of 1888, music lessons kept her occupied — no small feat, given her restless energy and her friction with her grandfather.

Maud suffered from being kept out of school. School was the métier of her success, and she missed the fellowship of her peers. She was embarrassed by community gossip that turned against her grandparents (mostly her grandfather). She had been caught in the crossfire following the year-long feud between her sharp-tongued grandfather and Miss Robinson, and was left feeling helpless and vulnerable and confused. In that crucial period when children should be learning their strengths, Maud was battered by these family tensions and felt humiliated within the community.

Quite early in her life, Maud developed an ability to abstract herself. This was a coping mechanism as well as a defence against her grandfather's criticisms. Those who remembered her as a child said she could be somewhat "uncanny" or "otherworldly." In local legend, and by her own account, she was remembered as "different" from the other children — sensitive, sometimes remote, often moody, but also capable of "stirring things up." Like so many children who are buffeted between intermittent approval and unpredictable criticism, she did not learn to be at ease with herself at this crucial stage of life. Self-doubts would plague her all her life.

Izzie Robinson was not the only source of tension within Maud's family in 1888. In her mid-thirties Maud recorded her memories of her Uncle John F. (John Franklin Macneill):

> His manner to me, and indeed to most children, except those of whose parents he had a salutary awe, was brutal, domineering and

insulting. . . . He had a remarkably harsh voice and on calm summer evenings when he raged at some of his children he could be
heard all over the settlement to the amusement of the dwellers
therein. . . . Yet uncle John was . . . intelligent, sober, and industrious. But his traits of selfishness, bad temper and tyranny over-
rode everything else. . . . Had Uncle John married a woman with
a bit of temper too I believe he would have been a much better
and more agreeable man because he could control his temper
when he had to. Like all bullies he was a coward at heart and never
attempted to domineer over a person who could and did confront
him boldly. . . . But Aunt Ann Maria was a placid, smiling, good
tempered *animal*. . . . She fostered all the worst elements in Uncle
John's nature by truckling to him to his face and then taking
her own way by guile and deceit behind his back and bringing her
family to do the same. (January 28, 1912)

That same summer, Grandfather Macneill had a terrible altercation
with his son. The trouble likely arose from dynamics between father and
son. Both could be very charming in company, but each took offence easily,
and both could be explosive. Maud recounts that Alexander Macneill and
John F. did not speak to each other all through the summer and into the fall
of 1888, in spite of attending the same church and being active in its management structure. The distance between the two houses was so small that
the anger between father and son made the air palpable with tension.

The entry about her Uncle John F., written in 1912 after Maud had left the
village of Cavendish, is one of the most powerful condemnations of her relatives in Maud's ten journals. Maud and her Uncle John's children had often
played together. But around this time, the relationship between Maud and her
next-door cousin, Lucy (Uncle John F.'s daughter), began to corrode, probably as a result of what each family was saying about the other family behind
closed doors. Finally, Maud had a falling out with Lucy, writing in her journals that she found Lucy to be a "false friend." Yet Lucy Macneill (later
Simpson) was remembered with great affection for her wit and merriment by
people who knew her over her lifetime. This was not the only time that family tensions poisoned Maud's recollection of her early life.[31]

These passages highlight an important feature of Maud's temperament:
people who did not meet her high standards were condemned and discarded.

And once she turned against someone, she was without charity forever. In rural, nineteenth-century Canada (and many other places), a rigid perspective was the norm, with "Good" and "Evil" polarized. The nineteenth century did not generally cultivate an "open mind," one ready to consider all sides of a topic. The judgmental mind of her era accentuated her emotional temperament, and a person who felt as deeply as Maud did not soon forget having been hurt, nor did she forgive.[32]

Maud's feeling for the place where she was raised was one of the most enduring loves of her life. It was the site of intense pains and pleasures. Although her adolescent years held tension, her childhood was vibrant and adventuresome. She would immortalize Cavendish in her fiction, making it an idyllic setting for her heroines. As previously mentioned, the picturesque "Green Gables" was based on the home of her elderly cousins, David Macneill and his sister Margaret, a house which Maud often visited by walking through her beloved Lovers' Lane. However, the spiritual centre of the fictional "Green Gables" came from her grandparents' home. "Anne," like Maud, wanted to be valued in spite of the fact she was a girl.

Maud was beginning to see herself hobbled at every turn by gender, as well as by the general restrictions of nineteenth-century attitudes that devalued girls and women. Her anger was expressed in rebellion. Although Maud always disliked open confrontation, adversity toughened her determination; by puberty, she was already developing the steel will that would propel her to success.

Feminine role models for Maud

Maud's grandmother was one role model for her, and soon a teacher would appear who would become both model and mentor. In September 1889, the Cavendish trustees hired another female teacher, Miss Hattie Gordon. Miss Gordon had probably heard about the trouble Izzie Robinson had suffered with Alexander Macneill and she wisely boarded elsewhere. And, equally wisely, she started out by making fast friends with bright, young Maud Montgomery. Maud, now age fourteen, thrived under her tutelage.

Miss Gordon was from the same branch of the Scottish Gordons (from Perthshire) as the Reverend Charles W. Gordon, also known by his pen name "Ralph Connor," who would become a best-selling Canadian author with the publication in 1902 of *Glengarry School Days*. The departure of Hattie's ancestors (her grandmother was Christina MacLaren) from Scotland is mentioned by Sir Walter Scott in a footnote to *Rob Roy,* and Christina's great-grandfather figures as the original of "Pate-in-Peril" in Scott's *Redgauntlet.* Hattie's brother was the internationally famous American archaeologist Dr. George Byron Gordon, F.R.G.S., of the University of Pennsylvania. Maud does not mention these connections in her journals, and it is not clear if she was aware of all of them (beyond Dr. George Byron Gordon, who appears in her scrapbooks), but she does describe in detail her great affection for the gifted Miss Gordon.

Miss Gordon brought fun back into the schoolroom—and normality into Maud's life. Maud's confidence would develop throughout the year as Miss Gordon praised her elocutionary and writing abilities. Energized by Miss Gordon's praise of her writing assignments at school, Maud began again to keep a genuine private diary of her life. She burned the derivative and affected "Dere Diry" that she had been keeping since age nine. When she began her new diary at age fourteen, she had little thought of it as a shaped document she would keep all her life. However, as Maud recorded school events and developing relationships, the diary began to take on a life of its own.

In Victorian times, keeping a diary was a trend among many middle- and upper-class women (and girls), who were normally confined to a life of narrow domesticity. It gave them an outlet in a culture that largely denied females a public voice and public life. Maud began using her diary as a way of hearing her own voice, as a "listening friend." It could take her into a world where she could create out of herself, around herself, and for herself. Later, when fictional "Emily of New Moon" is told that she is a little girl of no importance to anyone, she makes the assertion—certainly startling for the time—that she is *important to herself.* Beginning a new journal at age fourteen, using her real voice instead of the fake persona of a "bad boy," is a sign of Maud's increasing confidence, that *she* was important enough to have literary aspirations, even if she was a girl.

Writing about a life is many steps removed from actually living it. The act of writing entails the shaping of raw experience. A diary puts the "self" at the core, and the raw experience of life is shaped around this self. Maud's extended family, her religion, and her community's social attitudes all fed into the inner person who lay at the core of her diary. And Maud's reading helped her shape the ways she described her experience.

There was lots of time for Maud to read and think, for winters were long and cold. Given the cost of fuel (for both lamps and heating), it was normal practice to keep warm by going to bed after supper, when the fire was dying down. Lying in the dark in the icy farmhouse, warm under her blankets and comforter, Maud could imagine herself as part of the stories she read. Soon her diary began to reflect this reading and dreaming experience, supplementing the reports of the day's doings at school.

As she entered adolescence, Maud developed an insatiable habit of reading, and she found models for womanhood in what she read. The book that imprinted itself most deeply on her adolescent style and imagination was Edward Bulwer-Lytton's mystical novel *Zanoni* (1842). It is a secularized and richly romanticized allegory, with a very different focus and style from *Pilgrim's Progress*, the book she read so many times as a child. In *Zanoni*, the principal characters are looking for mystical purity, truth, goodness, and learning (rather than for Bunyan's straightforward salvation and entry into Heaven). The "ideal" life in *Zanoni* is something that only men have the strength to achieve; women would have balked before the "Dweller on the Threshold" and the "Terror."

Zanoni's narrative focuses on a passionate love story—not of man for God, but of man for woman. The beautiful Viola has an extraordinary power of evoking emotion through her musical gifts. These gifts attract Zanoni, a handsome and mysterious wanderer, a member of the ancient Rosicrucians, and a mystical figure able to move in and out of human time. He gives up his immortality in order to marry Viola, whose haunting songs he loves. But in the end, misguided and weak Viola betrays him—after all, she is both *human* and *woman*. Both die, and their baby is left untended in a hostile world. (An orphaned baby was a tragedy that Maud responded to with passion and pity.) Typical of Victorian fiction and art, *Zanoni* associates men with the spiritual realm and women with the physical one.

And the notion of a world "beyond the veil," a mystic world of spirituality, was fascinating to Maud. *Zanoni* gave her a lush and ornate poetic language for expressing her own imaginative interest in an alternate world, shrouded in mystery. Echoes of *Zanoni* appear constantly throughout her adult writing, both in phrasing and in images.

As with much nineteenth-century fiction, *Zanoni* contains conflicting messages about women: although weak and easily led, they can also be unusually talented, like Viola. They are vulnerable to male exploitation, but one character has a significant line: "Heaven did not make the one sex to be the victim of the other" (*Zanoni*, Chapter 6, p. 353). In the nineteenth-century world, with increasing debate over women's roles, this was a powerful statement. This book helped Maud formulate her idea of female selfhood.

Maud fantasized herself as Zanoni's dream-lover, not failing him, as weak Viola does. Rather, in her dreams, she would have the strength to be the first woman to pass the "Ordeal"; she would be admitted to that select group of men living purely in the mind. She determined to choose the life of the mind over a life devoted to earthly pleasures. (These ideals were compatible with the teachings of austere Scottish Presbyterianism and other puritanical Protestant religions.)

But there was a dark side to her fascination with *Zanoni*. Maud shivered over Viola's fear of being "marked out for some strange and preternatural doom; as if I were singled out from my kind." Maud identified with this fear— she had sensed from an early age that she was somehow set apart from other children by her intelligence, her greater power of imagining and of expressing herself, and by her passionate, volatile nature. (Later in life, this motif of being "marked"—not unlike the Presbyterian concept of Predestination—would increasingly haunt her in destructive ways.)

Around her fourteenth year, Maud encountered another book that fed her adolescent fantasies: Friedrich Heinrich Karl La Motte Fouqué's *Undine* (written in 1811, translated into English in 1818). Undine is a "mer-child" exchanged at birth and raised by a human fisherman and his wife. (The idea of non-human and sexually alluring females emerging from the sea was prevalent in the oral tradition of many countries, and fed into the written literature. These beings, called "kelpies," "mermaids," and so on, reinforced the idea that females tempted males.) The little female changeling in *Undine* is a child of extraordinary beauty and charm, but she lacks, as children from the world of faerie do, a human soul. As a result, Undine is without the ability to feel emotion, which makes her capricious, unpredictable, and self-absorbed. Human men are drawn to her, not realizing that she comes from the sea. Her form is completely human (unlike Hans Christian Andersen's little mermaid, who is part fish). Undine entices a knight to marry her in order to gain a soul. It is a magic and happy transformation, achieved through love. Maud loved this book, with its romanticized ending (much happier than *Zanoni's*).

The dualistic worlds of *Pilgrim's Progress* and *Zanoni* reappear in *Undine*, and again the protagonists must combat a perilous landscape of evil to progress into a world of good (this, of course, is a very common literary structure). All three books reinforce the idea that there are two kinds of time (eternal time and human time) and two modes of human existence (spiritual and material). In different ways, they all depict the world as a struggle between Good and Evil. And in each, women are the weaker sex. But in *Undine* there is more potential for women: given the chance to acquire a soul, a female can become powerful and good. Maud liked this message.

Her imagination was greatly inspired by these stories, with their mystic worlds, ethereal creatures, and dream visions. This imaginative realm, reinforced no doubt by the otherworldly look of her native landscape in a rolling fog, could feel as real as the world she actually lived in. Later, in *Anne of Green Gables*, she would depict in comic mode the interplay between the book world and the real one. Romance is destroyed by sober reality when Anne, playing Tennyson's fair lily-maid Elaine, sinks into muddy water and nearly drowns when her "bark" springs a leak.

Early flirtations and gossip

Between the ages of twelve and sixteen, Maud began to be interested in real flesh-and-blood males. She began to imagine the pleasures of love that she read about in *Zanoni* and *Undine*. She was attracted to Nate Lockhart, the Baptist minister's stepson, and the cleverest boy in the school. They competed in school and writing competitions. He had an added allure: his uncle, who went by the *nom de plume* of "Pastor Felix," was a *real* author who published sentimental verse and essays in the American periodical press. Notes passed between Maud and Nate, schoolyard tongues wagged in jealousy, and Maud kept people guessing about the state of her heart—a lifelong trait. She had learned quite early in life that it was much safer to hide her emotions, which often fluctuated to extremes.

In childhood Maud had been free to associate with friends in Cavendish, a safe, close-knit, rural community. But as she approached puberty, her grandmother could see that a budding young woman with such an impulsive temperament might make mistakes. When young girls were candidates for scandal by virtue of family history, temperament, or class, the entire community watched them carefully. A girl who got herself "talked about" compromised her chances of a decent marriage. Her misbehaviour could also lower a

The "Old Home," where Maud was raised by her maternal grandparents, Alexander and Lucy Macneill, in Cavendish, PEI.

Maud around age 12.

Maud's "Lovers' Lane" in Cavendish.

Two images of Maud's bedroom in the "Old Home."

Maud's paternal grandfather, Senator Donald Montgomery (1808–1893).

Maud's grandfather's contemporary, the thirteenth Earl of Eglinton, of Scotland.

Hugh John Montgomery, Maud's father, and his second wife, Mary Ann.

Maud's mother, Clara Macneill Montgomery.

Alexander and Lucy Woolner Macneill, Maud's maternal grandparents.

Maud's birthplace at Clifton (New London), PEI, with Dr. Stuart Macdonald, her son, taken a few weeks before his death in 1982.

Left: Professor Murray Macneill (Maud's cousin), Uncle Leander Macneill, and Grandmother Macneill and grandchild.

The home of David and Margaret Macneill, and the model for "Green Gables," in 1935.

The John Campbell home in Park Corner, PEI, home to the "merry Campbell cousins."

Maud's beloved teacher, Miss Hattie Gordon.

Maud's uncle John F. Macneill and his wife.

John A. Mustard, while he was Maud's teacher and suitor in Prince Albert, PEI.

family's standing in the community, and the Macneills had great pride of family. Maud was lively and witty, with an attractive sparkle. And although she had a petite and girlish figure, rather than the full, voluptuous one that was desirable at the time, her flirtatiousness and spunky wit drew male attention. The Macneills watched closely, prepared to clamp down if too much "hot" Montgomery blood began to appear. She had hitherto enjoyed unsupervised walks in the woods, along Lovers' Lane, and down to the shore, but as she grew older, her grandmother began to restrict her freedom of movement. A spirited young girl, Maud resisted and rebelled.

Perhaps Maud's cousin Lucy told some tales at home about Maud's behaviour with boys, but whatever Lucy may or may not have said, Maud's stubbornness, rebelliousness, and flirtations were much discussed within her clan. Her journals do not tell her grandparents' side of this story, although she admits her aunts and uncles talked about her. Some tales lingered in PEI nearly a century later suggesting that Maud had been somewhat "boy-crazy" and "high-spirited" as a young girl. Adolescents often have a difficult time controlling their impulses and emotions. Naturally, as a high-spirited girl wanting freedom to manage little flirtations, she rebelled against any restriction of her activities.

Reflecting on her adolescent years much later, Maud complained that if she slipped out for a walk in the woods her grandmother would suspect she had been out to meet a young man and would make remarks that made her "hate living" (January 2, 1905). This is bitter language. When she complains that her grandparents frowned on her interest in attending all the Baptist evening prayer meetings and community hall lectures, she makes them sound rigid and unreasonable. Maud's journals pretend to be candid in self-analysis, but she skips lightly over the taboo subject of sexual behaviour. However, on three separate occasions when she admits she was deeply attracted to certain men, she vigorously denies in each case that she gave in to her sexual impulses. The very force of her denial—probably written into her journals after 1919 when she began recopying them—suggests that she wanted to counter gossip that she feared might linger years later when she was world-famous and expected her life to be scrutinized. She alludes in her journals to future biographies.

Gossip was not just entertainment. It was a powerful form of social control when Maud was young. Gossip went from one end of the 145-mile-long Island to the other in record time, often travelling faster than people did, especially after the Island adopted the telephone that Alexander Graham Bell had patented in 1876. Men outwardly disdained gossip as a woman's vice, but women understood—as Maud did—that gossip could bring the mightiest down, men included. *"What will people say?"* was always the dreaded question. Maud's grandmother used it with her, and she would later use it repeatedly with her sons.

Female sexuality was a source of enormous anxiety in that era; indeed, all human sexuality was seen largely as a shameful, secret activity. Raising a girl like Maud would have been a nerve-wracking process in an era when a female's reputation for chastity set her social value, her marriage potential, and hence her future happiness. Relatives who resented that she was cleverer than their offspring would have been ready to chastise her behaviour with young men, especially since any indiscretion on her part would reflect poorly on the entire clan.

Fortunately, Maud's beloved teacher, Hattie Gordon, was the model of an ambitious young woman who had gained some education and was practising a profession. Like many young men, Maud wanted to take teacher's training in order to put aside enough money to finance a real university education at a school off the Island. But there was a catch: school teaching was much more poorly paid for women than for men, even when they did the identical work. Once again, she could see that her gender was a disadvantage. And anyone could point out that the women who proceeded through the Prince of Wales College to become teachers quit teaching the minute they found a husband. (In fact, teaching in a different community was often a means of obtaining a husband.)

A woman who was not lucky enough to marry stayed with her parents, or she might move in with a married sibling, where she had a very low social status and hence had to work doubly hard at domestic chores to justify her use of space. Or she could move to town and clerk in a store. A few women, like Charlottetown's talented Angie Doiron, had their own commercial shops, but this was rare. An unmarried woman could move around as a dressmaker, or could work as a maid in someone else's home, but these options were beneath Maud's social class. The Scots regarded going out "in service" as fit only for the Irish or the French Acadians. As she grew older, Maud was terrified that she would become a lonely and pitied old maid.

Yet, when Maud looked at women like her aunts and her grandmother, she could see that married women's lives were hard: the saying that "a man must work from sun to sun, but women's work is never done" was clearly true. Women's lives were given over to incessant child-bearing and work—and if they married a difficult husband, to suffering in silence unless they could "manage their man." If they could not produce children they were pitied, while today we might be more inclined to pity the fertile woman of that era. There was no effective birth control. With six to eighteen children to care for in primitive conditions, motherhood was no small task. Women frequently died in childbirth or developed medical problems from overwork or from merely giving birth to so many children.

Maud was beginning to understand her rather tenuous position within the structures of her clan and village. There was no easy escape from her position as a clever but plain young woman without an inheritance or the means to a good education. Her Uncle Leander, a minister, could have done much for her at this period. He could have invited his talented but restless niece to New Brunswick and introduced her to culture there if he thought she was getting out of hand in Cavendish. But his family visiting went in one direction only. Maud could again see that if she had been a boy, there would have been more interest in her career.

During these tumultuous years, it was Miss Gordon who helped Maud develop a belief in herself. Very soon after her arrival, Miss Gordon organized her students to give a "Literary Concert" in the Community Hall. Here Maud gave her first public recitation, "A Child Martyr." Her excellent memory made learning set pieces easy, and she knew from her grandfather how to make her voice perform. She was a big success, and this was just the first in a lifetime of public performances. Her stature in the community went up several notches. Meanwhile, Miss Gordon began to foster Maud's talent in other ways. She asked her students to work on essays for entry in the *Montreal Witness* school competition. In February 1890, Maud's essay on the wreck of the *Marco Polo* placed third in the county. As the year unfolded and Miss Gordon constantly praised her elocutionary and writing abilities, Maud began to dream of becoming an author. She believed that she could only achieve this goal through higher education. She wanted to become famous, and to prove to her clan that she was talented and worthy—even if she was only a girl.

CHAPTER 3

The ugly stepmother: Prince Albert and disillusion

During the winter of Maud's fifteenth year, the possibility of an escape from the scrutiny of her strict grandparents presented itself. It was mooted that she travel to Prince Albert, Saskatchewan, to live with her father. She felt certain that she would be happier there. It never occurred to her that her father might want her to come for any reason other than deep paternal affection.

As a senator in Ottawa, Maud's Grandfather Montgomery had access to political perks like free passes for railway travel, and he was hankering to make a trip all across the country on the newly opened transcontinental rail service. (Before the Last Spike was driven on November 7, 1885, railway lines had already branched in many directions on the prairies.) He planned to visit his son Hugh John in Prince Albert, Saskatchewan, on his way to the west coast. He could easily drop Maud off at her father's house. She would be a lively travelling companion, and the magnanimous gesture would cost him nothing.

The Macneills were willing to release Maud to her father's family, though not without mixed feelings. Despite their difficulties with their spirited granddaughter, they did care for her deeply. Moreover, they had raised her to an age at which she could now be useful. Daughters and granddaughters who stayed close to home were expected to look after their elderly parents and grandparents. Of Alexander and Lucy's children, John F. Macneill was at odds with his father, and their two living daughters were some distance away. Lucy Macneill could hardly be blamed for hoping Maud might be a source of practical help and future comfort. If she were now whisked off to the distant interior of the great continent, might she marry there, and stay? Never kindly disposed to Hugh John—especially given that he had contributed almost nothing to the costs of raising Maud — the Macneills likely felt he was now arrogating to himself the benefits of their labours. But Maud's increasingly tempestuous nature had caused enough turmoil, and her grandmother was undoubtedly weary from buffering the clashes between Maud and her grandfather.

Much had happened in Hugh John Montgomery's life since his departure from the Island. Grieving after Clara's death, he had gone first to his sister in Boston, a natural destination for many Maritimers. Then, after returning to the Island to maintain contact with his young daughter, he had left to seek opportunities in the west, like thousands of other Islanders. He worked in Winnipeg, Manitoba, and then moved to Prince Albert, Saskatchewan, a boom town, where his father's political connections helped him find a lucrative $700-a-year position as a Forest Ranger and Homestead Inspector. When he began moonlighting as an auctioneer to supplement this rich salary, his supervisor disapproved and punished him by transferring him to another town, Battleford. This was inconvenient: Hugh John had acquired a house in Prince Albert, pretentiously naming it "Eglintoun Villa" in honour of his putative connection with the Earls of Eglinton.

This house now had to be put up for rent. The entrepreneurial Hugh John rented to the Agent for Dominion Lands, a Mr. McTaggart. McTaggart's stepdaughter, Mary Ann McRae, twenty-three years old, was the niece of the railway millionaire William Mackenzie (1849–1923; knighted in 1911). Hugh John took notice. Perhaps the chemistry of his loneliness and her connections to wealth helped him see beauty in Mary Ann's slightly sour face.

Hugh John Montgomery and Mary Ann McRae were married in 1887, back at her home in Cannington, Ontario; they were fêted in Ottawa at a viceregal reception in the Senate Chamber; and they lived in Battleford for three years before moving back into "Eglintoun Villa" in Prince Albert. Hugh Montgomery resumed his auctioneering, sold life insurance, ran a conveyancing business, dabbled in real estate, and became a purchasing agent for the growing railway network of his wife's wealthy uncle, William Mackenzie. Described in the Prince Albert *Times* as a popular and buoyant character, he somehow never managed to become a man of substance.

By 1890, he and Mary Ann had a two-year-old daughter and were expecting a second child. Bringing Maud out to help his peevish wife with the work must have seemed a good idea to Hugh John (and it is doubtful that he was fully apprised of what a handful his daughter could be). Maud would gain experience in homemaking while she looked after her half-siblings, and Mary

Ann would have more time for the socializing she enjoyed. He may also have hoped that an adoring daughter in the house would offset Mary Ann's bad temper. With his little "Maudie" about, he could share tales about people on the Island.

On August 11, 1890, when Maud and her grandfather left for Saskatchewan, Senator Montgomery arranged to be taken briefly into the private railway car of Canada's prime minister, John A. Macdonald, who was just then touring the island by rail. Impressed, Maud wrote in her diary that the prime minister was a "great crony" of her Grandfather Montgomery. Maud described Sir John A. Macdonald as pleasant, "a spry-looking old man — not handsome but pleasant-faced," and his wife as "stately and imposing, with very beautiful silver hair, but not at all good looking and dressed . . . very dowdily" (August 11, 1890).

Travelling some three thousand miles in nine days, Maud rolled past the picturesque New Brunswick riverbanks, the steep, wooded hills of Maine with clusters of ragged children in the clearings, the northern wilds of Ontario (a landscape of tree stumps along the Canadian Pacific Railway tracks), the "cold Superior's rockbound shore," the monotonous prairies of Manitoba and the "desolate" city of Winnipeg, which looked "as if someone had thrown a handful of streets and houses down and forgotten to sort them out afterwards," and the Saskatchewan bleakness around Regina. The last part of the trip was in a caboose and then in a buckboard pulled by a team of horses. They arrived on August 20, and her grandfather was then ready to hail ceremoniously the first train that came through, extending the line to Prince Albert.

Prince Albert had been founded in 1866 as a Presbyterian mission but was now incorporated as a "pretty" but "straggly" town along the riverbank. It had one bank, a town hall, tailor, gunsmith, dentist, taxidermist, barber shop, millinery shop, and sash and door factory; two hotels, bakeries, drugstores, blacksmiths, photographers, jewellers, breweries, gristmills, printing offices, and doctors; three sawmills, purveyors, and butchers; four painters and law firms; five carpenter shops; and seven bricklayers and stone masons.[33] There was also a division of the North West Mounted Police, several churches, a public school, and a convent school for girls. The 1890 census reports Prince Albert as having 1,090 inhabitants; this included a visible population of natives and many "half-breeds." The Riel Rebellion of 1885, in which Maud's father claimed to have been a volunteer, had culminated in Batôche, twenty-seven miles away. Maud came to a booming, raw frontier town with a totally different character from the staid, settled, and cultured Cavendish.

But there was disappointment for Maud. Only three days after her arrival in Prince Albert, she became desperately homesick. Her homesickness was only partly for the beauty of Prince Edward Island. She had quickly taken the measure of her father's new wife. "[A]lready my eyes have been opened by several little things," she wrote in her diary. Mary Ann, pregnant and dyspeptic, insulted her husband. Maud wrote that her father "asked me to put up with some things for his sake . . . she picks and nags at him unceasingly and on some days he cannot make the simplest, most harmless remark but she snubs him. . . . For example—at dinner time today father and I were talking about Aunt Emily and Uncle John Montgomery. Father said he did not think Aunt Emily cared a great deal for Uncle John when she married him. 'Oh, I suppose you think she wanted you,' sneered Mrs. Montgomery, in her most insulting tone" (August 26, 1890).

Mary Ann clearly resented the bond between her husband and the nearly grown child of his first wife, who was starved for her father's love. By the time Grandfather Montgomery came back through from British Columbia on September 20, Maud wrote her cousin, Pensie Macneill, that she would have given anything to go home with him.

The younger McTaggart children (Mary Ann's half-siblings) apparently confided to Maud that they did not like Mary Ann either. Nor did Edie, the young girl from Battleford who had been hired to help in the house, and who was quickly dispatched back home after Maud's arrival. When Mrs. Montgomery, resenting the girls' friendship and chatter, quizzed Edie about why Maud "put her hair up" (a sign of a young woman's adulthood, and premature for a fifteen-year-old), Maud fumed in her journal: "To ask such a thing of a girl in Edie's position—household help. It has made me feel absolute contempt for her" (October 20, 1890). Maud had brought her own snobbery from her family, as well as her reading of British novels. Ironically, the easily displeased Mary Ann, who was only twenty-seven, now insisted that Hugh John quit calling his daughter "Maudie" because it was "too childish."

Hugh John, who had not seen his daughter since she was nine. He hadn't anticipated that his daughter, expecting to be the apple of his eye and craving the affection he had to parcel out to his younger family, would be seen as competition by his wife. Maud was expecting to be treated as a princess, but Mary Ann saw her as an unpaid household drudge.

Maud had looked forward to continuing her education in Prince Albert, but the school system in this raw town was far more crude than that of

Cavendish. School classes were held in a former hotel. The classroom was directly beneath a public ballroom and doubled as a ladies' dressing room on ball nights. On days following a dance, the children found hairpins, feathers, and flowers strewn on the floor. The police patrol headquarters were in the same building; drunken men and petty criminals were locked in cells adjacent to the classroom, according to Maud's journals from this period.

When Maud started school in September, there were eight boys in the class, four of them "Nitchees." This Algonkian term meant "friend" but had become derogatory slang. To keep order in class, the teacher was expected to use a five-foot rawhide whip. Recess consisted of watching people on the street: "Indians for the most part—'braves' with their dirty blankets . . . or chattering dark-eyed squaws with their glossy blue-black hair and probably a small-faced papoose strapped to the back," wrote Maud. She described the native people again in letters to Pensie, saying that there were many Indians, but they were much handsomer than the ones in PEI.[34] Another letter described how the women swaddled their infants in strips of flannel rolled tightly around the baby, then fastened the swaddled baby to their backs with a shawl.[35]

Maud's teacher was a rather handsome young man from Ontario, a graduate of the University of Toronto. Born in 1867 in Uxbridge, Ontario, John Mustard was the promising and gifted son of prominent farmers and churchmen of Scottish descent; coincidentally, he had gone to school with Mary Ann, Maud's stepmother, in Uxbridge. His position in Prince Albert had been obtained with glowing recommendations from his former professors. However, Mr. Mustard, with what Maud called his "carefully cultivated moustache," did not have the aggressive and commanding presence needed to handle the motley crew in his wild classroom. Raised by his devout Presbyterian parents to take life seriously, he was earnest about life and mild in personality. Maud commented, "Mr. Mustard is not a good teacher and the work seems to drift along without any 'go' or life in it" (Sept. 19, 1890). Letters to Pensie complain of dull lessons—drill, drill, and more drill. For a quick student like Maud, this was exceptionally boring.

John Mustard soon took more than an academic interest in his bright, vivacious new student. She had poise and excellent manners; it was clear that she came from a cultured family, like his own. He started making regular visits to chat with his old schoolmate, Mary Ann, at the Montgomery home. Maud, who would turn sixteen on November 30, was approaching a marriageable age, and she saw the motive behind his visits. Full of ambition, she did not want a serious suitor—and certainly not Mr. Mustard.

In November she secretly sent a poem on the legend of PEI's Cape Le Force to the Charlottetown *Patriot*. (This story was from her Grandfather Macneill's oral repertoire, and, given his ongoing friction with Maud, he may have been more annoyed than proud to see that his enterprising granddaughter had poached his material.) On December 7, 1890, she wrote in her journal that it had been accepted for publication:

> Well, this has really been the proudest day of my life! I *feel* at least
> three inches taller than I did yesterday. . . . Today when I came
> down, ready for Sunday School father came in with last night's
> mail and among it a *Patriot*. I seized it with a beating heart and
> trembling finger and opened it. . . . The letters danced before my
> eyes and I felt a curious sensation of choking—for there in one of
> the columns was my poem! (December 7, 1890).

And she adds: "Mrs. Montgomery looks as if she considered the whole thing a personal insult to *her* and has never mentioned the poem at all." At age sixteen, Maud saw that even a "chit" of a girl could become more powerful by taking up her pen.

With this personal success, life became more enjoyable. Mr. Mustard, the teacher and suitor, became a comic figure for her character-sketching. She encouraged him, perhaps as a cat plays with a mouse, to make good copy for her diary. By her account, Mr. Mustard's best topics of conversation were Predestination and other dry points of theology. If he thought his knowledge would impress Maud, he was wrong. She scorned the doctrine of Predestination as medieval and outdated, and she had read too widely to accept narrow dogmas. "As for me," she writes haughtily, "a million Mustards could never make me believe that God ordains any of his creatures to eternal torture for 'his own good-will and pleasure'" (April 6, 1891).

As Mr. Mustard intensified his attention, Maud found a new interest. A girl named Laura Pritchard became her best friend, and she had a brother named Will. Will had red hair, green eyes, and a crooked smile; he was relaxed, unpretentious, and funny. Maud had always been drawn to people with a sense of humour, like her Campbell cousins. Laura was equally fun-loving.

The Pritchards had a large farm outside of town, but they stayed in town during the harsh winter. Laura attended a different school (the convent school) but they became fast friends anyway.

Maud's easygoing repartee with her young friends may have annoyed Mr. Mustard. When Mr. Mustard spoke to her about her "haughty manner" of speaking back to him, she retaliated by giving him her excessively formal treatment: "I froze up and was as chilly as an iceberg to him all afternoon, while taking particular care to keep all the rules. I can tell you he found me 'haughty' with a vengeance!" she wrote in her journal (January 7, 1891).

In early 1891, Maud's father inexplicably jumped from the Conservative Party of his father's politics to the Liberal ticket, and ran for federal parliament. He lost his election bid, and she was heartily glad when the worry and excitement was over. The fact that Mrs. Montgomery had given birth in February to a colicky baby, Donald Bruce, who required constant walking, added to the general turmoil in the household.

Hugh John hired a new "servant girl" in March (a "breed," Maud notes, reflecting the attitudes of her era). Maud's stepmother gave this girl Maud's room, putting Maud in the spare room. The hired girl left in a few days, complaining that Mrs. Montgomery was too cross. Not a gracious personality at the best of times, Mrs. Montgomery was also contending with a new baby, a child of two, a husband who was humiliated in his public defeat, and a resentful stepdaughter all under the same roof.

Maud then had to leave school to attend to the housework. She enshrined herself in her diary as a long-suffering victim. "I do not say a word, however, because it would make father feel so bad" (March 28, 1891). By this time, it was painfully evident that her father's life did not revolve around her. By the end of April, she had missed two months of school to help out at home, a source of tremendous frustration and resentment. In her regular letters to Pensie, not once does she mention her father, except to comment that he is out or away.

With all these tensions, Maud began having the headaches—as though a tight band were constricting around her head—that were to plague her for the rest of her life. She also began the lifelong pattern of confiding to her journal that writing in it was the only comfort she had.

Even though she was no longer at school, she remained busy in the community: church and school concerts, Sunday school (which she taught), recitations (the local paper raved about her ability in elocution), and "frolics" such as tobogganing parties. These events were described in letters to Pensie;

her grandparents probably heard everything she wrote second-hand. She went about, unsupervised and unchaperoned, on picnics and excursions, on drives in the country, and to dances in the nearby army barracks. Her grandparents would have been appalled that her father was exerting no supervision to protect her reputation, if not her virtue.

Yet, with all this freedom, Maud was not happy. In every letter she wrote home to Pensie, she complained about Prince Albert and described her longing for Cavendish. She had come west in 1890 hoping finally to find a happy home, with her father. Her jealous and pettish stepmother was eager to see the end of resentful young Maud, and Hugh John agreed that she would return to the Island.

Her grandparents in Cavendish must have thought she would at least be cured of her idolatry of her father. But Maud never acknowledged — either during or long after her trip to Prince Albert — that her father was weak and rather less than successful as a parent. Like Maud herself, Hugh John was presented as being constantly victimized by his wife. We will never know for sure if Mary Ann was as nasty as Maud made her, but as a literary creation, she is expertly pinned to the pages of Maud's journal as the archetypal specimen of the wicked stepmother.

Maud's writing was progressing splendidly. Her descriptive piece on Prince Albert, focusing in part on the native people, was published on June 18 by the *Prince Albert Times and Saskatchewan Review*. By age sixteen she was already a skilled writer, able to write to Pensie, her chum back home, in a naïve, simple style, yet easily able to elevate her tone for her newspaper audience:

> The river is a sheet of silver . . . and on the opposite side the poplars sway eerily in the gathering gloom — all so weird and mysterious that one half expects to see a dusky warrior, clad in all his ancient panoply of war-paint and feathers, spring from their shadows. . . . [W]e look at the poor Indian now, clad in ragged garments . . . with a dirty blanket flung over his shoulder, as he shuffles through the busy streets . . .[36]

The piece drew great praise from her father and everyone else — except, of course, from Mary Ann, who was counting the days until Maud's departure.

For her own part, Maud could not wait to see the seashore, her "dear room," Lovers' Lane, the mackerel skies, the green fields—all now vested with romance and nostalgia. Better to be with strict grandparents who cared for her than with a father who was too busy for her and a stepmother who was truly hateful.

Her imminent departure forced Mr. Mustard's hand; she puns in her journal that "Mustard actually *mustered*—oh, forgive the pun. It just *made itself*—up enough courage to put his fate to the test . . ." Maud's journals record that he stammered out,

> "Do you think, Miss Montgomery, that our friendship will ever develop into *anything else?*"
>
> And his look and tone plainly revealed what he meant by "anything else."
>
> "I don't see what it *can* develop into, Mr. Mustard." (July 1, 1891)

And that romance was over. John Mustard was not to disappear from her life, however.

The year had been a great disillusionment. But it provided fodder for fiction. Her sense of exploitation would be used in her later writing, most notably in *Anne of Green Gables:* Anne similarly encounters selfish people who want her as a servant. Maud's experience with colicky baby Bruce would also be echoed when Anne saves a child. Her father may have served as partial model for the lovable and henpecked Matthew Cuthbert, afraid to talk back to his forceful sister Marilla. Maud had learned from her stepmother how to drop poisonous innuendoes. This, too, she added to her fictional arsenal.

Maud's father's weakness had inflicted the pain on her that most of her future literary heroines were to suffer from—a father's absence or death. Maud claimed that her father fought back tears when she left Prince Albert—tears that she was sure reflected his love for her. But in reality she had lived under his roof for a year and had been disappointed many times over.

More shockingly, Hugh John allowed his sixteen-year-old daughter to travel across the continent without the protection of a chaperone. Respectable young women simply did not make such long journeys alone. An unaccompanied woman was at risk, both to her person and to her reputation, and one so young was particularly vulnerable. Maud's unchaperoned return was an extraordinary breach of custom and propriety. Worse, it was downright unsafe.

Maud had to change trains at Regina and Winnipeg and to disembark at Fort William, find overnight accommodation on her own, and then catch a morning boat to Sault Ste. Marie, going through locks on the canal, and travel down the St. Mary River to Lake Huron. At Owen Sound, Ontario, on Georgian Bay, she caught a train for Toronto, transferred to another train to Smith's Falls, and yet another on the short run to Ottawa. She spent overnights in rough little junctions along the way, in rowdy hotels with saloons that served the local brew to those who wanted relief from hard work, the bush, and the boredom of life in a primitive area. The disembarking of an unattended young female would have caught the eye of every sex-starved logger, unattached local, and drunken barfly. Maud was small, slight, and by now more shapely. No decent father would have allowed his sixteen-year-old daughter to make such a trip alone in that era. Why Hugh John permitted it, and why Senator Montgomery sanctioned it, defies understanding. If Maud felt hurt by the lapse in protocol, she did not say so. Given the mores of the time, however, she must have noticed the lack of concern, whether she could admit it or not. It was only another sign that she was not very much valued.

In Toronto, Maud called on the family of the wealthy William Mackenzie, Mary Ann's uncle. No one had bothered to tell the Mackenzies that she might come, apparently; they were away, and she spent her five-hour wait between trains with the governess. When she arrived in Ottawa at five in the morning, her Grandfather Montgomery was not there to meet her: he had overslept. She took a streetcar to his hotel, only to find that by then he had gone to meet her. "He soon came back in a great flurry, bless his dear old heart, but calmed down when he saw me safe and sound." One puzzles to think what danger he expected her to face at five in the morning in Ottawa that she might not have met some night in a rough hotel on her trip home.

After whisking her through the Parliament Buildings, the Library, and showing her a session of the Senate (where she found the debate on the 1890 census dull), Grandfather Montgomery dispatched her to Prince Edward Island. She had hoped to stay longer with him, and see more of Ottawa, but a sharp-eyed granddaughter underfoot apparently did not suit either his schedule or his lifestyle. Travelling this time with proper chaperones, she took the famous "Intercolonial" train through Montreal, Quebec City, and New Brunswick. She caught the train ferry and arrived at Summerside, PEI, mid-afternoon on September 5, 1891. Again, no one was there to meet her, and here her journal mentions surprise: "It *did* seem a rather chilly home-coming for there was not a face in all the crowd that I knew. Never mind—it was home and that was enough."

After two hours waiting in the station, she took another brief train ride to the Kensington station; again, no one was there to meet her. Postal service in that era was both fast and reliable, and it is improbable that no one knew she was coming. Was her Grandfather Macneill vexed with her? Did no one care about her?

Maud's independent spirit asserted itself. In spite of her year of desperate homesickness for Cavendish, she now hired a wagon team to take her to Park Corner, where she always felt welcome, important, and valued. She stayed three days with Aunt Annie and her Campbell cousins rather than returning to her grandparents' house. The laughter at the Campbell house always helped cure bruised feelings. Perhaps she was also making a point with her Macneill grandparents: she was now a much freer agent, a young woman who made her own decisions.

She was ecstatic when she finally reached Cavendish. The description of her drive from Park Corner to Cavendish sounds like a model for Anne of Green Gables' first entrance into Avonlea: "my excitement increased all the rest of the way as I gazed my eyes out at all the familiar spots until Uncle Crosby must have thought he had a crazy girl on his hands" (September 8, 1891).

It was, in the end, a joyous homecoming for a prodigal granddaughter. She came back with new status: as a girl who had travelled halfway across the continent in an era when many Islanders rarely travelled more than thirty miles from their birthplace. And even more important, she was now a writer who had published in papers in Prince Edward Island and the west. Her year had confirmed her goal of becoming a writer. She knew in her heart she could never count on her father, *ever*, although she always spoke of their undying affection for each other. She would either have to marry or make her own way in life. These were sobering realizations. She was now determined to get the education that she believed she needed to develop her writing talent.

Prince of Wales College and after (1892–1895)

Maud's tight-fisted Grandfather Macneill had no intention of wasting money on further education for her. For one thing, he disapproved of "lady-teachers."

Also, it was generally accepted that women taught only until they married, so educating a young woman was a waste of money. Alexander Macneill had already tied up some of his cash reserves in providing a mortgage for the faltering farm of his daughter Annie's husband, John Campbell, a lovable man who managed money poorly. And he would not be able to rely on his estranged son, John F., to look after him, either. In that era there was no social safety net: the records of Legislative Acts in Charlottetown authorized some relief money for destitute people, usually widows with young children, but this was rare. Churches and neighbours helped those who fell on hard times, but basically people had to look after themselves. Alexander Macneill knew it was prudent to hang on to his remaining cash reserves.

Maud's aunts and uncles were not keen to see money spent on her, either. Alexander and Lucy had not educated their own daughters, so why should they educate a granddaughter? Money spent on Maud would be money others would not inherit. A year at Prince of Wales College in Charlottetown would cost seven dollars for rural students, and room and board would have to be added to that. (A teacher at that time was paid about thirty dollars a term.) And many people still believed that too much education was dangerous for women. The Charlottetown papers carried regular advertisements for patent medicines like Lydia Pinkham's vegetable compound, which ensured that "the young girl is safe from the dangers of school years and prepared for a hearty womanhood." These advertisements were placed cheek-by-jowl with news items on the front page. Because the format was no different, the ads looked like hard news.[37]

Maud saw that her only hope lay in getting help from her grandmother. In the fall of 1891, she mapped out her own course of independent study to prepare for the entrance exams to the college, while remaining informally involved with the Cavendish school, helping with concerts and giving public recitations. She stayed in Cavendish until February, studying hard. On February 13, 1892, her grandmother went up to Park Corner for a visit—a sudden trip for a woman who almost never left home. Three days later, Maud found herself installed at her Aunt Annie's house, hired to give a quarter-year's worth of music lessons to the Campbell children. What was behind all this? Was it necessary to separate Maud and her grandfather again? Or had Lucy arranged a way for Maud to earn money that would not antagonize her grandfather? It would not be surprising if Lucy Macneill had slipped her daughter Annie the money to pay Maud. Lucy was always practical: she had already paid to give Maud organ lessons, and now the benefits of those music lessons could be passed along to her other grandchildren at Park Corner, who were genuinely musical.

Whisked away from Cavendish, Maud spent three intensely happy months in the household of the "merry" Campbell cousins, all younger. In Uncle John at fifty-nine, Aunt Annie at forty-four, and the cousins, ages fifteen, thirteen, eleven, and nine, Maud gained the model for a happy family. Aunt Annie was a warm, affectionate woman who loved her sister Clara's daughter, even though she disapproved of Maud's preference for "scribbling" over housework. Across the road lived Grandfather Montgomery (then eighty-four, in the last year of his life) and his second wife, Louisa (age seventy-one). And there were more Montgomery cousins and relatives who lived in the surrounding area: Jim and Lewis McIntyre; Jim, Louise, and Russell Crosby; and Will Sutherland. There were also outings to visit Aunt Emily and Uncle John Montgomery in Malpeque. During this visit, she met another cousin, Edwin Simpson of Belmont.

Maud's diary descriptions of the "young fry's" junkets are vivid social history. They show the problems of mobility in pre-macadam and pre-automobile days. Rain made the red soil on the Island turn greasy—not just muddy, but as slippery as axle-grease. In the dark, the landmarks vanished. In winter, the snow-covered dirt road itself vanished, and veering off the road at night was an ever-present danger. It was possible to unwittingly stray onto the snow-covered bay where the ice could plunge horse, sleigh, and occupants to an icy death in the sea. In a field, stumps might break sleigh-runners, leaving one stranded in sub-zero temperatures. If a horse broke through deep-crusted snow or ice, it could flounder and get stuck. Uneven terrain could tip the sleigh and its occupants into drifts. Smash-ups could be fatal.

Attending family festivals and several marriages, Maud became better acquainted with the Montgomery clan. It was, overall, a happy visit, which cemented a lifetime of close connections with Aunt Annie Campbell's clan. On June 8, she went reluctantly home to Cavendish.

Fame was beginning to reach Maud in small ways. In the summer of 1892 she learned that the lieutenant-governor of the Northwest Territories had admired her newspaper piece on Saskatchewan and had asked her Grandfather Montgomery for her photograph and anything else she had written since. If she hoped that this recognition might persuade her well-to-do Grandfather Montgomery to help fund her further education, however, she was wrong.

Nate Lockhart, her old chum (and, for a time, a childhood boyfriend), came home from Acadia University for a brief period, but he remained strangely and disturbingly aloof. Miss Hattie Gordon, beloved teacher and friend—and the only person in Cavendish sympathetic to Maud's ambitions to become a writer—left Cavendish for Oregon, the home of her parents. Murray Macneill, son of Uncle Leander, came over again for a summer vacation, irritating Maud with his supercilious attitude. More to her liking was a visit from her old chums Wellington and Dave Nelson, not seen since they'd left her grandparents' home after boarding with the Macneills. Following their visit, she wrote a long entry in her journal, which dipped back to the many happy hours they shared, and concluded: " . . . one day the boys went away suddenly for good and all. But youth forgets speedily."[38]

Behind the scenes, Maud's grandmother wrote the negligent Hugh John again and asked him to contribute some money towards Maud's education, but he was little help. At last, Grandmother promised the balance for Maud's education herself. Maud could now take the entrance exams for Prince of Wales College. She was thrilled.

She had missed much of her year in Prince Albert when she had been kept at home by her stepmother. As a result, she needed another year of preparation. She was once again anchored in the structured life provided by her grandmother's steady routine and temperament. Maud studied, she read every book in the Cavendish lending library, and she practised her writing continuously (producing poetry, literary sketches, and journal entries). At school, she tangled with a red-haired classmate, Austin Laird, and teasingly wrote a poem about "The Boy with the Auburn Hair." He sulked; after two months, his dignity still prevented him from addressing Maud directly. This tiff may be the model for Anne and Gilbert's feud in *Anne of Green Gables*, a decade later.

Nate Lockhart, home again in June 1893 to visit, informed Maud condescendingly that she "had a fair intellect" and if she could take a college course, she "might attain to some success in the world of letters." The comment rankled, and years later, when she was world-famous, she noted smugly that Nate had become an "obscure" lawyer on the prairies.

The month of June also brought a letter from Mr. Mustard, her former teacher in Prince Albert. Now a fledgling minister in Ontario, he wrote that he was "seriously thinking of retiring and becoming a sort of college recluse and celibate" (June 8, 1893). She wrote tartly in her journal that it would be no great loss to the world if he did retire from it. But to him she wrote a polite response. Already her public utterances were very different from her private musings. (The newly minted Reverend John Mustard gave up his hopes of marrying Maud, as well as his notions of celibacy: in 1896 he married Catherine Agnes McFarlane of Thamesville, Ontario, beginning a long and happy married life.)

Maud went to Charlottetown in July 1893 to write her week-long entrance exams. Two weeks later, she learned that she had ranked fifth out of two hundred and sixty-four candidates. Students' grades and test scores were always printed in the newspapers, which made for a competitive climate. How other people's children performed was a subject of endless gossip, and those who did poorly were publicly embarrassed, as were their families. Maud did not say if either grandfather was impressed, but there was no offer of financial help.

A month later, Maud learned that Grandfather Montgomery had died. She wrote no sad effusions in her journal. It had taken three days for the news to reach her, and she did not attend the funeral, held at Park Corner some thirteen miles away. But the rest of the Island paid homage. The Charlottetown *Examiner* of August 1, 1893, praised him and summarized his distinguished career.[39]

Bypassing Hugh John, the Senator left his 275 acres of prime farm land to his youngest son, James, with the provision of a portion of the property to the late Cuthbert's son, and, in the event that son should die, to Hugh John's son, Donald Bruce, the colicky baby Maud had helped pacify in Prince Albert. Although Maud was older than Bruce, she was a *female* grandchild and thus not in line for any inheritance. Her grandfather gave no thought to the talented and ambitious granddaughter who needed his help the most, although he himself had basked in public recognition of her talents.[40]

Maud knew that the Macneill farm would be willed to her Uncle John F. Macneill, despite the bad blood between father and son. Her own father had a new family to look after, so she would not get much, if anything, from him. She would be on her own financially. Unless she succeeded in her studies at Prince of Wales College and worked as a teacher to maintain herself until she was established as a writer, she faced a bleak future.

On September 4, Maud travelled to Charlottetown to begin her studies. Interestingly, it was her grandmother—not her grandfather—who drove her the distance of twenty-five miles over dirt roads. Almost as soon as she arrived, poetry began welling up in Maud. She submitted a poem, "The Violet's

Spell," to *The Ladies' World* in New York; it was accepted for publication some two weeks later, and she received two subscriptions to the magazine in payment.

Maud arranged lodging at a boarding house at 187 Fitzroy Street. Her roommate there was Mary Campbell of Darlington, PEI, and they would remain lifelong friends. Other roomers included a quarrelsome wife and her oft-drunken husband—again, good copy for the journal. Boiled mutton was served day after day, and the kitchen and food were unsanitary. The landlady, Mrs. MacMillan, skimped on heating oil and the house was often below freezing. But Maud and Mary Campbell and their many friends—most notably her tall, handsome Sutherland cousins—kept busy with fun and work. They enjoyed extracurricular activities, in addition to other diversions: the opera, boating trips, and public lectures (notably the preaching of the evangelist B. Faye Mills, who drew 2,700 people under one roof with a lecture on the importance of people recognizing their emotions). Another friend, Ida, "got converted" at the church revival meeting, but Mary Campbell was restrained from coming out by fear of what Maud herself calls her "sarcastic tongue and unfailing and unsparing raillery" (May 6, 1894).

Maud studied English, French, Greek, Latin, Agriculture, Mathematics, Geometry, Algebra, Trigonometry, Chemistry, Horticulture, Roman History, Hygiene, and School Management—a double load, so that she actually completed two years of college in one. Her favourite teacher, Professor Caven, a "whiskery" and "tobacco-y" old man, praised her writing and gave her public "puffs" about it. (He may have been the eventual model for the likeable Mr. Carpenter in *Emily of New Moon*.) Conditions for studying in the MacMillan boarding house were trying, and the succession of fun-loving friends was a distraction, but Maud's excellent memory served her well for exams, in December and again in May. With a little cramming, she ranked sixth out of one hundred and twenty students in her finals, despite the fact she'd taken on double the usual number of courses. Forty-nine students failed.

Maud did so well that she was selected to speak at graduation. She gave a sensation-making speech on Portia in Shakespeare's *The Merchant of Venice*. The Charlottetown papers printed it prominently, giving secondary billing to the class valedictorian and to the adult speakers, including the premier and lieutenant-governor of the province. One newspaper article said that Maud's splendid address:

was a character study such as might have come from the pen of George Eliot in her teens. . . . It was not only a subtle literary study; it was a literary gem. . . . In phrases of almost perfect art, Miss Montgomery praised the beauty of the Portian type of heart and mind and soul. Especially heart; for that was where the humanity lay, was it not? . . . To say that Miss Montgomery in this analysis did justice to Portia's intellectual worth may seem a strong statement and undue praise, but it is a simple truth.[41]

In her writing, Maud was focusing on the role of "heart" and emotions in human behaviour. The tenets of the Scottish Enlightenment of the eighteenth century had travelled with Scottish emigrants, stressing the importance of man's reason over his other faculties, including his emotions. The Presbyterian intellectual inheritance also emphasized the use of learning to bolster reason and good sense. Maud was a keen observer of human nature, as well as a reader of the English romantic poets, and she could already see how the mind very often chose and justified what the heart had already dictated.

Maud's Macneill grandparents did not attend her graduation; her achievements during this year did not change her grandfather's opposition to her obtaining a teaching licence. She passed her License Exams, gaining a First-Class Certificate. When it was time to return to Cavendish, again it was her grandmother who drove in alone to bring her and her trunk back.

Her cousin Jack Sutherland, who had squired (and kissed) her through the later part of the year, simply disappeared when the year was over. She was disappointed. Marriage between cousins was common but Maud herself had seen the bad effects of intermarriage in Cavendish, where there was, as Aunt Mary Lawson put it, "too much of one breed" in many families. She also consoled herself with the knowledge that if she wanted to pursue a writing career, marriage would have to wait. She had seen enough babies in Malpeque and Prince Albert to know how much time they required.

Maud had a difficult time obtaining a teaching position. Many graduates had been able to afford a three-year course at Prince of Wales College, while she had been there for only one year (albeit doing two years of work in that time). Positions were scarce, in spite of the fact that young men often taught only long enough to fund a university education off the Island.

A letter might procure an interview for a teaching job, but the trustees insisted on meeting the candidate before hiring. And this was a problem: Maud's intransigent grandfather refused even to lend her the horse and buggy to attend interviews. The trains did not go into remote rural areas, so if the male head of the household refused access to the family carriage, the women were effectively grounded. Because she could not get to interviews at better schools, the only school available was at Bideford, a North Shore community of farming and fisher-folk with a local shipbuilding business. The pay in this rural school was poor for the work involved. Maud received thirty dollars for her first term, and approximately forty-five dollars for the next quarters.

On July 19, 1894, at the age of nineteen, Maud began teaching in Bideford. The school was a short walk from the Methodist parsonage, where she arranged to board. The barn-like one-room school was "bleakly situated on a very bare-looking hill." The previous teacher had been a disaster, and students had quit attending. Maud began the year with twenty children in the class, ranging from six to thirteen years of age. But as her reputation for good teaching spread, the twenty students increased to forty-eight by October, eventually peaking at sixty. One girl began studying for entrance to Prince of Wales College. This gave Maud the extra burden of teaching at a level near her own. Many of the boys now coming to school were bigger than their diminutive teacher. A few were fully grown young men who had quit because they had not been learning under the previous teacher. Maud had to work extra hard so that the students could catch up by the next time the inspectors came around. She complained that the trustees in this district were "skinflints"; she had to use some of her money for school supplies.[42]

At school she was responsible for starting the stove fire each morning, stoking it all day, and putting it out at night. She also had to keep the classroom clean and neat, ordering and maintaining all supplies, teaching all students in the one room all day long with no relief. Some students came from civilized and orderly homes, but others were from rough backgrounds. She also had mentally challenged students. When she wanted students to learn a dialogue for a concert, she had to spend the evening copying it out by hand.

Maud taught well, used her quick verbal skills and her sense of humour to keep order, and she soon became popular with her students. But it was truly hard work. In the long evenings, preparing classes, grading papers, and making copies of materials in her drafty boarding house, using a candle or kerosene lamp, was a miserably cold business. More than once, Maud arose to find the water in her washbasin and jug frozen. In those days, before bathrooms and running water, the simple matter of keeping one's person clean was hard work.

The bright spot in Maud's life was her room in the manse. The manse was a large house, and her landlady, Mrs. Estey, gave her young boarder a large room—drafty, to be sure, but with a commanding view of the ocean bay. Mrs. Estey was a good-natured and lively woman who was happy for the companionship. Maud liked her, and her little daughter, Maudie, very much. The Reverend Mr. Estey was less congenial: he was insensitive and authoritarian, too much like her grandfather. He often asked her to fill in as organist in his church. Given her mediocre musical skills, she disliked playing in public. Furthermore, when she did help, she could not attend her own Presbyterian church at Tyne Valley. Mr. Estey took her for granted and was not obliging in return—for him, a woman's wishes meant little.

Maud presented a courageous face to the world. After her first visit home in October, she wrote two accounts of her homesickness, one in a letter to Pensie on October 28, 1894, the other in a journal entry of October 27, 1894. The stylistic differences between the two passages again reflect how she adapted her tone to her audience. To Pensie she wrote in a childish way, so that her friend, who lacked Maud's ease with words, would feel comfortable writing back.

Leaving her home in Cavendish always brought on homesickness, making Maud vulnerable to fits of tears. She fought hard to maintain her psychological equilibrium, helped by an extraordinary ability to focus her mind on the task at hand, whether it was teaching, reading, or writing. In particular, writing helped to manage her moods. As Maud matured, she began to suffer more intensely from mood swings. Every emotion—pain or pleasure—was experienced with a fierce intensity, sometimes resulting in volatile, impulsive behaviour.[43] Alternations between emotional lows and highs affected her outlook on the world, sometimes making her see it as clouded and dark, and other times as rosy and bright. All too often, the clouds began to block out the sunshine. During her Bideford years, she began to be more analytical about herself. She also began to suffer more from these mood swings, which would trouble her greatly throughout her later life.

Soon after she arrived, the local Ellerslie paper noted: "Miss M. Montgomery is proving herself a good teacher." A little later the Bideford notes read: "Our school is doing grand work under the guiding hand of Miss Lucy

M. Montgomery, who although only a few weeks in charge, is fast becoming popular with both scholars and ratepayers." Newspaper puffs talked about her elocution skills when she was called on to perform in nearby communities. Her presence made any gathering an "event." When a Montgomery relative in a nearby community was installed as a Mason, the newspaper account cited the many recitations and songs, and noted, "Where all did [go] so well, it may seem invidious to particularize, but the recitations given by Miss Montgomery, teacher at Bideford, were so well rendered as to deserve special mention."

There were constant rounds of social activities: church functions, private parties, Sewing Circle meetings and bazaars, magic-lantern shows, dances, and private "suppers," where she was invited to recite. She needed transportation to these events, and the young man who drove Maud around most of this year was Lou Dystant. "[H]e does very well for somebody to drive me about" (November 13, 1894), she wrote dismissively. Lou, skimming over the brilliant snow, warmly wrapped, with cutter and horse, hoped for romance with Maud, not just friendship. Maud had no interest in marriage to a commonplace young man, and she tried to keep these friendships platonic. Her lively personality brought her unsuitable suitors who were dismissed.

During her winter at Bideford, she made trips across the frozen bay to Malpeque to visit her Aunt Emily and Uncle John Montgomery. Maud was very fond of her uncle for his warmth, kindness, and soft-spoken manner—and especially for his sense of humour, a welcome relief after her Grandfather Macneill's sharp and hurtful wit. However, this beloved uncle, stricken suddenly, in the prime of life with a brain tumour, died in February 1895. When the news was telephoned (the earliest mention of a telephone in Maud's journals) she was profoundly saddened. One newspaper stated that there were over one hundred sleighs in the funeral procession. Eulogies praised her uncle, John Malcolm Montgomery, who had been the local representative in the provincial legislature for four years, as an exceptional man: "He would not stoop to promote party purposes when he felt his party was in the wrong." This was fine praise in the politicized atmosphere of Prince Edward Island. Maud nowhere comments on the tragedy of his death to her Aunt Emily, who at thirty-nine, after only thirteen years of marriage, was widowed with five children to raise by herself.

An event farther away, but also with great impact, was the engagement of Laura Pritchard, her friend from Prince Albert. Other lives were moving ahead; Maud was unwilling at this point in her life to follow Laura's course of action, marrying a kindly but undistinguished and dull man because he was the best available.

In early 1895, the *Toronto Ladies' Journal* accepted her poem "On the Gulf Shore" and sent her a subscription. Elated, she redoubled her efforts at writing. By this time she thought she might achieve modest success by writing out of her own experience, but she hardly expected to rival great female English writers like George Eliot or Charlotte Brontë. Although the sharp Macneill wit and the determined Woolner grit might have been unpleasant to live with in aging grandparents, those qualities would become increasingly useful to her.

After a whirlwind year, Maud had saved almost $100 from her salary of $180, in spite of paying board (unlike many other young teachers who managed to teach in their own home districts and thus save extra money). But her $100 was not enough to finance a year at university. She would need to teach for a second year. She thought bitterly of Murray Macneill, younger than she and also very gifted, whose father happily funded all his education costs not covered by scholarships (and ministers' sons had much support). Perhaps her grandmother was thinking about the same inequities. In the summer of 1895, she offered to add $80 to Maud's $100. Grandmother's contribution was a considerable outlay for a seventy-one-year-old woman from a farm community where cash was scarce, but her grandmother had some of her own money from taking in boarders. She would help her granddaughter because Hugh John either would or could not.

Nothing in Lucy Macneill's experience would have led her to believe that throwing scarce dollars into further education for a young woman was a good investment. Yet, despite her husband's disapproval, she asserted herself this way. Strangely, Maud does no more than mention her grandmother's contribution in her journal. She merely complains that her grandmother did not understand *why* she wanted university training so badly.

On Maud's last day at the Bideford school, the traditional public exam went off very well; following the well-attended final program, the pupils presented their "Dear and Respected Teacher" with an address and a little silver and celluloid jewel box. All the girls cried. Maud returned to Cavendish until it was time to depart for Dalhousie University. On September 16, 1895, it was her grandmother who again drove Maud across the Island to catch the ferry to Pictou Harbour, Nova Scotia.

CHAPTER 4

Climbing the Alpine Path

As her aging grandmother returned to Cavendish alone, twenty-year-old Maud spent a merry last evening in Charlottetown, entertaining three young men: Lou Dystant, from Bideford; Norman Campbell, brother of her former roommate, Mary; and John (Jack) Sutherland, cousin and sometime escort from college days. The next morning Maud took the boat for her new adventure at the university. Her journal entry for this year begins in big, bold caps: "HALIFAX SEPT. 17, 1895."

Dalhousie University was located in a beautiful old city, founded in 1749. Halifax, Nova Scotia, boasted one of the largest harbours in the world, with both commercial and cultural connections to the British Isles, Europe, the West Indies and the United States. Stately buildings recalled its 150-year history, and its frequent fogs gave it the otherworldly mystery that had charmed Maud in Cavendish.

Dalhousie, modelled on the University of Edinburgh, was a progressive school that advertised itself with pictures captioned, "Dalhousie College, Halifax, The Doors of Which Are Wide Open to Women." The debate over women and higher education continued to rage in the United States and Canada, but, in spite of public prejudice, Dalhousie was taking a firm stand. The Maritimes in general had high female literacy: in the 1891 census, Prince Edward Island had a 91 percent literacy rate for young women under nineteen, with Nova Scotia and New Brunswick at 90 and 85 percent respectively.[44]

Some young women went to college to prepare themselves to become cultured wives of successful men. Maud's friend Edith England of Bideford had enrolled at Sackville College (later Mount Allison University) to study music and painting. Maud wrote condescendingly about Edith: "She has been a petted only child, surrounded by luxury all her life" (September 25, 1895). Edith, with no real aspirations, was being given an education, with no effort to earn it; Maud had worked exceedingly hard for every inch of advancement. Her goals were far more than marriage: she wanted to write "a woman's humble name" in the halls of fame.

Maud moved into the dormitory of Halifax Ladies' College, which offered young women a solid training course in secretarial and domestic arts. There the Ladies' College "girls" and the Dalhousie women students were well chaperoned by imposing women who brooked no nonsense. Maud wrote about the principal: "Nature must have meant Miss Ker for a man and got the labels mixed . . . She is guiltless of corsets and her dress is in strict conformity with the rules of hygiene and ugliness. Her iron-gray hair is always worn in a lopsided coronet and she possesses a decided moustache. She is a 'Girton' product and no doubt very clever. But she has not one ounce of charm or magnetism" (December 24, 1895).[45] Another matron, Miss Claxton, Maud describes as "a fussy, nervous little old maid, with a hooked nose, an inquisitive expression and a thin rattling little laugh that sets my nerves on edge."

Young women like Maud saw few appealing female models in the world of educated women. The examples of Miss Ker and Miss Claxton seemed to support the widely held scientific belief that studying made women either "mannish" or pathetic old maids. Still, Maud was not dissuaded from her desire for education.

Ten days after arriving in Halifax, Maud took a biography of George Eliot (Mary Ann Evans) out of the library. Two biographies of Eliot had come out in the previous decade: Mathilde Blind's in 1883 and J. W. Cross's in 1885. The first was a biography by a leading British feminist writer, and had been reprinted in numerous editions. Many of the words, phrases, and patterns in the Mathilde Blind book appear later in Maud's journals. Blind describes qualities in Eliot that Maud later finds in herself.

Blind's biography begins with an introduction that gives straightforward advice to women authors, presumably inexperienced young ones. Blind quotes George Eliot as saying that the women of France have had an unusually vital influence on the development of literature: "For in France alone the mind of woman has passed, like an electric current, through the language, making crisp and definite what is elsewhere heavy and blurred." Frenchwomen had "the courage of their sex":

They thought and felt as women, and when they wrote, their books became the fullest expression of their womanhood. By being true to themselves, by only seeking inspiration from their own life-experiences, instead of servilely copying that of men, their letters and memoirs, their novels and pictures, have a distinct, nay unique, value for the student of art and literature. Englishwomen, on the other hand, have not allowed free play to the peculiarly feminine element, preferring to mould their intellectual products on the masculine pattern, creating absurd exaggeration of the masculine style, like the swaggering gait of a bad actress in male attire.[46]

Blind uses the term "The Alpine Path" to describe the difficult course that women writers must follow if they are to achieve, like George Eliot, their highest potential. Years later "L. M. Montgomery" would use the phrase as title for an autobiographical essay, attributing the term "The Alpine Path" to a poem entitled "The Fringed Gentian," which she found in *Godey's Ladies' Book*, pasted in her scrapbook, and later copied into her journals on several occasions (October 21, 1916; January 5, 1917; November 22, 1926). The poem concludes:

> Then whisper, blossom, in thy sleep
> How I may upward climb
> The Alpine Path, so hard, so steep
> That leads to heights sublime,
> How I may reach the far-off goal
> Of true and honoured fame
> And write upon its shining scroll
> A woman's humble name.

Blind's 1883 biography may have been the source for the phrase "The Alpine Path," both for Maud and the poem's author. The metaphor of a difficult journey in the quest for success recurs in her writing; for example, "Emily of New Moon" also talks about "the alpine path."

For more formal education, Maud enrolled in Latin, French, German, Roman History, and both first- and second-year English at Dalhousie, and for Shorthand at the Halifax Ladies' College. Of her professors, Dr. Archibald

MacMechan was the most influential. An encouraging and concerned teacher, he had been trained at the University of Toronto and at Johns Hopkins University. He was a scholar with wide abilities: he published poetry, essays, scholarly editions, and critical studies. He was a pioneer in the field of Canadian Literature, and his *Head-Waters of Canadian Literature* (1924) remains an important milestone in the development of Canadian criticism. He argued that Canada should move beyond the colonial mould and develop its own "native literature."

He recognized Maud's exceptional talent, and his praise encouraged her immensely. He wrote that her first writing assignment on the prescribed subject "My Autobiography" was "particularly good and interesting." Her second essay, titled "My Earliest Recollection," recalled the memory of her mother lying in her coffin. Maud knew that this essay was first-rate, and she incorporated it into her journals in April 1898. MacMechan's next assignment took her to the Halifax Public Gardens to prepare a descriptive landscape piece: rendering nature was already Maud's forte, given her wide reading of eighteenth- and nineteenth-century landscape word-painting. In January, at the end of the semester, she got a "first" in English. Later, in 1924, after his pupil was world-famous, MacMechan praised her writing in his *Head-Waters of Canadian Literature* as a good example of Canadian "regionalism."

Maud looked forward to Christmas and the return to Cavendish, with her tales of university life. Her journal records sore disappointment: "My fare would not cost any more than my board here but grandma wrote that she thought I had better not go home for fear the roads might be bad for getting to the station etc." Maud added, "I know what that means. Grandfather doesn't want to be bothered meeting me or taking me back" (December 23, 1895). She was perhaps petulant: her seventy-five-year-old grandfather might have had legitimate worries about travel by horse and sleigh in the dead of winter, when huge drifts could obscure the roads, even if he only had to drive to the nearest railroad station.

Maud's sketches of Miss Ker and Miss Claxton were written during this holiday, and her account of a small confrontation with Miss Claxton is vintage Montgomery, dramatizing her ability to deliver arch or sarcastic comments with impeccable and saccharine politeness:

I went into the teachers' parlour and seeing Miss Whiteside and Miss Tilsley there alone, as I supposed, I said, "Isn't this a lovely morning, girls?" Up popped Miss Claxton from a low chair where she had been squatted unseen. "You should not call us girls," she piped frigidly. "It is not respectful." "Oh, I beg your pardon, Miss Claxton," I said politely. "I did not see you there. Of course I would never refer to *you* as a girl." Miss Claxton liked it very little, for she does not relish an allusion to her age anymore than ordinary people, but she had to take it, for my apology was perfectly courteous in tone and matter and she had no excuse for resenting anything in it. (December 24, 1895)

Christmas, which Maud had expected to be very dull, was a "rather pleasant one" after all—pleasant for Maud, who was practising her writing.

Everything at Dalhousie excited her: lectures, repartee, operatic productions, walks, lively novels, academic competitions (in which she excelled). It all brought a surge of physical and mental activity. She pasted into her scrapbook a picture of a handsome, craggy stag, expressing sexual energy in a subtle way. She giggled with the girls, flirted with the boys, attended many parties, prepared "papers" for club meetings, "buckled to" her studies with "all due grit," and gave music lessons to make money. And, of course, she wrote.

But this manic upswing began to manifest itself in sleeplessness, a problem that would recur throughout her life. When Maud awoke, unable to sleep, she wrote. The harvest from her feverish brain was astonishing. She sent poems and stories away to magazines and entered whatever local contests she could find.

February and March 1896 brought success: three pieces were accepted, earning her a total of twenty-two dollars (for comparison, in 1889–90, Dalhousie had charged students six dollars tuition for each course they took in a year). First was a five-dollar prize for best entry in a contest sponsored by the *Halifax Evening Mail*: a response to the question "Which has the more patience under the ordinary cares and trials of life—man or woman?" She made two submissions to the contest. Both entries were about gender, but from different angles. The first is a succinct parable about a Guardian Angel (male) who wheedles a gift for women from the Benign Giver (also male): the gift is not justice, but instead a "long-suffering, all-forgiving divine patience" to deal with men. Serious, but with a gently sarcastic undertone, this witty allegory did not answer the contest's question. Maud submitted another entry under the name "Belinda Bluegrass": a witty, lighthearted poem on male and female varieties of patience. It makes the same point as her first entry: women are socialized to be patient with men. The "Belinda Bluegrass" poem won first prize and the parable won honourable mention for literary merit.

In her journal, Maud writes that she had "small interest" in the contest until a friend prodded her to enter—the standard female disclaimer of the era, implying that a "proper" woman is so modest that she would move into the public domain only after someone else's urging. But the disclaimer is hardly convincing, given that she woke up in the night with the second poem almost formulated in her brain—female modesty notwithstanding, the contest was clearly very much on her mind, and she wanted to win.

Five days later, *Golden Days*, a magazine from Philadelphia, sent her five dollars for a short story called "Our Charivari." In another three weeks, another well-known magazine, *The Youth's Companion*, accepted her poem "The Fisher Lassies"—for twelve dollars! A year's tuition at the Prince of Wales College had been seven dollars in 1893, and she had made twenty-two dollars from her writing in one month in 1896. Flush with cash and ambition, she bought elegant bound copies of Tennyson, Longfellow, Whittier, and Byron, as a self-reward for having arrived. She particularly enjoyed Whittier and Longfellow, committing many of their poems to memory, and underlining the books heavily, particularly the poems about nature.[47]

She loved seeing her name in print. Continued success brought another three-dollar cheque in April from *Golden Days* for her poem "Apple Picking Time." She must have chuckled over the story of her success reaching the ears of the "grim cats" in Halifax Ladies' College, her arrogant cousin Murray Macneill, who was also at Dalhousie, and eventually all of the village of Cavendish. Pique and pride must have squeezed her grandfather in equal measure. There was no more eloquent statement to a parsimonious Scotsman than that made by money.

Maud was ready to take on wider challenges. Among her many pieces for the Dalhousie college paper was a remarkably mature article entitled "A Girl's Place at Dalhousie College."[48] This was picked up by the *Halifax Herald* for a special supplement on Dalhousie. It sets forth all the traditional arguments about why women should not be educated, and refutes them. After giving examples of women's success at Dalhousie and elsewhere, she argues that the real worth of an education is not to prepare a woman for a specialized career, but to broaden her mind and increase her powers of observation.

The year at Dalhousie was invaluable in building her confidence: was she (as the Charlottetown *Examiner* had called her) a "young George Eliot"? The comparison was heady. By April 1896, when she finished her college year, having published in real, paying magazines and having placed first in her class in English, she knew the year had been worth the effort.

There are interesting points of comparison between Maud's career and that of her first cousin, Murray Macneill, son of her mother's brother, Leander. Born in January 1877, Murray was two years younger, but he would be graduating from Dalhousie with his B.A. that spring; unlike Maud, he had lost no time having to work to finance his education. A brilliant polymath, he had started studying at Dalhousie in fall 1892, at age fifteen, and completed the course with little effort. Maud reflected bitterly that Murray would go on for graduate training while she would have to go back to exhausting country school teaching after her single year of freedom.

Everyone on campus knew Murray. Maud was resentful that he ignored her, his poor country cousin. In her scrapbook Maud pasted a newspaper clipping: "Murray McNeill, son of the Rev. L. C. McNeill, Saint John, is one of our best students. He toiled not, neither did he spin, but First Classes always came his way." The Convocation Roster for 1896 shows that twenty-eight students received B.A.s (five of them women), and Murray, nineteen years old, won the top graduation prize. At no place in her journals does Maud note that Murray won the William Young Gold Medal when he graduated from Dalhousie, in 1896. The second-best award was the Avery Prize, and it went to another student.

Years later, when Maud wrote *Anne of Green Gables*, she calls the most prestigious prize "the Avery Scholarship," immortalizing the name of Dalhousie's Avery Prize, the award that Murray did *not* win. In 1908 she sent Murray a copy of *Anne* after it became a best-seller. He then held the "Chair of Mathematics" at Dalhousie. What did he think when he read the description of the "fat, funny, little upcountry boy with a Bumpy forehead and a patched coat" who had won the "mathematics prize"? Murray's specialty had been mathematics. He had a protruding forehead (a distinctive Macneill forehead like his father's) that could easily have been called "bumpy" by an unkind satirist. And from the perspective of sophisticated Halifax, New Brunswick was certainly "upcountry." But it is certain that Murray never wore a patched coat. Murray, a sophisticated reader of literature (but without Maud's talent for writing it), must have sniffed over this gratuitous piece of mischief on Maud's part.

Murray and Maud were not kindred spirits. Maud kept hearing of Murray's amazing progress in the academic world. Scholarships pursued Murray and hung themselves around his neck: following graduation from Dalhousie, he went to Cornell (which offered him a slightly better scholarship than had Harvard, Yale, Columbia, and Clark). Math came to him so easily that he spent most of his time reading history and politics, or attending art galleries and cultural events, though he professed he could never learn to like poetry. To fill out his education, the young Murray made grand tours of Europe and Britain. To make matters worse, his achievements appeared to be largely effortless: he complained that math offered no challenge and was boring. Maud knew she was every bit as clever as Murray in her own field and that, had she been a boy, her proud clan would have seen that *she* got the best education.[49]

Maud was bitter that after a single year in university, where she had been happy, admired, and immensely productive, she had to go back to the hard, dreary, underpaid, and undervalued work of country school teaching. Still, her whole orientation in life was to make the best of whatever circumstances occurred. Like grandmother's Woolner family, she sized up the situation, considered her options, and laid careful plans to make her name in literature.

Returning to Cavendish for the summer of 1896 was a letdown, but Maud revelled in the sanctuary of her little upstairs room in the old home, aloof from the household below. Another pleasure was "Lovers' Lane," the heavily shaded and fragrant path beside the freshwater stream that tumbled along year after year. The sound of the water calmed her frayed nerves. Breezes swept in off the ocean and over the fields, buzzing and humming insects added variation, and frogs made their strange music. The moist air and the smell of balsam soothed her. Her rambles were full of visual beauty, perfumed and spicy fragrances, a caressing atmosphere, and comforting sounds.

"Lovers' Lane" had special associations for Maud, backing on the school area where she had played as a child. Children had fished, cooled their milk in the brook, plotted, laughed, and shared secrets there for years. When an older Maud wanted a "passport back to fairyland," she only had to walk through "Lovers' Lane" to feel herself a renewed spirit. Like the Sea-Kingdom of *Undine*, the lane fed Maud's imagination with wild, passionate, and often undirected images of longing. It also soothed her.

But if "Lovers' Lane" stayed the same, the rest of her world was changing. Laura Pritchard had married in Prince Albert. Maud felt the call of romance and sexual desire in many of her moods. Yet, she clung tremulously to the stability of the repressed lifestyle she knew, with her grandparents' regularity of habits and the community's resistance to change. In her dreams, she craved escape—romance, love, fame. Tensions were building. In a picture of Maud with her Uncle John's children and Fanny Wise (the pretty young teacher boarding with the John F. Macneill family) Maud looks cross and unhappy; so do Uncle John's children. Only Fannie Wise looks at peace with herself.

That fall, a new teaching opportunity came up in the community of Belmont. Its teacher, Maud's cousin Edwin Simpson, had saved enough money living at home to leave for university. He took a special interest in Maud and helped her secure the position he was vacating. Maud had been actively searching for a position again, and this one came to her easily.

Belmont was a small community on the Malpeque Bay, about thirty miles from Cavendish. It was near the part of the Bay where Maud's original Montgomery forebears had settled nearly one hundred and twenty years earlier. Maud called it a pretty place, because of the Bay, but expressed "a creepy crawly presentiment" that the inhabitants might not be as attractive.

During her visits to Park Corner, Maud had become acquainted with Ed. Both his parents were Simpsons and related to each other. This Simpson family produced six children: Fulton, Edwin, Alfred, Burton, Milton, and Sophy. Ed was two years older than Maud, good-looking, and brilliantly talkative.

At Park Corner, Ed had once walked Maud home from a Literary Society meeting and they'd talked about books all the way. She wrote, "I don't know whether I like Ed or not. He is clever and can talk about everything, but he *is* awfully conceited—and worse still, *Simpsony*" (March 26, 1892). The Macneills of Maud's generation generally disliked the Simpson clan, thinking them windy, pompous, and full of themselves. Ed, however, was much attracted to the witty, clever Maud.

Ed's parents, although living in Belmont, were both descended from the original Simpsons and Macneills who settled Cavendish. Through intermarriage over five generations, the blood had grown increasingly "congested." When Alexander Macneill railed against cousins marrying cousins, he could point to bad results. The Simpson family was a prime example. Intellectually, the offspring ranged from brilliant to mentally defective; emotionally, they ranged from normal to totally unhinged.

When Maud went to Belmont, she stayed temporarily with the Simpsons. She wrote, "Mrs. Simpson—who was also a Cavendish Simpson and married her cousin as a matter of course—seems like a kind, mild woman, but of a somewhat melancholy disposition." Maud's identification with "melancholy" in the Simpson family should have warned her to stay away from romantic entanglements with them; she knew by now that she herself was also given to moody, depressive spells. But in her experience, eccentric and mentally imbalanced people were common and did not necessarily stand out as abnormal. The Simpson family was kind to her, not only because she was a relative, but also because she was a new teacher.

Ed's interest in Maud increased. Her willing imagination transformed him into a darkly handsome Byronic hero. And he had promise. When he graduated from the Prince of Wales College, he was described in the college paper as "Editor-in-Chief of the College Observer . . . in debate he was a Hercules. Notwithstanding his many scruples, Ed will, without doubt, be a star in the legal professions."

Coming from a family that included successful lawyers, Maud took note. Marrying a lawyer would enable her to afford enough household help to pursue a writing career. And she did want to marry, eventually: a single woman was a social pariah, and she wanted children; she also wanted the physical and emotional affection of a man. As she assessed this attentive cousin, she was still decompressing from the stimulating, heady Halifax year. She felt a terrible loneliness. She ignored Ed's annoying personal mannerisms—a perpetual moving, twitching, lifting, or tapping of feet and fingers—focussing instead on his brilliant discourses. Apparently, Ed judged that Maud had an intelligence adequate to the sizable task of appreciating his own.

At this time, Maud's Great-Aunt Mary Lawson (her grandfather's sister) was a temporary resident in the Simpson house. Widowed and childless, she lived around with relatives, as poor relations were forced to do. She was generally welcomed for her fine storytelling abilities. She turned human observations into non-malicious anecdotes, and harmless gossip into an art form. Like all good storytellers, Aunt Mary Lawson had learned to read body language and to analyze personality. To Maud, who had seen how eighteenth- and nineteenth-century British women writers transformed human social interaction into novels about domestic manners, Aunt Mary Lawson was the model of an able storyteller.

Maud shared a bedroom with her Aunt Mary Lawson. Maud and Aunt Mary bonded quickly and of course began to gossip about the odd personalities of some of the Simpson progeny: Ed was undeniably talented, if pompous and self-important; Fulton was a giant in size and likewise in emotional imbalance; Alf had the Simpson trait of dominating all conversation, but was otherwise pleasant; Burton was quiet and withdrawn, an aberration among loquacious, self-absorbed Simpson males; and the daughter, Sophy, was a "lifeless mortal," retreating from her merely slow-witted self into periods of withdrawn and silent sulks (October 21, 1896).

This compendium of oddities might have remained simply an entertaining mix had not the three eldest Simpson boys all started courting Maud at once. Ed's absence was his best suit, for his "Simpsony" traits were diluted through distance; and Maud, who loved corresponding and missed the stimulation of university, enjoyed his letters, even if they were stilted and turgid. The other Simpson sons were still at home. The giant Fulton, later described as "sulky, jealous, meddlesome, querulous" (January 2, 1897), tried to attract her attention. When his brother Alf offered her rides, Fulton became angry and agitated, taking on a wild and "unearthly" look.

As soon as possible, Maud left this household, ostensibly to board closer to the school, with the Simon Fraser family. They were kind, and they served a clean if unexciting table. Elsewhere in Belmont, she found the people "rough, poor, and illiterate" (November 7, 1896).

Although the Frasers gave her an upstairs room, with a view of beautiful Malpeque Bay, the old farmhouses were neither insulated nor heated during the night, and her room proved unbearably cold. By mid-November, Maud would rise to find snow blown onto her pillow from the leaky window. The Frasers did not go to church, and so lacked the normal reason for weekly bathing; Maud complains of the Fraser men's lack of hygiene. She always kept herself immaculately clean, even though this meant washing herself in a frigid room in a hand basin, uncovering only a part of her body at one time. Periodic forays into the Fraser kitchen—the only warm room in the house—were the only way she had of warming her hands. Later, the kindly Mrs. Fraser prepared a room with a warm stovepipe running through it, which made bathing and writing more comfortable.

Maud's only consolation in this "dead-and-alive existence" was writing in her journal, and that had to be kept under lock and key, since the Frasers poked through her things when she was out. "I wonder how some people live at all—they seem to get so little out of life. It must be a bare, starveling existence for a vast number," she wrote on December 17, 1896. In this atmosphere, Maud's diary records her vision of an increasingly bleak world, which mirrored her own growing sense of loneliness and despair.

Whenever she heard from Ed in Halifax, the memory of her Dalhousie year sent her into a deeper low than she had ever experienced. She began to brood obsessively on the barrenness of her life. Maud had always used laughter to defuse low spirits, but the Frasers were too prosaic for repartee. In her short stay with the eccentric Simpsons, she had at least enjoyed laughing at them with Great-Aunt Mary Lawson.

Maud was beginning to feel the symptoms of a full-blown depressive episode: she had previously suffered from sleeplessness, but this recurred alongside an inability to feel pleasure in anything. For Christmas, she went to Bideford to visit Edith England, home from Sackville College and engaged to a brilliant young man preparing for law. Again, Maud felt excluded from the happy, forward march of others' lives.

In February, Aunt Mary Lawson left the Simpson household. Maud had visited the Simpsons through the winter, but with Aunt Mary's departure, she lost the last salubrious force in her battle against loneliness and depression. On February 2, 1897, in one of Ed's lengthy, stylistically tedious but clever epistles he stated that he loved her and wanted them to become engaged. She deliberated. Her heart felt no stirrings, but she lived in a society where women often made marriages for other reasons. She began to think she could perhaps tolerate Ed.

As she sank into depression in the first quarter of 1897, the spectre of the disintegration of her personality spooked her. Suicide was frequently and graphically reported in Island newspapers — one particularly gruesome form of suicide was to drink carbolic acid or Paris Green (a rat poison) and suffer a horrible death as tortured loved ones looked on. Other imbalanced people murdered family or friends, or went on sprees shooting animals. Mental breakdown was common, and the provincial insane asylum, Falconwood, built in 1879, was well supplied with inmates.

By March, Maud complained of feeling "fearfully tired," a symptom of depression. She recognized her own abnormal state, and wrote about it in her journals. This helped her recognize repetitive patterns, and she identified specific activities that helped her deal with depression. Long, vigorous walks provided some relief, but walking was difficult in the winter. Lively company also lifted her spirits, as did keeping a regular, structured routine. Given her pleasure in language, the act of writing sometimes edged her into a better mood. The paucity of stimulation shows in Maud's journals; when she had nothing to write about but hoped that the act of writing would give her a lift, she resorted to mechanical exercises. One typical example was a long, flat description of her room in the Fraser house. In a deep depression, she was entirely unable to write, either on her creative work or in her journal. She formed the habit of making notes for her journal, and writing these up later when her spirits improved.

In April 1897, Laura Pritchard wrote her from Prince Albert that her brother, Will, had died after an attack of influenza. Maud and Will had corresponded periodically ever since their Prince Albert friendship, and she had retained a spot in her love-starved heart for him. Now, hearing of his death, Maud opened the ten-year letter that he had given her to open in 1901 — why keep it after he was dead? In her journal, she reported that it was a love letter.

Such a stressful loss tilted her further towards a major depressive episode. It reminded her of other losses, most notably her mother's death. No one really cared about her now, she felt. For a young woman who had always been surrounded by an extended family, she was getting perilously close to being orphaned as an adult. She felt adrift in a cold world.

Ed now professed his love constantly. She associated him with happier settings: Park Corner, Prince of Wales College, Dalhousie. In May 1897, she heard that Laura Pritchard (now Mrs. Willard Agnew) had given birth to her first child, and she received the news with mixed emotions. Thinking about her own life's journey through an uneven mental landscape, she drew on her childhood favourite, Bunyan's *Pilgrim's Progress*, for the language to express her depression:

> I wanted love and protection. Life at times lately had worn a somewhat sombre aspect . . . I was run-down and inclined to take a rather morbid view of my prospects. Hence, I was all the more tempted to grasp at what promised to lift me out of my Slough of Despond. (June 30, 1897)

In this frame of mind Maud accepted Ed's proposal. She wrote him that, given time, she might learn to care for him. Ed's letters became more effusive. She began recoiling from them. She ceased to enjoy her teaching, and then even her writing, which was carved out of sleeping time, in the early morning in her icy room. Only the discipline and sense of duty that she had learned from Grandmother Macneill kept her going.

But life was not without some uplifting moments: pushing herself to write, she continued making some sales. In March, she sold "The Prize in Elocution" to the *Philadelphia Times* for $8.75; in April a story to *Arthur's Home Magazine* for $3; and in May "Extra French Examination" to the *Philadelphia Times* for $7. Her basic salary was approximately $45 per school term. Selling three stories for $18.75 was very encouraging. She had written these stories quickly, but in the grip of a depression, writing was a challenge.

In early May she closed the school for the standard three-week holiday between terms. Her mental state was precarious. She became physically ill. Her muse grew alliterative: for herself, "sniffle, sigh, and sneeze"; for Belmont, "mist, mud, and misery" (May 3, 1897). She suffered from disturbed sleep, brooding morbidity, general irritability, fluctuating emotions with tears ready to embarrass her at the slightest provocation, severe headaches, a sense of terrible soul-loneliness and isolation, an inability to make decisions, and a perpetual "spiritlessness" and "tiredness"—all symptoms of a full-blown depression. She decided she simply could not take another year in Belmont. When Ed Simpson proposed in person on June 8, 1897, Maud accepted.

Ed's kiss to seal the engagement brought her no emotion. "I did not feel at all unhappy—but neither did I feel happy—certainly not as a girl should feel who has just parted from the man she had promised to marry" (June 30, 1897). Her only genuine emotion was a strong revulsion to this new fiancé, but the self-centred Ed did not observe this. By mid-June the physical and mental repugnance she felt was overwhelming. Returning to Cavendish, she spent the rest of the summer wrestling over her promise to marry a man whose mere touch made her feel physically ill. Normally, she suffered from wildly oscillating moods; now she describes herself as feeling emotionally dead.

Ed gave out the wrong signals as a lover when he was courting Maud: "He was far too self-conscious, too fond of saying and doing things for effect, and—in plain English—far too conceited" (June 30, 1897). His fingers constantly twitched and tapped. Did Maud's super-sensitive radar detect something amiss other than excessive self-absorption? She wrote in her journal much later that he married twice, but had no children, "which did not surprise me"—whatever that means. Her growing reservations were sensible: in their shared bloodlines, each had ample genetic inheritance to produce psychological disorders.

Additional problems arose. Ed told her, after their engagement, that he planned to become a Baptist minister. She had thought his plans were to become a lawyer. The Presbyterians of Cavendish had always looked down on

Baptists. Furthermore, Maud had serious reservations about marrying a minister. Other professions, such as law, were equal to the ministry in social prestige, but did not make so many demands on a wife. A parson stationed in some small town or out of the way place would expect his wife to act as unpaid helper. Nor did Maud fancy a peripatetic existence. She was a person who put down deep roots.

When she was ready to leave Belmont, she wrote, "I *will* be sorry to leave — as I always am to leave an old room. . . . How many more am I fated to leave yet in my wanderings!" (June 30, 1897). Here was a new theme, one that would become part of her interpretative framework from then on: a belief that she was cursed to be a rootless wanderer, never permanent, always forced to move on.

She worried incessantly. Her journal records one long entry on June 30, shortly preceding her engagement to Ed; no entries follow this until October 7, 1897.

That autumn, she read Olive Schreiner's *The Story of an African Farm*[50] (1883). This book, which had already sold some 100,000 copies, questioned the moral certainties of Christianity, and had been denounced as "blasphemous" from church pulpits across America and Great Britain. It was also a feminist book: it overturned the traditional assumption that women, as sexual beings, entrapped men; rather, the novel depicts men trapping women. The heroine of this book eventually chooses *death* over marrying a man by whom she is pregnant, and to whom she is sexually attracted. The book was a revelation to Maud, reading it, as she did, during her entanglement with Ed. Like Schreiner's heroine Lyndall, she felt tortured; she was certainly close to implosion, if not verging on being suicidal.

Another young woman with Maud's ability might simply have left the Island to clear her head, and to find a life elsewhere. Hundreds of young men and women were leaving the Island every year. The Island newspapers of the period talked about the exciting opportunities off the Island. The 1890s had seen a remarkable change in the status and freedom of women. In the 1895–96 period, even the Island papers were full of talk of the assertive "New Woman" who was transforming society. Maud could have set off to be a newspaperwoman in London, as did Sarah Jeannette Duncan of Brantford, Ontario, or an editor for an American publishing house, like Jean McIlwraith of Hamilton, Ontario. Some exceptionally adventuresome and gifted Canadian women did leave their hometowns for professional work in urban centres in Halifax, Montreal, Toronto, in the States, or in Great Britain. Maud knew a Miss Arbuckle in Summerside, PEI, who had gone to work for an American publisher, L. C. Page of Boston.

Maud was certainly talented enough to have worked her way up in the publishing world. Gifted in teaching, she could have found work in either community schools or private academies anywhere. She did not stay rooted in Prince Edward Island because she was provincial in outlook: she had already travelled to the Canadian west, Ottawa, Halifax—much farther than the norm for young women of her time. Nor did she stay because of her love of the landscape.

Instead, it was at this watershed time that her mood swings began to seriously affect the choices she made in her life. Depression had led her to accept Ed's proposal, and that decision had deepened her melancholy. Her experience with mood swings in Belmont had left her feeling out of control, and her confidence was eroded. From Belmont onward, she became increasingly afraid of being "struck down" by her dark moods. As the victim of uncontrollable depression which made her increasingly anxious, she was unable to take the risks that equally gifted women with stable moods could take. She instinctively began to seek out situations where her life would be rigorously structured and predictable. She became fearful of cutting loose from the society she knew, lest she spin out of control, with no one to look after her. School teaching was hard, but it was safer than leaving the Island. The adventures she craved would have to take place in her reading and imagination.

Not privy to any of these thoughts, Ed was quite ready to organize her life around his own. He was leaving for another year of university, and he told Maud of a teaching position coming up in Lower Bedeque. He suggested that she apply for it, and he put in a good word for her there with Alf Leard, a friend of his who was vacating the post to study dentistry on the mainland. Maud obtained Alf's position, and moved into one of the most traumatic periods of her life.

The question of Herman Leard

When Maud left Cavendish for Lower Bedeque in the fall of 1897, she wrote "I feel like a prisoner who has shut the door on all possibilities," quoting a phrase from *The Love Letters of a Worldly Woman* (1891), by Lucy Lane

Clifford.[51] She felt she was in Ed's clutches, under his surveillance, waiting for the dreary day when he would claim her.

Lower Bedeque was a small community on the South Shore of the Island, across from mainland Canada. The farms in this area were large and fertile, and the community long settled. Maud's teaching position would start in October. She arranged to stay with Alf's people, the Cornelius Leard family. They had a comfortable home right across from the school building. She would room with their daughter, Helen, who was her own age. It would be a huge change from miserable, lonely Belmont.

As soon as she settled into the very sociable Leard household, her prospects began to look brighter. Their home was as tidy as her grandmother's. Mrs. Cornelius Leard, daughter of a Baptist minister from Nova Scotia, was cheerful and efficient. The Leards were people of substance in the community. Cornelius Leard's farm was much larger than Maud's grandfather's.[52] As a family, they were prosperous, articulate, well-dressed, self-directed, intelligent, and refined, although not intellectual and literary in the way Maud's Macneill family was. They were also a relaxed family who enjoyed each other's company, playing practical jokes and sharing merriment. They were skilled in many crafts, busy and happy in creation, and active in community affairs. The cheerful, easy atmosphere in the home began to make her feel comfortable and relaxed, just as visiting the Campbells of Park Corner always did.

Maud brought her own gifts to the Leard household through her storytelling ability and wit. She could make funny stories out of almost anything, and she was full of interesting book-talk. In the appreciative audience of the Leard family, she began to blossom again.

Of the Leards' eight children—three boys and five girls—two of the daughters, Georgina and Millie, had grown up and left home. Both lived nearby in Central Bedeque, and they dropped in often to see their parents and younger siblings. Georgina had married Thomas Moyse, raising two sons who eventually became medical doctors; Millie, universally admired and very active in church and community, raised a large family of affluent, solid citizens.

The other six Leard children still lived at home. Herman, the eldest, was the son designated to take over the prosperous farm. Born on July 2, 1870, he was four years older than Maud. The next son, Alpheus, studying for a career in dentistry, was the one Maud replaced, taking his teaching position from October 1897 until May 1898 so he could study further.

Helen was dating Howard McFarlane, the man she would eventually marry. A noted craftswoman, whose exotic and original creations were exhibited and much admired, she eventually became a leader in the Women's Institute. The three youngest children were Calvin, Mae, and "Fed" (Frederica). Calvin, a skilled carpenter, eventually inherited the farm, doing some fox-farming when that came into vogue. Frederica, who was a young girl during Maud's residence in the house, grew up to run a fashionable tourist business in Fernwood. Mae became the dietitian in the Prince County Hospital. The Leards were a genteel and talented family, competent in all they did.

They had none of the unbalanced intensity of the Simpsons, the lifelessness of the Frasers, or the sharp twists of her Grandfather Macneill. Maud had grown up in a family whose tone was set by complicated, volatile people like her grandfather. The Leards sailed through their lives in less turbulent barks. Maud thoroughly enjoyed living with these happy, productive people.

Pursued by memories of Ed Simpson's intense self-absorption and nervousness, Maud immediately took note of Herman's unaffected openness. He was courteous, good-tempered, relaxed, and at ease with people. He listened to her talk and laughed at her witticisms and jokes. This was new for Maud — her grandfather and Ed had always demanded to be the centre of attention. For once, she felt appreciated for *her* personality. Maud began to feel Herman had an indefinable charm, and she spoke of being fascinated by his "magnetic blue eyes" (January 22, 1898).[53] Maud had come into this house in the throes of a depression, and romantic feelings were predictable for someone who was lonely, emotionally vulnerable, and unhappily engaged.

Maud's reputation as a very successful teacher had preceded her, and her travels off the Island gave her additional glamour. Her descent from two fine old families provided a nice pedigree in a culture that took especial note of "who you were." Although no one would have called her beautiful, she dressed attractively and stylishly and had an extraordinary amount of poise. By her own account in her journals, verified through family memories, she and Herman "talked and jested and teased each other continually and kept the house ringing with mirth and laughter." Her depression lifted, and her spirits soared to the other extreme, helped by her new circumstances and love interest.

Maud was susceptible to Herman's romantic overtures, and undoubtedly encouraged them by flirting — a skill at which she was very adept. Soon he was entering her bedroom on the pretext of bringing her mail. Although Maud shared this bedroom with Helen, Helen was often away on dates. Herman lingered to talk. He brought her chocolates. Ed's kisses had left her "cold as ice," but she soon reports in her diary that "*Herman's* sent flame through every vein and fibre of my being." Next, she was fighting to control her emotional highs just as much as she had fought to control her lows.

She tried to dampen her romance with Herman, knowing she was engaged to Ed. She wrote dramatically, "for the sake of my self respect I *must not* stoop to any sort of an affair with another man" (April 8, 1898). She could not help herself, however:

> If I had—or rather if I *could* have—kept this resolve I would have saved myself incalculable suffering. For it was but a few days later that I found myself face to face with the burning consciousness that I *loved* Herman Leard with a wild, passionate, unreasoning love that dominated my entire being and possessed me like a flame—a love I could neither quell nor control—a love that in its intensity seemed little short of absolute madness. Madness! Yes! (April 8, 1898)

The feelings Maud describes are consistent with clinical accounts of people gripped by a "manic" high, struggling to rein in overwhelming impulses that may at times feel overwhelming. Individuals with mood disorders are notorious for impetuous affairs of the heart that lead to extramarital affairs. However, the language she uses may also echo that in the "racy French novels" that the Charlottetown papers periodically railed against.[54]

Herman may have been confused by Maud's actions, especially when she continually welcomed him into her bedroom when his family was out, but she says that she hustled him out as soon as their preliminary lovemaking reached a dangerous point. She wrote that the only reason that she did not succumb to her desire for Herman was the knowledge that he would have despised her if she did. Intercourse before marriage (especially without an avowed intention to marry) certainly laid a woman open to a man's contempt in her culture; if it led to pregnancy, as often happened before birth control was available, it led to lifelong public shame. Maud's lovemaking with Herman went against her own sense of morality. Brought up a strict Presbyterian in a culture that believed sexual activity outside of marriage was a very serious sin, Maud was playing with fire, and she knew it. What's more, a betrothal was serious business in that era, and she was engaged to another man. Her behaviour could only have been construed as shamefully "loose" by the values of the time.

According to Maud's account of her romance with Herman in her journals (which she recopied, and undoubtedly retouched and reshaped, some twenty years later when she had become world-famous), very early in the Bedeque year she decided that Herman was beneath her socially; although she was physically attracted to him, she would never consider marrying him. Later, she would claim that she discounted him because "he had no trace of intellect, culture, or education—no interest in anything beyond his farm and the circle of young people who composed the society he frequented. In plain, sober truth, he was only a very nice, attractive young animal!" (April 8, 1898). But in actual fact, Herman was considered the "best catch" in the community of Bedeque. Popular and well liked, he was a fine young man who stood to inherit the large and successful family farm. His family was different from hers, but they were in no way inferior. They produced very successful professionals—dentists, doctors, businessmen, and teachers—and were pillars of the community.

By early spring, Maud was positive that she wanted out of the engagement with Ed. Her physical caresses with Herman had intensified her awareness of her revulsion to Ed. She wrote Ed, asking to break off the engagement, after nearly a year of agonizing over it.

Ed Simpson's response was that of a stubborn, strong-minded man. When she asked him "to release" her from her engagement, he told her that he would only under certain conditions.[55] Perhaps in his own conceit he could not fathom why any woman in her right mind would reject *him*. Perhaps he thought that as a "weak woman" Maud could not possibly understand herself and her feelings. She wrote a series of increasingly firm letters before he would consent to liberate her from her promise to marry him.

Alf Leard was returning from his educational leave to take up the Bedeque school again, and Maud knew she would have to leave the Leard home. She was heartily tired of teaching and wanted to spend all her time writing. During the school year, with all of her emotional turmoil over matters of love, she had somehow still managed to write, likely energized by the sense of well-being that comes from a hot romantic affair. She published approximately five poems and five stories between October 1897 and April 1898, making some $25 from her writing. (Alf Leard's salary was $56.25 for each of the four quarters of the year, but Maud was paid only $45.00 per quarter for her Bideford teaching.) She believed that if she could only write *full time*, she could make enough to live on.

But there was a dilemma. She could not admit to her grandparents that she was tired of teaching; she had argued for an education on the grounds that she wanted to teach. Her grandfather's sarcasm on hearing that she now wanted to quit would have been insufferable. In addition, her relationship with her aging, cranky grandfather was so tense that she knew returning to live with him in Cavendish would be impossible. Her mood swings made her feel too vulnerable to live on her own, even if she could have afforded it. She had no place to go.

And then fate intervened. On March 6, 1898, a telegram informed Maud that her Grandfather Macneill had dropped dead the previous day. She went home for the funeral, then returned briefly to finish her term. She could now live in the Cavendish home that she loved, with her grandmother, who, de-spite her faults, had always been remarkably supportive. And Maud hoped to rein in her turbulent emotions once back in her grandmother's routine-bound orbit. Since Grandmother was still reasonably fit and active, she could con-tinue doing most of the cooking and housework, and Maud could write on a regular schedule. Others would see that she was returning the care her grand-mother had given *her*, and she knew that the community would think ex-ceedingly well of her for doing so. The approval of the Cavendish community was extremely important to Maud, given that she had spent so much of her adolescence feeling she did not have it.

And what about her "mad" love for Herman, the "nice, attractive young animal"? That romance ended, by Maud's account, when she returned to Cavendish. The real end of this love story, however, came a year later, after Maud and her grandmother had settled into life together. One day in June 1899, it was reported that Herman Leard had died of the complications from influenza.[56] Maud was stunned. Her attraction to him had been hard to sub-due even in absence. To learn that he was dead when the memory of his phys-ical presence was still so strong was ghoulish. Because she did not attend the funeral, Maud lacked the visual imagery to place Herman firmly under the sod. She was stricken with grief—and relief—all at once, caught in a longing that could never be satisfied, and one that would intensify in memory. She wrote much later: "I did not shed many tears. . . . No agony could ever equal what I once endured. It is easier to think of him as dead, mine, *all* mine in death, as he could never be in life, mine when no other woman could ever lie on his heart or kiss his lips." (This comes from her diary entry of July 24, 1899, which she recopied into her journals after 1919.) Herman had loved *her*, she declared, "or pretended to—with a love passionate and sensual enough, of no very lofty or enduring type; but never, never as I loved him" (July 24, 1899). This last statement is a curiously discordant one; by Maud's own account, *her* "love" for Herman had been rooted solely in sexual attraction. The comment not only reveals a crack in her own story, but suggests that she may have known he was trifling with her while planning to marry someone else.

Maud carried the memory of Herman in her heart long after he was buried—nourishing, burnishing, and cherishing it in a highly romantic fashion. She found gripping pathos for her diary in her account of falling in love with someone who was not "worthy" of her.

When *The Selected Journals of L. M. Montgomery: Volume I (1889–1910)* was published in 1985 (nearly ninety years after the events they recount), Maud's account of her love affair with Herman Leard raised eyebrows of old-timers in the Bedeque area. To begin with, the Leards had been a respected family, not crude people beneath Maud's "class." (Maud, who had read many, many nineteenth-century British novels, did have a sense of being in a privileged class—one to which the titled Montgomerys and the literary Macneills belonged, and possibly from which the Leards were excluded.) But her account did not square with the memories of the Lower Bedeque community in another important respect—in that of her romance with Herman Leard. Descendants of third parties, as well as those of the Leard family, tell a very different story.

Local legend says that when Maud Montgomery arrived in their community, Herman was already seriously courting Ettie Schurman, one of the most beautiful and eligible young women in Prince County. The Schurmans were a very prominent family, with large, prosperous farms, and the match between Ettie and Herman would have been seen as very suitable by both families. Herman often went off to Baptist church events, as described in Maud's journals, and the reason he did not take Maud with him, as might have been expected, was because he went to see Ettie.

The love affair that Bedeque remembers was not between Herman and Maud, but between Herman and Ettie. (Maud's romance with Herman was carried on secretly, and under the circumstances, it is highly unlikely that

Herman told any stories out of the bedroom.) Herman and Ettie were apparently engaged to be married in 1899, the year that Herman died. With his death, the community experienced the loss of one of its most popular young men. Over one hundred carriages carrying people from the surrounding area came to his funeral. Afterwards, Ettie grieved long and hard, and she is remembered for her sorrowful planting of blue forget-me-nots on his grave.

Much later, Ettie married a dashing war hero named Munsey who had moved from Alberta to Prince Edward Island. They had two little girls, Pril and Doris. Then, tragically, only ten years after Herman Leard's death, Ettie Schurman Munsey died.[57]

Constance Carruthers, a family friend of Ettie's children, said that when Herman took Maud, the incumbent teacher living in the Leard house, to local church socials, he would have done so out of courtesy. Mrs. Carruthers noted that by Maud's own account in her journals Herman did not take her "with him on his trips to the 'Corner' or to Central Bedeque. Nor was she [Maud] invited to drive across the ice to a Summerside church with him on Sunday evenings." These were his times for Ettie, the girl he was seriously courting and planned to marry. Ettie's acceptance of such invitations from him, given the customs of that era, indicated that Herman and Ettie were either already engaged at that point or at the least had serious "intentions of matrimony," both before and during the time when Maud was living with the Leards. It is inconceivable that Maud did not know of his attentions and attachment to Ettie.

As adults, Herman's younger sisters told stories about how amused they had been to observe "Miss Montgomery," their teacher, flitting from window to window, watching for Herman to return from events to which she had not been invited. They sensed that Maud was very fond of their brother, and that she was jealous when his attentions went elsewhere. They remembered her as being "pouty" and "moody" when Herman went out on horseback to see Ettie, but lively and fun when he was home.

Maud's journal account of her romance with Herman mentions no other woman in his life. Maud's attachment to Ed was known (Ed visited the family at Christmas to see Maud, and Maud did not break the engagement with Ed until spring). If Herman was already attached to Ettie Schurman at the time, then he was trifling with one person while engaged to another, just as Maud herself was doing. Perhaps Herman felt that Maud, being engaged, was behaving immorally, and so he was free to do the same. Or, perhaps he was trying to see, in good faith, which woman he liked better. If Herman was genuinely interested in Maud for awhile, Ettie won out: she was much prettier and welcomed his courtship outright.

As we read her journals, we must keep in mind that Maud was an avid consumer of all kinds of literary romance, and she probably embellished the story of her entanglement with Herman when she recopied her journals after 1919. A convention of nineteenth-century romance is the "two-suitor" plot, in which a young woman must choose between two men who offer totally different prospects.[58] Polishing up the Herman "affair" years later, prior to committing it permanently to her journals, Maud may have utilized this structural convention—she is the passionate woman who has to choose between two men: one whom she loves but cannot marry because of his class, and another who is suitable, but whom she does not love. Framing her own situation in these literary terms, Maud wrote, "There was I under the same roof with two men, one of whom I loved and could never marry, the other whom I had promised to marry but could never love!" (April 8, 1898).

In fact, Maud's account in her journals gives the impression that *she* rejected Herman. But local history says his heart was elsewhere and that Maud knew it. What is posterity to make of this discrepancy between Maud's account of her thwarted romance with Herman Leard and local memories? A close reading of Maud's version—told in a very convoluted way in her journals—reveals that Herman Leard did *not* actually propose to her. This section of her diaries is one of the most carefully written sections in the entire ten volumes. It is so carefully constructed, in fact, that casual readers will not even notice at first that Maud is still very much engaged to Ed when she nuzzles with Herman. Maud's pride no doubt motivated her to tell the story as she did, implying that she rejected Herman. She would have believed that no one could gainsay her years later, particularly since she stipulated that her full journals could be published only after her own death.[59]

A poem written by Maud in February 1921 can be reread in light of the story of Herman Leard and Ettie Schurman. This poem is entitled "The Bride Dreams." Recall here that Maud was small and dark, and Ettie Schurman was fair and beautiful. In the poem, a young couple has married. The bride, small and dark, records a nightmare in which she has died and been buried in her wedding gown. In the grave, she can see the living folk above. Her husband is being pursued by a wheaten-haired young woman who resembles Ettie.[60]

IV

Then I felt a thrill the dank earth through
And I knew—Oh, I knew
That it came from your step on our path from the dale;
Almost my heart began to beat!
Proud of her golden ring, at your side—
That slim white girl who lives at the mill,
Who has loved you always and loves you still,
With her hair the colour of harvest wheat
And her lips as red as mine were pale.

How I hated her, so tall and fair
And shining of hair—
Love, I am so little and dark!
My heart, that had once soared up like a lark
At your glance, was as a stone in my breast:
Never once did you look my way,
Only at *her* you looked and kissed—
My eyes were sunk in cruel decay
And the worms crawled in the silk of my vest—
(Keep me from death, Oh, my lover!)

Maud says that she finished this long poem in February 1921; and she thought it very good. The dream motif was a natural one for Maud: she had vivid dreams all her life that either reworked past experiences or were visionary dreams that she used to read the future. In February 1920—a year before she finished this poem, and at a time when the memory of her passion had been stirred up again—Maud had just finished reworking, polishing, and recopying the story about Herman Leard into her journals (see entry of March 3, 1920). Significantly, another man who appreciated her talents had entered her life by that point, and his admiration fostered another burst of creative energy—not only in the production of fiction, but also making a permanent record of her life by recopying her journals.

CHAPTER 5

The Golden Decade, 1898–1911

Maud's grandfather's death closed the book on Bedeque. It ended, in a dignified way, the tortured affair of Herman. In life, Grandfather Macneill had given Maud the love of word and story; in death, he gave her the freedom to write.

Although Alexander Macneill was seventy-eight, his death was unexpected. Maud wrote, "The shock was terrible." Then she added, "[I]n all truthfulness, I cannot say that I have ever had a very *deep* affection for Grandfather Macneill. . . . Nevertheless, one cannot live all one's life with people and not have a certain love for them" (April 8, 1898). Perhaps a more honest and (and less gracious) version of Maud's feelings appears in her semi-autobiographical novel, *Emily of New Moon*. There Emily's stern maiden aunt reflects on her father: she "involuntarily remembered the ashamed, smothered feeling of relief when old Archibald Murray died—the handsome, intolerant, autocratic old man who had ruled his family with a rod of iron all his life and had made existence at New Moon miserable with the petty tyranny of invalidism that closed his career" (Chapter 6).

Maud had acknowledged that there was much to admire about her grandfather, citing his "rich, poetic mind, a keen intelligence and a refined perception" (January 7, 1910)—but as she looked at her grandfather in his coffin, her grief was tempered by her many memories of fearing his stinging sarcasm. Seeing her grandfather in his coffin made her recall her youthful mother's still sadder funeral in that same room.

> I was very young at the time—barely twenty months old—but I remember it perfectly. It is almost my earliest recollection, clear cut

and distinct. My mother was lying there in her coffin. My father was standing by her and holding me in his arms. I remember that I wore a little white dress of embroidered muslin and that father was crying. Women were seated around the room and I recall two in front of me on the sofa who were whispering to each other and looking pityingly at father and me. Behind them, the window was open and green hop vines were trailing across it, while their shadows danced over the floor in a square of sunshine.

I looked down at the dead face of the mother whose love I was to miss so sorely and so often in after years. It was a sweet face, albeit worn and wasted by months of suffering. My mother had been beautiful and Death, so cruel in all else, had spared the delicate outline of feature, the long silken lashes brushing the hollow cheek, and the smooth masses of golden-brown hair.

I did not feel any sorrow for I realized nothing of what it all meant. I was only vaguely troubled. Why was mother so still? . . . I reached down and laid my baby hand against mother's cheek. Even yet I can feel the peculiar coldness of that touch. The memory of it seems to link me with mother, somehow—the only remembrance I have of actual contact with my mother. (April 8, 1898)

Maud's allusion to "shadows" that "danced . . . in a square of sunshine" were surely not part of her genuine memory as a small child. They are the writer's artistic touch, added later. But they catch the life Montgomery would live— a watchful one, with a constant shifting between brilliant sunshine and deep shadows.

Alexander Macneill's women did not bury their troubles when they buried him. The consequences of his will were a torture to his widow and an outrage to Maud. He had apparently left the writing of his will until he was too infirm to wield a pen. Written by another hand, it misspelled words and names, including his own wife's, and was signed "Alex M. McNeill [sic]" in a shaky, stiff signature. In the will, he left all his farm real estate to his estranged son, John F. Macneill. To his "beloved wife, Lucyan [sic]" he left only his personal property, "all monies, mortgages[,] household furniture."[61] Nothing was left to his sons Leander or Chester, but he bequeathed one hundred dollars each to his living daughters, Annie and Emily; he left nothing to Maud, even as a token of affection, despite the fact that she was his late daughter Clara's only child, and despite her lack of other prospects. She would be out of a home to live in as soon her grandmother died—or as soon as John F. claimed the house and Maud's grandmother was sent to live with another daughter.

Although Alexander Macneill had been executor of his own father's will—a model in its protection of the widow's ownership rights and other powers, not surprising given Speaker Macneill's legal training—he failed to use his father's will as a guide for his own. His will does not specify who will inherit the actual house where his widow lives; arguably, the house was more in the category of "real estate" than "personal property." On the basis of this will, John F. could (and did) claim the barn; he could (and did) claim the horses and carriages, leaving his mother and Maud without conveyance. Maud suspected that next he would claim the house (and, in time, he did). The will either manifested Alexander Macneill's chauvinism, insensitivity, lack of foresight, or his cruelty—or, perhaps as Maud tartly put it, his foolishness. However, at first John F. Macneill made no attempts to oust his mother from her home. For the time being, Maud and her grandmother had a place to live.

Maud's grandfather's death was in other ways a blessing. Maud could now return to a home she loved and devote herself full time to writing. She was not like the many nineteenth- and early twentieth-century women writers (in Canada and other countries) who had to toil with their pens all night to earn money for their families' upkeep—women like the nineteenth-century Susanna Moodie. Maud's mental energy was boundless, but her physical stamina was not: she had always been very susceptible to colds, flu, and other infections whenever she went without sufficient sleep.

Virginia Woolf's famous 1928 treatise *A Room of One's Own* states that women writers were disadvantaged by not having "wives" to take care of practical matters for them. (Like most male writers in history, William Wordsworth had a wife to pamper and feed him—plus, in *his* case, a gifted sister for companionship.) Maud saw she would now have exactly what she needed: the comforts of home, her quiet grandmother's non-intrusive companionship, the stabilizing force of her grandmother's routine, a room to write in where there were no minefields of sarcasm or sexy young men straying into her private space offering chocolates and affection. She would return the "debt of gratitude" to a grandmother who had made sacrifices for her. Maud had found stability, space, and respect—all under the rubric of "doing her duty."

The village post office had always been in the Macneill kitchen, and this was another benefit. She could submit stories and poems, and any rejection slips sent in return could be kept secret. The post office also offered an ongoing window on life in Cavendish, as well as an opportunity to hear regular gossip from the steady stream of mail-fetchers. In her time away, Maud had learned to see her community in greater perspective, and she was ready to mine it for literary subject matter.

Maud was still only twenty-three years old. Ever her organized grandmother's child, she planned out routines for writing and stuck with them. Her discipline with her writing would become legendary. Now she had time and space to learn more about the book, magazine, and newspaper markets.

She had more time for reading, too. She helped select books for the Cavendish Lending Library and subjects for discussion at the Cavendish Literary Society. She read biographies of women writers and discovered that many had led lives as circumscribed as her own. She reread the Brontë sisters' stories about dark and brooding human passions, and Jane Austen's cool analyses of sexual politics. She admired George Eliot's novels, which set women within complicated social networks. And she remembered the Mathilde Blind biography, arguing that women should write about women's preoccupations, their means of getting what they wanted, and their talk about their lives. Blind had said of Eliot's early years: "Such was the place where the childhood of George Eliot was spent. Here she drew in those impressions of English rural and provincial life, of which one day she was to become the greatest interpreter. Impossible to be in a better position for seeing life . . ." Maud had only to think of the Macneill kitchen and post office where she had heard so many stories, the natural landscape she knew so intimately, and her affection for her "own people." She hoped to immortalize Cavendish in literature, as Jane Austen, the Brontës, and George Eliot had all done before her, writing of the areas that they, as women, knew best. She would anchor herself in her community, and create a history for a rural society already in rapid transition; just as Sir Walter Scott, James M. Barrie, and Charles Dickens had done from a male perspective.

In 1890s periodical literature she had read the essays of reformist women and reactionary men who took different sides on "The Woman Question." She would record the lives of women and children on her beloved Island. "To dwell among my own people" and to write their story became her goal. Later, around 1920, she wrote fondly of them:

They live in a land where nature is neither grudging nor lavish; where faithful work is rewarded by competence and nobody is very

rich and nobody very poor, where everybody knows all about everybody else, so there are few mysteries; . . . where the wonderful loveliness of circling sea and misty river and tree, fairy-haunted woods
is all around you; where the Shorter Catechism is not out of date;
where there are still to be found real grandmothers and genuine old
maid aunts; where the sane, simple, wholesome pleasures of life
have not lost their tang; where you are born into a certain political
party and live and die in it; where it is still thought a great feather in
a family's cap if it has a minister among its boys; where it is safer to
commit murder than to be caught without three kinds of cake when
company comes to tea; where loyalty and upright dealing and kindness of heart and a sense of responsibility and a glint of humour and
a little decent reserve — real solvents of any and all problems if given
a fair trial — still flower freely. . . . Such are my people.[62]

After Maud moved back home to Cavendish in May 1898, she literally wrote
"with a passion." She sent out floods of stories and poems, and when many
of them came back, she simply sent them to other magazines. Her persistence and diligence paid off, and the acceptances grew steadily.

At this same time, she experienced more turbulence in her personal life.
Her sense of isolation from her own age group once again began to trouble
her. On January 16, 1900, she received another devastating telegram: *"Hugh J.
Montgomery died to-day. Pneumonia. Peacefully happy and painless death."*

Maud was paralyzed. She did not write about her father's death in her
diary until May 1, 1900, when sunshine had started to coax life back into the
landscape. Then she wrote about her feelings:

No words to describe how I felt! For weeks I only wished to die.
The news was a thunderbolt from a clear sky. Only a short time
before I had had a letter from him written in the best of health and
spirits. The next was that brutal telegram. . . . How we loved each
other! . . . We always remained near and dear in spirit. . . . Have
you left your "little Maudie" all alone? That was not like you.[63]

But the urge to write returned eventually. The force of an upswinging
mood comes vigorously through as she moves through her grief to eulogize
her father, and then focuses on her own position: "Well, I must henceforth

face the world alone. Let me see what my equipment for such a struggle is."
Then she enumerates: she has youth, a superficial education, three hundred
dollars (her father left her two hundred in his will), no training for anything
save teaching, and no influence. But she has "something else—my knack of
scribbling." Then a proud announcement: "Last year I made exactly ninety-
six dollars and eighty-eight cents by my pen!"

Certainly her income from writing had been climbing. She kept account
books, and she recorded her sales from writing. Collating the amounts she
recorded in her financial ledgers (now in the University of Guelph Archives)
with the listing of stories and poems in the *Preliminary Bibliography* of stories
and poems compiled by Rea Wilmshurst, calculations indicate: $4 in 1895,
$72 in 1896, $80 in 1897, $90 in 1898, $73 in 1899, $89 in 1900.

By 1900, after two years at home, writing constantly, she still was not doing
much better financially than she had when teaching at Bideford in 1894–95.
But there was an upward progression. She was feeling more free and cheerful,
and, living at home, was able to keep what she made instead of paying it out
for room and board.

In January 1901, she became depressed again. January was always a bad
month for her, and the anniversary of her father's death seems to have acti-
vated another bout of depression. Even the death of remote and aged Queen
Victoria in 1901 felt like "a very decided shock." When Maud's old friend
Edith England in Bideford became "a bundle of nerves" on the death of her
father (who had paid for her education), Maud described this as "arrant nonsense." A strange lapse of sympathy this is, coming from one who was often a
bundle of nerves herself, especially when feeling vulnerable.

As always, Maud recovered as the weather warmed and she could get out
to garden and walk. During the summer of 1901 she produced a sizeable number of stories and poems. A new Presbyterian church was being constructed,
giving the whole community an uplift. Maud ended the summer in such a
good frame of mind that she took the initiative of planning a trip to Halifax to
see the September Exhibition.

Hearing of this plan, Lottie Shatford, one of Maud's acquaintances from
Dalhousie who now worked for the Halifax *Echo* and knew that they needed
a proofreader over the winter, recommended Maud to the editor. Maud ac-
cepted the job, and arranged for her Uncle John F. Macneill's eldest son
Prescott to stay in the Cavendish house with her grandmother. Her "visit" to
Halifax turned into an extended stay from September 1901 to June 1902.

Experience in a newspaper would seem useful for someone wanting to be a writer. Furthermore, Maud was paid five dollars a week, more than she had made in teaching. It turned out that she could find time to continue writing, often while actually working in the *Echo* office. She wrote a series of bright news articles, mostly for the women's pages of the *Echo*, which was the evening edition of the *Chronicle*. During her nine months in Halifax, Maud published steadily: twenty-two poems for a total of $67, and seventeen stories for a total of $123—a grand total of $190. In the same period she made about $180 in salary. She had made more by her pen than by her newspaper work.

In spite of this success, she again suffered from an episode of depression in January. She now knew there was something wrong with her that was independent of location. In Belmont, she had been able to blame the dreary company and a cold, bleak landscape. But in Halifax, in the middle of a humming newspaper office, depression again robbed her of all forms of pleasure and made her life hellish for six weeks. In her diary, she dismissed Lottie Shatford, the friend who had obtained the job for her, as *not* being "a kindred spirit."

When she was "down" she felt that she had to pretend to be her fun-loving self. This was a terrible struggle, and she began seeing herself as wearing a "mask of gaiety." Another pervasive reading of her life took hold: the idea of the double self, one face for the public world, and a very different face in private.[64] Maud realized that it was easier to conceal her moods in the privacy of her own home than in a newspaper office. And living in rooming houses with a grungy view (at 23 Church Street, and then later at 25 Morris Street) was hardly the same as living in beautiful Cavendish. Moreover, there were problems brewing at home between her grandmother and Prescott.

Maud had suffered such excruciating homesickness that when she was offered the option of keeping her job at the *Echo*, after a summer break, she declined. Instead, she returned home as eagerly and precipitously as she had left. She knew that her grandmother truly needed her now. Predictably, her Grandmother had fared poorly with Prescott, a selfish lad with his father's personality. Prescott, twenty-two, wanted to marry; and he needed a house.

More trouble was on the horizon in the wake of Alexander's "foolish" will. John F. decided to claim the house, given that the will had not specified Lucy Macneill's residence in it for the rest of her life. John F. saw no reason why his mother could not do what a widow often did, which was to go to live with a married child—not with him, but with daughter Annie at the Campbell farm, or with Emily, now a widow with a partly grown family at Malpeque.

There was only one problem: Lucy Macneill did not want to be pushed out of her own home in which she had raised all her children. She was a very respected member of the community and the church. She also wanted to provide a home for Maud.

Maud knew that it would be more difficult for her uncle to claim the house if she were living there with her grandmother. Maud was a formidable opponent in any battle. And, as far as clan battles went, this was to be an epic one. Maud and her grandmother eventually won, but the atmosphere was poisoned between Grandmother Macneill and her son for the rest of their lives. John F. was so angry that he ceased speaking to his mother and Maud.

Meanwhile, Maud again settled into her grandmother's methodical routine. By walking through old haunts she revived childhood memories; talking to old friends (even those she had outgrown intellectually), she felt the comfort of shared experience. In 1902, a contact in Philadelphia named Miriam Zieber, who wanted to create a literary club of pen-friends, put her in touch with two other writers. One was Ephraim Weber (1870–1956), an Alberta teacher, writer, and homesteader, with whom Maud began a lifelong correspondence. The next year she would begin a similar one with George Boyd MacMillan (1880–1952), who became a professional journalist with the *Alloa Journal* in Scotland. Maud quickly dropped the uninteresting Miss Zieber, but stayed in touch with each of the two men, gaining a sense of connection with other professionals. These pen-pals were stimulating and sympathetic intellectual companions who made no emotional demands on her.

Life at home with her aging grandmother picked up when a new teacher, named Nora Lefurgey, came to the Cavendish school in the fall of 1902. Unlike Lottie Shatford, Nora was a "kindred spirit," sharing intellectual interests and values. Nora was a reader with an excellent memory, and, like Maud, she loved to quote poetry and favourite passages from writers like Scott, Burns, Wordsworth, and others. Nora possessed a strong and irrepressibly positive life force, and she energized those around her — just what Maud needed. They became such fast friends that in January 1903 Nora moved from the John Laird house, where she was boarding, to live with Maud and her grandmother.

Maud and Nora began a joint diary in February. In these diaries, like two giddy, adolescent girls, they tease each other about potential suitors. In fact, most of the young men in Cavendish who had not inherited farms, but who had any ambition and energy, had already left the Island to seek their fortunes. Maud and Nora accused each other of chasing those who remained. It is strange to compare this shared diary—silly and shallow—with some of Maud's lugubrious entries in her private journal of the same period. It is stranger still to compare them with the polished but lighthearted fiction and poems Maud was steadily publishing through this period.

The joint diary, for all its affected silliness, at times gives a better sense of what was happening in the community in 1903 than Maud's journal does. On May 17, Maud wrote:

All this week I have simply had a fiendish cold. Nora has pretended to have one, too, and made it an excuse not to go to prayer-meeting Thursday night. But I went for I wanted to get a good look at our new "supply." Who knows but that he is the "coming man."

On June 21, she wrote again in an exaggerated tone:

This morning we had a Highlander to preach for us and he was "chust lovely" and all the girls got stuck on him. My heart pitty-patted so that I could hardly play the hymns. It's weak yet so I shall stop short.

The young "Highlander" was named Ewan Macdonald. When this unattached young minister "preached for the call" to fill an empty pulpit, every unmarried young woman in the area took interest. To marry a minister was to marry very well indeed. As the most educated person in a rural community, the minister had instant respect and status. Ewan Macdonald's name would appear only once again in Maud's journals before 1906. But the record of Maud's publications shows that with the appearance of this new minister, she began to ramp up energy in her professional writing.

Nora finished her teaching in late July and left Cavendish for good. On September 1, 1903, the thirty-four-year-old Reverend Ewan Macdonald was inducted as minister in the Cavendish church. Maud does not even mention this event in her journal, although the entire community would have turned out for the occasion. Ewan was installed by his acquaintance from Pine Hill Seminary, the Reverend Edwin Smith, an exceptionally handsome and gifted (and newly married) minister.

Also attending the induction was a young man who refused to get out of Maud's life: her cousin and former fiancé, the Reverend Edwin Simpson, now himself a Baptist minister. He remarked to Maud that Ewan looked like a "boy whose mother had told him to put on his best suit" for the occasion, a comment that infuriated Maud (October 12, 1906). Ed was perhaps hoping to show how much Maud had lost when she rejected his suit; he kept turning up in Cavendish, visiting, preaching, or attending social occasions such as this induction service. However, each additional contact only repulsed Maud more.

CHAPTER 6

The impact of Ewan Macdonald

Ewan Macdonald was born in Bellevue, PEI, on July 18, 1870, four years before Maud. After taking a teaching licence from Prince of Wales College,
he taught school in his home district long enough to fund a degree at the
Presbyterian training college, Pine Hill Divinity School, in Halifax. His father's farm at Bellevue was at the other end of the Island from Cavendish.
Ewan's grandparents had emigrated with his father (age seven) from the Isle
of Skye, Scotland, possibly escaping impoverished conditions brought on by
the 1840 potato famine. A very handsome man, Alexander Macdonald
(1833–1914) had married another Skye emigrant, Christie Cameron (1835–
1920), after his first wife had died, leaving him a young daughter named
Flora. Christie Cameron was the daughter of Ewan Cameron, a ship's captain from Point Prim, PEI.

Alexander and Christie Macdonald raised a large family. Their lives were
concerned with survival, not with the display of fine manners. Although
Ewan's father owned land in PEI, their household was decidedly rougher than
Maud's. Furthermore, as Highlanders, the Macdonalds came from a Gaelic-
speaking tradition. It is unclear whether or not Ewan's father, who in infirm
old age signed his will with an "X," was literate in English. (Although there
had been a system of public education in Scotland since 1696, it was very uneven, and often nonexistent on the islands.) Ewan's family may have come up
from poverty, but they were kindly, gentle people, not judgmental like Maud's
family. They believed strongly in education, and had intelligence and ability.

Ewan himself was a good-looking man, with a warm and dimpled smile,
good teeth (particularly valued by Maud because hers were so small and

crooked), and dark but "rosy" skin. It is likely that his parents spoke Gaelic at home because Ewan retained a pronounced Gaelic accent all his life. Maud found his Gaelic accent charming, even though it might have denoted a lower social class to many of Scottish and English extraction.

A minister needed a wife, and Ewan was looking for one, preferably with musical and social skills. He had already had one secret, failed romance: he had once been engaged to an older woman in his home community, but he had backed out, breaking the engagement. Now he was looking again for a suitable mate. At the point that Ewan became the new Presbyterian minister in Cavendish, the church also needed a new organist. Maud's musical talents were mediocre, but she had noted the pleasant Ewan, as did several other spinsters in the area, including (as Maud believed) her friend, Margaret Ross of Stanley. The competition for the minister's attention made the organist's job more appealing. At twenty-nine, Maud was perilously close to the social scorn of spinsterhood. She accepted the position of church organist.

In the same year that Ewan was inducted, Maud's cousin Frederica ("Frede") Campbell turned nineteen. She was nine years younger than Maud, and they had not been close friends earlier. But now that Frede was older, she and Maud discovered that they were also "kindred spirits." Frede was exceptionally gifted academically, with a unique combination of Macneill brilliance and Campbell vitality. She had met Ewan, and admired him, and this influenced Maud.

Subject to vacillating moods herself, Frede understood Maud, and a powerful sense of trust developed between them. With Frede, Maud could discuss her deepest fears: that she would have to leave Cavendish after her grandmother died and the house finally went to Uncle John F.; that she might not find a man to marry; that if she did, she would be too old to have the children she wanted; that she might have a mental breakdown like those regularly described in Island newspapers. With her cousin Frede, Maud found that she could "rinse out her soul" in a way not possible with anyone else.

From 1898 onward, the "black dog" of depression had intermittently stalked Maud, resulting in sleepless nights, restless agitation, skittery thought processes; at times she even reported an inability to make sense of words on a page. Her journals provide some remarkable descriptions of these episodes, written after they had passed. Only from a distance could she shape and treat them artistically. For example on June 30, 1902, she wrote:

[I] did not sleep until dawn. Every trouble I ever had came surging
up with all its old bitterness—and all my little present day worries
enlarged themselves to tenfold proportions and flew at my throat.
Life seemed a horrible, cruel, starving thing and I hated it and
wished I were dead. I cried bitterly in sheer heart sickness and
loneliness. Anything like that wrings the stamina out of me.

In April 1903, before Ewan had come to preach for the call, she recorded
brooding, feeling constantly tired, and wanting to "fall asleep and never wake
again." Old friends like Mary Campbell (now Mary Beaton) had married and
were expecting babies. The year 1903 saw still more weddings: notably the
marriage of the Reverend Major MacIntosh, the Cavendish minister before
Ewan, to Mabel Simpson, church organist; and the marriage of Maud's
cousin, George Campbell of Park Corner, to Ella Johnstone. In 1904 Maud's
friend Fanny Wise married R. E. Mutch, and Maud's cousin Murray
Macneill (who was now a professor at Dalhousie) married Dorothy Holmes
of Halifax. Then, in 1905, Myrtle Macneill, Maud's younger "cousin," married Ernest Webb and Maud was also a bridesmaid at the wedding of her
friend, Bertha MacKenzie, solemnized by the new minister, the Reverend
Ewan Macdonald.

Between September 1903 and May 1905, Ewan Macdonald boarded at
Stanley, one of his three ministerial charges (Stanley, Rustico, and
Cavendish). All the unmarried spinsters, including Maud, had their eyes on
him. During this period, Maud made several trips to Stanley to visit Frede.
Now that this unmarried minister was in the picture, Maud began romanticizing the cozy little house in New London where her parents had started
housekeeping together. At home, she rummaged through her memories of
past male friends: Nate Lockhart, Herman Leard, Will Pritchard. She read a
packet of Will's letters in March 1904, and felt,

as if a cruel hand were tightening its clutch on my throat. . . . I
don't know why Will's letters should have such an effect on me . . .
they were not such as would be expected to stir up such a riot of
feeling in me. But I've been lonely and sick at heart all day, and I
just long wildly for his bright friendliness again . . . I cannot understand my mood at all. (March 16, 1904)

In January 1905, she wrote poignantly in her journals of how unloved she had felt in her childhood. Although the childhood she describes was not the childhood that might objectively be recognized from her other accounts, it does reflect how she re-visioned her childhood when she was depressed. Now, in 1905, her moods cycled rapidly: she was a "winged spirit" on March 16; she was "a caged creature" March 23; the following week "a prisoner released." But change was coming.

On April 14, 1905, she began to have pleasant dreams. Rumours had been afloat that Ewan Macdonald was moving from Stanley to Cavendish, which meant to Maud that she had perhaps caught his eye. As soon as this move was in the wind, Maud's spirits ascended rapidly. She started planning her first full-length book. (She had by this time published at least 168 short stories and 192 poems in periodicals.)[65]

In early May 1905, Ewan moved to Cavendish, taking a room with the John Laird family. This was easy walking distance from the Presbyterian church, and the church was next to the Macneill homestead. From her bedroom window, Maud could see people walking up their lane to the post office, or hear them enter if they came into the kitchen from the back of the house from another direction.

The first evening that Ewan came to call for his letters, Maud—who normally did her writing in the privacy of her upstairs bedroom as soon as it was warm enough in spring—was suddenly positioned in the kitchen, apparently admiring the last rays of light and ready to engage him in cheerful conversation. By her account he entered just as she had finished the first lines of this first full-length novel, to be named Anne of Green Gables. She put her writing aside to chat with the amiable minister. Her new duties as church organist provided matter for discussion.

Perhaps it is true that her basic idea for the novel—as she claimed in one account—originated from a newspaper clipping about a couple requesting an orphan boy to help them, but instead being sent a young girl by mistake. What is certain, however, is that the narrative flowed smoothly out. The main character in this novel was as lively as Maud herself, and resembled her in other ways. The heroine, Anne Shirley, was an unwanted orphan, just as Maud had felt herself to be when she revisited her childhood in January 1905. The first third of the novel presented Anne—a child of wildly fluctuating moods—as the most lovable creature imaginable. She would find love and acceptance in her new home, and then she would sacrifice herself at the end by doing exactly what Maud had done when she'd come home to stay with her grandmother. At the novel's conclusion, a more mature Anne would sit, as Maud had so often done, looking out her window, wondering what was around the "bend in the road." The novel was a version of Maud's own emotional and spiritual autobiography, a blend of her childhood as it was and as she had reconfigured it in the entry of January 1905, followed by the high brought about by the happy anticipation of Ewan's impending move to Cavendish. Only the facts and names were changed. Maud manufactured a history for Anne in order to obscure her heroine's origin in her own life. (Anne is the orphaned daughter of two schoolteachers who died of a fever, and her subsequent life includes misery and abuse in various homes and an orphanage until she is adopted by the Cuthberts.) In fact, Anne was a creative rendition of the volatile and lovable child Maud herself had been—not an orphan, but one carefully raised by a loving and supportive grandmother and a difficult, judgmental grandfather whose harsh words had made Maud feel like a charity case at times.

In May 1905 Maud had published a story called "The Hurrying of Ludovic." In this story, a courtship fails to advance because sluggish Ludovic Speed will not propose to his lady, the thirty-something Theodora. Ludovic is characterized by his "unhesitating placidity" and his eyes "with a touch of melancholy in them" as he shambles down the long road to visit the ever-hopeful Theodora. He has "a liking for religious arguments: and talks well enough when drawn out." Theodora plots to get this "big, irritating goose" to propose after fifteen years of courting. There were about fifteen months between the time Ewan was inducted as the Cavendish minister and the time Maud sent this story off for publication. The *Canadian Magazine* published it in May 1905, the month that Ewan strategically moved to Cavendish and started actively courting her. Fifteen months may have seemed like fifteen years to a woman like Maud, who was thirty and had been hopefully encouraging the clueless new minister since the day he preached for the call in spring 1903.

Before she wrote *Anne of Green Gables*, Maud had been doing better and better financially. Her yearly income from writing was already climbing towards the astonishing sum of $500 a year from short stories and poems. (For comparison, Ewan's salary in his triple-charge parish was $765 in 1909, and ministers were well paid professionals.)

Maud wrote her *Anne* manuscript in a flowing hand that seemed to skim the story off a teeming brain. Luckily for Maud, her aging Uncle Leander and his wife did not come to the Island for their usual two months of summer vacation that year. In the absence of this interruption, Maud wrote *Anne of Green Gables* with manic energy throughout the entire year of 1905, apparently completing the book by January 1906. There was no time to write in her journals in that period—and not much need, either, since they were, on the whole, the place where she vented her unhappiness, and in this period, her life was looking more promising, with a suitor on the scene.

Anne of Green Gables was written in the most positive and forward-looking part of Maud's life, and it is her most sparkling novel. Anne is a fictional character, of course. Yet, she is as much the result of the coming together of a real man and a real woman as if she were a real flesh-and-blood child. Lucy Maud Montgomery is certainly the "mother" who conceived, carried, and delivered Anne. But Ewan played—literally—a seminal role in the production of this book: he was the catalyst that pulled Maud out of a period of depression, providing the energy to take on a full-scale book. His attentions sustained her spirits so that she wrote with a "wingèd" pen, producing the entire novel in approximately ten months, in longhand, between spring 1905 and early 1906.[66]

Maud's "gift of wings" had finally enabled her to take flight, thanks to the astonishing effect of the dimpled and rosy-cheeked Ewan. In spite of—or perhaps because of—the afflictions in her life, Maud had written her first novel, the one that would make her famous throughout the English-speaking world.

Anne of Green Gables (1908)

Anne of Green Gables is only one of many novels about orphans written in this era, but it has outshone all of them. Part of the book's power comes from the way Maud draws on her own emotional experience, and reconfigures her own past. Anne is a sensitive and very bright orphaned child who has had disastrous experiences in homes where she was unloved and exploited. By accident, she is sent to the home of two elderly people, brother and sister, who had asked for a boy to help them on their farm. Matthew Cuthbert loves little Anne from the start, but dominant, rigid Marilla plans to return her to the orphanage since she isn't what they'd asked for. When Anne wails, "You don't want me because I'm not a boy," she is expressing Maud's lifelong sorrow.

One third of the way through the book, Matthew and Marilla Cuthbert decide to keep Anne because their sense of duty tells them they can do something for this little waif. Marilla trains her to behave in acceptable ways, and as she grows up Anne enriches their lives and endears herself to the entire community. As the novel ends, she is a young woman poised to take flight. But then death claims Matthew. Because aging Marilla can stay in her home only if someone stays with her, Anne curtails her ambitions in order to repay to Marilla her debt of gratitude.

Anne and Marilla are as different in temperament as emotional little Maud and her Grandmother Macneill had been. When Anne comes to Avonlea (a community like Cavendish), she is a little chatterbox given to extravagant language and excessive emotions. She is either in the "depths of despair" or overexcited with her enthusiasms. She is impulsive and gets into all kinds of funny scrapes. Her most noteworthy trait is her fertile imagination. Staid, sensible Marilla guides Anne into curtailing her wild, romantic excesses of words and actions. Anne wins Marilla's love, just as Maud did her grandmother's, as she matures.

Matthew and Gilbert play supportive roles in the novel that mimic Ewan's role in real life. Ewan was as much taken by Maud's charming talk as Matthew is by Anne's. Matthew is as kind and nonjudgmental as Ewan was. And Ewan Macdonald, as suitor, was waiting in the wings, just like Anne's beau, Gilbert Blythe. In Ewan's attentions, Maud finally found what Anne sought: to be loved and valued.

Maud's own community of Cavendish had known her as an impulsive and sometimes otherworldly child, as a difficult-to-control and flirtatious teen, and as a moody young woman who seemed suspiciously off-balance at times. Maud took all the difficult qualities of the child she had been, things that would have been the subject of community gossip, and she turned them into endearing traits in little Anne. By the time Ewan Macdonald appeared on the scene, Maud, approaching twenty-nine, had new self-understanding. In creating Anne so like herself, she was creating a new way of seeing the difficult child she had been as a lovable, engaging one. Perhaps she even hoped to counter village gossip and give people (and possibly this new minister) a way of understanding her. Maud made a great many superficial alterations in the fictional transformation—Anne was given red hair to symbolize anarchy (and perhaps a Scots-Irish heritage), whereas Maud had brown hair. Anne came to an elderly, unmarried brother and sister, not to elderly grandparents; Anne was sent to the Cuthberts by mistake, whereas Maud stayed with her grandparents because her mother had died and her grandmother had a strong sense of duty.

Some of the more literal-minded people in the local community fell to looking for models as soon as *Anne* was published. A few saw elements of the youthful Maud in her creation. However, others claimed that they themselves were the model for lovable Anne. Ellen Macneill, a little orphan girl who had been adopted by Pierce Macneill and his wife, wanted a piece of Anne's immortality and went to her grave claiming to be the model because she, too, was adopted. However, of this rumour, circulating during her lifetime, Maud wrote "The idea of getting a child from an orphan asylum was suggested to me years ago as a possible germ for a story by the fact that Pierce Macneill got a little girl from one." But, she added in total exasperation on January 27, 1911: "There is no resemblance of any kind between Anne and Ellen Macneill who is one of the most hopelessly commonplace and uninteresting girls imaginable."

Montgomery acknowledges that the prototype for Anne's home with Matthew and Marilla Cuthbert was that of Maud's Great-Uncle David Macneill, a "notoriously shy" man like Matthew. He lived with his Marilla-like sister, Margaret, and they raised the illegitimate daughter of their niece, Ada Macneill, a young schoolteacher who was considered by the community to have been "badly used." This niece's child, Myrtle Macneill, was a great comfort to them, and in 1905 she married Ernest Webb. Ernest and Myrtle inherited David and Margaret's farm and raised their children there. It is now a provincial park, with the "Anne of Green Gables House" and the adjoining "Lovers' Lane" open to the public. Myrtle Macneill Webb and Maud were good friends all their lives, but neither ever claimed that Myrtle was the model for Anne, despite the fact that she was raised in the house that was the model for "Green Gables" and she had done for her elderly surrogate parents what the fictional Anne did for the Cuthberts.

Maud would never admit that her heroine Anne was partly based on the child she herself had been, or at least one of the complex little girls who lay inside her. She rightly thought this was irrelevant and that people would use the idea to discredit her creativity. Over her lifetime, Maud created heroines very different from Anne, and yet each of them is in some way drawn out of the complex person that she was. Nothing made Maud angrier than hearing people say that they knew the originals of her characters, as if all she had to do was to transcribe them from life to make a book. She admitted that her characters had some resemblances to people in real life, but it was her imagination that made them live in fiction.

The book takes its power from Maud's ability to word-paint landscapes, her skill at characterization, her understanding of how human beings interact in a small community, her trenchant social criticism, her sense of irony, and her sly erudition. Most of all, it is energized by her sense of humour. Readers laugh at the honesty of children, and the foolishness of adults. The book also captures with realism and nostalgia the tranquil nineteenth-century rural life that would disappear after World War I. Maud succeeded in capturing the culture, the history, and the times of her own people—and perhaps even much of the country of Canada—in her first book.

When the Muse descended on Maud Montgomery in that spring of 1905, coming in the company of the kindly Ewan Macdonald, a good-looking but unimaginative suitor, the effects flowed both ways. Ewan's attentions energized Maud, but in turn her high spirits also stimulated Ewan, who was by nature a bit phlegmatic. For a man like Ewan, whose childhood had been poor and culturally deprived, whose education had been endless hard work, and whose emotional life had been flat, Maud must have seemed like a creature of fancy ready to fill the void. Maud was undeniably a lady in manners, deportment, and dress. He must have been flattered that she would consider a romance with him, a somewhat backward and stiff Highlander. That Ewan chose her over other aspiring women, given her rather plain looks and near spinsterdom, certainly delighted Maud. She used every charm she knew to win him when he came for the mail and she had a chance to talk to him, amusing him with her sparkling wit and stories about the community and her activities in it and the church. Later, in her journals, she would tell this story in a very different way, even razoring out and replacing the pages that originally described their courtship. She would make it sound as if Ewan sought her, and she merely accepted him because there was no better, her "Hobson's Choice"—which was, of course, at least partly true.

Inspired and invigorated by finding love, Ewan became a very competent minister in Cavendish. He gave interesting sermons. People liked him. Maud gave him entertaining walks through the cemetery, narrating entertaining stories of the departed. He moved into action and mobilized the community to clean up the graveyard where a century's collection of ancestors lay, including Maud's mother and the rest of the family. (This beautifying project would be used later in *Anne of Avonlea*, where Anne encourages the "Avonlea improvement Society"—an idea generated by the popular press of that day, which was devoting much coverage to landscape and garden developments.) As his tenure wore on, and his courtship infused him with energy, his ambition surged. He began to think that he might become an even more successful minister if he took more training.

On October 12, 1906, Ewan drove Maud up to visit married friends, Will and Tillie Macneill Houston. On the way, he told her of his new plans: to leave Cavendish and take additional schooling at the famous Trinity College in Glasgow, Scotland, the most prestigious centre for studying Presbyterian theology in the world. Ewan's father had fled Scotland to escape abject poverty; now Ewan would go back, triumphant in his calling as a minister of the Lord. Ewan was not wrong in thinking that a brilliant future might stretch before him. He was highly intelligent, and also had the instincts of a "good shepherd": he was a gentle, well-meaning man. Shrewd and low-key, he was a skilled negotiator when tempers were ruffled, a necessary trait in a minister. He was also an effective organizer and mediator when he was in top form. Energized by romance, he showed great promise.

Ewan had been increasing his presence in the newspapers, preaching in important venues, as befitted ambitious young ministers. The *Examiner* stated that on September 5, 1906, he preached in the prestigious St. James Presbyterian Kirk in Charlottetown. By September 25, the paper announced that the Cavendish pulpit had become vacant. (He had already announced his intention of going to Scotland.) On October 7, Ewan again preached in St. James Church in the morning service and at Zion Church in the evening. He was preaching in Charlottetown's most notable churches, in partnership with the distinguished Reverend T. F. Fullerton, a very prominent minister who frequently made the news. This burst of activity was spectacular for Ewan Macdonald after his competent but mediocre academic career. It appeared that his trajectory was that of a successful young minister ready to climb clerical ladders.

Seen in the context of his lifetime performance, his sudden show of activity suggests that he was riding an emotional high induced by his new romance. Had this been his standard and stable mode, his career would have been very different. But he would prove to be a man whose moods rose and sank, like the energies within him, and his performance was uneven.

As they drove along, Maud considered this good-natured man who was modest, yet dedicated and seemingly ambitious. She had read in the newspapers about his preaching in important churches. *Anne of Green Gables* had been completed some ten months earlier and was still making the rounds of publishers. Maud had no idea that it would become an international best-seller. But she did feel warm and hopeful in Ewan's presence. As she and Ewan drove by horse and buggy that night, the weather was ominously dark and stormy. He proposed. Maud accepted. Both were very private people by nature, and they agreed to keep the engagement secret.

Ewan left to begin his advanced training in Glasgow around October 20. After she accepted Ewan, Maud wrote her cousin Ed Simpson a letter that made their breakup irrevocably final. Ewan promised to wait for Maud until she was "released" from her duties caring for her grandmother. Meanwhile, she was putting jewels in her own crown. Her grandmother was in relatively good health for her advanced age, and Maud could keep writing. It was a satisfactory arrangement for everyone — except, of course, Uncle John F. Macneill, who wanted the house.

Ewan had no sooner arrived in Scotland than he began to deflate. His departure from Cavendish had been quite a send-off: the community had put on a big celebration for their minister and given him a "purse" to help with his studies. He had crossed the ocean with great confidence, but as soon as he reached the University of Glasgow, he found himself in association and competition with brilliant, cultured, and highly articulate scholars from all over the globe. In Prince Edward Island his Highland roots and heavy Gaelic accent had been a slightly negative social marker among more sophisticated English-speaking Scottish immigrants, but in Glasgow, where the theology school was full of highly educated young Scots, Ewan found himself not only regarded as a backward Highlander but also as a provincial bumpkin from Canada. In Cavendish, Maud — immersed in the literary images of the Highlanders as brave and exotic — had romanticized his Highland roots, and this had bolstered his confidence. He got no such treatment in Scotland.[67] Ewan's name is written on the Glasgow entrance roll with a strong hand, but he soon began to collapse psychologically, skipping classes. He was out of his depth with the urbane and broadly educated students at the theology school. Moreover, he lacked the social graces that would have helped him feel comfortable with the others. This earnest young man soon began to feel inadequate. Within a month, his letters to Maud took on a morbid tone. He spoke only of discouragement.

Maud urged him to see a doctor, but he wrote back that a doctor couldn't help him. (He was right — there was no medical treatment for depression in that period.) Perhaps he was counselled; perhaps some theologian told him that he was committing the "unpardonable sin" of doubt. At any rate, this idea took hold of his mind. In the theological terms of Presbyterians, the unpardonable sin was a failure to put all one's trust in God. Believing himself shut out from complete faith, Ewan, now an engaged man, must have felt trapped in a future profession and a life. It is hard to fathom the depths to which his disturbed and disordered mind led him. He left Glasgow in the spring, sometime around March 4, 1907, when he sent a strange, blank, message-less postcard to Maud.[68] There are no records in Glasgow of his academic performance at Trinity College beyond his matriculation signature, and no records to show he completed any work whatsoever.[69]

When Ewan went off to Scotland, his successor in the Cavendish church was another eligible bachelor, John Stirling. Stirling had a chiselled and ruggedly handsome face, a very sharp mind, and a refined manner. He came from a "good family" and was stable as a rock. All considered, with the benefit of hindsight, he was a much more promising man than Ewan.

Ewan returned from Scotland to Prince Edward Island at the end of March a sadly deflated man. After a lot of trouble in finding a charge, he accepted a less than desirable position in another small rural community, the remote Bloomfield-O'Leary parish, a very long way from Cavendish. Only rarely did he visit Maud. In his depressed state, he must have worried about his engagement and whether he himself was suitable for marriage. But he admired Maud too much to play the role of a cad and back out, as he had from his first engagement. Ewan was apparently doing satisfactorily in his new position when *Anne of Green Gables* was released and became an astonishing success.

Maud's sudden fame may have inspired Ewan to attend the Presbyterian General Assembly off the Island, apparently looking for better opportunity on the mainland, as so many other ambitious young ministers did. For instance, the Reverend Edwin Smith, who had inducted Ewan as a minister in Cavendish, had already resigned (as recounted in the *Patriot* on May 1, 1909, p. 8), and had left the Island for greener pastures, and perhaps greater adventure, along with thousands of young people in other walks of life. According to the Charlottetown *Patriot*, in September 1909 Ewan resigned at Bloomfield, to the regret of his parishioners. He headed to a double-charge parish in Ontario, where he would live in Leaskdale, Ontario, patiently waiting for Maud to be free to marry.

The bitterness between Maud, her grandmother, and John F. Macneill's family began to take its toll. Lucy Macneill came from an extremely long-lived family. Her sister Margaret lived to be nearly one hundred, and as a clan, the Woolners were normally very long in the land. But her son's estrangement preyed on her mind, and, as she failed, Maud's grandmother fell into periods of weeping and sadness.

There were problems at John F. Macneill's house, too. His lovely daughter Kate had caught pneumonia and died in 1904 at the age of twenty. Maud had liked her. But Maud did not like the other daughters—Maud's former playmate, Lucy, and Annie, the youngest. Lucy had incurred Maud's anger for a perceived transgression, probably by tattling on Maud's flirtatious behaviour, and Maud cut off all association with her, later reporting in her journals that Lucy had married beneath herself. As for Prescott, when his grandmother tartly told him he could wait to have her house after she died, he snapped, "You may live ten years yet."[70] Prescott developed health problems in 1906 and went into painful decline with tuberculosis of the spine, dying before his grandmother.

Maud's use of language is deadly, and she wrote damning descriptions of most of her Uncle John's children—Prescott, Frank, Lucy, and Annie. She was more kind to Ernest, the one son she liked, and the one who would indeed eventually inherit the farm. Of Lucy, she wrote:

> Lucy was their oldest daughter . . . I kept on believing Lucy to be my true friend until I had unmistakable evidence of her falseness and deceit. When once my eyes were opened I investigated the matter thoroughly and a sickening tale of underhand malice and envy was revealed. . . . She had not stopped with distorting facts and insinuating malicious opinions. She had employed absolute falsehood. . . . Lucy was false to the core.[71]

 Cavendish might have seemed idyllic, but it had the same passionate hatreds in it that fuelled wars on a national scale elsewhere. Until Maud's journals were published, it was assumed that she knew only the rosy and romantic sides of life, but her devastating character sketches of people in the journals demonstrate otherwise.[72]

Despite the tensions with Uncle John's family, Maud kept up her publishing efforts. She wrote and wrote, and read and read, while taking long walks to relieve her own anxieties. She suffered increasingly from headaches.

———

It appears that Maud circulated *Anne of Green Gables* to publishers throughout 1906, as soon as she had it typed. She reported later that the novel was rejected by five publishers—in order, Bobbs-Merrill of Indianapolis; MacMillan of New York; Lothrop, Lea & Shephard of Boston; Henry Holt of New York; and L. C. Page Company of Boston—and then it lay in a hatbox for a considerable time before she reread it, liked it herself, and sent it out again to the L. C. Page Company of Boston.[73] They wrote a letter accepting the novel on April 8, 1907, typed up a contract for the book by April 22, 1907, and Maud received it by post and signed it on May 2. In at least one speech during the 1930s, Maud said that *Anne of Green Gables* got special attention at the Page Company because a friend of hers from Summerside was a reader there and lobbied for the book.

Perhaps this history of the multiple rejections is accurate, perhaps not. The mail service was admittedly faster then. But if the handwritten manuscript was finished in January 1906, it had to be revised and typed, activities that normally took Maud several months; and if it was then sent to five publishers, one after the other, they would have had to return it almost without reading it, if we are to believe her story of its journeys—which in some tellings had the rejected manuscript reposing in her old hatbox until she had half forgotten it and found it during spring cleaning. Whatever the truth was, Maud was undeniably persistent in the face of manuscript rejection. As soon as any short story, poem, or other manuscript came back, she sent it out again.[74]

Maud expected *Anne of Green Gables* to be released in fall 1907, and wrote both of her correspondents, Ephraim Weber and George Boyd MacMillan, to that effect. Page apparently encountered delays with the internal artwork.[75] In January 1908, she again wrote MacMillan that she expected it soon. On March 2, 1908, Maud wrote to Ephraim Weber that she had been busy for a month correcting the proofs of *Anne of Green Gables*, and it was to be out shortly ("around the 15th," presumably of April). On April 5, 1908, she told Weber that she was expecting the novel any day, and that Page had sent advance publicity for it. On June 12, 1908, *Anne of Green Gables* was entered for copyright by L. C. Page under the number A-209449, and on June 20, her own copy arrived from Boston. By June 30, L. C. Page had announced that *Anne* was in a second printing. (The true first impression of the first edition of *Anne of Green Gables* bears an April 1908 date, and has two garbled sentences in it; Page soon corrected these errors and passed off the June impression as a first impression, first edition.)[76] Reviews and letters about *Anne* began to pour in. Five months after the book was published, Maud reported having received sixty-six reviews.

Long before *Anne* was published, Maud was regularly written up in Island papers as a gifted poet and short-story writer. By mid-summer 1908 there were further write-ups about the success of *Anne of Green Gables*. The *Examiner* carried a long and laudatory review on July 10, 1908. The *Patriot* followed with a long, favourable review on July 13. On July 29, 1908, the Summerside *Journal* raved:

> *Anne of Green Gables*, the latest literary effort of Miss L. M. Montgomery, of Cavendish, has made an instantaneous hit. The story throughout is most entertaining and the quaint and delicious sayings of Anne are bound to become household words. The book could only have been written by a woman of deep and wide sympathy. The humorous touches are most captivating. Beyond doubt, *Anne of Green Gables* is well worth reading. If you wish to see how really clever an Island girl can be just get this book. (p. 5)

Major papers in the United States also carried glowing reviews of the novel. The sales were phenomenal. Soon fans from all over the United States began to descend on Cavendish, wanting to meet Maud. The book was reprinted each month for the rest of the year, and almost as frequently the following year. By 1914, it had gone through thirty-eight impressions, and was still selling well.

When the book became an instant best-seller, Maud's fragile temperament found sudden fame disorienting. To make matters worse, in July 1908 their house roof caught fire, a portentous event that devastated her nerves. By October she complained of feeling "deadly tired all the time." Ten days later she complained about uncontrollable hyperactivity in her brain: "vexing thoughts began to swarm through it like teasing gnats." She had bouts of unexplained weeping, and she began reliving every failure in her life (all symptoms of depression). Her behaviour upset her elderly grandmother even more.

Uncle Leander and his family were again at the family farm. He was a reader, and to his credit, he was impressed by *Anne of Green Gables* — and even more so by the way the book was selling. He began to treat Maud with new respect, deeming her intelligent enough to discuss men's topics: politics, literature, history. Her Uncle John F. Macneill read the novel too; he is reported to have sneered that "anyone could have written it."

Maud dedicated *Anne of Green Gables* to the memory of her father and mother. One of her greatest disappointments was that her late father would never know that she had "arrived." Mary Ann McRae Montgomery did live to hear of the book's phenomenal success. If she resented her stepdaughter's fame, however, she did not have long to do so. The Charlottetown *Examiner* reported on April 19, 1909, that "Mrs. Mary Montgomery, who made a fortune in real estate speculation, died at Prince Albert, Sask." She was forty-six. This was one death Maud did not lament.

Still, amid all this emotional upheaval, Maud was pushing herself to write. L. C. Page had set her to writing a sequel, *Anne of Avonlea,* a continuation of Anne's story, even before *Anne of Green Gables* came out, and the new book was published in 1909 to immense sales. Page now urged her to get on with another book. She cobbled together *Kilmeny of the Orchard* for publication in 1910, basing it on material published earlier. At the end of 1909, when she was trying to write *The Story Girl,* she turned once again to herself as a partial model for her heroine, Sara Stanley.

Sara, the "Story Girl," has an absent father and lives with relatives in Prince Edward Island. She is a local legend for her ability to tell spellbinding stories. Sara actually tells many of Maud's own set-pieces. The cousins Sara lives with—Dan, Felicity, and Cecily—exhibit the happy qualities of the Campbell cousins, George, Clara, and Stella. Sara's chief admirers are two young boys, relatives from Toronto. In the year before she married a minister, Maud had fun writing mock-sermons for the characters in her book to deliver, with farcical seriousness.

By January 1910, as she wrote *The Story Girl,* Maud spiralled towards a complete breakdown. "I thank God I do not come of a stock in which there is any tendency toward insanity," she writes on February 7, 1910.[77] Maud did not lose touch with reality (as in insanity), but her mood swings into depression were debilitating, and they disrupted her life. Maud describes in 1910 how she had a month of nervous prostration: "an utter breakdown of body, soul, and spirit." The symptoms she describes include sleepless nights, and dreadful mental restlessness when she walked the floors with a fury, like a caged tiger. Talking to people coming to their house for their mail was a torture. She could not read or write or think. People noticed her distraught appearance.

I wanted to die and escape life! The thought of having to go on living was more than I could bear. I seemed to be possessed by a

morbid dread of the future. No matter under what conditions I pictured myself I could only see myself suffering unbearably. . . . I had
no hope. I could not realize any possible escape from suffering. It
seemed to me that I must exist in that anguish forever. This is, I believe, a very common symptom of neurasthenia. (February 7, 1910).

She added that when she felt that way she could understand why people
committed suicide to escape their feelings of torture. Her words are a classic
description of a person's feelings in a severe depression.

With her newly found fame, she now developed many worries about her
fiancé: his sinking moods, his irregular performance, his awkwardness in polite society, his narrow range of knowledge, and, worse, his lack of intellectual
curiosity for anything outside of his profession. The man who had been so solicitous before now seemed incapable of understanding or comforting her in
any way. She told him of her despondent spirits, and he suggested that she
give up her writing. He was unable to see that her writing was an integral part
of her spirit and sense of self, and that it was, in fact, what sustained her. He
simply thought it made her nervous.

Yet he was a very kind man, a trait that, having lived with her Grandfather
Macneill, Maud valued highly. She had already backed out on Ed Simpson,
and she didn't want the reputation of being a "jilt." If she rejected Ewan, who
was willing to wait patiently for her until her grandmother died, she might not
find someone else. And she did *like* Ewan a great deal. Maud had sought out
Ewan's love when her prospects were minimal, and she would have felt it dis-
honourable to back out as soon as she saw a chance for success and wealth.

In February 1910, Maud received a royalty cheque for $7,000. To put this
in perspective, the prime minister of Canada made $14,500 in the same year.
She had accepted Ewan when she thought he was headed towards a successful career in the ministry. Ewan's brief blaze of glory had fizzled out after his
return to the Island, but she was becoming a wealthy, famous woman. On
November 19, 1910, for instance, the respected American periodical *The
Republic* gave her a full page. The second paragraph read:

Less than three years ago the name of L. M. Montgomery was unknown to the reading public of the United States. Today she is in
the forefront of our popular authors, not only in this country but in
England, Canada and Australia. It is true, of course, that the author

had a modest repute for excellent apprentice work . . . but doubtless those who knew her best little dreamed that her bud of promise was to have so early and splendid development. (p. 5)

Maud's doubts about the man she was engaged to continued to grow.
During her engagement, which they kept secret, she had watched, probably
with frustration, as the very attractive John Stirling courted Margaret Ross of
Stanley—a woman she believed to have been one of her early rivals for Ewan's
attention. In her journals Maud remained absolutely silent about this budding
courtship. After the Stirlings were married in 1910, she stated with some tartness
that he was one of those men that women marry for reasons other than love, and
she unjustly labelled him as homely.[78] John and Margaret Stirling made a happy
marriage, remaining friends with Ewan and Maud throughout their lives. By
1911 Maud would look back on this earlier period and meditate on why we "seldom give our love to what is worthiest" (February 5, 1911).

Another friend was married that year. Nora Lefurgey, the vivacious
teacher who had boarded with Maud and her grandmother, married Edmund
Ernest Campbell, an Island son who was by then a very successful mining en-
gineer in British Columbia. (He appears to have been one of Maud's older
students at Belmont.) This once again reminded her of her age.

Maud was now suffering from the excessive demands of her publisher, L. C.
Page. He wanted more books as quickly as she could turn them out. She was
expected to produce one book after another at breakneck speed. But at least
the frantic pace of her writing kept her from thinking about other worries,
like her future marriage to Ewan. She discovered that writing could often
help her block out worries in her real life. It was a pleasant way to escape.

Kilmeny of the Orchard (1910), written quickly to satisfy Page, was the expansion of a story published between December 1908 and April 1909 as "Una
of the Garden" in a Minnesota-based magazine called *The Housekeeper*. It
tells the story of a young woman bearing a curse, who cannot speak until a
suitor arrives and releases her voice. Similar to fairy tales like "The Sleeping
Beauty," it also parallels Maud's own story: Ewan's courtship allowed her to
move beyond formulaic short stories and sentimental poems. Only then was
she freed from a harsh grandfather's curse. By freeing her from the fears of becoming a pitiful and voiceless old maid, Ewan's love made her imagination

soar and her pen sing. The style of *Kilmeny* is different from Maud's other novels, and in style reflects her rereading of Hans Christian Andersen's stories shortly before expanding "Una" into a novel.

Maud was not writing her novels in a vacuum. This was a period of great Canadian nationalism. An article in the *Examiner* notes that a host of other Canadian writers—Bliss Carman, Archibald Lampman, Wilfred Campbell, Frederick George Scott (father of Frank Scott, the famous jurist and poet), and Marshall Saunders were all born in 1861 and were now in their prime, creating an indigenous Canadian literature. Maud's books were admired by the general public as part of this new burst of creativity. On one level, *Anne of Green Gables* tells the story of how an orphan found a happy home, but on another, it also captures the colonizing experience, especially the story of Canada's settlement: an outsider (or immigrant) comes into a new territory, transforms it by naming it and changing it, makes it his or her own, and is rooted there—a classic pattern, but the difference was that this outsider was a little *girl*. Whatever the appeal, in 1910, new impressions of *Anne of Green Gables* continued to roll steadily off the Page presses; a British edition had been published and was already translated into Swedish and Dutch.

The Earl Grey Affair

Maud's reputation as a writer was spreading internationally. In the summer of 1910 the popularity of *Anne* carried Maud further into Canadian history, when she drew the admiration of the Governor General of Canada, Earl Grey, who made a trip to the Island especially to meet her.

Sir Albert Henry George Grey (1851–1917) was Governor General of Canada from 1904 to 1911. During this period of extensive social change, he was an active reformer, supporter of Canadian culture, and traveller. Known also for his tireless promotion of unity within the Commonwealth, he sought to address as many "ordinary" Canadians as possible. Wilfrid Laurier (then prime minister) said Lord Grey gave "his whole heart, his whole soul, and his whole life to Canada." Earl Grey was an articulate, gifted diplomat, without pretense or affectation.[79] Respected throughout Canada, he took his duties seriously and was the first Governor General to travel to Hudson Bay and Newfoundland.

Towards the end of his office in Canada (the next Governor General was sworn in early the following year), at the age of fifty-nine, Earl Grey undertook an expedition from Manitoba to Hudson Bay and the Maritimes. The members of the expedition had been largely chosen by Grey himself, and included geologists, journalists, and constables of the Royal Northwest Mounted Police. Several notable academics from McGill University included the expedition doctor, Dr. John McCrae (1872–1918), lecturer in Pathology and Medicine, and Professor John MacNaughton (1858–1943), a distinguished professor of Classics noted for his wide-ranging literary knowledge and his sociable personality. These men were colleagues of another prominent McGill scholar, PEI native Dr. Andrew Macphail (1864–1938), who was then one of the Island's most famous native sons. He was not part of Earl Grey's party.

The expedition was to evaluate the possibility of a rail link from the prairies to Hudson Bay. The expedition started at Norway House at the mouth of the Saskatchewan River; around August 10, 1910, they set off, travelling in twelve twenty-foot canoes, each paddled by two Cree guides, several hundred miles across north-eastern Manitoba. The group faced lengthy portages and rapids in their journey to York Factory, on Hudson Bay. Here they boarded the *Earl Grey*, a 250-foot steamship that had been built in 1909 for the Canadian government. This boat was an icebreaker as well as a passenger and freight ship that could cross the Northumberland Strait, from the mainland to PEI, in winter. The steamship, with a specially appointed suite for the Governor General, took them through the Hudson Strait, around northern Quebec and Labrador, to the Maritimes. They kept in touch with land through marine dispatch.

On July 16, 1910, when first hearing of this planned venture from his colleagues, Dr. Andrew Macphail wrote to the Honourable Earl Grey, graciously inviting him to visit the Macphail ancestral homestead in Prince Edward Island on the last leg of the expedition. Earl Grey wrote him on July 23, 1910, to say that if they *did* have time to visit PEI, it would be,

> for the express purpose of offering the tribute of my homage to Miss Montgomery. I shd. like to thank her for *Anne of Green Gables*. I have not enjoyed a book more for a long time than I did hers—a *Classic*. I recommended all my friends in England to read it—but they nearly all were before me. They had read the book before I had![80]

By late August it was clear that the expedition had made good time, and the group could dock in PEI so that the Governor General of Canada, Earl Grey, could meet Maud.

Dr. Andrew Macphail is an interesting character here.[81] An important figure in PEI history, he was a high-profile academic at McGill. He was also devoted to improving the standard of living on Prince Edward Island, where he lived part of every year at the Macphail homestead. In 1907, Dr. Macphail was appointed McGill's first professor of the History of Medicine, and in 1911, he founded the *Canadian Medical Association Journal*. A Renaissance man in the fullest sense, he was also a man of letters, founding and editing for over a decade *The University Magazine*, which discussed literature, philosophy, politics, industry, science, and art. He also published several books on a range of subjects. (His 1939 semi-autobiographical novel, *The Master's Wife*, is his best-known work today.) His scientific study of agriculture on his farm in Prince Edward Island led him to scientific innovations that started the seed potato industry on PEI. At age fifty, he would enlist in World War I, in spite of having been blinded in one eye, and serve on the front for nearly two years in the medical corps where he helped found the Canadian Field Ambulance Service to provide care for injured soldiers.

If Maud knew anything about this expedition, she had no inkling that it was being routed through Prince Edward Island strictly so that Canada's beloved Governor General could meet *her*. Because of Macphail's standing on the Island, the newspaper depicted it as a visit to Dr. Andrew Macphail's impressive homestead.

On September 6 Maud was absolutely astonished to receive an invitation from Lieutenant-Governor Benjamin Rogers, saying "His Excellency Earl Grey will be in C'town on Sept. 13th and wishes to meet you." The same post brought a letter from Dr. Macphail telling her that *he* would be entertaining the Earl's party at *his* home in Orwell, and *she* was invited to come. Maud wrote in her journal entry of September 7, 1910, that it "speaks something for 'Anne' . . . that she should have been sufficiently delightful to a busy statesman to cause him to single her out in his full life and inspire him with a wish to meet her creator."

With only seven days' notice between the telegram and the event, Maud was thrown into a panic over what to wear. There were no clothes in her wardrobe appropriate for a viceregal occasion. She hastily engaged a local dressmaker (Bertie Hillman) and hurried to Charlottetown, where she bought a length of silk in one of her favourite colours, brown.

She also bought and read a book published early that year by Dr. Andrew Macphail, *Essays in Fallacy* (1910). Dr. Macphail's status on the Island ensured that this book had received front page attention in the *Examiner* of September 10, 1909, with the headline: "Dr. Andrew McPhail's Essays Praised in England: Contemporary Review Recognizes Ability of P.E. Island's Gifted Son."[82] The article goes on to state that "Dr. Andrew MacPhail's essays on imperial policies and the future of Canada will materially affect the attitude of responsible thinkers throughout the Empire and in the United States . . ."

Macphail was an outspoken social critic and had a great deal to say, among other topics, about women. One essay in his 1910 book, titled "The American Woman," urges women to stop asserting their rights and instead remain submissive, quiet, long-suffering, and attentive to their husbands. Another, "The Psychology of the Suffragette," condemns women agitating for women's voting rights. (Island women would not obtain the right to vote until 1922.) Such behaviour "makes a man impatient and finally contemptuous of all femininity," wrote Macphail.[83] Macphail also criticized the proliferation of young female teachers, arguing that young males needed male models for their teachers. The increasing presence of women in schools, he argued, was undermining educational standards. Maud wrote respectfully in her journal that his book was "stimulating" with much "unpleasant truth" in it, but she goes no further, perhaps intimidated by the *Examiner*'s comment that "Dr. MacPhail's incisive prose style reveals a mind of extreme ability stored with the best literature and trained by direct observation."[84]

Maud must have wondered nervously before she went to the Macphail homestead if the much venerated Dr. Macphail had indeed read *Anne of Green Gables*, which had been published two years earlier. If he had (as was likely), he would have seen that she had depicted the *male* teacher, Mr. Phillips, as a fool. By contrast, Anne's other teacher, Miss Stacy, based on her own Miss Gordon, was a model for all young women to follow: this "lady teacher" inspired her students, touching their lives. At Dalhousie, Maud had published a serious essay on the importance of education for women. Still, she was well aware that her Grandfather Macneill and others like him (including the venerated Andrew Macphail) still disapproved of women teachers. Maud was not one to attack public opinion stridently—instead, she used humour in her novels, feeling it was more effective for ridiculing outdated ideas.[85]

Maud attended the events in her new brown silk dress, hastily made for the occasion. The *Earl Grey* dropped anchor at 3:00 p.m. on September 13, in

Charlottetown, off the Marine Wharf. Lieutenant-Governor Rogers went on board and brought the party ashore. At 4:00 p.m. they took a train to Uigg, where the guests enjoyed a reception and repast at the Macphail homestead in Orwell. This party included, among others, Lord and Lady Grey, Lord Lanesborough, Lord Percy, Dr. John McCrae, Professor John MacNaughton, Lieutenant-Governor and Mrs. Rogers, the Honourable John Agnew, and "Miss Maud Montgomery." Later that evening, the group returned to Charlottetown by special train, returning after 10:00 p.m. The next day, they dined on board the *Earl Grey*. After the dinner, the boat sailed for Pictou, where it would anchor again, and Earl Grey and his party returned to Ottawa by rail.[86]

Maud's description of the reception at the Macphail homestead in her journals treats only on comic aspects of the encounter. She recalls how she and Earl Grey strolled out to the orchard to talk in private about her writing. There, they sat on the steps of the outhouse, which had been fixed up with dainty curtains for the occasion. She speculates that Earl Grey was perhaps unaware of the purpose of the outside toilet when he preferred its steps to the Macphail house for unaffected, unpretentious "real" talk.

Strangely, Maud wrote little about the people she met at this reception. Dr. John McCrae was the official physician for the expedition. Born and raised in Guelph, Ontario, he would later make his name known internationally by writing "In Flanders Fields," the most famous war poem to come out of World War I. At the time of the Earl Grey reception, Dr. McCrae was a thirty-seven-year-old bachelor, two years older than Maud, sharing her birthday of November 30. Maud does not mention meeting this handsome, charming, and distinguished fellow Scottish-Canadian, although she certainly would have been presented to him. After his death in 1918, Maud paid tribute to him by using his poem as the model for Walter Blythe's famous poem in *Rilla of Ingleside*. Anne's son, Walter Blythe, shares McCrae's literary sensitivity, modesty, idealism, and devotion to duty—all traits and values Maud admired.

Maud *did* comment on Dr. Andrew Macphail, a man so venerated on the Island that the Island papers carried accounts of his every publication, of every movement he made either on or off the Island, and every off-Island guest who came to his homestead. (For instance, at one point an Island paper announced that Dr. Macphail's friend, Rudyard Kipling, would be visiting him on the Island the following year, a visit that seems not to have taken place.) Of Macphail, Maud wrote, "the doctor himself is a strange-looking man—[he]

looks like a foreigner" (September 16, 1910). Macphail was very high-minded, noted for his principles, his strong views, and his seriousness, and Maud's characterizing him as a "foreigner" was certainly *not* a compliment. In a xenophobic era (and Island) that even feared little orphan children like "Anne," this gratuitous tag in her private journal was in fact little less than insulting.[87]

It is no surprise that the visit of the revered Earl Grey was headline news in the Island papers. The Charlottetown *Examiner* announced on September 14, 1910: "EARL GREY, GOVERNOR GENERAL NOW VISITING PEI." Maud is mentioned only in the third paragraph. Similarly, the *Patriot* ran several articles before the visit, and the front page on September 14, 1910, charted the "movements of the vice regal party," mentioning only in the second paragraph that "Miss Lucy Maud Montgomery" was one of the guests. Maud recalls how many of the people in Cavendish were stunned to hear about her invitation to meet Earl Grey. (Her dearest relatives—her Aunt Mary Lawson and cousins Bertie McIntyre and Stella Campbell—were thrilled by the honour.) Although Islanders often saw her name in the newspapers for poetry, and she had received attention for the success of *Anne of Green Gables*, she still had a small profile on the Island compared to a man like Dr. Andrew Macphail. The "Earl Grey affair" raised Maud's status throughout the Island.[88]

Later, the *Patriot* of October 10, 1911, ran an account of a sketch in another magazine in which Maud informed a journalist that Earl Grey told her he "had determined when he came to the Island to see at least two persons, the authoress of 'Anne of Green Gables,' and Dr. Andrew Macphail and his potatoes." She must have had a twinkle in her eye when she repeated this characterization by Earl Grey, linking her name to books and Macphail's to potatoes. This article also attributes to Earl Grey the opinion that "Canadians were a very fine people, but one thing he had against them was that they were so apt not to appreciate the work of one of their own until it had been admired by others."[89]

Maud and Earl Grey continued to correspond for several months, improving her mood and self-confidence considerably. He had asked for copies of her books and she sent them. He advised her against writing sequels, saying they were "never as good." He sent her the current *Bookman* so she could see its portrait of Mrs. Gaskell, the English writer, whom both of them admired. He wrote:

Like Mrs. Gaskell you possess what *The Bookman* describes as the three fairy gifts of the English Novelists, viz: knowledge of human Nature, Imagination, a natural love for a good story, and a pretty style.

Then he adds, with playful seriousness, in this letter of September 20, 1910:

I see I have endowed you with 4 as against *The Bookman's* 3 gifts. I must consult *The Bookman* again to see where we differ. At any rate this triple or still more this quadruple possession gives you great power, and consequently the burden of a proportionate responsibility.

He cautions her to "withstand the temptations of publishers who will want you to sell your unborn soul for their advantage" and advises her,

to keep your undeveloped influence as a sacred lamp, which shall be a light to yourself, the Island, Canada, the Empire and to the English-speaking peoples of the world. Young as you are, you have already been able to make the name of Prince Edward Island known wherever the English tongue is spoken. That is much: but having got so far, that is only a stepping stone to more important accomplishments.

He forecasts in his letter of September 20, 1910, that if she can only be "sufficiently inspired" from her "sea-girt nest in Prince Edward Island" she will "touch the heart and fire the imagination of the whole Empire."

Maud replied to Earl Grey on September 26, with the characteristic modesty of a woman writer who could not admit to ambition, since women were supposed to have none. Part of her long letter reads:

I do not think I am a very ambitious woman. I do not care much for fame; and from its attendant shadow of publicity I shrink. But I do wish to give back to the world something of the joy and pleasure I have received from its heritage of "the thought of thinking souls" of the past. I think I know my limitations. I am not a genius. I shall never write a great book. But I hope to write a few good ones . . . (September 26, 1910, Public Archives of Canada, Earl Grey papers)

Earl Grey's influence, or attempted influence, did not end there. On September 27 he wrote to Professor John MacNaughton at McGill suggesting that he write an article on "Miss Montgomery." MacNaughton was a highly respected scholar, and when on the Island, he had expressed admiration for Maud's literary skills.[90] Grey wrote:

> I wish you would write a review of Miss Montgomery's novels for the "University Magazine," if MacPhail [*its editor*] approves; but being an Islander I expect he will reserve that appreciation for his own pen . . .

Earl Grey promised to send *Kilmeny, The Story Girl,* and Maud's poems to MacNaughton, adding:

> You can introduce into your review, if you like, the incident at MacPhail's Farm, where I pointed out that her open volume, on which young MacPhail's 3 candles were resting, evidently had formed the basis of all his illumination. As you pointed out at the Consolidated School, her candle is going to illuminate the Island in every land where the English language is spoken. (Letter of September 27, 1910)[91]

MacNaughton replied promptly:

> Your Excellency, I am very much indebted to you for the kind and gracious letter which I got yesterday. I saw Dr. Macphail last night and found him not as enthusiastic about Miss Montgomery's work as we are but perfectly willing to let me write about it . . . (Letter of September 29, 1910)

We can only speculate about Macphail's private response to Earl Grey's adulation of Maud. Maud Montgomery and Andrew Macphail were as different as could be in personality and style. Was his pride piqued to hear Earl Grey suggest that Maud's humorous novels were the basis of so much international "illumination," a term that had been used in reviews to describe his own collections of thoughtful and serious essays?

Professor MacNaughton never wrote the article on Maud, whether because of Macphail's disapproval or because of other demands on his time.[92]

Earl Grey was deeply interested in the fledgling Canadian cultural and liter-ary world, and sympathetic to it. He would have known that a serious article by a major male scholar at McGill would have influenced the course of Maud's career. Sensing her talent, he wanted to encourage it, providing her with the same kinds of puffs and praise that academic and professional men regularly gave to each other.[93]

Whatever the underlying politics of Earl Grey's visit to the Island, and its aftermath, his admiration of Maud was a significant boost to her self-respect, raising her confidence at a low point in her life. However, writing a best-seller had not wiped out the damage from her childhood—her underlying sense that she was of little importance.

The 1910 trip to Boston

Only a month later in 1910, Maud was entertained by another prominent man, her publisher, Lewis Coues Page, of Boston. Page had good reason to in-vite Maud to visit him, his firm, and his impressive residence: her books were earning him a fortune. Page was a shrewd businessman, exactly the kind of publisher Earl Grey had had in mind in his warnings to Maud. The first con-tract (for *Anne of Green Gables*) had specified that Maud's royalty would be 10 percent of the *wholesale* price of her books, rather than the more custom-ary 10 percent of the *retail* price. This was her first novel, and she had no ex-perience with book contracts and publishers.[94] Like many new authors, she was so keen to be published that she took what was offered, assuming that as standard.

The further "binding clause" in the *Anne of Green Gables* contract spec-ified that Maud had to give subsequent books to Page *at the same rate* for a specified period. It was not unusual for publishers to put binding clauses into their contracts, but to insist her forthcoming titles remain at the same rate was both cunning and unfair. A decent publisher would have given her 10 percent of the *retail* price, or more after she established herself as a successful author. A writer of continuous "best-sellers" might have hoped for an escalating per-cent of the retail price. He repeated the same clause in contracts for her next two books, *Anne of Avonlea* and *Kilmeny of the Orchard*. By 1910, Maud had learned that she was being shortchanged, and she wrote to him that she did not intend to sign that binding clause in subsequent contracts.

Agents and writers' unions were fairly new phenomena at that time, so writers were at the mercy of the publishers. Women writers were especially exploited, as they had little experience at defending their rights in public or in initiating legal challenges. Page knew his advantages and pressed them. He also knew that women fell readily for his personal charm.

Page had two motives for inviting Maud to Boston. The first was to show his quaint little Canadian country lass to the curious Boston press, introduce her to Boston socialites, and thus stoke the market for her books with the reading public. The second was to persuade her to sign another contract extending the same binding clause to all books written in the next five years.

Maud had been fighting depression in the autumn of 1910. While meeting Earl Grey in mid-September had been a boost, it was not long before her mood started sinking again. Also, being thrust into the public eye had been disorienting. The invitation to visit Page came on October 13. At first she decided against the visit, and started a letter to Page explaining that she could not come, but then, suddenly, she recalled experiencing a sudden "inrush of energy and determination"; she "felt strangely blithe and joyous" as she had "not felt for years," and she decided to go after all.

She travelled to Boston by train, accompanied by her cousin Stella Campbell. Both women spent their first day, a Sunday, with a cousin, George Ritchie, and his family. On Monday a taxi arrived to take Maud, Stella, and Lucy Ritchie to Page's office on Beacon Street, where Maud finally met Lewis Page and his brother, George Page, and others in the firm. The rest of the day Maud spent shopping in the Boston department stores in order to have a suitable wardrobe for the rest of the visit. She had never seen anything like the stores in Boston. She bought herself a brown broadcloth suit, as well as a beautiful hand-embroidered pink silk afternoon dress costing eighty dollars (an amount that would have been approximately half of her year's teaching salary in Bideford).

She was to be a personal guest of Lewis Page and his wife, Mildred, at "Page Court," their elegant home at 67 Powell Street in Brookline, Massachusetts. On arrival, she was met by a maid who took her to a guest room. Seeing herself in the bedroom in a full-length mirror was a new experience. She described the visit in her journal entry of November 29, 1910. As she descended the stairs, the "polished hardwood staircase" was "lined with a collection of prints" of the Page ancestors—a very impressive group. She was ushered into the library for tea with Mildred Page, who was "fairly good-looking but utterly without 'charm.'" The library was the most elegant room she had ever seen: built-in shelves filled with expensive books, large casement windows, and comfortable easy chairs before a large fireplace. On the wall hung the original painting of the cover of *Anne of Green Gables*. Later she enjoyed a formal dinner with the Pages and other houseguests, a couple on their honeymoon with connections to Italian royalty, the Boston banking world, and an American senator.

Of Page himself, Maud wrote:

> Lewis Page is a man of about forty and is, to be frank, one of the most fascinating men I have ever met. He is handsome, has a most distinguished appearance and a charming manner — easy, polished, patrician. He has green eyes, long curling lashes and a delightful voice. He belongs to a fine old family and has generations of birth and breeding behind him — combined with all the advantages of wealth. The result is one of those personalities which must be "born" and can never be achieved. (November 29, 1910)

Most women reacted to Page in this way: he was tall, urbane, elegant, and charming. According to Page's literary executor and cousin, the late W. Pete Coues, when Page entered a room, he attracted everyone's attention with his commanding presence and distinguished carriage. An "outstandingly handsome man," he was always "well-dressed and avant-garde." Still athletic, he exuded masculinity in a way that disarmed women. He was five years older than Maud. He had always moved in the top echelons of Boston society and was the embodiment of the aristocrats Maud had read about in British novels.

The entire setting was intoxicating. Maud asked if she might take photographs of the Page home, both inside and out. Her grandfather, Senator Montgomery, had owned a nice house, but it was nothing like "Page Court," the North American equivalent of the splendid homes on great country estates of British royalty.

During her visit, Page treated Maud like royalty, with luncheons and receptions arranged in her honour, side trips to historic sites and museum tours, as well as book-signings. Boston journalists were invited to "Page Court" to interview Maud, and they wrote about her: "As the young author entered the Pages' beautiful library one thought came to us: 'It is a repetition of history: Charlotte Brontë coming up to London.' By-and-by we found we

were not alone in the idea." One journalist, writing in *The Republic*, described Maud as,

> . . . short and slight, indeed of a form almost childishly small,
> though graceful and symmetrical. She has an oval face, with deli-
> cate aquiline features, bluish-grey eyes and an abundance of dark
> brown hair. Her pretty pink evening gown somewhat accentuated
> her frail and youthful aspect.
>   . . . For all of her gentleness and marked femininity of aspect and
> sympathies, she impressed the writer as of a determined character,
> with positive convictions on the advantage of the secluded country
> life with its opportunities for long reflection and earnest study. . . .
> Bostonians are charmed with her unique personality no less than
> with her books; but for ourselves we should be more interested to
> know just how the pageant of our strenuous life has recast itself on
> the mind of this quiet but observant and philosophical sojourner.[95]

Page, who was skilled at fanning public interest, made sure that this magazine (and others) featured the "best-selling" status of *Anne of Green Gables*
in the Boston media:

> Every discerning critic realised that in "Anne" a new and original
> character had come into the world of fiction and would abide until
> she had become a classic. In these fickle days when of making
> books there is literally no end, six months is a long popularity for a
> book, but after over two years "Anne of Green Gables," now in its
> twenty-fifth large edition, is selling as well as ever, and is known in
> every land of English speech.

By the time she left Boston, however, Maud was less impressed with Page.
She had written him *before* she went down that she was unwilling to sign another contract with the "binding clause" in it. She knew that he was reaping
huge profits from her books, and also that he should give her better terms. But
Page was shrewd, intuitive, and used to getting his way with women—whether
they were authors, employees, maids, waitresses, or clerks.
    Towards the end of Maud's visit, Page asked her if he could bring home
the next contract for her to sign. She agreed, assuming that he would have

omitted the offending binding clause. On her final night, however, he came *up to her bedroom* with the contract. It would have been appropriate for him to ask her down to the library to read and sign the contract; but, cunning man that he was, he no doubt felt that an awed, repressed "spinster" of thirty-six, who was out of her element in his house and under the spell of his charm, would feel her most vulnerable in the intimacy of her bedroom. Maud was distressed to find the offending clause still in the contract. She wrote later:

> Did Mr. Page reason thus: — "She has been my guest; I have been exceedingly good and agreeable to her; in my house and as my guest she won't want to start a discussion which might end in a wrangle and stiffness; so she will sign it without question."
>
> If he did, I justified his craft for I decided to sign it for just those reasons. (November 29, 1910)

In forcing Maud's hand, Page got his way in the short term. But he also made a fatal mistake. Maud would never trust him again. With her innate sense of morality, she felt that she had been cheapened by acquiescing to a business deal that diminished her. She would soon be hearing alarming tales from other people who dealt with Page and considered him unscrupulous.

Yet, the trip had been exhilarating. She had spent wildly for some expensive clothes. She had drunk "Chateau Yquem" for the first time and loved it. She had taken wonderful trips to historical sites. Boston was a place of immense culture and elegant living, and she envied the life of the elite. She began to dream of a new life — if her income and celebrity continued, and if Ewan became a successful minister, eventually moving to a large urban centre where she could be part of a literary world.

Back on the Island, it was more apparent than ever that life was changing. The population demographics of Prince Edward Island were undergoing a significant transformation: the well-educated younger generation, finding more opportunity elsewhere, had for some time been leaving for mainland Canada or the United States.[96]

Maud's father's generation had left the Island in droves when the railways opened up the Canadian west, and the exodus from the overpopulated

Island was continuing. In a speech reported in the *Examiner* on February 16, 1911, Andrew Macphail claimed that in just one single day in September 1908 exactly 5 percent of the adult male population had left the Island. Although this is almost certainly an exaggeration, the Island's population did decline significantly in the four decades following 1891. By 1910, the desire to leave the Island for opportunity elsewhere was a contagious fever raging through the younger generation. The Island had seemed an idyllic, changeless place in Maud's childhood, but now it felt increasingly like an isolated backwater.

As previously mentioned, after Ewan returned from his studies in Scotland in spring 1907, he had trouble obtaining a good parish on the Island. Many other ministers were leaving for the mainland, some merely to find work and others to find new experiences. One who had taken this step was the very successful Reverend Edwin Smith, who had trained at Pine Hill Seminary like Ewan, and had inducted Ewan at Cavendish. Smith had resigned at Cardigan, PEI, in May 1909. In September 1909, Ewan resigned at Bloomfield and obtained a parish in Ontario; in so doing, he positioned himself with the other adventurous go-getters on the move.

Island newspapers lamented that the best and brightest young Islanders were departing for greater opportunity elsewhere. Maud had been worried about Ewan's fizzle in Scotland, but she took some heart when he showed this initiative. The town Ewan was moving to—Leaskdale, Ontario—was close to Toronto. Maud had already met journalists from Toronto: Marjory MacMurchy and Florence Livesay (wife of the distinguished journalist J. F. B. Livesay, and mother of the future poet Dorothy Livesay). They had sought her out in PEI, and she had enjoyed the contact. Her taste of the culture in the big city of Boston had enlarged her "scope for imagination."

Maud loved her Island, but she knew that she would not be able to stay on the Macneill homestead when her grandmother passed on. Like her Uncle Leander, Andrew Macphail, and her cousin Murray, she could return to the Island for summer vacations. The Island papers treated her with respect, but they were prouder still of Islanders who drew attention on the world stage— especially if they always attributed their success to their Island beginnings, as Andrew Macphail had done. If you were born on the Island and moved away, you were always an "Islander." Maud's successful cousin, Murray Macneill, was actually raised on the mainland, but he regularly visited the Island with his parents as he grew up, and was always considered to be an "Islander" by virtue of lineage. Moving away did not mean loss of your Island heritage and identity. Ewan's move excited Maud.

But although Ewan had showed this initiative, Maud continued to worry. His letters from Leaskdale were stiff and dull. By January, the excitement of Earl Grey's visit was wearing off, and Maud had slipped into another depressive episode. "I cannot even write my worries out here—they go too deep and cut too keenly," she wrote in her journal at age thirty-six. "I write continually, with a gnawing worry at my heart all the time. . . . If I had anyone to share the worry with me—to talk things over with—to assist—to encourage! But I have no one" (January 15, 1911).

She felt anxious about what would happen when her grandmother died and she would be obliged to embark on a life with Ewan. She liked him very much as a person, but what would their marriage bring? She had seen by his experience in Scotland that he could slump into depression; they had no mutual intellectual interests; being a minister's wife was unpaid servitude; and she wondered if she would be able to keep up her writing career.

Another writer with her income and success might have moved alone to a big city to work, hoping to meet a man more suitable for marriage. But she had already known loneliness and terrible depression in Halifax; she felt she could not risk that misery again. Moreover, she did want to have children, and a normal life as a married woman and mother. At thirty-six, time was running out for her.

Ewan was not without virtues: he was relatively good-looking (important to her); being a minister gave him social standing (also important); he was gentle and kind (a welcome relief after her grandfather); and as the minister at Cavendish, he had been a jolly, easygoing man who did not get upset over little things, as she did. These attributes all had a calming effect on her own high-strung nature. Weighing all in the balance, she did not have the courage to break yet another engagement after Ewan had waited so long for her.

The next few months were lived between writing happy fictions and writing bleak journal entries. Her incredible discipline kept her going professionally. She continued writing the novels that Page requested, while still finding time to send stories and poems to periodicals. At least twenty-six short pieces were published in 1909, and at least ten in 1910, including some with such suggestive titles as "A Soul That was Not at Home," "The Dream Child," "The Courting of Prissy Strong," "A Valentine Mistake," and "A Garden of Old

Delights." As long as she was able to access her imaginative worlds, she could temporarily escape the real one. In Maud's worst moods she suffered constant headaches, wrote compulsively in her journal, and dreamed of death. In better moods, she was hopeful. She could not see around "the bend in the road," but she had dreams.

In March 1911, the inevitable happened: Lucy Woolner Macneill died. She and Maud had both contracted a deadly influenza. Lucy developed pneumonia, called "the old person's friend" in the days before antibiotics, when it meant almost certain and peaceful death for the elderly. As she wished, Lucy Macneill died in her own home, cared for till the end by Maud. Lucy's son, John F. Macneill, who had not visited or spoken to his mother in five years, visited her when she was dying, and was said to have left with "bowed head" (Maud's retrospective journal entry of January 28, 1912). He would finally have his house, but he had estranged his mother in pressing for it. Lucy's oldest son, Leander, came home for the funeral. He was himself declining with a debilitating nerve disease, which had made Lucy's final years particularly sorrowful: Leander was her favourite son, the one who had always doted on his mother.

The death of her grandmother seemed inconceivable to Maud, even though for some time Lucy's health had been failing. Her grandmother had always been there: although strict and at times firm with her oversensitive grandchild, she had also supported Maud in important ways when Grandfather Macneill would not, making sacrifices even in the face of his disapproval. Maud felt a deep sense of gratitude to the dignified, quiet, but strong grandmother who had taken her in when her father wanted to find a home for her after her mother's death. Maud knew that her grandmother's stability, discipline, and training had enabled much of her literary success.

With her aunts and friends helping, Maud cleared out the house. Most of the furniture went to her Aunt Annie Macneill Campbell in Park Corner (where it remains in the Campbell home and museum). Maud gave her organ to Cavendish Presbyterian Church (where it still is, although the church is now a United Church). Her spool bed went to Ernest and Myrtle Webb (and was passed down through Myrtle's daughter Marion to her daughter, Elaine Laird Crawford of Norval, Ontario).

When everything else was distributed or burned as rubbish, Maud closed up the house so that her Uncle John F. Macneill could finally claim it. He must have done so bitterly, for Prescott, the son for whom he had wanted the house, had died the previous year. John let the house stand empty and eventually fall to ruin. Some time later he tore it down to prevent tourists from overrunning his property in search of L. M. Montgomery's childhood home. (His grandson, John Macneill and his wife Jennie have restored the foundations and grounds, and they are now a tourist site of tasteful, peaceful, and genuine authenticity in Cavendish.)

Lucy Macneill's death was followed five weeks later by the death of Tillie Macneill Houston. Maud felt this death, of unspecified causes, was suspicious. Just over a month after Lucy's death and burial, Tillie contracted measles, recovered from them, and then suddenly died. Maud recorded in her journal that this was deeply disturbing, partly because of her fondness for Tillie, and partly because Tillie's husband had made an unwanted pass at Maud some five years earlier. When repulsed by Maud, he had asked, "And what if I am not always married?" (February 9, 1911). Maud wondered with a shudder if Tillie had really died of natural causes, but she dismissed these doubts as best she could.

And now, her own future was looming. Too busy and disorientated to make journal entries, she kept notes, and later wrote up the course of events: "Now that poor grandmother had gone, there was no longer any reason for delaying my already long-deferred marriage and it was arranged that Ewan and I should be married early in July" (January 29, 1912). Preparations got underway.

Weddings at that time were held in homes, not churches. Maud had invitations printed and sent them to a small group of selected family and friends. She arranged for her wedding trousseau to be made in Montreal. Her cousin Frederica ("Frede") Campbell came home for the wedding (she was studying at the Macdonald Institute in Montreal, where she was working towards a degree in household science). Frederica planned the wedding dinner. Frede photographed Maud in each of the outfits she would wear on her honeymoon in Scotland and England. No pictures were taken of Maud in her wedding gown, either then or later. (The dress has been restored and is available for viewing at her birthplace.) Maud's gown was of what she described as white *crêpe de soie* with a chiffon tunic and pearl-bead trim. Her veil was tulle, with orange blossom wreath. Her bouquet was of white roses and lily of the valley. Ewan's present to her was a necklace of amethysts and pearls.

Framing her future

Maud's moods and thoughts through this time of upheaval can best be viewed through photographs that she herself staged. Since purchasing her first camera, Maud had been an avid amateur photographer. On June 25, 1903, and again eight years later, on May 24, 1911, she went to the seashore with her camera and a good friend: in 1903, the friend had been Nora Lefurgey, and in 1911, it was her cousin Stella Campbell. Each time, Maud carefully arranged a photograph of herself, framing herself in symbolic terms.

In 1903, the photograph was taken in the flush of her excitement a few days after Ewan (the "chust lovely" Highlander) had first preached in Cavendish on June 21, 1903. The second photograph was taken around May 24, 1911, some six weeks before her marriage to Ewan and her departure from the Island.[97]

In 1903, Maud and Nora had walked down to the shore to take each other's picture on the rocks. Maud says that they stripped and put on their "bathing dresses." Nora's picture survives and *she* is fully clothed. For her own photograph, Maud is wearing a scanty diaphanous wrap that she later called an improvised "bathing costume." It would hardly stay in place in the water, but the symbolism is subtle and ambiguous, carefully worked out for the picture-taking session.

Maud's picture reveals and celebrates the sensual body, its curves, its desires. Her shrouded white figure is positioned before the mouth of the dark cave. Here the sea-nymph can tryst with her lover when he rises out of the sea. The contrast between white figure and black background provides drama. So does the angle: Maud is seen from behind, her face out of view while she looks out at the sea. The mystery question: What does she look for? Her lover? A ship to carry her away? The composition is carefully constructed: Maud's body is full of triangles and peepholes, as mysterious as the cave itself.

Yet there is something virginal about her as she scans the horizon. The picture shows a woman capable of passion, but there is a certain spirituality about it. Maud's averted gaze makes her inscrutable, elusive, unreadable. Imagine the effect, by contrast, if she turned her head and looked over her shoulder at the camera, with her head tilted submissively and seductively. . . . Or if her body were turned towards the camera, with her head tossed back.

Maud has carefully positioned herself in the 1903 picture as both a sexual woman and a spiritual being, and in both cases a female form of haunting beauty. She could be a nymph, mermaid, kelpie, part human, or part from the world of faerie. The photograph recalls Maud's earlier description of herself as a blend of the passionate Montgomery blood and the Puritan Macneill conscience (April 8, 1898). Maud admitted that after they took this picture, she hid it away.[98]

On May 24, 1911, Maud staged the second photograph by the sea, a companion to the first. (See photos opposite page 151.) In less than two weeks, she would be a married woman. She and Stella went down to the ocean. She sets the scene for this photograph in her diary:

> Tonight. . . . I did what I dreamed of doing all through the years of childhood. . . . I have written before . . . of the charm New London Point always had for me, when I looked at it from Cavendish across New London Harbour—in childhood, when it was for me the end of the world and beyond it seas of faery—in youth when it was beautiful as an outpost of sea sunsets—and in later years when the revolving light bejewelled it every evening. It has always been my dream to walk out on it to the very tip and look off from there to the wide, ocean wastes beyond.
>
> Tonight. . . . I climbed down the steep rocks by the aid of a ladder and walked out to the tip of the headland. On my right lay the harbour and away beyond it the misty Cavendish shore. To my left was a sunset sea, veiling itself in twilight shadows. Before me lay the open ocean, purple, murmurous, wind-visited, where the ships came and went on their blue pathway. Over me were early stars. The poignant beauty of it all cannot be put into words—the thoughts and feelings of my heart then cannot be expressed in symbols of earth. I seemed to be caught up into eternity. But the pang that came when I looked across to the distant homeland shore was of earth: and I was sad when I drove away, although my long dream had come true and brought to me all I had dreamed into it. (May 24, 1911)

This second picture of Maud shows none of the sexuality, the longing, the mystery of the other. She is no longer the young woman who yearns for romance, adventure, or even, possibly, a spiritual life in the mind. She has put the nymph-of-the-sea behind her, and the cave is gone.

Maud's Cavendish cousins and friend Fannie. Back row: Frank Macneill, Fanny Wise, Lucy Macneill Middle row: Maud, Kate Macneill, Prescott Macneill Front row: Ernest Macneill, Anne "Tot" Macneill.

Edwin Simpson, Maud's cousin and first fiancé.

The Leard family of Bedeque: Back row: Georgina, Herman, Helen, Calvin Middle row: Alpheus, Mr. and Mrs. Leard, Millie Front row: Frederica ("Fed"), Mae.

Ettie Schurman, who was widely believed to be engaged to Herman while he courted Maud.

Nora Lefurgey (Mrs. Ned Campbell).

Maud around age 24.

Maud around 1903 (perhaps hamming with Nora Lefurgey).

A handsome Ewan Macdonald at the time Maud met him.

The Webb family: Margaret and David Macneill (the brother and sister who lived in "Green Gables" and were the partial models for Matthew and Marilla); their adopted niece Myrtle Macneill Webb, Ernest Webb, and their baby daughter.

Cover picture on the 1908 Page edition of *Anne of Green Gables*. Its original publication was clearly aimed at an adult audience.

Dr. Andrew Macphail of PEI and McGill University.

Lady Grey and Earl Grey in PEI, with party at the Macphail Homestead, including Dr. John McCrae (seated left).

"Page Court," the home of L. C. Page, at 67 Powell Street, Brookline, Massachusetts.

Lewis Coues Page of Boston, Maud's unscrupulous publisher, in 1908.

Maud in 1903, photographed by Nora Lefurgey, after Ewan became minister in Cavendish.

Maud in 1911, when her marriage to Ewan was imminent.

She is a mature woman who will be a pillar of rectitude, discipline, strength, courage. Maud frames herself as a black silhouette against a white background, not as a white figure against a dark background. Her resolution is clear, despite the fact she is facing away from the camera. The feminine triangles of the nymph are replaced by an upright column of powerful woman; the diaphanous wrap has been replaced by a sombre encasement that obscures her sexuality (and her feelings of vulnerability). Her hat clamps down on her so there is no escape from her armour. This is a woman who has reined in her yearnings and put "duty" foremost.

Sadly, there is little sense of possibility in her horizon: there is only the image of a Maud who has literally "girded up her loins" and looks as formidable as a nun in black habit. Again, she looks into an unknown distance. This time, there is no sense of her world being a joyous, mysterious one. The picture is stark and stiff. She stands alone, poised for the future. There are no props like the cave to divert us, or tell a secondary story. She has on her walking clothes, and is ready to leave one life, one identity, for another. She has made up her mind: the Macneill conscience has won the struggle over the Montgomery hot blood.

There is a more subtle contrast, too: the 1903 nymph sat on a solid rock, but the Maud of 1911 stands on shifting sands. This artistic image represents her life from now on: she will stand alone on these shifting sands and resolutely face whatever is in the unknown future.

Maud says nothing in her journal entry about taking her camera, but the real reason for her walk out on the New London point seems to have been to take this haunting picture for posterity. She leaves it to us to interpret. She shows that she is earthbound, for better or worse, and the ocean is described as one of "wastes" rather than a place to escape into the land of mythic kelpies and faerie. She is ready for marriage.

Marriage to Ewan Macdonald

Maud's marriage to Ewan took place at noon on July 5, 1911, in the Campbell home at Park Corner, with the Reverend John Stirling as the officiant. The night before her wedding, Maud said that she cried herself to sleep. She recalled that threatening rain clouds showed in the morning, but they blew away. The Park Corner home was already renowned for its feasts. One elderly guest exclaimed, "Gad, they never had the like of this at Government House!" (May 23, 1911, in a retrospective entry dated January 1912). But Maud was unable to eat following the wedding. She described the day:

> I had been feeling contented all the morning. I had gone through the ceremony and the congratulations unflustered and unregretful. And now, when it was all over and I found myself sitting there by my husband's side—my husband!—I felt a sudden horrible onrush of *rebellion* and *despair. I wanted to be free!* I felt like a prisoner—a hopeless prisoner. Something in me— something wild and free and untamed—something that Ewan had not tamed—could never tame—something that did not acknowledge him as master—rose up in one frantic protest against the fetters which bound me. At that moment if I could have torn the wedding ring from my finger and so freed myself I would have done it! But it was too late—and the realization that it was too late fell over me like a black cloud of wretchedness. I sat at that gay bridal feast, in my white veil and orange blossoms, beside the man I had married—and I was as unhappy as I had ever been in my life. That mood passed. (May 23, 1911, in a retrospective entry of January 1912)

It is important to realize that she described her July 1911 wedding in a retrospective entry dated January 1912, but that Maud recopied her PEI journals into final form after 1919. We cannot know what was a genuine feeling at the time, and what is later reshaping. However, we do know that the pictures she took in 1903 and 1911 could not have been reshaped.

Perhaps somewhat ominously, Maud and Ewan followed a hearse part of the way en route during their departure from the Island, or so she wrote in her journal entry of September 1, 1919, when she thought back to that day and invested it with symbolic mood.

The 1911 honeymoon in Scotland and England

Now married, Maud and Ewan left the Island. Maud could look back on the first half of her life with great pride and a sense of accomplishment. She had been dealt hard lessons and challenges, and she had met them with courage and grace.

Maud began her life as "Mrs. Ewan Macdonald" by fulfilling her long-held dream of travelling to Britain, and particularly to Scotland and England. Her childhood had been filled with hearing her own relatives and other Scottish expatriates speak of their ancestral homeland as the "Old Country." From her extensive reading of history, poetry, and fiction she imagined a landscape of romance and adventure amidst craggy mountains, cascading waterfalls, glens, inland lakes, and medieval castles. She planned a "literary tour" as so many others had done—from Samuel Johnson in the late eighteenth century to more recent Victorian tourists. Her marriage gave her a travelling companion, and her royalty income paid for a lengthy and expensive honeymoon.

Following the wedding, Maud and Ewan travelled to Summerside; they sailed the following morning on the *Empress*, a ferry piloted by Ewan's uncle, Captain Cameron, to Pointe-du-Chêne, New Brunswick, where they boarded a train to Montreal. On July 8, 1911, they sailed on the White Star ocean liner, the *Megantic*, reaching Liverpool, England, nine days later. After a brief visit to Chester, England, they travelled by train to Glasgow, Scotland, the site of Ewan's short-lived theological training.

Maud and Ewan undoubtedly had very different outlooks on the trip to Scotland. For her, Scotland was a romantic culture-scape with complex literary roots, as well as the ancestral seat of her titled forebears; for Ewan, there was a harsher, more ominous reality. His family had left the Highlands in desperate poverty, and in more recent memory his year at the Glasgow seminary had been overshadowed by a bewildering and enervating clinical depression. For him, Scotland undoubtedly embodied danger and defeat.

How painful was it for Ewan to return there? Maud wrote next to nothing about his presence—or his emotional state—during the trip. On this honeymoon, there was no travelling to the Isle of Skye, the ancestral seat of *his* Highland family and kinsmen. Instead, they visited her points of interest. While in Glasgow she described the thrill of seeing historical artifacts: a letter written by Sir William Wallace, and the cradle of Mary Queen of Scots. (Most Montgomeries had been Jacobite supporters, followers of the line of contenders for the monarchy, Mary Queen of Scots and Bonnie Prince Charlie: a romantic but doomed history, easier to romanticize from a distance than to have lived in reality.)

From Glasgow, they went up to Oban, and then sailed to the Island of Staffa to see "Fingal's Cave," itself a natural wonder of enormous pillars of black basalt. The cave is a long cavern into which the ocean flows, creating an otherworldly effect that gripped many travellers before and after Maud. They returned via the historically important island of Iona, where, among other things, Maud visited the grave of the Scottish King Duncan, who was murdered by the legendary figure Macbeth.

Their next trip was to Ayr to see the home of Robert Burns. Maud could claim a somewhat tenuous affinity with Burns through her nineteenth-century relative Hector Macneill, a friend of Burns. Burns's poetry had rallied nationalism at home and throughout the Scottish diaspora, and, like so many Scots, Maud knew much of his poetry by heart. She visited his birthplace and the "old haunted kirk," the scene of drunken Tam O'Shanter's adventures. She viewed Burns artifacts, including a lock of his lovely "Highland Mary's hair and the Bible they swore their troth on when they parted." They walked his pathways, and over the stone "Auld Brig."

A side trip up the Trossachs allowed Maud to see some Walter Scott territory, including Loch Katrine, the setting for Scott's "The Lady of the Lake," which, as previously noted, she could recite by memory. They went from there to Edinburgh (where Maud's Uncle Leander had attended university), visiting Edinburgh Castle, Holyrood Palace, and other famous sites. Travelling next to Abbotsford, Walter Scott's home, was one of the high points of her trip. She saw the immense library, his writing study, and the great hall where he kept a collection of old armour and swords from medieval times. Other artifacts were the crucifix that Mary Queen of Scots carried to her execution, a lock of Bonnie Prince Charlie's hair, and Rob Roy's original purse.

Another favourite author of Maud's was J. M. Barrie, a novelist and playwright who had lived in Kirriemuir, a quaint little town that was the prototype for his "Thrums" novel settings. Although Barrie is best known today for his novel and play *Peter Pan*, Maud's favourite works were his "Kailyard" novels, such as *Sentimental Tommy, Tommy and Grizel, A Window in Thrums*, and *The Little Minister.* These novels idealized Scottish country life, and Barrie's treatment of this landscape is in many ways similar to her own romanticization of "Lovers' Lane." She walked through the "wild glens" of "Sentimental Tommy" and wrote that Tommy's paths were "the very red of our own Island roads, and this made me feel very much at home in 'the den.'"

They travelled on to Aberdeen, and from there to the battlefields of Culloden, where Bonnie Prince Charlie "made his last stand for the crown of his fathers." They saw "Tomnahurich" ("hill of the fairies") in Inverness, one of the world's most magnificent and unusual cemeteries, shaped like a gigantic cone, with a road winding around it to the small plateau on top. The honeymoon continued down the Caledonian Canal to Fort William, and then by train to Edinburgh again. "All over Scotland," she wrote her friend, Fannie Mutch, "wherever there were mountains, the everchanging effects of cloud and mist and sunshine on their lofty brows were wonderful. If I were to live near mountains for any length of time, I should become as fond of them as of the sea."

Maud and Ewan then linked up with George Boyd MacMillan, the journalist in Alloa who had been her Scottish pen-pal since 1903. Engaged to be married, MacMillan brought along his fiancée, Miss Jean Allen, to sightsee with Ewan and Maud. Jean was younger than the three of them, and her conversation did not interest Maud. Maud and MacMillan, who had much in common, enjoyed talking extensively, and they walked and chatted together. Jean Allen was left to walk with Ewan, a dull conversationalist at the best of times.

The foursome was a disaster. Miss Allen became rude, pouty, and quarrelsome. Ewan helpfully suggested to Maud that Jean's temper-tantrums might be caused by jealousy because Maud spent all her time talking with MacMillan. Eventually, after Maud and Ewan returned home, MacMillan and Jean Allen parted ways, and he remained a lifelong bachelor, but he and Maud exchanged letters and Christmas gifts for the rest of her life.

Maud was especially fascinated by the old town of Stirling, site of Stirling Castle ("the finest relic of its kind in Scotland") and the Wallace Monument. "It was a steep climb to the top of it, but such a view as we had! . . . Beneath us, like a map, we saw half of Scotland, and every acre of ground on which we gazed was saturated with historic interest. We could see seven famous battle fields from where we stood." They left Scotland via Berwick-upon-Tweed, Scott's *Marmion* territory, and in this region they visited Flodden Field, Holy Island, and Norham Castle.

Maud's honeymoon was not all joy: their sightseeing had stopped briefly several times because Maud was afflicted with medical problems. An ulcerating tooth gave her considerable discomfort, and she suffered from a painful case of "honeymoon" cystitis. Before antibiotics, such ailments could cause enormous misery.

The journey continued to England, with a trip to the Lake District (Wordsworth country), Haworth (Charlotte Brontë's home), London (staying at the famous Russell Hotel), Kenilworth Castle, Warwick Castle, Shakespeare's home, the Salisbury plains, Stonehenge, and Oxford. In England, they saw their first airplane ever.

Their last major side trip was down to the Suffolk Coast, to Dunwich, Lucy Ann Woolner's home territory. In Dunwich, they stayed in the "Ship Inn" and explored the site of the old Woolner house, where her grandmother and Aunt Margaret Woolner MacKenzie had lived as little girls before their emigration to Prince Edward Island. (Both the Ship Inn and the house, called "Corporation Farm," were still standing at the end of the twentieth century.) Maud found a man with a key to the house, and since it was then temporarily empty, she was able to enter it. Maud had grown up hearing stories of her grandmother's childhood. She looked for relatives left behind but did not have much time or much success.

It is interesting that, in spite of her cherished Scottish ancestry, Maud did not try to locate either her Macneill or Montgomery clansmen during this trip. (In November 1904, she had written to MacMillan, her Scottish correspondent, asking if he had ever travelled to Eglinton Castle, the seat of the Montgomeries, Earls of Eglinton, adding that "we claim descent from them," proving she had some information about them.) All contact with these families had been lost. Her real knowledge of her Scottish forebears began with her great-great-great-grandfathers, Hugh Montgomery and John McNeil, who both came from the Argyllshire area, but she did not even seek out clansmen with the name when she was in the immediate area visiting the Burns home, which was very near Skelmorlie, Scotland, the likely seat of her Montgomery clan. Her immediate connection to her East Anglian grandmother was far more real than the romanticized Scottish ancestry of her paternal lines.

Whatever her reasons for a more personal exploration of family ancestry in Dunwich, England, than in Scotland, Maud would always remain publicly and privately proud of her Scottish ancestors: the titled Lowlanders who spoke English rather than Gaelic. How did Ewan feel about his own Highland family's lack of cultural refinement? We can only speculate. He was not a reader and did not know how these landscapes had been represented in literature. Nor was his family one of accomplished storytellers. His wife's feelings for Scotland came from envisioning it as a literary landscape, full of tales of enchantment and mystery, peopled with characters (often lords and ladies) from the fiction, ballads, and narrative prose she had had access to in her family and community. His family's stories would have been of near starvation.

The social and cultural gaps between these two Scottish-Canadian Presbyterians from Prince Edward Island were as wide as the ocean. In Maud's glowing description of their honeymoon in her journals, Ewan is almost invisible.

PART TWO

————

The Leaskdale Years

1911–1926

CHAPTER 7

As her honeymoon in Scotland and England drew to a close, Maud's mind was arranging furniture in the Leaskdale manse. She was almost thirty-seven, and she wanted to feel settled in her very own place. She had felt unwanted in a succession of homes—Aunt Emily Montgomery's in Malpeque, her father's in Prince Albert, and even her own home in Cavendish, after she had become old enough to understand that she could live there only until her grandparents died. Her insecurity had been intensified during her grandfather's declining years, and again after his death when her Uncle John F. Macneill attempted to claim the house. It is no wonder that longing for a home is a major theme in *Anne of Green Gables* and other novels. Anne Shirley's ongoing desire is to be "of a place," to find a permanent home where she feels wanted and secure. Maud wanted more than anything to be permanently settled as mistress of her own home and the mother of a happy family.

Throughout her honeymoon, Maud had been searching for decorations for her new home. She particularly wanted spotted china dogs like those she had admired as a child in Grandfather Montgomery's Park Corner house. She found two sets of dogs and bought both. Her favourites were the two larger ones, antique Staffordshire china, with gold spots. She planned for them to reign over the hearth, in her mind a hallowed space in any home. She named them "Gog" and "Magog."

There was a touch of waggish irreverence in their naming. In the Bible, Gog and Magog are the two evil kings of the north who attack the kingdom of Israel. Led by Satan himself, they fight against God. There is no record of what Ewan thought of these imaginative names in a Presbyterian manse. The manse, as it turned out, had no hearth, so Gog and Magog stood guard by

Maud's bookcase, instead. Perhaps she saw the dogs as protecting her corner of the room against too much theology.

A woman could prove she was refined, a cut above the "common herd," if her home was attractively appointed. Most women in Maud's era lived their lives predominantly in their homes, with little real power outside them. The decoration of their house—their one sphere of influence—was a major focus, satisfying their aesthetic needs. In a society not yet driven by consumerism, there was little money available for decorative frills in the home. Young women from cultured families used their leisure time to learn needlework and other artistic skills. Magazines were available to them in the new world of print culture: new ideas and fashions, patterns, and materials to order. For more than twenty years, Maud had been laying up her handmade items in her hope chest: crazy quilts, knitted afghans, fancy pillows, crocheted antimacassars and doilies, and fancy embroidered linens. (Much of this survives in the University of Guelph Archives, and Maud's largest crazy quilt is in the Campbell house in Park Corner.)

Maud was in an unusual situation: her hope chest was full, but she also had her own royalty money to spend on purchasing more substantial items. She intended to buy fine china and silver, nice furniture, and to live in style, after a decade spent in a deteriorating farmhouse. Her future home might not be as big and elegant as "Page Court," but it would be as impressive as taste would allow in a Presbyterian manse in the Ontario countryside.

Her first view of the manse, however, was somewhat disappointing. Built of pale-yellow Ontario brick, in a common L-style that she considered ugly, it was far from ideal. In addition to the absence of a fireplace and hearth, there was no indoor bathroom and toilet (though this was not unusual for the era). Another problem was that the manse was not in "move in" condition. She wanted to paint the worn floors and do some redecoration. She and Ewan had to board next door, where Ewan had lived for the past year, with two elderly spinsters. Although these two women might have "delighted Dickens," as Maud noted, they were overly solicitous, unsophisticated, and extremely curious about the minister's new wife.

Ewan preached on Sunday, October 1, 1911, the morning after they arrived from their honeymoon. A church reception was held the following Tuesday for the newlyweds; it was widely known in the congregation, of course, that their diffident minister had married the famous "L. M. Montgomery," and this was a focus of immense local interest. The Uxbridge *Journal* reported that:

Despite torrential rain the Leaskdale church was filled to capacity Tuesday night to welcome the Rev. Ewen [*sic*] Macdonald and his bride, the well known writer, Miss Montgomery of Prince Edward Island. Supper was served in the basement with such opportunity for social chat and pleasantry that it was after nine o'clock before people went upstairs. . . . Mr. Macdonald has already won a firm hold of the people by his manly character, sound judgement and loving zeal in his high calling. With his gifted and charming wife Leaskdale may call herself happy.[1]

A few days later, even though the house was not quite ready and the new furniture had not arrived from Toronto, the Macdonalds moved in, sleeping on the floor on feather cushions—anything to be out of earshot of the curious old maids. On October 24, they "really" moved in. Maud had had all the wooden floors painted dark tree-green, rather than the traditional grey. Her favourite wallpaper pattern was always one with sprigs of green ferns. She described each room of the house lovingly in her diary and pasted in photographs of the furniture, the family heirlooms, and her own household "gods," feeling that she had given her home class, in spite of its plainness.

Upstairs were five rooms: in the master bedroom she installed pearl-grey furniture, set off by a crimson rug. A second bedroom was decorated in pink with white furniture, and the third in blue with fancy Circassian walnut. A fourth room was allocated for storage, and a fifth set aside for a maid. The large landing at the top of the stairs was set up as Maud's sewing area.

The first floor held the kitchen, the dining room, the library, and parlour. The dining room was awkward, containing an ugly stovepipe, and there was little space for her new sideboard. It was a poor location for entertaining, but handy to the kitchen at the back of the house. The parlour was brightened by creamy-yellow wallpaper and enriched with green brocade drapes, a moss-green rug, furniture in a light Hepplewhite design, and a small bookcase guarded by Gog and Magog.

Her most treasured family heirloom was the "Woolner jug," which she used to hold potpourri. This decorative jug, brought by Maud's great-grandmother from England to Canada, had been filled with blackcurrant jam made from her English garden. Later, the jug's function was to hold cream—and for Maud's grandfather to entertain visitors with stories about its history. This prized object now provided a link to Maud's distinguished ancestors, showing that she came from a "family with traditions." She placed the jug on a small curved table to catch visitors' attention, which would often lead to her telling its story.[2]

Because this was a minister's house, it contained a library. Ewan's library was unusual in that it was shared with a working novelist. For the first time in her life, Maud had bookcases for all her books as well as a new desk, full of cubbyholes, where she could store her writing utensils. Above this desk she hung copies of the paintings of "Anne," "Kilmeny," and "The Story Girl" that had decorated the covers of her books. On the other walls hung enlarged and tinted photos of "Lovers' Lane" and other Cavendish scenes. It was in this room that she would get back to work—but not until the new year.

A minister and his wife were expected to visit in all the homes of parishioners, and to receive in their own. On October 11, 1911, Maud advertised in the "Personals" column of the Uxbridge *Journal*:

> Mrs. E. Macdonald will be at home at the Manse, Leaskdale, on the afternoon and evening of Thursday, Nov. 2 and Friday, Nov. 3, and thereafter in the afternoon and evening of Tuesday each week.

Maud liked the look of Leaskdale. She described it to George MacMillan as "a very pretty country place—would be almost as pretty as Cavendish if it had the sea . . ." (65). Leaskdale was a tiny village—a grouping of some ten to twelve houses, with a church, blacksmith, general store, and a mechanic's garage. The church was small, but it was an attractive red-brick structure. It was located partway up a hill, across the road from the manse. The surrounding fertile farmland held beautiful rolling hills and forests reminiscent of Prince Edward Island. Beyond Leaskdale proper there were small rivers and lakes, in addition to other locations with red soil (also like that in Prince Edward Island). Seven miles to the south lay Uxbridge, with a rail connection to Toronto.

Maud was not as pleased when describing her husband's parishioners. She asked her diary: "Is *this* the kind of people I must live among?" (September 24, 1911). She had fondly cherished the eccentricities of all her Cavendish kinfolk back home, but was less tolerant of the same kind of people in Leaskdale. After receiving in her home for the first time, she wrote: "To all I try to be courteous, tactful and considerate, and most of them I like superficially. But the gates of my soul are barred against them. They do not have the key" (October 24, 1911). This was the initial reaction of a very private woman,

in whom reserve was an instinctive and protective mechanism against judgmental clansmen. She had enjoyed her fame as a writer in a community
where she was already known, but now it made her the object of curious and
prying eyes among strangers. What Ewan's parishioners actually met in Maud,
however, was a friendly, witty, gracious, and refined woman with a poised social presence. They took her into their hearts, and in time she grew very fond
of most of them.

Maud knew how important it was for a minister's wife to work with her
husband. As Mrs. Lynde in *Anne of Green Gables* remarks, "sound doctrine
in the man and good house-keeping in the woman make an ideal combination for a minister's family." But as an unpaid helper, the minister's wife was
also expected to provide leadership for women's activities in the church. Men
may have done the preaching and decision-making, but women were the real
workers, organizing fundraising events; preparing decorations and refreshments for social events, meetings, and funerals; gathering or making all the
items to be sent to foreign missions; and helping those in the community who
were sick or the victims of bad luck.

Leaskdale women were delighted to discover that the famous "L. M.
Montgomery" was accessible, prepared to help in all these activities. She
could give fascinating talks on books, could recite dramatic poems and passages for fundraising church programs, and was a superb cook and housekeeper. She quickly gained their respect. Only a month after Maud's arrival
as a new bride in Leaskdale, the Macdonalds began working with the Young
People's Guild in the church. On November 16, 1911, the social part of the
program included a duet, a dialogue, a reading by "Mrs. Macdonald," and
ended with a floral contest and refreshments. Maud's intent was to give
young people practice in conducting these meetings and performing in
them. She made fun out of learning social graces and other skills in a public
forum.[3]

When Maud moved to Leaskdale, she energized the entire community.
She had more than professional elocutionary skills; she was a natural enter-
tainer who loved telling stories and jokes. She was also skilled at drawing others out. Her smile was warm and encompassing. Her chit-chat brightened
every social occasion, at church or in homes. Years later, one of the parishioners would remember that "her conversation was frequently pointed up
with, 'That reminds me' and off she would go with some 'yarn' for there was
always a funny side to things. Because she was witty and gay, young and old

enjoyed her company. Rarely one missed hearing some tale about her beloved Island or its people."[4]

She was soon elected to official positions, given her organizational skills and other abilities. She noted in her diary that the women's mission society had three different branches: the Foreign Missions (for China, India, etc.), the Home Missions (for the Canadian west and north, among native peoples), and the Missions Band (organized to involve young children in mission-mindedness). Maud had some private reservations about the proselytizing aspects of missions, but approved strongly of their medical and educational functions. She was expected to take a leadership role in all aspects of the meetings (which consisted of hymn-singing, standard prayers, business reports, the reading of a chapter from a missionary's often dull memoirs, another hymn, collection, and refreshments). None of the members guessed that she complained in her private diary about these time-consuming meetings. But she did enjoy "making things go" and she quickly grew into her new role.

There was soon an excuse to slow down her busy pace: in early November, she discovered that she was pregnant. One of her main reasons for marrying had been to have children. Nearly thirty-seven, she was thrilled that a baby was coming.

At the end of November, there was more happiness. Daffy, her cat, had been shipped from Prince Edward Island. She had not intended to bring him, but she had found that she missed him too much. To her, a house without a cat was incomplete. Dehydrated and frightened after three days riding in a crate, Daffy was delighted to see his mistress again. He found more freedom in this home than he had in her grandmother's house: he lay on Maud's writing table as she wrote, on the dining table as she ate, on her lap or curled up beside her when she read, on her bed as she slept, and he even claimed his very own chair in the parlour.

Despite her pleasure in her new home, Maud enjoyed escaping from Leaskdale for meetings in Toronto. On December 6, 1911, she accepted an invitation to a Canadian Women's Press Club in Toronto, where she and Marian Keith (another novelist) were honoured at a reception. On December 7, Maud went to another reception at the National Club and stayed at Marjory MacMurchy's home for the night.

The well-connected Marjory MacMurchy was immensely helpful to Maud in providing an entrance into Toronto society; among other things, she arranged for Maud to give talks to organizations and literary groups. Marjory was a journalist, an occasional novelist (with a series of books between 1916 and 1920), a social activist, a crusader for women's and children's rights, an early member of P.E.N., and the long-time president of the Canadian Women's Press Club.[5] Marjory had first known Maud as a member of the executive of the Women's Press Club in the Atlantic region. On a visit to the Island in 1910, she had interviewed and written an article on the best-selling author of *Anne of Green Gables*. Marjory had then welcomed Maud and Ewan upon their arrival in Toronto following their honeymoon. Marjory's extended family of jurists, doctors, teachers, and activists were important members of the Toronto elite, and through Marjory, Maud learned who was important in the Toronto cultural, business, and social worlds, and she began to move among them.[6] Yet, Maud's entree into Toronto's cultural life meant that she had to put extra effort into her church work at home, in order to remain "visible" in the performance of her duties as a minister's wife. And getting to Toronto—by horse and buggy over dirt roads to Uxbridge, and then by train—took considerable planning and effort.

She soon began to get a sense of the families in Leaskdale. Sober, intelligent, and successful farmers, they shared the Scots-Presbyterians work ethic Maud knew so well from Prince Edward Island. Mr. and Mrs. George Leask—descendants of the Scottish family for whom the village was named—lived in a large and impressive red-brick house near the manse.[7] Other substantial houses and farms belonged to members of the Mustard family, Hugh and James. Their forebears had also come from Scotland, settling in Scott Township in 1832; their descendants would become prominent doctors, educators, theologians, and nurses.[8] Ten or twelve other families held property on the grid of side roads around the village: the Shiers, Lyons, Lapps, Cooks, Colwells, and others.

Ewan's parish was a double charge: Leaskdale and Zephyr. The small village of Zephyr was some eleven miles away—a long trip with a horse and open buggy when the rutted dirt roads were either muddy, dusty, or icy, or in a sleigh in winter when the snow was blowing in streaks across the flat, icy fields. Most members of the Zephyr congregation were also successful and sober people. But the church, a modest frame structure built in 1881, was beleaguered by several troublesome families, truculent members who often caused friction. Ewan's amiable tact would be invaluable. In Zephyr, there was a Methodist church as well as the Presbyterian one, and there was some antagonism between them.[9] Since churches were the main social organization—and organizing force—in a community, the two denominations in Zephyr created a less unified community than in Leaskdale.

The Macdonalds spent their first Christmas dinner at the home of the Hugh Mustard family. The gathering included Hugh's brother, the Reverend John A. Mustard, who was visiting with his wife and son. By a strange twist of fate, this was the same "Mr. Mustard" who years earlier had been Maud's teacher in Prince Albert. John Mustard, so disparaged as a hapless suitor in Maud's early diary, was now an exceptionally successful minister in Toronto. He was seven years older than Maud and three years older than Ewan. He was trim, fit, robust, and distinguished-looking (his thick black hair had turned a striking silver-white). Maud's comments in her private diary are less than kind about the "same slow John Mustard" who, she says, still presents commonplace incidents as "awfully funny." She adds with a pinch of mischief that his jolly wife could "talk enough for two" and that, though pretty, she is very "fat."[10]

The Macdonalds had their own guests at Christmas, too, including Maud's dearly loved cousin Frede, now finishing her degree at Macdonald College near Montreal. To be equitable, Frede's sister Stella had also been invited.

Stella Campbell was now, at thirty-two, an aging "spinster." Most of her siblings at Park Corner had left, but Stella was forced to live on in her child-hood home—which she would have left in a flash if she had been able to find a man willing to marry her. Her unhappiness manifested itself in temper-tantrums, sulks, bossiness, hypochondria, and rudeness. Although Stella could be fun when in a good mood, she was generally unhappy, and her noisy, aggressive presence could quickly fill a household with tension. She and her brother George fought constantly, and George had a temper as explosive as Stella's own. Stella often pushed George beyond his limits: he would roar angrily out of his home, and return in an even worse temper. Stella took out her frustrations on her mother (Maud's beloved Aunt Annie) and Ella (George's pretty and gentle wife).

Maud hoped that an extended trip to Ontario at Christmas might give Park Corner some peace, and perhaps Stella a new lease on life. In hopes of promoting romance, Maud also invited an old beau of Stella's—Irving Howatt, now a barrister in the west (Edmonton)—to visit Leaskdale over Christmas. (Maud does not mention this in her journals. The romance did not work out, despite Maud's efforts to promote it by lending large amounts of money to Stella, some of which Stella then funnelled to Irving Howatt in unsecured loans.) After Christmas, Stella asked Maud if she could stay the entire winter. Maud, caught off guard, was appalled, but she felt unable to face a row with her cousin. With apprehension, she acquiesced—but persuaded Frede to speak to Stella beforehand on the proper behaviour expected in someone else's house. Maud *did* need a housekeeper now that she was pregnant as well as very busy. She offered Stella a salary for housework, hoping that remuneration would signal to Stella that she "should not presume too much." As Maud put it, "I made a virtue of necessity and hoped against hope" (September 22, 1912).

Maud hoped in vain. Stella became a tyrant. It was not long before she grew impossibly bossy, insulting Ewan and embarrassing Maud before the parishioners. (Remembering Stella years later, Leaskdale old-timers recalled discreetly that people did not warm to her as they had to her sister, Frede.)

But Stella, hard-working and capable, did the cooking and housekeeping. Food preparation was a full-time job in itself, and then there was the washing, ironing, and housekeeping when that was done. Stella's help was valuable. The Macdonalds fetched their fresh milk and cream daily from the Leasks, across the road, and churned their own butter. Maud kept her own hens for eggs and dressed chickens for meat. In the Leaskdale community, there was a "beef ring" in which a different farmer would slaughter each week and distribute fresh meat to each family in the ring, but generally meats had to be canned, pickled, salted, dried, or cured in smokehouses, and then reconstituted in recipes. Maud had salted herring shipped up from Prince Edward Island each year. Making fresh bread was a daily chore.

Whatever her other faults, Stella was a very good cook, like all the Campbells. She made excellent desserts, the one thing easy to vary in family menus: Maud's handwritten recipe book contained pages and pages of cookies, cakes, and pies, balanced by only a few recipes for meats or vegetables. Houses were very cold then, lacking insulation, and people needed energy from food to keep warm. Even the Macdonalds' carrots were candied. One maid remembered Ewan saying to his wife quite often: "Maudie, when are you going to make some plum pudding?" Like most Scots, the Macdonalds always had cooked oatmeal for breakfast, often with bacon and eggs. The Macdonald household indulged in one luxury many others did not: on their cereal they put thick, fresh cream. What they did not use, they churned into butter. (Generally, farmwives saved most of their cream to sell.) Stella grew "fat as a seal." Despite her pregnancy, Maud grew thinner.

Maud planned her meals and housework each weekend, and gave Stella the daily schedule a week in advance, as she would do with all her maids. (Her first maid, Lily Reid, recalled being handed a weekly schedule of "washing on Monday, ironing on Tuesday, Wednesday for baking and extras, Thursday for upstairs cleaning, Friday for downstairs, and Saturday to make all preparations for Sunday.") Washing was done either on a washboard, or in a machine with a paddle that was manually agitated, and it was hung to dry on an outside line, even in the freezing cold. Most women ironed on kitchen tables padded with blankets, but Maud was more modern and bought an ironing board. Two irons were kept in rotation, one heating on the wood-fuelled cook stove while the other was in use. Ironing required extreme care, since an overheated iron would scorch and instantly ruin valuable clothes or linens, especially when cotton was starched to give it more body.

Stella "is an odd compound," Maud reflected: "She would work her fingers to the bone for you, complaining bitterly of it all the time and furiously resentful if she is not allowed to do it. She insults and derides you to your face, but behind your back she is the most loyal of friends and would defend you against the world. But everyone who ever has to live with her will be miserable—there is no doubt of that" (September 22, 1912).

Having a cousin as helper seemed normal to the community women, since they could see that Maud spent much time in church activities. The extra help also meant that Maud could return to writing. Every morning she shut herself in the library and worked for two hours. She had never been quite as busy as she was now. In January 1912 she resumed work on *Chronicles of Avonlea*. Her publisher, L. C. Page, was hounding her for more "Anne," so she gathered a group of stories she had written before her marriage, changed their setting to that of "Avonlea," and brought "Anne" in as a spectator, commentator, or minor actor in each story. She cobbled these stories together and sent a group of them to the publishing company in late March to make a selection of the best. They returned their selection and she signed a contract on April 26, 1912; the book was in print in late June, just three months later. (She did not realize at the time that Page had retyped and retained copies of the extra stories rejected for this volume, something that would cause much trouble later on.)

In January 1912 Maud also found time to catch up with writing in her old diary, abandoned, except for rough notes, at the time of her grandmother's death. Now she wrote out a long, retrospective entry on her final days in

Cavendish, giving her comments on most of the people there, her marriage and honeymoon, and her arrival in Leaskdale. She also found time to maintain her correspondence with her long-time pen-pals, George Boyd MacMillan and Ephraim Weber, whose lively, intelligent letters helped fill an intellectual void that her husband and community did not.

When Maud and Ewan went on their expected rounds that winter, taking evening tea in parishioners' homes, she always carried her bag of needlework. She could knit and crochet, without even watching her flying fingers. Her skills at "fancy-work" were much admired by the farmwives, themselves adept at basic needlework. To these women, she was "Mrs. Macdonald," and she seemed to be one of them. Her life as a world-famous writer was largely out of sight.

In February 1912, however, it was as "L. M. Montgomery" that Maud was invited to the Hypatia Club in the nearby town of Uxbridge. This group had been formed in 1907 by seven women (Mrs. Beal, Mrs. Sharpe, Mrs. Gould, Mrs. Urquhart, Mrs. Vickers, Mrs. Willis, and Mrs. Chinn) to discuss books and authors. The meeting was held at the home of Mrs. I. J. Gould. Maud and Mrs. MacGregor (the writer "Marian Keith") were invited as honoured authors. A newspaper write-up of this February 1912 meeting praised a "Club Magazine" compiled on the occasion and read by Dr. Horace Bascom, a local medical doctor. This "showed much talent on the part of the contributors," with news items, health notes, advertisements, and jokes, but the "chief interest was centred in the short stories written especially for it by the authoresses. The object of the Club is to promote a study of English Literature and they are fortunate in having associated with them, as a member, Mrs. McDonald [sic] of Leaskdale," continued the newspaper. The Hypatia Club would be a great pleasure to Maud during her fifteen years at Leaskdale, and she contributed innumerable items to their program.[11]

In March 1912, Maud read a paper on Longfellow's "Attitude to the Sea" at the Zephyr Presbyterian Guild.[12] Two days before that, she and Ewan had been to the Zephyr Women's Christian Temperance Union meeting. In May she gave them a lengthy paper on Ralph Connor's *The Sky Pilot*.

Maud was in her element as mistress of the manse in Leaskdale and as literary celebrity in the larger communities of Uxbridge and Toronto. Little time elapsed between finishing *Chronicles of Avonlea* in March and starting *The Golden Road* on April 30, 1912. In this sequel to *The Story Girl*, Maud again modelled the teller of tales on herself, though declaring that many of the stories were ones she had heard from her Great-Aunt Mary Macneill Lawson, now eighty-nine years old. (Mary Lawson would die in October 1912.)[13]

Looking back at her youth with the detachment of distance, Maud began to realize what a rich childhood she had enjoyed, growing up in a unique rural community with a strong oral culture. She knew that with developments in communication and transportation the sense of safe isolation, which Cavendish had retained, was fast disappearing. Maud continued writing this nostalgic story of childhood in Prince Edward Island through her pregnancy. Maud felt overstretched at times, but she had an extraordinary ability to compartmentalize her life. She made a schedule for her writing every morning, and kept faithfully to it. When things became too oppressive, she drew on her ability to "shut the door of my soul on the curiosity and ignorance by so many and retreat into a citadel of dear thoughts and beautiful imaginings" (April 4, 1912). No one guessed that when she re-emerged, refreshed and renewed, she found many of them tiresome.[14]

Maud took enormous pleasure in small things: seeing trilliums in the spring woods, growing flowers and vegetables in her summer garden, preparing desserts for church socials, telling a story and making everyone laugh, looking at farmers harvesting crops, watching a winter sunset throw purple and mauve shadows over the snow, skimming over the rolling hills in a sleigh pulled by "Queen" (the Macdonalds' black mare), reading inside while a storm howled outside, and most of all, listening to the purring of her cat Daffy. It was Maud's basic nature to see the world as a luminous place, and she wrote glorious passages about it in her diary. When people wondered how she managed to do so much, she laughed that her cat rested for her.

In June 1912 the Leaskdale church celebrated its fiftieth year with a huge party and reunion—plenty of work for a minister's wife, who was by then eight months pregnant. Attendance was so good that many could not fit into the church. A few days before her first baby was due, Maud read a paper on *Paradise Lost* at the Women's Foreign Mission Association of the church. The first copies of *Chronicles of Avonlea* were in print by June 30, 1912. At this point, she was only a week from the delivery of her first baby.

Maud had worried that the quiet life with her grandmother in Cavendish would "unfit" her for any other kind of life. She found, on the contrary, that the busier she was, the happier she felt. With relief, she wrote that she had been free of nervous attacks the whole year. She was very contented, and by all accounts so was Ewan.

A son is born: Chester Cameron Macdonald

"It has always seemed to me that a childless marriage is a tragedy—
especially in such a marriage as mine. . . . I want to have a child—
something to link me with the future of my race," Maud had confided to her
diary on October 24, 1911. "I want to give a human soul a chance to live this
wonderful life of ours. I want something of my very own—bone of my bone,
flesh of my flesh, to love and cherish." Reopening her diary on January 28,
1912, Maud Montgomery Macdonald wrote: "I am to be a mother. I cannot
realize it. It seems to me so incredible—so wonderful—so utterly impossible as happening to *me!*"

But it was also frightening. She was a diminutive and delicate woman,
halfway through her thirty-seventh year, at a time when childbirth could still
threaten complications leading to death. (Statistics on mortality in childbirth
in 1912 are not easily available, but by 1921 the rate had dropped to 419 deaths
per 100,000 cases. By 2000, the rate was less than 1 in 100,000.) Planting her
spring garden, Maud wondered if she would be lying "beneath the sod" when
the next spring came around. Consequently, she hired a professional nurse
recommended by Dr. Helen MacMurchy, Marjory's sister, and she arranged
for Dr. Horace Bascom of Uxbridge to attend the birth. Normally, experienced
women from the community helped with childbirth, calling in a doctor only
if there were complications (when it was sometimes too late). Maud's preparations were unusual for the times. But she could afford it. In 1910, she had
made $6,449, and $5,578 in 1911, from her books' sales alone. (Compared to
Ewan's yearly salary of $900, this was a small fortune.)

On Sunday, July 7, 1912, just after twelve noon, baby Chester Cameron
Macdonald was born, a fine, healthy baby. That Chester's was an easy birth
seemed a miracle, boding well. (Maud ascribed the ease of the birth to exercises she had been doing, as well as to a form of self-hypnosis she had been
practising every night.) Motherhood brought her a new kind of joy, a pleasure
beyond anything she had experienced. She had read about mothers failing to
bond with their babies, and she worried that this might happen to her. After a
good night's rest following the easy delivery, and a momentary feeling of estrangement, her "whole being . . . [was] engulfed in a wave of love for that little blinking mite of humanity."

Chester was all that a mother could have hoped for in a baby: he was
sturdy, alert, and exceedingly cute. She watched him sleep, move, and coo to

himself. She wrote rapturously about cuddling him. She described his shrieks when the nurse bathed him, until he learned it was not "a fatal affair." She melted when he looked at her with an expression of "intelligent wonder" in his eyes, and she thrilled to the knowledge that the "little mind" was starting to develop:

> I gaze at my child with an aching wonder as to what germs of thought and feeling and will and intellect are unfolding in that little soul. I can see what he is externally. I can see that he is plump and shapely and sturdy, with long-lashed dark blue eyes, chubby cheeks, lacking his father's dimples but with dear wee waxen fingers and toes. But I cannot peep into that baby brain and discover what is hidden there. He is my child—"bone of my bone and flesh of my flesh"—but his little individuality is distinct from mine. He is the captain of his own little soul and must live his own life as we all do from the very cradle. (September 22, 1912)

Her journal entries describing her newborn are extremely moving: they capture the amazement a new mother feels over her first baby. "There is nothing on earth so unutterably sweet," she wrote touchingly, "as a sleeping baby." And Chester was a contented baby—again, a blessing in a first child.

Maud dismissed her earlier worries, which included a frightening dream at the time of Chester's birth:

> I dreamed that I wakened in the night, sat up, and looked over the footboard. . . . On the floor . . . lay a big empty black coffin, with a man standing at the foot and another at the head. As I fell back on the bed, overcome with the horror of the sight, the men lifted the coffin and laid it on my bed across my feet. . . . That dream haunted me. From that hour, I saw that hideous empty coffin waiting for me at the end of my months. (September 11, 1912)

All her life, Maud had had vivid dreams. She felt in them a psychic power, not uncommon in a Scottish culture that believed in "second sight." She mulled over her dreams, believing that they sometimes foretold the future. She wrote off this dream, however, for Chester had not died, nor had she. But she did not forget the portentous black coffin associated with his birth.

Part of her joy over her new baby was in sharing it with Frede, who had come to Leaskdale to help after Chester's birth. Frede stayed through the summer. Another bonding: Frede not only liked Ewan and had encouraged his and Maud's courtship, but she also shared intensely in the baby-worship. With their similar outlooks on life, Frede and Maud together found fun in everything. Frede, like Maud, had the famed Macneill memory and could quote poetry for every occasion. They also composed poetry together, in high spirits. In the 1970s and 1980s, people still remembered how the whole Macdonald home rang with laughter when Frede was visiting—laughter shared by Ewan and anyone else present. It was a joyous household, aside from Stella's presence. Still entrenched in the manse, it looked as if she might stay forever. She assumed a proprietary air with respect to Maud, Ewan, and the house. Ewan suffered in silence, unwilling to reply in kind to her bullying.

Frede and Maud conferred. Frede agreed to tell Stella how much she was needed at home, a lie that Stella somehow believed. Stella departed on August 21, 1912, and she was not missed. Frede, who had graduated as valedictorian from Macdonald College, was looking forward to her first job at Red Deer College in Alberta. She stayed on in Leaskdale until December 1912. After she left, Maud hired Lily Reid, a young widow from a nearby farm, to help with the housework.

The easygoing Ewan had been finding life with such a talented, vibrant, and energetic wife at times exhausting. In a house that was overrun with women—Maud, the nurse, Frede, Stella—he remained in the background, leaving all baby and child management to his wife. As Maud rhapsodized over her new baby, Ewan began to see that fatherhood could marginalize him further. When Maud departed for Toronto to visit friends in their first year, he felt a little too happily abandoned. As soon as Maud had recovered from childbirth, she went straight back to her writing. Ewan saw that she could block everything out when writing—everything except the baby, of course.

There were other pressures for Ewan. He began to sense that his powerhouse of a wife was hoping he would do well as a minister so that they could eventually move to a bigger community with a better manse, ideally in Toronto, where her book life was. He was annoyed when Maud received fan letters addressed to "L. M. Montgomery," rather than to "Mrs. Ewan Macdonald." (He once became testy over this, but later apologized.) According to the accounts given by the Macdonalds' maids, however, during these initial years the manse was a happy household. These women remembered Maud and Ewan arguing "with spirit," but the arguments were amicable, and sometimes just in fun. Maud did not write about this in her journals. Nor did she say, as the maids did, that she won all the arguments of any substance and, in the country phrase, she increasingly "wore the pants in the family."

Maud continued to develop her connections with Toronto's bustling literary society, usually under the aegis of Marjory MacMurchy. Marjory was not a true "kindred spirit"—she was too absorbed in her own multifaceted career to be a close friend—but she was happy to be the link between Maud and the Toronto book world. The staid colonial society of Toronto found Maud's Prince Edward Island storytelling refreshing. She was greatly admired in literary circles as a native-grown Canadian talent with an international audience. (By this time, *Anne of Green Gables* had been translated into Polish, Dutch, and Swedish, as well as being sold throughout the English-speaking world.)

Maud's polished refinement and her sparkling wit made her a favourite at Toronto social gatherings. At one private tea, Maud was herself the guest of honour in a group that included M. O. Hammond (she had already been in contact with him in his role as arts and literary editor and photographer at the *Globe*); the Venerable Archdeacon Cody (Henry John Cody, an Anglican canon who became Ontario's minister of education and then president of the University of Toronto from 1932 to 1945); literary anthologist and gadfly John Garvin and his wife Katherine Hale (a minor novelist who had nonetheless climbed high in literary social circles); and several distinguished professors at the University of Toronto (all male). Maud was intrinsically reserved, and this slight shyness made her likeably modest and unassuming. But she was also very poised, and she could rise to occasions well. Toronto saw her as a fresh personality, at once quaint and sophisticated, dignified and unaffected.

The Toronto visits were, however, a decidedly solo venture. Ewan would have been totally out of his milieu in the Toronto literary world, even if he had wished to seek the social enticements of Toronto without appearing to neglect his congregation. And there was no doubt that Maud enjoyed her independent outings. Except in the periods when she was tied to her home with small, nursing babies, Maud could escape into another role in Toronto, enjoying her own celebrity, rather than deferring to her husband before his parishioners.

———

In Leaskdale, Maud had far less access to community gossip, and this she missed. In the presence of their minister's wife, women remained on their best behaviour and talked about "non-combustible" topics. In Cavendish, Maud had profited from the best location in the community for hearing local news—her grandparents' home, with the post office in its kitchen. Here in Leaskdale, she was cut off from the gossip that had fed her fiction. She could not even make a confidential friend of any of her husband's parishioners without arousing the jealousy of others. At Uxbridge, in the Hypatia Club, she found one new friend, Mary Beal (Mrs. Norman Beal). A gifted, socially prominent, and well-to-do woman, raised in Uxbridge, she was the daughter of one of the founding members of the club, but now lived in Toronto.

In February 1913, the Hypatia Club put on a dramatic presentation that followed a script they had used before. The "Goddess of Fame," played by Mary Beal, summoned a series of women who acted out the parts of historical women who deserved the "laurel wreath of fame": the Dowager Empress of China, Ruth (of the Bible), Laura Secord (Canadian heroine in the War of 1812), Helen of Troy, Jenny Lynd (the Swedish "nightingale"), Pandita Ramabai (female revivalist in India), Elizabeth Barrett Browning (poet), Mrs. Winsloe (who pleaded the merits of her soothing patent medicine for infants), Hypatia herself (as a Grecian oracle), Harriet Beecher Stowe, Marie Antoinette, Flora Macdonald (who saved the life of Bonnie Prince Charlie), Shakespeare's "Portia," "Madame Butterfly" from Puccini's opera of that name, Queen Victoria, Miriam (of the Bible), Madame Emma Albani (Canadian opera singer), Florence Nightingale, Pauline Johnson (a famous half-native Canadian poet who performed on the stage, transforming herself from white to native), Miss Canada, and a generic "Mother." Maud came as herself, along with "Anne of Green Gables." The laurel crown was given to the generic, idealized "Mother," who played, no doubt, the role of the Victorian "angel in the house." The group raised $241 for library purchases that year.

For all such outings Maud could safely leave Chester in the care of Lily Reid, the manse's maid since Stella's departure. Lily's two young children, Edith and Archie, were cared for by Lily's mother.[15]

A daily stint of writing remained an inviolate part of Maud's morning routine. By May 1913, she had finished *The Golden Road*, which picked up and continued the story of the King family and their friends. Its heroine, "the Story

Girl," continues to recount old folk tales and myths, sharing this role now with the "Awkward Man," a dreamy recluse who is also a writer. In place of the hellfire sermons of the *The Story Girl*, Montgomery offers the equally terrifying experience of confronting a "witch," old Peg Bowen. There are many echoes of Louisa May Alcott's *Little Women*: sweet Cecily, like Alcott's sweet Beth, will not live beyond the golden road of childhood.

A more personal echo appears at the climax, when Sara Stanley is reunited with her beloved father, absent since his daughter was eight years old. The motif recurs again later in *Jane of Lantern Hill*, marking Maud's endless longing for her idealized father. Brown-bearded Blair Stanley in *The Golden Road* is described in terms that identify him with Hugh John.

Shortly after she finished *The Golden Road* in May 1913, Maud started work on her third "Anne" book. She was being urged by L. C. Page to produce more money-making "Anne" novels. The story of young college girls setting up house together and fully enjoying the warmth of friendship took her into a period of creative energy. The memories of Prince of Wales College days and the recent closeness with Frede furnished the tone for "Anne of Redmond," later to be published as *Anne of the Island*.

When Chester was one year old, in July, Maud proudly took him to Prince Edward Island. Whenever she went home to visit on the Island, her arrival was major news—a striking contrast to her return from Prince Albert, when no one had bothered to meet her train. The papers reported her every movement on and about the Island, giving her a similar kind of attention to that received by Andrew Macphail. The adulation she received on the Island always recharged her. Although her life was now in Ontario, she felt that her roots would always be in the Island. She was now living through the happiest period of her life, right after Chester's birth, with success in all areas of her professional and personal life. She was speaking the truth when she said, "I haven't time to *be* because I have so much to *do*" (December 1, 1912).

As Maud worked feverishly on her next book, Ewan, too, showed a burst of energy. An ambitious plan to support a foreign missionary took possession of him. Many large parishes, Roman Catholic as well as Protestant, particularly urban ones, counted it a distinction to support the work of "their own missionary." It gave the parish a rallying point, and in a pre-television era, letters from a good missionary stationed in India or some other still-exotic place made wonderful entertainment when read from the pulpit. Missionaries coming home on furlough brought incredible excitement if they were good speakers. A minister who obtained his congregation's support for a missionary underlined his own success as a pastor. In autumn 1913, Ewan Macdonald began canvassing his parishioners, pressing them to support a missionary. The necessary amount was $1,200 a year, more than Ewan's own salary.

Maud disapproved of Ewan's plan. She knew that cash was never a plentiful commodity, even on a successful farm. Nor did industrious Scots farmers really like being parted from too much of their hard-earned money, sympathetic as they might be to redeeming "heathens" in foreign parts. Maud felt this enterprise would be doomed to failure, and she told Ewan so. But Ewan was stubborn, and determined to assert himself in this instance.

By 1914, Ewan had engaged a young ministry student, Stuart Forbes, B.A., to travel to Honan, China. Ewan (with Maud's help) gave considerable money to support his missionary. They also gave another $1,100 for the building fund of Knox College, also clearly coming from Maud's funds, since Ewan's salary was only $900 that year.

Maud must have hoped that the ambition she had witnessed in Ewan's early days in PEI was returning, even if she disapproved of the missionary project. She had witnessed temporary bursts of energy before: for example, when Ewan spurred the improvement of the Cavendish graveyard (an act that endeared him to the community), and when he preached in two large Charlottetown churches just before he left for Scotland. He could be very effective at these times. (In fact, she would have been impressed by the account of his preaching in these prestigious churches in the *Examiner*, October 6, 1906, right before she accepted his proposal on October 12, 1906.)

Maud herself had embarked on a new career as a riveting platform speaker. On October 13, 1913, under the auspices of the Women's Canadian Club, she addressed eight hundred women in Forrester's Hall, Toronto, on the subject of Prince Edward Island. All the major Toronto newspapers carried accounts of "Mrs. Macdonald" and her speech. She copied one of these into her diary entry of November 1, 1913, obviously pleased with its characterizations:

> There is something quaint and taking in her whole personality. She is quiet, with a great deal of reserve force and strength. Few writers impress one to the same degree with the conviction that she lives in a mental world of her own where Anne and Kilmeny and the Story Girl and other characters as yet unknown to her readers pursue adventures of absorbing interest. Mrs. Macdonald has a

voice of admirable carrying quality. . . . One of the many favourable comments heard on every hand was to the effect that she was absolutely natural and unaffected.

She did not copy two other revealing parts of the journalists' comments. First, on her positive influence on her audience:

The audience was as interesting in its own way as the speaker. As those listening women were drawn more closely into the mould of the speaker, as they became informed by her insistence on every-thing that is normal and happy and beautiful in life, their faces changed . . . to the look that people wear when they are living again their happiest moments. . . . They smiled and laughed and applauded and to all intents and purposes were girls again in their old homes. It is indeed a magical power to be able to call back all that is wholesome and lovely and unforgettable in one's childhood and this magical gift is Mrs. Macdonald's. The loveliness of sim-plicity, the greatness that is fostered in quiet lives was the subject of her address. But it was not delivered in abstract or lofty terms. It was told as a story should be told without much comment and the audience was left to find the lesson.

Second, on her topic:

The first part of the address was a lyrical, passionate praise of Prince Edward Island. . . . This was no ordinary geographical traveller's tale of a familiar country, but a lover's praise of a heart's country. As she piled sentence on sentence to explain to inland folk the mystery and the beauty and the love of the sea, it began to be plain that those who heard this address perhaps would never forget it.[16]

Maud's new acquaintances in Toronto sent her these glowing newspaper accounts. She was secretly delighted, but already she was noticing that Ewan did not share the same pleasure in her success. What did Ewan feel like when he delivered weekly sermons in front of a wife who, after her first formal pub-lic address ever—to eight hundred people in Toronto—had received rave re-views in at least *seven* Toronto newspapers? Ewan had been taught to believe that all gifts came from God; why, he must have brooded, did he not have speaking powers equal to those of his wife if God wanted him to succeed in the ministry? Was God set *against* him? He had not anticipated what it would be like to live with such a gifted and articulate wife. He could not fault Maud as a wife and helpmeet in his ministry, but her extraordinary abilities somehow diminished his. Old-timers remembering Ewan in the late 1970s all used the same term to describe him: he was "deep," they said. He began brooding, keeping his feelings and thoughts to himself, and a number of people noticed this.

Maud was caught up in her own success, and she confided in her private diary: "I really believe I would like very much to live in a place like Toronto— there I could have some intellectual companionship, have access to good music, drama and art, and some little real social life. I have *no* social life here—none at all, not even as much as I had in Cavendish" (November 1, 1913). There was reason to hope that Ewan might advance up the clerical ladder, just as John Mustard had.

In November 1913, Maud found that she was pregnant again. Delighted, she hoped for a girl. This pregnancy was as difficult as the first had been easy. Constant nausea alternated with long stretches of compete mental lethargy. She recalled with alarm the severe depression she had suffered before her marriage and feared a recurrence. She continued working as best she could on *Anne of the Island* (she used a garden metaphor—doing "spadework"— to describe the process of planning out plot and characters for a novel or story), but the difficult pregnancy made her feel increasingly out of touch with the fictional world of her girlhood. Her life was moving on, and other shadows were emerging in the road "around the bend."

After finishing her morning stint of work, she spent the rest of the day on her family, her house, or her community duties. Her maid, Lily Reid, commented that Maud was extra-conscientious: she was a serious person who "did more than most minister's wives."[17] That was her nature—she was caught up in the notion of duty—and she also felt that she strengthened Ewan's pastoral service, which would help his career.

One personal pleasure through the long, cold winter of 1914 was reading. Maud averaged at least a book a day. She read new books her publishers sent her alongside her old favourites (which she read again and again). On trips to Toronto, she purchased new books. She was an exceptionally fast reader, and blessed with a near-photographic memory. On successive readings, she underlined her favourite passages in her books (some of which have survived) and made jottings of reactions into notebooks (which are often copied into her diary, although her notebooks themselves have not survived). To her, books were the centre of a cultured person's life. Books were also a companion—one that an intellectual husband might have been. She accumulated more and more books; when she cleaned the Leaskdale library one spring she counted 1,200. (Books bearing her inscription still turn up across Canada.)

Ewan's initiative with the missionary drew attention. "It was worth travelling a good way to see the love and respect of the people for their minister, and the minister's pride at the generosity of his loyal people," wrote a Toronto lawyer named Mr. John A. Paterson, K.C., describing the country parson's magnificent effort in a 1914 publication called *The Presbyterian*. For a time after Ewan undertook this missionary activity, it did look as if he might rise beyond the role of country parson: some of Maud's spotlight was temporarily diverted to him. In June 1914, he had the pleasure of welcoming "his" missionary. All went well, until the young missionary came to visit and turned out to be rather a dull fellow. He had no personal charm, and no understanding that he should make an effort to connect with those who were paying his salary.

It was fortunate that Maud had kept her own finances separate from Ewan's after her marriage—a departure from the custom of the time. She might *give* him money for his missionary project, but he could not *take* her money without her agreement. As a man of the old school who believed that God vested all authority in males, Ewan was initially troubled by her independence—this was not his idea of wifely submission as set forth in the Bible—yet he also understood that he had married an exceptional woman. He enjoyed the trips and conveniences that her income made possible. He recognized her abilities in planning and organization. He reluctantly came to see that she had been right about the ill-advised missionary project. More and more, Maud made the real decisions in the family, although she always pretended to defer to Ewan in the process.

Despite tensions in this marriage, Maud was content. Ewan was a good and kindly man. Her book sales were still strong, although they were dropping off from the highs of *Anne of Green Gables*: in book royalties alone, she made $3,599 in 1912, $3,959 in 1913, $2,817 in 1914, and $3,586 in 1915 (when Ewan still made $900 a year).[18] She had gained the admiration and appreciation of the parishioners in Leaskdale and Zephyr. She had met and become a part of Toronto's elite literary world. Although Toronto was not Edinburgh, or London, or Boston, these were times of growing Canadian nationalism, and Maud felt that she was on the ground floor of an edifice that would eventually develop into a great Canadian literature. She underlined a section from Sir Walter Scott's "The Lay of the Last Minstrel" about his pride in his native land:

> Breathes there a man, with soul so dead,
>   Who never to himself hath said,
> This is my own, my native land!

In 1914 she seemed on top of the world. No one could have known that she—and the world—were rushing madly into a future that would soon change everything they knew.

CHAPTER 8

The darkening plains

On August 5, 1914, Maud wrote in her journal, "England has declared war on Germany." Like most North Americans, Maud had paid scant attention a few months earlier when she had read that a Serbian had shot the Archduke of Austria and his duchess. The previous century had been filled with many assassinations and political skirmishes, but the fighting was usually localized. People in Canada, and indeed everyplace else, expected this war to be over quickly, perhaps in months, or even weeks. No one foresaw that it would spread, devouring an entire generation of young men.

On that August in 1914, Maud could not have imagined how much the war would eventually affect her husband, her community, and her own life. The war would also have a significant effect on the atmosphere in which writers worked: it would transform literary styles, alter the subjects deemed appropriate for literature, and create a new kind of reading public.

The "Great War" was to drag on for four years, killing more than 10 million young men worldwide and drawing sixteen nations and their colonies into conflict. Some 628,736 Canadians served in the war, and 66,573 were killed, with another 138,166 wounded. Many were maimed for life from gas attacks and other injuries. Over 10,000 men from the Toronto area alone were killed.

Against this international backdrop of death and destruction, Montgomery's smaller world suffered its own pain and catastrophic events. On August 13, 1914, only eight days after the war was declared, Maud suffered the first of her personal tragedies: her second baby, Hugh Alexander, died at birth. She was overwhelmed with sorrow, and with so much grief close at hand, the Kaiser of Germany seemed far away. Little Hugh (named after her father and

Ewan's) was quietly buried in Zion Cemetery, outside Uxbridge. She wrote in her journals with the same power about her sorrow as she had written about her pleasure after Chester's birth.

By August 31, 1914, Maud's fierce discipline sent her back to her desk. She found herself in the grip of a lethargic depression and had to force herself to work. She finished *Anne of the Island* on November 20, ten days short of her fortieth birthday. "Never did I write a book under greater stress," she recorded on November 20, 1914. Yet, in the writing, her spirits had recovered, and in spite of everything, she wrote in her journal: "Life is much richer, fuller, happier, *more comfortable* for me now than it was when I was twenty. I have won the success I resolved to win twenty years ago. It is worth the struggle . . ." (November 20, 1914).

Anne of the Island (1914)

Anne of the Island had been conceived as the saga of Anne's college years, but when Maud was planning it back in August 1913, she found it increasingly difficult to re-enter the mental frame for this book—it seemed to belong to another century and life. As her spadework progressed, Anne's happy college years did not have any room for the death of her baby, Hugh. But once she started, the act of writing the book was pleasurable, giving her escape from her sorrowful present. Still, it lacked what *Anne of Green Gables* had: the sense that she was living it, feeling every emotion, as she wrote it.

In *Anne of the Island*, Anne sets off to "Redmond College." The story is loosely based on Maud's own year at Dalhousie. Maud had herself lived in Halifax Ladies' College, under the watchful eye of grim old maids, but Anne and her friends rent a charming little house, "Patty's Place," from two older women (aged fifty and seventy) who decide to cut loose from their circumscribed life to sightsee together in Europe. The "household gods" who come with this cottage are Gog and Magog, china dogs modelled on the ones Maud purchased on her honeymoon. These pagan deities seem appropriate in the house owned by two spunky older women who have flouted convention by refusing to marry and procreate. As Anne and her roommates at "Patty's Place" laugh and study together, Maud creates a world in which young women enjoy each other's fellowship instead of being pitted against each other in the search for desirable mates. There is a strong sense of female community and solidarity in this book. Men enter these young women's world as potential suitors to be discussed and laughed over—just as Maud had done with Frede and Nora Lefurgey.

The book chews over some of the contemporary attitudes about female education. Older women remark that younger women just go to college to get a man, but Maud gives this a new twist: her college girls see marriage as a fate to be put off as long as possible. They acknowledge that they must eventually settle down, but they intend to have a good time beforehand. Maud depicts higher education for women as both improving and enjoyable, an activity that only old fuddy-duddies would disparage. At the end, the novel appears to reaffirm the prevalent view that a woman's duty is to marry and procreate, not to seek an education, but at the same time it offers new views on the subject. This is a typical strategy we find in Maud's novels: affirm the status quo, so conservative readers will not be upset, but suggest subtle and attractive alternatives to other readers.

The suitors themselves are creative variations on young men Maud had known. Anne has to choose between suitors: Gilbert Blythe shares some of the characteristics of Maud's friend from Saskatchewan, Will Pritchard; Royal Gardner has a tendency to manage other people's lives, not unlike Ed Simpson.

Anne of the Island seems a book out of sync with the troubled times, and in one sense it is. In it, Maud is returning to a lost world for consolation. However, judging from its lively sales during the war, thousands of readers found it comforting. Maud was good at sensing the public mood. Part of her continuing popularity arises from her ability to recreate happy and recognizable worlds where people have fun together. But *Anne of the Island* also prepared young women for what was coming: learning to take responsibility for themselves instead of depending exclusively on men.

Maud's spirits improved after she finished writing *Anne of the Island*, though she complained of frequent fatigue. Still, exhaustion was better than the debilitating depressions that had beset her before her marriage. Frede came for Christmas again that year, and together she and Maud analyzed the war news: "We flayed the Kaiser every day and told Kitchener what he ought to do . . ." (January 1, 1915).

Immediately after Christmas 1914, Maud heard from her half-sister, Ila, in Saskatchewan—one of the three children born to her father during his second marriage to Mary Ann—that her half-brother Carl had enlisted. The war was coming closer to home, affecting her own family as well as her community. Patriotic fervour was spreading, especially in newspapers and in the pulpits. The newspapers urged Canadians to feel a duty to the "Empire" and to Great Britain (the "dear old mother country"), as well as a duty to uphold the values of the civilized world against the forces of the Kaiser and the German army. Ministers urged patriotism as a means to save Christian values from the "forces of Evil."

Religion had been losing its hold on people in the first part of the twentieth century. By World War I, the power of the ministry was already in decline, even in rural parishes like Leaskdale. Religion had always provided a source of shared assumptions about social order that located and bonded people in time and space. The late nineteenth century's assault on religion—in the name of "higher criticism" and scientific inquiry—had greatly weakened the Church's authority. Increased literacy had enabled people to read more and think critically about their own culture and history, and with the rapid development of science, the clergy no longer held the *only* keys to the "great unknown."

To the clergy, the war now provided a way of demonstrating the materiality of evil: it was embodied in the German Kaiser (who was "raping little Belgium"). Those who fought against Germany were soldiers of the Lord saving the world for future generations. The soldiers who "went west" or "over the top" were likened to Jesus, dying so that others might live. Serving in war was the supreme "self-sacrifice." Even if this war was not fought over religion, the language and rhetoric of religion was used to mobilize people to fight.

"There were few stauncher supporters of the war than Canada's clergy. For them, the atrocities committed by the enemy demanded that the Allied nations become agents of divine retribution, cleansing the earth of those who defiled Christendom with their crimes," writes historian Jonathan Vance.[19] Ministers preached that enlisting was "a duty of conscience, of religion." Like so many wars of ancient history—and modern times—this one was depicted as a holy war against "Evil" and "Evil-doers."

While religion appealed to young men's moral sense, there were other reasons they enlisted. Some were motivated by a genuine sense of patriotism and principle, outraged by the descriptions of barbarism they read in the newspapers. Many other young men rushed to sign up for the war in hopes of adventure, seeking a "piece of the action" before the war was over; people speculated that Britain and the Allied Forces would bring Germany and the Kaiser to their knees in short order, possibly in a matter of weeks. Still others were drawn to the war through recruiting rallies stage-managed to pressure them into signing their names. Ministers like Ewan assisted at these rallies, and, in many cases, conducted them.

These recruiting meetings were held in local venues, usually churches. Entire families attended them because they were informative and entertaining, and such diversions were in short supply in rural communities before the development of radio and television media. Once there, people heard visiting speakers talk of the brutality of the Germans, the savagery of enemy attacks, and the glories of serving one's country. Women sang patriotic and inspirational songs. "Signing officers" were positioned at the exits to take signatures. Ministers hovered, too, as symbols of God's authority. Able-bodied young men could not exit without feeling shame if they had not signed their names. Once a young man had put down his name, he was committed. Signing up was easy, even a little unreal; no one wanted to be called a "slacker." And the war had truly stirred up deep feelings of loyalty for the "Old Country," as well as a renewed reverence for the God of Righteousness in a world that had begun to secularize.

In 1915, *Everywoman's World* asked certain high-profile authors to answer two questions about war: "What will be the outcome of the war for the world at large?" and "What will it be for women in particular?" They introduced Maud's comments with the note that "L. M. Montgomery, writer of graceful romances, strikes a sterner note in her message to . . . [our] readers." Maud felt much quiet skepticism over religion—she saw it as a social institution more than a religious one—but she retained a deep-seated reverence for the idea of God. Her comments on these two questions are interesting:

> I am not one of those who believe that this war will put an end to war. War is horrible, but there are things that are more horrible still, just as there are fates worse than death. Moral degradation, low ideas, sordid devotion to money-getting, are worse evils than war, and history shows us that these evils invariably overtake a nation which is for a long time at peace. Nothing short of so awful a calamity as a great war can awaken to remembrance a nation that has forgotten God and sold its birthright of aspiration for a mess of potage. . . .

In regard to women, I do not expect that the war and its outcome will affect their interests, apart from the general influence
upon the race. But I do hope that it will in some measure open the
eyes of humanity to the truth that the women who bear and train
the nation's sons should have some voice in the political issues that
may send those sons to die on battlefields . . . [20]

Although much of this statement seems to be appropriate for a minister's
wife, there is also the hint of a quiet call for women's suffrage. Maud was not
a public crusader for women's rights like some women activists—Nellie
McClung, for example—but in her writing and speaking she often con-
tended for women's interests with hushed but eloquent force.

Another son: Ewan Stuart Macdonald

In March 1915, Maud was delighted to find she was pregnant with a third
child. But hard on the heels of the good tidings came frightening news. In
April, Maud received a telegram saying that her cousin Frede, now an instructor at Macdonald College (and regarded as one of their best teachers),
was dying of typhoid fever. Maud rushed to Montreal. A miracle—as soon as
Frede saw Maud, she began to recover. This was Frede's *second* brush with
death: in 1902, she had been so sick that one Prince Edward Island paper
carried a notice that she was mortally ill. The already powerful bond between the cousins was now stronger than ever.

Maud did not start another novel during her third pregnancy in 1915. Perhaps
she feared that too much stress might result in another stillborn child. Instead,
she began to collect and write material for a book of poetry. She treated herself
to a restorative six-week trip to the Island through June and the first half of July.
It was a summer of bad weather and she was uncomfortable with her pregnancy.
Her life seemed less settled because of the war, and she was often overwhelmed
by wildly fluctuating mood swings. She visited her old home in the moonlight
(in the dark, so her Uncle John F. Macneill would not see her) and wrote:

For a space the years turned back their pages. The silent sleepers
in the graveyard yonder wakened and filled their old places.
Grandfather and grandmother read in the lighted kitchen. Old

friends and comrades walked with me in the lane. Daffy frisked in
the caraway. Above me my old white bed waited for me to press its
pillow of dreams. . . . I could hardly tear myself away from the spot.
Perhaps the charm it had for me was not a wholesome one . . . It
may not be well to linger too long among ghosts, lest they lay a
cold grasp upon you and bind you too closely to their chill, sweet,
unearthly companionship. (June 27, 1915)

She was glad to return in July 1915 to her busy life in Leaskdale.

In Ontario, Maud could remember the best of the old life and write
about it, but when she was back in Prince Edward Island in person, she increasingly found herself pulled in two ways: when she was with people—and
this was most of the time—she enjoyed herself; but when she was alone, she
was easily drawn back into the past, remembering her morbid unhappiness
during periods of debilitating depressions. The resurging memories dogged
and alarmed her.

On October 7, 1915, Ewan Stuart Macdonald was born. From the very
first, everyone declared that he took after Maud and her family as much as
Chester had taken after Ewan's side. This delighted her, and she believed that
he favoured her own late father (whom she continued to idealize). But she
had little time to rhapsodize over Stuart as she had over her first-born son.

Maud felt a lingering depression through the fall of 1915 and the winter of
1916. Perhaps it was an aftermath of childbirth; certainly it was accentuated by
worry over the war, as well as over her many responsibilities. For a woman who
was nursing a new baby, her schedule was very busy. She was president of the
local branch of the Canadian Red Cross Society, which met every second
Tuesday in Leaskdale Church. She worked hard with the local Presbyterian
Women's Guild, using her performance skills at fundraising events.

The Uxbridge *Journal* noted: "Nearly every battalion in France has a
woman's club at home working directly for it." Women were very active in the
war effort in rural communities like Leaskdale. They *cared*—they knew each
boy who had gone overseas. They organized patriotic meetings to raise money
for supplies for the battalions from their area. Registration was taken for
"Women's Emergency Corps," recording the names of women ready to do the
work at home of men who had enlisted. Maud's friend Mrs. Norman Beal organized a large benefit for the support of the 116th Battalion. The proceeds
purchased supplies. The Women's Red Cross Society put on fundraising box

socials, pie socials, and concerts so they could buy materials to make bandages and yarn for knitting socks. The war effort consumed the community. Maud taught her Sunday School classes, went on pastoral visitations with Ewan, and entertained as necessary.

When Stuart was three months old, his exhausted mother did not have enough breast milk for him. She had been beset by repeated breast inflammations, he was not gaining weight properly, and she feared for his survival. And for weeks Ewan had suffered from bronchitis—a very serious illness before the advent of antibiotics, given that it could develop into pneumonia. He was unable to preach.

It was not until March 1916, when Stuart was six months old and had been put on cow's milk, that he began to thrive. Then Maud was able to resume the literary activities that she enjoyed. She travelled to Toronto for a string of festivities: an afternoon tea given in her honour by the Canadian Women's Press Club; a reception and tea hosted for her by Mrs. Norman Beal and her mother-in-law; a reception honouring her by the Salisbury Chapter of the Imperial Order of the Daughters of the Empire (I.O.D.E.); a special tea for her given by Mrs. Talling, with the Reverend Dr. Marshall Talling doing the "honours of the house."

Meanwhile, the war was beginning to make a deep impact on Canadians. The German army was rolling across Europe, seemingly unstoppable on its way to world domination. People were frightened that if Germany conquered England, Canada would become a German colony. Older men, as well as boys, now wanted to fight. Frederick George Scott, Canon of the Anglican Church in Quebec, a man well over fifty, was one of the many older men to enlist and serve on the front as a chaplain.[21]

The Reverend Edwin Smith—Ewan's acquaintance, who had left the Island shortly before Ewan did—took a leave of absence from the Presbyterian ministry to serve in the British Navy. Other mature, married men of Ewan's generation also enlisted. Sam Sharpe, the Uxbridge town solicitor, divested himself of his business interests and mobilized a county battalion in the Uxbridge–Scott Township area. Sharpe had been a prominent lawyer and businessman in Uxbridge and a Member of the Provincial Parliament. A graduate of Osgoode Hall Law School and the University of Toronto, Sharpe was married (but without children). By Christmas 1915, Lieutenant-Colonel

Sharpe had enjoined 20 young men to enlist in this 116th Battalion, and he trained them for war. He eventually commanded over 250 men.

The example of a prominent man like Sharpe, who gave up a comfortable life and business, inspired others in the community. Canadians wanted to do their bit for the "Old Country"; loyalty to Britain was everywhere. In Zephyr, Robert F. Brooks was one of the most successful farmers in the area, with a hundred-acre farm. He noted that he had no wife or family dependent on him: "They need me 'over there,' and I've got to go." Newspaper clippings describe the auction sale of his top-quality farm animals and equipment. Brooks's sacrifice was the talk of the entire county. Neighbours bid up the prices to show their own patriotic spirit.

Even Stuart Forbes, the lackadaisical missionary supported by Ewan's parishes in Honan, China, simply vacated his post and headed to Europe to fight. He did not bother to notify Ewan of his departure, and the whole missionary business ended as a defeat and a humiliation for Ewan.

Ewan's contribution to the war effort thus far had been to organize or to help at recruitment meetings.[22] He soon had a new task, however: comforting the heartbroken families when their sons were maimed or killed. The bad news came by telegram, and the telegram's arrival was normally announced over the telephone. Because all the country homes were on "party lines," every time a phone rang, everyone on the party line could listen in. The mere ringing of a telephone began to fray already taut nerves. Nearly twenty young men from Scott Township were killed before the war was over.

In the case where a son had been slated to take over his father's farm and look after his parents, the death was more than emotionally devastating—it was a disaster for the entire family. Maud suffered over the loss of local boys as much as Ewan did: she had taught many of them in Sunday School or directed them in church programs, and every loss was personal. And each time she and Ewan had to comfort families over their loss of a son, she relived her own intense grief at the death of her second baby.

Maud's faith was increasingly tortured: although she believed in the concept of sacrifice, she found it hard to believe that this was God's plan for these young men. She knew she would not want her own sons to go and was thankful that they were so young, a sentiment that wracked her with shame. These feelings resulted in considerable internal conflict, which she dealt with by turning her powerful emotions into stories or poems.

Newspapers were full of the war news, and Maud's vivid imagination was fired by the exaggerated propaganda. Maud's diary entry of January 1, 1915, states that Frede, who had visited again over Christmas, had returned to Montreal, and Maud would miss talking to her about the war. "Ewan refuses to talk about it. He claims that it unsettles him and he cannot do his work properly." She follows up this revealing—and totally unexplored—statement about Ewan with, "No doubt this is so; but it is rather hard on me, for I have no one else with whom to discuss it. There is absolutely *no* one around here who seems to *realize* the war." She adds: " . . . it is well they do not. If all felt as I do over it the work of the country would certainly suffer. But I feel as if I were stranded on a coast where nobody talked my language." Fortunately, the women with sons dying in the trenches could not read Maud's private thoughts about their seeming complacency.

Despite her doubts, Maud continued to see the war in dramatic terms, and she believed those who sacrificed their lives were heroes, no matter how much personal pain the war caused. Increasingly, the war was all that *she* thought of and wanted to talk about. Her journals show that she was absolutely consumed by it, wracked by it, tortured by it, obsessed by it—even *addicted* to it. All Ewan could do was walk to the local store to fetch her the newspaper every day, and he did this faithfully. But what did Ewan feel? Why did he refuse to talk about it, when he otherwise tried to please his wife? His refusal could not have been just because he was "busy." Did he feel guilty because he was not one of the older men, including ministers, who had enlisted, like Canon Scott and Edwin Smith? Did he squirm over his complicity in sending young boys to war while he stood safely in his clerical collar in the pulpit, *preaching* the virtue of giving one's life to destroy evil? He did believe that the German Kaiser was evil incarnate and that fighting was necessary, but it could not have been easy for a thoughtful man like him to comfort families whose sons were now dead. As a minister who had studied religious wars in history, he could see how religion had been used throughout history, especially in Scotland's bloody past, to urge people to battle, and justify murder and killing.

Ewan made his own small war effort: in August 1916, he helped found a War Resources Committee, partly to aid bereaved families. He became more subdued, obviously troubled deeply about the war, his relation to it, and the impact on those he knew. Whatever the complexities of his marital situation, the husband who had been displaced by a baby was now displaced by the war.

———

In November 1916 that Maud's first book of poetry, *The Watchman*, was published. "The Watchman" was the name of the highest sand dune on the Cavendish shore, the local topographical peak, and the title poem presents a "watcher of the world," looking over the onslaught of war. She finished the poems collected in *The Watchman* at the end of March 1916, after working on the collection for some time. This was her own personal response to the war—to enfold it in poetic metaphor, which provided a feeling of control over a frightening new world. She was deeply involved with this book on an emotional level.

During the war years, she read and reread many history books, seeking historical perspective on the repeated occurrences of war throughout the ages. Maud's vivid imagination led her to visualize war's horrors and feel tormented by these images. She agonized over what appeared to her to be humanity blindly repeating the same mistakes. She was obsessed with the war, but she could not stop herself. She put up a map of Europe and followed each advance of "the Enemy." Towns in Poland with names she was unable to pronounce became as familiar as Toronto, Uxbridge, and Leaskdale. When she became too overwrought, she locked the door of her bedroom and paced the floor. Once again she was a helpless prisoner of her agitated moods.

Nevertheless, the Macdonalds' Christmas Day in 1916 was a very happy one. Frede was with them again, as she so often was. *The Watchman* had been published in November. The church enjoyed its annual Christmas concert. For a week, the Macdonalds had a wonderful time, laughing, eating good food, visiting, and playing with the babies. Again, laughter filled the house. One maid said of Frede, "She was funny as all get-out." After Frede's departure, Maud wrote in her journals, "We had a delightful week and I think I can live comfortably on it through the winter" (January 4, 1917).

Her overall mood, however, remained anxious and contemplative. She wrote the next day that "I have been contented in my marriage, and intensely happy in my motherhood. Life has not been—never can be—what I once hoped it would be in my girlhood. But I think, taking one thing with another, that I am as happy as the majority of people in this odd world and happier than a great many of them."

One suspects that Ewan had many similar feelings—content with his family, but at the same time unconnected to a woman whose intensities were so powerful, and whose broader inquiries into the human heart left little time for worrying about what was in his. And what *was* there, in his heart? Confusion? Shame? Jealousy? Disappointment? Were there only flat, impoverished emotions, with something truly missing (as Maud had come to believe)? Or was his flatness a function of an underlying depression? Ewan was merely discouraged by the demands that were made on him: writing sermons to make sense of a confusing, changing world; producing erudite sermons that could take him to bigger and better parishes to please Maud; and finding some way to feel heroic himself, since his wife lived in a world where heroism was important. He saw that Maud was a model to many people, and he was just a country parson—a good enough man, certainly; an intelligent man without question; but a man lacking the gifts of self-assurance, the boundless energy, and natural charisma to take him where his wife wanted him to go. He no doubt felt threatened by it all, and yet he stood in awe of the woman he had married.

CHAPTER 9

Maud's focus was not only on the war abroad. There was also a war brewing in her professional life. A royalty report from her publisher, L. C. Page, in February 1916 was worrisome: he claimed that the sales of *Anne of the Island* amounted to only 3,200 copies. This was considerably fewer than she had expected, and she suspected Page of dishonest accounting.

Maud had initially offered *The Watchman* to Page, but Page had brusquely refused it, on the grounds that poetry did not make money. She was furious: he had already made a fortune on her novels, and this book was especially important to her.

By now, Maud had been chafing for several years at Page's insistence on the initial "binding clause" that held her later books to the same paltry royalty rate of *Anne of Green Gables*. Her contract to give Page subsequent books had run out with the publication of *Anne of the Island* in 1915. She could now leave Page with good conscience, and his insensitive refusal of *The Watchman* was the last straw.

On her literary jaunts in Toronto, she had met John McClelland, of McClelland, Goodchild, and Stewart (soon to be McClelland and Stewart), and she had engaged the company to publish her poems. Page's refusal to publish *The Watchman* would prove to be a costly mistake for him. John McClelland's decision to take on a book of poetry that would itself make no money was undoubtedly the best business decision he ever made. With it, he acquired "L. M. Montgomery" as his author, and the sales of her best-selling books helped his firm become Canada's pre-eminent publisher of Canadian authors for the rest of the twentieth century.

Maud promised McClelland her next novel, *Anne's House of Dreams*. On his advice, she joined the Authors' League of America, an association that would be able to offer her legal help if her disagreements with Page ever went to court. Lewis Page was well known as a man who used intimidation to get his way—first angry threats, then lawsuits.

In February 1917, while she was reading the proofs for *House of Dreams*, Maud received a threatening letter from Page: he was furious that she was moving to another publisher, and he had found a pretext to withhold her royalties. In May 1917 she engaged a lawyer through the Authors' League to deal with Page.

Anne's House of Dreams (1917)

Anne's House of Dreams is a story of pre-war Prince Edward Island, but it introduces events and emotions more troubling than ever before. In it, Anne's first child dies at birth, an experience Maud knew all too well. Anne becomes pregnant again, and another baby is born. The "house of dreams" now has a dream fulfilled. At first, it appears to be a book about happiness in marriage—Anne's and Gilbert's—and fulfillment in child-bearing. On the surface, the book reinforces romantic attitudes about marriage. Yet Gilbert is always out of sight, and Anne finds a community of other friends.

The book introduces several new characters: a handsome young journalist with the sophisticated authorial skills to turn traditional Island tales into a sellable work; and Captain Jim, a retired sea captain, whose best stories, Maud wrote in her journals, came from her own grandfather. And there are new women characters, as well: Susan Baker, a funny, warm-hearted helper and friend, the housekeeper that Montgomery must have dreamed of; and Miss Cornelia, sharp-tongued gossip and "man-hater," able to vent some of Maud's own less "respectable" feelings. The novel provides another glimpse into the comfort that friendship and shared storytelling can provide.

The real focus of the book, however, is the mysterious woman whom Anne sees in the distance one day. She is beautiful, closed off, and tragic. Her name is Leslie Moore—the initials "L.M." are Maud's own, of course. Leslie Moore is tragically yoked to a man who is, literally, an emotional zombie, one of the walking dead. Leslie was forced to marry this man, Dick Moore, by her controlling mother, even though she did not love him. On one of his trips abroad, he had a debilitating accident and was shipped back, a shell of a man. Leslie is held in her marriage by a sense of obligation. Inside the lonely and depressed Leslie—who must be a wife to this dead-in-life man—lies a smouldering vitality and near-explosive frustration.

This ill-advised marriage is a startling new theme for Maud, one undoubtedly drawn from her anxiety about her own marriage. Dick is human only biologically. He is unable to connect emotionally to others. The tragic marriage of Leslie and Dick Moore is ended by medical intervention. When his human side and memory return after an operation, Leslie finds that Dick is not her husband after all. He is simply a cousin of her husband, a man who bears a remarkable resemblance to Dick—and Dick, it turns out, is long dead. The repressed, frustrated Leslie is suddenly free to marry again.[23]

By then Maud was no longer living with the man she *thought* she had married. Ewan's capacity for pleasure seemed somehow crippled: he did not take the kind of joy that she did in nature or in other kinds of beauty. He had been lively in her presence when they were courting and during the early part of their marriage, but increasingly he exhibited a curious emotional flatness in his relationship to the world around him that she could not understand. He fell into abstracted moods, was subdued and lethargic. He looked sad. In this era, husbands and wives often lived in different intellectual spheres, but Maud had hoped for a marriage where there would be at least some companionship.

In the novel, an outsider falls in love with the emotionally starved Leslie's new lover. This young man is a talented journalist named Owen Ford. He speedily wins the repressed heart of "L.M." The beautiful Leslie Moore eventually moves into a marriage as happy as that of Anne and Gilbert, after being freed from her husband.

Perhaps Maud remembered one of the ministers at Ewan's induction, Edwin Smith. Smith was very active as a journalist, and he could easily have provided a partial model for Owen Ford. Edwin Smith had the same kind of easy charm as Owen, the same interest in many things, including a notorious fascination with boats and sailing, and the storytelling ability of Captain Jim. After his war service, he would be known as "Captain Smith."

Anne's House of Dreams was dedicated to Laura Pritchard Agnew, Maud's childhood friend in Prince Albert, "In Memory of the Olden Time"—a puzzling dedication. Laura married her childhood sweetheart, a man who adored her, and she apparently had a happy marriage, at least to Maud's eyes. But Maud privately thought Laura's husband a dull, insipid man—nothing quite as bad as Dick Moore, but still not worthy of the lively Laura, except in his devotion to her. Perhaps this novel was dedicated to Laura for no particular reason other than to deflect attention away from its real subject: the pain of Maud's own emotional loneliness in a marriage.

By 1916, Ewan had become largely absent in his wife's diary. He was rarely mentioned in the first half of 1916, for instance, unless he was ill. In this year, he was sometimes away at recruiting meetings (December 10, 1916; January 5, 1917), and these had begun to depress him. Maud's diary does not record much joy in her own relationship with Ewan, an absence made all the more noticeable because she does write extensively about her love of her children. In fact, it could be argued that her journal was beginning to substitute for the emotional closeness that might be found in a satisfying marriage. Maud writes on March 16, 1916: "How I love my old journal and what a part of my life it has become. It satisfies some need in my nature. It seems like a personal confidant . . ."

It is a curious fact that when the Polish army chose one of Maud's books to issue to their fighting troops in World War II, they chose *Anne's House of Dreams*. It was supposed to inspire the young men to fight for the ideal of happy married love, a peaceful hearth, and a safe home. The book implies such pleasures. But its real power comes from Maud's powerful depiction of the longing for that love and home.

Only Maud's storytelling ability makes this book compelling. The novel's plot is as far-fetched as a Gothic romance. Its happy ending strains credulity. But the novel works as a strangely moving read because Montgomery has reached inside herself and externalized her feelings, showing the misery of a lonely soul, and the hope for a better future.

Less than three weeks after finishing *Anne's House of Dreams* Maud began writing a version of her life called "The Story of My Career" for publication in *Everywoman's World*, a popular magazine for women. Nothing could present a more different view of her life from the depths sounded in *Anne's House of Dreams*. Now available as *The Alpine Path* (Fitzhenry and Whiteside, 1975), it provides a sanitized account of her childhood—retelling many anecdotes from her diaries—and ends with her move to Leaskdale, presumably to be forever happy as the contented wife of a clergyman. However, her journals give a different narrative:

I was never in love with Ewan—never have been in love with him.
But I was—have been—and am, very fond of him. He came into
my life at its darkest hour when I was utterly lonely and discouraged with no prospects of any kind, and no real friends near me. At
first I thought I could never care at all for his type of man; but I
did; and I married him—and I have not regretted that I did so. . . .
But I write not of these things for the Editor of *Everywoman's*. My
grandchildren may include what they like in my biography. But
while I live these things are *arcana*. (January 5, 1917)

In the "Story" of her career, she tells how she always wanted to be a writer,
and focuses on the perseverance that allowed her to climb "the Alpine Path"
to success and fame. The touch is so light in this version of her life that the
public believed that she had lived an uneventful and wholly satisfying life
until her personal journals began to be published in 1985.

Memories about the family dynamics in the Leaskdale manse were few
by the 1980s, but the succession of maids employed by Maud from 1912 on-
wards did have some superficial observations.[24] Maud treated her maids as
members of the family, and they all ate meals together. All the maids liked
Ewan very much, although many viewed him as rather "stodgy." Some commented on his inactive nature and his "fleshiness," but they thought him very
fond of his wife (and her very fond of him!). To them, he was a "typical man,"
though unnaturally maladapted to the tasks most men should have been
doing in the house. However, the Leaskdale maids all regarded the
Macdonald family as a very normal and typical family, with the standard family "devotions" after breakfast ("standard Presbyterian fare" at the time, said
one maid). These consisted of Ewan reading a passage from the Bible followed by prayers, the entire ritual lasting from five to ten minutes. Maud they
remembered for her unfailing sense of humour and companionable nature.

After Maud received a cheque for $2,500 (half her advance) from the
Frederick Stokes Company (who became her American publisher after she
left L. C. Page, and to whom she had sold the rights to *Anne's House of
Dreams*), she began looking in her notebook for ideas for her next novel. The
plot of *Rainbow Valley* began to emerge, with the sound of impending war in
the background.

The great Halifax Explosion was in early December 1917. Maud's first
thought, like that of many others, was that it was a German attack. This ex-

traordinary tragedy—2.5 square miles of Halifax levelled and 1,600 people killed by the explosion of a ship carrying munitions—seemed to bring the war onto Canadian shores.

By now, stretched between her duties as a minister's wife, a mother, and a writer, and her worries about the war, Maud's physical health began to suffer. She was continuously sick with colds or the flu, or other ailments. People noticed that her hands were never still: they were knitting socks for soldiers, crocheting, or otherwise in perpetual motion, nervously wringing or grasping each other. Maud always lived on the edge with her nerves, and her emotional fragility increased during this time, both because of the war and because of her looming legal dispute with her publisher, which had the potential to ruin her financially.

Rainbow Valley (1919)

In *Rainbow Valley*, started in early 1917 and finished in December 1918, she found her own memories of an idyllic childhood irrelevant. She had grown up thinking that wars in other countries were as far away as the moon. It seemed beyond comprehension that the world could have shrunk so fast. National boundaries and oceans of space no longer protected people from war in other lands. In this novel, Maud made a transition from the isolated and lovely atmosphere of Avonlea to the horror of war in Europe.

Maud finished *Rainbow Valley* the day before Christmas, some six weeks after the war had ended. The novel is set before the war, but as she wrote it, she knew the outcome of the war, who would die, and who would return. Her half-brother Carl Montgomery had lost part of a leg at Vimy Ridge; Edwin Smith had been decorated for service by the British Navy and demobilized; and many of the young men she had taught as boys in Sunday School were now lying beneath the poppies in Europe. She dedicated her new book to three of the young men in the Leaskdale and Uxbridge parishes who died in the war: "To the memory of Goldwin Lapp, Robert Brookes [sic], and Morley Shier, who made the supreme sacrifice that the happy valleys of their home land might be kept sacred from the ravage of the invader."[25] The language of the dedication reflects the language of the pulpit, the Bible, and World War I propaganda.

In this book she introduces the Meredith family: a sad, dreamy widowed minister and his neglected, unruly children. Another new character is the orphan Mary Vance, fostered first by the Merediths, and then by Miss Cornelia. Mary Vance, coming from an abusive background, is coarse and must be nurtured into acceptability. A range of personalities interact: dreamy, bossy, or managerial, lovable or not. Anne and her husband, Dr. Gilbert Blythe, are so mature and respectable now that they are dull. Mary Vance, Miss Cornelia, and Susan Baker (the Blythes' cook) are the most piquant and forthright. Anne's son Walter is developed as "different," a sensitive child who prefers aesthetic interests to rough-and-tumble fighting with other boys. He sees "beyond the veil," glimpsing into a world that others cannot see.

The setting is "Glen St. Mary," not far from "Avonlea," but the people of Leaskdale still point to the Ontario valley that they believe was the basis for Rainbow Valley. Like so many of Maud's novels, *Rainbow Valley* gives a sense of a tightly knit, repressive-but-lively-and-bustling Presbyterian community. The sylvan glen that the children call "Rainbow Valley" is a woodland haunt where they escape their hidebound and judgmental community. From its secluded and bubbling spring, they drink pure, cool water. The path from "Rainbow Valley" (recalling "Lovers' Lane" in Cavendish) leads through the adult community to the wider world outside, and in this future world looms "the shadow of the Great Conflict . . . in the fields of France, Flanders, Gallipoli, and Palestine."

On one level, the story provides comfort when John Meredith finally marries, giving his motherless brood someone sensible and practical to love and guide them. Amiable, good, and level-headed only when called to attention, Mr. Meredith spends much of his time thinking about the imponderables of theology. He is an endearing and wistful version of Ewan, an intelligent, abstracted, and generally ineffectual man.

The war precipitated another event. Frede Campbell, Maud's cousin and treasured "kindred spirit," had been dating a young chemistry instructor at the Macdonald College named Cameron MacFarlane, but told Maud several times that nothing would come of her relationship with him. He joined the Princess Patricia's Light Infantry. Cameron, home on furlough and now a lieutenant, suddenly proposed on May 16, 1917. Six hours later they were married, just before he left for overseas. Maud described her response to the news as: "Dumbfoundered, flabbergasted, knocked out and rendered speechless."

However impulsive the marriage, Maud was deeply hurt that Frede had married without telling her first—so much so, in fact, that Maud wrote her correspondent, George Boyd MacMillan, that she had been present at Frede's wedding, when in fact, she had only visited Frede after the wedding.

Frede had been approaching twenty-eight when Maud married at thirty-six. Several of Frede's romances had not worked out, and by the time the war came along, reducing the pool of men, Frede was in her mid-thirties, beginning to acquire the derogatory designation of "spinster." Frede was an intelligent, strong-minded, and independent person. Moreover, she appeared to be launched on a brilliant career as a Home Economist at Macdonald College in Montreal. When women married, whether educated or not, they were expected to give up their professions and tend to their families. Frede joked in the summer of 1918, after her wedding, that she wished she "could have both the 'job' and the husband." This meant that Frede's education, which Maud had paid for, would essentially go to waste. Of course, many marriages were made in haste during wartime. In 1916, Maud's younger half-brother, Donald Bruce Montgomery, had married quickly and unwisely in Winnipeg, and Maud saw both of these marriages as further casualties of war.

The war that everyone had expected to last only months dragged on for four years until November 11, 1918. The death of so many young men brought a psychic loss to all of Canada. Many of those who did return came back with missing limbs or with lungs damaged by poison-gas warfare, which shortened their lives. Others returned as psychological cripples, from shell shock or "survivor guilt." The distinguished Colonel Sam Sharpe of Uxbridge was one of these latter: he committed suicide on his way home from the war, jumping out of a two-storey window in the Royal Victoria Veterans' Hospital in Montreal. His funeral was huge and attended by many government dignitaries. "Survivor guilt" was not a concept at that time, and people could not understand why he had taken his own life, or imagine how he would have felt if he had been forced to resume life in a community where he would see the parents of young men who had died under his leadership. How could he forget those country roads where he had led his marching battalion of young boys, piping and beating their drums, expecting to return in glory? Many of them were now dead in unmarked graves in Europe, while he had survived.[26]

Maud, with a mind that ran to literary tropes, became consumed by the image of the "Piper," an ambiguous figure who at first seemed to be a Scottish bagpiper leading men and boys nobly into battle, but who morphed into a trickster figure: the Pied Piper of Hamelin, leading children to their death. Her imagination was tortured by this shape-shifting character, who had had a very real incarnation in their own community of Scott Township, a bagpiper marching right through the centre of Leaskdale.

In these early post-war months, Maud was finding it increasingly difficult to maintain a positive outlook. In her journals, she expressed growing frustration with a world that did not reward noble thoughts and good deeds. She did not fully understand this changed atmosphere. She accepted religion's loss of authority, but she was unwilling to relinquish her own belief that justice and goodness should prevail.

Back on June 17, 1916, when the war was well underway, she had voiced in her journal what so many in her generation felt, a feeling that intensified for her as time passed: "Our old world is passed away forever—and I fear that those of us who have lived half our span therein will never feel wholly at home in the new."

For one thing, the war had reshaped the relationship between men and women. Before the war, and especially in Maud's own younger days, newspapers and magazines had been full of articles and advertisements depicting women as the "weaker sex." During the war, women had taken over much of men's work—everything from running farms to working in munitions factories—and had proved themselves highly capable. Moreover, the war had shrunk the world: people would never again feel safe from the turmoil taking place on distant shores. The technology developed for war would itself transform communication and transportation, speeding up the pace of civilian life, demanding another huge adjustment for the population. Maud, already catapulted from rural Prince Edward Island to urbanizing Ontario, felt the change with particular intensity.

The war's effect on technology was seen locally. In August 1917, the first flying machine ever seen in those parts had been spotted over Uxbridge. In November 1917, a small aircraft came down unexpectedly in a local field. The whole community converged on the plane and pilot to inspect the strange contraption before it took off again for Camp Borden in Ontario. The local paper gave it a long write-up, concluding:

> The Great War has revolutionized the manufacture of air craft. . . .
> It is predicted that when the war is over they will come into general

use for the conveyance of passengers and mail matter . . . but we doubt that a very large percentage of our population will trust their lives to any machine that flies through the air. (Uxbridge *Journal*, July 26, 1917)

The development of automobiles had also been facilitated by the war. In 1918, the Macdonalds bought a car with Maud's income, a five-seater Chevrolet. Many of the parishioners now had automobiles too. Of course, in the days before snowplows, a car could still not be taken out in winter as it could not get through the drifts; nor could it be used in the spring when the dirt roads were "breaking up," because it would get mired in the mud. So while travel in winter and early spring was still by traditional means (horse and cutter), there was a general recognition that the world had entered a new mechanized age.

But most of all, the war had undercut the very structures of human belief. The old view of the world, ruled by an omnipotent God who took an active and benevolent interest in all human affairs, was for many nearly impossible to maintain. Decimating a generation of young men hardly seemed benevolent. People might pray just as much, but many were no doubt wondering if God was listening—or if He even existed. If not, then ministers were playing a game of charades, and the Church was nothing but a social institution. Maud herself had already come to this view of the Church. Her pagan china dogs, Gog and Magog, must have smirked in the dark, dead hours of night.

When Ewan Macdonald chose the ministry for a profession, he entered one of nineteenth-century society's most important and prestigious professions. In the twentieth century, he felt a loss in status, in light of the diminished power of and respect for his profession. Ministers in both large and small communities felt the impact of this changing outlook. The fiery rhetoric of war had turned to ashes in their mouth. Some of the contemplative personalities like Ewan, who had preached for sacrificial heroism while standing safely in his pulpit, were vulnerable to as much "survivor guilt" as the soldiers who returned safely.

Maud would later refer to the "spring of 1914" as the "last spring of the old world" (March 18, 1922). After that date, she said, *the world changed.* Her own intense sense of personal loss and tragedy were to intensify after the war, and her world view would darken.

The 1919 Influenza Pandemic

On September 1, 1919, Maud wrote in her journal that "1919 has been a *hell-ish* year." For most people, the mere fact that the war was over made it a good year. For Maud, it brought more grief. In 1919, death and mental disturbance deprived her of the two people closest to her. Neither tragedy was directly caused by the war, but both were part of what she described poetically as the poisonous red tide that flowed in its wake.

The "hell" of 1919 had actually started in October 1918 for Maud when she contracted the "Spanish flu" that killed seven thousand in Ontario alone. For two months after, she suffered the languor and depression that followed this illness. This particular flu was unusual in that it often killed the young and healthy, not just the old and sick. Maud reported that so many people died in a short time in Ontario that corpses had to be buried in mass graves because there were not enough coffins.

The Campbell family in Park Corner, Prince Edward Island, also came down with this influenza. George Campbell and his young son died, leaving his mother (Maud's Aunt Annie) and his young and pregnant wife, Ella, to raise six children all under the age of eleven.

In November 1918, before she was herself fully recovered, Maud left Ewan and the boys in Lily's care and went to Prince Edward Island to help Frede, who was caring for the entire Campbell family. "Frede and I can always laugh, praise be!" Maud once wrote. "I can't conceive of Frede and I foregathering, even at seventy, and not being able to laugh—not being able to perceive that sly, lurking humour that is forever peeping round the corner of things" (July 22, 1918). Now, even in a time of enormous distress, after disinfecting the Campbell house, when all were in bed, Maud and Frede shut themselves up to "talk and laugh at our pleasure" (November 9, 1918). Maud was still at Park Corner when the November 11 Armistice was signed. She describes walking down the lane with Frede in the darkness, and across the Park Corner pond bridge "on a grim, inky November night." They had skipped over that bridge in childhood, but the new world they were in was changing and darkening.

When the flu killed George Campbell, his widow and mother lost their breadwinner—a devastating situation. But at least Frede had a good job at Macdonald College in Montreal and could be expected to help them.

On January 12, 1919, following a dreary Christmas, Maud, still feeling weak and exhausted, went to Boston to appear in court against her publisher,

L. C. Page. Relations with Page, who had been such a gracious host in 1911, had turned decidedly sour. Maud was now suing him for the royalties he was withholding out of spite after she moved to a Canadian publisher. He seemed , to revel in needling her in every way he could. On Christmas Day 1918, an expensive history book from his firm came to her with a personal note in his own handwriting that read: "Merry Christmas and Happy New Year. L.C.P." The book was named *Sunset Canada*.[27] "Quite free and easy," she snapped about the unwanted gift. "Especially for the man I'm suing in the Massachusetts Court of Equity for cheating and defrauding me!"

When she arrived in Boston that January, she took an undisguised pleasure in seeing that L. C. Page had aged considerably in the eight years since she had seen him. His appearance showed evidence of the dissipated life she had heard that he had been leading—an observation that suited her sense of justice. She gave her testimony, but the trial continued. On the way home, she looked forward to stopping by Montreal, where Frede was teaching at Sainte-Anne-de-Bellevue and supervising the Women's Institutes in Quebec. She was considered a rising star in her profession. But just as Maud was finishing her business in Boston, she got a wire that Frede had contracted the flu and was seriously ill. The war was over, but this virulent flu was still sweeping the western world, and would eventually kill more people than the war itself had killed. Ominously, this was Frede's *third* life-threatening illness.

When Maud arrived at the Macdonald College infirmary, Frede's condition was desperate: she already had the deadly pneumonia that so often followed this strain of flu. Maud slept in the infirmary, comforting and nursing Frede along with the nursing staff. Frede deteriorated over the next few days. She became too sick to talk, and then to laugh.

Maud and Frede had always been held together by the bond of laughter. Humour allowed them to share problems, re-energize themselves, and pull themselves out of dark moods. Even the *memory* of jokes shared with Frede helped to steady Maud's nerves. Now at her bedside in Montreal, Maud tried to cheer her with a tale of little Stuart's struggle with a pancake. It had been "crisped" at the edge in frying. After trying to cut it with a spoon, he'd asked in a plaintive tone: "Mother, how do you cut *pancake bones?*" That was the last time Maud heard Frede laugh. On January 25, 1919, Maud waited beside her bed as Frede's life ebbed away.

It would be months later that she described Frede's death. "She 'went out as the dawn came in'—like old *Captain Jim* in my *House of Dreams*, just as the eastern sky was crimson with sunrise." When Maud was able to write again in her journals, she anguished over the prospect of a life without Frede.

> How *can* I go on living when half my life has been wrenched away, leaving me torn and bleeding in heart and soul and mind. I had *one* friend—one only—in whom I could absolutely trust . . . and she has been taken from me. (February 7, 1919)

Maud's pain was so intense that she did not actually write up Frede's death in her journals until the following September, entering it as a retrospective entry. She had been so overwrought with emotion at the actual time of the death that she was unable to cry or grieve. To her utter mortification, she instead broke out in uncontrollable and hysterical laughter. A friend of Frede's, Miss Anita Hill, and the nurse held her tightly and comforted her. For two days Maud paced in nervous agitation in the living room of Frede's residence. Tears finally came, but brought no relief.

Frede's sister-in-law, Margaret MacFarlane, came to help pack her possessions for dispersal. They found in Frede's drawer a letter that she had written at the beginning of the flu epidemic directing how to divide her affairs in the event of her death—the wedding gifts from her husband's friends were to go to his people, everything else to hers. Maud took back the silver tea service she had given Frede at her wedding for Chester's use when he became an adult. Frede had adored little Chester. Maud also took several other items: a bronze statuette called "The Good Fairy" that had special meaning (she remembered Frede's joy when it was the first wedding present); a pendant; and earrings of peridot and pearl, which an old beau had given Frede. She thought they might eventually go to Stuart's future bride, or to one of the Park Corner nieces.

Long before her death, Frede had told Maud that she had a fear of "being buried alive" and a "horror of the slow process of decay in the grave" (January 19, 1919). She had insisted that if she died first, Maud would see that she was cremated. Maud knew that many people, and perhaps even Frede's own mother, would be upset over cremation, but she followed Frede's wishes. She put red roses on the casket—Frede's favourite flowers—for the brief funeral service in the reception area of the "Girls' Building." There was another brief ceremony in the crematorium at the top of the mountain in Montreal. Maud wrote:

To see those doors close between us was far harder than hearing
the clods fall on the coffin in the grave. It symbolized so fearfully
the truth that the doors had closed between us for all time. I was
here—Frede was there—between us the black blank unopening
door of death. (September 1, 1919)

Emotionally depleted, Maud returned to her life in Ontario. The entire
community of Leaskdale mourned Frede's death. Many years later, people still
talked of Frede's joyous laughter, the genuine, hearty kind that comes from
within a person at ease with herself and her life. She made an impression on
all who met her.

For weeks after returning home from Montreal, Maud suffered from disturbing dreams and headaches. Well-meaning neighbours sometimes said the
wrong things to her. Ewan was unable to comfort her, perhaps because his
own demons were depriving him of the ability to empathize. For the rest of
her life, Maud would mourn Frede. Every January on the anniversary of her
death, memories flooded back. Periodically she would read all Frede's old letters and feel disbelief that such a vivid personality could be dead. Often when
she heard or saw something humorous, she felt a momentary stab of pain
because she could not share it with Frede. For a private woman like Maud,
one who had been conditioned all her life not to reveal inner worries, the loss
of her one trusted best friend was catastrophic.

She and Frede had developed very strong bonds, partly from kinship, and
partly from shared experience. They both felt "different" from the rest of their
family, that they were the "cats that walked alone." Each had been a sensitive
child who felt misunderstood. At school, each had been clever, leading to a
feeling of exclusion from the circle of other schoolgirls. Frede had been a
plain, almost ugly child, but, like Maud, she had been radiant with personality and *joie de vivre*. Each had suffered unrequited love affairs, despairing together that they might never find a mate. Both were ambitious women who
wanted to take full university degrees, but neither had a family who could or
would pay for them, despite their exceptional intellectual gifts. (Maud had
paid for Frede's training at Macdonald College in Montreal.) Their volatile
temperaments were similar, and Frede understood Maud's rising and falling
moods. They shared everything—and when they did, their fears, insecurities,
and anxieties turned into laughter. They were both widely admired for their
competence and uniquely refreshing personalities, but each had a deep inner,

reflective life. Maud was twenty-eight in 1902, and Frede nineteen, when their friendship began to develop, and they had seventeen years of "beautiful friendship" before Frede's death. Maud wrote:

> Well, I must make an end now and face life without her. I am forty-four. I shall make no new friends—even if there were other Fredes in the world. I have lived one life in those seemingly far-off years before the war. Now there is another to be lived, in a totally new world where I think I shall never feel quite at home. I shall always feel as if I belonged "back there"—back there with Frede and laughter and years of peace. (February 7, 1919)

Ewan's illness

Frede's death seemed to have a domino effect: next, Ewan began to suffer from a deeper bout of serious depression. Ewan had always basked in Frede's warm approval, and her death deprived him of someone who boosted his confidence.

When he was well, Ewan was a smart, cheerful, practical man, with dimples and sparkling dark eyes. His sense of humour was a very different kind from Maud's dry, wry, razor-sharp wit—he teased, bantered, and enjoyed playing practical jokes. When trying to tell a clever anecdote, he usually got the timing or punchline wrong. But his general affability made him lovable. Most of all, he was a kind man—the "kindest man who ever lived," his son Stuart Macdonald said to me repeatedly. After years of dodging her Grandfather Macneill's sarcastic digs, Maud valued kindness.

In many ways, Maud and Ewan complemented each other. Maud was a driven "hard worker" in every respect, while Ewan "took things easy." She was "high-strung," living daily on her nerves; he was phlegmatic. This might have been a good combination, with Ewan able to calm Maud when she was overwrought, and her boosting him when he was too full of lassitude. There were complications, however: Ewan was subject to depression and Maud to wide mood swings. And there was little space in Ewan's stern Scottish-Presbyterian culture for open discussion of his private feelings. Ewan had been raised in a world where men discussed actions and beliefs, but not their feelings. These he hid under his reserved exterior, brooding darkly. After the war, a major depressive episode washed over Ewan.

Ministers had to cope with especially hard adjustments after the war ended. Society seemed adrift, and religion no longer acted as a compass. To reorient people to religion, church leaders started a sweeping ecumenical crusade called "The Forward Movement," the aim of which was to bring congregations back to church, to allow faith to "heal the wounds of humanity." The most dynamic ministers in various denominations were engaged to travel across the country, giving weeks of inspirational speeches to counter the general drift of society towards secularism.

Ewan's first major breakdown started the week that the first of these high-powered ministers descended on his parish to speak to his two congregations: the week between May 25 and May 31, 1919. Each night there was to be a different preacher in the area. Ewan was to meet them at the Uxbridge station, ferry them about, introduce them, and listen as they gave energizing speeches to parishioners. Then he and Maud were to host and entertain them at home before they set off again to speak elsewhere.

As soon as the series started, Ewan's first symptoms manifested themselves in a severe headache and insomnia. His behaviour became increasingly erratic. By mid-week he was morose and withdrawn, still complaining of his headache. He only went through the motions of hosting his guests. Once, he rose before dawn to walk the roads in agitation. Later, he wrapped a bandana around his head and lay in the hammock, moaning. After the men left, his symptoms varied from agitation to a catatonic, glassy-eyed state. This was a new and alarming development.

At the end of that week, Maud insisted that Ewan see the doctor in Uxbridge. Dr. Shier diagnosed his problem as a "nervous breakdown" and prescribed rest, believing that Ewan was overtired from his busy schedule. Ewan was always glad to rest. He sought medical palliatives, such as were available then, to help him relax. Maud gives a spotty anecdotal account in her journals of the drugs that Ewan was taking then and later. However, throughout the rest of the year, Ewan was given various medications: barbiturates like Veronal, and bromides, all central nervous system depressants that doctors of the era prescribed as general sedatives.

Ewan's trouble came from a deeper source than Dr. Shier recognized. Although he seemed calm enough on the surface, Ewan was a deeply sensitive man. In addition to the guilt he may have felt over persuading young men to join the war, he felt greater pressures resulting from the Church's waning influence. Another more threatening movement was afoot—this one supported by the government as well as the Church—to merge a number of the Protestant Churches and consolidate congregations into a "United Church." Many Presbyterians saw it as the destruction of their Church by the Government of Canada, something that seemed unbelievable.

This "Church Union" was going to put many ministers out of a job. Ewan had reason to fear for his own future. He knew he was not as dynamic as the Forward Movement preachers, or as many other ministers he knew. Depressed as he was, he felt inadequate to the challenges ahead. His feelings of inadequacy deepened his depression. It was a downward spiral.

After his visit to Dr. Shier, Maud says that she pried out of Ewan what was really upsetting him. It was, he said, the conviction that he was "*eternally lost*—that there was no hope for him in the next life. This dread haunted him night and day and he could not banish it" (September 1, 1919). Maud interpreted this as a sign of "religious melancholy," the term used at that time to indicate a depressive mood disorder that afflicted religious people who would naturally interpret their affliction within their religion's conceptual framework.

A long medical history was associated with the specific symptoms of the mental disorder that Ewan now exhibited. "Religious Melancholia" dated back to the Middle Ages, possibly earlier. Nineteenth-century texts about mental illness discuss it. Religious melancholics believed that they were doomed to go to eternal Hell after they died, regardless of their behaviour during life.

The Presbyterian doctrine of Predestination—which taught that God had "predetermined" who would go to Hell before they were even born—was an outmoded doctrine in Ewan's time, but old beliefs die slowly. Predestination was firmly lodged in Ewan's mind: as a boy, he had heard it preached by old-fashioned rural preachers, and preached again in Charlottetown by an evangelist around the time he was leaving Prince Edward Island for Ontario. It provided him with the explanatory concept to understand precisely why he felt so miserable and depressed.

He linked this to another theological concept: Ewan felt that because he had doubted that he was one of the "Elect" (chosen for Heaven), he had therefore committed the "unpardonable sin" (of doubting God and His power). This idea of the "unpardonable sin" was, like Predestination, an older religious tenet but a powerful one in people's minds.[28] Ewan was caught up in circular reasoning within a complicated theology. Maud railed against the "damnable theology" that had taught him these concepts, but she also

Ewan and Maud on their honeymoon in Scotland, in the summer of 1911.

The Leaskdale, Ontario, manse, circa 1911 (Maud's first home after her marriage).

Leaskdale Presbyterian Church (Ewan's primary charge).

Zephyr Presbyterian Church (Ewan's other charge).

Maud and Stella Campbell at Niagara Falls.

"Gog and Magog," Maud's china dogs, in Leaskdale.

Dining room in the Leaskdale manse, with Maud, cousin Frede Campbell, and Ewan, holding Chester.

Marjory MacMurchy, a Toronto writer and journalist.

Marshall Pickering, who sued
Ewan after a 1921 car accident.

Maud and her first son, Chester Cameron Macdonald, circa 1914.

Justice William Renwick Riddell
(1852–1945), who presided over the
Pickering-Macdonald decision.

The Reverend Edwin Smith.

Ewan in the Leaskdale garden circa 1914.

Picture from Maud's PEI scrapbook, showing the young Edwin Smith.

Ewan and Edwin Smith.

The Rev. and Mrs. John A. Mustard and son Gordon.

believed—probably correctly—that these ideas had taken hold of him so readily because his mind was already disturbed.

Maud says that she dragged more details out of Ewan—confirmation that
this mental disorder had first appeared when he'd reached puberty (at age
twelve). It had surfaced again at Prince of Wales College when he was eighteen, and again at Dalhousie College. He had been well until his trip to
Glasgow in his mid-thirties, in 1906–07. In Glasgow, however, he had been
overwhelmed by fears and a sense of inadequacy.

Each breakdown in Ewan's life had taken place at a pressure point in his
life, and had grown from the belief that he somehow did not measure up. This
"proved" to him that he was an outcast from God: again, that he had committed the "unpardonable sin" of insufficient faith that God had given him the
strength and courage he needed for his profession.

After the war, Ewan's doubt that religion was the cure to all human woes
again proved he was guilty of the "unpardonable sin" and doomed to Hell,
where he would burn forever. His saw his fate as having to pretend to his
parishioners that he was God's representative and faithful servant when he in-
wardly believed he was cursed.

In his breakdown of 1919, Ewan developed all the secondary symptoms of
severe depression: social withdrawal, loss of cognitive functions, insomnia, hes-
itant speech, low energy, constipation, irritability, loss of interest in family and
life in general, and obsession with ideas about worthlessness, guilt, and self-
destruction. Maud now suspected that the matter was a recurring problem,
and that it was serious mental illness. She wrote in her journal: "I was horror-
stricken. I had married, all unknowingly, a man who was subject to recurrent
constitutional melancholia, and I had brought children into the world who
might inherit the taint. It was a hideous thought . . ."

Mental illness had always been a subject of community gossip on the
Island, intensified by the local newspapers of her childhood, which detailed
frightening stories of people either "going melancholy" or turning "violently
insane." Those in the first category were likely to destroy themselves, while
those in the second were a danger to others. William C. Macneill, a prosperous farmer and father of one of Maud's many cousins (Amanda), went
"melancholy" and drowned himself.

Shortly after 1900, the Island newspapers began expanding their coverage of mental illness, as a result of the new communications technology, the
telegraph, which was able to relay news from all over the North American

continent. People read, for instance, of cases like that of John E. Sankey, son of the famous revivalist Ira D. Sankey, who was declared insane in New York because he thought he had created the world (covered in April 16, 1908). There was extensive ongoing coverage after 1907 when the New York millionaire Harry Thaw murdered the famous New York architect Stanford White, after White seduced Thaw's wife, Evelyn Nesbit Thaw, a well-known chorus girl and actress (later immortalized in the movie *The Girl in the Red-Velvet Swing*). Thaw's plea was not guilty by reason of "insanity"—a new category of plea in law. For three years the Prince Edward Island newspapers covered his trial and its appeals, and people were riveted to this story. There was wide public disapproval of the fact that Harry Thaw was ultimately acquitted. (Maud pasted a picture of Evelyn Nesbit into her journals, and claimed that she had pinned it up as the visual model for her "Anne of Green Gables.") Later in that year, a man in Prince Edward Island escaped a murder conviction by pleading insanity and was sent to Falconwood, the province's insane asylum. After this legal shocker, the province (and Montgomery herself) had an even greater fear of mental illness. Patent medicine firms fanned the flames by advertising in every issue of the paper that they had treatments to "Bring Health to Despondent People."

Maud wrote in her journals of eccentrics like "Mad Mr. MacKinley" and "Peg Bowen" who roamed around the countryside. They were harmless "crazy people," present in some form in every community. It is no surprise, then, that Maud's novels make many references to mentally ill people: recall "Mad Mr. Morrison" who chases "Emily of New Moon" inside a church. This scene was written in the 1920s, following Ewan's mental breakdown, and is highly symbolic and eroticized. Emily (a heroine based on Maud herself) is accidentally locked together in the darkening church with Mr. Morrison, a hoary old man, who has in his insanity gone seeking his long-deceased young wife. Maud builds up the terror and revulsion that the fictional Emily feels as she flees through the maze of pews in the darkened church, taking flight from the clutches of this crazed but agile madman. Maud registers her revulsion to this old man's attempt to grasp Emily's young body. Maud comes perilously close to suggesting the subject of sexual violation by a man who is insane.

Generally, eccentrics and people with mental illness were kept in their communities and tolerated, like "Mad Mr. MacKinley" in Maud's childhood. Sometimes, if they became too much of a problem or danger, they were sent off to Falconwood. In 1892, when Maud was eighteen, the provincial insane asylum had 137 inmates, committed under the grouping of either "Moral" or "Physical" categories of insanity. "Moral" causes or symptoms included domestic trouble, adverse circumstances, religious excitement, or love affairs. "Physical" causes or symptoms were intemperance (either with alcohol or sex), sexual self-abuse, sunstroke, uterine or ovarian disorders, hereditary or other diseases, and congenital problems like epilepsy. By 1908, with so many astonishing categories to draw from, Falconwood had 223 inmates, ranging from people who had tried to kill themselves (or others) to those who indulged in public masturbation and needed to be put out of sight.

Because Maud had been raised in a print culture of "yellow journalism" that sensationalized and pathologized mental illness, Ewan's breakdown was particularly distressing to her. Giving front-page coverage to the Harry Thaw trial in Prince Edward Island, the *Examiner* of February 19, 1907, editorialized: "The vivity with which the American and Canadian People scan the reports of the Thaw trial—loaded with pruriency as they are—is not creditable to the moral tone of the North American continent . . ." The paper then proceeded to detail all the salacious matter that it so haughtily condemned people for reading, and other local newspapers for reporting.

In the Island society—where most people were born, lived, and died in one place, and everyone knew the family history of everyone else—mental illness simply could *not* be concealed, and people observed that it did tend to run in certain families. They also noted that while it might be a fleeting occurrence, aroused by passion or despair, and shed with equal swiftness, often the illness recurred. Maud always commented with disapproval when her relatives or friends married into a family that might potentially pass on the "taint" of mental illness.

She began to watch her boys for signs of their father's instability. Chester and Stuart, who had been her great joy, now became an ongoing source of anxiety. Maud had always puzzled over Ewan's lack of strong feeling for anything: people, places, things, and especially beauty. His flat response to the physical world now appeared to suggest something missing in his makeup. She noticed how much Chester favoured his father: she described him as "reserved" and "harder to understand than Stuart." Stuart, however, was frank and open: "Stuart gives the impression of beauty and charm. Physically he is a very lovely child, so clear and rosy his skin, so brilliant his large blue eyes" (February 24, 1919). But she had worries about Stuart, too. "Alas, I fear he has inherited from me something besides my love of beauty—my passionate intensity of feeling and my tendency to concentrate it all on a few objects or persons unspeakably dear to me" (February 24, 1919). The boys were indeed very dissimilar. This was apparent from their earliest childhood.

Maud often lived at the edge of stability herself, but at no point did she lose her hold on reality. In her Prince Edward Island years, she suffered serious depressive states, often quite debilitating. However, she recognized them as abnormal. When she shut herself in a room to pace the floor, or suffered "white nights" of sleeplessness and anxiety, she had perspective on herself. She knew her depressions always coincided with too much solitude and externally depressing circumstances. She also knew what helped her recover: vigorous exercise, good company, and laughter.

Ewan, however, had no perspective on what was happening to him and little memory of his state of mind afterwards. When he had delusions, he believed them. Sometimes he heard voices telling him he would go to Hell and that he should destroy himself. Ewan's symptoms varied in intensity but usually started with severe headaches accompanied by an expression of profound gloom. He began "pawing at his head" or tying a handkerchief around it. He became very lethargic, taking pleasure in nothing. He would look vacantly into space in absolute silence, or chant doleful hymns, unaware of those around him. If spoken to, he became hostile, refusing to do "his duties as the man of the house" (stoking the fire, carrying out ashes, caring for the horse, and cleaning the stable). His memory became badly impaired, a frequent symptom of depression, and his speech became puerile. Usually, depressed people lose their appetite for food and sex, but Maud states ambiguously that Ewan did not lose his interest in eating, avoiding a comment on his interest in sex. His malady, Maud recorded, cut him off from the "intimacies" of normal life and left him imprisoned by his delusions.

Maud knew that one telltale sign of mental imbalance was self-obsession. Maud characterized her cousin Stella Campbell, on March 12, 1921, as a borderline mental case: "Like all mentally unbalanced people she is completely centred on self." Maud also remembered with revulsion her cousin Edwin Simpson. He, too, had been totally self-absorbed, despite his intellectual brilliance. When ill, Ewan was completely indifferent to Maud and to his children.

Even Ewan's appearance changed when he was ill. His facial features developed a "repulsive expression." His eyes became "shiny," "wild," and "haunted." Maud says she couldn't "bear to look at him" (January 6, 1923) when he had a "horrible imbecile expression on his face" (March 16, 1924).

Sometimes his face turned livid, and he raved obsessively over the idea that he was dying without anyone caring. In other phases of his illness, he would sleep continuously, refusing to get up for several days except to eat. When insomnia overtook him, he fled the house in the early hours, pacing up and down the roads. This alarmed Maud even more: farm folk were early risers and likely to see him, and suspect something was amiss with their minister. When he had visions or heard voices, he muttered out loud to himself, a sure giveaway of his problems. Maud wrote in her diary that aspects of his illness seemed "so unnatural that it fills me with such horror and repulsion that . . . it turns me against Ewan for the time, as if he were possessed by or transformed into a demoniacal creature of evil—something I must get away from as I would rush from a snake. It is terrible—but it is the truth" (August 31, 1919).

Maud worked hard to keep his mental condition secret, lest her children become social pariahs. Publicly, she attributed his illness to headaches and indigestion. In an era when much of what went on inside the body was largely a mystery, people accepted her explanations. At his worst, she kept him out of sight. When he was only slightly affected, he could keep up a minimal conversation, and they carried out some pastoral visits together, with her carrying the visit through cheerful banter. His malady had one very strange aspect, which was quite atypical of a clinically depressed person: his problems seemed to come and go, quickly and unpredictably. In the space of a half hour, he could change from normal to unbalanced and vice versa. This suggests a more complicated medical issue than mere depression.

Ewan's first attack, in May 1919, lasted throughout the entire summer. He took medications as prescribed. In desperation, Maud sent him to Boston in June, to the home of his half-sister and her husband, Flora and Amos Eagles. Maud joined him as soon as she could. Boston then had the most advanced North American treatment centre for mental illness, and Maud arranged for Ewan to consult a famous specialist, Dr. Nathan Garrick. Garrick puzzled over the diagnosis: was it, he wondered, "simple melancholia" (a reactive depressive episode largely precipitated by external circumstances), or was it "manic-depressive-insanity" (a serious mental illness that was inherent and would recur again and again)?

There was at that time no effective treatment for either, and Dr. Garrick intensified Maud's concerns by telling her never to let Ewan out of her sight, lest he attempt suicide—something that he had already spoken of on occasion.

Dr. Garrick gave Maud sleeping pills (chloral) for Ewan and told her to make him drink lots of water as his kidneys were not functioning properly. (Slowed body functions often accompany depression.) After a two-month absence from Leaskdale, with their children under the care of the young maid, Ewan inexplicably and spontaneously got better and they returned home. Maud told everyone that Ewan had had "kidney poisoning." People believed this rather vague diagnosis because she had consulted the best doctors in Boston.

From 1919 onward, Ewan was a new anxiety in Maud's dark closet of worries. He would recover, and then relapse. He would be treated with sedatives. His changes were unpredictable and dramatic. During some attacks Ewan could function, even if he was dull and miserable. But many other times, he was so mentally disoriented that it was necessary for substitute ministers to fill in. She never knew what a day or week or month would bring.

The Leaskdale congregation remained patient and solicitous throughout Ewan's recurring illnesses and periods of absence from the pulpit. They had always liked him as a minister, and did not see him in his worst states, so they assumed he had a physical problem. Maud worked so hard for them, and for a long time she placated those who might otherwise have complained. However, the sixty-six parishioners in Zephyr, who paid Ewan $360 a year in 1919, eventually began grumbling that their minister was not worth his salary.[29]

After the Macdonalds returned from Boston in 1919, Maud hauled out her writing and began working up a plot for a new book, *Rilla of Ingleside*. Her emotional reserve was depleted, and it would take her nearly nine months just to figure out a plot. "I am the mouse in the claws of the cat," she wrote in August 1919, after hosting an editor of *Maclean's* magazine who had come to interview her for a story. "I talked brightly and amusingly—and watched Ewan out of the corner of my eye. . . . That is my existence now."[30]

Marriages often fall apart when there is serious depression in one partner. Maud says in her diary that she thinks "incurable insanity" is justification for divorce, but that divorces are not part of her family tradition (October 18, 1923). Maud and Ewan had grown up in a culture and time where divorce was considered a scandal. In the 1890s, Queen Victoria's vigorous condemnation of divorce was reported in the Prince Edward Island newspapers. Other newspaper articles lamented that divorce was becoming a scourge in the United States. On March 6, 1901, *The Daily Patriot* had crowed that Prince Edward Island had "not [had] a single decree of divorce granted . . . in . . . 33 years," adding proudly that it "is extremely doubtful if any other province or state in the English-speaking world can furnish such a record as this." The paper noted that in this same period there were 268 divorces in the rest of the Dominion of Canada, with its population of 6 million people. In 1911, the year of Maud's marriage, Prince Edward Island still held its head high as a province unsullied by divorce, crediting the low divorce rate to good education and a morally upright population.[31] They did not comment on the fact that in this same period various murders, poisonings, and spousal abuse cases on the Island, resulted in one of the marriage partners being tossed into Falconwood or jail.

On May 16, 1918, the Uxbridge *Journal* noted that the Canadian Parliament was debating whether the Senate or the courts should grant divorces. Although attitudes were changing, Maud could not have coped with either the emotional upheaval or the scandal of a divorce, even if she had wanted one—which, apparently, she did not.

As Maud came to contemplate the troubled life stretching endlessly in front of her, she could see that she had shown enormous strength thus far. She had fashioned herself into a very respectable woman by marrying, and in particular by marrying a minister. She had, in her maturity, a will of steel, a genuine affection for the man she had married, and a determination to live her life with dignity. She had become famous, and was widely admired and revered, and she enjoyed her fame and reputation. To abandon a sick husband would have been unthinkable to her, no matter how she might have wished to be freed of his problems. She knew her marriage had its tragic dimensions. So, it appears, did Ewan. He suffered under the additional pressure of fearing that he was a leaden weight in the soaring heart of his exceptionally gifted wife.

CHAPTER 10

More troubles with L. C. Page

Though the Great War had ended with the signing of the Armistice on November 11, 1918, Maud was engaged in an epic battle of her own.

In 1917, she had gathered the courage to bring her first lawsuit against the L. C. Page Company of Boston. She was now positive that Page had been cheating her. For nearly a decade, she would fight him through five separate suits and countersuits, until the final decision in 1928.

"If Page is not honourable I am no match for him," Maud had written nervously in her journal on July 26, 1915. She had been hearing troubling tales about his business practices ever since 1911, the year after her visit to his home in Boston. By April 12, 1916, Maud had confided in her journal, "I am afraid of Page."

She had very good reason to fear this Boston Brahmin. She had already seen that he was a cunning manipulator. She would learn that Page was also a man of astonishing arrogance, able to crush others through mere intimidation. He was a bully with very deep pockets, not to mention a love for litigation. Maud's instincts warned her that he was also vindictive. Had she known beforehand just how spiteful he could be, her courage to take him on might have failed.

There were many tales about Page from those who had done business with him. Gossip travelled fast and far: he was both a colourful personality and a high-profile publisher. Maud had asked her cousin Bertie McIntyre in Vancouver to check out his reputation with some booksellers in 1916, and she later reported that the tales that came back were so "ghastly" that she could not confide specific details even to her journals. Another of Page's best-selling authors confided Page had cheated her, and she had left him, unfortunately leaving her best copyrights behind. Marshall Saunders had more to say. Clippings and gossip about Page's private life were circulated throughout Canada and the United States among the author-publisher-bookseller community, with details supplied by the many salesmen and office staff who had worked for him and left, often in disgust or following unfair treatment. Mr. McClelland, who had angled to become Maud's Canadian publisher, eagerly passed along every tidbit to Maud.[32]

Lewis Page was the first-born son in one of Boston's most privileged families. His father, Charles A. Page, chief war correspondent for the New York *Tribune* under Horace Greeley, later became U.S. Consul-General in Switzerland. Lewis's mother, Grace Darling Coues, was descended from Elliott Coues, the famous ornithologist who had founded the American Ornithological Society. Lewis Coues Page was born in Switzerland in 1869. His father died, leaving his widow and several children: Lewis, Charles F., Charlotte, and George.

In 1884, Grace married again, this time to widower Dana Estes, co-owner of a prominent publishing firm in Boston. Estes had been instrumental in founding the International Copyright Association in 1887, and counted Lord Tennyson among his acquaintances. With Estes as a stepfather, Lewis Page learned at an early age about high society, books, business, and power.

Lewis Page attended private schools and graduated from Harvard in 1891, where he was a track letterman. Tall, athletic, handsome, and suave, he was considered one of Boston's most eligible bachelors. He would marry three times. His first wife died. He then married the beautiful and charming Kate ("Kitty") Stearns, daughter of James P. Stearns, a prominent fixture in Boston financial circles. After several years of marriage, Kitty hired a private detective to shadow her philandering husband. She divorced him in 1904 and won a rich settlement. Kitty was a much respected and admired Boston society woman, and public sympathy went to her. The other party in the divorce was one of Page's employees, Mildred Parker—the wife Maud met in 1911. Lewis married Mildred in May 1904, soon after his divorce, and built the elegant "Page Court" home. (When Maud stayed at "Page Court" in Boston, she did not know Page's marital history. She was given to understand that Mildred Page was his second wife, not his third.)

In 1897, after several years working at his stepfather's publishing firm, Page acquired the subsidiary firm of Joseph P. Knight and renamed it "The L. C.

Page Company." He set himself up as president, and installed his brilliant but less dashing brother George as treasurer and head of the manufacturing department. He took over established best-sellers like *The Little Colonel* (1895) by Annie Fellows Johnston, which became a series. Then he hit the jackpot with *Anne of Green Gables* in 1908. It was reprinted twenty times by April 1910, and thirty-eight times by 1914 (this May 1914 popular edition was advertised as "limited to 150,000 copies"). Another bestseller in 1913 was Eleanor H. Porter's *Pollyanna*. He had started his firm with inherited money but soon was doing very well on his own.[33]

In 1910, when Maud first met him, his reputation was well established as owner of one of the more prestigious publishing firms in the United States. *Anne of Green Gables* had continued an extraordinary success ever since its 1908 publication; by 1911, Page was flush with money from it. Seeking to improve his social stature after bad publicity from his divorce, he partnered with another man to buy a baseball team, the Boston Braves, paying some $100,000. Soon the Boston papers were carrying accounts of his lawsuit to wrest full control of the Braves from his partner. Other skirmishes reflected on his character. He frequented the Boston Club for men, but was eventually expelled for being "insufficiently a gentleman," after he seduced a young female employee in a brazen manner that the other men could not ignore. Undaunted, he then started a club of his own, according to his cousin and literary executor, W. Peter Coues. Even to Bostonians, he was a larger-than-life figure.

Located at 53 Beacon Street in Boston, the L. C. Page Company headquarters were in a five-storey brownstone that was exceedingly chic and palatial. In 1914, he bought out his deceased stepfather's firm, Dana Estes and Company. (His stepfather had died in 1909, and the firm had gone downhill. Page waited until its value dropped, and then bought it.)

Page cleverly singled out a very good niche market—popular fiction—at a time when literacy was skyrocketing as a result of the promotion of universal education in the United States and Canada. His books were beautifully made, and he took pride in his reputation as the "best book-maker" in the States.

Maud says in her journals that she did not know the firm when she sent *Anne of Green Gables* off to them, but she was probably disingenuous. Page had published the famous Maritime poet Bliss Carman since 1902, and Sir Charles G. D. Roberts, another famous Maritimer in 1903. In 1908, Page published Carman's *The Making of Personality*, and Ewan gave it to Maud as a gift at Christmas. Later, she claimed that she sent the manuscript for *Anne* to Page because a friend of hers from Summerside worked for Page who accepted it only because Miss Arbuckle talked it up (July 30, 1916).

Booksellers across the United States and Canada complained that Page was a hard, and often unfair, businessman. He would deliberately overship, and then refuse to take returns, and then refuse to ship anything more until all old bills were paid, regardless of whether the booksellers had sold the extra books that they had not even ordered. He would arbitrarily deny terms and vary discounts so that booksellers never knew what to expect. Booksellers loathed him, but Maud was so popular across North America that they had no choice but to deal with Page. Although Page published other best-selling books, Maud proved to be his most successful author, and Roger W. Straus projected that she made him more money over his sustained career than anyone else. When Farrar, Straus & Giroux purchased the L. C. Page Company in 1957, Straus and his chief financial officer, Robert Wohlforth, said that they purchased the firm *primarily* to get the rights to *Anne of Green Gables* and the other L. M. Montgomery books.[34]

Page was not only tough with booksellers. He was a "stern employer," said one person, and you worked hard there. Within his own firm, there were unusual practices. Almost all of his employees were women. He was notorious for hiring clever young women to work in his firm because he could pay them far less than men. There was no employment equity then, and women often made one-quarter to one-half what men did in the professions open to them.

He had other reasons for favouring women employees. "He *liked* women," his cousin Peter Coues recounted in the 1980s. William Pearce (Peter) Coues was much younger than L. C. Page, and became his executor.[35] Page's personal allure was such that many women employees vied for his attention. Tales of his seductions, occasionally rebuffed but more often successful, were the stuff of legend and titillating amazement in his day. While there undoubtedly were women who worked for him who did not attract his advances—or who managed to escape them—the firm is remembered as having the atmosphere of a harem: it was said to turn alive with excitement whenever he walked through a room. That he kept and managed multiple mistresses at the same time was a source of gossip among women and envy among men. "Women gave him comfort," as his cousin tactfully put it, "and he took advantage of this."[36]

Page also manipulated his authors. He bought copyrights outright from authors if he could. He also offered smaller royalties than the industry standard, as with Maud.[37] In contracts, Page put in his "binding clause" to hold his authors to the same exploitative terms forever (i.e., royalties on the *wholesale* rather than *retail* price. Maud got seven to nine cents per book, instead of the nineteen cents that might have been more reasonably expected).

Page's widespread reputation as a powerful and vindictive man frightened people. To Page, authors were like common workers in factories, and he rode roughshod over them. A large number of his best-selling authors were women, and women at this time were socialized to be submissive to men. Page was accustomed to getting his way by charm; he used his temper when his charm failed; and if both of these failed, there was the threat of a lawsuit.

Page had a working business relationship with his brother, George, a *summa cum laude* graduate of Harvard, but even with his own family members, Lewis could be a bully. George was the physical opposite of his brother—shorter, softer in appearance, and less imposing. Maud believed that he was a much nicer man when she met him, and her opinion was shared by others who remembered the Page brothers. George and Lewis quarrelled a great deal, according to the employees. It is the general consensus that in every difference of opinion, Lewis dominated.

Page was a sportsman who liked the trappings of wealth, the high life, and especially gambling. His gambling debts were often substantial. In 1913, when *Anne of Green Gables* was in its thirty-seventh printing, making big money for Page, he made the papers with yet another lawsuit: he brought suit against a New York gambling house to stop payment on a $1,500 cheque written at 5:00 a.m. to cover some money he had lost during the evening. He asserted in his court papers that when he sobered up the next day, he discovered he had been "cheated," being too drunk to be in possession of his faculties. He used good lawyers, and won his case.

Tales of Page's life in the fast lane spread rapidly; in 1916, his third marriage started unravelling in an ugly public fight. Mildred told the court that Page had ordered her out of their home, and when she and her baby daughter returned against his will, he closed her accounts, shut off the gas and electricity so that she had to use candles, and forced her to sell her jewellery to buy food, at a time when *his* yearly income was $35,000. (In the same year, the Canadian prime minister made $14,500, Ewan made $900, an average working Canadian man $800, and an average woman $400.) Mildred obtained a settlement for $4,400 a year in alimony, plus $50 a month for an infant named "Mildred."[38] Page's second wife (Kate Stearns) was already receiving $1,600 per year in alimony, which meant that between the two women, he was liable for $8,200 per year to his two former wives (not the $10,000-plus figure Maud heard through the grapevine).

Hearing all this gossip about Page's divorce and business practices, Maud certainly realized that Page would be a tricky adversary. Between his gambling debts, his need for alimony money, his expensive social life, his purchase of baseball teams, his founding of clubs, his generosity to mistresses, and his love of costly wines and food and attractive female servants, Lewis Page had a great need for more cash, and, as Maud noted later on, a need to "cheat his authors." According to Mr. Wohlforth, the publishing world was full of stories about Page, "who contrived a lot of stress in everybody." In the 1980s, Roger W. Straus, of Farrar, Straus, and Giroux, characterized L. C. Page as one of the most colourful characters in the publishing world over a sixty-year period.[39]

In the ensuing decade there would be *five* lawsuits and countersuits between Maud and the L. C. Page Company. These lawsuits would cost Maud a small fortune. The lawsuits cost Page even more, as well as the reputation of his firm. The terrible irony is that he was able to finance his legal cases against Maud easily out of the profits he made from selling her books and, later, from the movie rights to *Anne of Green Gables*.

If Page had thought that Maud was just a country lass from a small Island province, easily intimidated because she was a woman and somewhat shy, he certainly misjudged her. She came to the Page fight in 1917 with no small amount of residual anger. After a childhood with difficult, bullying men, Maud had a strong sense of herself as a person—she was, after all, descended from the prominent Senator Donald Montgomery and Speaker Macneill. She may have been over-sensitive and emotionally fragile, but she also possessed a toughness and determination that was equal to Page's meanness. Nothing pulled her out of a depression more quickly than a worthy opponent. And Page was certainly that.

The legal action between Maud and Page started after the contract that bound her to Page had expired, and she chose John McClelland of McClelland, Goodchild, and Stewart (founded in 1906) as her new publisher and literary agent. Mr. McClelland had taken her new book of poetry, *The Watchman*, which Page had refused. Although she had originally wanted McClelland to let Page have the American rights to her next new novel, *Anne's House of Dreams*, Page's threats to sue her and McClelland if they did not give him these rights worked against him. McClelland sold the American rights to the Frederick Stokes Company. Stokes, in turn, granted the New York firm of A. L. Burt reprint rights for this same work.

Page, enraged that Maud had had the gall to offer the poetry book he had refused to another publisher, and then to switch publishers (which was within her rights, of course), continued to threaten her and McClelland, Goodchild, and Stewart with lawsuits if they did not give him the American rights to *Anne's House of Dreams*. Page cunningly sent Maud an advance on her next set of royalties; she cashed this cheque, thinking it was for his royalty payments on her other books (December 31, 1916). Later, when she read the cleverly worded letter more carefully, she discovered that it included payment in advance for *Anne's House of Dreams*, which allowed him to argue that her cashing the cheque constituted proof that he was in his rights to assume he would get those rights. Then, in February 1917, Page, angry that the rights had gone to Stokes, wrote Maud that he had discovered an "error" in accounting from three years earlier, and thus was withholding $1,000 from the royalties due her. This was a barefaced lie—*she* knew it, and *he* knew *she* knew it, and would be furious. This was his way of being spiteful, and of giving her a threatening warning at the same time. There was no way for her to get the money except to take him to court. Both knew that it would cost her far more than $1,000 in expenses to get that $1,000 out of him. She realized that he was trying to intimidate her into returning to him, and she was not going to buckle.

L. C. Page proceeded to sell reprint rights for a cheap reprint edition of *Anne's House of Dreams* to Grosset & Dunlap. This action was astonishing, considering that the rights to publish this book had gone to Stokes. Page's arrogance in selling property that was not his is incomprehensible, but he covered himself through the "advance" he had sent, tricking her. If he did not have a legal right to something, Page apparently intended to bully and bluff. He had sufficient money and clout that other publishers, as well as booksellers, feared him.

It is an unfortunate fact, both then and today, that people's legal rights are only as good as their ability to enforce them. Page knew this very well. He had a deep purse, and Maud (like most authors) did not. He knew that Maud would have to sue him in *his* jurisdiction, adding yet another expensive burden for her. Where would she even get a lawyer? He banked on Maud expecting that if she started a lawsuit against him and *won*, it would cost her more in expenses and legal fees than she would get out of it. On the other hand, if she *lost*, she would have to pay damages, as well as her own court costs and possibly his. This could ruin her financially. Since she had moved to another publisher, Page did not care if he destroyed her, or at least worried her so much she could not write.

Maud knew, too, that the stress of the lawsuit would keep her in constant turmoil, and affect her writing and work, as well as her pleasure in her children and social life. However, if she did *not* sue, she knew she would stew and smoulder and hate her victimhood. It was a no-win situation. Page knew that, too, and he did not expect her to sue him.

Page not only threatened Maud with lawsuits, he also kept threatening Stokes, her American publisher, and McClelland, Goodchild, and Stewart, her Canadian one. While they all believed he was bluffing, they were nevertheless nervous, given his power base and reputation. They heard through the grapevine — for the Canadian legal world was very small — that he had engaged the Toronto firm of Blake, Lash, & Cassells to represent him in Canada. This frightened both Maud and McClelland.

What L. C. Page did not anticipate was Maud's incredibly strong sense of justice. Truth was a very strong component in her moral code, and when angry, she became much tougher. Page must have been surprised when he learned that in May 1917 she had engaged a lawyer in the United States through the American Authors' League and had entered suit against him in the Massachusetts Court of Equity.

Maud was suing for two things: the $1,000 in royalties he had withheld on the reprint of *Anne of Green Gables*; and damages for fraudulently selling Grosset and Dunlap the rights to *Anne's House of Dreams*. She expected to lose the second point because she had made the mistake of cashing the cheque he had sent her for the Grosset and Dunlap sale.

The first lawsuit was heard between January 11 and 22, 1919, in the Suffolk County Court in Boston by Judge Charles Francis Jenney. Frank Nelson Nay represented the Page Company and Weld Allen Rollins represented Maud. As anticipated, the judge gave the second point to Page, but he gave Montgomery the first point, ordering Page to pay her the $1,000.

Knowing the value of her work, Page then offered Maud $10,000 for her rights. She refused. She had seen enough of Page by this time — his bullying and his mendacity, even in a court of law where he had sworn to tell the truth — that she wanted no further association with such a man. She had been startled, for instance, to discover that when John McClelland's firm sold her books in Canada, a very small market, comparatively, the *Canadian* orders were for thousands more copies than Page had reported selling in the United States. This indicated a longtime fraud in their accounting. She estimated that she had lost some $50,000 to him from his beggarly royalty on the "wholesale" rather than the "retail" price, alone. (Stokes was giving her 20 percent of the retail price, instead of Page's 10 percent of the wholesale price.) She began to wonder how many more thousands she had lost if the Pages fiddled their books.

This all made Maud give serious thought to how much money she should ask for, for the sale of her rights, and she came up with the figure of $18,000. After some dickering and bluffing, Page agreed to the sum of $17,880, with a condition: that she allow his company to publish one more book of "Anne" short stories, the stories that had been left over after they had made their selection for *Chronicles of Avonlea*. This new book would be called *Further Chronicles of Avonlea*.

Here, the Page deviltry becomes very complicated. Maud wanted to sever *all* relations with the Page company, but they had reminded her about these leftover stories, saying that since most had been published in Canadian magazines, no copyright had been taken out on them in the United States. Therefore, any American publisher could hunt them up and publish them without her permission, or without paying her any royalties whatsoever. This threat was blackmail.

Maud was aghast. This meant Page could bring out this book, falsely packaging it as a new "Anne of Green Gables" book, in a year when she was bringing out a truly new "Anne" book with Stokes in the United States and with McClelland and Stewart in Canada. Because Page's name was so well known as her publisher, people would buy his book, assuming it was her newest one, and undercut her sales with her other publishers. The new publishers would be justly annoyed. To tie the Page Company down to bringing this book out in a year when she was not bringing out another "Anne" novel, she agreed to let them have these stories and the copyright. But she imposed conditions: that the book would not be fobbed off as another "Anne" book. The name "Anne" or "Anne Shirley" and Anne's picture were not to appear on the cover, and in the promotion they were not to advertise the collection as an "Anne" book, although they could say it was by the author of "Anne." She stipulated various other conditions, as well.

Here the plot becomes even more complicated: in 1912, when Maud had prepared the collection for *Chronicles of Avonlea*, she had used many stories, many which had already been published in periodicals. To satisfy Page, who was trying to make *Chronicles* look like another "Anne" book, she had revised these stories, inserting the character or name of Anne wherever she could. She had sent these off to Page, who made the selection for *Chronicles of Avonlea* and then supposedly returned all the typescripts and magazine clippings of the stories to her. In the days before photocopiers, when the only way to make a copy of something was to reproduce it by typewriter or by hand, Maud assumed that they had not kept copies of the rejects. She was wrong.

The Pages had actually typed up their own copies of *all* these stories before returning them to her, and secretly kept these copies in their vaults. If they had admitted to having these copies with "Anne" inserted throughout, Maud would have flatly refused to let them publish a second book entitled "Further Chronicles of Avonlea," knowing full well that they would market it as another new "Anne" book.

Instead, Page led her to believe that he did *not* have copies of the stories. He asked her to retype all the material from her original magazine copies. She was willing to undertake this work for three reasons: because she knew the name "Anne" did not appear often in the magazine versions and she could remove it if it did; because she knew she could cut out the descriptive material she had used elsewhere; and because this would prevent Page from bringing out a book in a year that she had another book coming out.

So on January 22, 1919, Maud signed an agreement in which Page purchased all rights to the income from contracts for *Anne of Green Gables* (April 22, 1907), *Anne of Avonlea* (February 16, 1909), *Kilmeny of the Orchard* (February 14, 1910), *The Story Girl* (November 15, 1910), *Chronicles of Avonlea* (April 26, 1912), *The Golden Road* (July 18, 1913), and *Anne of the Island* (January 26, 1915) for $17,880. (Technically, they had always held the copyright, but they'd had to pay her royalties. What they bought now were the entire "rights," so that they could keep all income from the books.) This agreement specified that the L. C. Page Company also secured the copyright to sixteen individual short stories that would become *Further Chronicles of Avonlea*. Montgomery was to furnish them with copies of these stories that she would type up from her originals. Page retained the right to make small editorial changes in the stories, but agreed not to insert the name "Anne" in any stories where it was not already, or to use the name "Anne" on the subtitle, or to put a picture of "Anne" on the book to lead the public to think it was another "Anne" book.

Maud signed the agreement, thinking it meant that she would be free of the Page firm forever. She also thought that the public might eventually get tired of her older books. And, being pragmatic, she thought "a bird in the hand was worth two in the bush."

She returned home and began preparing the sixteen stories, which took two months of non-stop typing and correcting. On March 20, 1919, she sent Page the retyped stories, having taken out references to "Anne" and various descriptive materials. She considered the matter finished.

She was in the dark about other actions behind the scenes. She did not know that Page had been negotiating the sale of film rights to *Anne of Green Gables* long before the January 22, 1919, contract was signed. The minute they had her signature on the document giving them the full rights to her books for the $17,880, they finalized the film deal, collecting $40,000 for themselves. The movie was finished by Realart in summer 1919. Evidently it had been under production while she was still negotiating with Page, and before she had signed the contract. Maud did not find out about the movie, and the loss of what should have been her share of the income ($20,000), until December 1919, *after* the film had been released, and had begun showing, to wild acclaim, in movie houses across America.[40]

There was a further jolt in store when the galley proofs of *Further Chronicles* came for her to check in January 1920. Not only was there an introduction that linked all these stories to *Anne of Green Gables*, but Page had ignored the 1919 versions she had sent. Instead, they had used the old 1912 versions that she had prepared for them when they were still on good terms, and into which she had inserted Anne's name wherever she could—copies they had not admitted that they still had.

Maud wrote them a furious letter, saying they could not use those 1912 versions. They informed her that since the stories were already typeset, they *were* going to use them, whether she liked it or not. They stated further that although the contract specified *they* could not add Anne's name, in the 1912 versions *she herself* had added Anne's name. Unfortunately, this was true.

Maud saw she had been tricked. Page had let her spend two months of tedious work typing and revising the 1919 copies in order to mislead her into thinking that his company did not have copies of the 1912 stories. They knew that she would eventually find out that they had had the copies all along, but letting his enemies know that he had bested them apparently gave Lewis Page particular pleasure. He figured that after the book was published, it would be too late for Maud to do anything about it.

It is perhaps a small mercy that Maud did not learn about another offensive manoeuvre by Page: on April 10, 1919, Page wrote the immensely popular Canadian poet and performer Bliss Carman—who had already published with them—asking if he would write the introduction to *Further Chronicles of Avonlea*. Carman was always in need of money, and Page would have expected him to jump at the opportunity, not only because being asked to write an introduction was an honour, but also because it paid well. However, Page showed his sleaze in the final paragraph of the otherwise fine letter, and Carman must have balked:

My Dear Bliss:

Would you like a commission of $25. to write an appreciation or foreword (on the lines that you did a while ago for Annie Fellows Johnston's TRAVELLERS FIVE) for a new collection of stories by your compatriot, L. M. Montgomery, author of ANNE OF GREEN GABLES, etc?

I recall that you have always been a real admirer of this writer, going back to the time when you said of ANNE OF GREEN GABLES something to this affect [*sic*]:—"It is a real tribute to the merit and charm of this story, that while the young people of the house are making a clamouring search from cellar to attic for the missing volume, they cannot appease their desire because the master of the house has taken the book to finish the reading on the way to town."

The new book is to be entitled FURTHER CHRONICLES OF AVONLEA, Avonlea, of course, being the charming little village in Prince Edward Island where the author lived, where Anne Shirley was created, and where the author resides and wrote of all of the characters she has pictured—from real life. In the forthcoming volume Anne Shirley only appears incidentally, the same as in the previous volume, CHRONICLES OF AVONLEA, but the atmosphere and charm is there, and I want this brought out in the appreciation, and I know that you can do it.

    . . .

It is possible, also, that we might arrange to let you do a little retouching or polishing of the stories if they need it, in which case we would pay $50. instead of $25.

    Very sincerely yours,
    [*signed*] Lewis C. Page[41]

Bliss Carman was an odd personality, but he was no fool. Why would L. M. Montgomery not polish her own stories? It is likely that Carman, well connected to the literary gossip of the day, had already heard of people's legal woes with Page. To Carman's credit, he did not touch this assignment. The introduction was done instead by Nathan Haskell Dole, a prolific American writer, editor, and translator, who was eminent in the Boston social and literary world that Page was part of.

George Page wrote Maud saying that their lawyer had advised them that they had every right to publish the 1912 versions since they had been "found" in the vaults after all. He added a postscript saying that he was acting under his lawyer's directions, which Maud interpreted to mean that he was uncomfortable with the way she was being treated. She speculated that he had to compromise his own integrity under pressure from his forceful older brother. Later events suggest she was right.

Maud instructed her American attorney, Weld Allen Rollins, to file suit, if necessary, to stop Page from publishing the 1912 versions, and another letter to the Pages telling them that they were to direct all further correspondence to her lawyer. Three days later, Rollins wrote Page that he was seeking an injunction against the publication of the book. George Page wrote back the next day that the Page Company believed it was acting within its legal rights. Five days later Rollins responded that the Page Company would be liable for heavy damages if they proceeded. On March 14, 1920, Page notified Maud that he was publishing the 1912 versions over her objections, and on April 8, the book appeared. Maud wired Rollins to proceed with litigation. Two days later she received her "author copies" of *Further Chronicles of Avonlea* and discovered that, although it did not have the same picture of "Anne" on the cover, it had a red-haired girl who looked very similar to the other pictures of "Anne." Page had won the first round by ignoring the injunction, but the fight was not over.

In her own copy of the Page first edition of *Further Chronicles*, Maud inserted furious comments. She bracketed the first three paragraphs of "Tannis of the Flats," saying that these three paragraphs were a Page interpolation. She was embarrassed that many of the descriptive passages from stories in *Further Chronicles* had since come out in other books that she had published with Stokes, and she bracketed these. No author would want to appear to be recycling her own material, as if her creative wells had run dry.

On April 24, 1920, Rollins filed a "bill in equity" on behalf of Maud in the Suffolk County Court requesting an injunction to prevent the Page Company from *further* printings of the *Further Chronicles* and an accounting of profits and damages for loss of reputation. This was Maud's second lawsuit against Page, and it dragged on until December 1928.

She had to make a trip to Boston, in May 1920, for the courtroom showdown. She soon received a brutal lesson in how simple matters can become unbelievably complex in a court of law. For nearly two months, the Pages and their lawyers nitpicked over details in the contract to obfuscate the real issues and to draw things out, creating more expense for Maud. Because the Pages had breached the 1919 contract's terms forbidding them from marketing the *Further Chronicles* as another "Anne" novel, this was one of the contentious points. Maud wrote:

> Those three grave lawyers and myself wrangled all day over the question of the exact colour of "Anne's" hair and the definition of "Titian red." Ye gods, it was funny! The big table was snowed under with literature and prints to prove or disprove. Years ago, when I sat down in that old kitchen at Cavendish, that rainy spring evening, and dowered "Anne" with red hair, I did not dream that a day would come when it would be fought over like this in a court room. It would be deliciously amusing—if it were not so beastly horrible. French [Page's lawyer] was determined to prove that Titian hair was dark red and that I knew it was dark red. I didn't. I always supposed Titian-red was a sort of flame-red and I stuck to it through all his badgering. Rollins dug up an encyclopedia in which Titan hair was defined as a "bright golden auburn" and the Master said it had always been his impression that Titian hair was the hue of burnished copper! And so on! (June 18, 1920)

For a person who by nature avoided direct conflict in her life, Maud stood up well in the trial. Her fighting spirit was aroused in the heated cross-examination, but her nerves fell apart as soon as she left the court. She could not sleep at night. She took prescribed Veronal and bromides to help calm her nerves. When she finally got back home on July 10, 1920, she was so agitated that she cried on and off for days. She had missed Chester's eighth birthday for the sake of the trial, and yet nothing had been resolved—wrangling continued long after her own testimony was finished and she came home.

In the meantime, Page decided that the best method of fighting Maud's first lawsuit was to counterattack. In a third lawsuit registered in the Massachusetts Supreme Judicial Court in October 1920, Page sued Maud for libel, alleging that she had impugned his business practices. The case was dismissed in that court on August 11, 1921. Not to be thwarted, Page then appealed it to the United States Supreme Court, where the same thing was argued on March 13, 1923. It was again denied in a judgment by Mr. Justice McKenna on April 9, 1923.

Page surely did not expect to win such frivolous libel suits, but he knew that while the case dragged on he would have the pleasure of harassing Maud now that swords were openly drawn. He was probably astute enough to know that although she could put up a tough front, she would have many sleepless nights of worry. For her part, she was realizing how easy it was to go to law, but how hard it was to extract yourself once there. Worse, she had to pay her lawyers every single day that the case dragged on. Rollins kept reminding her, too, how unpredictable the results of any lawsuit could be. Maud had also seen how convincingly a dishonest person could lie in court and how easily a smart lawyer could obfuscate the truth. Rollins periodically lost his own courage and urged her to settle. She flatly refused each time.

Her second lawsuit against Page (which had started in 1920) continued to drag on and on. From time to time she sent Mr. Rollins payments for several thousand dollars. Page was now represented by an exceptionally able and aggressive lawyer named Asa Palmer French, who had been the U.S. Attorney for the District of Massachusetts. He had an aggressive style, like Page: he was insulting, unpredictable, and intimidating.

This second suit was very complicated, and the conflicting statements (or "lies," as Maud called them) made it difficult to follow. As a result, the case was handed over to a "Master," whose job was to sort through all the documentation and file a report for the judge. This Master's report, handed down in August 1921, was largely adverse to Maud. By this time, she had paid Rollins $6,000 on the case, and nothing had been determined. However, Rollins was able to appeal and secure a more favourable report from the Master. What had seemed to Maud a simple case of bullying and fraud had turned into something incredibly convoluted.

Maud, Mr. Rollins, Stokes's attorneys (who were helping Rollins), and John McClelland were given an unexpected boost in the middle of this dreary litigation. Maud learned in late March 1922 that Wanamaker's—the most prestigious department store and book-selling chain in America at that time, and certainly Page's best customer—had shut down all its accounts with the Page Company. This was an astonishing move, and a devastating financial blow to Page. John Wanamaker was fed up with Page's unethical business practices and simply refused to deal with him any more. Mr. Wanamaker was a formidable businessman with a huge fortune of his own, and he was one of the few who could stand up to Lewis Page.[42] Being dropped by Wanamaker's damaged the L. C. Page Company's reputation, as well as hurting their bottom line. This was big news in the American book world—the biggest retailer and book chain in American dropping one of the most powerful publishers of popular books.

The Wanamaker's cancellation began to empty Page's deep pockets. (When Maud received the typed evidence from the trials in late 1928, she learned that without Wanamakers the Page firm receipts had dropped from close to half a million dollars in 1921 to roughly $250,000 in 1926.)

By now, the strife that Page had brought into others' lives was starting to take a serious toll on his own firm. Lewis and his brother were fighting more. The milder and less litigious George Page saw the larger picture: that his brother's bullying ways were costing the firm enormously, both in profits and reputation. Maud did not know this, however. She simply saw in Page a man who seemed impervious to destruction. She lived in a constant state of tension, without the alleviation provided by a stable and sympathetic husband's commiseration. Ewan was preoccupied with his own problems.

On April 14, 1923, Maud received joyous news from her attorney: Judge Hammond had given a favourable decision on the second lawsuit after three years. He wrote that although Page had *thought* he was within his rights in publishing the book from the 1912 versions of the stories, he did not in fact have these rights, and as a result Page was directed to pay Maud *all* the profits from *Further Chronicles of Avonlea.*

Page, not one to capitulate easily, instructed Mr. French, his lawyer, to appeal Judge Hammond's findings. Maud and her lawyer found this bizarre: typing and printing up all the material for the appeal would cost Page more than the judgment against him. But Page still had money, and even if his lawsuits were eventually dismissed, he clearly intended to harass and perhaps destroy Maud as they dragged along to their conclusion.

Incredibly, Page next flatly asserted that there were *no* profits whatsoever from *Further Chronicles of Avonlea*. Everyone knew that there must have been profits, but to prove this Maud's lawyers would need to examine the L. C. Page financial books, which would involve more expensive litigation. Weld Rollins was quite sick of the Page firm, and now he had to nickel-and-dime with Page, who was charging up all the expenses they could find against the gross profits.

This delaying tactic did not promise Page any success in the end. There were profits and they would be dug out. But Page knew that Maud would have to keep paying her lawyer while an expensive forensic accountant located the profits. Maud understood by now that Page would rather pay his own lawyer $10,000 than pay her $1,000. Rollins saw that she was going to be paying so much for his services that he again suggested she simply settle at this point. She would not. All her Presbyterian rectitude stiffened her resolve. She believed that injustice should not go unpunished. She could not fight the demons in her own husband's mind, but she could battle the devilish Page.

In January 1924, Page and his lawyers took another step: they moved their ongoing (but thus far unsuccessful) libel suit against Maud into a New York jurisdiction. This started the fourth of their lawsuits. In December 1925, after two more years of wrangling, Page appealed the case all the way to the New York Court of Appeal, but this decision came down against him. Still, Page knew that if he wasn't winning, he was nevertheless wearing out his adversary and draining her bank account into her lawyer's pocket. Page often said that he wished he had been a lawyer himself.

Page's purchase of all of Maud's rights in 1919 had been a good move: it now gave him plenty of money to continue funding lawsuits against her. In the post-war 1920s, her books enjoyed a surge in popularity. The early L. M. Montgomery titles owned by Page had the pre-war pastoral Prince Edward Island charm in them. By the end of 1914, *Anne of Green Gables* alone had been reprinted thirty-eight times. All the sequels that he had bought were also being reprinted. In 1920, Page—ever the skilful merchandiser—brought out a new edition, filled with pictures of the silent movie featuring film star Mary Miles Minter.

In the meantime, Page and his lawyer developed another devious scheme—they persuaded the courts to freeze Maud's U.S. royalty payments (up to the total of $30,000) from Stokes. The argument was that if they won the libel judgment, the money would be there to pay them. Page's motive was to strangle Maud's income. Then he would have her where he wanted her— she would be without any funds to pay her substantial legal bills for fighting him. Any savings she had would soon be exhausted. Maud wrote: "There is no end to the deviltry the Pages will attempt and no end to the kinks in U.S. law that enable them to do it. It is an iniquitous law that allows a person's property to be attached before a case is even tried" (January 5, 1924). But there was nothing she could do about it.

Poor John McClelland, Maud's gentlemanly Canadian publisher, who was accustomed to civility, decency, and honesty, was horrified and not a little frightened by the wrath of Page. When Mr. McClelland himself had gone down to testify on her behalf he had become so addled on the stand that Maud and her lawyers doubted that he helped her case. Now, fretful about Page, McClelland told Maud that he was sending her the Canadian royalties *in advance* in case Page should try to "attach" them in Canada. This was the last straw for Maud: she did not think Canadian law would allow such a thing, and wrote McClelland ("who ought to know" she fumed on February 4, 1924) to find out *for sure* whether the Pages could reach up to Canada to attach her royalties.

Maud had one very tense week waiting for clarification from McClelland. He had bothered her for nothing: he found that the Page Company could *not* attach her royalties in Canada. But the fact that they *believed* that Page was urging a Canadian firm to act against them nevertheless lingered as a threat with both Maud and John McClelland. They feared that the lawyers might still come up with some other damaging plan.

Maud's American publishers began to develop cold feet as well. Frederick Stokes thought Page outrageous and corrupt, but his firm was fed up with this costly fight. They were also afraid they might lose, given the fabled unpredictability of the courts. So once again Maud received a letter from her American attorneys suggesting she settle. She refused, knowing that if she capitulated because she was intimidated, she could not live with herself.

In October 1924, she received a blithe letter from the Page Company asking for her help in putting out a booklet on her life and career. "I can't understand the psychology of those men," she fumed. "Here they have been hounding me through the U.S. courts for years and at this very moment have

a suit against me in New York—a mere 'spite' suit—and have tied up my royalties and have worried me half to death. And yet they coolly ask *me* to help
them get up something solely for their own benefit and convenience—for I get
nothing out of it" (October 30, 1924). Page knew his victim well. This was just
another form of harassment, and it worried her out of more sleep. Maud was
very alarmed about her husband's mental health at this point, too.

The Pages continued to do very well with all their L. M. Montgomery titles. In April 1925, they gave an exclusive licence to George Harrap &
Company of London, England, to supply eight of Maud's works to the British
market. They received $9,000 for this licence—and Maud nothing, since she
no longer owned any rights. But she had to keep paying her own attorneys,
and in May 1925, Rollins sent her another bill for $1,000, with a warning that
he would be spending a lot more time on the case before it was over.

In October 1925, she heard that the New York libel case (the fourth lawsuit) had gone against the Pages, by a unanimous ruling. In December 1925,
Frederick A. Stokes finally sent her the cheque for all her royalties that they
had been forced to withhold.

The battle with the Page Company was not over, however.

Ewan's lawsuit with Marshall Pickering

While Maud was battling Page in American courts, Ewan was drawn into a
local lawsuit that was equally enervating. His troubles started in 1921, escalated into a court case in late 1922, and dragged on for a long time after that.

When the Macdonalds first moved to Leaskdale, cars were still a novelty; when villagers heard the noise of an approaching car, they ran to the
window to watch. But by 1917, many in the village owned cars. In 1918, when
Maud's royalties came in at $45,725, she decided that the time had come to
purchase a car, and that Ewan could assume the role of chauffeur for his
family. She had wanted a car since her first ride in Lewis Page's in Boston. So
the Macdonald family purchased a five-passenger Chevrolet from Mr. Ivor
Law in Zephyr, who had set up a business selling both cars and gas in that village. At age forty-eight, Ewan found himself learning how to drive, and a new
world opened up to the Macdonalds.

Ewan was maladroit when it came to anything practical or mechanical.
Still, he learned how to crank the car to start it, then hustle back to the driver's

seat very quickly to keep the motor from dying. His family grew accustomed to lurches when he tried to get the car moving forward without killing the motor. Like many other drivers at that time, he had trouble remembering that the car was not a horse, and if he needed to stop quickly, his first impulse was always to yank backwards on the steering wheel, as if he were holding the horse's reins, and yell "Whoa! Whoa!" Some found this endearing, others found it funny, but his young sons found it very embarrassing. Since Maud never learned to drive, a car was the one place where Ewan felt superior to his talented wife. A drive often blew the cobwebs of Predestination and damnation out of his mind, making him feel the distinguished family man he had it in him to be.

Early automobiles were quite unpredictable objects. They sputtered, jerked, and died, and all too often their wheels or entire axles fell off while being driven. But there were few drivers on the dirt or gravel roads, and cars did not go very fast. At top speed, they might achieve a burst of thirty miles per hour. (Just ten years earlier, in 1911, the world's speed record for an airplane was set by a U.S. Army aviator who went 106 miles in two hours and seven minutes.)

Ewan's difficulties with his automobile had resulted in several minor accidents. Maud soon decided that their jumpy Chevrolet was inferior. On May 12, 1921, Ewan traded the Chevrolet for an elegant Gray-Dort touring car that they christened "Lady Jane Grey."

A month after the purchase of the new car, the real trouble started. On June 12, 1921, after church on a fine bright Sunday in Zephyr, the Gray-Dort was loaded down—with Ewan, Maud, Chester, Stuart, parishioner Mrs. Jake Meyers, and her young daughter, all on their way to the Meyers' house for tea. Ewan stopped at Ivor Law's gas bar for fuel.

Zephyr was not much more than a crossroads, with Mr. Law's establishment located in the middle of the little village. Unfortunately, the crossroad had a blind corner. After purchasing gas (something a minister should not have done on a Sunday, some might have said), Ewan looked to see if anyone was coming before he started onto the road again, but he didn't take a second look—as usual, he was focused on moving the car forward before the motor sputtered and died. As they turned out into the road, Maud yelled for him to stop—a car was coming. Ewan did not hear her. "Lady Jane Grey" often jerked and died for no reason at all, but this time she took a lively lurch straight into the path of an oncoming car. There was a noisy crash. Fenders crumpled. Glass flew.

The driver of the other car, a Chevrolet, was Marshall Pickering, an elder in the Methodist Church. His wife, Sarah, had a cut on her face that produced much blood but proved superficial. No one in the Macdonalds' heavier car was at all injured, despite the fact that the impact had whirled their car around into the opposite direction. The Laws, who had witnessed the crash, ran to help.

When the dust settled, it was clear that both cars were damaged. "Lady Jane Grey" had a bent axle, smashed fender, and broken lamp-post (repairs costing fifty dollars). The Pickering Chevrolet, a lighter car, sustained eighty-five dollars in damage. Maud thought that they were equally to blame: Ewan for careless driving (pulling out without looking a second time), but Pickering for speeding. Moreover, Pickering had not been on his own side of the road, as he should have been. He also admitted that he had seen the Macdonald car before crashing into it. (He reasonably expected Ewan to stop, but Ewan instead pulled into the road.) Normally people drove in the middle of these old dirt roads unless someone else was coming. Then they moved over. Cars were so few that road signs weren't yet necessary. There were *some* rules of the road, however, including that a driver should slow to twelve miles per hour and toot the horn before proceeding around a blind corner. And drivers were always supposed to look twice before proceeding onto a road. It indeed seemed that both drivers were at fault.

The day after the accident, Mrs. Ivor Law called the Macdonalds to tell them that Marshall Pickering had been taken to the hospital that morning for "stoppage of urine." She noted that he had had several of these attacks before. In fact, he had had prostate trouble for a number of years, but had told people in the community that he had put off having the operation because his father had died as the result of a prostate operation (before antibiotics, patients often died from post-operative infections).

Ewan visited Mrs. Pickering to commiserate the next day. She made snappish remarks about Ewan's bad driving, but she did not link her husband's prostate trouble to the accident. Shortly after that, Ewan paid Marshall Pickering a courtesy call in the hospital where he was recovering from a successful operation. While there, Ewan met Pickering's son Wellington, who, in the course of an amiable chat, told him that his dad had intended to have the operation the following week, and had written him four weeks ago to come home for the summer to look after the farm while he was recuperating.

Maud wrote in her diary a week later, on June 16, 1920: "Everywhere we go we have to talk of it [the accident] and explain. A hundred exaggerated reports have gone abroad concerning it." But talk died down, Pickering recovered, and that was the end of the affair—or so everyone thought.

In early December, Maud reported having one of her "queer 'symbolic' dreams," and this worried her. She dreamed that she had come home from a trip to find that Ewan had been hanged but had come back to life after being cut down (February 28, 1922). She thought this presaged trouble.

Some ten days later a letter came to Ewan from Pickering stating that the operation would not have been necessary had it not been for the accident, and that Ewan should pay $500 of the $1,000 it cost. This was one-third of Ewan's yearly salary (which had risen to $1,500 in 1921) for his combined charge of two churches. But of course Pickering knew that Ewan's wife was "rich"—her royalties had paid for the fancy Grey-Dort.

The Macdonalds were outraged, particularly by the demanding tone of Pickering's letter. They knew that enlarged prostate glands were a problem that came on over time, not as the result of a single car accident, and they knew that he'd needed the operation well before the accident. However, Maud observed that "*he* didn't know we knew that . . . not having heard his son's conversation with Ewan. I suppose he thought it could 'put it over us' quite easily" (February 28, 1922).

The Macdonalds felt there would have been some justice in Pickering's asking that they pay for his car repairs, for he'd already been in the road when they'd pulled in front of him. However, if he had been on his side of the road, the accident would not have taken place. Similarly, if he had slowed and beeped at the corner, as a driver was supposed to, then they would not have collided. But they balked over the medical bills.

Ewan wrote back to Pickering that they were both at fault for the accident and that it was therefore fair that they each pay their own expenses. He told Pickering that many people had heard him talk about his need for the operation before the crash. Maud observed: "Probably this put Pickering into the rage of a man who has tried to do a detestable thing and has been found out. He is a very conceited, arrogant, bumptious man who cannot brook contradiction in anything" (February 28, 1922). His wife (a third wife) she had already characterized, quite critically, as a "very ignorant, insolent, vulgar woman." Maud does not soften the punches in her private diary—an understandable reaction, perhaps, for someone who always had to be impeccably polite in her public role as a minister's wife.

The Macdonalds heard nothing more for over two months. On February 28, 1922, when they assumed that the matter was over, they were surprised to get a response. According to Maud, Marshall Pickering's letter to Ewan Macdonald "raved . . . abusively through several very badly written and badly spelled pages," saying that he had never been sick before, could prove by doctors that the accident had both caused his prostate problem and necessitated the ensuing operation, and demanding that Ewan pay $500 within the month or the matter would be "settled" in the courts. At the beginning and the end of the letter, he wrote boldly "Written Without Prejudice." Clearly he had composed the letter himself—as the spelling and grammar revealed—but that he had consulted a lawyer was evident through his use of the specialized legal term.

Maud wrote: "I suppose he imagines that Ewan, being a minister, will submit to blackmail rather than be dragged into the worry and notoriety of a lawsuit. If so he does not know either of us. We will not be frightened into paying his bills." Maud was still fighting her own lawsuits in the United States and the letter upset her. "Ewan never worries over anything—except eternal damnation—but I do. . . . Just as soon as one thing passes, or grows easier, something else comes" (February 28, 1922).

For once, Ewan did not dither over what to do: he flew into action. By April 2, 1922, he had met with a lawyer, Mr. McCullough of Toronto, who told them that if they could prove that Pickering had planned to have the operation before the accident, the case would be easy to win. Ewan would have to find witnesses to disprove Pickering's statements in the letter.

On April 25, 1922, the Macdonalds received an official letter from Pickering's lawyer, Mr. Willard W. Greig, of Uxbridge, demanding "$1,500 under threat of a writ." Greig was a young lawyer at the beginning of his long and successful career in Uxbridge.[43] The letter from Pickering's lawyer gave Ewan a focus for action.

Galvanized into action, Ewan was tireless in his search for testimony to support his case. He saw himself as the victim of a greedy opportunist, and he wanted to believe, like his wife, that God favoured those who steadfastly fought injustice. Ewan covered immense amounts of ground looking for people to testify that Pickering had talked about his need for prostate surgery before the accident. He was quite successful: Marshall Pickering was a garrulous man who travelled far and wide in his car.

Ewan was very good at canvassing, and he showed ingenuity and excellent networking skills. People embraced the opportunity to talk to him because they welcomed a chance to hear more details about the accident. And when he went farther afield, everyone knew his wife was a celebrity. Interesting gossip was hard to come by, and tales of this affair had spread for many miles around, even as far as Kingston, Ontario.

Ewan's manner was amiable and homespun but gentlemanly, so people welcomed him into their homes. Pickering, by contrast, was often arrogant: even in his own church, many people found his attention-seeking irritating. A well-dressed and handsome man, he was said to be *too* aware of the fine figure he cut. He had a habit of coming to church after the minister had started the sermon and tiptoeing ostentatiously up to his pew in the front, grimacing for comic effect as each step elicited creaky squeaks from the floor. Expecting the performance each Sunday, children giggled in expectation and parents gritted their teeth.

But whatever his faults, Pickering was also a substantial citizen. His family had been early settlers in the area, and he farmed one hundred acres right outside Zephyr. He had been on the building committee when the Methodist church was established, and he remained a significant force in its management. He was a great talker, a talented singer, and a cocky show-off—a quality the Macdonalds loathed. At age sixty-two, Marshall was still a vigorous man behind the wheel. He was much more alert than Ewan, who would be fifty-one in 1921. Whatever these personality differences added to the affair, in a rural community where lawsuits were exceedingly rare, the entire Leaskdale-Zephyr community and the surrounding counties were mesmerized by the spectacle of a public altercation between a Presbyterian "man of the cloth" and a well-to-do farmer who was a powerful force in the Methodist Church.

Maud was delighted to see Ewan rouse himself to action after the prolonged mental distress following his May 1919 breakdown. Relieved that he was taking up his cudgel against injustice, she was nevertheless skeptical. She had already had enough experience in the American courts to know how convincingly people could and would lie.

The stakes in this lawsuit kept rising. On September 25, 1922, the Macdonalds learned that Pickering was now suing them for $8,000: $1,000 for his operation; $5,000 for his sufferings, and $2,000 for his wife. Now there was a new charge: he alleged that Mrs. Pickering had developed "sugar diabetes" as the result of the accident. Old-timers interviewed in the 1980s said that Marshall Pickering was not a sophisticated man for all his "snap," and they did not fault him for thinking that if he had stoppage of urine after an accident, there was a connection. Nor, they said, would he and his wife have understood what caused diabetes. She claimed she had had to keep her daughters home from paying jobs in order to keep house for her. Maud knew that a lawyer often sued for more than he hoped to get as a strategy for getting part of it, but the inflated amounts were still worrying, especially since Maud was already deeply concerned about her American lawsuits. The sum of $8,000 also stunned this rural community. One man gasped, to Maud's delight: "Eight thousand!! It's more than his whole damned carcass is worth, let alone his prostate gland" (October 1, 1922).

On September 27, 1922, Maud opined that "poor Ewan has begun his task of getting all possible evidence." Mr. Law was willing to give testimony that "Pickering was in the middle of the road, did not turn out, did not sound his horn, [and] was going very fast and was equally to blame." Two "respected and reputable" men at Mt. Albert agreed to testify that Pickering had told them after the operation that he had needed the operation anyway.

The lines of battle were drawn, but the pressures that would come to bear on the outcome were many, complicated, and insidious. In a community in which the Pickerings were long established, a subtle force was enacted through the bonds of kinship, marriage, and community entanglements. Although many people had casually mentioned to Ewan that Pickering had talked about his need for the prostate operation long before he had it, and promised to testify to this, they backed out when they realized what testifying actually meant. Ewan would then discover that a potential witness's uncle or brother was married to someone who was a distant cousin or sibling of someone related to the extended Pickering family. In Cavendish, Maud had always been an "insider"; she would have understood instinctively how these tangled webs would affect testimony. In Leaskdale and Zephyr, the Macdonalds were effectively "outsiders."

Another complication was the denominational rivalry between the Presbyterians and the Methodists. Ewan could not count on any Methodist testifying publicly against Pickering, no matter what people were willing to tell him privately. Presbyterian ministers like Ewan came and went, but Marshall Pickering and his family would stay in the community. Proving the truth would be more difficult than they had anticipated.

The community speculated on every aspect of the situation. "Many people in Zephyr think that it is Mrs. Pickering that put Pickering up to this,"

Maud wrote in her journals, but "other people think it is Greig" (September 30, 1922). Many more were horrified that a minister was being sued, and observed that the lawsuit would never have come to pass if Ewan had not had a "rich wife." Because there were many people on a rural telephone party line, everyone flew to the phone to listen in whenever anyone's phone rang. Generally, the Methodists rallied against the Presbyterians, but there were always splits and defections. The only thing most people agreed on was that both men were bad drivers—Pickering went too fast and Macdonald went too slow. Even Maud admitted that Ewan was a poor driver.

In preparing for the trial, Ewan remained focused and determined. He not only canvassed everyone to whom Pickering had spoken, he also checked out all the doctors in the area. He found a Dr. Boynton in Sutton, whom Marshall Pickering had consulted about his enlarged prostate long before the accident. Dr. Boynton was willing to testify to that effect. But as soon as Pickering heard through gossip that the doctor was going to testify, he confronted him, boldly claiming that the consultation had never taken place. Taken aback, Dr. Boynton showed Pickering his notes, with Pickering's name and the details of the visit. A quick thinker, Pickering paused, then shot back that it must have been his young nephew, another "Marshall Pickering." Fortunately for Pickering, that nephew was no longer around, so this could not be confirmed. Although the doctor knew that prostate problems were not a young man's ailment, he backed out of testifying because he said that he had to admit that he could not honestly remember Marshall Pickering's face.

Next, Ewan talked to the doctor who had diagnosed Mrs. Pickering's diabetes prior to the accident, and had sent her to Toronto specialists. Since insulin had just been discovered by Drs. Frederick Banting and Charles Best (and John Macleod and James Collip) at the University of Toronto in the winter of 1921–22, it should have been easy to discredit Mrs. Pickering's claim that her diabetes had been caused by a car accident—especially given that the diagnosis of diabetes had already been made before the accident.

Maud groused on November 16, 1922, that as the trial drew near, their lawsuit was the talk of the communities for a twenty-mile radius. "I can't exactly blame people. The fact of a minister being sued is a dramatic event to them— a veritable god-send in their humdrum, colourless lives. It is only natural they should make the most of it. But it is hard that Ewan and I should be butchered to make a Roman holiday! I feel all raw and bleeding, mentally and physically" (November 16, 1922). Her own Page lawsuits were still pending, but no one in her community knew anything about them.

The Macdonalds were not aware that Marshall Pickering had hired a new Toronto lawyer, Thomas N. Phelan, to assist Greig. Phelan was one of Canada's sharpest lawyers in the emerging field of automobile law. A King's Counsel (K.C.), Phelan was very prominent in the Toronto legal community. He suggested a trial in front of a judge, not a jury. The Macdonalds happily agreed to this, thinking that a jury might be prejudiced against an educated clergyman with a rich wife, and would feel more sympathy for Pickering, an unsophisticated farmer. They did not think of the fact that the impressive Phelan was, of course, well acquainted with all the judges where the case would be heard, and a top-flight lawyer would command respect in the small legal world of Toronto.

The trial was set for November 23, 1922, in the Assize Court in Toronto. Maud noted that Ewan had been well throughout the entire fall, although he looked very tired by the time of the trial. "I think if we win the trial the sense of success will scatter that dark complex of inadequacy in his subconscious mind which I believe is responsible for much of his trouble," she wrote hopefully in her journal on November 21, 1922.

The Macdonalds expected to win, with both facts and medical evidence on their side. Maud worried that Ewan's lawyers, brothers named McCullough, were more affable than sharp, but Ewan had done a good job gathering all the evidence. Even if many witnesses had fallen away, he still had found several courageous people willing to testify that Marshall Pickering had said he needed the prostate operation long before the accident. As well, the Macdonalds had doctors to testify that enlarged prostates and sugar diabetes came from pre-existing conditions, not from car accidents.

The courtroom was stuffed with people from Leaskdale and Zephyr, which boosted the Macdonalds' morale. Some, of course, came out of curiosity, but most were there in sympathy with the Macdonalds. Even those who were afraid to testify wanted to see justice served. There was also a reporter from the *Globe* at the trial.

The judge presiding over the case, the Honourable Justice William Renwick Riddell, was one of the most eminent legal lights in Toronto, if not Canada. He was a Scot who proudly claimed ancestry, as Maud herself did, from a knight who had accompanied William the Conqueror to Britain. Justice Riddell, the son of a prosperous farmer in Cobourg, came with impressive credentials. Winner of the Gold Medal of the Law Society of Upper Canada, he had been called to the bar in 1891, at age thirty-one. He had married the wealthy Anna Crossen, whose father owned the Cobourg Car Works, which manufactured railway cars at the time of Canada's railway expansion. By age forty-one, William Renwick Riddell and his wife had acquired a fine house next to Sir Oliver Mowat's home where they entertained elegantly. In 1906, he was appointed to the Supreme Court of Ontario, where he served until 1945. He had been elected as a Fellow of the Royal Society of Canada and would receive, by his death, eleven honorary degrees from all over North America.

Riddell was part of Toronto's elite society. An accomplished orator, he was much in demand as a speaker in Canada and the United States. He hobnobbed with the best and most powerful in the legal and political world, counting among his acquaintances Sir Wilfrid Laurier and William Lyon MacKenzie King, both prime ministers of Canada. He was very well versed in history and law, and had written the first history of Canadian jurisprudence. He wrote prodigiously on a range of topics, medical and literary: venereal diseases in the Middle Ages, hiccups, Virginia Woolf's books (he didn't like them), ancient dentistry, Freemasonry, Ontario history, insomnia, legal matters, and so on. Justice Riddell seemed a perfect judge for the Macdonalds, considering his Scottish background, his attraction to famous and successful people, his extensive knowledge of medicine, and his wide experience in law.

Maud gives a blow-by-blow account of the courtroom testimony in her journals. Judge Riddell's handwritten notes have survived to confirm her account, and they shed even more light on the dramatic proceedings and astonishing judgment.

The trial began on a Thursday afternoon. Maud had watched Justice William Renwick Riddell through the morning and had misgivings. Intuitively, she sized him up as a "colossal egotist . . . who thinks his own judgment quite infallible" (November 26, 1922), and for once in her life, she may have been understating the case.

Marshall Pickering was the first to testify. He had said in discovery that he had seen the Macdonalds' car some one hundred rods away, but he changed it now to twenty rods, saying he had been mistaken before. Maud acerbically comments that if he was "mistaken" in this, one would assume he might be "mistaken" in other things. He swore he was going only twenty miles per hour, and that he had sounded his horn four times (witnesses denied both those assertions). He said that he was operated on for a "congested" prostate gland, not an "enlarged" one, and he swore that he had never spoken of having prostate trouble before the accident occurred. When he was cross-examined by McCullough (Ewan's lawyer) who cited names of their witnesses who would testify that he had spoken beforehand of the need for an operation, he admitted that he "might have said he had a burning sensation at times" when urinating.

When McCullough asked if Mrs. Pickering had ever been treated for diabetes (which everyone in the community knew she had), he said, by Maud's journal account, "She *had a little* of it a few years ago but she got some medicine from the States that cured her."

McCullough next elicited an admission from Pickering that *if* he had slowed to twelve miles per hour at this blind corner, he could have avoided the accident. When McCullough confronted Pickering about tampering with a witness, Judge Riddell cut off the questioning, saying it didn't matter. When Pickering's testimony was finished, Justice Riddell advised McCullough not to call Ewan's witnesses—the ones who would testify that Pickering had told them before the accident that he needed an operation—because he would "give very little attention to such evidence." When McCullough explained that he wanted to call them to "test the credibility of the witness," Maud reported that Justice Riddell replied, "Oh, I believe the witness. He is an honest man."

Riddell then asked McCullough to call some of the doctors. Dr. Johnson, Pickering's own doctor, said he had found some "congestion" in the gland, and supposed the accident had caused it. Dr. Robinson, a pathologist at the University of Toronto who had dissected the gland after the operation, testified there was no congestion in the gland at all, and he "had the section of the gland there to prove it." Further, he stated that the "operation would have been necessary in any case in two or three months." Two more experts in kidney disease testified "that diabetes was incurable" and the accident would not have caused Mrs. Pickering's diabetes.

In testimony the next day, Mrs. Pickering denied that she had ever been treated for diabetes before the accident, even though her husband had said the opposite on the previous day, and their doctor (Dr. Johnson) had also testified that he had diagnosed her diabetes and sent her to a specialist in Toronto *before* the accident. In cross-examination, she admitted that she had not consulted a doctor *after* the accident. McCullough picked up these discrepancies and questioned her further about seeing the specialist before the accident.

Maud reports that Judge Riddell cut him off by saying, "I don't believe she ever had diabetes or if she had she is cured."

More people testified. Finally, Ewan and Maud testified and were cross-examined. The Macdonalds' lawyers did not put on the rest of their witnesses, for fear of antagonizing the impatient Riddell. They believed that on the basis of testimony already given he could do nothing except find in Ewan's favour anyway, given that experts had contradicted the Pickerings' testimony and that the Pickerings had contradicted themselves. Maud, however, was not so sure.

She was right. Justice Riddell incomprehensibly found in favour of the Pickerings, awarding Marshall Pickering $1,000 for his operation, $500 for his suffering, and Mrs. Pickering $500, plus expenses (which amounted to over $1,000). Ewan's lawyers and many from the community who had witnessed the trial were astonished. Maud reported that the court clerk had indiscreetly confided to the Macdonalds before the judgment came down that anyone could see "it was just a conspiracy to get money out of" them.

How could such an eminent judge as Justice Riddell—an undisputed polymath, president for twenty-five years of the Health League of Canada—have come to such a conclusion? He had written widely on medical matters—ranging from a translation of a sixteenth-century work on syphilis to articles on the history of medicine.[44] Clearly, the Macdonalds were at a disadvantage in having the case tried in Toronto, where the judge did not know the community standing of the various witnesses—who was truthful, and who was not. However, cross-examinations had revealed lies in testimony, so that should not have mattered. A man of such substantial wealth as Riddell could not have been "bought off." Nor could Pickering have offered him enough to make an under-the-table handshake worthwhile.

There are other explanations, none of which occurred to Maud and Ewan.

First, Judge Riddell's own notes, taken during testimony at the trial, reveal factors that may have influenced his judgment. At the time of the Macdonald trial, Justice Riddell was in his seventieth year, and the notes he took indicate that he was hard of hearing.[45] In 1922, there were no hearing aids, and he simply could not hear all that was said in the courtroom, and may have been too proud to admit this. His notes are riddled with errors: Pickering's Uxbridge lawyer, Willard F. Greig, he recorded as "Gray"; Dr. McClintock he called "Clintock"; Dr. Stevenson he called "Stephens"; Mason Horner becomes "Mason Marner." The sketchy notes appear to be taken by someone having a hard time keeping up with the testimony.

The transcript also suggests that Riddell simply was not listening attentively. Perhaps he was tired or bored. Or he had already made up his mind, and only heard selectively. For instance, he did not record the actual detailed testimony of any of the specialist doctors who testified on the Macdonalds' side—he just entered their names—but he *did* record the testimony of the Pickerings' local doctor. And he recorded only the part of Dr. Johnson's testimony that was in the Pickerings' favour. For instance, he wrote "prostate enlarge[d] and congested by blow." Yet, he did not record the University of Toronto pathologist's expert testimony and note the final clinical report that the prostate was *not* congested and that the enlarged prostate itself was *not* caused by the blow. The expert testimony should have trumped a country doctor's initial diagnosis.

In the case of Mrs. Pickering's diabetes, Riddell records no medical testimony at all, especially none of the specialists' comments that contradicted her allegations. Nor does he record the discrepancy between her and her husband's testimony in respect of the onset of symptoms. It is possible that Phelan, a Toronto lawyer who would have known that Riddell was hard of hearing, had advised his witnesses to speak softly. But other factors may also have come into play.

Riddell's notes show that he was very much aware of the reputation of the lawyers presenting the cases. He wrote clearly in his notes that T. N. Phelan was a "King's Counsel" lawyer, a designation of importance. Older lawyers like Riddell saw Phelan as an up-and-coming power in the legal world.[79] The McCullough brothers were competent but undistinguished. The "old boy" network was strong in law, just as in other professions, and Riddell had a long history of cultivating connections within it for reasons related to his own personal agenda. He still powerful ambitions for himself. Riddell had basked in the limelight of power through his truly distinguished career, and now, late in life, he lusted for much more recognition. He needed the support of the old-boy legal network, especially of outstanding lawyers like Phelan, to get it.

In 1923, the year after Judge Riddell decided the Macdonald-Pickering case, he wrote to Prime Minister Mackenzie King, asking for appointment to the position of Chief Justice in the Supreme Court of Canada. His not very subtle letter, dated April 1923, read: "Unless my claims receive sympathetic consideration from yours, my loss of three-quarters of a million [dollars] and seventeen years faithful—I think I may add successful as well as honourable—service go for nothing."[46] But the appointment he so coveted was never to be his, and at age ninety-one, he was still writing to Mackenzie King, begging for recognition. One final letter stated that a friend of his "assures me that it requires but a *hint* from you to Churchill to have me made a Member of the Privy Council," and a little later he says, "Or I would take a Knighthood."

Maud was fond of saying, "The mills of the Gods grind slowly, but they grind exceeding small." She puzzled in her journals over Riddell's decision—one that changed her life immeasurably for the worse. In her bewilderment, she rescued Riddell's name from the obscurity he feared, but not in the way he might have liked: her journals gave him a spicy page in her own life story, even though he made Pickering the courtroom winner.

As Maud herself knew all too well, winning a legal judgment and obtaining the payout were two separate matters. The Macdonalds felt rage and injustice after the judgment. But there was more fallout. When they read the *Globe* account of the trial, Ewan found himself identified as "husband of the novelist better known as L. M. Montgomery." Ewan rarely took strong positions, but this time he set his foot down: since he himself did not have the money to pay the judgment, he informed Maud that he would not allow her to use a penny of her savings to pay it for him. He had been driving the car, not she, so the judgment was against him, not her. The car was registered in his name, not hers. Fortunately, Maud had always kept her money separate from Ewan's, an unusual practice for a woman of that era. There was no legal recourse for Pickering, to his and Greig's disappointment, for they could not extract money from Maud's own bank account. Ewan's Presbyterian congregations were likewise outraged by the judgment. They rallied behind him and arranged to pay his salary in advance so it could not be garnisheed.

As so often happens with lawsuits, all participants would be losers. Pickering earned nothing but frustration. Rather than obtaining any money, Pickering had to lay out money himself to keep bringing Ewan to court over the next few years to testify that he, Ewan, was still unable to pay the judgment. Pickering knew that many villagers were snickering behind his back, and others in the community shunned him. They were unwilling to testify against him, but they knew that his condition had existed before the accident. Shortly after the trial was over, he himself developed diabetes, prompting Maud to comment wryly in her journals that it was enough to make one believe in "judgements from God." Pickering died in 1930.

The consequences of Riddell's judgment followed the Macdonalds to their graves. Maud had hoped that winning would dispel Ewan's feelings of "personal inadequacy." When he did not win, despite working so hard, Ewan took it as one more sign that he was an outcast from God. Before long, he sank into depression again. After the trial, gloom began to hang on him, and his posture and manner gave it away. He needed medications once more. The cheerful, sweet man that Maud had married was again replaced by a sad, morose one.

Maud's equilibrium was also upset by the Pickering affair. The case had poisoned the community atmosphere. Still, she managed to write all of *Emily of New Moon* between August 1921 (two months after the accident) and February 15, 1922 (before the trial came up in court). She wrote, "I have had more intense pleasure in writing it than any of the others—not even excepting *Green Gables*" (February 15, 1922). One can only be amazed at her discipline, and be thankful that she found exhilaration in writing fiction.

But as always in Maud's life, more was going on than was visible on the surface. Years earlier, the entrance of Ewan Macdonald as a promising suitor had fuelled the creation of lovable "Anne." Now, Maud put the same energy into *Emily of New Moon* that she had put into *Anne of Green Gables*, and felt the same intense pleasure in writing it. But it was not because of Ewan's presence this time. Now, the attention and admiration from another man helped bring "Emily" into being. That man was the Reverend Edwin Smith, now called "Captain Smith," a returning World War I war hero.

CHAPTER 11

Captain Edwin Smith

In Maud's ten volumes of personal journals, the name Edwin Smith appears only fourteen times, sometimes as a passing reference. He makes even fewer appearances in her scrapbooks. Yet in this period, he provides an interesting episode in the Macdonalds' history, allowing us to speculate on complexities in Maud's and Ewan's relationship. To understand the especial significance of Smith's very limited appearance in Maud's journals—and his disproportionate impact on the Macdonalds' life—we must loop back to the Island years, when Maud and Ewan were courting, and then leap forward again to 1919, when Edwin Smith re-entered the scene.

Maud gives only a cursory history of Captain Smith in an entry of September 1919, when he seems to reappear out of nowhere. She jauntily tells us that she had first heard of him when he was the Presbyterian minister in the Kensington parish. She says that she had never met him before he preached at Ewan's induction in Cavendish in 1903. She observes that he was then young, "lately married, very handsome and clever." She attributes to her friend Fanny Wise the observation, "That man is too good looking to be a minister."

In 1919, Smith came to Leaskdale to see them. Maud observes that by this time Smith has had "adventures galore." He is living in Oshawa, Ontario, with his family, working as an agent for the Imperial Life Insurance Company.

> I had expected to see a good deal of change in him. He is by now
> fifty years old. But he looks about 35. There is not a thread of gray
> in his thick black hair, not a line on his lean, handsome, almost

boyish face, not a trace of stoop or stodginess in his slender upright figure.

He entertained us brilliantly with his tales of adventure. He is certainly a rather universal genius, for he can preach, talk and write wonderfully well, is a Fellow of the R.A.S. of London, and is full of personal charm and magnetism.[47]

Then, she adds:

I rather think he lacks steadiness of purpose, with all his gifts, and so has been surpassed in his professional career by men who were far his inferiors in mental capacity.

This last line about Smith is dated September 21, 1919, but we do not know when she actually wrote it. (There was always a time-lag between events and their being recorded in her journals. Maud's procedure was to jot dated notes onto stray pieces of paper, and then, in the next stage, write them up into her formal "journal." Sometimes there was another intermediate stage where she did a preliminary write-up into an informal account that could be recopied, particularly if the subject was "delicate." At many points in her life, she was months, or years, behind in writing up events, as was the case here.) Maud's editorial comment about Smith's "lack of purpose" sounds strange in the context of their *first* reunion after an interlude of many years. However, the delay before this story of Smith's return was actually transcribed may help account for this slightly incongruous comment. (She only started recopying her journals in 1919 and it took her a long time to move from the beginning in 1889 to 1919, so she could shape her entries with the benefit of some hindsight.)

Edwin Smith is an enigma in Maud's saga. He and Ewan were approximately the same age, and both were graduates from Pine Hill Seminary in Halifax (then a Presbyterian training school, now the ecumenical Atlantic School of Theology). Edwin graduated in 1897, and Ewan in 1903. Both men were Scottish in descent, and their careers ran along parallel courses as Presbyterian ministers on the Island, their paths crossing many, many times in church meetings, according to the PEI newspapers, which gave extensive coverage to ministers' activities. But there was one major difference between their early careers: Smith's was as dazzling as Ewan's was undistinguished.

Smith was from Merigomish, Nova Scotia, and had been educated at Pictou Academy (1887–89), Dalhousie College (1891–92), Manitoba College (1892–96), and at Pine Hill Seminary (1896–97). At a time when Master's degrees were far more rare than Ph.D.s are today, he had taken his Master's degree at Manitoba, writing a short but solid thesis on "Heredity." He had then spent a year abroad in Britain, travelling and undertaking study at Oxford University. He started his preaching career at Shediac, New Brunswick, then moved to Kensington, PEI, where he came to Maud's attention through newspaper articles and relatives' accounts. When he preached at the induction service for Ewan Macdonald in Cavendish, Maud was not the only young, unmarried woman who noticed his good looks and buoyant carriage. But, sadly for them all, he had already married the pretty Grace Chambers of Tatamagouche, Nova Scotia, in 1897.

Smith was spectacularly successful in the ministry in Prince Edward Island. A mesmerizing speaker, a charmer with his warm and outgoing personality, and an unusually dynamic man of action, he also had an uncommon knack of seizing opportunities for adventure. In early 1903, his adoring parishioners in Kensington gave him a return train ticket to Vancouver and back — a first-class ticket, no less — so he could attend the Presbyterian Church's General Assembly. From this trip, the enterprising Smith developed a lecture called "Canada: From Ocean to Ocean," in which he lavishly praised and described the natural beauty of Canadian scenery, linking it all to God's bounty. But Smith did more than speak. He illustrated this lecture with stereopticon views. The stereopticon was an exciting new technology at the time, when only a few people had cameras and there were few means to see pictures of other places in the world, except in expensive books, themselves a rare commodity.

Talk of Smith's narrative gifts spread fast around the Island — the *Patriot* called him "eloquent, forcible, and effective" (June 2, 1903). He travelled around the Island giving his illustrated lecture, showing the landscapes of the rest of Canada. The newspapers carried constant and glowing accounts of his shows. He was so newsworthy that in December 1903 the *Guardian* even reported as news that Smith had driven from Kensington to Charlottetown in "four and a half hours." On December 21, 1903, his picture occupied the centre of page one in the *Guardian*, and the article there summarized his entire first sermon at Cardigan, where he had just moved. Newspapers claimed that he had been a brilliant student, a claim that was overstated.

Smith was notable for more than his speaking ability, however. He was also an accomplished yachtsman, a fact that gave him dash and glamour. The Island newspapers dubbed him affectionately the "nautical clergyman." He received province-wide attention when he purchased a new thirty-six-foot yacht called the *Volunte* before moving to Cardigan in 1903. During his years there, Smith continued sailing off the Island, lecturing about his travels (eventually charging admission to his lectures), and producing travel writing for various magazines.

On the Island, before radio and television, Islanders read their newspapers eagerly and attentively. These newspapers reported everything that happened across the Island, whether it was important or inconsequential: who came off of the ships from Boston, who was staying in what hotel, who had visited whom, whose horse had bolted, who had been born, married, or died. They talked about what they read. Ministers were the most important people in a community, and religion and politics were always newsworthy items. There was competition for good ministers, and parishioners basked in reflected glory when their ministers made the news. The dashing Reverend Smith was so well known that *The Daily Patriot* even carried the item that there had been several bidders when he offered his cow, "Dainty Lass," for sale in June 1905.

But on January 20, 1906, the *Examiner* did the unexpected: it carried a short and sharply critical editorial piece on Smith's popular lectures, saying that his "From Ocean to Ocean" talk was not in the "true interests of the Province" because it encouraged young people to depart by making the rest of Canada so appealing. Young Islanders had long been leaving the overcrowded province for advanced professional education, but now they were migrating permanently to the Canadian west. This loss of an educated, energetic young generation was becoming a serious political issue.

Smith, always a good sailor, took measure of the wind and quickly adjusted his sails: he cleverly refocused his lectures from the beauty of Canada *beyond* the Island to the beauty *within* Prince Edward Island. This was timely and smart.

The government of PEI had started organizing a campaign to promote tourism. Smith's new lectures on Prince Edward Island were so successful that the Island's Tourist and Development Association soon recruited him to speak about the Island's beauties in the United States. *The Daily Examiner* and *The Daily Patriot* gave him big write-ups when he delivered a series of "illustrated lectures on P.E. Island in New York, Providence, Boston, and other Eastern cities." He drew huge audiences. On June 23, 1907, the *Examiner* reported that the Island expected an influx of tourists after Smith's lectures in the United States. The tourist board suggested that if the Americans "seeking the restful shade of rural P.E. Island" were "well received, accommodated, and pleased, they will come again."

Between 1903 and 1906, while Smith was getting so much Island newspaper attention with his travels, talks, and activities, Ewan was the minister at Cavendish and courting Maud (who was busy writing *Anne of Green Gables*). Ewan rarely made the papers.

After some years at Cavendish, and buoyed by Maud's affections, by 1905 Ewan felt the need to distinguish himself in some way, too. There were different paths to success in the ministry, and one was through further education. Ewan—who could not have hoped to compete with someone like Edwin Smith for sheer *dazzle*—chose the route of further study, making the decision to take a postgraduate course of study in Scotland. On August 20, 1906, the *Patriot* describes his send-off from Cavendish with the typical laudatory write-up in the newspaper. But as we have seen, the schooling in Glasgow was not a success. The same week that Ewan sent Maud the blank and unsigned postcard from Scotland (March 4, 1907), Maud and other Islanders were reading that Edwin Smith had just addressed over four thousand people in the United States, about the beauty of Prince Edward Island. "This [talk by Edwin Smith] is the greatest advertisement this Island has ever had in the great Republic," the *Patriot* effused on March 6, 1907.

Maud had also been very alert to the province's desire to develop tourism in the 1903–1907 period, and she had sung its praises in her first novel, emphasizing its natural beauty. Between late 1906 and early 1907, she was quietly sending out *Anne of Green Gables* to publishers.

Smith continued to draw extravagant media attention: on April 21, 1907, the *Patriot* bragged that he was one of the best speakers *on the continent*.

The following day, April 22, 1907, the contract for *Anne of Green Gables* was being typed and mailed to Maud. She signed it on May 2, 1907. Maud and Edwin Smith seemed on parallel tracks to success and fame, towing their entire province behind them. Ewan, who was by then struggling to find a parish, was left behind in the dust.[48]

On January 25, 1908, Smith's second two-month speaking tour in the United States was announced; the *Patriot* published a handsome picture of him on the front page. Maud clipped it and pasted it into her scrapbook. On this same page in her scrapbook she placed a poem, with a maple leaf below it; Smith's picture is directly beneath these two items. The poem, "Winter in Lovers' Lane," by Clinton Scollard, begins:

> In Lovers' Lane 'tis winter now
> Will springtime never come again?

The poem ends:

> Those tremulous trystings, are they done. —
> The meeting joy, the parting pain?
> Will hearts no more be wooed and won
> In memory haunted lover's lane?
>
> Ah, wait till April's bugle call
> Reigns, rich with rapture, up the glen.
> Till may once more her flower thrall
> Weave amorously—and then—and then!

Although Maud pasted Smith's picture in her scrapbook, she does not even mention him in her (recopied) diary of this period. However, the proximity of these three items—the poem about "Lovers' Lane," the maple leaf of patriotism[49] and passion,[50] and Smith's picture all come together on one important page of her scrapbook: he is the man of a maiden's dreams, he is famous for advertising the landscape of Prince Edward Island and Canada, the country of the maple leaf, and he is linked to the intimate Island lane that Maud most associated with romance, dreams, and awakening.

While Smith had been off promoting Prince Edward Island tourism in the United States in the early months of 1908, the L. C. Page Company of Boston had been preparing to publish *Anne of Green Gables*. By June 1908, Maud's little red-headed girl was launched as the Island's greatest ambassador ever. Ewan's courtship had figured prominently in the creation of little "Anne," but Edwin Smith, whose eye had seen (and speeches had touted) the beauty of the Island so effectively, alerting Maud even more to the possibilities of speaking and writing evocatively about landscape, was also a fellow traveller in her imagination. They were kindred spirits through their joint promotion of her beloved Island. It was, in the curious and complicated way that Maud's affections worked, a creative *ménage à trois*.

The rest is history: no fictional character has ever done for a province's tourism what little "Anne" did for the Island. Smith's public speaking skills initially promoted Island tourism, heightening Maud's awareness of the romantic possibilities in its unique landscape, and then her literary skills embellished, in words, the enchanting picture of the Island. Maud's "Anne" became the Island's foremost tourist icon, first reinforcing, and then completely overtaking Smith's efforts. Almost immediately after *Anne*'s publication, newspapers reported an influx of tourists in search of its heroine.

This all should have thrilled Maud, who had been ambitious to write a "woman's humble name" on the scrolls of fame. However, she focused on another worry. No longer facing a bleak, impoverished existence after Anne's success in 1908, Maud now wondered if she had committed herself to an unwise engagement. She knew that Ewan had come into her life in its "loneliest hour" and had given her the affection she had needed to write in a positive state of mind, but in the ensuing period she had seen that Ewan was a man of disturbing limitations. His slump in Scotland had alarmed her. She could not help comparing him with a man like the dashing and already married Smith, whose success by that time only underlined Ewan's failure to rise in the ecclesiastical world. It is no wonder that she herself suffered a nervous collapse after *Anne* was published, partly from the overwhelming public attention, but partly because of her ambivalence about the engagement.

The Island was not quite ready for the influx of American tourists brought in by Smith's speeches and by Maud's book. Smith had urged the well-heeled millionaires to motor to the Island for their summer holidays in 1907 and 1908, but as soon as the tourists came en masse in their cars, neither the Islanders—nor their horses—liked these noisy newfangled contraptions. This heated up an issue simmering on the Island. Public opposition to automobiles grew more forceful as the belching and sputtering machines proliferated. Angry letters blitzed the newspapers, both pro and con them. The April 4, 1908, issue of the *Patriot* announced a bill to "prohibit the running of all motor vehicles upon the streets and roads of this province under a fine of $500 or 6 months in jail." Five hundred dollars was a year's salary—a very stiff fine.

Someone wrote to the *Patriot* to point out that abolishing automobiles from Island roads would damage all Smith's good work in promoting the province: would the well-heeled tourists even come to the Island, this writer asked, "if they had to leave their automobiles behind"? But, incredibly, in 1908, a complete ban on automobiles was instituted in Prince Edward Island.[51]

The 1908 law undercut all of Smith's promotion of the Island as a tourist destination, and Smith was undoubtedly annoyed. A restless adventurer, he soon decided that it was time to move on. On May 11, 1909, Smith resigned as pastor of St. Andrew's Presbyterian Church in Cardigan, and this again drew newspaper attention, although less than one would expect. When asked to reconsider his resignation, he told people that he had already accepted a position as assistant editor with the *Presbyterian Witness* and would leave the Island at the end of June. "He wields an incisive and vigorous pen, and will no doubt achieve success in his new position. He will not forsake the pulpit, but will preach frequently in different churches, where his work calls him," wrote *The Daily Patriot*, graciously. Smith had been steadily supplementing his income with travel writing for various magazines, and he continued this, travelling by his yacht to places—Newfoundland, for example—that he wanted to write about. By June 28, 1909, Smith had bought himself a newer and bigger yacht, this one sporting both sails and *a gasoline engine*. He was always one of the first to make use of new technology in travel, photography, and communication. His move to the mainland took him out of the Prince Edward Island newspapers, but it focussed attention on the fact that ambitious ministers were leaving the Island.

It was only *after* Smith's departure from the Island that Ewan took the initiative of attending the Presbyterian Church General Assembly in Toronto, looking for a new position and a fresh start off the Island. He got his position in Leaskdale and Zephyr, Ontario, and was inducted on March 15, 1910.

Smith first moved to Nova Scotia, then to Alberta, and finally returned to Ontario. In November 1915, he accepted a call to be minister at the very beautiful Avondale Presbyterian Church in Tillsonburg, a small town between Toronto and Detroit. Maud does not mention this in her journals, but she does paste a picture of the handsome church and Smith in her scrapbooks. (How or where she got the clipping is unknown, but she could have cut it from a church publication.)

At the time the war broke out, Canadians of British extraction were deeply patriotic. Like most ministers, Smith depicted the war as a struggle against the dark forces of evil. Like Ewan, he assisted at recruitment or "patriotic" rallies.

Unlike Ewan, however, Smith was a "man of action." He and his wife, Grace, had produced seven children since their marriage in 1897. At age forty-six, in 1916, Smith did an astonishing thing: he obtained a leave of absence from his congregation and, leaving his family, volunteered for military service, travelling to England to train at the Royal Naval College. He won first-class honours in all subjects (with much better marks than he had scored in theology school, where he had been a good but erratic student). From then until 1918, he served in the British Navy.

The Toronto Star of September 22, 1917, carried a big article about Edwin Smith entitled "Canadian Parson, Naval Officer: First man from this country to win commission in British navy / A Thorough Briton / When war began he left his church in Tillsonburg to Command a Patrol Boat." He became famous for being the only ordained clergyman who ever commanded one of His Majesty's ships of war.[52]

After the war was over, in 1919, Smith returned to Canada and to his family, moving to Oshawa. Ewan and Maud had spent much of that summer in Boston, where Ewan had had treatments with Dr. Nathan Garrick. Shortly after their return in September 1919, Smith—now known as *Captain* Smith of the British Royal Navy—turned up in Leaskdale to visit them. He was now very famous as a war hero. He came to visit Maud and Ewan at the precise time that Ewan's mental health was at its most vulnerable.[53]

Of course, Smith knew Ewan reasonably well, having associated with him frequently in church meetings before they left the Island, but there was no other strong bond between them. (In fact, these earlier church meetings had often been chaired by Smith, with Ewan only a participant.) But Captain Smith, like every literate reader in Canada, knew that Maud had become famous, and without doubt he was impressed by her success. A man of wide-ranging literary and intellectual interests himself, he had always written for periodicals. No doubt he thought it would be interesting to talk about old times on the Island, to hear how celebrity had affected Maud, and, most of all, to regale both Maud and Ewan with his war adventures. Smith was a superb raconteur in private, a spellbinding speaker in public, and a treat to have as a guest.

Smith was also a guest who came with a long history. The past successes of this astonishing speaker would now be repositioned in Ewan's fragile present, threatening him again. Maud speaks several times in her journals of Ewan's deep-seated sense of inadequacy, but she does not say how flattered and pleased *she* is that the famous Captain Smith is now seeking them out.

Maud felt anxiety when Ewan first went to Uxbridge to pick up Smith on September 13, 1919. He was depressed, and they had words just before he set out for the station. Maud tried to reason him into banishing his "false and blasphemous ideas" about being "damned." In exasperation, she told him he had "responsibilities": he "had brought two children into the world." He retorted: "Yes, and I wish from the bottom of my heart I never had." This was unlike Ewan.

Then he added, "Well, I must go to meet Smith I suppose. Your idea is that I must go on till I drop." With these bitter words, he left for the station.

To Maud's surprise, when Ewan returned from Uxbridge he was a different man. According to her journal, he was chatting amiably about "old times" with the engaging and irrepressible Smith. On Sunday, September 14, Smith acted as supply minister, after a summer of supply ministers, in the ailing Ewan's pulpit. Smith spoke to both of Ewan's congregations. He had fascinating stories to tell about his own heroic experiences as captain of a fleet patrolling the German-infested waters of the English Channel. Promoted to lieutenant in the war, Smith was proud that his men were personally "inspected" and praised by the King of England.

As a special token of thanks after the war, the British government had given him his own personal copy of the film they made from footage of the war. A copy of this historical film, *The Empire's Shield*, is in the British War Museum in London, England. (Smith himself does not appear in it.) Riding on his fame after the war, Smith resumed his travels and speeches, but now in the capacity of a "war hero." He travelled throughout Canada and the United States, talking about the war, and using the novelty of the silent film to illustrate his talks. Ewan's parishioners could now hear this charismatic speaker in person. In a religious setting, Smith's battle stories seemed to prove that God was always with *him*, supporting the righteous side, and that he was one of God's many brave warriors. This must have been hard for Ewan to hear, feeling that he was himself one of God's outcasts.

Smith stayed on with the Macdonalds on that visit in September 1919— and on and on—for almost five days, telling them of his adventures. This was a long time to leave a wife and seven children who had not seen him during the entire time he was at war. Maud was an avid listener, starved as she was for good conversation and companionship after a summer of Ewan's depression and withdrawal. Smith's illustrious career again shone a bright light on Ewan's dingy one, but the immediate effect of his visit was stimulating, probably because it distracted Ewan temporarily from his demons.

After Smith's first visit to the Macdonalds in September 1919, Ewan stayed reasonably well until mid-November. Then he slid into depression again. This prompted more visits from Smith, who was always happy to put on his minister's gown and preach for Ewan. The Reverend Edwin Smith, now out of the ministry, missed having an audience. Maud loved his company—he pulled her out of her own preoccupation with Ewan's condition. Smith always came without his wife, who stayed home with their family. Smith became a frequent visitor throughout the next four years, bringing much needed intellectual companionship to Maud's constricted life.

In December 1917, Maud had hired a new maid named Lily Meyers, the sister of the earlier maid, Edith Meyers (and no relation to Lily Reid, the first maid). She was a lively and temperamental young woman, but a hard worker. She came from Zephyr, where her family lived close to Marshall Pickering. She was also a gossip, and an indiscreet one. At first, Lily did well as a maid. She was cute and funny, and had a number of possible suitors. She seemed satisfied with her work, expecting no doubt to leave as soon as she had found a young man to marry. But romances came and went, and several years later, when no proposals had come to rescue her, Lily became increasingly cross and disgruntled. (See Maud's journal entries of April 8, 17, 1921; May 8, 1921; March 29, 1924.)

An unrestrained rumour-monger, Lily began to prattle on in the community about the Macdonalds' friendship with Smith. This friendship would have been seen as normal by most everyone, given that Ewan and Edwin had known each other on the Island, and "down-easterners" were known to be clannish. But Lily could see something different in the dynamic between Smith and the Macdonalds. Maud came to life when Smith arrived. Increasingly, Ewan sat in silence, listening during their animated and witty conversations. Lily could not have understood that Ewan was ill with depression, and merely saw that he looked sullen and morose. Each time Lily went home, she took gossip to Zephyr, and when she returned, she brought that village's gossip back.

To people in the Leaskdale and Zephyr community, it would have been unthinkable for a minister's wife to carry on with another man—and a married minister at that. Maud would certainly never have done anything disreputable, but she was human enough to enjoy Smith's attention and admiration as well as his stimulating conversation.

Smith continued selling insurance for the Imperial Life Insurance Company of Oshawa, and Maud bought a $20,000 life insurance policy from him. By July 1920, the Smiths had moved to Whitby, even closer to Leaskdale. Maud notes that on July 24, 1920, Captain Smith motored in, and in no time had them all "cheered up." She adds: "There is something infectiously healthy about his personality—you simply *catch* optimism from him. He stayed all night and we had a very pleasant evening . . ." She adds that since they live only thirty miles apart, "we can be neighbourly."

On August 28, 1920, the Macdonalds motored to Whitby to visit the Smiths. Upon their arrival, Ewan began complaining of headache and exhibiting symptoms of depression. Maud added to her August 1920 account of this particular visit to Whitby: "Mrs. Smith is a nice matronly person but not especially stimulating. I liked her, however." As she damned with such faint praise, Maud knew very well that she herself was *never* boring.

In May 1921, Smith drove to Leaskdale to collect Maud, who was giving a speech at Whitby's Ladies' College. Sounding not unlike "Anne" entering Avonlea for the first time, Maud effused as they travelled to Whitby: "We motored through a spring world of young leaf and blossom and had a wonderful drive." She stayed overnight with the Smiths. Ewan and the boys drove in to retrieve her the next day.

This time Ewan came looking morose and bearing tales of their increasingly cantankerous maid, Lily. He expected Maud to come home and deal with the "Lily problem." Lily had always alternated between being "amiable and well behaved" and sulky and insolent (September 13, 1923). Moreover, she had been working in the manse nearly five years now (since 1917), and was bored with her job. Maud resented Lily's untidiness and increasing failure to do the required work. Maud had plenty of other things on her mind, including the ongoing lawsuit with Page. But she was afraid to scold Lily: "Lily is the sort of girl who, if sent away from a place, would revenge herself by telling lies everywhere about the ménage she had left" (October 24, 1922). Maud was quite sure that Lily had been gossiping about Smith's visits. This embittered her further. There was no way that Maud could discuss this gossiping with Lily, who would have turned any mention of it into even juicier gossip.

It was shortly after Maud's speech at Whitby Ladies' College, accompanied by Smith, that poor, distracted Ewan had crashed into Marshall Pickering on June 11, 1921.

Later that month, the Macdonalds and the Smiths were planning a joint drive to Prince Edward Island. They would each drive their own cars, traveling in tandem, with the Macdonalds in one car, and the Smiths and another couple in the Smiths' car. Such a plan seems bizarre: the front car would throw up dust from the roads, and the car behind, with open windows, would harvest it all. Motoring with open windows in hot weather would make conversation all but impossible. And the dust that blew through the cars would stick to sweaty bodies and clothes. This trip, in July 1921, was predictably a nightmare. (See description of it in journal entry of August 11, 1921.)

Maud, ever the photographer, took a picture of the three couples picnicking along the way. It shows Smith as his usual vigorous self, but Ewan looks pitifully estranged from the circle of friends, and both angry and sad. In the photo he removes himself from the group, and even though he hides behind his dark glasses, he is no doubt feeling considerable internal pain.

That November (1921), Ewan and Maud again motored to Whitby so that she could speak in the Methodist church. Ewan's state of mind had further deteriorated. Right before they left on November 6, Maud had a terrible session with him. She again pried out of him a frightening admission: that he wanted to commit suicide, but was too much of a "coward" to do so. She wrote in her journal:

> He is no more like the man I married than—he is *not* the man I married. An altogether different personality is there—and a personality which is repulsive and abhorrent to me. And yet to this personality I must be a wife. It is horrible—it is indecent—it should not be. I feel degraded and unclean. (November 1, 1921)

Smith's next recorded visit seems to have been on February 28, 1922. Ewan was away once again "preaching for a call" and Captain Smith came to fill in for him. Maud casually and jauntily writes:

>Captain Smith . . . was here both Saturday and Sunday nights and
>we spent both evenings talking of a thousand subjects. It is such a
>delight to have a real conversation with a companion of intellect
>and sympathy. Captain Smith is one of the few people I have met
>with whom I can discuss with absolute frankness, any and every
>subject, even the delicate ones of sex. Sex is to men and women
>one of the most vital subjects in the world—perhaps *the* most vital
>subject since our total existence is based on and centres around it.
>Yet with how few, even of women, can this vital subject be frankly
>and intelligently discussed. It is so overlaid with conventions, inhi-
>bitions and taboos that it is almost impossible for anyone to see it
>as it really is. (February 28, 1922)

This evening of free-ranging discussions, on topics like "sex . . . as it really
is," must have kept Lily's ear to the keyhole, especially given Ewan's
absence.

To make matters more suspicious to Lily, the next day Maud and Smith
left alone together for Toronto, leaving her behind to watch over Stuart and
Chester, now aged seven and ten. In Toronto, Maud and Captain Smith met
up with Mrs. Smith, as well as with Ewan, who had been away preaching "for
a call." They all went to Massey Hall to hear the controversial Mrs. Margot
Asquith, Countess of Oxford and Asquith, lecture on her very frank memoirs.

Mrs. Asquith was the outspoken second wife of Herbert Henry Asquith, the
British prime minister from 1908 to 1916, who had led Britain into war. Mrs.
Asquith was a noted wit, a society woman, and "personality." She was uninhibited to the point of being scandalous, and full of often indiscreet gossip about
her friends in the literary and political worlds, with a reputation that had travelled around the British Empire. Like Maud in that she kept a diary, Mrs.
Asquith had written and published, from 1920 to 1922, a two-volume autobiography that shocked readers, including Maud. But Maud had read in Mrs.
Asquith's memoirs that Henry James had read her diary in 1915 and told her that
she was the "Balzac of diarists," catching the essence of people, and pulling the
secrets out of "crooked lives." (Maud's entry of December 13, 1920, gives her
less-than-impressed comments about Mrs. Asquith's autobiography.)

It is not hard to imagine the tales Lily could have spun in her own head
about Maud and Captain Smith driving off to Toronto together, knowing that
would make juicy gossip in Zephyr.

There is no mention of the Smiths again until July 1922, when the Macdonalds stayed over with them on their way to Niagara. By this time, the Macdonalds were very preoccupied with the Pickering lawsuit, with the court date set for the trial on November 23, 1922.

In the second week of May 1923, Smith filled in for Ewan again when he was away in Prince Edward Island, and Maud accompanied him to the Zephyr service. Maud and Ewan had long felt tension with some of the Zephyr congregation. Maud particularly disliked a woman named Mrs. Will Lockie who was adept at delivering gratuitous and subtle insults to her. (Entries of April 6, 1922, and November 16, 1922, show Maud's views on Mrs. Will Lockie. Maud was fond of some other women also named Mrs. Lockie.)

On the way out of the church that Sunday, an amiable parishioner remarked to Maud that the congregation missed Ewan; Mrs. Will Lockie quipped within Maud's hearing, "Oh, well, we had a very good sermon. Captain Smith seemed to take so well with the young people" (May 13, 1923). Maud fumed silently over the implication that Ewan did not, even though she knew it was true. Mrs. Lockie's greater insult, however, lay in the subtle inference that Ewan and Smith were somehow competitors. The congregations of Leaskdale and Zephyr could not help feel the difference between these two preachers: a depressed and stiff Ewan and a dynamic Edwin Smith. Maud was only too aware of Ewan's deficiencies, but hearing Mrs. Lockie's putting them out in the open was demeaning. Maud knew Ewan had never been good with young people; he was, as his son Stuart later said, the "kind of man who is born old." But Maud was loyal to her husband.

Smith continued to come to supply frequently when Ewan was going elsewhere to preach for a call, and time after time, the call went to someone else. The congregation surmised in time that Ewan had not gotten the appointment he was likely seeking. Maud grew increasingly angry with Lily's prattles, and complained vigorously about her in her journals. But she did not identify the real cause for her anger at Lily for feeding the gossip upon which people like Mrs. Will Lockie dined.

The next time Smith came to preach for Ewan when Ewan was away, Mrs. Smith came also. Perhaps Maud had urged it, hoping to lay to rest Lily's gossip. For this visit, Lily had been sent home. Maud writes in her diary with an airy nonchalance that obscures the underlying nuances:

For a wonder this was a fine Sunday and Mrs. Smith came up with the Captain. We had a pleasant day, for Lily went home last night. In spite of the extra work this entails I am always heartily glad when she is out of the house, when I have my own friends here. We are free then to talk as we please with no outsider to *hear, tattle, and pervert.* [*Italics added*] (May 27, 1923)

Maud and Mrs. Smith went over to Zephyr *together* for the service on May 27. Afterwards, Maud greeted Mrs. William Lockie as people filed out, and she took the magisterial high road, saying, "as usual . . . most graciously, 'How do you do, Mrs. Lockie?'" Maud reports that the surprised Mrs. Lockie stammered out, "I'm glad to meet you," as if they had just met for the first time in their lives.

Maud's method of letting certain people know they displeased her was to treat them with extremely courteous formality. Mrs. Lockie's inappropriate reply shows that Maud accomplished exactly what she had intended with her frosty civility: she rattled Mrs. Lockie, making her feel foolish. Maud chuckles with satisfaction that Mrs. Lockie in her awkward reply "surpassed herself."

Many years later, in 1986, when Lily was an old woman, but still very lively, I interviewed her about her time with "Mrs. Macdonald." When asked if she remembered "Captain Smith," she certainly did. Looking quite smug, Lily lowered her voice, and leaned forward so that another woman who was present (Mrs. Wilda Clark, a strong admirer of Mrs. Macdonald) could not hear her words. Lily then whispered in a salacious and conspiratorial tone: "*He* was *her boyfriend.*" She added a smutty and dismissive, "*Hmmmph.*" Her tone was that of someone in possession of gossip she intended to withhold, knowing that suggestive innuendoes are more damning than specific allegations.

For Maud to dabble in an extramarital affair would have been impossible in a fishbowl like the Presbyterian manse, with a gossipy and inquisitive maid constantly eavesdropping. And people who remembered Smith said that, for all his charm, he was not a "ladies' man." He was "a man's man"—one who liked adventure, new technologies, and the kind of intellectual discussions few women were educated enough to participate in. He had his faults, too, and Maud could see them, summing him up as lacking "steadiness of purpose," thus being "surpassed in his professional career by men who were far his inferiors in mental capacity." (Her assessment seems accurate in light of Smith's subsequent career, but this would not have been immediately apparent in

1919. Her comment would have been interpolated later when she had more idea how to shape her story, and after she wanted to reduce Smith's significance in her journals.)[54]

This is not to say that Maud didn't *dream* about other men making more exciting husbands than the one she had married, or that she didn't appreciate Smith's company. Her life would obviously have been very different if Ewan had been a vigorous man, sharing her range of interests. But Maud knew that as a minister's wife she must be an impeccable role model. She also had a will of steel, however volatile her emotions might be, and she knew from painful childhood experiences that nothing escaped community eyes very long. Gossip had been the strongest force of social control during her youth, and whatever other monumental changes had occurred in the world since the war, this was not among them. She had lost her unquestioning belief in all the tenets of her ancestors' stern Presbyterian religion, but she had not lost her sense of propriety and dignity.

Even in her nineties, Lily was a pretty woman with much vitality, a quick eye, and a decidedly down-to-earth orientation. She had been brought up in a Victorian world where men and women lived in different and unequal spheres, and she could not have understood how a man and a woman could have a friendship based on mutual intellectual interests. She would not have understood the appeal of intellectual companionship for someone like Maud, especially when Smith admired her professional accomplishments— admiration she craved but had received from no other close acquaintance except Frede. Lily lacked intellectual depth and experience of life outside her small rural community, and it was much later in the twentieth century that non-sexualized friendships became possible for men and women.

However, as limited as Lily was in understanding, she understood that everyone in the community had an insatiable interest in what went on inside their minister's household, with his famous wife. If Lily, who was the type of person who traded in gossip and would therefore have made an effort to listen to Maud and Captain Smith conversing, heard Maud and Smith discussing any aspect of sexuality, she would have drawn damaging conclusions. She would have been very willing, as Maud puts it, "to tattle and pervert," especially after Maud had "dressed her down" (October 24, 1922), which must have rankled for a long time. Lily's vacuous prattles, no doubt given salacious embellishment, did enormous damage to Maud's peace of mind in the Leaskdale community and made her willing in the end to leave it, even if she attributed their move to other factors. Gossip that Maud had been a high-spirited and flirtatious teenager had hurt her when she was young. Gossip about the Herman Leard affair had embarrassed her when she was a young woman. Now idle and untrue gossip infuriated her in her married years.

Had Maud been less sensitive, and less beset in other areas of her life, she might have ignored it, rather than letting it rankle. But it was a problem to deal with in her journal, since stories might linger long after her death, as indeed they did in the case of Herman. Hence, Maud wrote a great deal about Lily's moral failures in her journals so that if any of Lily's damaging gossip lingered years later, people would understand that Lily was just a speculative and low-minded maid with a prurient curiosity and tongue.

After 1923, the Smiths moved to Williamsburg, below Ottawa on the St. Lawrence River, and they are not mentioned again. Why? We do not know, but it is surprising since Maud normally kept up with good friends all her life. She was a dedicated letter-writer, and distance did not normally affect her friendships. Ewan and Smith were on different sides of the "Church Union" debate, but this is not likely to have caused a rupture, since the Macdonalds did not let disagreement over Union break up their other long-standing friendships, with John and Margaret Stirling, for example.

It is more likely that Maud herself cut off the relationship with Smith, once Lily's gossip was abroad in the community and Mrs. Smith had made her appearance to shut it down. It is also plausible that Ewan heard some gossip from malicious parishioners and complained to Maud that people were getting the wrong idea. Gossip could also have come home through Chester. His classmates made vicious sport at school by saying hurtful things to upset and rile him. Maud would have terminated her friendship if she felt it was hurting her family. Whatever the cause, there is a profound silence around the Smiths' departure, and "Captain Smith" vanishes from the journals after 1923.[55]

We do not know when Maud gave Captain Smith the typewriter on which she had written *Anne of Green Gables*, but it was an extraordinary gift, considering that she kept every object associated with her own fame. This old typewriter was one of her most sentimental possessions. In this symbolic gift to Captain Smith, Maud recognized their joint professional beginnings in Prince Edward Island, their individual roles in making it a tourist destination, and their shared emotional experiences through the power of words. He was a valued "kindred spirit" of hers, at least for awhile.[56]

When the Smiths moved out of the Macdonalds' lives so suddenly and apparently permanently, it was a serious blow to Maud. She lost a friend who provided friendship, good conversation, and admiration of her talents, and who had much in common with her. First she had lost Frede, then Smith. While his presence is briefly glossed in Maud's journals, his force in the Macdonalds' lives is erased, and he remains a mysteriously silent topic.

CHAPTER 12

Maud and her journals

Maud was fourteen years old in 1889, when she started keeping little "diaries" in assorted notebooks. Thirty years later, she decided to copy these diaries into uniform legal-size ledgers, pasting in pictures, making a record of her life. These journals would become an essential part of her life—as joyful companions, as therapy, and finally as compulsion.

By the end of 1919, Maud had become a very lonely woman. Although she had her children, Frede's death and Ewan's illness had left her feeling isolated, and again mourning the early loss of her own parents. Her journal gave her a fellow traveller in an increasingly troubled terrain. She wrote in her journals that, "It is the *lonely* people who keep diaries. . . . When I have anybody to 'talk it over with' I don't feel the need of a diary so strongly. When I haven't I must have a journal to overflow in. It is a companion—and a relief." Her journals were "the other side of a conversation that began in reading" (an observation coined by historian Nick Whistler). She could record what she was reading and add her mental musings about it, as well as jotting down phrases and aphorisms she especially liked. Finding comfort in her journal brought dignity to a life disturbed by personal loss and crushing loneliness.

As a minister's wife—and as a very judgmental person—her more frank private thoughts had to be carefully hidden from view. Her tendency to sarcasm and irony needed management. She wrote, "Temperaments such as mine *must* have some outlet, else they become morbid and poisoned by 'consuming their own smoke,' and the only *safe* outlet is in some record as this" (February 11, 1910). The journal kept the two sides of her persona—the public and the private—well enough connected that she did not implode.

She also wanted her journal to be a social record of an era that was undergoing rapid transformation. After World War I, Maud realized that massive social changes were underway, and she realized that her own life was strad-dling this divide. As an amateur historian, she wanted to preserve the memory of the old, and record her life's trajectory into the new.

As she created these journals, she found another use for them—she could once again visit her childhood through the mere act of recopying and re-thinking the story of her life. She used her early journals to spin her early memories of rural community life into new novels and stories.

Her novels required happy endings—that was expected by her publishers and readers—but there were deeper soundings in her own life, and her jour-nals provided the counterpoint for her sunny novels. When Maud began the project of writing out her own life's record, she did it partly to bring sanity and control back into her life, but she also wanted a record of what her life had re-ally been like—the darker side that was largely kept private. The journals be-came her space for self-display and self-examination.

By 1919, when she started recopying her journals, Maud's books were fa-mous all over the English-speaking world.[57] She knew that she was an author whose life would be scrutinized by later biographers. If she wrote her own life in her journals, she hoped to have some control over how her story would eventually be told. There were grievances she wanted to air, and other things she wanted to conceal (or reshape). She had succeeded against enormous odds in her professional and personal life, and she wanted the world to see how admirably she had negotiated her way through innumer-able minefields.

When the massive re-copying project started in 1919 progressed, Maud saw that there were minefields of another kind in the actual process of writing up a journal. When diaries become the place to express the repressed side of a personality, they are likely become an unbalanced repository. Maud noticed this when she reread what she had written in periods of sadness and gloom, saying that her journals gave:

> . . . the impression of a morbid temperament, generally in the throes of nervousness and gloom. Yet this, too, is false. It arises from the fact that of late years I have made my journal the refuge of my sick spirit in its unbearable agonies. The record of pain seems thus almost unbroken; yet in reality these spasms came at long intervals. . . . Between these times I was quite tolerably happy, hopeful and interested in life. (February 11, 1910)

Maud was, however, a person of many moods, and the mood she was in when she recopied an old diary entry into her journal could affect its retelling. She often looked back on things recorded long ago and saw them in a different light. Sometimes she would even change her take on certain events already recorded in her finished journals—for instance, the pages that tell of her courtship with Ewan are razored out and replaced so neatly that the alteration is hard to spot in the handwritten volumes.

She began her recopying with the month of September 1889, when she was not quite fifteen. In other words, all the journal entries (which are the reconstruction of material from her earlier notebooks and notes) are written in retrospect, by a woman in her mid-forties. Her journals may *appear* to be a seamless, continuous narrative of a life, written easily in dated entries, as her life itself unfolds, but her process is far more subtle than one of making artless jottings that miraculously transform themselves into an engrossing narrative. Still, while she may shape her narrative, she tells us that she intended "as far as in me lies, to paint my life and deeds—ay, and my thoughts—truthfully, no matter how unflattering such truth may be to me. No life document has any real value otherwise." She added that "the worst as well as the best must be written out—*and* the best as well as the worst, since we are, every one of us, whether we own to it sincerely or not, angel and devil mixed up together . . ." But shaping, pruning, shading, and amplifying would be any writer's prerogative.

On April 16, 1922, she finished copying her childhood diaries into the formal journal ledgers, and from that point on she made daily jottings on pads or pieces of scrap paper, dating these and giving enough information to remind her of the events once she was ready to expand them into a journal entry. At several particularly troubled periods in her life, she stopped writing altogether, but she always resumed when she found her footing again in a few years. There was usually enough time-lag that she could select what was worth recording and shape things in her mind. Because her entries were written from notes, and because her memory was so good, her journal entries always have great immediacy. But it is always important to consider how the time-lag affects their reliability, and adds to the overall complexity of her journals.

Real life is untidy, unshaped, with loose ends. Her journals have no loose ends, no pointless stories, no catalogues of the boring effluvia of life, no people of importance to her narrative who have not been introduced. Each descriptive or narrative unit always becomes part of a unified whole.

As an artist, Maud had a strong instinct for literary shaping operating at both an unconscious and a conscious level. Each of the ten *early* recopied journal ledgers took on a shape of its own. For instance, her second volume gives a fierce resumé of her distresses in childhood, which shifts the reality of the relatively happy childhood of the first volume into a myth of symbolic orphanhood. But the myth would remain an important fixture in her own self-image. *Anne of Green Gables* was the glorious result of her mostly happy childhood, as described in Volume One, but *Emily of New Moon* grew out of the later myth of the orphaned, unloved child, fighting obstacles the whole way to success.

When she began recopying Volume Three of her journal sometime between 1920 and 1921, she was finishing the retrospective of her life in Cavendish. She began this third volume as if it were a book in its own right, not a continuous narrative of a life. The shape of her journal, with its blank pages from one to five hundred, had already begun to interact with—and perhaps mediate—the way she was shaping the story of her own life. She described a "curious feeling of reluctance" as she began the new volume. With the benefit of hindsight, she comments on Volumes One and Two of her earlier journals.

> The first volume seems . . . to have been written by a rather shallow girl, whose sole aim was to "have a good time" and who thought of little else than the surface play of life. Yet nothing could be falser to the reality. As a child and young girl I had a strange, deep, hidden inner life of dreams and aspirations, of which hardly a hint appears in the written record. This was partly because I had not then learned the art of self-analysis . . . and partly because I did not then feel the need of a confidant in my journal. I looked upon it merely as a record of my doings which might be of interest to me in after years . . . (February 11, 1910)

She vows to achieve a better balance in Volume Three.

As Maud, now in her forties, wrote up her childhood, a new character, "Maudie," began to emerge. Maudie resembled aspects of all her heroines, but was far more complex than either Anne, Emily, Valancy, or Marigold. Maud's writerly instincts told her that emphasizing early hardships would make adult achievement more impressive. This is an autobiographical technique long used by writers, politicians, and other successful professionals. But this involved a certain amount of refiguring the actual facts.

In her journals, "Maudie" fights great odds: she is an unusually sensitive, precocious child, easily hurt, with no parents to stand up for her. She was isolated and lonely in her childhood, raised by two old grandparents who had little understanding of or sympathy for her. She was persecuted by some of her teachers and jealous cousins, scolded and berated by her relatives for her ambitious "scribbling," but she persevered in spite of every discouragement. In fact, however, Maud's real childhood was, for the most part, happy. Although she suffered from a sense of difference as she grew up, this difference came from being an "elite" member of the community (and a child who was better dressed and smarter than others).

Maud had read an enormous amount by the time she began rewriting and shaping her own journals. Keeping diaries was a fad in the late nineteenth century. It allowed women of intelligence and leisure to express themselves when they had no public forum. Male statesmen in the corridors of power also kept diaries, but these were naturally very different from women's private, domestic diaries. Maud complained that Edward Gibbon, following the male Victorian model of objective, rational, controlled writing, had put none of his personality into his memoirs. She determined to map new territory for women: she would write a life history with the emotion and personality deliberately left in.

Still, all this said, there are only rare glimpses of how Maud actually *thinks* and *feels* about *herself*. We learn how she sees herself through the eyes of others, including her husband, her children, her husband's parishioners, and her fans. We also hear what she does, what she thinks about others, and how she feels about everything, but we see little of what she truly thinks about herself. Maud was a very guarded and private person, even in her journals. Playfully, she pasted in a picture of herself, taken in the Leaskdale kitchen, which shows her intuitive understanding of the ways an autobiographical writer operates, and how pictures can be read as texts. She holds a fan up to conceal her face, which is in turn covered with a veil.

Towards the end of 1920, Maud indulged in a piece of self-analysis. Prompted by "Mrs. Asquith's Autobiography," Maud asks herself whether a truly frank and incisive self-analysis is ever possible, and she writes that *she* is the one person in a thousand who *does know* her own weaknesses and strengths. "But I could not, even in these diaries which no eye but mine ever sees, write frankly down what I discern in myself," she admits (December 13, 1920).

In another paragraph of her journals written up at the same time, she writes that she has "not yet found anything much pleasanter than talking with the right kind of a man—except—but I won't write it. My descendants might be shocked." Speculating on love in that same long entry (January 31, 1920), she mentions Herman Leard—"a memory which I would not barter for anything save the lives of my children and the return of Frede."

At this point in late January 1920, and perhaps at the time of the "fan" picture, she was recopying the 1898 section of her journals concerning Herman. Were all of her raptures about her unfulfilled love with Herman really about Herman? Or did she displace some private feelings for the attractive and virile Captain Smith, a man seen so often during Ewan's breakdowns, onto Herman Leard? Did the poem "The Bride Dreams," finished in February 1921, come wholly out of her *imaginary life* with Herman—or partly with Smith? Or did the memory fuse both?

More important, did the actual man matter? Maud did suffer from thwarted passion and unfulfilled desires, but the specific men who aroused her dream life may have been immaterial. Maud felt her every emotion with intensity, but she had learned from her self-contained British grandmother to maintain an aura of dignity and reserve. To betray your raw passions in front of people was "cheap"—and dangerous, too, for it made your weaknesses visible to your enemies. In her fiction, Maud took emotions she knew and attributed them to a spectrum of imaginary characters. In her journals, she appears to have reversed the process, taking her emotions and attaching them—sometimes arbitrarily—to suitable real-life characters.

Since Maud intended her journals to be truthful, she was unable and unwilling to falsify the emotional core of her experience, but sometimes she gives us only part of the picture in cold, hard, truthful facts. As Emily Dickinson puts it: "Tell all the Truth but tell it slant—."

A case in point is the story about her love affair with Herman Leard (entry of October 7, 1897). As we know, she did not tell this tale as others have since told it—that Herman was already engaged, just as she herself was, and that they were both acting scandalously in terms of the mores of the time. She omits all mention of the existence of Herman's girlfriend, Ettie Schurman.

Her infatuation with Herman is undoubtedly true, and her feeling of frustration—the emotional core of the story—is also true. But she shapes the story in such a way as to divert the reader from much that is culpable on her part. There are at least four reasons for her shaping the story as she did.

Her first reason was purely aesthetic. Maud wanted a narrative shape that would allow her to turn a rather sprawling story into a compelling narrative. The narrative pattern she knew best was the one in *Pilgrim's Progress*. (In John Bunyan's story, the "pilgrim" going through life has to sidestep dangerous spots like the "Slough of Despond.") The "Herman affair" was a large pothole on her precarious road through life, but John Bunyan's structural pattern was too one-dimensional to use, so she looked for a more complex narrative pattern.

Her second reason proceeds from the first reason, but has to do with morality. The literary convention of the two suitors made a much more complex and dramatic story, and it allowed, in addition, something of a cover-up. The account of the Herman Leard affair in her journals is designed to lay to rest any lingering stories about her. Though Herman was caressing her in the bedroom while she was engaged to Edwin, by insisting that she drew a line in love-making *beyond which she would not go*, she establishes that she had the kind of moral fibre expected in proper young women in late-Victorian society.

Her third reason had to do with her own complicated psychology, and the art of displacement. In 1920, when she recopied the Herman story into her entry of October 7, 1897, her marriage to Ewan was unfulfilling—intellectually, emotionally, and physically. She could not have lovers in real life, but she could collect other men in imaginary positions of romance in her "waking dreams," her "dream lives," and (of course) in her fiction. But she could never say that a married woman might still feel unmentionable longings; those would have to be displaced into "story."[58]

The fourth reason is related to how she perceived the trajectory of her own life. Wishing to give shape and continuity to the story of her life, Maud looked again and again for a controlling narrative or life-myth. She wrote in an entry dated October 7, 1897, and recopied in early 1920: "Some lives seem to be more essentially tragic than others and I fear mine is one of such."[59]

Knowing that she was world-famous in 1920 enabled Maud to reveal some of the really "secret" aspects of her inner life. She was able to admit, now that she had *made* it up the "Alpine Path," that her inner self often felt insecure. She writes of giving a speech to the Women's Canadian Club in Chatham, Ontario,

When I rose from my seat on the platform to begin my readings the whole large audience rose to its feet. The tribute thrilled me — and yet it all seemed as unreal as such demonstrations always seem to me. At heart I am still the snubbed little girl of years ago who was constantly made to feel by all the grown-up-denizens of her small world that she was of no importance whatever to any living creature. The impression made on me then can never be effaced — I can never lose my "inferiority complex." That little girl can never believe in the reality of any demonstration in her honour. (December 11, 1920)

This is a very telling comment, but her journals do not have many other such overt revelations. Her life is truly a game of smoke and mirrors.

Maud filled ten volumes of these handwritten journals — nearly five thousand pages and more than one and a half million words in total — by the time of her death. She stated in April 16, 1922, that she would like to see her journals published in one hundred years without any omissions, but, if her heirs wanted, they could publish an *abridged* version after her death (as a "good financial proposition"), so long as they cut out "anything that would hurt or annoy anyone living." She also wrote:

> *I desire that these journals never be destroyed but kept as long as the leaves hold together.* I leave this to my descendants or my literary heirs as a sacred charge and invoke a Shakespearean curse on them if they disregard it: There is so much of myself in these volumes that I cannot bear the thought of their ever being destroyed. It would seem to me like a sort of murder. (April 16, 1922)

Maud creates the same intimacy with readers of her journals that she does in her fiction. When her journals were first published, starting in 1985, reviewers and readers felt they now truly knew the real Maud: a tormented, unhappy, judgmental woman who lived a life of terrible frustration. However, the people who still remembered the woman herself in the late 1970s and early 1980s — as their relative, their minister's wife, their employer, their friend — recalled yet another Maud Montgomery. She was an empathetic person who was deeply interested in others and sympathetic to them; a very witty conversationalist who liked to socialize, tell stories, gossip; a lively woman who liked to attend movies, discuss books and ideas, and take joy in the beauty of the natural world around her. She was full of jokes and the ability to see the funny side of anything. Many people who knew her simply could not believe what they read in her journals, and one maid even accused the editors of her journals of completely fabricating them.[60]

Maud's journals show her compulsion to write, her love of words, her sense of humour, her varying moods and passions, her intellectual engagement with the world around her, and her sly ways of recording her triumphs without exposing the pride she had been taught to regard as a sin. However, they contain little that is embarrassing, and when there are damaging stories, they are there only because there is no way to avoid them.

One reaction to her journals needs to be recorded, however—that of Maud's first daughter-in-law, a very astute woman, who read Maud's first nine handwritten journals in the early 1980s *before* they were published, and then remarked to this effect: "So many pages, so much information, but when all is said and done, she has not *really* revealed a lot about her inner self, what she is *really, really thinking and feeling down deep.*"

That said, there is no question that after 1919, Maud's journal did become her best friend. Using her "gift of wings," she was able through her journal to enter a private discursive space where she could communicate—on her own terms—with future generations. To a future great-granddaughter, she wrote:

> I lived a hundred years before you did; but my blood runs in your veins and I lived and loved and suffered and enjoyed and toiled and struggled just as you do. I found life good, in spite of everything. May you find it so. I found that courage and kindness are the two essential things. They are just as essential in your century as they were in mine. . . . I hope you'll be merry and witty and brave and wise; and I hope you'll say to yourself, "if Great-great-Grandmother were alive today, I think I'd like her in spite of her faults." (April 16, 1922)

Escaping the fetters of time, she managed to escape from the loneliest place on earth, a life lived in "the solitude of unshared thought" (March 29, 1935).

CHAPTER 13

Maud's life was like a three-ring circus. As a minister's wife, she was a Sunday School teacher, a tireless organizer for the many women's church organizations, and a director of young people's plays and educational programs. As a fundraiser, her abilities as a public performer kept her in wide demand in neighbouring communities. As a professional woman, she was involved in the newly founded Canadian Authors Association and was a stalwart member of the Canadian Women's Periodical Association. Time-management was a necessary skill. She wrote every morning for a set block of time. Her inner life may have been tempestuous, but her public life was always disciplined and controlled. She was the consummate professional.

A narrator in one of her later novels would say, "Life cannot stop because tragedy enters it. Meals must be made ready though a son dies and porches must be repaired even if your only daughter is going out of her mind."[61] Only two weeks into the new year of 1920, at age forty-five, her journal offers a glimpse into the tension between her inner and outer world:

> A missionary meeting this afternoon and one of Stella's letters full
> of growls and complaints spoilt today. I led the meeting and tried
> to put a little life and inspiration into the programme but the sight
> of that circle of stolid, fat, uninteresting, narrow old dames would
> have put out any poor little fire of my kindling. They just sucked
> all the animation out of my soul. (January 13, 1920)

She finished this numbing day as she usually did—by turning to books to improve her frame of mind. She reread a book that was "excruciatingly funny and the laughter it gave me was a boon. It flooded my drab soul with a rosy light and entirely headed off the fit of nervous crying with which I had expected to end the day" (January 13, 1920).

At the same time that Ewan had been suffering so intensely from his first mental breakdown in fall 1919, *Maclean's Magazine* carried an article entitled "The Author of *Anne*." It stated: "She is a woman of personal charm and winsomeness, as broad-minded and practical as she is imaginative, with a keen sense of humour, happy in the keeping of her home and the interests of the parish."[62] This is the public woman people saw, reacted to, and admired, and it was all genuine — every bit as genuine as the woman who dissolved in private tears at the end of discouraging days, or who wrote sharply about the dull and narrow-minded women in her husband's parish. She carried on with dignity, no matter what she grumbled in her journals. The private Maud stayed well hidden when the public Maud went on stage.

Finding new heroines: Rilla of Ingleside, Emily of New Moon, and more

In February 1920, Maud saw the Mary Miles Minter silent movie of *Anne of Green Gables*. People wanted more "Anne" books, but if she wrote them, Maud knew that would only increase Page's sales of the earlier ones. Instead of more "Anne," then, Maud was planning a new heroine who would reflect the social change wrought by World War I.

Maud felt the accelerating wheels of progress in both positive and disorienting ways. The war had spurred science and technology, speeding up the transmission of information. She read about new ideas, and introduced her Sunday School classes to names and theories. Newspapers were becoming more sophisticated and influential, and they had introduced "women's pages." The production of knowledge was moving into the universities. Occupations were becoming defined and professionalized, and women were starting to move into public forums and professions. Cars increased people's mobility, and airplanes were now finding all kinds of commercial uses. Women's daily lives were being altered by the development of electric appliances — refrigerators, stoves, washing machines, and irons. As the world spun forward, people began feeling unsettled by what came to be known as "future shock." All this called for a new focus in fiction.

Maud wanted to write a book about how the war changed women's lives, moving them from the private spaces in their homes into public spaces.

Women's wartime success in working outside of the domestic sphere had contributed to voting enfranchisement and opened the door to professions that had always been exclusively male. Maud wanted her novel to focus not on fighting men, but on the support women had provided to soldiers, and their sacrifices and suffering at home. Captain Smith had made the war vivid from a man's point of view, but she had experienced women's pain on the home-front in her own community. War was bravery on the European front, but it was also courage at home.

Rilla of Ingleside (1921)

In March 1919, shortly before Ewan's first serious breakdown, Maud had started plotting *Rilla of Ingleside*, her tenth novel. She was feeling constrained by the popularity of her former books, knowing that readers expected more of the same. Although she would have to use the old containers of domestic romance, she determined to pour into these some serious new themes, written from a female perspective, including women's suffering and grieving, as well as their learning to perform in a public forum. Continuing with the tale of the Blythe and Meredith children of *Rainbow Valley*, she now moved the young men from their pastoral childhood in Prince Edward Island into the trenches in Europe. She wanted to retire Anne, who was now the staid and proper wife of a doctor, with little dramatic potential; the new heroine was Anne's youngest daughter, Rilla, who undergoes a complex maturation alongside the inevitable transformation of the old pre-war world.

Rilla is also about the maturing of Canada as a nation. Canada's soldiers—like Captain Smith, Maud's half-brother Carl, and the young men of Leaskdale—had fought bravely alongside men from Great Britain, the "mother country." Now Canada could proudly take its place in the world, moving from thinking of itself as a colony to seeing itself as an emerging, strong nation.

The novel opens with a scene in the living room of Gilbert and Anne Blythe's house. After a morning of housework, their maid, Susan Baker, sits down for an hour of "repose and gossip." She opens her copy of the *Daily Enterprise* and she sees big black headlines about the assassination of Archduke Ferdinand in Sarajevo. Susan, however, is after some more interesting "local gossip," and says:

"I never take much interest in foreign parts. Who is the Archduke man who has been murdered?"

"What does it matter to us?" asked Miss Cornelia [a neighbour], adding that murder was common in the Balkans, and that Island papers should not print such sensational stories."

By the time of the novel's publication, most readers would have recognized the Archduke's assassination as a localized event that set many larger forces in play, eventually leading to World War I. They would have understood the symbolism in the next chapter when Miss Oliver, the local teacher, an intense and gifted woman with an uncanny prescience, recounts a dream she has had the previous night:

"far in the distance, I saw a long, silvery, glistening wave breaking. . . . I thought, 'Surely the waves will not come near Ingleside' . . . before I could move or call they were breaking right at my feet— and *everything* was gone—there was nothing . . . where the Glen had been. I tried to draw back—and I saw that the edge of my dress was wet with blood."

The image of the "blood red tide" that rolled up on the shores of Prince Edward Island expressed how the war had been *felt* by women.

As the book opens, Rilla, a pampered, fun-loving young teen, is looking forward to a party. When she hears her teacher's dream, she merely worries that the dream might portend a storm that will spoil the evening. The sharp and intense Miss Oliver responds with a light sarcasm that Rilla would have missed: "'Incorrigible fifteen,' said Miss Oliver dryly. 'I don't think there is any danger that foretells anything so awful as *that*.'"

Over the course of the novel, the red tide invades peaceful Prince Edward Island, destroying people's sense of protected isolation in Canada. It carries their sons and brothers and husbands to Europe. The women cope bravely. Rilla herself assumes the care of an orphaned war baby. She and the other women throw themselves into the war effort through organizing Red Cross auxiliary units, just as Maud had. Rilla's two beloved brothers leave to become soldiers. One of Anne's sons, Jem, returns triumphantly, but the other, the sensitive and poetic Walter, does not. Just before Walter is killed, he writes the moving poem that takes his name round the world—a poem that echoes John

McCrae's "In Flanders Fields," the most famous poem to come out of World War I. At the end of the novel, Anne's other son Jem returns, saying:

> The old world is destroyed and we must build up the new one. . . . we've got to make a world where wars can't happen.

Rilla is a sentimental novel in one sense. Maud tries hard to shore up people's belief that the war was truly a fight against evil. When Walter's last letter arrives after his death, it tells them that he has died that others may fulfill their lives in freedom and happiness. It urges them to "keep the faith." This echo of the war rhetoric is what Maud *wants* to believe—indeed, what she *must* believe: that this war was one that would end all wars.

As a woman who read history books constantly, Maud was well aware of mankind's repetitive engagements in war. When Captain Smith swept into Leaskdale in fall 1919, telling first-hand tales of his heroism in war, they were exciting to hear, but Maud could fit these into the context of her historical reading. In December 1919, for instance, she had finished reading Edward Gibbon's *The Decline and Fall of the Roman Empire* for the third time. In April 1921, she finished rereading George Grote's twelve-volume *History of Greece* for the second time. In October 1921, she finished rereading Justin McCarthy's *A History of Our Own Times*. In May 1922, she was reading another kind of history, William Lecky's two-volume *History of European Morals*. (She had read his *History of Rationalism* in 1917.) By 1924, she stated that she believed that all events were governed by the Darwinian concept of "blind impersonal Chance," not by a deity. Her doubts about the role that God and religion played in human affairs were already beginning to show as she wrote the first draft of *Rilla of Ingleside* in the first eight months of 1920.

She brings ambiguity into the novel through her symbolic use of the "Piper." This mythic figure had appeared first in *Rainbow Valley*, leading the boys out of the sylvan glade of childhood towards their future in European battlefields. When the image of the Piper appears again in *Rilla*, he seems to be the same Scottish bagpiper whose music instills bravery in soldiers, pumping them up with courage, and leading them valiantly into battle. Walter, for instance, has been a gentle, poetic boy who shies from aggression, fearing both war and death, but this admirable Piper gives him resolve, purpose, and courage.

However, as the story progresses, the Piper of *Rainbow Valley* morphs into a more mysterious figure in *Rilla*. He resembles the deadly "Pied Piper" of the children's fairy tale—the Piper who pipes to innocent children, leading them away from their parents into a cavern. When the door closes behind them, they disappear from earth and are never seen again. This latter Piper, from the Underworld, has fooled them with his seductive music.

Maud's reading of Gibbon demonstrated all too clearly how the religious concepts of Good and Evil had been used throughout history to mobilize people to fight. Why should innocent boys from rural Canada have had to die in European trenches to fight *God's* war? She had started to see religion more as a social organization than anything else, and she thought that the real power lay in science and knowledge, not in a literal and omnipotent God sitting on high. Like so many other reflective people of her era, she was conflicted and confused. But she *knew* that people had to continue to believe the war rhetoric, or they would think that their sacrifices had been in vain. Certainly, evil was real.

The shifting Piper imagery betrays her confusion, as does her conclusion to the novel. At the end, Rilla, has grown into a mature woman. She has shed her symbolic childhood lisp in the process, but in the last chapter, she suddenly slips back into her insecure, dependent, lisping childhood self as soon as her soldier-lover comes home and proposes to her. Many find it a frustrating, unsatisfying conclusion for a serious novel. The message is what Maud's readership wanted to hear—that the war had defeated barbarism and evil, once and for all, and that women could now happily revert to being wives and mothers. Rilla's returning lisp marks symbolically the end of women's performance on public stages. They retreat into domesticity.

When Maud had begun planning *Rilla* it was about six weeks after Frede's death, and when she finished it, on August 24, 1920, the dedication was to "Frederica Campbell MacFarlane, who went away from me when the dawn broke on January 25th, 1919—a true friend, a rare personality, a loyal and courageous soul."

Maud heard from the Island in April 1920 that her Uncle John F. Macneill was tearing down the house that she had been raised in. After the publication of *Anne of Green Gables*, tourists had descended on Cavendish, with hordes of sightseers trespassing all over the Macneill homestead, peering into the windows of the empty house and trampling all over his planted fields—from Uncle John F.'s point of view, a maddening invasion of his property. People came to his door and pestered him with inquiries about his famous niece.

Maud's crusty Uncle John F. did not believe that *Anne of Green Gables* was *that great* a novel in the first place. He came from a family of naturally gifted storytellers, and this novel sounded just like the rest of the stories told by his family. Any one of them could have put it onto paper, he said, no doubt believing what he said. Maud's adulation by the reading public goaded him to end the trespassing and intrusions. He tore down the now decrepit "old home."

The news that the house was being razed caused Maud no end of distress. She had always been deeply attached to houses and places, and to that home especially. To someone already feeling the discomfort of too much *change* in her world, this was a powerful blow. The irony did not escape her, either. Her books had brought the coveted tourism to PEI, and now invading tourists were destroying what she valued most: the peaceful Cavendish she loved, and her old home.

No one would have suspected, however, as she worked on her manuscript of *Rilla of Ingleside*, that there was so much turmoil in her life. She had, for instance, been in Boston from May 17, 1920, until around July 9, 1920, to face Lewis and George Page in the court battle to stop their distribution of *Further Chronicles of Avonlea*. While that court case dragged on, they continued to sell all the books they could, effectively thumbing their noses at her.

She came home from her Boston session in a ragged state, and she steadied herself in her long and lonely hours back at home by continuing to copy her diaries into her journals. Ewan was often in bed in those days, suffering from his attacks of melancholy. Somehow, though, she finished *Rilla* in August 1920.

Maud was restless after the war ended, and she would have liked living in a bigger city where there was more intellectual stimulation. Ewan was still "preaching for the call" at other larger churches. One place he had tried for— the Columbus-Brooklyn parish near Whitby (where Captain and Mrs. Smith lived)—had a much larger and less drafty manse, features Maud wanted. She thought he might get it. But in the end, J. R. Fraser, an old friend who had helped Ewan settle in at Leaskdale in 1910, suddenly resigned his Uxbridge position and got the charge instead of Ewan. Ewan became more depressed as he repeatedly tried unsuccessfully for other churches.

Early in 1921, Maud had given a series of talks to publicize the forthcoming *Rilla of Ingleside*—first in Toronto, then in London, Ontario, where she gave readings and lectures at the Canadian Club, the Girls' Canadian Club, and the Women's Press Club. A London journalist, one of the Blackburn family who owned the *London Free Press,* expressed a general impression: that L. M. Montgomery was "too full of humour and philosophy" to ever feel blue. It was an irony Maud felt worth recording in her journal.

Maud tells of the trip to London in her journals, but she does not mention the striking coincidence that Captain Smith lectured in London the same night she was there, close to where she was. Possibly they drove down together, since they were in frequent contact. When she returned home, she found that Ewan had bought a new car, the Grey-Dort, to replace their Chevrolet.[63]

It was this July in 1921 that the Macdonalds and the Captain Smith family made their long-planned tandem trip to Prince Edward Island. Captain Smith went about the Island showing the eleven reels of the silent movie (*The Empire's Shield*) in a two-hour-long production, talking about his war service to the mother country.[64] This was reported in the Island newspapers, but again Maud does not mention it in her journals at all.

Things went better for Ewan once he was in Prince Edward Island with his own family. After first visiting John and Margaret Stirling, then Ewan's sisters at Kinross, then Maud's old Prince of Wales College chums in and near Charlottetown, Ewan and Maud and the boys drove on to Cavendish, visiting Alec and May Macneill, and Ernest and Myrtle Webb and their children. The next stop, at Park Corner, brought back all the old remembered happiness for Maud in that house. Chester and Stuart engaged in boisterous fun with the rollicking new generation of merry Campbell cousins, Ella's and the late George's children.

On the way home, the Macdonalds stopped over in Saint John, New Brunswick, staying with Maud Estey Mahoney, one of Maud's former students from Bideford. Maud, as a celebrity passing through Saint John, consented to let a local journalist come to interview her. Chester and Stuart were obstreperous while she was being interviewed, but it never occurred to Ewan to distract them or take them out for a walk. He just grew impatient to end the interview. Maud had been revitalized by the trip, but Ewan was turning "morose and cranky" again as they approached home.

After finishing the *Rilla* manuscript on her return, Maud wrote in her journals on August 24, 1920, that she would never write another book in the Anne series.

> I am done with Anne forever—I swear it as a dark and deadly vow.
> I want to create a new heroine now—she is already in embryo in
> my mind—she has been christened for years. Her name is "Emily."
> She has black hair and purplish gray eyes. I want to tell folks
> about *her*.

This story, which had been incubating for quite some time, marked Maud's
serious attempt to ditch the "Anne" series. "Anne" had begun to feel like an
incubus that hung around her neck, thanks largely to Page.

In addition, Maud noticed that all her books were now being marketed
only for children, including *Anne of Green Gables*. The rapidly increasing literacy rate in North America was creating a huge marketplace for "children's
literature," and there were not enough books to fill the demand. Many books
with a child protagonist were now being moved down into the children's literature shelves, with altered cover art and illustrations. The pictures on the
covers of all of Maud's books show how the heroines grew ever younger as
time advanced.

Maud had not written her books specifically for children; they had been
written for a general popular audience. It was a happy coincidence that they
were equally successful with children. After writing *Anne of Green Gables*,
Maud had indeed told her correspondent Ephraim Weber in 1907, before it
was published, that she had written a novel for juveniles—"ostensibly for
girls"—and in 1908 she had sent a copy of *Anne* to her cousin, Professor
Murray Macneill, with the same message. At the time she made these remarks,
she was downplaying her writing career to show "womanly modesty." Later,
when attitudes towards women writers changed, Maud would boldly assert the
truth—that she had not written *Anne* for children, but for herself and other
adults. After all, hadn't sophisticated men like the Honourable Earl Grey and
Mark Twain been delighted with *Anne of Green Gables?* Frustrated by being
pigeonholed as a children's writer, Maud wrote in her journals:

> I want to write . . . something entirely different from anything I
> have written yet. I am becoming classed as a "writer for young
> people" and that only. I want to write a book dealing with grown-
> up creatures—a psychological study of one human being's life. I
> have the plot of it already matured in my mind. The name of the
> book is to be "Priest Pond." (August 24, 1920)

Her next book had some "Priests" in it, but it started out with a young heroine, too. This novel would be about a little girl's having the world—her world—all against her. Maud wanted to show how women had to fight against cultural expectations that curtailed their aspirations. Throughout the war, she had seen women move into the public sphere. The Victorian ideology that women should be mere "angels in the house" no longer defined them. Women had shed their white angels' wings during the war, taking up dirty jobs in fields, in factories, in business—places where only poor, working-class women had been before, and then in terrible conditions. Maud's books were moving in the direction of portraying serious themes, and her creative energies were surging.

Emily of New Moon (1923)

On August 20, 1921, Maud wrote the first chapter of her new novel, *Emily of New Moon.* It dealt with the upbringing of a young girl who wants to become a writer. Emily was the *new* heroine designed to replace Anne. Still, there were many similarities between Anne and the new Emily. Each has been orphaned, and ends up with two elderly caretakers, one stern and the other sympathetic. Each girl has to struggle to be loved and to be valued. Both girls came out of Maud's own multi-faceted personality, and were much indebted to Maud's memories of her own childhood. Yet Anne and Emily are dramatically different.

The 1908 Anne is an engaging little waif, with her focus on finding a home where she will be loved and secure. Maud features Anne's winsome talkativeness and her response to the beauties of nature in Avonlea (Cavendish). But when Maud dreams up Emily, she wants to show a talented, ambitious girl who knows that she wants to be a writer in spite of all the impediments to authorship a young woman faced in the late-nineteenth and early-twentieth centuries.

Maud wrote *Anne* in the 1904–1905 period, when, buoyed up by her courtship with Ewan, she accessed her relatively happy childhood. When Maud was brooding up *Emily* in 1919–20, and writing the first draft in 1921–22, she was revisiting her childhood through a new lens, and she was once again reconfiguring her childhood in her journals. *Emily of New Moon* was written in six months—a phenomenal burst of élan—and perhaps reflects the energizing effects of Smith's admiration of her achievements, intelligence, and personality.[65] Serious Emily, always watchful of others, is a very different child from the impulsive and talkative Anne. When her father dies, Emily is reluctantly claimed by her mother's Murray clan, who feel it their "duty" to raise her. In the first third of *Anne of Green Gables*, the anxious Anne waits to see if the Cuthberts will adopt her. In *Emily of New Moon*, Emily likewise waits, while the relatives all try to shift the responsibility for Emily onto others in the clan. But Emily, hiding under the table, overhears it all. Instead of being damaged for life by what she hears, she is angered to the point of indignation, and bursts out from under the table — much to the shock of those adults who have been discussing her.

When the housekeeper, Ellen, tells Emily she should consider herself lucky to get a home *any place*, she adds the frank assessment that Emily is not of much importance to anyone. Emily retorts in indignation, "*I am of importance to myself.*" This is an extraordinary assertion in an era when young girls were socialized into domesticity, subordinating their identity to their husbands and family.

Like Anne, Emily is raised by surrogate parents, only in Emily's case they are two sisters, Aunt Elizabeth and Aunt Laura. Also in the house is Cousin Jimmy, their brother. Elizabeth is as stern as Marilla, Laura as indulgent as Matthew, and poor Jimmy is a testament to Elizabeth's fierceness: he is brain-damaged because when he was a child, the bossy Elizabeth pushed him head first down a well.

In her journals Maud acknowledges that Emily's inner life is partly hers — a rare admission. Maud details the psychological hardships that Emily suffers in a restricted, contained, and confined life, drawing heavily from her own memories. Heir to the entire clan's criticism, Emily longs for her dead father's unconditional love, and she suffers terribly from her clan's ridicule of her writing ambitions.[66]

Despite all the repressive forces in this surrogate family, Emily survives. At the beginning of the novel, she writes letters to her dead father, but at the end of the novel she is writing for herself. Her last words at the end of *Emily of New Moon* are written in her diary: she says that she is going to keep a diary so that it may be published when she dies.[67]

Even Anne's and Emily's boyfriends are quite different. Anne's boyfriend is Gilbert *Blythe*, a name suggesting happiness. Emily's first male admirer is an older man named *Dean Priest*, double-barrelled, imposing clerical name.

Dean comes into her life, offering her the kindness, protection, and fellowship she lost when her father died—exactly what the newly minted Ewan had offered Maud in 1903 to 1904, shortly after the death of her own father.

In the first book of the *Emily* trilogy, Dean Priest seems wholesome and exciting when he meets Emily and offers her his companionship. However, his characterization shifts to something sinister, like the Piper in *Rilla*. In the two *Emily* sequels, Dean Priest morphs into a creepy personality nicknamed "Jarback Priest" (because of his deformed back). It was in November 1921, when Maud was in the middle of writing the first novel in the *Emily* sequence, that she was herself experiencing a physical repulsion to Ewan, which she described as making her feel "degraded and unclean." Dean Priest also begins to exude a disturbing sexual aura in the novel.

Emily shares another important trait with the young Maud: she has immense imaginative talent. Emily differs from Anne, however, in having a mystical power that she calls "the flash"—"the wonderful moment when soul seemed to cast aside the bonds of flesh and spring upward to the stars" (Chapter 8). It is then that her soul can see "behind the veil" of surfaces to transcendent beauty and realities beyond (reminiscent of the novel *Zanoni*). Maud models Emily's "flash" on a feeling she described herself having in a series of 1917 articles which are gathered into *The Alpine Path*, and again in her journals in January 1905 (which period was recopied and possibly rewritten in the early 1920s):

> It has always seemed to me, ever since I can remember, that, amid all the commonplaces of life, I was very near to a kingdom of ideal beauty. Between it and me hung only a thin veil. I could never draw it quite aside but sometimes a wind fluttered it and I seemed to catch a glimpse of the enchanting realm beyond—only a glimpse—but those glimpses have always made life worthwhile. (January 2, 1905)

Anne, Emily, and the young Maud(s) of the journals all flowed out of the same pen, from the same fluid reservoir of memory. Maud's fertile imagination needed only the germ of a feeling or idea to begin sketching out a character. She would brood up her character, then methodically plot out actions for each chapter of a book. She sometimes did this out loud while working or walking—many people remember her talking to herself as she walked. This was not seen as odd; they knew she was plotting her books. When the "spade-work" was done, Maud began writing the book. She envisioned scenes in her mind as she wrote with great intensity and speed, laughing out loud at smart retorts made by her characters who were, in some cases, saying things that she herself would be too reticent and polite to say. She was dead to the immedi-ate world around her when she was writing, but she probably lived more in-tensely in that "dead" state than in any other.

Once she dreamed up her characters, and plotted out the book's chap-ters, she slipped into a watching mode—watching them live out their lives on her own private screen. In Leaskdale, one little boy, Fred Leask, played with Stuart around the time that *Emily* was being written. He remembered how he and Stuart could do anything "while Mrs. Macdonald was writ-ing"—steal cookies, slide down the stair banister, race through the house chasing each other. Fred described how Mrs. Macdonald would look into space, smiling or chuckling as if she were watching actual people, then bounce in excitement and laugh softly as she scribbled down what she was seeing. "She was off in another world," he recalled in the early 1980s, "and her pen really flew."

Maud had written her first chapter of *Emily* on August 20, 1921. She fin-ished the entire first draft on February 15, 1922. By August 1922 she was read-ing the proofs.

> It is the best book I have ever written—and I have had more intense
> pleasure in writing it than any of the others—not even excepting
> *Green Gables*. I have *lived* it, and I hated to pen the last line and
> write *finis*. Of course, I'll have to write several sequels but they will
> be more or less hackwork I fear. They cannot be to me what this
> book has been. (February 15, 1922)

While Maud was writing *Emily of New Moon*, her lawsuits with Page con-tinued to simmer. At the same time, the Pickering affair was boiling up into the lawsuit against Ewan, and Ewan was doing his best to find another parish.

On March 25, 1922, Maud wrote in her journal that the Leaskdale women had arranged a program with a tribute to her. They would have known that Ewan was trying out for another church, and they undoubtedly had heard bits of Lily's gossip about Smith. The women, who were very fond of Maud, would have been outraged that any rumours were circulating about a minister's wife, and especially one they loved and respected.

The community did not want the Macdonalds to leave because they genuinely *liked* Ewan and they *loved* Maud. She made their church work interesting and fun as well as profitable, and brought a sparkle to every gathering she was in. There was much appreciation for her efforts with the young people of the parish. She taught them public performance skills through the Young People's groups and she told them of inventions, ideas, and other currents in the world outside their isolated area. (In the early 1980s some remembered her telling them about Freud and Einstein.) A young woman, Margaret Leask, wrote the tribute, presented it, and saved it for posterity. It read, in part:

> Dear Mrs. Macdonald,
>   The members of the guild decided that since this was to be "Canadian Authors" night, it would be a most fitting time to pay tribute to you as a Canadian Authoress and also to show in some degree our appreciation of the wonderful interest which you take in our welfare. As an Authoress, celebrated throughout the world, we are proud to know you and honoured in having you as leader of our activities. Your leadership is a source of inspiration to all of us, and under your leadership the meetings are both interesting and instructive. The outside world knows you as a brilliant writer, but we know you not only as a writer, but as a woman who has deservedly won our respect and admiration . . .

Later, Maud caught a glimpse on Ewan's face that she interpreted as anger over her tribute. She felt that Ewan was jealous of her work, and she commented on his attitudes in her journals (March 25, 1922), deftly deflecting attention from other areas of his anxiety:

> Ewan's attitude toward women—though I believe he is quite unconscious of this himself—is that of the mediaeval mind. A woman is a thing of no importance intellectually—the plaything and servant of man—and couldn't possibly do anything that would be worthy of a real tribute.

Maud had written about Ewan in 1921:

> Poor fellow, he is good and kind and never did willful harm or
> wrong to anyone in his life. Yet he is most miserable. (May 18,
> 1921)

Yes, poor Ewan. Very little was going right in his life either, and whether or
not he was jealous of his wife, or merely disappointed in himself, he certainly had cause to feel ineffectual amid the powerful forces swirling around
him. Maud could transmute her turbulent emotions into art, but Ewan had
no such release, except to bury them deep within himself and brood. In
those hidden fastnesses of his mind, problems festered, and the medicines
prescribed to flush out his anxiety only added to his woes.

As 1922 ended, Maud wrote about another advance in technology that was
beginning to make its way into the homes of ordinary people: the radio. Dr.
Shier, the Macdonalds' doctor in Uxbridge, had one, and had told them that
on a recent Sunday he had actually heard sermons being preached in
Pennsylvania and Chicago over this new device. Maud commented again
on how life was speeding up after the war. More and more events were
crowded into each week. Home was becoming the base from which you
operated your life, not a private sanctuary in which you *lived* your life. She
ceased hearing in memory many of the sounds of childhood—the birds, the
wind, and in her particular case, the sound of the sea—because there was
the constant inner voice telling her what had to be accomplished before
day's end. The world was, indeed, changing.

Maud's activities in the Toronto book world helped release her from tedium and worries at home. She had always believed deeply in public service,
and that those with ability should use their gifts to better others. She frequently
promoted the books of less established writers in speeches. She had given of
herself unstintingly in her role as minister's wife, and she put an equal amount
of effort into promoting the Canadian book trade as a speaker, organizer, and
idea-person on executive committees. The success of her books allowed her
publishers, McClelland and Stewart, to invest in other young Canadians, and
she gave John McClelland promotional blurbs to use in his advertising. She
also wrote reviews of other writers' books. Newspaper accounts of her speeches

recount her telling her audiences repeatedly to "buy Canadian books and magazines." She also wrote encouraging personal letters to other new Canadian writers.

Canada had performed well in the war, and was now in a period of nationalistic enthusiasm. Back in 1910, Maud had written in a PEI newspaper about the fledgling industry of Canadian literature, saying a period of "sturm and drang" was needed for Canada to develop a sense of itself and a national literature. She recopied this article in her journals after the war ended:

> I do not think our literature [in 1910] is an expression of our national life as a whole. I think this is because we have only very recently—as time goes in the making of nations—had any national life. Canada is only just finding herself. She has not yet fused her varying elements into a harmonious whole. Perhaps she will not do so until they are welded together by some great crisis of storm and stress. That is when a real national literature will be born. I do not believe that the great Canadian novel or poem will ever be written until we have had some kind of baptism by fire to purge away all our petty superficialities and lay bare the primal passions of humanity. [Quoted in her journals on August 27, 1919, slightly abridged from an article she earlier wrote for the Toronto *Globe* that was reprinted in *The Island Patriot*, January 6, 1910.]

The Great War had been this catalyst. In the 1920s, Canadians began to position themselves on the world stage of nations and national literatures. Historian Carl Berger says of this period: "the desire for a national culture that would reflect the character of Canada in imaginative literature, art and history became a master impulse in the intellectual life of the twenties."[68]

Maud was irked in March 1921 when her American publisher, Frederick Stokes, wrote her complaining that there was not enough American experience in *Rilla of Ingleside*. She stated angrily in her journals that she "wrote of Canada at war—not of the U.S." (March 5, 1921). Like many Canadians, Maud bristled at what they saw as American cultural imperialism, and she had enough stature to refuse to alter her book.

A great deal of Canadian resentment had been developing against the United States: for one thing, its copyright laws allowed Canadian writers to be exploited. The copyright situation for Canadian authors had long been vexing. To begin with, the United States had not joined the Berne Convention that bound it to respect copyright registered in other countries. Maud had herself been caught by this when Lewis Page threatened to locate and re-publish the stories she had already published in Canadian magazines, using them in *Further Chronicles of Avonlea*. Canadian authors were justifiably furious over this, given that American publishers could pirate their work without compensation. Canadian writers banded together to address this issue.

The result was the official founding of the Canadian Authors Association (CAA) in 1921. A magazine called *The Canadian Bookman*, first published in January 1919, fostered the CAA and became its spokesman. In 1921, over one hundred Canadian authors and academics attended a founders' meeting in Montreal on March 11 and 12. They established a copyright committee and hired lobbyists to send to Ottawa. Maud was too busy with her parish and family duties to attend this meeting, but she followed events with great interest. Active in the Toronto branch of the CAA, she was elected its vice-president in early fall 1921. Eight months after its founding, it boasted eight hundred members. Maud gave speeches in the fall to promote the CAA message: buy Canadian books and support Canadian authors.

It was in this period that Maud did a great deal to promote Frederick Philip Grove's new book, *Over Prairie Trails*, for McClelland and Stewart. She wrote Grove several encouraging letters in the 1920s. Grove did not return the admiration: in 1926, he wrote his friend, Professor Arthur Leonard Phelps, "I've often wondered how a woman like Mrs. Macdonald [Lucy Maud Montgomery] can write the books she does write: not that those books may not have their readers who profit from them: I have found that out. But how a woman who judges so accurately can stand *writing* that stuff. For she does have a remarkable scent." (Since Maud admired and encouraged Grove's novels, he naturally admired her ability to discriminate.)

Maud was also involved in new promotional development. The CAA organized the first "Canadian Bookweek" for November 19 to 26, 1921. The motto was "More Readers for Canadian Authors" and the object "To suggest to every Canadian that he buy more Canadian books." For weeks before the event, she wrote publicity items and letters on behalf of the CAA, and when the time came, she stayed with her friend Mary Beal in Toronto for the week. Maud had promised to appear as part of the program, and she frankly confessed that she wanted to escape from the manse for a few days.

Nellie McClung was the guest of honour at the opening CAA dinner for some eighty people at the Arts and Letters Club. Maud sat at the head table next to McClung, along with J. M. Gibbon (President), B. K. Sandwell (National Secretary), and numerous other important people in the fledgling organization, including the Reverend Basil King, another famous Islander, author of moralistic and popular novels. (King had been the pastor in a prestigious church in Cambridge, Massachusetts, when Maud visited Page in 1911, and he and Mrs. King had hosted a reception for her.) She was delighted to see him again, but of Nellie McClung, Maud wrote snippily: "Nellie is a handsome woman in a stunning dress, glib of tongue. She made a speech full of obvious platitudes and amusing little stories which made everyone laugh and deluded us into thinking it was quite a fine thing—until we began to think it over . . ." (November 18, 1921).

Maud's own speeches for many occasions were also light productions full of amusing little stories that kept people laughing. Her comment seems to have arisen from their difference in style and personality: Nellie McClung was an extrovert who sought and revelled in the public spotlight, and used her writing to advance political ideas, whereas Maud was a much more reserved and private person. Basil King made a speech she pronounced "full of good ideas, with no superfluities or frills or gallery plays" (November 18, 1921). He, of course, had been an early endorser of Maud's own books.

The Bookweek was a huge success. Some twelve hundred people attended a reception that the Canadian Press Club gave for the CAA. Maud recounted being smothered by those praising *Anne of Green Gables* and asking her if "Anne was a real girl." Later she enjoyed some plays at Hart House. She met again a friend of Frede's, Jen Fraser, and they gossiped about Cameron MacFarlane, Frede's husband. Maud spoke to eight hundred girls at Jarvis St. Collegiate, the school run by Marjory MacMurchy's father, Dr. Archibald MacMurchy. She next spoke to a large group at the Parkdale I.O.D.E. At Victoria College, she "spent a very dull evening listening to a couple of literary papers by erudite authors who could not stoop to be interesting as well as erudite." Maud had little patience for those who took themselves too seriously or lacked a sense of humour.

The week whirled by with swamped appearances, readings, and speeches: at Moulton College, with hundreds seeking autographs; at the Simpson's department store; at the Dunn Avenue Methodist Sunday School (to 600 students); at Oakwood School (to 1,300 young people); at the School of Commerce (to 1,500); and at the Cloke Bookstore in Hamilton. She attended

receptions and luncheons honouring her at Mary Beal's house; at the National
Club; and at the Business Women's Club, where she and Mrs. Emmeline
Pankhurst, the famous English suffragette, were both guests of honour. At a
Women's Press Club reception she met Lady Byng, the wife of the Governor
General, sponsor of the Lady Byng Memorial Trophy for gentlemanly behav-
iour in hockey. She also saw two movies, *Quo Vadis* and *Biff-Bing-Bang*.

After this flattering, exhausting week of honours and socializing, Maud returned to the gruelling conditions at the manse, fearful of the state in which
she might find Ewan. However, he was fine. But there was a letter full of
"woes" from Aunt Annie in Park Corner. The crop had been poor that year.
Maud decided to surprise her beloved aunt with a cheque at Christmas. She
was extremely fond of the fatherless Campbells at Park Corner, and she continued to be their salvation in times of need.

Shortly after, at the request of Stokes, she ventured on another outing to
Ohio, to read and speak in several places. There she escaped her role as minister's wife and visited a cabaret, where she and her hosts dined, listened to
"jazz music," and watched some modern dance (which was regarded as a
scandal by conservative magazines). This time she returned to find Ewan
heading into another attack. It was in early December 1921 that Maud had
had the unsettling dream of Ewan being hanged in the church and then
resuscitated.

The outside world guessed nothing of Maud's rich but often tortured
inner life. She was to them a successful author, a dynamo in her community,
a powerful speaker in public, a performer for charitable causes, a woman
whose intellectual range made her a fascinating conversationalist in social
gatherings, and a warm and likeable human being with a very fine sense of humour. (For example, her service to the book community during the fall of 1921
led to her being honoured by the Canadian Women's Periodical Club in
Toronto in January 1922.)

Changes in the literary climate

The founding of the CAA was one more sign of the changing times. There
was much talk again (as there had been in the 1880s) of an evolving "national
literature." The CAA, initially dominated by older men, had expanded to
contain many supporting members whose approach to literature was more

enthusiastic than discriminating. For all its good work on copyright law and promoting the writing of Canadian authors, the CAA still struck some ambitious younger writers as a social club where the stuffy old guard mingled and schmoozed, proud of a handful of unimaginative poems they might have published in newspapers and magazines.

The young poet Frank R. Scott—later to be one of Canada's most impressive legal minds and a professor whose thinking influenced, among others, Prime Minister Pierre Trudeau—emerged as a key member of the new school of young Montreal poets in the early 1920s. This group began an attack on what came to be dubbed the "Maple Leaf School"—poets who "warbled" over themes like Canada's beautiful scenery and its patriotic affiliation to the "motherland." (In 1927, F. R. Scott wrote a brilliantly satiric poem about the CAA entitled "The Canadian Authors Meet." It skewered those he saw as literary wannabes who wrote sweetly sentimental and patriotic verse imitating Romantic and Victorian poetry.)

Maud had published many poems that were fairly romantic in tone. In this new climate, even *Anne of Green Gables* seemed a bit too positive and sentimental, too much like *Pollyanna* the insufferable "Glad Girl," who resolved to be "glad" even after the worst catastrophes. At the conclusion of *Anne of Green Gables*, Anne believes that "God's in His Heaven, all's right with the world," a view very different from the post-war outlook. After the devastation of a war that had killed millions, how could anyone believe that except sentimental, foolish young girls? Even Maud saw *Anne* as belonging to a time before the war.

As 1922 opened, literary styles had already begun to change. Modernism exploded in literature, as well as in visual art, architecture, music, and many other cultural fields. It signalled the dying gasp of all things Victorian and the evolution of a new fiction in Europe and North America. Young writers described the emptiness of the "modern" world. T. S. Eliot wrote his famous poem *The Waste Land*, a vision of a sterile, suffocating world, in 1922. Experimental writers like Virginia Woolf and James Joyce challenged traditional literary styles with their "stream of consciousness" technique. In the United States, young novelists like Ernest Hemingway pared down their style to a "virile" tautness. Anti-heroes replaced conventional protagonists. Skepticism and cynicism, alienation and isolation, were frequent tones in literature.

Maud did not like this new cynical view, or the style of writing. Ironically, after she had worked so hard to give support to other younger writers in her speeches and in the executive of the CAA, she herself became the target of younger professional critics, who saw her style of writing as both outdated and banal. It was no longer trendy to write "regional romances," sentimental "idylls," or humorous novels—all tags attached to her books by various of the "new" critics. She defended her books against the charge that they were sentimental by arguing that there was a huge difference between "sentimentality" (which she loathed) and "sentiment" (which she saw as the impulse that held societies together). She praised Charlotte Brontë, one of her favourite authors, for her "absolute clear-sightedness regarding shams and sentimentalities" (September 22, 1925). Later, she would be pleased with the reviewer who wrote that her first *Emily* book was full of "sentiment that never gets over the line into sentimentality" (March 1, 1930).

Her trademarks as a writer were still "local colour," with a good frosting of "purple prose" to describe beautiful natural landscapes; girl heroines who were full of passionate emotional responses to life; humorous treatment of the vagaries of human nature; an affectionate view of humanity shown in the characters' zest for life and concern for each other; and tidy happy endings— which were labelled "sentimental" by the critics. Unfortunately, all these features were on the Modernists' scorn list.

Maud clung resolutely to the idea that a writer should be uplifting, rather than mired in the world's "pigstyes." She loathed the depravity, defeat, and destruction in modernist writing. She determined that she would never show the "shadows" of her own life in her fiction, but would hide it away in her private diary. She believed that the best way to reform people was with humour, not cynicism. While Maud had increasing doubts about God's omnipotence, she still believed that He would reward His faithful servants. With desperation, she clung to that weakening conviction.

No one in the middle of this seismic shift fully understood what was evolving. But as the early 1920s wore on, Maud saw that her style of narrative was coming under attack. She had not been disturbed over the occasionally churlish reviewer, but this was a systemic attack on the foundations of her fiction. If the disappointments in her personal life were not enough, she now faced the diminution of her celebrity in the literary world—the respect that she had laboured so hard to achieve, and which had given her such pleasure.[69] As soon as *Emily of New Moon* was finished in 1922, Maud worked ever harder recopying her diaries into her journals, while continuing to record current events in her ongoing diaries.

Her journalizing kept her living in several time frames at once: the past was being reconfigured in her "journals" (and being relived while being transcribed on the page); the present was being lived (and being recorded in daily notes in her diary for future transfer into the journals); and the future was being anticipated in her imagination (as she worried about her husband and Chester).

Her ability to both remember and imagine were so powerful that the past and the future could fuse, squeezing out the present. Her son Stuart, in fact, commented in the 1980s that his mother lived too much of her life in the past and the future, and not enough in the present. Chester's first wife put it another way in the 1980s: she said that Maud lived too much in fictional worlds and not enough in the real one. Both were reflecting on Maud in her last decade, not on the young or middle-aged Maud. In retrospect, others might say that because Maud was not one to live complainingly or disreputably in her real life, her imaginative world was her only safe alternative. She did not just live to write, she wrote to live. By her ability to live in several different time frames all at once, she could divert herself from discomfort in her present. Her friend Captain Smith might have been an adventurer in life, but she could be one only in her imagination.

At the end of December 1921, Maud wrote some curious passages about "dream lives" in her journals. She had just returned from a busy evening of hosting the church Women's Guild executive, and she reports that Ewan attended and was unsociable, rather than trying to "slip away and indulge his broodings." They had spent considerable time with the Edwin Smiths through the summer and fall, listening to Smith describe his adventures.

In the entry for December 29, 1921, Maud muses over the "dream lives" she had in her childhood. She confesses that she lives them still. She describes one from her childhood in which she imagined herself a female member of the British Parliament named "Lady Trevanion." When someone made a "contemptuous reference" to her "as a *woman*," little Maud always leapt to her feet as Lady Trevanion and, adapting "Pitt's Reply to Walpole," she "hurled" back:

> Sir, the atrocious crime of being a woman which the honourable
> gentleman has, with such spirit and decency charged upon me, I
> shall attempt neither to palliate nor deny but shall content myself

with wishing that I may be one of those whose follies cease with
their *sex* and not one of that number who are ignorant in spite of
manhood and experience. (December 29, 1921)

She describes another dream life in South Africa during the Boer War, one
shared with Cecil Rhodes, a man her generation greatly admired. These
"dream lives" were imagined so vividly that she claimed that she could live
in them completely. She describes a current one:

> It is a curious thing that all through my life when some great strain
> or crisis came and all my old dream lives, lived so often that they
> had at last grown stale and flavourless, failed to give these escapes,
> some new, vivid, and exhilarating dreamlife would come into
> being. For months I have been a member of a party seeking in the
> mountain deserts of South America the jewels hung on a stone god
> in a great underground cavern. I have gone through the most
> amazing adventures, risks, terrors, hardship, have found the jewels,
> outwitted foes and traitors and returned in triumph. How silly it all
> seems written down. Yet it has been a wonderful, breathless, excit-
> ing existence as lived, and seems now in retrospect as real as life I
> have actually lived . . . (August 13, 1925)

She goes on to explain that these dream lives are completely different from
"stories I 'think out.' When thinking out a story I am outside of it—merely
recording what I see others do. But in a dream life I am inside—I am living
it, not recording it."

In Maud's journals, there is far less evidence of these "dream lives" than
the above passage would suggest. Although the word "dream" appears with
enormous frequency in the journals, and is used in various capacities, it is
rarely used in relation to "dream lives." More often she refers to "day-dreams."

These references to dreaming "day-dreams" numerically cluster in three
spots in her journals: during the "affair" with Herman Leard; during her romance with Ewan; and during the period when Captain Smith was living
nearby and visiting often.

When Ewan was courting Maud in 1905, for instance, she says she went
out for a walk and "wandered happily along. . . . Later on I began simply to
dream. One can dream into one's life everything that isn't in it, so fully and

vividly that for the moment the dream seems real . . ." (March 16, 1905). The period of their courtship is filled with references to dreams and waking dreams. These kinds of vivid nighttime dreams, "waking dreams," and more especially "dream lives" re-emerge in the period when Smith's visits and conversation give her a lift. But of course she never links them to him, nor the earlier ones to Herman or Ewan.

With the exception of Cecil Rhodes (1853–1902), whose picture is visible in a photograph of her room in Cavendish before her marriage, Maud is quiet about her accomplices on these "dream-life adventures," but one can assume she was *not* a solitary explorer. Nor is it likely that the stodgy, depressed Ewan metamorphosed into an adventurer. It is far more plausible that Smith, an adventurer she did know, was the type of companion she found for her imaginary dream lives in this period.

Gossip

The flip side to Maud's ability to dream and imagine is represented by her often tense interactions in the real world. Here, public opinion, and particularly gossip, was a constant threat. As noted, Maud rages in her journals about her housemaid, Lily—her messiness, her foolishness, her general incompetence. Rather than dwell on Lily's gossip, Maud deflects attention to the swirl of community gossip. Of her gossipy neighbours, she writes: "They know the exact moment our washing is hung out, the number of pieces, and everything else that is done in our back yard. As to what goes on indoors, where they can't see, I fear their agony of curiosity about it will shorten their lives" (entry dated October 18, 1921, but written later). The underlying suggestion is that Lily, who was privy to all that happened inside the manse, enjoyed satisfying their curiosity. Of course, the Macdonalds enjoyed the gossip that Lily brought back from Zephyr and were curious to hear the details. They had a good laugh when Lily informed them that some of Marshall Pickering's Bible class students had dropped out because they didn't want to be taught "by a perjurer." But it is also likely that Pickering had found out the names of the Macdonald's witnesses from Lily.

Once she starts on the subject of gossip, Maud explains that idle gossip does not necessarily start with enemies. One of the Macdonalds' close neighbours in Leaskdale, Mrs. Alec Leask, a good friend, invented stories about the

Macdonald family based on snippets of information she had picked up, including conversations overheard on the telephone party lines. On one occasion she put out the word that Maud was writing a book on "stepmothers" to be published after she died. Since Maud's stepmother had originally lived in this area of Ontario, this idea drew much attention. (Lily may also have been involved in this tale, after hearing Maud tell funny stories about her stepmother in Prince Albert. Possibly Lily took a quick peep in Maud's diaries when she was recopying the part about her stepmother, and assumed it was for a book.)

In another entry (June 8, 1922) Maud recounts more local gossip. Supposedly Mrs. Leask had heard in Toronto that an unnamed Canadian author had just inherited a lot of money. She decided it must be Maud, and spread the word through the community that Maud was now an heiress. Maud worried that this gossip, if believed, would suggest to the parishioners that they did not really need to pay Ewan. Such stories take their own narrative life in Maud's journals because she is so maddened by gossip in this period. Gossip was entertainment in a small community, but it was also the means to carry out family feuds. There was no better way to "get even." She also knew that in a rural community, a time-honoured way for adults to test the truthfulness of gossip was to repeat the stories directly to a person, and then to watch for his or her reaction.

In Zephyr, Mrs. Will Lockie continued to prick Maud with various thorns. Maud had long chafed over Mrs. Lockie's remark that Maud kept a maid so she could "live without working," unlike the rest of the farmers' wives who *had* to work. In 1922, Mrs. Lockie further angered Maud by referring to a nurse Maud had hired for the births of Chester and Stuart: "We country women can't get a trained nurse. *We have to die*," she said on November 16, 1922. Maud says that she itched to retort, but did not dare say: "*You* have three children. Yet you are alive." Maud's only retaliation was to repeat gossip about Mrs. Lockie in her journal—that when she was younger and working as "a servant girl" she stole jam and preserves (very valuable commodities then) from her employer's pantry. Maud took some comfort that her journals would give the last word in the Lockie-Macdonald feud.

Gossip was often indirect, and Maud reacted sharply to innuendos like this, from a friend: "Nobody ever need say anything against you or Mr. Macdonald to me. . . . They don't say anything—they don't dare to." This, she noted, suggested that people *had* indeed been saying things (June 12, 1922). In better times, Maud would have laughed off these remarks. But she was raw from many other problems, including Lily's gossip, and she was finding it harder to laugh.

By March 1922, Lily had been with Maud for four years. When she had first come in 1918, Maud's home had been a cheerful house with little children; by now, Lily was bored with her job and generally unhappy.

To Maud, the most trying thing about Lily was her indiscretion, not her other faults. Maud demanded loyalty from employees and friends, but Lily, feeling sour, used gossip as revenge. On several occasions, Maud heard that she had told bold untruths about inconsequential matters, saying, for instance, that Maud *slept in* while she, Lily, did the work. Maud was livid: an outright lie, it reinforced the opinions of women who were jealous that Maud had a maid. Furious, and unable to write in her journal about the real source of her anger—Lily's gossiping about Maud's close friendship with Smith—Maud tells all the other stories about Lily, and gossip in general, to neutralize any stories that might linger in future years. Maud wanted to prove that where there was smoke there was not always fire—sometimes it was just the burning underbrush of gossip.

Gossip had always been a component of Maud's books. In fact, some of her books have little plot, they just move forward through talk (which is largely gossip). Now, gossip became a major subject in the *Emily* trilogy, reflecting Maud's own sense of victimization. Chapter 21 ("Thicker than water") of *Emily Climbs*—written in less than five months between August 29, 1923, and January 17, 1924—shows Maud's full fury at the power of gossip to destroy reputations. Raised in the small, closely knit community of Cavendish, where gossip regulated social behaviour, Maud would be pursued to her dying day by her grandmother's question: "What will people say?"

After May 1923, the Smiths departed from both Maud's journals and the Macdonalds' lives.

Amid all the pettiness over gossip, Maud was delighted with an unexpected professional honour. At the end of January 1923, she received a letter from the Secretary of the Royal Society of Great Britain, inviting her to become a Fellow of the Royal Society—the first Canadian woman ever to be offered the honour of putting "F.R.S.A." after her name. Now that literary tastes were changing and in some quarters her books seemed to be falling out of fashion, public recognition was especially important to her. She was proud of her long climb up "the Alpine Path."

Spring 1923 brought a Canadian Authors Association convention celebrating a new copyright law. Maud was so pleased when Professor John Daniel of Acadia University greeted her with, "Hail, Queen of Canadian novelists!" that she recorded this in her journals. Logan, with co-author Donald French, was preparing a new study entitled *Highways of Canadian Literature*, to be published in 1924, and they treated her with respect. Maud's springtime public speeches included a trip to Stratford and Mitchell, this time to speak to an audience of 150 that included many men, a new experience for her. In March, she would have another perk: *The Toronto Star* published a survey they had done, asking people: "Who Are the Twelve Greatest Women in Canada?" She was chosen as one, and recorded that in her journals.

CHAPTER 14

Maud and her boys

An early *Maclean's* article in 1919, entitled "The Author of *Anne*," stated that Maud was "a mother who mothers her children personally; they have always been considered before her books . . ." This was not quite true.[70] An objective observer would probably have seen her actual time allotment otherwise: her writing came first, her church work second, and her boys third. Ewan and her housework would likely have vied for number four. She *loved* her boys immensely, but with so many demands on her time, she was not able to *enjoy* them much. Loving children is not the same as enjoying them; children who are *enjoyed* feel secure in their parents' love. Her children were left to find their own amusements, something easily done in a small, safe, rural area like Leaskdale. Even when she did things with them, her mind was preoccupied by other matters. Maud puts in small anecdotes about her sons in her journals; while these reflect great affection, the reality is that she spent relatively little time with them due to the heavy load she carried—a rather sad state of affairs for a woman who had wanted children so badly.

Towards the end of his life, Stuart still recalled trying to attract his mother's attention when he was a child. He told of pushing wildflowers under the door when she was writing in the study. That brought his mother to the door to acknowledge the flowers and thank him, only to disappear behind the closed door again. Another time, when he was older, he memorized a poem she loved, Sir Walter Scott's *The Lady of the Lake* (some fifty pages of very small print). This had more of an impact. Oddly, Maud does not mention this feat in her journals, yet for Stuart, it was one of the most vivid memories of his childhood, one of those events that bonded him to his mother in a way nothing else could. He knew how much she liked reciting poems and had often heard her recite long sections from Scott's poem. Like his mother, he had an exceptional visual and aural memory and could memorize very easily. Years later, he still remembered the look of surprise on her face as he started reciting, and her mounting excitement as he continued, page after page, canto after canto. About halfway through his recitation he forgot a line, and his mother quietly prompted him. He said that he never forgot his astonishment that she knew the poem so well that she could prompt him at any place. He got extra attention for those efforts, for a very long time.[71]

As the boys were growing up, a pattern had been emerging. Stuart favoured his mother, not only in looks but also in personality and disposition. Chester took after his father. Maud consequently worried a great deal about Chester. Sunny little Stuart charmed the community with his smile and his recitations at church events. He had his mother's sense of timing and showmanship when reciting on the stage. He created no disturbances at home or school, and he made friends easily. Chester was just the opposite. From the beginning, something seemed amiss.

When Stuart reached his sixth birthday in 1921, Maud wrote assessments of her two sons. Stuart she characterized as smart and lovable, Chester as having some troubling qualities. "There is the same curious little streak of contrariness in him that there is in Ewan . . . its presence has always made him an exceedingly difficult child to train. . . . [H]e is a blunt reserved little fellow while Stuart, with his angel face and joyous pervasive smile, is the friend of all the world" (October 7, 1921).

Chester, in his ninth year, was already creating trouble in school. He was undeniably bright, and, like Stuart, he usually led his class. Chester had also inherited his mother's good memory, and he was an excellent reader, but his failure to socialize well with the other students produced constant mayhem. His mother initially blamed his troubles on inexperienced teachers. She remembered that when she had been teaching, she had been able to keep all the students in line.

However, according to Chester's former classmates in Leaskdale — interviewed in the early 1980s before the Montgomery journals were published and people's memories became tainted by what they had read in the journals — Chester was *always* getting into trouble at school. The students loved "to get him going" because he created such a lively uproar. Children teased and tormented him because he would react angrily to provocations and retaliate by lunging at offenders, and his clumsy attempts to catch his skinny, fast-footed classmates created a comic delight. They all said, independently, as adults looking back, that he was by nature a "loner." He wanted desperately to be accepted, but he was socially inept and ostracized.

Chester's classmates also recounted that he began showing precocious interest in girls long before anyone else, but the result was that the girls banded together to tease him. Girls would taunt him at recess, and he would erupt and chase them. Disturbances in class were also common, with kids throwing surreptitious spitballs at him to get a reaction. Failing a provocation, he would act up to become the centre of attention. The teacher would say, without even turning, "Is that you, Chester?" He often "got the strap" (a rubber belt about fifteen inches long, one quarter of an inch wide, with which the palm of the hand would be struck several times). As soon as he was old enough to walk the distance by himself, he was frequently sent home from school by exasperated teachers. Something seemed amiss with this boy.

There were no programs then for identifying and working with children with behavioural problems. A relatively inexperienced young teacher would have found it largely impossible to discuss the difficulties with Chester with Canada's most famous author of books that featured the trials of childhood. However, Maud did not need to be told about Chester's problems (e.g., as with impulse control): she saw them, but did not know what to do. She was alarmed and admitted to punishing Chester at home. She complained that Ewan was ineffective for training and discipline. For Ewan, as for many men in his generation, child-rearing was a woman's job.

Indeed, Ewan was no good with small children, nor did he connect with the older youngsters in his parish. Stuart remembered how his well-meaning father tried to relate to children by carrying hard candies called "humbugs" loose in his pocket. These he offered to children—who popped them in their mouths even if they had grungy pocket lint stuck to them.

Ewan left everything to Maud, including the boys' sex education. Maud says that she made a point of answering the boys' questions frankly and openly, and she got Chester a book about sex that explained details to him. She wrote that she was resolved not to turn sex into the "dirty" topic it had been in her youth. Her Victorian training, however, had left *her* exceptionally anxious over matters associated with sex.

Quite early in his development, Chester developed impulsive habits of sexual self-gratification, and he made no effort to conceal this. Maud was alarmed.

She certainly did not want Chester pleasuring himself in the bedroom he shared with his younger brother, nor did she want a maid—or visitor—to see it. "I have had to talk to Chester lately about certain habits to avoid," she wrote euphemistically on January 11, 1924, expressing irritation that Ewan would not do this. However, her talks did not stop Chester's behaviour, which continued to cause alarm. Chester was a very impulsive child—and later an impulsive young man—who could not postpone any kind of gratification.

For a woman so given to worry, Maud now had many sources of anxiety. Were Chester's problems with his peers related to Ewan's apparent inability to bond strongly with anyone? She remarked in her journals that Ewan had never had a close friend in all his life. Despite the pretext of friendship between Captain Smith and Ewan, she knew that it was really *her* conversational ability and celebrity that prompted Smith's frequent visits. His parishioners, and most people in general, had always *liked* Ewan, and thought him a good and kind man, but there was never a bond of strong friendship. As a minister, Ewan needed to maintain a certain reserve with all parishioners, but it was a fact that he, too, had always been a "loner." Although he was sensitive and brooding himself, he often seemed to lack the capacity for deep empathy with others. His bouts of depression only increased his self-absorption.

Chester looked like his father, was built like him, and now was showing signs of being like him in other ways that were poorly understood and poorly defined. Maud fretted over what she believed to be a hereditary taint in Ewan's family. One of Ewan's brothers, a well-to-do rancher in Montana, at some point late in his life went missing in a state of melancholy after saying he was going to kill himself. He was never found, according to Maud's journals.

Ewan and Chester begun to clash early in Chester's life. Ewan was apparently tormented by the fear that he had replicated himself and all his weakness in Chester. Maud had more than a premonition that there might be future trouble with Chester. She guessed that if Chester were going to inherit his father's melancholy, it would be manifested at puberty. This was a family whose problems were only beginning.

Ewan had remained anxious over himself since his first serious mental episode in 1919. In October 1921, he had driven himself down to Warsaw, Indiana, to visit his brother, a very successful medical doctor, hoping to get advice about his mental condition. After Ewan's return from Indiana, he had a particularly bad "melancholy" spell. He fixated on the idea that he was an "outcast from God," a soul lost to Satan and eternal damnation. In one of these depressions, he told Maud that he contemplated suicide. (When Maud reads Lecky's *History of European Morals*, she comments on suicide in her journals, picking up his ideas. Seen in her entry of May 10, 1922.) What little peace of mind Maud still had was lost with that admission: suicide would brand their children with shame for their entire lives. On November 1, 1921, Maud wrote in her journal that when he was ill, Ewan was "a personality which is repulsive and abhorrent to me . . ." Yet, at Christmas that year, Maud reported that Ewan was perfectly normal for the first time since 1918. These sudden and disorienting ups and downs seemed her new reality.

Finances were also a worry. Maud had been surprised that her October 1921 payment from her U.S. publisher, Stokes, was the smallest she had yet received from them. She blamed it on the financial depression in the United States at that time, and worried that she would have to draw on her capital. She thought ruefully of all the thousands of dollars that she had wasted on Stella Campbell, giving her money to lend to a suitor (Irving Howatt) and later money to buy a farm in California. The pressures on her increased, and with Ewan's mental health being so unpredictable, she was beginning to worry about whether she could maintain her income sufficiently to support them. She felt vulnerable in almost every aspect of her life now, and that would in turn affect her ability to write.

The vacation in Bala, Ontario

In the summer of 1922, there was no chance for the Macdonalds to drive down to Maud's beloved Prince Edward Island. (Ewan was busy talking to people, organizing witnesses for the Pickering lawsuit.) Instead, in July they made a shorter trip to the beautiful lake district of northern Ontario, an area Maud remembered from her return train trip from Prince Albert some thirty-one years earlier. On July 24, 1922, they packed their car and motored the eighty-five miles to Bala, Ontario. Maud took her imaginary "dream lives" with her.

In the jazz age, Bala was one of the most popular vacation spots in Ontario. A charming resort town on the lake some 125 miles north of Toronto, it was a favourite destination for Torontonians wanting to escape the summer heat in pre-air-conditioned times. Well-to-do people usually drove up in their own cars, but others came by train. Waiting to see who might spill out of the train (or steamboat from other ports) was the main excitement of the day for the younger folk in Bala.

Bala lay at the edge of Lake Muskoka, where the Musquosh River flowed into Bala Bay. Large American bands came in the summer, playing for all the vacationing city people who congregated there to mix, eat, drink, dance, and have a good time. At night, a part of the town was lighted by lanterns, and the large dance pavilion down by the lake gave Bala the atmosphere of a carnival. In the day, it was a beautiful place with lawns sloping down to the lake water, making it easy to swim or canoe. When the music died down and night fell, the roaring waters cascaded over the jagged rocks with a thunderous roar that sounded much like the surf in Prince Edward Island. Wealthy people built beautiful summer homes on the larger islands, which were reached by stately mahogany launches, some of them so large that their decks were used as dance floors. Bala was a magical place in those years between the end of World War I and the onset of the Great Depression, and both Ewan and Maud needed some magic in their lives.

Ordinary tourists stayed in guest homes near the shore of the lake. The Macdonalds stayed at Roselawn Lodge, located on Bala Bay, right below the waterfalls. Maud fell in love with the area. The twinkling lanterns reminded her of the carnival setting of the canals at the base of the famous conical Tomnahurich Mountain in Scotland.

When fogs arose, Bala had the same otherworld quality of Prince Edward Island and Scotland. Maud particularly liked the evenings, when she could sit on the porch, looking through the mists to the lights at other cottages, with campfires blazing, and escape into imaginings of warm fellowship in these private places. When Ewan took the boys out one afternoon, she described one of her "waking-dream lives":

> I picked out an island that just suited me. I built thereon a summer cottage and furnished it *de luxe*. I set up a boat-house and a motor launch. I peopled it with summer guests—Frede, Aunt Annie, Stella, Bertie—Mr. MacMillan (to whom I engaged Bertie!). We spent a whole idyllic summer there together. Youth—mystery— delight, were all ours once more. I lived it all out in every detail; we swam and sailed and fished and read and built campfires under the pines—I saw to it that I had an island with pines—and dined gloriously at sunset *al fresco*, and then sat out on moonlit porches

(well-screened from Muskoka mosquitoes!)—and always we talked—the soul-satisfying talk of kindred spirits, asking all the old, unanswered questions, caring not though there were no answers so long as we were all ignorant together. (July 31, 1922)

Maud continues describing their "dream life" adventure. Ewan does not make the first list of names above, but she tucks him into the second paragraph, maybe as an afterthought, adding that in her dream he is "*not* a minister." The people she chose for her dream were all people who made excellent company. Of course, the best conversationalist and storyteller she knew in 1922 was Edwin Smith who loved lakes, oceans, and water. His ability at sailing was legendary and his yacht from his Prince Edward Island days would have been a classy companion for the motorized mahogany launches in Bala. Significantly, he is not named in this waking dream. He has been all but erased from the narrative in her journals.

While Maud was in Bala, she checked the English proofs of *Emily of New Moon* and did restful fancy-work. The family took their meals across the street with a Mrs. Pyke, "a lady cumbered with much serving."[72] In a picture of herself in a canoe, which Maud has entitled "Dreaming," she looks extremely happy.

On this Muskoka vacation, the Macdonalds made a day-trip to see John Mustard and his wife. For $100, John Mustard had purchased a wilderness spot on Lake Muskoka a few miles north of Bala. John and his teenage son Gordon had recently finished building their own modest wooden cottage, amid mature maples and oaks on a long, sloping bank that ran down to the lake.[73] John Mustard's rural retreat was a paradise, just what Maud might have dreamed of owning herself. With the $10,000 she had wasted on her feckless cousin Stella Campbell, she could have bought the largest and most romantic island in Muskoka.

But what would that have availed her without a soulmate to enjoy it with? Nature—water, trees, flowers—all made Maud feel wholesome, but Ewan did not even notice them. The lake would only have been a place for Ewan to drown himself when a melancholy spell descended on him. Ewan's figure had thickened with age, inactivity, and too much food. By contrast, the trim and distinguished-looking Reverend John Mustard shed his formal clerical garb and turned into a woodsman when he came to Muskoka. John had nailed up a nice little cottage for his family, but Ewan was so clumsy that he could not have clapped two boards together. In this little cottage in the backwoods, one could go to sleep to the call of the whippoorwill and wake to the call of the loons. It was a dream spot. Maud must have felt unspeakable envy when she first saw it nestled amid the trees.

Needless to say, John Mustard did not make it into Maud's waking-dreams. He was too genuinely and irritatingly *good* to be interesting. But she could not have helped comparing the man she had spurned to the man she had chosen. John Mustard was healthy and optimistic; Ewan was sluggish and gloomy. John Mustard had far less income than they had, but he had far more joy in what he had.

John Mustard was a compassionate man who undoubtedly saw the depressive aura around Ewan. From his brothers, Hugh and James Mustard, mainstays in Ewan's parish, John would have known that Ewan was well liked but that his health had been troublesome. No doubt he sensed Maud's inner worries. When Mrs. Mustard took Ewan and the boys out for a little fishing expedition, John Mustard played the good host and stayed behind to keep Maud company. This was not appreciated—Maud would never have discussed her husband with him, or their past encounter in Prince Albert. And she despised pity. Their conversation was stilted. His friendly kindness annoyed her. In her journal, she presents the Reverend John Mustard as the same "tedious man" who had been her teacher in 1890–91, and she says nothing to indicate his sterling qualities. The Reverend John Mustard's career path had been steady, solid, and upward from the beginning. Maud was well aware of all this, but she does not write anything about it in her journal. Nor does she tell us what she very well knows—that he has become one of the most successful and respected Presbyterian ministers in all of Toronto.[74]

Maud had asked earlier in her life why people could not always love that which was most worthy. Certainly John Mustard was as worthy as men come, and he was unfailingly kind to the Macdonalds, and genuinely solicitous over Ewan's health until the end of Maud's and Ewan's lives. In a thoughtful frame of mind during this Bala vacation, Maud must have compared Mustard to the other minister of her ken, Edwin Smith. Smith had the personal charisma and dazzling oral skills that left people admiring *him*, whereas John Mustard exuded sincerity, solidity, and generosity of spirit towards *others*. But Maud could not bring herself to give John Mustard his due in her journals.[75]

Maud's visit to Bala, and to the Mustard cottage, got only a small write-up in her journals, but her trip gave her new ideas. She tucked away this magical

landscape—and the waking dreams she had had there—in her memory bank
for a future novel.

The following spring, in 1923, Ewan had bad news from the Island. His sister Christie's son, Leavitt, had embezzled a large amount of money, and the
only way for his family to avoid public shame in the province was to make
silent restitution. Ewan's distracted and heartbroken sister begged for a
$5,000 loan on her mortgage. Since Maud had just received profits from
Further Chronicles of Avonlea, Ewan wanted her to lend them to Christie.
Maud balked. She doubted she would ever get the money back, and she had
already lent a great deal of money to other family members that would not
be repaid. She wanted Christie to go to Ewan's two brothers for the money.
One brother, Dr. Angus Macdonald, in Indiana, was very well-to-do, and he
had no children, so he could well afford to help. Ewan decided to take a
quick trip to the Island to see what else he could do for his sister; Maud approved, knowing that Ewan always performed well in negotiating situations
where he had a focus.

Ewan came back from the Island with hopeless news: Leavitt had run up
a $13,000 debt and embezzled $1,500 from the post office, a federal offence.
He had now absconded to the United States, leaving his dying father and distraught mother to cope. Ewan worked it all out, asking for some of Maud's royalty income. "To get his parents in a mess like that!!" Maud exclaimed in her
journal, but then added, "But I must not be too harsh. I don't know how my
own boys will turn out yet" (May 21, 1923). She had plenty of reason to worry
about Chester.

A month later she noted another sounding of this theme: a family's disappointment in a son. John Mustard's only son had "broken his parents' hearts,"
she wrote, "by suddenly presenting them with a French Canadian Catholic
wife whom he picked up in the mining regions up north." Maud felt, like
most of her Presbyterian contemporaries, that marrying a Catholic, especially
a French-Canadian one, was a big plunge down the social ladder. Scotland's
history was full of clashes between the Presbyterians and the Catholics, and
the enmity ran centuries deep. It had carried across the Atlantic, and Maud
had been brought up to believe that Catholics were even worse than "heathens," who were merely ignorant. This was embedded as deeply within her
as the fear of what people would say or think. (Yet, intellectually, Maud rose

above her deep prejudice in her *Emily* novels, portraying a Catholic priest with respect.)

By late summer 1923, Maud herself wanted to travel to Prince Edward Island for some renewal. She was having trouble writing. This time, she left Ewan at home, taking only her two sons, now eleven and seven. But the visit was bittersweet. In spite of the still-strong charms of the sea wind, the hearty meals, the twilights in "Lovers' Lane," and the warmth of renewing friendships, Maud realized sadly that the Prince Edward Island she loved was as much a *time* as a *place*. The landscape might be the same, but many of the people she loved, like Frede, were gone. In addition, the character of the Island was changing as a result of tourism, for which she was largely responsible. (Once the law against cars had been repealed, American tourists had flooded in again.)

The only thing that had not changed on the Island was the superior quality of its cats. At Park Corner she picked out a wonderful little striped kitten with an "M" on its side to ship back to Ontario. She named him "Good Luck" and called him "Lucky." Of all the cats that she would have in her life, Lucky was to be her favourite.

As soon as she returned from the Island, in late August, Maud resumed the task of writing *Emily Climbs*. She felt little interest in it. Her readers would demand that Emily grow up, marry, and live happily ever after. Maud had been in a state of heady excitement when she wrote both *Anne of Green Gables* and *Emily of New Moon*, but it was only her personal discipline that got her through the sequels, where her feisty heroines had to be tamed.

The family tension in Maud's life, combined with the steady writing and revising of her books, compounded by a too-busy round of social obligations, was beginning to take its toll. She had gained forty pounds in the previous two years. She was suffering from muscle spasms in her shoulders and neck, and these were expanding into headaches. She was now forcing herself to write three hours per day instead of two, which aggravated this condition. She revised "Emily 2" during the next two months, and had it ready for a typist by March 8, 1924. She dedicated *Emily Climbs* to "Pastor Felix," the pseudonym of a long-time correspondent, the Reverend Arthur John Lockhart (c. 1850–1926), a poet who was the uncle of Nate Lockhart, her first "beau" from schooldays.

The formula for popular fiction required young women to marry. Young men could light out for new territory and adventure (like Huckleberry Finn), but women were usually destined for matrimony. Maud complained in her journals that she could never write of young girls as they really were, very interested in boys and with growing sexual urges: "*Love* must scarcely be hinted at—yet young girls in their early teens often have some very vivid love affairs. A girl of *Emily's* type certainly would . . ." (January 20, 1924). As Maud watched Emily's sexuality developing (while remembering her own development, and keeping one eye on the real-life turmoil in Chester's pubescent life and the other on her aging, troubled husband), she must have wondered where to take her story. Emily had to be taken through her teenage years into marriage without any hint of improper thoughts along the way.

Maud was in her forty-ninth year, still full of vitality, locked into a marriage to a man who, when he was depressed, she found repugnant. Maud's maids recounted that although Ewan wore relatively formal attire most of the time, he always looked slightly slovenly; his rumpled look was accentuated by his swarthy skin. Some people compared Maud's impeccable cleanliness and wondered how she could tolerate such an unkempt husband.

Emily Climbs (1925)

In the first *Emily* book, Dean Priest is an older man, widely travelled, who becomes a friend to Emily. In the second *Emily* book, he becomes the hunchbacked "Jarback" Priest, who develops a romantic interest in her. An adult reading *Emily Climbs* feels discomfort with the change: Dean may be a "Priest," but to adult readers he begins to feel unwholesome, more like a sexual predator than an older friend.

The *Emily* trilogy had begun in 1921 as a Künstlerroman, a story about the education and development of an artist figure—in this case, a female artist. It loses its direction as Maud negotiates the dark waters of sexuality, unable to depict either the abnormal or normal kind. Dean's nickname of "Jarback" signals that something is wrong with this man. "Jarback" then slips into the skin of a predator—he is quite willing to destroy Emily's self-esteem and her writing in order to persuade her to marry him. Ewan had counselled Maud to give up her writing after she had a nervous attack early in their relationship. As we saw earlier, Maud once complains in her journals that the otherwise kindly Ewan has a "medieval" attitude towards women, seeing them as a man's possession (March 25, 1922). The adult reader hardly knows what to make of this fictional character, Dean Priest, who suddenly shifts from being a father-figure to a lurking menace, interested only in Emily's body, not her creativity or soul. The fictional world of sexuality has become as unstable as Montgomery's real one. Maud seems to be writing out of her own emotional turmoil, and although the young reader stays interested in finding out what will happen to Emily, the novel seems to have lost its focus. Maud often said that she intended to keep the "shadows" of her own life out of her fiction, but they appear here in strangely twisted form.

By March 1924, when Maud was finishing *Emily Climbs*, she had the "tight" feeling in her head again. Her Canadian income was down. *Rilla* had sold, but only 12,000 copies; and *Emily of New Moon* only 8,500 in Canada. And there was ongoing aggravation over Ewan's lawsuit. Ewan could be hauled into court anytime that Pickering thought he might have enough money to pay the judgment. The letters from Lawyer Grieg kept insulting Ewan for his "inability to pay." The mere reminder of the lawsuit stirred up one more failure for Ewan—his inability to get justice in a court of law—and seemed once more to prove that God had rejected him.

At one point Greig sent an affidavit, implying that Ewan was hiding his real income so he would have more money *"wherewith to enjoy himself* and to spend in *unnecessary ways."* Both Maud and Ewan thought this statement a howler. The idea of a staid Presbyterian minister, particularly a depressive one, enjoying himself in *"necessary"* ways was funny enough, but "in unnecessary ways" was beyond imagining, even to Ewan. It is one of the few times in her journals where Maud tells of having a good laugh with Ewan (although maids and relatives said they did have a good time together in the early years).

The whole Pickering affair continued as a strain on the Macdonalds, even if they could laugh over aspects of the case—including the fact that the court required Pickering to pay thirty dollars, then a substantial amount of money, for Ewan's expenses every time Ewan was summoned for a court examination of his financial state. The procedure wore Ewan down, and he relapsed into melancholy after almost a year of being fairly stable. Maud wanted to pay the debt from her income and be done with Pickering, but Ewan stubbornly refused.

On a Sunday in the first week of March 1924, Maud went into the library to find him, with a bandana tied round his head, suffering another attack: "unshorn, collarless, hair on end, eyes wild and hunted, with a hideous imbecile expression." He preached a puerile sermon, reducing her to tears of humiliation. Ewan was soon too ill to preach at all. In mid-April, their newspaper, the

Northern Ontario Times, carried the Leaskdale note that "Mr. Macdonald is improving after an attack of neuritis. Mr. Edmunds of Uxbridge occupied the pulpit on Sunday." Maud was using neuritis to explain her husband's problems at this time; it is a vague term suggesting inflammation of the nerves. Soon Maud was again in pain from a tight feeling around her head, undoubtedly caused by stress, a symptom that would afflict her during tense periods for the rest of her life.

When Ewan did manage to sleep, he found himself frightened by his dreams. Once he woke in a terror, having dreamed of murdering a good friend. This was apparently the second time Ewan had had the dream of killing a friend, and Maud began to be frightened of him, for herself and for the boys. He had begun to hear voices in his attacks telling him "he was going to be lost—God hated him—he was doomed to hell" (March 25, 1924).

Whenever Maud saw Ewan start to "paw" at his head, she knew the malady was starting up again. She could not imagine where things would end. She had been giving Ewan a steady course of chloral or Veronal when he had symptoms or when he could not sleep—drugs that were recommended by Dr. Shier, as well as the Bostonian Dr. Nathan Garrick. (Ewan may have medicated himself on top of what Maud gave him.) In these attacks, Maud reported that Ewan had abnormal physical symptoms: his breath smelled of urea and his skin turned a poor colour.[76] This time, his attack intensified as the days wore on, and he paced the floors, shaking, his eyes haunted. One day his illness reached a peak, and he fled the house and strode up the road in mud and slush, in full view of the neighbours, and then returned, muttering that he was dying. Maud took his pulse, which was fine. She brought him to the library so the boys would not see him. After bursting into tears and crying for some time, he improved.

When he was at his worst, she kept him out of sight of the community. When he was only slightly affected, and they had to go visiting, he was able to keep up a minimal conversation, and she would carry it. Once, by "devilish felicity" a lady they were visiting in Zephyr regaled them with tales of the "suicides of the unsound in mind." A Zephyr neighbour had just tried suicide by Paris Green, but had not taken enough to kill her, only enough to furnish "gruesome details" for gossip (April 20, 1924). Maud watched Ewan's increasing agitation until he got up and left the room, at which point she managed to change the subject.

———

Maud finished *Emily Climbs* on March 8, 1924. Since the *Emily* books were to be a trilogy, it would have been natural for her to start the third and final *Emily* novel next. Instead, she started a novel called *The Blue Castle* on April 10, and then the third Emily book, *Emily's Quest*, on May 26, 1924. This was unprecedented—having two novels going at the same time. *The Blue Castle* seems to have been a "one-off" novel, demanding to be written, pushing aside the third and final *Emily* book. *The Blue Castle* is set in Muskoka.

In late April 1924, Maud took a break from her writing for her "semi-annual orgy of household shopping" in Toronto. She brought home a little puppy for her boys, an Airedale they named Dixie, hoping it would be a happy distraction in a troubled household.

She made some speeches, and local newspapers carried accounts. The *North Bay Nugget* reported: "Mrs. McDonald [*sic*] paid a glowing tribute to the high character of Canadian writing." In all her speeches she now routinely made a plea for Canadian support for Canadian writers, books, and magazines. She was carrying the Canadian Authors Association message everywhere she spoke. The Hamilton *Spectator* found her:

> an altogether delightful person—rather above medium height [*not accurate*], and with thick hair, slightly graying, which she wore waved and coiled becomingly about her well-shaped head. Her face was unlined and she smiled easily, and to the reporter who had once fancied that the lovable Anne of Green Gables was none other than the author, she seemed indeed the embodiment of that wholesome, refreshing type of Prince Edward Island womanhood. . . . When asked her opinion of the modern "teenage girl"—the ultra modern young person who smoked and went everywhere unchaperoned, and who contrasted rather sadly with Anne of Green Gables, Mrs. McDonald defended the modern young girl. . . . Speaking of the too popular sex novel of the present day which the young girls read, Mrs. McDonald admitted that it was not until the other day that she had read *Flaming Youth*, the most flagrant of the fast sexy novels. She had been disgusted by it, for it neither pointed a moral, nor had it any excuse for its existence, like some of the really great sex novels, such as Tolstoy wrote.

Some days later, Maud wrote again in her journals how much she was en-joying writing *The Blue Castle*. It touched on taboo themes: she gave an un-married mother a brief but sympathetic treatment in it, depicting her as an innocent, gullible, and psychologically needy young woman who got pregnant out of innocence. The main heroine fantasizes wildly about the perfect lover.

Maud's life seemed in some sort of choppy turmoil. In May 1924, she in-explicably set *The Blue Castle* aside and prepared to start "Emily 3." She fin-ished her annual month-long ritual of spring-cleaning, followed by cleaning layers of manure and straw buildup out of the horse stable with pitchforks in preparation for a new batch of chickens. Maud could not count on Ewan to do work like this, so she did it herself, with help from Lily—who was a hard worker, good at pitching manure, whatever her other faults might have been.

Finances were a problem because of the ongoing Page lawsuit, but Maud's financial state eased when *The Delineator* asked her to write four Emily stories, with payment of $1,600. On the first of June, Ewan left for a long vacation in PEI, a relief after three months of gloom.

Sadly, as soon as Ewan returned from PEI, Maud learned that her Aunt Annie had passed away; she went to the Island for the funeral. Maud experi-enced her beloved Aunt Annie's death as she would have that of her own mother—she remained deeply attached to the Park Corner farm as a beacon of happiness from her childhood. Her Aunt Annie Campbell's nonjudgmen-tal love had been a source of great comfort to her when she was young, and now one more person she loved on the Island was gone. She came back with nerves frayed, and decided they all needed a holiday.

Mammoth Cave in Kentucky

Now, Maud planned a different vacation for her family: a car trip to see the unusual underground formations in Kentucky known as Mammoth Cave. Being behind the wheel always cleared Ewan's mind. Maud's cousin Bertie McIntyre came from British Columbia to accompany them. Bertie had the Montgomery sense of gaiety and was good company. The boys, now twelve and nine, were the right age for such a car trip.

There was something symbolic in Maud's desire to see this cave. She herself lived partly on the surface of life and partly in another world, out of sight, where she walked in the alternate byways of literature, creativity, and imaginative adventures. So, in a sense, she was drawn to the subterranean. She had grown up with Scottish and Irish mythologies, which held that there was an alternate world of fairy folk beneath the earth's solid surface. To her imagination, this pagan Celtic legacy of subterranean folk was no more fantastical than the Christian belief in a God and singing angels above the earth's solid surface. She wanted to see, in real time, in real life, a place where there was an alternate world that was out of this world but that nevertheless had physical existence. Powerful emotions that no one could know of were churning in her.

So the Macdonalds packed their bags, loaded their car, and started off on the morning of July 28, 1924, to Kentucky. Ewan drove their new car "Dodgie" without accident for a total of 1,817 miles, over an eleven-day period—a remarkable feat of concentration, considering that most of the roads they travelled over were dirt and gravel, full of ruts and potholes that could knock off the tires or axles of those fragile, early cars. It was an endurance test for all. When a storm came up near Sarnia, the Macdonalds quickly drove their car off the road into a nearby barn until it was over, and they were lucky to encounter no more rain on the trip. Their only other mishap was finding a single bedbug in an Indiana hotel. Maud was amazed to find red roads in Kentucky, just like the ones in Prince Edward Island.

Mammoth Cave cast an indescribable spell on Maud. Even Ewan was captivated—"and Ewan seldom seems to take much pleasure in the things that please others," she wrote. Each day they donned "cave costumes" and walked down into the mouth of the chilling cave (fifty-four degrees Fahrenheit), then followed guides with gasoline lanterns through two to three miles of subterranean paths, past underground lakes and rivers, along precipices, down steep steps, and through long, lofty "rooms" with strangely formed grotesque figures looking like birds or animals or people, in a world without sight or sound. Maud mused over the totally white eyeless fish that she had heard about in sermons all her life—an example of what ministers said happened when living creatures didn't use their powers and descended into a "degenerate state." When the tourists rose to the earth's surface again, it seemed unreal for the moment, the ground she stood on an illusion.

The trip both pleased and "spooked" her. She never wanted to return: this mysterious underworld world, beneath the lush rolling green fields of Kentucky, was too close a reminder of the double life she led herself.

The profound identification she experienced in the hidden worlds of

Mammoth Cave proved to be curiously restorative. She again felt pleasure in the world around her, and her love of sharing that pleasure with others bubbled up again, with its healing powers. After she returned home, she spoke to many groups about the wonders of this experience, including the Hypatia Club and the Guilds of Leaskdale.

Church Union turmoil

A new concern had been percolating in the Macdonalds' lives for a number of years: the subject of "Church Union." It had been mooted before the Great War, and approved by the General Assembly in 1916, but was not taken up again until after the war. In 1924, a Church Union bill went before the Canadian Parliament for debate. It proposed that the Presbyterian Church, the Methodist Church, and the Congregational Churches (and a few already amalgamated Protestant denominations) join into one church, to be called the "United Church of Canada." The doctrinal differences between various Protestant churches were compatible. Canada's population was diverse and scattered, and the increasing use of cars, giving people more mobility, made it unnecessary for there to be so many tiny rural Protestant churches with very small congregations.

Many farmers were sympathetic to the economic aspect of Church Union. They struggled to support their churches in the depressed times after the war. From a financial point of view, Church Union made sense. There would be a larger congregation supporting a single minister, and only one church building to maintain. There would be social benefits, too—people could see many more of their neighbours in the community every time they worshipped or attended a church function. Churches were still the dominant social organization in every community.

From other points of view, however, Church Union spelled trouble. Old loyalties to specific denominations and sects would die hard. Although the war had lessened the hold of the Church on people, congregations were still very loyal to the specific churches of their fathers. Both Ewan and Maud knew that if Union went through, amalgamating several denominations into the "United Church," the weaker ministers would be pushed out. The unspoken truth was that Ewan was likely to be one of these, given his erratic health. Maud knew that if he lost his profession, she could still support them well enough on her income, but she feared that the psychological impact on him would be devastating.

Church Union was particularly favoured by parishioners in Zephyr. That tiny village not only had Ewan's Presbyterian church, but the Methodist one as well. (The Methodist church was the one Marshall Pickering attended—although he himself was in hospital now with the diagnosis of diabetes.) The national government planned to ask each congregation in Canada to vote on whether the parishioners wanted to amalgamate churches, either to endorse Church Union or stay out as Continuing Presbyterians. This vote at the community level became an incredibly divisive agent, splitting families, and pitting neighbours against each other.

In summer, after the Church Union bill passed in Parliament, setting the stage for local votes on whether to go "union" or not, Ewan mobilized himself again to persuade his two churches to remain Presbyterian rather than become a "United Church." He and his Scottish forebears had all been Presbyterian, and he wanted to stay Presbyterian, rather than go "Union." For her part, Maud decided that she didn't much care which way things went, writing in her journals:

> The Spirit of God no longer works through the church for humanity. It did once but it has worn out its instrument and dropped it. Today it is working through Science. That is the real reason for all the "problems" we hear so much of in regard to the "church." The "leaders" are trying to galvanize into a semblance of life something from which life has departed. (December 14, 1924)

She said nothing like this in public, however.

With Church Union boiling up, Ewan could focus his considerable persuasive and negotiating skills. But by the end of the year, the tension over the Union question made everyone feel frayed. There was much politicking, much gossiping about others' motives, nasty power-wielding within congregations, and in some cases, some real skulduggery in voting procedures, as ministers devised ways to deny the vote to those whose preference they did not like.

By Christmas, Maud felt exhausted. She was coping with the general anxiety over Union, endless youth dialogue practices for the Christmas concert, letters from people asking her for financial help, mail from her Boston lawyer, the start of a bad cold, and Lily's claiming to have a dozen illnesses—

a "new one every half hour." Maud felt, she said, "like a cat one jump ahead of a dog" (December 28, 1924). A new physical symptom bothered her: roving and immobilizing muscle spasms.

When the votes were all counted in January 1925, both of Ewan's congregations had voted to remain Presbyterian. Leaskdale was solid, voting 63 to 11, but the results in fractious Zephyr had a smaller margin, 23 to 18. Some of the Zephyr people left the church anyway. This placed even greater financial strain on those who remained. Maud was cross with those who left, but the Macdonalds laughed to hear a report of the Methodists complaining that the Presbyterians had sent all their "cranks" over to them.

All across Canada, the aftermath of the Church Union vote was acrimonious. Many Presbyterian ministers quit speaking to former friends who had taken the other side. The Macdonalds had been very close to John and Margaret Stirling in Prince Edward Island, visiting each other whenever possible. Church Union did not completely destroy this long-time friendship, but it did cause serious strain, because John supported Union. Church topics were off limits when they met. It also caused rifts between many of the Presbyterian ministers in the Ontario circle that Ewan knew. Maud mentions nothing in her journals about Edwin Smith's thoughts on Union, but church records show that he later became the minister at a United Church some distance away in Ontario.

Ewan's position as minister in Leaskdale and Zephyr was now—thankfully—reasonably secure. This cheered him enough that he kept trying for a new "call" to a different congregation. They were still in a moving mode. The bickering and cash-strapped parish of Zephyr, the Pickering affair, the incessant small community gossip over Maud's personal life and business affairs, and the Church Union fighting had left them both convinced that it was time for a change. It seemed that as soon as Ewan smoothed over one problem in Zephyr, another issue arose. When Maud went to women's meetings—and there were many of these—she claimed to feel an undercurrent of tension.

Ewan had received a number of invitations to "preach for the call" in the post-war period—after all, it was widely known that he was married to the famous authoress, L. M. Montgomery, and that she was an excellent "helpmeet" in his church work. Ewan could rise to the challenge of giving fine sermons when he preached elsewhere, but there must have been something subtle in his demeanour or appearance that turned people off. Or, given the speed at which gossip spread, perhaps rumours of his intermittent illnesses preceded him. Again and again, over several years, he lost the call to someone else: at Pinkerton and Priceville, at Columbus and Brooklyn, at Markham, Orangeville, Hillsburg, Whitby. All were rural or small-town parishes—a Toronto charge was beyond him—and even the rural places seemed not to want him after they saw him. One reputedly did not want him because he came with a *car*: ministers with cars were apt to go gadding off to Toronto. Each rejection laid him lower. Ewan's continuing failure to get a new call sent him to bed with his old, debilitating depression once again.

In February 1925, a new maid, Elsie Bushby, came to replace Lily Meyers. Maud had wanted to dismiss Lily for a long time, but she had been afraid of what an angry Lily might say. Even when Lily finally left on her own, Maud still worried that she would "tell all kinds of falsehoods about me and my household all over the country" (February 27, 1925). There were few stories, of course, that Lily had not already told, but Maud makes the comment to emphasize in her journals—for future readers and biographers—that Lily was nothing but an unreliable troublemaking gossip.

Elsie Bushby, her replacement, was a bright and perky young woman who brought enormous cheer into Maud's life. By her own account, Elsie came from a very poor farm family and had grown up in a household where there rarely was enough food to go around. Elsie was nevertheless rich in vitality, with an irrepressibly positive attitude towards life. She was a hard worker, a quick learner, and a spunky young woman very glad to get the position.

As soon as the bouncy, bright Elsie was established in the household after the end of the first week in January, Maud's spirits soared and her pen started flying again. She went back to writing *The Blue Castle* with renewed vigour. She could write and enjoy it again, even if Ewan was struggling mentally and taking bromides. In less than a month, she had finished the first draft of the novel, calling it a release from her cares and worries.

This novel is her most revised novel, perhaps an indication of the stress she was under when she wrote the first part of it. It is also a novel that changes greatly in tone from beginning to end, so much that it almost seems to have been written by two people (an indication, perhaps of Elsie's effect on the household). In early March, after a whirlwind but immensely detailed revision, Maud pronounced the novel finished.

The Blue Castle (1926)

Maud first began to unpack her emotions from the 1922 trip to Bala into fiction in April 1924, immediately following Ewan's worst mental attack since 1919. Bala remained in her mind as the terrain for private dreams. She could imagine trysts with a lover on one of the distant, misty islands. Their private cottage among the trees would be visible only when its lights twinkled over the water at night. They would be there alone and together, wildly in love, enjoying each other. She began to fashion an imaginary lover—he would be a mysterious man, believably ordinary in some ways, but with the mystique of a fascinating demon-lover in others. She would use elements of the Bluebeard fairy-tale myth to give him a sinister aura. These creative stirrings completely obsessed her, and this was the book that shoved the final *Emily* novel into the background.

Anne's House of Dreams had removed a zombie-like husband from a passionate young woman's life. Reversing this situation, *The Blue Castle* produced a romantic lover for its unhappy, lonely heroine. *The Blue Castle* was drawn from deep in Maud's reservoir of imaginative wishes. Ewan's apparent "madness" and murderous dreams certainly heated up her febrile imagination. She could not help wondering what her life would have been like had she married a man who was a confident, intellectually stimulating, responsive partner, a composite of the best qualities of men like Ewan, John Stirling, John Mustard, and Edwin Smith.

The heroine of *The Blue Castle*, the plain and depressed Valancy Stirling, is a spinster of twenty-nine who is as desperate for marriage as Maud herself was at the same age. There, on an imaginary island in Lake Muskoka, Maud put her most passionate writing into the story of Valancy Stirling, who "wakened early, in the lifeless, hopeless hour just preceding dawn. She had not slept very well. One does not sleep well, sometimes, when one is twenty-nine on the morrow, and unmarried, in a community and a connection where the unmarried are simply those who have failed to get a man."

Valancy's mother, Mrs. Stirling (an Anglican, by the way, not a Presbyterian), is the kind of overbearing and pinched mother who would "sulk for days" when crossed. Living with them is "Cousin Stickles," a whining widow with a "mole right on the end of her dumpy nose, bristling hairs on her chin," and "protruding eyes." Cousin Stickles never tires of bragging to Valancy that *she* was married at seventeen. And Valancy's mother—a woman who can

make her anger felt in every room of a house, and who feels daily embarrassment over the fact that her daughter has failed to marry—never tires of telling
Valancy, who wants nothing more in life than to get married and have "fat little" babies, that it is "not *maidenly* to think about *men*." Mrs. Stirling does not
know that Valancy, "so cowed and subdued and overridden and snubbed in
real life, was wont to let herself go rather splendidly in her day-dreams."

Valancy's escape is to her "blue castle" in Spain. In it she keeps many
lovers, though "only one at a time." She had one at age twelve, another at fifteen, and another at twenty-five. By age twenty-nine, Valancy often feels a pain
around her heart. She would like to see a doctor about it, but is afraid to—
afraid her mother will find out she has gone without permission, afraid of what
the doctor might tell her.

Valancy's only escape from the dreariness of her life is to read books by
John Foster, a popular writer who mixes nature description with philosophy.
Her life is changed the day she comes across the line in his *Magic of Wings*
that says: "Fear is the original sin. Almost all the evil in the world has its origin in the fact that someone is afraid of something" (Chapter 5).

Mrs. Stirling has instilled in Valancy the terrible fear of "what people will
say" about her. Valancy's mother, as well as her aunts and uncles and cousins,
all say cruel things to her. If Valancy ever speaks back to anyone, her mother
chides her that it is "unladylike to have feelings." Her mother polices her every
moment; she is not allowed solitude and privacy even in her own bedroom,
lest she do unmentionable things there.

After reading Foster's statement about "fear," and articulating to herself
that "Despair is a free man—hope is a slave" (Chapter 8), Valancy begins to
free herself. She goes to see a doctor. Through a mistake, the doctor tells her
that she has only one year to live. She is seized with a new attitude to life, and
decides to move out of the family home. To the shock of her clan, and as an
act of compassion, Valancy moves in with a young woman who is dying of
consumption, the daughter of the disreputable town handyman, "Roaring
Abel." "Cissy" Gay has had a baby out of wedlock, and the baby has died. To
make the Gays even worse social pariahs, Roaring Abel Gay, though
Presbyterian, is a profane inebriate who always manages to reduce to shambles the theological arguments of every minister who tries to reform him.
Valancy has always liked Abel, "a jolly, picturesque, unashamed reprobate"
who "stood out against the drab respectability of Deerwood and its customs
like a flame-red flag of revolt and protest" (Chapter 9).

While living at the Gays', Valancy meets their friend Barney Snaith, who roars around town in his Grey Slosson car (named "Lady Jane Grey," like the Macdonalds' own car). Cissy dies (the predictable fate in Victorian literature for any woman who has sinned sexually). With a shocking lack of propriety, Valancy herself proposes to Barney Snaith, the dashing mystery man whom the town believes to be a criminal on the run, explaining to him that she does not have long to live. They marry hurriedly and move to his small cottage on a secluded Muskoka island. They have a year of more bliss than she has known in her entire life. Maud concludes with a surprise ending that is, of course, happy for everyone. Barney Snaith is, of course, the famous John Foster, a millionaire from the sales of his popular books. Her family, who have been so ashamed of Valancy's behaviour that they disowned her, rush to reclaim her.

This book is wonderfully implausible, but readers willingly suspend their disbelief. The hard-hitting but hilarious verbal exchanges between well-sketched characters expose all of Maud's disdain for social sham and hypocrisy, and must have left many of the readers of her time gasping for air—some in shock, others in laughter. The book defies classification, even as a "romance," because it is so full of wisdom about life, laughter at human foibles, and powerful emotions. A 1926 review in Great Britain's famous journal *Punch* notes that the plot of the book is like "sentimental fiction," but hastens to add that although the "plot is as threadbare as could well be imagined . . . [,] the odd thing is that in the telling it acquires a surprising semblance of freshness."[77]

At the end, we find that John Foster has become a writer because he experienced emotional deprivation in childhood due to his mother's early death. Both he (and Maud) offset the feelings of isolation and loneliness by finding an alternate world where they write novels in order to create their own happiness. Foster is slightly embarrassed by his books, which are full of purple prose (like Maud's own). Maud structures the book in a way that consciously exposes the psychological necessities behind her imaginary writer's actions and his stratagems for coping in life. The imaginary heroine is given the same treatment. The book provides genuine insights about how personalities are moulded. It also captures and defuses the corrosive and explosive rebellion in its author's soul.

Once again, Maud had caught the spirit of her era in creating characters who challenge religion and give human hypocrisy a rough ride. Maud gave away nothing personal, however, when talking about her novels and her own life. Later, in 1929, she said about the setting for *The Blue Castle*, the only novel she ever set in Ontario: "*The Blue Castle* is in Muskoka. Muskoka is the only place I've ever been in that could be my Island's rival in my heart. So I wanted to write a story about it."[78] No one would have guessed that she gave her own subterranean emotions a life in her imaginary places—in this case, her "Blue Castle," the island where she escaped her own prison, and lived through her heroine the fantasy of being married to a man she was wildly in love with. He might tell her that "There is no such thing as freedom on earth . . . Only different kinds of bondages," but she would counter, as Maud herself might have, that the "prison unto which we doom ourselves no prison is" (Chapter 29). And, when Maud closed off this book, she resolutely returned, with dignity, to her own personal prison.

The Blue Castle sold very well in its day, from England to North America to Australia in English, and in other languages as well. It has stayed in print. Its plot took on political overtones when it was made into a musical comedy in Poland in 1982, and well over a decade later that show was *still* a box-office success there. In 1992, it was made into a successful play in Canada, authored by Hank Stinson, and it was performed in both Muskoka and Prince Edward Island. In 1987, the Australian writer Colleen McCullough wrote a book, *The Ladies of Missalonghi*, which had so many similarities to *The Blue Castle* that she was accused of plagiarism. (In the resulting international furor, McCullough acknowledged that she had read Montgomery so many times in her childhood that she might have unconsciously internalized the plot and characters.) Maud herself probably had a literary model in mind for Barney Snaith: his prose sounds much like that of John Burroughs (1837–1921), a famous naturalist whose works she enjoyed. Barney's writing also echoes Maud's own purple prose.

When Valancy Stirling thwarts convention and marries Barney Snaith, his shack of a cottage recalls the cottage of John Mustard. No doubt John Mustard read this novel after it came out. He would have recognized the physical landscape of the novel, and the cottage, but he must have puzzled over its dashing, freewheeling, and raffishly charming Barney Snaith, who bore no resemblance to him, except in his love of escape into the deep woods. Nor would there have been any clear visible connection between Mrs. Ewan

Macdonald—who had always been staid, distant, and formal with him, even as a girl in Prince Albert—and the sexually vibrant Valancy Stirling. As a minister who dealt steadily with the parables, metaphors, and symbols in biblical messages, he must have puzzled over the magical transformations of fiction and the secret thoughts that lay deep in Maud's heart.

If "Captain" Edwin Smith read the novel—and he undoubtedly did—he would have seen many of his own characteristics as adventurer and raconteur in the hero, Barney Snaith, who sweeps repressed Valancy off her feet. Both he and Snaith had travelled extensively, both loved driving on the open road, and he, like Barney, could be a charmer with blarney. Smith wrote well, too, about travel, beauty, and nature, and had published in various Canadian magazines. Would he have been flattered—or alarmed? Likely, he would have seen many of Maud's traits in Valancy Stirling, for they had revealed some of themselves to each other in their late evening talks.

Another man who would have read the novel was the egotistical Edwin Simpson, Maud's former fiancé. He kept up with Maud's novels and always bragged to others that he knew the sources of Maud's characters. Did he fancy that he had only to look in the mirror to see some of the mysterious and deeply alluring Barney Snaith in himself?

But the man who must have been most puzzled of all by the novel was the man to whom it was discreetly dedicated, a man whom Maud had never met in the flesh: Ephraim Weber, M.A., the quiet, earnest, stiff, intellectual Alberta teacher who had been her pen-pal for nearly twenty-five years. The dedication reads: "To Ephraim Weber who understands the architecture of blue castles." Weber, a strict Mennonite by upbringing, must have been both flattered and deeply puzzled by this dedication. He may even have wondered, or fantasized about, the depths she could see in him that were not readily apparent to others, even perhaps to himself. Yes, he had dreams, but Weber's dreams in life had remained in the architectural drawing stage. This dedication tweaked Ephraim Weber's curiosity enough that he and his wife made a trip from the west and stopped to meet Maud just two years later. Maud found him a likeable but earnest bore. No record remains of what Mrs. Weber thought of Maud's insight into her husband's "blue castles."

This novel was certainly not written for children. It was even banned from some church libraries. First, it has an unwed mother in it, but, worse, when Roaring Abel skewers religious hypocrisy, he is so funny that readers cannot help laughing. Apparently, no one saw that this novel was close to being

Maud's own spiritual autobiography, a spillover mid-life crisis. It is ironic that at the same time Maud was choosing older heroines and mature themes for her novels, she was being demoted to the children's shelves of bookstores and libraries by changing literary styles and other forces. This novel was the first to be banned in some libraries.

Writing *The Blue Castle* was emotionally draining for Maud. To calm and restore herself, she now took out the old diary of Charles Macneill that she had borrowed from Alec and May Macneill on her recent trip to the Island, and began copying it straight into her journal. It reminded her of how things were between 1892 and 1898: "it took me back again in a world where happiness reigned and problems were non-existent—for me at least . . . Pensie was alive to run with me under the moon and together we slipped back into . . . the Eden of childhood" (March 1, 1925).

The act of copying helped her to begin reliving these years in preparation for picking up and finishing "Emily 3." Copying the old—and dull—diary also took her mind off herself. She felt on the brink of a nervous collapse—she felt morbid, as if imprisoned. She knew she was in an abnormal state. She had spells where her hands began trembling uncontrollably (a common symptom of depression, as well; possibly a sign of too many of the medications the Macdonalds were prescribed). She had not felt such despair since her 1909–10 depression. There was no privacy from the children, Elsie, or Ewan. She started waking up at 3:00 a.m. (the classic time for depressives to wake) "in the grip of silly, senseless, gnat-like worries" (March 27, 1925). On March 29, she wrote: "I can't see any chance of happiness or even of peace again. . . . I can't help crying." The next day she came down with the flu, and convinced herself that this was the cause of her fits of crying, but found no real consolation in that theory. Yet, by April 20, she had pulled herself together and she gave her unforgettably wonderful lecture on Mammoth Cave and its subterranean world to the Hypatia Club ladies in Uxbridge.

As spring came, Ewan's depression lifted. He was able to get his car out after the winter and go out visiting his parishioners. The Macdonalds now heard that Marshall Pickering had been confined to bed with a serious paralytic stroke. The accident and its aftermath had been equally destructive to each family. Pickering had been a vigorous man when the accident occurred in 1921, but the aftermath of public disapproval had been a strain, and his failure to get his money in spite of winning the lawsuit had caused further aggravation. It must have felt like salt being rubbed in the wound when he could see that Ewan was not going to pay the judgment because he "had no money," while Maud herself continued to lend money to local people in need (something she does not record in her journals, but which old-timers in the community all remembered in the 1970s and 1980s). Whenever a parishioner had bad luck financially, "Mrs. Macdonald" would help out. Mrs. Isobel Mustard St. John recalled in the 1990s, for instance, how Maud had lent her uncle money to get through medical school. He paid Maud back every penny he borrowed, and was proud to do so because "most people never repaid Mrs. Macdonald."

Elsie, the new maid, continued to be a delight in the Macdonald household with her sunny disposition. She was eager to learn and eager to please, even though she suffered from recurring and painful chronic appendicitis. Elsie had a facility for making work into fun; she took great delight in simple things, like getting out the wash earlier than anyone else in the village. Late in her life, Elsie spoke affectionately about Maud as an employer. She said that Maud taught her how to plan meals, to cook many different dishes, to serve guests properly—in general, how to manage a good kitchen and run a tidy, well-organized house. Elsie said her own family had often subsisted through the winter on a skimpy diet of mostly potatoes. The many techniques for vegetable, fruit, and meat preservation and cooking that Maud taught her were a revelation in that era before electric refrigerators and freezers. She believed that she learned more from Maud than she would have from taking a full college course in Home Economics, a developing field of studies then for women. She said, in fact, that the knowledge she acquired at Mrs. Macdonald's home had allowed her to become "a lady" and "marry above her class."

Maud's spirits began to rise steadily, too, when the days lengthened and warmed. A fundraising play she directed in the church was a big financial success, and her group was asked to present it in surrounding communities. But the winter had taken its toll: she wrote tersely in her journal, "Went to Guild tonight and conducted a programme on 'Canadian Humour.' Did not feel humorous."

The next phase of the Church Union vote loomed in the parish, and several families were still wavering between remaining Presbyterians or going over to the newly created United Church. Some people would sign a promise to support the "salary list" and then defect. The loss of a single family hurt the weakening Zephyr Presbyterian Church. The reasons that parishioners left a church did not generally arise from religious convictions; instead, they were financial, political, social, and personal. For instance, the Methodists had a nicer church and better Sunday School facilities. On the June day after people had to declare themselves definitively for one church or the other, Maud wrote: "The papers are full of flamboyant accounts of the 'birth' of the Great United Church. . . . It is rather the wedding of two old churches, both of whom are too old to have offspring" (June 11, 1925).

There was a lot of ministerial traffic through the Macdonald manse in the aftermath of Union, and Maud thoroughly enjoyed squaring off against some offending ministers. She could not insult her husband's parishioners, but when a pompous minister crossed her threshold and then patronized her, he was fair game. Maud had many traits that made her an excellent minister's wife, but her need to trim people down to size occasionally was not one of them.

Chester was now ready to start high school, but there was no high school in tiny Leaskdale. He might have boarded in Uxbridge, but Maud had very high aspirations for her sons, and this meant giving each boy the best education that she could afford. After surveying the possibilities, she chose St. Andrew's, a boarding school in Aurora, north of Toronto. Chester studied for the entrance exam and made the grade. He was a gifted student, and although he still had serious problems relating to his peers, he had learned superficial social skills.

His departure on September 10, 1925, was a sad day for Maud. Like many mothers, she felt anxiety when her first little fledgling left the nest. But she had more legitimate worries than most mothers: she remembered how Ewan's malady had manifested itself every time he went off to a new school—to high school, to Prince of Wales College, to Dalhousie, and then his final and terrible breakdown in Glasgow. Chester's behaviour, she wrote in her diary, was "on the knees of the Gods." After depositing Chester at his new school, they stopped to visit Elsie's grandmother on the way home. Maud was astonished when one of Elsie's "rough" uncles told her he had read all her books. Ewan, Maud's own husband, did not read them. When Chester came home for Thanksgiving she and the boys celebrated by going to see the new movie The Birth of a Nation. Ewan did not enjoy the new "moving pictures" that were becoming increasingly popular. Maud loved them.

In the fall of 1925, the *Delineator* asked Maud for four more stories (about a new heroine, "Marigold"). For these four stories she would again be paid $1,600. (This was $100 more than Ewan was paid for his full year of work in two churches.)[79] It was on October 30 that she got the news from her lawyers that Page's lawsuit against her in New York had been denied. This meant that L. C. Page had exhausted his options and he could no longer hold up her royalties from the Stokes company. This was a huge relief.

In November 1925 she was still trying to draft her third *Emily* book, but her heart was not in it. Emily was growing up. Her marriage was the foregone conclusion, demanded by the genre and the era. Maud's fans were so involved in the story that many wrote her anxious letters, pressing the case for or against the various potential suitors. One fan wrote imploring her not to let Emily marry Dean Priest. Maud had no intention of this, of course. But another candidate for marriage—Teddy Kent—struck most mature readers as an unsatisfactory choice, too. Perry, the hired boy, despite his brilliance and potential, was socially unacceptable "for a Murray" (like Emily was). How to resolve this novel was a problem, so she put it aside in frustration.

Finally, Evan had some hopeful news. The Reverend W. D. McKay, then moderator of the Toronto Presbytery, came to preach at their church for its anniversary service. He told Ewan about an opening in Norval, Ontario, a small town halfway between Guelph and Toronto. Maud caught certain remarkable details: that the large brick manse was outfitted with electricity, that it had an indoor bathroom, and that it was on a radial railway line that went to Toronto. Ewan was invited by the moderator to preach for the call in Norval just before Christmas in 1925. A few days later he received the news that he had been chosen. After years of trying for another parish, he was elated.

Not surprisingly, Maud felt some ambivalence about leaving Leaskdale, and she began to feel sentimental about the manse where her children had been born, and where she had written all her books since *The Golden Road*. But she knew it was time to move on. Most of all, she hoped that the change would lift Ewan's melancholy permanently. If that happened, she would be able to resume a social life with the literary groups in Toronto, and from Norval she could get to Toronto more easily. She was starved for the intellectual companionship and fellowship that she had enjoyed in Toronto before Ewan's breakdown in 1919. Now it looked as if Ewan might be getting a new lease on life—and with that, she and her family would, too.

Ewan accepted the call to Norval shortly after Christmas. They planned to move in February 1926. Both parishes were distressed over the Macdonalds' departure, particularly over the loss of Maud, who had brought so much to the community: intellectual input into the women's meetings and clubs, and outstanding work with the young people in both churches.

Maud sorted and started packing their belongings the first week of January, continuing steadily for the intervening weeks. Some furniture was sold, as the Norval manse was much larger and required bigger pieces of furniture. As Maud packed, she sorrowed over each room she dismantled, particularly the parlour, so full of memories of her little babies and of Frede. Various men helped Ewan crate up the furniture they were taking, and it is a measure of his improved mental health that he was able to help pack.

Many parishioners came to tell them how sad they were to see them leaving. Sessions often ended in tears. In the third week of January, Maud wrote a paper for the Guild on Marjorie Pickthall and noted that it was the last one she would read there. In 1911, when she had first arrived in Leaskdale and was still unpacking, she read them a paper on England; now she was reading them another paper, this one on a Canadian poet.

On February 9, 1926, the Leaskdale Women's Missionary Society honoured Maud at a meeting attended by all seventy-five members. Their address thanked her for the "honour you have conferred upon our place, it has become known as the home of L. M. Montgomery Macdonald, the world-known Authoress . . ." The feeling was so genuine that Maud found she had to fight tears during the meeting. On February 11, the Zephyr church gave a farewell reception, presenting her with a golden pen and Ewan with a leather-bound copy of *The Book of Praise*. She had not expected to feel sorry to leave Zephyr, but she did. At another farewell occasion at Leaskdale Church on February 12, they were given more presents and one hundred dollars in gold. February 14 was Ewan's last Sunday of preaching in these congregations. He did well. In the end, Maud found parting a bittersweet experience. She had put down much deeper roots than she realized. Ewan, however, felt no attachment to Leaskdale, and had no regret at leaving. That was Ewan, flat in the kind of emotions that nearly swept Maud off her feet.

February 14 was also their last night in the manse. Ewan was out late trying to wrap up loose ends, and he returned after Maud had fallen into bed in exhaustion. He woke her with the news that he had been handed a note from a friend in Zephyr saying that Pickering was telling people he planned to seize the railway car with their possessions *if they were shipped in Ewan's name.* The movers were coming at eight o'clock the next morning. Maud sprang out of bed, and she and Ewan worked frantically until four in the morning changing all the name tags from "Rev. Macdonald" to "Mrs. Macdonald."

They hoped now to leave the Pickering affair and Zephyr problems behind. Maud knew that if Ewan should only stay well, all would be fine. Life looked hopeful again.

PART THREE

The Norval Years

1926–1935

CHAPTER 15

The movers came early on February 15, 1926, taking the re-labelled crates without incident. (Pickering's tale, it seemed, had been floated only to scare them.) They spent the next two nights with Leaskdale parishioners, allowing Ewan time to finish up church business. On Wednesday, February 17, at 9:00 a.m., the Macdonalds left Leaskdale in three cutters; they stayed overnight at the Walker Hotel in Toronto. The next day they were met by Ernest and Ida Barraclough, parishioners who would host them until their furniture arrived in Norval. Maud felt heartened when they settled in the Barracloughs' well-appointed house to a warm supper and good conversation.

Ewan would again serve two parishes: Norval and Glen Williams. (Each congregation had voted to remain Presbyterian rather than become part of the new United Church.) Each little village lay in a glen with a river curving through it. The Presbyterian churches themselves were huge, stately edifices, very unlike the modest little structures of Leaskdale and Zephyr. The Norval manse, a two-storey, red-brick house, was a large and handsome one, a big step up from Leaskdale's plainer yellow-brick manse.

The Barracloughs, who lived in Glen Williams, seemed like old-world aristocracy to Maud. Ernest Barraclough, a small, dapper man with patrician manners, was a prominent elder in the Union Presbyterian Church of Glen Williams, and reputedly the wealthiest man in either congregation. Originally from England, he owned and ran a large and prosperous woollen mill. His large brick house at 25 Mountain Street stood atop a hill overlooking his mills and the town below. His wife Ida Stirrat came from a prosperous local family. The gracious Ida was much larger than her slim husband—indeed, she was stylishly ample in size, with regal carriage, and was always tastefully and handsomely attired. She was well liked in the community. The Barracloughs had no children.

There was much to learn about the new community and parish. As talk rambled, Ewan and Maud shot to attention upon learning that the treasurer for both churches, a young man named John Russell, had a connection to Zephyr: he was engaged to a woman whose brother was married to one of Marshall Pickering's daughters. They were horrified. Now Ewan would have to explain the whole lawsuit to the church managers, requesting to be paid in advance. People here would not know the circumstances of the case and would assume that their new minister had skipped out on a bona fide legal judgment against him. *What would people say?* The Macdonalds did not sleep well that night.

As soon as their furniture arrived a few days later, the now-anxious Macdonalds returned to Norval to set up their new home. From the top of the hill at the radial train station stop, they surveyed the dark village below, and saw the church spire rising out of the gloom, with the manse beside it.

Maud knew that Norval and its surrounding area was considered one of the "beauty spots" of Ontario, and although it was a cold February night with whipping winds, she was thrilled with her new home. She could live in this self-contained rural community, and yet hop on the "radial" train (an electric train much like a streetcar) and go to Toronto. The radial station was adjacent to the home of John Russell's parents' farm at the top of the glen, an easy walk from the manse. Norval itself resembled a Scottish glen as envisioned in novels by J. M. Barrie or Sir Walter Scott. The Credit River reminded Maud of the tumbling mountain streams she had seen in Scotland. It was far more romantic than the quiet little brook that bubbled through "Lovers' Lane" in Cavendish. She wrote her Scottish pen-pal, G. B. MacMillan, that Norval was more like an "old-world" village than a Canadian one. She could not have found a place in southern Ontario more to her liking. She was prepared to put down deep roots here.

Norval was nestled in a long valley, with steep hills on each of the four sides. The Credit River curved into town from the north-west and exited through the south-east part of the glen, on its way down to Lake Ontario.

The picturesque village was anchored by two imposing structures: the red-brick Presbyterian church at the west end and a huge stone gristmill straddling the river at the east end. Topping the mill roof was a small cupola, with a gnome-like weather vane. The main street—with its hotel, general store, hardware store, bank, butcher shop, bakery, and candy store—was lined with both small and large homes. In the middle of the village, a road came down

Stuart in sailor's suit.

The Macdonald family after the move to Norval in 1925.

University of Guelph Archives

Isabel Mustard St. John

Captain and Mrs. Smith on left, the other Smiths, and a depressed Ewan, with Stuart and Chester.

University of Guelph Archives

Ewan around 1930.

University of Guelph Archives

Ethel Dennis (maid from August 1934 to
March 1937).

Elsie Bushby (maid from January 1925 to
June 1926).

Mrs. Faye Thompson (maid from April 1931
to August 1934, and again from March 1937
to June 1939) and daughter June, with Joy
Laird's mother, Josie (in light dress).

Mrs. Mason (maid from January 1927 to
April 1931) and daughter Helen, with Stuart, Ewan, and Chester Macdonald.

Mrs. Lily Reid (maid from December 1912 to January 1916) with Chester Macdonald.

Edith Meyers (maid from January 1916 to December 1917) with Stuart Macdonald.

Lily Meyers (maid from March 1918 to February 1925).

Anita Webb (maid from July 1939 to early 1941).

The Union Presbyterian Church.

The Norval manse.

The spire of Norval's Presbyterian Church, where Ewan was a minister, reflected in the Credit River.

Ewan with Ernest and Ida Barraclough of Glen Williams, Ontario.

the south hill (named "Cemetery Hill") from the cemetery and close to the radial station at the top of the glen, crossed the main street and then the river, and curved up the facing northern hill ("Station Hill") past the rail road station, then headed through the scenic countryside of farms towards the Union Church, which lay at the top of the glen above Glen Williams.

Norval had been founded on land that had been purchased from the chiefs of the Otter and Eagle native tribes around 1818 by a Loyalist of Scottish descent named Alexander McNab, and was soon joined by his brother James. They saw the potential in the Credit River and built the first gristmill in the 1820s. By 1827 James was offering free land grants to tradesmen who would settle there.

Tradition said that the village took its name from a line in a Scottish play by John Home (1722–1808) called *Douglas*: "My name is Norval; on the Grampian Hills . . ." The area was rich in oak and white pine trees which could be floated down the Credit River to Lake Ontario. The original gristmill supported other industries: a cooper shop to make barrels for shipping flour, an ashery that burned hardwood cleared for farmland and produced the potash from which soap was made, and the Gooderham & Worts distillery. Later, Norval included a tannery, brickyard, bakery, woollen and flax mills, a broom factory, brass foundry, and a carriage works. Norval was a main stagecoach stop along the earlier plank road between Guelph and Toronto, and had several hotels and inns. At its peak in the nineteenth century, it was a thriving town of four hundred people.

The Norval gristmill, said at one point to be the largest in Canada, produced some three hundred barrels of wheat flour per day during World War I. Wheat was shipped from the west for processing in Norval, and by the late nineteenth century Norval billed itself the "wheat processing capital" of Canada. Traffic came through on the railroads, and immigrants from the United States were said to "flow like a flood towards the golden acres of the setting sun" out west on the railway. Norval grew into a thriving village with three churches, a Mechanics' Institute, and an Orange Lodge.[1]

When the Grand Trunk Railway had come through in the later nineteenth century, however, farmers near town held out for a too-high price for their land, and the railway was subsequently laid out one mile north of the village. This distance was fatal, and the main train made its last stop at the Norval station in July 1926. When the Macdonalds moved there, Norval had shrunk to about two hundred and fifty inhabitants.

The Toronto-Guelph electric suburban radial railway, opened on the south side of Norval in 1917. Maud could travel to Toronto on her own, for shopping or to attend literary meetings and events, or in the other direction, to Guelph, where she made shopping trips to see her favourite millliner to buy the fancy hats she had always loved. For a woman who never learned to drive a car, accessible public transportation was a godsend.

Because Norval lay in a valley, it was an echo chamber. Maud loved the double echo in Norval. When she called her cats, the sound echoed back twice, first from the buildings, then from the hills.

At Ewan's induction, nearly three hundred people braved three-foot-high snowdrifts to attend, some arriving two hours early to get a good seat in the large church. The local paper noted that one of the important ministers attending was the Reverend John Mustard of Toronto. The paper also boasted that "the Rev. Ewen McDonald [sic] was married to Anna [sic] Montgomery, author of Green Gables." Maud was now fifty-one years old, author of fifteen internationally acclaimed books.

Ewan soon met John Russell, the church treasurer. To Ewan's astonishment and relief, Mr. Russell revealed that he already knew about the Pickering case, and had told the Session managers that it was "a framed-up job to extort money" from the Macdonalds. He had *already* arranged for Ewan's salary to be paid in advance. Ewan and Maud were mystified by this loyal support, given before Russell had even made their acquaintance, but they nevertheless welcomed it. The Russell family became their fast and loyal friends. Their house was visible at the top of a hill with a picturesque fringe of pine trees; Maud would always affectionately call "Russells' Hill" the "hill o' pines."

Ewan and Maud felt immediately at ease with the people in both parishes. The earliest settlers there had been mostly Scots or Scots-Irish (many from County Antrim in Ireland).[2] The first Presbyterian worship group had been founded in 1833, with a circuit minister riding to Norval on horseback and holding church services in people's homes. The Presbyterians had built a frame church around 1839, but a quarter century later replaced it with the splendid Gothic brick church, costing the huge sum of $7,000 in 1879 (The Anglicans had built themselves a modest frame church in 1846 and the Methodists had built their little church in 1850.) By the 1860s, Norval had erected a fine brick school to replace its wooden one. Norval had even had its own militia group and drill shed during the Fenian raids. The land around the village was so scenic that Upper Canada College of Toronto purchased five hundred acres of land on the Credit River upstream from Norval, to be used for student retreats.

It secretly pleased the Macdonalds that the church and stately manse (built ten years after the church at a cost of $2,700) were the most outstanding buildings in the picturesque little village, and far nicer than most others in Ontario villages. Several other houses were beautifully landscaped with trees, shrubs, and flowers.

Maud had loved the natural beauty of Cavendish, and she thrilled that their new home was a youngster's paradise, for the sake of her boys. Upstream, the Credit River wound down through much higher hills, cascading, twisting, and turning through rugged bush until it forked and flowed peaceably into Norval. The river's tributaries and branches meandered in a leisurely way through town, making an extensive riverbank for play and picnics. The Credit was then gathered by a large dam that provided the water power for the flour- and gristmills in the south-east part of the village (where Highway 7 runs now). In summer, youngsters could fish, sit along the bank and talk, or swim in the large reservoir of dammed-up water. In winter, they cleared the snow off the dam to make a large rink for skating. The girls figure-skated or played "crack-the-whip" and the boys played tag or "shinny-hockey," using wads of Eaton's catalogue pages to pad their shins. Mindful of the hazard posed by rapids, which did not freeze-over solidly, children could skate for miles on the river. On bright starry nights, parents sometimes built a bonfire on the shore and the skating continued. According to old-timers reminiscing in the 1980s, some of the families brought organs, guitars, and mouth-harps, and after outdoor activity on the river, they would congregate in one of the homes to sing, play games, or make pull-taffy.

The roads coming down the hills at each side of the glen made wonderful sledding for the children, too. The main road through Norval was paved around this time, since it was the only provincial highway from Guelph to Toronto, but the lack of snow-clearing equipment meant that cars were rarely taken out after winter snows began in earnest. Horses and sleighs moved more easily through the snow and they went slowly enough that children could hitch their sleds to a farmer's sleigh as he left town, getting a ride up the steep hills, then slide back down the hill. Or sometimes they went "hookeying" — hooking their sleds to the sleigh of a farmer leaving town, and when they met another farmer coming in, switching sleighs to get pulled back. For those who wanted even more speed and danger, there was a toboggan chute down Russells' Hill.

Glen Williams had as much charm as Norval. Its huge grey-stone Union Presbyterian Church, even more striking than Norval church, stood at the top of the hill that climbed out of Glen Williams. The countryside between the two parishes was filled with expansive farms, and in some areas there was some red soil, as in PEI. The well-to-do farmers maintained their two parishes well, and were very glad to get a minister because, after a bitter fight over Church Union, their pulpit had been empty for five months.

Ewan felt proud to have secured this idyllic location for his family. As for Maud, she could live in the kind of scenic country setting she loved, in a place with extensive walking areas as beautiful as "Lovers' Lane." Her boys were growing up fast, and if Ewan only remained reasonably well, she would get her life back again.

Maud had brought her maid, Elsie Bushby, from Leaskdale. For all her good housekeeping qualities, however, Elsie was inexperienced with men, and easily flattered by any attention. Trouble began when a young man named Rob began courting her. He hung around the Macdonalds' manse all day, staying (uninvited) for meals, talking incessantly, and bad-mouthing many in the church and community. The Macdonalds found his presence intrusive, but since his parents were in the congregation, they had to endure him. When Rob and Elsie started coming in late after rides in his car, people talked. Maud knew that if Elsie got herself "in trouble," Elsie's family would hold her responsible.

Heating systems in a house like the Norval manse were a great conduit for conversations from other rooms. One evening after Elsie returned home late, Maud sat by the heating grate above the kitchen and listened to Rob encouraging Elsie to come to work in Toronto, where he had recently taken a job in a garage. She then heard Rob abuse her and Ewan for using their living room for their own guests when Elsie was entertaining there. Carried by Rob's volubility, the easily led Elsie declared that she "hated the Macdonalds." (June 11, 1926).

Maud prided herself on treating her employees well, and she had often heard Elsie tell others how much she liked working for the Macdonalds. Maud was particularly fond of Elsie, but her code of behaviour demanded absolute loyalty and honest dealing from others. She retreated to her bedroom, feeling furious—and deeply hurt.

A few days later she heard angry voices downstairs at 2:00 a.m., and she crept down the back stairs to listen. Elsie and Rob had come in late, made a snack for themselves, and ransacked Maud's private desk. They were reading her notes—the dated daily jottings of factual events to write up in her journals when she had time. She kept these in a private desk in the library. That they had rifled through her private desk was the last straw for Maud. Although Maud blamed Rob for everything, Maud would never trust Elsie again.

The next day she summoned Elsie, gave her two weeks' severance pay, and told her sharply to go home to her mother. Elsie was floored, not being privy to what Maud had overheard, and also not knowing that Maud objected to her boyfriend, since he was, after all, in the congregation. Elsie went home to her family in total confusion, feeling disgrace and shame. For many years people in both communities speculated about why she had left the manse so suddenly, without explanation. No one knew.

The greater loss was Maud's. She missed Elsie's *joie de vivre* for a very long time afterwards, feeling a mixture of indignation, betrayal, and, most of all, the loss of a young person she had genuinely liked. Finding a good maid was difficult: business was booming after the war, and locally, the Glen Williams woollen mills offered employment to young women. Maud contacted an agency in Toronto and interviewed a woman named Margaret MacKenzie who had just arrived from Scotland. Maud did not like her, but decided to try her anyway, given the lack of other candidates. She could not do without help and continue in her professional life.

At the end of June, the Canadian Women's Press Club (CWPC), which now had four hundred members and had been going for some twenty years, sponsored a massive meeting called a "Triennial." It was a conference of high-powered professional women, with about a hundred delegates from across Canada. The Honourable G. Howard Ferguson, Premier of Ontario, opened the Triennial Congress with a speech arguing that Canada would disintegrate without the pull of "the Empire," and extolling imperial virtues.[3] Next, selected delegates spoke about their provinces. A newspaper article continued that "Prince Edward Island was represented by a charming speech by Mrs. Ewan MacDonald," singling her out alone for praise. The many male speakers in the CWPC Triennial Program included Mayor Lorne Pierce, Donald G. French, F. J. B. Livesay, Norman McIntosh, H. Napier Moore, Newton McTavish—all distinguished publishers, literary critics, and journalists of the era.

Newspapers covered the event and listed the important women journalists and writers attending: Judge Emily Murphy of Winnipeg, Agnes Swinnerton, Cora Hind, Madge MacBeth ("Gilbert Knox"), J. G. Sime, Charlotte Whitton, Isabel Ecclestone MacKay. Maud was one of the speakers: she attended functions at the Toronto Press Club, the Grange, and the Royal Canadian Yacht Club. Her old friend, journalist Marjory MacMurchy, gave a tea in her honour. Maud loved circulating once again in the literary culture of Toronto, and enjoyed the role of a successful older writer who promoted new Canadian writers. The good fellowship improved her spirits for weeks afterwards.

Maud enjoyed these trips to Toronto events, staying over with Marjory MacMurchy, Mary Beal, or her Montgomery cousins, Cuthbert and Ada McIntyre. Her publishers, Mr. McClelland and Mr. Stewart, were always ready to take her out to dinner. They discussed new titles and sent her free books, hoping for her promotional blurbs. And she loved shopping at Eaton's, her favourite department store.

As for Ewan, he had a slight mental slump in April and May after their move, but he soon improved, and it became clear that the parishioners were pleased with their new minister. He left in early August for a month's holiday with his own relatives in Prince Edward Island. Maud looked forward to having a little solitude in her new home. She wanted a rest—from packing, from stress, and from Ewan himself. She wanted to "own" her new landscape through long, appreciative, often solitary walks.

Chester, now fourteen years old, was continuing to worry her. Maud confided to her journal that he made a "fool" of himself over "every pretty girl he sees" (August 14, 1926). She wondered if this "girl crazy" phase would pass, or if it would cause serious damage in his life. She was relieved that he did some work in the gristmill for part of his summer, hoping that would keep him out of serious trouble. It was great comfort that his reports from St. Andrew's were good. He clearly had a fine brain.

Maud turned back to her work on the third *Emily* book, which she had set aside in 1924 when she started *The Blue Castle*. Between Chester and Elsie, she felt out of patience with young love, but she had to deal with it in the next stage of Emily's life. Maud had no interest in the inevitable — consigning Emily to marriage. In Toronto, she had met talented professional women like Marjory MacMurchy, who had married only late in life, and her sister, Dr. Helen MacMurchy, who had stayed single. Both had fulfilling and self-supporting careers. But Maud's reading public was not ready for Emily to choose a career over marriage, even though "companionate marriages" were a hot topic in the media at the time. (These marriages, in which a couple married to have companionship and conjugal rights without intending to have children, were generally condemned. Conservatives and clergymen argued alike that it was God's plan for women to marry and procreate.)

While the writing of *Emily's Quest* progressed, there were tensions in the manse. Margaret MacKenzie, the new Scottish maid, proved to be eccentric and morose, with few skills in either housekeeping or cooking. Worse, she resented all instruction. But Maud decided to keep her for a short period of time because she was afraid of what people in the new community "might say" — namely, that she herself was "a difficult mistress." An alien presence like this sullen maid, so different from the cheerful Elsie, had a dampening effect on Maud's own moods. She fought depression. She worried when Chester was often caught lying. She took both of her sons aside at this time and made them promise never to smoke, but Chester started smoking anyway (and was soon caught). Maud's overwrought reaction was to weep disconsolately, creating a scene that her younger son remembered vividly to the end of his life.[4]

Late summer brought the interruptions of making jams and pickles for winter, painting the floors in the manse, giving the occasional speech, and attending missionary meetings. There was also a stream of guests. Maud's half-sister Ila came to visit with her three children. Maud liked Ila, who, she thought, was much more like their father, Hugh John Montgomery, than her other step-siblings, who resembled Mary Ann.[5]

In September Maud had a very welcome guest from Cavendish, Myrtle Macneill Webb. She was not the special soulmate that Frede had been, but she was discreet and a "kindred spirit" — someone with whom Maud could both laugh and reminisce. They shared a love of gardening, nature walks, cats, and gossiping about family and people in Cavendish. Ewan drove Maud and Myrtle to Aurora so that Myrtle could see St. Andrew's, Chester's private school. They visited old friends in Leaskdale, saw the movie *Ben Hur* in

Toronto, made an outing to Niagara Falls, visited Brampton's Dale Greenhouses near Norval (said to be the largest greenhouse in the world at that time), toured the University of Toronto campus, particularly Knox College, and then drove around the beautiful Caledon Hills north of Norval, coming home through Belfountain, one of the most picturesque little towns on the winding Credit River. It was a restorative visit for Maud, Myrtle, and Ewan, who enjoyed chauffeuring them around.

The fall of 1926 was busy. The Macdonalds joined in local community fun such as corn roasts, sitting on boxes around the fire by the river, eating candy and roasted corn, telling jokes, singing songs, and generally having a good time. In October, Maud and Ewan had a happy reunion in Galt, Ontario, with the Reverend James K. Fraser, one of her favourite former elementary teachers in Cavendish. Maud and Ewan restarted Young People's groups in their new parishes, and she was delighted to find that there were talented "organizers" in this parish who did not rely solely on her for ideas. She had time to catch up on her correspondence.

To Lorne Pierce, Toronto's most influential editor and publisher, she sent some items at his request: a picture of herself, of the Norval manse, and of her old home in Cavendish, plus a manuscript he had asked for, her poem "The Choice" (which she said expressed her philosophy of life). She added a short biography which ended with the information that she had married a Presbyterian minister and had "two sons, aged 14 and 17 respectively, two cats and seventeen hens."[6]

Lorne Pierce (1890–1961) was a founding member of the Canadian Authors Association (CAA), the Bibliographical Society of Canada, and the Art Gallery of Ontario. The editor of Ryerson Press from 1920 to 1960, he devoted his career to the development of Canadian literature, culture, and history. Being noticed by Lorne Pierce meant a great deal, and Montgomery desired nothing more than to be recognized for her achievement on both the national and international stages.[7]

There were more church activities: for one "Fowl Supper" Maud baked, brewed, made cake, jellies, salads, and "mock chicken," and then performed as entertainment. After the rain took the fall leaves and the world buckled down for the winter, she still had her beautiful pine trees. She could lie in bed looking at them standing guard at the top of Russells' Hill, in a "delicate, unreal, moonlit world," or wake and see them talking "to the sky against the fires of sunrise" (November 1, 1926). Maud's dreams always reflected her state of mind. She started re-imagining an old dream of discovering, in a house that she had been living in for years, a new and unexpected suite of beautiful rooms. A dour Presbyterian might have predicted that happiness would soon give way to trouble.

Between fall 1926 and 1927, two items were published that Maud does not mention in her journals. The first was a high-profile study of Canadian writers that denigrated her books as the worst writing Canada had produced — an attack that had enough influence that it inflicted a long-festering wound. The second was a small typographical error that opened the old wound of gossip from her childhood and her Leaskdale years.

The first assault, in 1926, on Maud's reputation was totally unexpected. An ambitious young lawyer named William Arthur Deacon had moved to Toronto from Winnipeg and had the goal of establishing himself in the powerful newspaper and magazine worlds as Canada's pre-eminent literary journalist. There were already several established literary journalists (such as Stanley Morgan-Powell of Montreal), but Deacon aimed to become the first *full-time* book reviewer in Canada. (Newspaper journalists had dominated the field of book reviewing and criticism before World War I, and they still had the most influential voice through the 1920s. Academic criticism began to develop only after the war, and became much more important in the 1930s.)

After World War I ended, Canada saw itself as a young country ready to develop a national literature. William Arthur Deacon, a man of huge ambitions, was "infused with a sense of mission for the establishment of an entire, self-contained, dynamic Canadian cultural milieu — a Canadian authorship, a Canadian readership, a Canadian literature — and sometimes he called himself its prophet," according to Clara Thomas and John Lennox in *William Arthur Deacon: A Literary Life*. Deacon wanted to develop the literary consciousness of Canadian readers, educating the Canadian public into more "sophisticated tastes." Like so many other literary nationalists (including Maud), he wanted Canada to develop world-class writers and its own literature.

Deacon regarded as hopelessly old-fashioned the writers who appealed only to "lowbrow" unsophisticates; among these he listed popular novelists like Montgomery and Ralph Connor, both widely read beyond Canadian shores. He described these writers as a national embarrassment. In particular, he regarded Maud's books as shallow sentimentalism and the "nadir" of

Canadian writing. Literary styles were indeed changing: "Victorianism" and "Realism" were going out of style, and "Modernism" was coming in. Deacon saw himself as *the* critical voice who would sweep out the old and bring in a new, modern criticism and literature.[8] (At the same time, a young generation of academic critics were establishing themselves in a parallel role in the universities, and articulating a more intellectualized approach called "Modernism.")[9]

A man of prodigious energy, Deacon worked hard writing reviews, promoting writers, engaging in political activism, and keeping in touch with everyone in the book world. He was literary editor of the influential Canadian magazine *Saturday Night* from 1922 to 1928. And in the autumn of 1926 he published *Poteen*, a book of essays on Canadian culture, politics, and literature, intended to provide "a concise literary history of Canada" and to demonstrate "justifiable pride . . . in an emerging literature that already has such worth and distinctiveness."[10] This book (which Maud read) helped establish his reputation as a growing power in the Canadian literary world.[11]

In *Poteen*, William Arthur Deacon did not damn with faint praise. Instead, he ended a major chapter with an open attack on Maud's popularity and reputation:

> Lucy M. Montgomery of Prince Edward Island shared the quick popularity of [Ralph] Connor in a series of girls' sugary stories begun with *Anne of Green Gables* (1908). Canadian fiction was to go no lower; and she is only mentioned to show the dearth of mature novels at the time (p. 169).

Maud is dismissed on other counts, too. Deacon provides two lists of noteworthy Canadian writers, first of adult fiction and then of children's literature. *Poteen* does not include Maud in the first category, although he does include other women writers like Mazo de la Roche, Mabel B. Dunham, Gilbert Knox (pseudonym for Madge MacBeth), Martha Ostenso, Marjorie Pickthall, and Laura Salverson. Nor does he include Montgomery among the Canadian writers who write for children, like (Margaret) Marshall Saunders (*Beautiful Joe*) and Catharine Parr Traill.

Poteen also includes a survey of the academics who had recently written surveys of Canadian literature. Deacon criticizes Professor Archibald MacMechan of Dalhousie (Maud's former teacher) for giving attention to

Anne of Green Gables in his *Head-Waters of Canadian Literature* (1924), and he slams MacMechan's summary chapter as "valueless" because he writes "on the 'best-sellers' of the period instead of on the works of literary merit regardless of commercial success" (p. 211). (Maud's writing is clearly in his sights here.) Deacon promoted the idea that "best-sellers" were usually inferior to serious works of fiction because the masses liked them. Although he disparaged both Ralph Connor and Montgomery, his greater contempt was for Maud. Later in his life, Deacon read Connor's autobiographical writing, and revised his opinion of Connor when he had more insight into the issues in his books.[12]

Maud was certainly accustomed to the occasional reviewer complaining that her books were too sentimental, or finding other faults with them. The war had undeniably changed public tastes. She saw that women were caught between the old attitude that they should subjugate themselves to their husbands and the new one that they could have independent ambitions for themselves. By the 1920s her books were beginning to reflect this new reality. *Rilla*, the *Emily* books, and *The Blue Castle*, for instance, all deal in subtle ways with the complicated social forces that impede women's advancement, achievement, autonomy, and authorship.

Maud's style was that of a storyteller, with none of the hard edges of Modernism. Her popular best-sellers, "idylls," and "romances," made her a ready target for Deacon.

Up to this time, Maud had had generally good press from newspaper reviewers and academic critics. In 1914, one of the earliest critics, Thomas Guthrie Marquis, wrote of Montgomery in his multi-volume *Canada and its Provinces: A History of the Canadian People and Their Institutions*:

> Sympathy with child life and humble life, delight in nature, a penetrating, buoyant imagination, unusual power in handling the simple romantic material that lies about every one, and a style direct and pleasing, make these [Montgomery's] books delightful reading for children, indeed, for readers of all ages.[13]

In *Head-Waters of Canadian Literature*, Archibald MacMechan quotes Mark Twain's praise for *Anne of Green Gables* ("In Anne Shirley you will find the dearest and most moving and delightful child of fiction since the immortal Alice . . ."). Although generally favourable to *Anne*, and undeniably impressed by its having sold a reputed 300,000 copies in the first eight years, he carefully qualifies his comments, saying the readers of *Anne* have "a great indifference towards the rulings of the critics" and that "the deftness of touch, is lacking; and that makes the difference between a clever book and a masterpiece." However, he does judge that "the story is pervaded with a sense of reality; [and] the pitfalls of the sentimental are deftly avoided . . ."[14]

Another more substantial 1924 study, *Highways of Canadian Literature: A Synoptic Introduction to the Literary History of Canada (English) from 1760 to 1924,* by John Daniel Logan and Donald G. French, makes many references to Maud as a regionalist who shows "the beauty, the humour, and the pathos that lies about our daily paths" (299):

> In Anne we have an entirely new character in fiction, a high-spirited, sensitive girl, with a wonderfully vivid imagination; . . . so altogether different from the staid, prosaic, general attitude of the neighbourhood . . . (p. 300).

The authors praise Maud's authenticity, and find a psychological depth in her characters that has wide appeal to adults:

> In *Emily of New Moon* (1923) Miss Montgomery created a new child character. . . . The chief difference . . . is that she employs a more analytic psychological method in depicting her heroine — a method that tends to produce an adult's story of youth . . . which makes equal appeal to the young in years and the young in heart (pp. 301–302).

Dr. Logan was a distinguished professor of Canadian Literature at Acadia University in Nova Scotia, with a Ph.D. from Harvard (at a time when most professors held only Bachelor's or Master's degrees). Donald French was a Toronto author and critic and honorary president of the Canadian Literature Club of Toronto. (Maud wrote proudly in her entry of March 5, 1921, that Dr. Logan had said in a lecture: "that Canada had produced 'one woman of genius'—that 'L. M. Montgomery' in the opinion of eminent critics 'equaled or surpassed Dickens in her depictions of child life and character.'")

Deacon enjoyed flying in the face of the prevailing public opinion (and most critical opinion) with his complete dismissal of Maud's books. By 1926, at age thirty-six, he was at the beginning of a long and influential career, and attacking a living Canadian literary icon was a useful tactic for a new critic who wanted to be noticed.

Maud knew Deacon personally. She may not have realized at first how much his negative assessment would affect her ranking in the canon of respected Canadian books, but his words were painful to read, and she said nothing about *Poteen* in her journals. She mentioned Deacon's name only twice in her journals, despite the fact that he dominated the literary scene in Toronto during her sixteen years in Norval and Toronto, and they were both active as executives in the Toronto branch of the CAA. Both entries express her dislike for him, but give no specific reasons why.[15]

Deacon consolidated his power in the CAA. He became an activist in reforming Canadian copyright law. He promoted books, authors, and cultural events. As Thomas and Lennox observe, "In these days before the CBC there was . . . no national communication network and Deacon's enterprise, combining reviews with literary news and gossip, was certainly devised to join together the book lovers of Canada and to give them access to books."[16] A tireless and lively letter-writer, Deacon was skilful at behind-the-scenes networking with others in the book world, mostly within the growing "old boy" network of publishers, periodical editors, anthologizers, and male professors who were starting to establish the "canon" of Canadian literature. He cultivated them, and they respected his growing influence. His ability to promote writers—or attack or ignore them—made him a very powerful figure, especially with writers and publishers. Occasionally he was obsequious in letters, but most often he was forceful and assertive and confident. He was kind to younger writers or to old friends, like Winnipeg's Judge Emily Murphy, but he could be abrasive. When the best-selling writer Mazo de la Roche sent him factual information about herself to help him in reviewing her new book, he responded: "Doubtless you were right to approach me, though nothing usually makes me quite so hostile as a request for a favorable review—no matter how subtly the appeal may be conveyed."[17]

He worked not through a specific argument so much as by labelling.[18] Both words ("sentiment" and "sentimentality") were highly pejorative in modern criticism. "Happy endings" were also a part of this critical discussion, and Deacon linked "happy endings" to sentimental writing. "'Unhappy endings' are often necessary artistically; and generally fatal commercially," he wrote in a letter.[19] Maud would introduce this discourse on "happy endings" in *Emily's*

Quest, finished in late 1926 and published in 1927, satirizing "unhappy endings" in the story about the writer "Mark Delage Greaves."

The Blue Castle's secrets

Maud's over-sensitivity made it easy for verbal thorns to prick her. Her grandmother's phrase "What will people say?" remained a lifelong incubus sitting on her shoulder. By the Norval period, she was repeating that line anxiously to her own sons, just as she had heard it in Cavendish during her own childhood when it was used as a powerful agent of social control. In 1927, her incubus found another sharp thorn for its arsenal.

In August 1927 a magazine called *The Canadian Countryman* began serializing *The Blue Castle*. This mass-market magazine would take her novel into rural homes all over Canada, including, of course, those in Leaskdale and Zephyr.

The magazine apparently typeset the novel from Maud's own manuscript, which, unfortunately, had a revealing slip in it, one which had been caught and corrected in the published novel. In just one place, she has called the dashing hero of *The Blue Castle*, Barney Snaith, by the name of "Smith."

The last thing in the world Maud would have wanted was for the good folk of Leaskdale and Uxbridge to suspect that the charismatic Reverend "Captain Smith" might have provided the model for the virile Barney Snaith, who roared about in his car rather like Smith did in his, and rescued the frustrated Valancy from her pinched life.

Maud was extremely skilled at concealing the origin of her novels. She maintained a façade of control which kept the passions in her heart out of everyone's sight. Her professional reserve ensured that no one saw the relationship between her heroines and her well-camouflaged multiple alter egos. No one around her fathomed how frustrated and bored she often was with the life she found herself in.

Maud's practice was to read each of her books or stories as soon as she received her personal copies. If there were errors, she corrected them in the margins. Her copy of the *Countryman* has not survived, so we can only conjecture that she felt consternation when she spotted her embarrassing slip, and realized that only one mean-spirited person in Zephyr needed to notice it in order to resuscitate Lily's gossip over the telephone party-lines.

In late November 1927, with the serialization well underway, Maud mentions in her journals that she suffers from a fierce attack of her "neurasthenia." She writes in her journals how "old wounds reopened and bled" (November 30, 1927). In an entry on November 28, 1931, the depth of her lingering anger at Lily resurfaces when she records with thinly disguised glee that Lily is pregnant out of wedlock and has to marry the widower who employed her after she left the Macdonalds. She adds about Lily: "The poor creature can't speak the truth even when she tries." Maud's suppressed rage over Lily had no real outlet except in her journals, and since they were intended for eventual publication, Maud had to be careful what she said there too, lest she give away more than she wanted to, rekindling any of Lily's stories. In 1926, William Arthur Deacon's attack on her writing had undercut her celebrity. Now, in 1927, this slip in the serialization could provide tinder for malicious gossips back in Zephyr.

When the glamorous Captain Smith had sailed into Norval as a dashing war hero, and was so obviously taken with her celebrity and her conversational skills, this was heady attention for the emotionally and intellectually starved woman she had become by then. Maud knew, as no one else did, that *The Blue Castle*, which had been such a joy to write, bubbled up from the high spirits that Smith's admiration had engendered. She obscures the fact that Captain Smith provided a model for the heroine's sexy and mysterious lover, Barney Snaith by all but erasing Smith from her journals. Yet, she left in many small similarities of the heroine, Valancy, to herself, not in the details, but in the fact that poor, plain 29-year-old spinsterish Valancy had been made to feel that everything associated with men and sex was shameful. For its era, *The Blue Castle* was quite an explicit book in its extremely subtle representation of sexual repression and then sexual satisfaction, helping it get excluded from some church libraries.

Emily's Quest (1927)

In 1926, while she worked on *Emily's Quest*, fear of gossip became a running subtext in the entire *Emily* series.

In *Emily's Quest*, Emily continues to pursue a writing career, but as Maud's readers were not fully prepared for full-blown career women, there was little choice but to end the trilogy with her marriage. Emily chooses—from three possible suitors—the young man who has become a world-famous artist, Teddy Kent. He is internationally regarded as a "genius," and every portrait he paints of a woman has something of Emily in it. This reflects another prevalent attitude: that women should live *through* their men. Emily's immortality will come through Teddy's achievements—a compromise, of sorts. (Frederick Philip Grove left an unpublished novel at his death that is built on the same theme.)

Readers pelted Maud with letters as she finished the novel; they weighed in on which suitor Emily should choose. Readers' responses also reflected the changing times. Many readers felt uneasy over the possessive Dean Priest and worried that he might re-enter the picture. Teddy Kent was hardly a perfect choice either; some readers picked up on his self-absorption, noting that he is devoted to his own career and his art. Emily's artistic abilities do not interest Teddy any more than they did Dean Priest, whose disparaging words were responsible for her destruction of her first novel manuscript. However, Maud had limited choices, and she married Emily off to Teddy Kent.

The intelligent and ambitious hired boy, Perry, is out of the question for Emily because of his low social status and his rough edges: he marries Emily's friend, Ilse. And, in fact, much of the book's focus is on Ilse, a high-spirited young woman who gets herself "talked about." (Her mother, accused of having a lover, has been the subject of truly lurid gossip, but in the first Emily novel, Emily has a "dream vision" that ultimately proves this to be false.)

Maud freely admitted that Emily was based on herself. But she did not acknowledge that the wild and rebellious Ilse came out of another part of her personality. Ilse is a free spirit, the embodiment of the energy and lawlessness that Maud might have exhibited if Grandmother Macneill had not reined her in so tightly. And Ilse's father is much like Maud's—useless as a protector or guide. Maud was relieved when she finished the book in December 1926. It had been a chore.

In late 1926, Maud had many other things on her mind. The Scottish maid, Margaret MacKenzie, had turned out to be untrainable. Maids lived with the Macdonald family, ate with them, and were included in family outings (with their way paid), so it was important for them to be companionable. Fed up with Margaret's surly behaviour, Maud fired her.

In January 1927, Maud hired Mrs. Mason, a widow with a young daughter named Helen. Mrs. Mason, like Maud, was a very private person. We do not know if she told Maud her story, but if she had, Maud would have felt sympathetic: it bore similarities to that of the heroine in *The Blue Castle*. Mrs. Mason (born Margaret Ruth Checkley), the favourite daughter of a very strict and authoritarian father with a large and successful farm near Arthur, Ontario, had run away with a farmhand from the neighbouring property, William Mason. Handsome and well dressed, he had come from England and taken a job as a menial worker in rural Ontario. He was middle-aged, received little or no mail, and told nothing of his past. People wondered if his name was really his own. Mrs. Mason fled her father's wrath, either before or after she married (if she was indeed married), and the couple left for the United States. In fairly short order, Helen was born (June 21, 1925), and William Mason reportedly died of cancer—or so Mrs. Mason told Helen when she grew up. Either unwilling or unable to return home, Mrs. Mason brought her baby back to Toronto, taking refuge with a sister while she sought some means of support. With no one to look after her daughter, factory work in Toronto would have been very difficult. For Maud, life eased again with a good maid in the house.

January 1927 proved an eventful month in other ways. The new year began with a letter from Marshall Pickering's lawyer, Mr. Greig, threatening to take Ewan's unpaid debt to the officials in the Presbyterian Church in Toronto. Given that the Norval church was $300 behind in paying Ewan's 1927 salary of $1,800. Greig could garnishee Ewan's salary if he found this out.

The Macdonalds were puzzled over why the salary was in arrears. In early January 1927 the mystery was solved when a nervous John Russell came to them, in secret. John, the church treasurer, had been "borrowing" from the church funds. He told the Macdonalds that he had expected a windfall of $500 for injuries suffered in a job some time earlier, and had been borrowing against that for some time. The year-end annual meeting of Session managers was approaching, and he did not have the funds to replace what he had taken. If the fact that money was missing was discovered, the congregation would be in an uproar; even worse, those in the United Church would enjoy a laugh over the Presbyterians losing God's money to a thief in their midst.

Rather than approach his own family, John Russell came to the Macdonalds and asked for a loan of the missing amount. That would pay Ewan's salary and replace the balance before Russell was found out at the annual meeting. He promised to give Maud a promissory note to repay her when he could—in other words, probably never.

Maud was no stranger to the ironies of life. She had no choice but to lend the money, noting gallantly that whatever John's motivations were, he had stood by the Macdonalds in the Pickering affair. John apparently felt no guilt over his "borrowing" church money, for he had firmly intended to repay it, just as he firmly intended to repay Maud. She grimly remarked that at least the situation would seal his loyalty to them. She had made $4,300 from royalties and investments in 1926, and would make $10,794 in 1927. She could afford to pay part of her husband's salary in this roundabout way. Such a turn of events could hardly have pleased poor Ewan, but what could he do? If Maud did not help cover up the thievery, it would create a huge disruption in the church and scandal in the community.

In the meantime, Maud's gift for "making things go" was energizing an entire community again. She organized a new fundraising adventure, the Olde Tyme Concert, a social event in which people dressed and performed as historical figures. Maud herself, appropriately costumed, recited "The Widow Piper." In a time before television, these theatrical ventures not only provided entertainment, but also gave local people with talent a creative outlet. And they raised money for church maintenance and charitable projects. Sometimes the Olde Tymers took their performances to other churches.

In mid-January 1927, Maud went to nearby Guelph, and spoke to a capacity audience at a Women's Club. The *Guelph Mercury* reported on her speech:

> [She made a] fervent plea for the support of Canadian authors as the means of establishing a Canadian national literature. "Canadian authors, having competition from both England the United States, were," she said, "at a disadvantage, and were frequently compelled to go elsewhere, in order to provide themselves with bread and butter and soap. If the departure of these young authors continues, there will never be a Canadian literature." . . . "Literature is not a sporadic gift from a capricious God. It is a slow growth, and cannot spring from a sordid, petty, and materialistic people. To establish a national literature, our ideas must be noble and enduring, our culture real and profound, because genius is the ability to grasp and give expression to all that has ever existed in the inarticulate soul of a people."

One might suspect that such high-minded sentiments would have bored the audience, but the report continued:

> Mrs. McDonald [sic], who has an international reputation for her books, proved to be one of the most entertaining speakers ever heard locally. Her address was characterized by a brilliant wit, and a charming undercurrent of sly humour, which made listening to her an unalloyed pleasure.[20]

She finished off her address by reciting some of her own poems and reading some amusing letters from her male readers, particularly what she called "freak" ones: one man wrote about how much he enjoyed her writing, adding judiciously that he was married and only writing out of "pure friendship"; and a Kansas city lawyer wrote her that he had had a dream in which he'd met "Paddy" (a cat in one of her books) in Heaven. And a serious young divinity student in North Carolina enjoyed her books but complained that he feared that her practice of "marrying off all her characters" would bring contempt to the holy state of matrimony. She told the group that she had written this divinity student that if he preferred, she would have her characters live together without benefit of the marriage vows. Then she finished with a reading from *The Golden Road*.

This basic speech format she used over and over in small towns, and invariably the newspapers reported on what a good speaker she was. She kept people laughing—she was a witty storyteller, with perfect timing. She made a point of reading letters from male fans to offset the growing perception that her books were enjoyed only by women and children.

By early February, Maud was catching up on her letter-writing. She got letters off to her old pen-pals G. B. MacMillan and Ephraim Weber. She answered every fan letter, handwriting each in a standardized format: she was glad they liked her writing so much that they'd taken the trouble to write and tell her; getting letters from her readers all over the world was one of her greatest pleasures; and she regretted that she was so busy she could only pen a line or two in reply. Then she answered questions they asked and told them about her newest book.

Occasionally someone's letter appealed to her, and she gave that person permission to write her once a year. To one such correspondent, a young man named Jack Lewis, she wrote in February 1927: "I am very glad my books have helped you to appreciate our world. But I guess the power of appreciation was there, though perhaps not awakened, or my books could not have put it into you." She added that she loved Prince Edward Island "more than any other place on earth. Someday I am going to write a book about legends and sea-stories of the old North Shore. And that will be a book boys will like!"

To another young fan named Evelyn Johnston, she wrote that Emily's story wasn't hers, but the *flash* was. Then she copied out a long description of an imaginary place called "The Land of Uprightness," which she had written earlier, in which she made note of climbing the "hills of firs" and looking "down over the fields of mist and silver in the moonlight."

In this airy passage (the kind of fancy-writing that Modernist critics deplored, but which might have intrigued later Freudian critics), she merges the landscape of Cavendish, the Island (where there is a harbour), and the landscape of Norval, where, from Russells' Hill, she could look down over the mists rising in moonlight above the forks of the Credit River. When the light was right, Norval was indeed a fairyland: there were times when this landscape produced in Maud the magical release of feeling that sent her imagination soaring, what Emily called "the flash."

Maud repeatedly puzzled over how the pine trees on Russells' Hill could transport her, and she reflected in her journal:

> My love for pines has always been a very deep and vital and strange thing in my life. I say strange because there is nothing in my life—or *this* life—to account for it. There were no pines in my early home. Very few pines in P. E. Island at all. One or two each in the woods. Yet I always loved pines better than any other tree. And I wrote scores of poems about them; and now that I have come to live in a place that is rich in pines I find that those old poems were *true* and expressed the charm and loveliness of pine trees as well as if I had known pines all my existence . . . (December 23, 1928)

Balsam firs she had had in abundance in PEI, but not pines. She may have forgotten that, as a little girl of about ten or eleven, she had studied a prose piece called "The Pine" by the English Victorian art critic John Ruskin, which appeared in the *Third Book of Reading Lessons* in the Royal Reader Special Canadian Series:

> The pine—magnificent! Nay, sometimes almost terrible. Other trees, tufting crag or hill, yield to the form and sway of the ground. . . . But the pine rises in serene resistance, self-contained; nor can I ever without awe stay long under a great Alpine cliff . . . looking up to its companies of pines, as they stand on the inaccessible juts and perilous ledges of the enormous wall, in quiet multitudes, each like the shadow of the one beside it—upright, fixed spectral, as troups of ghosts standing on the walls of Hades . . .

Ruskin goes on to describe the strength, shape, and power of the pines in this ornate rhetorical style, focusing on how Nature (and pines) can inspire the viewer.

When Maud read Ruskin in school, he gave her a "grand" way of *seeing* and *responding to* Nature. She, in turn, writing in her own style, taught millions of her young readers like Jack Lewis to *see* and *appreciate* and *respond to* the world of nature around them. Her word-painting provided filler, mood, and atmosphere in her novels, but it also gave aesthetic pleasure to many, taking them beyond the more prosaic realities of life. Other people in Norval looked up at Russells' Hill and saw a few ragged pine trees. Maud saw the hill with its pines as a portal to another world—one of beauty, of enchantment, of inspiration. In practical terms, her way of describing nature brought a never-ending stream of tourists to Prince Edward Island. She would need this romantic and imaginary escape increasingly as the "wheel of things" began to spin faster and faster.

The real world always reasserted itself, bringing Maud back down from her rhetorical highs. In February 1927, eleven-year-old Stuart disappeared after going out ice-skating on the Credit River with a friend. Carried away with the glories of the "wingèd heel," the boys had found themselves far from home when darkness fell and sensibly decided to walk home on roads, unaware that they were the object of a huge search. (A child could easily fall through the ice where the water was shallow and fast-running, especially after dark when the hazards were hard to spot.) Maud's fright took a toll on her fragile nerves.

In addition, the L. C. Page and Company lawsuit dragged on. In early February 1927, the Master's report had awarded her $16,000 of Page's profits from *Further Chronicles*, but she knew that actually getting the money out of the publisher would be a long, expensive process.

Then, on the Island, the Campbells continued to need Maud's help. Ella's daughter Amy borrowed money to study nursing (she would become one of the few people who paid Maud back). Over the years, the hapless Stella Campbell had borrowed thousands for her wild schemes and repaid nothing. In Ontario, Maud had lent money to a Leaskdale widower, Will Cook (later Lily's husband), who failed to repay her. And a friend from Leaskdale times, Mary Gould Beal, had borrowed money in 1925, and again in 1926, as her husband's business suffered a downward spiral. Money issues were beginning to trouble Maud: Chester was attending an expensive private school, and she planned for Stuart to go there as well.

But there were happy moments, too. In April, Chester stood third in his class at St. Andrew's, and he declared that he wanted to study mining-engineering for a profession (April 19, 1927). Stuart, still in Norval, was a constant delight to her. The Young People's Guild play Maud had directed was a smash hit, bringing in $78 for the church. A New York theatre company took out an option on *The Blue Castle*. *Anne of Green Gables* was translated into French. Her royalties seemed better. And Norval's natural beauty continued to be enchanting. With spring and summer coming, her spirits were rising. She wrote in her journals:

> Norval is so beautiful now that it takes my breath. Those pine hills full of shadows—those river reaches—those bluffs of maple and smooth-trunked beech—with drifts of wild white blossom every-where. I love Norval as I have never loved any place save Cavendish. It is as if I had known it all my life—as if I had dreamed young dreams under those pines and talked with my first love down that long perfumed hill. (May 26, 1927)

In July, Maud travelled back to her beloved Prince Edward Island, her first real vacation there in four years. While there, she received a letter from the Prime Minister of England, Stanley Baldwin:

10 Downing Street
19th June 1927

Dear Mrs. Macdonald:

I do not know whether I shall be so fortunate during a hurried visit to Canada but it would give me keen pleasure to have an opportunity of shaking your hand and thanking you for the pleasure your books have given me. I am hoping that I shall be allowed to go to Prince Edward Island for I must see Green Gables before I return home. Not that I wouldn't be at home at Green Gables!

I am yours sincerely,
[Signed] Stanley Baldwin

Maud received this letter when she was visiting in Cavendish. Taking a walk into "Lovers' Lane," she read it "to the little girl who walked here years ago and dreamed—and wrote her dreams into books that have pleased a statesman of Empire. And the little girl was pleased" (July 14, 1927).

With the happy heart of a young girl, she went to a spot on the shore at Cawnpore to speak to a group of Campfire Girls. With surf pounding in the background, she told them old sea stories, including that of the *Marco Polo*, wrecked at that very spot. Yet changes were taking place in the Cavendish of 1927, and these changes did not please her. The Cavendish Presbyterian Church that had nurtured her as a little girl was now a United Church. The old manse where she had had so many happy visits with her friend Margaret Stirling was gone. The Macneill clan itself was disappearing—in her youth there had been twelve Macneill families, but now there were only six, and four of these had no children. The old community hall was in disrepair, and the books of the old library were unattended and mouldering. Carloads of tourists now descended on Cavendish, crawling about the haunts made famous by *Anne of Green Gables*. The inhabitants of 1927 Cavendish were losing the quiet rural quality of their village—as a result of *her* books.

Her Uncle John F. Macneill was now seventy-six, and the bad feeling between him and his famous niece still rankled. But she liked her Uncle John's son, Ernest—a much gentler and kinder man—and she secretly hoped that the farm would stay in the family. (That wish was eventually fulfilled. Ernest's son, John Macneill, born in 1930, inherited the farm, which remains in the family.)

During the summer of 1927, a Toronto writer, Florence Livesay, spent her summer holidays in Cavendish, largely as a result of *Anne*'s popularity. Maud knew her from the Toronto Press Club. Mrs. Livesay (wife of J. F. B. Livesay, general manager for the Canadian Press for Canada, and the mother of future poet Dorothy Livesay) was preparing an article on Maud, and queried how she got a start in such a remote and quaint place as Cavendish. Incensed, Maud snapped in her journals that she thought "the 'literary atmosphere' of the old Macneills and Simpsons would not have been too rarified for even Mrs. Livesay to breathe" (July 17, 1927).

The newspapers of late-nineteenth-century PEI demonstrate that the literacy level of Maud's childhood culture was indeed impressive. It is to Mrs. Livesay's credit that she saw the importance of the oral tradition in Maud's writing. The Island newspapers crowed that "Mrs. Macdonald and Mr. and Mrs. Livesay are intimately acquainted, and there have been great 'foregatherings' at the shore during their present visit—nights of story-telling which will long be remembered by those privileged to be present."[21]

When Maud returned to Ontario after this three-week visit in July 1927, Marion Webb came back with her. All of Ernest and Myrtle Webb's children were growing up, and one farm could not support them all. Like so many other young Islanders, many of them would have to look elsewhere for a livelihood. Marion was a very pretty girl, with a sweet disposition and a good sense of humour. Both Marion's mother and Maud wanted to enlarge her horizons by having her visit in Ontario.

Very soon after her return to Ontario, Maud attended the formal garden party in honour of Prime Minister Stanley Baldwin and the two princes, the Prince of Wales and his youngest brother, Prince George, held on August 6, 1927, at Chorley Park in Toronto. She bought a new dress of lace and georgette in a light cocoa-brown colour, with trimmings of brown and a brownish salmon pink. She wore a hat of leghorn straw, trimmed with a feather of burnt orange, and had a professional photographic portrait made of herself in this dress.

Ewan did not accompany his wife. He had gone for his own holiday on the Island, with his people. Maud went to the reception, met the royal party, and observed that the Prince of Wales (who would later abdicate the throne) looked "tired, bored, blasé, as no doubt he was and small blame to him," considering that he had to greet four thousand people. She noted that of the two princes, Prince George was "far more chipper looking and seemed to be enjoying himself hugely."[22]

Maud did not have to wait in the receiving lines; she was sought out by an attaché and was taken to the Honourable Stanley Baldwin and his wife for a chat of nearly half an hour. Another newspaper account called the length of the visit "a significant tribute at any time but the more notable under the exacting circumstances and one to stir the pride of the most unself-conscious."[23] When Maud arrived home, she put away for her grandchildren the gloves she wore when she shook hands with the prince.[24]

When Ewan returned from Prince Edward Island, the Macdonalds bought a new "closed" car, a Willys-Knight, for $2,000. During September Ewan drove them around, showing Marion the sights of Ontario, such as Niagara Falls. Later in the fall, Marion returned to the Island. She was the kind of daughter Maud would have liked. Maud would miss her so much that she would encourage her to return later, changing the course of Marion's life.

In early October 1927 Maud had another welcome visitor, her beloved old teacher Hattie Gordon, who was on her way to visit her married daughter in Philadelphia. Sadly, the talented Hattie was now a tired, impoverished old woman, divorced from an abusive husband, with children grown and dispersed. Maud noted that the entire world had changed in the thirty-five years since they had parted. "The girl of 1892 and the woman of 1892 have not met again. They do not exist. And in that realization lies my loss," Maud wrote on October 14, 1927.

In mid-October 1927, Maud had learned that *The Delineator,* which had commissioned her to write four stories for them in January 1927, had changed editors, and the new editor, a man, had pronounced Maud's stories about a child named Marigold "too old-fashioned." They paid her the promised $1,500, but only as a kill-fee. She was deeply hurt and offended. This was one of the first indications that her writing was falling out of favour with more people than Deacon. It was one thing for critical tastes to change, but was the reading public going to change, too?

It was that November that the Countryman magazine came out with the error citing Barney Snaith as "Smith." By her birthday on November 30, 1927, feeling battered on several fronts, Maud began obsessing about the past. Her work with the young people's group had been extraordinarily successful for the past year, and she knew her depressed feelings were abnormal, but she could not shake them. When her Sunday School Bible class gave her a basket of roses at Christmas, she noted that Ewan turned away without a word.

In mid-December, she wrote in her journals that she thought we "are just entering . . . the age of Science—an age of wonderful discoveries and development. . . ." (December 17, 1927). Science did not yet understand affective mood disorder, or know how to treat it. When Maud felt depressed, she reread old favourites that suited her mood, like Nora Holland's sentimental poem "The Little Dog Angel," and *Undine*, the novel about a sea-sprite who is adopted by humans. Feeling estranged from her own world, she mused about the book, wondering what in it kept it from going "stale." It was, she noted, a fairy tale, the sort of story at which the modern world may sneer, but without which people cannot live.

She looked at her son Stuart and saw a tender boy in a brutal world, and brooded that a future world might attack him, as she saw it attacking her (December 23, 1927). He had her personality—and her heightened sensitivity. Early in January 1928, Maud began to worry seriously about her own emotional fragility and the effect that a complete breakdown would have on her writing and her earning capacity. She tried unsuccessfully to call in some of her outstanding debts.

Maud had remained an active member in the Canadian Authors Association, which continued its fight to establish copyright laws that would better protect Canadian authors. Her feeling of Canadian nationalism had increased now that she lived in Ontario. (The Maritimes had always had closer ties with the New England seaboard than it did with Ontario or the rest of Canada.)

The extent of her growing financial insecurity after Deacon's attack and the rejection of her stories by the new editor of *The Delineator* is evident in a letter she wrote to the Toronto novelist Katherine Hale on January 9, 1928. Maud told Katherine that she was rereading her husband John Garvin's *Canadian Poets* and had come across a poem of Katherine's there. Maud thanked her for its beauty and poignancy.[25] This letter was a well-calculated piece of flattery: John Garvin was an aging but still influential fixture in the CAA. He was an anthologizer of Canadian literature, and he was exceedingly proud of his wife. He was also the chief organizer for the CAA's fifth annual Canadian Book Week.

In February 1928, Maud spoke at the CAA meeting in Toronto. (She was amused when Garvin, a good-natured windbag, told her that *he* was responsible for the publication of the *Canadian* edition of *Anne of Green Gables*—at that time, there had not yet been a Canadian edition of *Anne*.) But in her journals, Maud compares John Garvin, who had such pride in his wife, with Ewan:

> Ewan secretly hates my work—and openly ignores it. He never refers to it in any way or shows a particle of interest in it. I certainly wouldn't want him to go about boring people publicly with his appreciation. But I would like him to *feel* a little. I have *never*, since I was married, neglected *any* duty of wife or mother because of my writing. I have done it at odd hours that were squeezed out of something else by giving up some of my own possible pleasure and *all* my leisure. So he has no justification for this attitude.
>
> However, let *me* be just. Would I want Ewan to be like old John Garvin in other respects? I certainly would *not*. Therefore let me not howl with indignation because he is not like him in this. (February 12, 1928)

Maud was resentful. In the previous year, her income had been six times that of Ewan's. With money made by the plays she had put on, the drama group had re-covered the cushions on the pews of the church auditorium, brought its Sunday School room a piano, and paid for the installation of electric fixtures. These were substantial achievements. But she knew that reason did not control human emotions.

Since coming to Norval, Maud had put forty pounds on her tiny frame. Women then did not mind a matronly, well-fed look. When they carried themselves well and dressed elegantly, it could make them look substantial and imposing, as was the case with Mrs. Barraclough. But the extra weight sapped Maud's energy. She tripped and hurt herself and took a number of weeks to recover in spring 1928, just when her young people were going to other towns to put on the play she had directed.

There was a bright spot in her spring—Chester had led his class at St. Andrew's. This allayed immediate fears about his behaviour and development. Soon another worry arose, however: the Barracloughs wanted to move to Toronto, so tried to sell the woollen mill Ernest owned. In the end, Ernest could not find a buyer, so they stayed. The Barraclough house had always been a sanctuary for the Macdonalds. They could count on Ernest and Ida to respect confidences when they talked over personal problems with them, especially their concerns about Chester.

Maud's spirits always rose with the first signs of spring. By June 1928, she was out in her garden again, feeling better. Ewan took off for the Presbyterian General Assembly in Winnipeg that year—a measure showing that he, too, was doing well. In the last three weeks of June, Maud spent three days in Toronto, again at the Triennial of the Canadian Women's Press Club. Back in Norval, she entertained Alf Simpson of PEI, Ed's more likeable brother.

Chester came home for the summer, proud of his academic achievement at school, but still clearly not well adjusted socially. The students at St. Andrew's had nicknamed him "Rat" (for stealing and eating). All the Norval young folk laughed about the nickname. Maud's maids over the years had all found his compulsive overeating frustrating: a maid was supposed to keep the cookie jar filled at all times, but Chester would eat an entire platter of cooling cookies at a sitting. He would smell the baking, sneak into the kitchen, steal the cookies, and then deny the theft. One incensed maid grabbed him and turned the pockets of his pants out to demonstrate through the crumbs that he was lying to her. But none of the maids over the years felt comfortable complaining directly to Maud about him, and if they had, it would have done little good. No one could control Chester.

In the summer of 1928, trouble began brewing between him and Ewan. A cryptic comment about Chester spilled into her diary: "something nasty and worrying that embittered life for many days and filled us with deep-seated fear of his future." She could not bring herself to give details: "There is no use to write much about it—no use tearing open a wound that has begun to skin over. But I have been very wretched over it and I cannot think about it without agony" (July 22, 1928).

The maids reported that his behaviour was unpredictable. When greeted in the morning, or whenever he came into a room, he might answer; but other times he rudely ignored their existence. When he was caught lying or smoking, he alternated between pretending to be extremely contrite and being angry and rebellious. Apologies and promises came easily, but Chester was caught again and again in lies. Most impulsive children (as Maud herself had been) reached an age at which they began to think about consequences and modify their behaviour, but he did not.

Chester's sexuality continued to be a concern. Although self-gratification and self-exploration is common with adolescents, in his case masturbation caused increasing distress. A maid or anyone else was in danger of accidentally stumbling in on an embarrassing sight. Stuart quit sleeping in the room he shared with Chester and moved outside to sleep in a tent, except in the winter.

Chester's behaviour around local girls was also causing alarm. According to his contemporaries (interviewed in the 1980s), young women in the community of Norval were very wary of him. Maud watched, paralyzed with mortification, unable to write or talk about it. When she was growing up on the Island, one of the behaviours for which people were placed in Falconwood, the mental institution, was public masturbation.[26] Ewan's increasing anger over Chester's behaviour may have reflected his memory of his own past—of his own sexual development, including his alleged window-peeping in Cavendish. Ewan was all too aware of the Bible's pronouncement: the sins of the fathers will be visited on the sons for many generations. Ewan saw this son as re-enacting the sins of his father, either imagined or real. It was an increasingly tense household.

In the athletic culture at St. Andrew's, Chester had remained an outsider, given his stiff and corpulent physique, lethargic disposition, general untidiness, and surly nature. He was also lazy about studying, but could do well academically in spite of a lack of motivation. Good grades did not endear a teen to a peer group that had already excluded him on other grounds. An outsider at school and an irritant at home, he was growing up an isolated and lonely young man.

At home, he constantly annoyed the maids, but he aggravated his father even more. Ewan had never spent much time with his sons, either talking or playing with them, and he had not built up a fund of goodwill and trust. Frustrated by Chester's behaviour, Ewan closeted himself more and more in his darkened study and brooded. In private, he complained to Maud about Chester—as if she could do something about this difficult son.

Friendless, Chester mostly stayed in his room and read. By 1928, when he was sixteen, he had solidified into a churlish loner who carried a lot of resentment—resentment towards a world that seemed to shun or dislike him; resentment towards the father he resembled; resentment towards a mother who was consumed by her own busy world of reading, writing, and church and social activities, whose interaction with him was full of frustration; and resentment towards a younger brother with a sunny disposition who was surrounded by friends.

Stuart played well with other children and had never been a problem; in Norval, he loved the river and spent most of his time there with the village youngsters. Stuart, unlike his father and brother, was very sensitive to his mother's moods. She noted in her journals that when she felt "down," Stuart would attempt to cheer her, for example by making her a cup of cocoa (February 14, 1928). Stuart loved sports and the outdoor life, and, left to his own devices, he was always busy, happy, and interacting with friends. The sedentary Chester's jealousy of Stuart increased.

A new kind of narrative began reasserting itself in Maud's consciousness, and in her journal. She began to obsess that *fate had put a curse on her and those she loved.* She had lost both her parents; she had lost her cousin and best friend, Frede, to premature death; she had married a man who became afflicted with intermittent mental problems; and now her older son seemed seriously troubled. In depressed moods, she revisited her negative thoughts. Why, she would ask herself, must everything she loved be cursed? The depth of her worry about her older son shows in the fact that she started to bring another theme into her journals, recounting in detail how others' children had disappointed them.

Maud soon had another jolt. Stuart was an excellent swimmer, but in July 1928 he had a narrow escape in the river. The Norval dam broke and he and his friends were swept over onto the sharp rocks below. They were bruised, but no lives were lost. This was the second scare over Stuart and the river, and Maud began obsessing that something was going to happen to her one "good son," as she began calling him. She felt that there would be a third catastrophe, just as Frede's third illness had carried her away.

Soon after that, a truly terrible tragedy occurred in the village, emphasizing how quickly lives could be snuffed out. The Macdonalds' neighbour, George Brown, had gone up to his farm with his children in the car, and he'd inexplicably driven directly in front of a radial railway train at the crossing. His three children—aged ten, eight, and five—were all killed by the collision, and the father was badly hurt. Stuart witnessed the entire tragedy and ran to help, but found only badly mangled bodies. The town was stunned and paralyzed.[27]

That summer the church had undertaken some construction on the manse to improve the bathroom. Ewan, preoccupied and inattentive at the best of times, fell headlong into the trench the workman had dug for the sewage system. He was shaken up, but not otherwise hurt. Ewan was frequently absent-minded (like the lovable Reverend Meredith in *Rainbow Valley*), and car accidents were becoming more common. Maud arranged for Chester to take driving lessons that summer. She wanted a second chauffeur in the family, and she hoped driving would help Chester to become more responsible.

To revive themselves, in early August the Macdonalds took a mini-vacation, motoring with the Barracloughs to Orillia, Muskoka, Cobalt, and North Bay, travelling on the new Ferguson Highway, and returning via Port Carling and Bala. It was a refreshing vacation, if short. Again, as in 1922, Maud lost herself in her reveries over the beauty of northern Ontario.

It was a sad day for Maud when Stuart left home in September 1928 to start secondary school at St. Andrew's. He would turn thirteen on October 5, 1928. He had actually completed his grammar school a year earlier, but his mother had kept him at home for a full year, without anything to do, claiming that he was still too young for secondary school.[28] In 1928, Maud wrote in her journals how she had been dreading Stuart's departure:

> Dear little Stuart. I have had him for thirteen beautiful years. And in all those years from the very night of his birth when he opened his big blue eyes and looked around the room as if he were two months instead of two hours old, he has never been anything but a joy and a delight and a comfort to me. I have never felt once ashamed of him—I have never had any reason to worry about him in regard to behavior or character. He has been the sunshine of the house and how I am going to live after he has gone I know not. (September 9, 1928)[29]

However, Maud's life was far from empty when both boys were at St. Andrew's. She continued working, as before, on activities for the Mission Band, the Missionary Auxiliary, the Ladies' Aid, the Women's Institutes, the Sunday School Teachers' Meetings, the Young People's Society meetings, and the drama programs for the Young People's Society and the Olde Tyme Concert. She attended as many social events in Toronto's literary world as she could manage. She kept daily notes for her journals, and wrote them up when she could steal a block of time. She maintained a voluminous correspondence. She spent a portion of each morning in writing—usually three hours—

while her maid got on with the housework, cooking, and washing. She managed to read or reread favourite books every day.

For social evenings, the Macdonalds repeatedly visited the Barracloughs. Other visitors in the Macdonald home during the Norval period reported that they sometimes felt embarrassed for Ewan at the dinner table. His table manners were very poor, revealing his background. Nor could he hold up his end of polite dinner conversation. He tried to tell stories when company was present—stories being a key part of Maud's idea of good dinner entertainment—but he had poor timing, rhythms, or formulas, and he usually mangled the punchline. This embarrassed his family, and a pained but tolerant look would come over Maud's and the boys' faces, as everyone prepared to laugh—albeit nervously—towards the end of the story. But for some reason, the dynamic with the Barracloughs was such that Ewan felt relaxed and valued there, and their home remained a haven for Ewan and Maud.

CHAPTER 16

The final *Emily* book, *Emily's Quest,* had been published in 1927. It was time to start another novel. Maud decided to expand the rejected Marigold stories into a novel, with Marigold Lesley as her new heroine. In June 1927, she began *Magic for Marigold,* and she finished it by October 1928.

Magic for Marigold (1929)

Marigold Lesley showed Maud making a conscious effort to modernize her heroines rather than to write out of her own experience, as she had with *Anne* and *Emily.* Marigold is born into a world where women can be successful medical doctors. In fact, Marigold's life is saved by a very capable woman doctor after the "men-doctors" have given her up. The well-known Dr. Helen MacMurchy of Toronto likely provided a model. Politically active as a crusader for women's and public health matters, she had a long and distinguished career as an author and doctor. She had also written an influential series of "little blue books" about child-raising and nutrition, published by the government.[30]

But besides a theory of child-rearing, *Magic for Marigold* presented an old-fashioned sense of mothering love. All her life, Maud had treasured the memory of Pensie's mother, Mrs. Charles Macneill, coming into their bedroom, bending over the children, and saying (when she thought the little cousins were asleep): "Dear little children." Maud echoes that line in *Magic for Marigold.*

The setting for *Magic for Marigold* is Prince Edward Island, but in fact the setting is drawn from both the Island and Ontario. The name "Lesley" paid honour to the many "Leslie" families in the Union congregation. Maud had dreamed up her new heroine as she sat at her Norval bedroom window and looked up at the "hill o' pines" on Russells' Hill: Marigold's home was "Cloud o' Spruce." And later in the book, when the "lady-doctor" marries, she marries an adventurer and prospector returned from prospecting in the Klondike, as one of Maud's friends had. For professional women to marry and continue in their profession was still unusual. But Maud wanted to show that she was moving with the times.

Lewis Page lawsuits resolved

Maud's lawsuits with her former publisher, L. C. Page, were drawing to a close. Back in February 1926, her lawyer had seen a small opening after the fourth case was dismissed (a case in which Page had tried unsuccessfully to sue her for libel in the New York courts). Mr. Rollins suggested that Maud sue Page for the costs of this New York libel suit. This became the fifth legal action between her and Page. She won this round and collected $2,200 from the publisher. From this settlement in July 1928, she had to pay her lawyers $1,200 for their services. But she had the satisfaction of finally extracting some blood out of Page, knowing how bitterly he would have hated to pay her.

In the same month (October 1928) that Maud completed *Magic for Marigold,* Rollins wrote that a favourable decision had finally been made in her *Further Chronicles of Avonlea* lawsuit, the one that had sought an injunction against Page's publishing *Further Chronicles.* It had originally been filed in early 1920. The decision rendered in 1925 was: that the Page Company had violated its 1919 contract with Montgomery when it published the 1912 versions of the stories; that Page could publish no more of these books; and that the profits thus far were to be turned over to Maud, subject to Page recovering his costs for publishing the books. The last provision, of course, gave Page a significant loophole. And he had appealed the 1925 decision every step of the way, dragging the case on until 1928.

In 1925, when Page had first appealed the injunction and the accounting of the profits, the business of establishing profits had been remanded to the County Court for accounting. Then the haggling had begun. Page claimed every imaginable expense against the profits. He also argued that his firm should deduct $3,000 for having bought the stories from Maud in the first place, plus the excess profits' tax they had paid in 1920 on them. And he claimed that 25 percent of the remaining profits had been paid to the United States government as tax. But things were coming to a close, as Page's options diminished.

An auditor assigned to the case in February 1927 said that Page owed her nearly $16,000 profits for *Further Chronicles of Avonlea* after his costs were deducted. She was astonished—she knew that *Further Chronicles* was one of her *weaker* books. This gave her some idea of what the income from her books meant to the Page Company—and led her to suspect that Page had not figured her royalties honestly on the better books in the *Anne* series. She was too weary to feel joy over winning the suit, and she merely wondered if she would ever see the money he owed her. She correctly predicted that he would spin out his delaying tactics through appeals.

But Page's game of intimidation and obstruction was playing itself out. She had already heard, on May 3, 1927, that George Page had retired from the firm, and a month later, on June 2, she heard that he was dead. Lewis's unhappy brother was only fifty-five when he died "suddenly of a heart attack" on May 28, in his summer home in Sherburn, Massachusetts. Maud heard an unconfirmed report (from Margaret Marshall Saunders) that he had shot himself. She quipped in her journal that Providence had made a mistake in taking George instead of Lewis.[31]

Two days later, on June 4, Maud received a bizarre telegram from Lewis Page saying: "Since, as advised, you like a good fight, you will be interested in knowing that George Page was buried today." Soon, she received a letter from Page with the same message, enclosing another copy of the telegram. All in all, she observed that she got three copies of the message, a baffling attempt to assign to her some responsibility for the death of George Page. In mid-June 1928, Mr. Rollins and Mr. McClelland both reported the gossip they had heard from a former Page salesman that Lewis Page had fought with his brother until George left the firm.

The story went that the fighting had worried Mrs. George Page (Mabel Hurd Page) until she had a mental breakdown. When George Page died, Lewis attended his brother's funeral, but was reputed to have sat by himself. Maud puzzled over Lewis Page's psychology—why would he send her, his most bitter legal antagonist, such inappropriate and inexplicable telegrams about family matters? Lewis Page was right in sensing that such messages would bedevil her.

But Maud's day of triumph was coming. In the last week of October 1928, a fat letter came from her lawyer. By this time, the mere arrival of these letters spooked Maud. Sometimes she would wait several days to get up courage to slit open the envelope. However, this one brought the good news she had been hoping to hear for a decade. The lawsuits were all over. Rollins told her that he had "attached" Page's property until he paid the judgment, and that the lawsuit had cost Page over a year's profits. Rollins also reported that Page had acquired heavy gambling debts and that he had been forced to lay off people in his firm and require the remaining ones to work longer hours to compensate.

Maud wrote in her journal on October 22, 1928:

> *It is over! Over!! Over!!!*
> *And— —I— —am— —free!*

Of course, Page had a few parting shots. In late November 1928, he sent her another telegram: "Mrs George Page has lost her mind after her husband's shocking death. She never recovered. She died yesterday." This puzzled Maud all over again. She thought it a sign of Page's mental imbalance. A more obvious explanation was merely that he had probably been drinking heavily when he sent her these telegrams.

Lewis Page had a phenomenal ability to get under people's skin. In the process, he damaged his own business. New authors who heard of his reputation feared signing with him, and although his old best-selling titles continued to generate income, he shifted his focus to reviving out-of-print classics. Without the Wanamaker's sales, his firm went downhill, although he hung onto it until the end of his life, and managed to die a well-to-do but not wealthy man. Even after his death in 1956, Page's will reflected his vindictiveness. He skewered various members of his family, but left substantial sums to all the women who had worked for him and garnered his favour. According to Roger Straus and Robert Wohlforth, the women's names were gleefully published in Boston, which caused local wags to joke that some women only found out who his other mistresses were when his will was probated.[32]

Page asked in his will to have only one thing inscribed on his grave: "*Qui libros bonos edendos curavit*" (Latin for "He took great care to publish good books"). Maud would have agreed with him on this point: he did make beautiful books. For her part, she would always regret that the man who had launched her career turned out to be such a scoundrel.

The battle against Page had brought Maud enormous strain for the eleven years between 1917 and 1928, keeping her constantly facing the possibility of complete financial ruin. L. C. Page was one of the foremost robber-barons in the publishing world, but he met a tough opponent in Maud. When her right-eous indignation was fully aroused, she had found more courage than even she knew she had. And stamina, too: she managed to publish six novels during the duration of the five lawsuits and countersuits.

The $15,000 settlement cheque came on November 7, 1928 (it was originally for over $18,000, but Rollins had extracted his well-earned final fee of $3,000). Maud observed that she had paid out about $14,000 in lawyers' fees over the years for the five lawsuits, so she really had netted only about $4,000 for all her trouble and worry after the various settlements were paid, "plus the satisfaction of thoroughly beating a man who tried to trick me. That second item, not the first, makes me feel that after all it was all worthwhile" (November 7, 1928).

Maud wrote in her journals that it was very handy to have that one big lump sum come in a lean year. She looked forward to investing it wisely so that it would pay for her children's university education and "make things easier."

Nora Lefurgy returns

In September 1928, a long-lost friend turned up: Nora Lefurgey, now Mrs. Edmund Campbell, re-emerged in Maud's life after an absence of twenty-four years. Back in 1903, the gifted and vibrant Nora—then the Cavendish schoolteacher—had boarded with Maud and her grandmother. Nora shared Maud's love of memorizing poetry and literary passages, as well as her love of nature. There was one very big difference, however: Nora did not have mood swings like Maud—she was unfailingly upbeat.

Nora had moved to Toronto so her two sons could attend high school there. Maud had known Nora's husband, Edmund Campbell, back in Belmont, PEI, when she was twenty-two. He had gone on to take a B.A. and an M.A. in Engineering, and had become a distinguished Canadian mining-engineer. He and Nora had enjoyed their nomadic life, travelling to the Canadian north and the American south and west, and had recently returned from a trip to western Canada. (Their stories of the Klondike inspired elements of *Marigold*.) Ed had now set up a consulting company in Toronto so that they could settle down and educate their remaining children.

Nora had already buried two of her four children: one had died at birth, and their only daughter had died of polio at age twelve. A third son, David, had survived polio, but was badly crippled and wore heavy iron leg braces. Their youngest son, Edward, known as "Ebbie," had been untouched by bad luck, and both sons were now enrolled in Upper Canada College, an exclusive Toronto secondary school for boys. Even though Nora had experienced the tragic loss of two of her children and the crippling of a third, she was as vital a life-force as ever.

Nora and family came out to Norval to visit Maud for Thanksgiving dinner. Out of touch for nearly a quarter-century, they "clicked" as before, and fell into an afternoon of reminiscing. Maud had a real companion again, like Frede, someone with whom to exchange good stories, even though they lacked the bond of kinship. Nora was trustworthy, of equal intelligence and learning with Maud, and she was happy in her own life, yet impressed by Maud's achievement and willing to acknowledge it. Nora's supportive friendship would help bring stability to Maud's life through the next decade.

In Prince Edward Island, Nora's family had outclassed Maud's—a detail left out of Maud's journals, although of course Maud would have been keenly aware of it. Nora's father, William Thomas Lefurgey, had been a parliamentary secretary; although he was a man of letters rather than a farmer, he also owned farmland in PEI. Nora was from French Huguenot stock—not Scottish—but her family was distinguished, and she had made a happy and successful marriage.

Nora's son Ebbie remembered vividly when he first met Maud during the summer of 1928, and his recollections give us quite another view of the world-famous author:

> She was seated in the sofa, Mother diagonally in front of her in a big armchair. I, ten years old, on the floor, small, skinny, fascinated at last to meet this woman of whom I had heard so much. To me she was a massive woman, formidable, with a strong voice which expressed her feeling of self-importance and superiority. My mother was ecstatic at seeing her old friend again but slightly hostile at Maud's air of superiority. I cannot remember what they talked about—all I remember is a feeling of relief when Maud at last left. I had my mother back.[33]

Young Ebbie saw another part of Maud's personality here, the woman who knew her books had made her a "household name" all over the English-speaking world. Justifiably proud of her attainments and honours, she wanted her hard-won achievement recognized, even by friends. She was, as the precocious Ebbie noted, very good at conveying her sense of dignity to others. Her carriage and nuanced use of language spoke her attitudes. A powerful presence was a real element in her person, a "persona," as real as her buried sense of inferiority—or, perhaps, just another expression of it.

Nora apparently could see both Mauds—especially the Maud who was insecure, who carried damaging psychological baggage from childhood, and who needed approval and respect. Nora gave that willingly.

In November 1928, Maud was a busy participant in the Canadian Book Week. The opening lineup of speakers in the fifth annual event were the big names of the day: Sir Charles G. D. Roberts, novelist Arthur Stringer, essayist and editor (of *Saturday Night*) B. K. Sandwell, and "L. M. Montgomery." In the public's eye, Maud was the biggest celebrity. Over two thousand people flocked to hear her in the program at the University of Toronto's Convocation Hall, with another thousand reputedly turned away. In a newspaper account of the gathering, "L. M. Montgomery (Mrs. McDonald), author of *Anne of Green Gables*, declared she could not speak, the only thing she could do was to tell her stories. To her, she asserted, amid laughter, the four most wonderful words in the language were 'once upon a time.' She then told a story of a Prince Edward Island shipwreck, and recited two poems . . ."[34] Montgomery's speech drew a standing ovation, with a call for an encore.

After the speech she was mobbed by young people wanting autographs, except for one who merely wanted a "handclasp" and "to touch" her. "Poor kiddy!" she wrote, "humanity can't get along without some god or goddess to worship. It is well that my young worshippers don't know what a very clay-footed creature their divinity is. Their lives would be poorer if they lost their illusion" (November 7, 1928). Maud's spirits improved greatly after Book Week—her success there offset the bruises to her professional ego elsewhere.

During this week, Maud spoke again, this time on a platform with Dr. Charles G. D. Roberts and (Margaret) Marshall Saunders, through the auspices of the Maritime Provinces Association of Toronto and McMaster

University. The newspaper account says that Roberts "deplored his 'propinquity with modernism.'" Saunders kept the audience of over five hundred people in a state of laughter with her amusing reminiscences of the Maritimes. Mrs. Macdonald also related stories of famous characters living down by the sea.[35] After she arrived home from the conference, she had more letters from her lawyer and Lewis Page. Her lawyer had mailed her the typed trial evidence. Then, incredibly, she had a letter from Page asking if he could "now" publish *Further Chronicles of Avonlea*, the book that she had waged the entire lawsuit to suppress. She was again bedevilled by his weird request.

The year 1928 ended much better for Maud than it had begun. The Macdonalds decorated their Christmas tree and enjoyed a turkey sent them by friends. Maud spent Christmas afternoon reading Morley Callaghan's first novel, *Strange Fugitive*, a Christmas gift from Nora. The book made her huffy. "Some 'sex' novels are interesting and stimulating, whatever may be thought of their wisdom or unwisdom," she wrote in her journal. But Callaghan dismayed her.

> Callaghan's idea of "Literature" seems to be to photograph a latrine or pigstye meticulously and have nothing else in the picture. Now, latrines and pigstyes are not only malodorous but very uninteresting. We have a latrine in our backyard. I see it when I look that way—and I also see before it a garden. . . .—over it a blue sky—behind it a velvety pine. . . . These things are as "real" as the latrine and can all be seen at the same time. Callaghan sees nothing but the latrine and insists blatantly that you see nothing else also. If you insist on seeing sky and river and pine you are a 'sentimentalist' and the truth is not in you. (December 30, 1928)

She added another paragraph dismissing Callaghan, who was then twenty-five years old:

> Callaghan is no newly risen star. He is not even a meteor. Merely a Roman Candle shooting up sparkiously and then sputtering out into darkness. He has neither wit, imagination nor insight. And he is deadly dull . . . (December 30, 1928)

Frustrated by what was happening to her own reputation through the latter 1920s, she began to grumble privately about being demoted to "only a children's author." She had written *The Blue Castle* in 1926, intending it to be a story for adults. Instead, it was often treated as a children's book and, as a result, its mature content got it banned for children in a number of places. While *she* was censored for mentioning an *unwed mother* (who dies, no less), young writers like Callaghan were earning *praise* for sympathetic treatment of down-and-outers and prostitutes. It did seem unfair. The only consolation was that, despite the fact that it shocked her Sunday School readers, *The Blue Castle* sold well, and her publishers wanted more of the same.

Maud had long been contemplating a novel about the tangled clan structure of the Scottish population in Prince Edward Island, and she saw a way to build this story around one of her own most prized family heirlooms, the old Woolner jug. The result, *A Tangled Web*, is probably her most intricate and complicated novel, and clearly intended for adults, not children. She took her title from Sir Walter Scott's *Marmion*, Canto xvii: "O, what a tangled web we weave / When first we practice to deceive!"

Maud had grown up hearing Grandfather Macneill tell how this jug had been brought by his wife's family, the Woolners, from England to Canada. Maud had given it a place of pride both in her Leaskdale home and in the Norval manse. In a subtle way, making the jug the centre of a new novel for adults would help solidify her credentials as belonging to one of Canada's "old families," a family with "traditions" and stability behind it. In Prince Edward Island, everyone knew her family's standing and pedigree. In Ontario, where it now mattered to her, they did not.

Maud knew much about the "tangled web" of family intermarriage in the small communities of Cavendish, and later Zephyr, Leaskdale, and Norval. During the Pickering trial and the Church Union fracas, the intricate patterns of kinship and marriage had caused a constant shifting of allegiances and realignment of loyalties. Now, with some perspective—and having Nora Lefurgey Campbell nearby, always ready for an exchange of funny stories—she could see the comic potential in this clan material. In May 1929, she began a new and very ambitious novel. She had already been planning the plot structure for nearly a year. It would take two more years to complete it.

In one interval between the recurrent bouts of flu and ulcerating teeth that plagued her throughout the winter of 1928–29, Maud travelled to

Toronto and spent a January night with Nora. Together they read over the "comic" diaries they had kept together back in Cavendish, laughing over their social life with the limited lot of available young men. This helped Maud immerse herself in the memory of the ups and downs of young love relationships, all of which fed into A *Tangled Web*.

In the Old Tyme Concert that she organized for January 1929, Maud stole the show in her performance as Mary, Queen of Scots. She had rented a theatrical costume from Toronto. The long, full dress was crimson velvet decorated with braid, ermine, lace, and pearls, topped with a ruff of lace. She wore her hair high, with a crown on it, and recited a poem about Mary, Queen of Scots. She got such an ovation that she gave an encore, "The curfew must not ring tonight."[36]

Maud kept up her speaking engagements, too, while she worked on her novels, directed plays, and organized women's church affairs. In May 1929 she addressed an audience of nearly five hundred young women at a banquet given during Girls' Conference Week in the Ontario Agricultural College Dining Hall in Guelph. It was the "final session of one of the most successful Girls' Conferences in the history of the Junior Women's Institute Movement."[37] She enjoyed her position as a role model for young women—she had combined professional success with marriage and motherhood—and her talks were both funny and inspirational.

Chester, now seventeen, and Stuart, fourteen, came home for the summer in June 1929. Chester had already had driving lessons, but she wanted him to learn how a car actually worked, so she persuaded the local garage to employ him for a month. Both Chester and Ewan objected to his doing any "manual labour," but her will prevailed. Ewan had been raised on a farm, but he felt he had risen above doing manual labour, and he also apparently felt that his sons were too good for it. Chester, by nature indolent, assumed easily the mantle of entitlement. But Maud did not want Chester sitting idle lest he get into trouble: he continued to "chase" girls.

That same summer, Nora Lefurgey Campbell went with her two boys to a cottage on Lake Temagami. In July, her older son, David, the one crippled by polio, accidentally turned over his canoe, and the heavy iron braces he wore pulled him down; he was drowned. They dragged the lake for four days before recovering his body. Three of the four children that Nora had given birth to were now dead. To distance herself from the heartbreak, Nora took a trip out west to see friends, and Maud did not see her again until December 1929.[38]

In September 1929, Maud took a long-awaited trip to the Island. She had been working on A Tangled Web since May and needed a break. A highlight of her trip to the Island this time was a reunion with Mary Campbell, Nell Dingwall, and Ida MacEachern, her old friends from the Prince of Wales College. The four women took a picture that matched one taken thirty-five years earlier. Maud could not resist remarking in her journals that Mary Campbell Beaton, who had been a "fine-looking girl" in 1894, had gone "to seed." Maud, who was still stylishly plump, was secretly pleased that she looked successful and well kept, no matter how ragged she felt at times.

Maud also spent time with Ewan's sister Christie, her favourite of Ewan's siblings. Of Christie's family of eight children, only one son was now left at home. Like the Campbells of Park Corner, Christie's family had been a financial drain on Maud. Christie had not repaid the $2,000 "lent" to the family by Maud to cover her son's embezzlement five years earlier (in addition to the $600 given to her by Ewan out of his $1,500 yearly salary).

Maud also made a visit to Angie Doiron's stylish dress and hat shop. Angie's buying trips to the States ensured that her Prince Edward Island customers were as well dressed as the best Boston ladies. Maud bought a dignified dress of brown lace, with a long tail—quite different from the above-the-knee dresses the young flappers were wearing. Maud had always admired Angie—who was beautiful, charming, and educated—and disparaged the English prejudice against the French. She noted that men of English ancestry would look down on Angie's French parentage, limiting her marriage choices. Maud was as inconsistent as others of her generation: she could feel prejudice against an entire ethnic group but admire a talented individual within it.

On this trip, Maud noted the change in the Island roads. Cars were everywhere, the roads were being widened, and the trees that lined the roads were being cut down. But inside the houses she visited, she reminisced, life was the same: in rooms lighted by kerosene lamps and warmed by wood stoves, they sat and did women's fancy-work, talked over family and friends, played with the ever-present kittens, and read. A good night's sleep had become a precious thing to Maud by this time, and here she slept peacefully again.

On this same trip, Maud went to visit Helen Leard MacFarlane, the sister of Herman Leard. Herman had been dead for many years, but he was very

much alive in Maud's memory. When Helen's son drove them past the cemetery where Herman lay, Maud later recounted in her journal that she was
gripped by the gruesome sensation that Herman was "reaching out to me from
his grave—catching hold of me—drawing me to him" (October 13, 1929).

Maud's vivid memory of intense emotions was both a blessing and a curse.
When she was home in Norval, her worries over the future roiled in her mind
in the middle of the night. In Prince Edward Island, her memories of the past
tormented her in the daytime.

Soon after Maud returned home from the Island in October 1929, women became "persons" in Canadian law, giving them the right to hold public office.
The milestone "Persons Case" had been brought forward by five women, including Judge Emily Murphy and Nellie McClung, and was finally settled
with the Canadian Privy Council's declaration that women would have the
same legal status as men did. The status of women had been changing rapidly
ever since they had taken on traditionally male roles during the war. Women
were entering the professions. Big newspapers had instituted "women's sections" and gave extensive coverage to women's activities.

Women had been becoming more assertive of their rights in marriage,
and in general. Maud had been asked to speak on this change to the Junior
Women's Institute. She gave a talk that said that the "modern girl was in no
respect worse, and in many respects better, than the girl of former generations" in wanting her rights and respect. She approved this advance.

But she would soon be thrust into a future that would test every strategy
she had for survival. By November 25, 1933, she would write in her journals:
"Not even a cat would care to haunt so changed a world."

CHAPTER 17

For much of her life, Maud had endured the feeling that she lived in a house of cards, apt to blow down at any time. After a series of homes in which she had felt like a temporary resident, in 1929 she finally reported feeling more secure.

Ewan was now settled. He had smoothed the lingering divisions from Church Union in Norval, the more troubled of his two parishes. His good nature and kind manner dispelled the inevitable small frictions that arise in any church. He worked up his own sermons instead of using a book of prepared sermons, as some ministers did, and he delivered them extemporaneously from memory. He used his knowledge of Greek and Roman history to make them appeal to young people, who still remembered and praised his "interesting" sermons in the 1980s. Finally, he was doing well. By 1929, Maud began to hope that they could remain in Norval or Glen Williams after Ewan's retirement. He was now fifty-nine. She was fifty-five.

Chester, age seventeen, was in his last year at St. Andrew's in 1929, and would start university in the autumn of 1930. Stuart, fourteen and in his second year at St. Andrew's, was leading his class. There were ongoing concerns with Chester, but Maud continued to hope that he would mature. Stuart, by contrast, was in every way a parent's dream. He fit in with people of all ages, earned top marks, did well in sports, and was always "joyous" and a loving, sensitive son. With the settlement of the Page lawsuit, Maud had enough money to give her boys the best possible education, no matter what ill winds of chance might blow.

Her feeling of financial security now allowed her to do something mundane that she had needed to do for years: have all her teeth pulled. People still died occasionally because of the gas anaesthetic given by dentists, so few

rushed blithely into such operations. Since childhood, Maud had suffered repeatedly from cavities, toothaches, and painful abscesses that burst and
drained. Her infected teeth had made her prey to other kinds of health
problems—her teeth were irregular, piled on top of each other in her very
small mouth and jaw, and she had never been able to clean them properly.[39]
She had known that the removal of her infected teeth would improve her general health, but the fear that she might die from the anaesthetic before she had
provided for her sons' education had kept her away from the dentist's chair.
The surgery proceeded smoothly. She stayed briefly to recuperate with Nora
in Toronto, but soon returned home. A doctor in Georgetown made her a set
of false teeth, and now she could smile in photographs, something she had
never done before.

The Great Depression

Maud wrote no entries in her journal on October 29, 1929, the "Black
Tuesday" that led off the great stock market crash. In communities like
Norval it was just another ordinary day—as ordinary as the June day in 1914
when Archduke Ferdinand was assassinated in Sarajevo. Maud spent it as
usual, with her morning stint of writing on A Tangled Web. It is likely, in
fact, that she did not even hear, at least for a time, about the pandemonium
that erupted in the New York Stock Exchange on that day, and of the suicides of ruined speculators, said to have jumped out of windows. Even if she
had, she would hardly have expected it to affect anyone's life in the country
villages of Ontario.

She was not a foolish speculator—the money she had just received from
the Page settlement was hers. She was not investing money borrowed on the
margin. When she invested it, she assumed that it would be safe. In
November 1928, Maud had invested the $15,000 in the most promising place
she knew, in the stock market. She did not know, of course, that the American
economic guru, Roger Babson, a friend and neighbour of the Page and Coues
families of Boston, had been predicting for some time that a stock market
crash was coming, and when it came, it would be huge. Babson had advised
his clients, his friends, and the subscribers to his "Babson's Reports" to take
their money out of speculative investments and put it in secure places. Those
who heeded his advice weathered the crash of 1929 much better than others,

and Page appears to have been one of them. Maud had no such advice: she invested her entire settlement in stocks right before the crash of 1929.

As 1929 drew to a close, Maud was reading of more bank failures. She remembered the crash of 1907, and how she had used a bank failure to cause Matthew's sudden death in *Anne of Green Gables*.[40] To add another dimension to her anxiety, Ewan was badly shaken up in a serious accident when the radial train he was on collided with a snowplow, and he was consigned to bed. By the end of 1929, she was complaining of headaches, insomnia, and "feelings of imprisonment." As she ended her seventh journal, she wrote, gamely, that she hoped that 1930 could be "better than its advent promises" (December 21, 1929).

By January 2, 1930, she discovered that a company in which she had invested heavily was skipping its dividend payments. From that point on, bad news about her investments cascaded down on her. She watched in horror as her investments began to plummet. By the time the stock market meltdown was over, all the money she had received in recompense after a decade of enervating litigation with Lewis Page was reduced to a handful of bills. A $14,000 sum invested in Simpson's was worth only $1,680 by April 1932, and by December 1932, only $840. Her $3,000 investment in a Toronto insurance company was completely lost. (In the late 1920s, the average yearly salary of an Ontario man was around $1,000.) By summer 1930, Maud was concerned enough about money that in her short letters to fans she asked them to recommend her books to others. By the end of 1932, she would be typing her own manuscripts again, for the first time since 1909. Her collapsed finances—so soon after she'd thought she was set up for life—took another toll on her nerves. Would her stocks rise in time to pay for her sons' educations? At the same time that her own investments were skipping their dividends in 1930, or simply disappearing, the financial situation of farmers and businessmen everywhere worsened. Her beloved Park Corner farm relatives desperately needed cash.

Like the rest of the world, Maud was moving into an uncharted realm, without the old landmarks of stability found in faith, religion, and social mores. This sense of impending upheaval, of destruction of the old order, took powerful symbolic form in a fire that hit the little community of Norval that winter. On the night of January 28, 1930, the beautiful old stone gristmill that lay in the heart of Norval ignited, exploded, and then burned like a raging inferno, spewing sparks for miles around. By morning it was a pile of ashes. The huge mill lay in the middle of the town, straddling the Credit River, a landmark for over a century. As it burned, threatening to engulf the entire village, the fire could be seen for at least five miles above the little glen, and, according to a contemporary newspaper account, "ice and snow surrounding the burning building was melted and formed a stream around the ancient structure like a moat." A fire brigade from Brampton, eight miles away, arrived just in time to confine the fire to the mill, saving the rest of the village.

The destruction of the mill hastened the demise of Norval. The mill was only partly covered by insurance, and it would have cost $100,000 to rebuild it, so it was abandoned. Mill families moved away to find other work, and all of the subsidiary local businesses suffered—the bank, grocery, bakery, candy shop, hairdresser. After the mill burned, the picturesque little Scottish glen of Norval was on its way to becoming just another one of Ontario's disappearing villages.

The only truly impressive remaining structure in Norval was now the stately brick Presbyterian church, with the handsome manse next door. Successful farmers in the region would continue to support the church, but as a student of history, Maud saw that even the Church itself, as an institution, was in serious decline.

The beautiful old mill had given the town much of its picturesque character. Maud missed the little beacon that burned all night in its cupola; it had been the first welcoming light she had seen in Norval when they'd arrived. And she missed the three weathervanes on the three chimneys. They had looked to her, against the night sky, like little trolls from Norse mythology. Their disappearance seemed a sad portent in a world whose beacons of light were everywhere being extinguished.

Only two weeks after the mill's burning, with people still reeling from the loss of their livelihood and landmark, Norval put on its annual Old Tyme Concert. People caught on the wheel of accelerating change could reverse time, at least for an evening: this year they celebrated the "life of the ancient village." There was a terrible irony to the theme they had chosen.

Perhaps it was Ewan's own sense of change and loss that partly motivated him to conceive and take on a major project: researching the history of his second charge, the Union Church of Glen Williams, which would celebrate its one-hundredth year as a congregation in 1933. The Presbyterian faith had drawn settlers into a cohesive congregation in 1833, and the Scottish stonemasons had finished the magnificent stone church in 1884. Doing something special to commemorate the centennial year was important to Ewan. The problem was that no one knew where to find the early records of the church. Somehow, with a historian's instinct, he thought to look in a nearby community called the "Scotch Block," where the congregation had initially worshipped in a small structure known as the "Boston Church." He found enough records of the pre-1883 history of the congregation to fill in the early years from 1833 onward.

From that point on, Ewan was consumed with collecting materials, and visiting farmhouses to interview the older people in the congregation, happily believing that he would establish the church's importance in history. Although he was a man of short-lived energy bursts, Ewan felt dedication to this—his— writing project. He carried it to fruition and was very proud of his accomplishment. The resulting thirty-six-page booklet was well done.[41]

Given that Ewan was Scottish, a reader cannot help but smile over the ambiguous characterization he offers of his predecessor: "Mr. Patterson was a good preacher and fearless debater. Like every Irishman he was warm in his sympathies and attached to his friends." Was Patterson a beloved and colourful preacher, or was he an opinionated, hot-headed man who favoured the members of the congregation who had Irish or Scots-Irish ancestry? Mr. Patterson had been extremely learned, perhaps more so than Ewan, although the congregation judged Ewan's sermons favourably. Ewan was said to "know his Greek and Roman history" very well, and to "have great intellectual insights into things." He "could give a very perceptive discourse on just one Hebrew word. He went into the background to a lot of things, using ancient history to illustrate, and he didn't just go on about stuff in the Bible," said one of his parishioners in the 1980s. His sermons grew much livelier in this period when he had his own writing project.

No doubt Ewan hoped the booklet would strengthen his congregation by praising their long tradition of worshipping together through several generations. The names of the church's founders were still in the congregation, names like Leslie, Stirratt, Henderson, Fraser, MacDonald, Reid, and McKane. But there were new names, too, for the church congregation grew through Ewan's early tenure. His predecessor, the aforementioned Mr. Patterson, with his "warm" Irish sympathies, had presided over a very divisive Church Union vote in Norval, one that split and riled the entire community. People were glad to have the calm "peacemaker" that Ewan was.

Strangely, there is almost no mention of Ewan in Maud's journals at all during this period, perhaps because he was happy and did not interfere with her life. She does not refer to Ewan's working on the history booklet, nor does she say how much help, if any, she gave in the actual writing. But even if she did possibly polish portions of his work, the writing style is not hers, and certainly the project was one he proudly felt to be his.[42]

Ewan ended his history with a vision of hope that "the glories of the church of the future will be greater than that of even the present." This was very different from Maud's own vision of the future, and from her phrasing. Of the actual centennial celebration, held Monday May 28, 1933, Maud wrote wearily that it was celebrated in the same old way, with "old ministers preaching, special music, crowds of people . . ." She offered a jaded prophecy about the *next* centennial and forecast that even if the physical church structure itself might still be there in a hundred years, it would be inhabited by "owls and bats and wandering winds." She added that if "Sunday services are held at all—they will not be held in little country churches. There will be just a few central churches in large cities and the services will be broadcast from them. Country people will sit in their homes, press a button and hear and *see*."[43] Ewan's view might be turned to the glories of the past, but Maud's vision was of a spiritually impoverished future. Memories remained years later in Norval of her offhand remark made in a rare unguarded moment—a remark shocking to the women who heard it—that religion had become nothing more than a social club in this era.[44]

Isabel Anderson—a different kind of fan

In the 1930s, Maud was nearly consumed by another inferno—the passion she had stirred in a young woman from a nearby town. It is one of the strangest episodes in her entire life.

Isabel Anderson had first introduced herself in a fan letter in 1926. She lived close by in the town of Acton, and she adored Maud's novels. Maud drew the conclusion that the writer was a young girl with a precocious writing ability. The letter had extravagant phrasing in it, such as Anne and Diana might have written each other in their pre-adolescent fancies. Maud had written back warm, encouraging words. Soon more adoring letters arrived. Next, Maud was invited to have an evening meal with Isabel and her family.

To her surprise, Isabel was not a young girl but a thirty-four-year-old elementary school teacher. She lived with her mother and sister. Both of them were normal and pleasant, but Isabel had the strange intensity of an unbalanced personality. A fluent writer, she was dull and gauche in person. Maud felt alarmed. Gushing letters that were cute if written by a young girl were something else if written by a grown woman. Maud's fears were well grounded: Isabel proved to be a different kind of fan, with a vengeance.

Maud had the novelist's fascination with unusual characters, but Isabel was not a type she could identify. There were some superficial similarities between Isabel and herself: Isabel's father had been the village postmaster, and Isabel herself was interested in writing poetry. Maud, having endured some very lonely periods in her own life, understood isolation. But there was no obvious reason for Isabel's loneliness: she had a very nice mother, a friendly, talkative sister, relatives in the area, and a job as a teacher.

After their first meeting, Isabel pelted Maud with letters, presents, pleading invitations, and phone calls. Later, Isabel's mother died and her sister escaped to be a missionary in the Canadian west. Isabel, already a social misfit, became even more estranged from other people, moved into a two-room apartment, and stepped up her pestering telephone calls. Maud felt sympathy for Isabel's increasing psychological isolation, not to mention her lack of friends, hopes, and ambitions.

Isabel was no beauty, but she was at least as physically attractive as many other women who found mates. Something else seemed to be wrong. Then Maud received a letter from Isabel saying that she thought she was "losing her mind." The only thing that would save her would be coming to the manse, and "sleeping with" Maud. By March 1, 1930, when Maud began writing Isabel into her journals, she was wavering between seeing Isabel as a lonely, neurotic young woman who merely wanted female friendship and seeing her as a woman sexually attracted to other women. Confused, Maud observed that the word "pervert" had been aired frequently in "certain malodorous works of fiction" (March 1, 1930).

Appalled by the thought of hosting Isabel, Maud wrote her that a friend was coming to visit so her spare room would be occupied, and that when the friend (Fannie Wise Mutch) left, Maud herself was going to the Island. That should have conveyed the message. It did not. As soon as Maud returned from the Island, Isabel continued her pleadings. No excuses worked. Isabel was entirely self-absorbed. At the end of February 1930, Isabel wrote Maud a "specially piteous letter." Maud decided that she should feel compassion for her:

> I had convinced myself that it was all nonsense to suppose Isabel a pervert. She was merely a lonely, neurotic girl who cherished a romantic adoration for me, thus filling a life that was otherwise piteously empty of everything that makes life worth living. And as such I wanted to help her if possible. (March 1, 1930)

Maud agreed to spend the night at Isabel's home. Staying overnight and sharing beds with people was common when families were large and houses small, and especially before people had their own cars, allowing them to drive home at a late hour after a visit. Thus, Isabel's request was not necessarily as strange as it might sound today.

The evening was a miserable one for Maud, as described in her journal entry of March 1, 1930. They ate with Isabel's landlady and then retired to Isabel's rooms. Maud found that Isabel was "as quiet, shy, restrained as—as— the simile *will* come into my mind—as a girl in the presence of her lover." She had no conversational topics. At bedtime, Isabel announced, "I do not mean to sleep at all tonight. I mean to lie awake and revel in my happiness." The bed they were to share was "fitted out like a bridal one—exquisite sheets, pillows, coverlet, blankets and puff—all evidently brand new and purchased for the occasion." In spite of her misgivings, Maud slept well because she was tired, and in the morning she looked forward to her escape. "I was still inclined to think, in spite of Isabel's queer speeches and queerer intensity of manner and personality that I had been utterly mistaken in my fears."

Shortly after she returned home, however, she received a letter from Isabel, who had wept at the station when Maud left her. It read:

> My Darling—
>
> It really is quite delicious to write that I ought to be washing a few things but it is really too romantic a night. But the sweet incense of your presence still broods around me like a dream from which I am only half awake.
>
> Darling, I love you so terribly, I do. I have a suspicion that if my chronic indisposition were accurately diagnosed much of it must be pronounced "love." To say that I worship you is a most colourless

statement of the fact. I can't tell you how much I loved having you. You are just as pretty as ever you can be with your lovely long braids and your sweet, sweet face, and the blue dressing gown, and I adore you. I want you again. I simply cannot endure not to have you again soon. It sounds quite ungrateful, I know, but I am suffering all the agonies of being in love. I have derived some comfort from sleeping in the precise spot you occupied half hopeful that some of the dear warmth might still be found to linger. But I crave something tangible. I want to hold in my arms what is dearer than life to me—to lie "spoon fashion" all through a long long night— to cover your wee hands, your beautiful throat and every part of you with kisses. I'm just mad with love for you.

She concluded:

Perhaps tomorrow I shall be sorry I wrote this. But it is true . . . And after this shameless confession don't you think I am a terrible creature? (March 1, 1930)

Maud certainly did. After reading the letter, she fled to the bathroom and scrubbed her hands with repulsion. She did not know what to do. It was hardly a situation to discuss with women in the church. She wrote in her journals that she was unable to discuss it even with Ewan, who would simply judge Isabel, rather ironically, as "out of her mind" (March 1, 1930).

Ewan had been in *his* right mind for nearly four years now, except for periods of minor depression, and for once, his response might have been more clear-headed than his wife's. Maud was now afraid to cut Isabel out of her life for fear that she might become totally unhinged and create a public scandal. Maud also recalled her own loneliness and depressed state before marriage, and knew that part of being a minister's wife was helping the lonely and sick. As a novelist and student of human behaviour, she was fascinated by Isabel's weirdness, but totally repelled by the inappropriate words and actions.

Maud reacted as she always did under extreme stress: she began a long writing project in her journals that was largely mechanical. She assembled all the reviews of her novels that her clipping service had sent her and lined up all the contradictory statements about each novel. This must have taken days. Then she embarked on a more extended project of going through her other scrapbooks and boxes of memorabilia and commenting on these (March 1, 1930).

But no escape was to be found from Isabel. By the next summer she was sending Maud veiled hints of suicide. Maud suspected that this was just self-dramatization, but she also recognized that someone as disturbed as Isabel was unpredictable and might commit suicide. She remembered the Prince Edward Island papers that published all the graphic and gory details of suicides, speculating on motives and causes. Maud also had seen Ewan's periodic mental problems, so serious that his doctor once warned her never to let him out of her sight lest he try to kill himself. Maud reflected tartly that Isabel was so miserable that she would be as well off dead as living (June 1, 1931). But she continued to worry, and in this case, felt cold terror imagining what people would say.

By this time Isabel possessed a sizeable cache of Maud's letters, dating back several years. The thought of Isabel's body being found with these letters on her breast and a suicide note saying she had killed herself because of Maud's failure to love her was simply too appalling to contemplate. It would make national and possibly even international news. Maud thought, not unreasonably, that people would find her continuing to tolerate Isabel so bizarre that they would imagine that there truly was a scandal under the story.

Maud and Isabel became locked in an ongoing battle: Isabel trying to manipulate Maud, and Maud determined to keep her at arm's length. Maud repeatedly wrote to Isabel, describing the kind of ordinary friendship she could give her. She forbade Isabel to write of "love." This brought protests from Isabel:

> I doubt you love anybody but your boys and your cat, and, I presume, your husband. . . . You love your cat; he knows it. You have a kiss—two kisses—for every creature in creation but not one speck of love for a hungry heart that has pleaded for it too long. You are like a lovely scintillating jewel whose radiant heart is cold and cruelly hard. (Isabel's letter of February 8, described in Maud's journal entry of February 11, 1932)

Isabel insisted that she was not a "freak" who turned to Maud to escape her own dreary life (as Maud had suggested). Isabel allowed that she needed to be "psychoanalyzed" and perhaps she should be "shot." Then Isabel dramatized her own death in the letter:

To die for the love of L. M. Montgomery! That would invest me
with glory and beauty and fame and I should have forever from the
hearts of the world what I craved from you and you denied.

Maud's response was a mixture of pity, scorn, and fear. She had already
tried plain speaking, telling Isabel frankly that her cravings were "lesbian" and
that she had lost her balance due to being "possessed." As Maud should have
known from her experience with Ewan in his spells, there was no reasoning
with a mentally disturbed person. Isabel alternated between abusive and pathetic responses, in letters and phone calls. Maud, in an increasingly poor
state of mind herself, described herself as "hag-ridden."

The existence of homosexuality had come to world attention some thirty
years earlier with the trial of Oscar Wilde in England, and his subsequent imprisonment for it. Radclyffe Hall's *The Well of Loneliness*, an exploration of
homosexuality, had set the world on its ear in 1928. Maud read everything on
the topic that she could find in Toronto libraries and bookstores, including
André Tridon's *Psychoanalysis and Love* (1922), which included a chapter on
"Unconscious Homo-sexualism." Maud did not see homosexuality either as a
crime or a sin; rather, she saw it as an attribute existing most likely from birth,
beyond conscious control. However, whatever Isabel's condition was, Maud
regarded her an unbalanced, obnoxious pest whose persistent demands for
"caresses" and "love" were disrupting her life.

One young woman who spent some time in the Macdonald house remembered Isabel vividly, and described how her visits to the manse annoyed
Maud, particularly when Isabel merely appeared without invitation. Maud
always scheduled her days, planning out every minute in advance, and an
unexpected visitor could disrupt a whole day. One visit stood out in memory: Isabel had come to Norval without being invited, and Maud had to stop
what she was doing. She took Isabel into the parlour with grim resignation,
to make polite, brief, and very formal conversation, intending then to send
her home.

In about fifteen minutes, Maud burst into the kitchen in a state of extreme agitation, saying in a shocked and disgusted voice, "She wants to hold
hands with me!" Maud washed her hands compulsively several times, and
paced around the kitchen. She said that she was "going to be sick," and was
so upset that it took some time for her to regain control of herself. After calming down, she returned to the living room, and said politely and smoothly to

Isabel that Chester would now drive her home because she, Maud, had to get back to her work.

Nora was the only person Maud felt comfortable talking to regarding the ongoing situation with Isabel Anderson. Nora, like Maud, kept a diary. In their respective diaries, they each give an account of Isabel. Comparing their versions illuminates Isabel's obsession with Maud, as well as her writerly interest in exploring an interesting psychological situation. Nora is more factual in her entry of August 12, 1932:

> Eb and I drove to Maud's the 12th and I came back yesterday [August 19]. Maud is a dear—with reservations . . . [*the ellipsis points are Nora's, and she does not explain, but she is likely referring to Maud's occasional "grandness"*]. The female pervert Isabelle [*sic*] Anderson visited Maud a whole day while I was there. Her ability for complete absence of all speech is phenomenal. How can Maud stand her? Is not even pretty . . .

Maud describes this same visit in her journals in August 20, 1932:

> Nora and Ebbie came out. Eb camped out with the boys by the river and Nora and I went on a voyage to some magic shore beyond the world's rim. . . . We joked—and talked beautiful nonsense—and did things just for the fun of doing them—and tried dozens of new recipes. And we laughed. Oh, how we laughed—and laughter as I have long been a stranger to. . . . And every evening after the supper dishes were finished, we walked four miles, in a lovely ecstatic freedom under a harvest moon, up the "town line road" to the station and back. I hadn't believed there was anything like those walks left on earth. From the moment we found ourselves amid the moon-patterned shadows of that road every particle of care and worry seemed to be wiped out of our minds and souls as if by magic. Hope was then our friend again—we were no longer afraid of tomorrow.

Then she describes Isabel's visit:

> One day I had Isabel Anderson down. Nora was full of curiosity concerning her. I, on my side, had promised to have her down

and had been dreading the martyrdom of a day spent alone with her. So I invited her to come . . . when I would have Nora to take the edge off her. . . . Isabel came on the bus. I suppose she had been looking forward to being alone with me, for a whole day and was bitterly disappointed on finding Nora here. For the first few minutes I really thought the girl was going to cry. At first Nora and I both tried to draw her out. . . . The most we could extract from her was a sulky yes or no. Nora and I finally reacted nervously and the spirit of perversity came upon us. We began to do what we had sworn we wouldn't do — rag each other before Isabel. . . . Isabel sat and listened to the insults and reproaches we hurled at each other as if she couldn't believe her ears. I'm sure it was a weird revelation to her of what friendship with me might be!! (August 20, 1932)

Maud goes on to say that the boys kept up the jests at dinnertime, after which Chester was deputed to drive Isabel home. Isabel went in smouldering silence. Through Nora's visit, Maud was pulled enough back into normalcy that she could register real annoyance at Isabel's rude behaviour.

I was simply very angry with Isabel. She had pleaded to be allowed to come down. I had asked her to come — given her the privilege of meeting one of my best friends, a brilliant woman of the world whom anyone should enjoy meeting. I had received her into the intimacy of my family circle. And all her thanks was this behaviour . . . (August 20, 1932)

Maud finishes her high-handed account of the visit with the comment that she would love to have given the bad-mannered, sulky "Miss Isabel" a good spanking. Isabel, however, was not to be put off. She soon wrote Maud again:

I love you so terribly. . . . My dear, don't you see that I need you more often than your other friends. I hope you realize under my bland exterior an undercurrent of fierce resentment. Can't I arouse in you the tiniest spark of pity for my languishing condition? (September 15, 1932)

Maud growled in her journal that she certainly did sense the resentment:

> Although I have told her repeatedly that I cannot and will not tol-
> erate physical caresses she coolly informs me that she is going to
> "save up" my kiss of greeting—a casual cool kiss I sometimes give
> her at meeting in the vain hope of satisfying her—by going with-
> out it until she can have twelve all at once! A regular Lesbian
> gorge. (September 15, 1932)

Isabel continued to bombard Maud with letters. Maud wrote her a bracing and patronizing letter on November 22, 1932, telling her that their communications must cease since Isabel would not be contented with "such
measure of friendship as is possible between a woman of my age and experience and a girl of yours."

> You call this "love," my dear. It is nothing of the sort. It is simply an
> obsession, as any psychiatrist would tell you. Their records are full
> of such cases, even to the wording of the letters, as you would real-
> ize if you had studied as many of them as I, in the pursuit of my
> profession, have done. . . . Some day you will suddenly awaken to
> the fact that you have recovered from it and are free once more.
> Then you will realize that this letter has been the truest kindness
> (November 22, 1932).

Maud growled in her journals that Isabel's letters showed that she was
more unhappy *after* the visits than *before*, so they did no good. Return mail
brought a piteous letter from Isabel pleading that she not be cut off into the
"darkness of despair." Isabel promised to think of Maud only as a "friend and
be sensible . . ." (December 1, 1932).

Next, Maud tried a new strategy, one most people would have tried much
earlier: that of ignoring Isabel's letters. Maud's silence was shattered by two
more letters from Isabel, to which Maud finally replied: .

> I am a woman of 58. At that age one does not form deep new
> friendships with anyone, even with those of one's own genera-
> tion . . . I have no time in my overcrowded life for more.
> (January 22, 1933)

Isabel fired back an intemperate, angry response:

> I see plainly that I am nothing whatever to you. . . . You have never
> tried to understand me or my point of view. You are stubborn and
> dogmatic and selfish and, like a spoiled child, have said, "If you
> don't play my game I won't play." . . . You would cry over the loss
> of a miserable cat and you would deliberately, ruthlessly, unneces-
> sarily crush a human soul struggling against what I sometimes feel
> is the approach of death. . . . I haven't enough spirit left to hate you
> but your unjust and ungracious treatment has left me only bitter-
> ness and contempt . . . (January 22, 1933)

This letter infuriated Maud, and she wrote a vigorous and sarcastic reply
in her own journal to each point in Isabel's letter. Maud felt sure that Isabel
would never bother her again, given the insults in her last letter. "I am free at
last, thank heaven. . . . The girl is not sane and I deserve all I have got for
being fatuous enough to think I could help her or guide her back to normalcy" (January 22, 1933). But Maud was wrong. Isabel's letters continued,
sometimes piteous, sometimes abusive.

"I can't set my foot on a writhing worm," Maud would write about one of
Isabel's more grovelling letters on February 9, 1933, adding, "I can't let a
human being suffer so when I can prevent it. Am not I suffering hideously,
with no one to comfort me and no prospect of any relief?" It was partly a
measure of Maud's own unsettled and depressed state of mind that she could
not shake Isabel loose.

Isabel's passionate crushes were not just on women. She later pursued
both married and unmarried men. Maud mentioned Isabel's name to another
minister's wife, and learned that Isabel had chased her husband until the wife
put a stop to it (May 3, 1932). Another minister from the area told Maud that
Isabel was a mental case, whatever her sexual proclivities (October 6, 1934).
This made Maud feel somewhat better, but she still could not completely
shake off her unbalanced fan.[45]

By 1930, Chester was ready to start university, at age eighteen. In her journals, Maud continued her ongoing narrative about children who disappoint
their parents.

One of Maud's best friends in the Prince of Wales College days was Mary Campbell, now Mary Campbell Beaton. Maud came from a culture that valued loyalty to friends and family even when that meant cover-ups, and in June 1930, a letter came from a Toronto lawyer asking Maud to put up $1,000 in bail for Sutherland Beaton, Mary Campbell Beaton's son. Sutherland Beaton had come to Maud earlier with a lie that persuaded her to lend him $100 — which she now knew he had no intention of repaying. This handsome and silver-tongued young man had a history of theft and forging cheques on the Island that Maud did not know about. His parents always made restitution to keep him out of jail. Now, having moved to Toronto where he was not known, Sutherland was up to his old tricks, and he had been caught red-handed by his employer.

The broken-hearted Mary Beaton spilled out the whole sad story of Sutherland's ongoing crimes, and came up to Toronto for his trial. Maud, always loyal to old friends, went along with her to the courtroom to give moral support. Toronto newspapers described the grey-haired mother crying as her son stood in the dock, but they did not learn (fortunately for Maud) that disconsolate Mary was sitting beside a very famous friend. With restitution made, Sutherland, only nineteen, was put on probation for a year and released to his mother's care. As Mary Beaton had to return to the Island, Maud was obliged to take responsibility for him until he found another position.

For three weeks, the handsome Sutherland stayed with the Macdonalds, driving about with Chester and another local young man, chasing the pretty girls in the community. Maud lived in terror that the parishioners would connect this young rapscallion with the newspaper story, and then blame her for allowing a convicted thief to squire their daughters about. Maud did not expect Sutherland to change his ways, and she was greatly relieved when he decamped for Toronto with the announcement that he had found a job. She suspected the job was a lie — which it was — but she was glad to be rid of him. Maud felt enormous pity for Mary Beaton's heavy heart. And she no doubt shuddered privately, given her concerns over Chester.

This was Maud's second experience with young men running afoul of the law. First there had been Leavitt, Ewan's nephew, caught when he embezzled in Prince Edward Island. Disgraced, Leavitt had emigrated permanently to the United States. Now, here was Sutherland Beaton, an engaging young man who was also a pathological liar. Maud was getting a taste of what could happen when a beloved child went "bad."

As for Chester, the maids grimly tolerated his messiness, laziness, and disrespectful behaviour, but they would not have voiced to Maud their other real reason for disliking him: that they could not leave any valuables or money in their room, or the items would disappear. It is not clear when Maud first discovered that he was stealing, but she had known for a long time that his word could not be trusted. Stuart simply avoided Chester now that they were older, and continued sleeping in his tent to avoid sharing a room with his brother.

The friction between Chester and his father intensified. Maud found herself in the role of a buffer between Chester and his father. She had no more control over Chester than Ewan did, yet she felt blamed for everything because of Ewan's belief that it was a mother's job to raise the children.

For Chester, morose and lonely, the summer of 1930 was particularly boring. He didn't want a job, but even if he had, there was no work available during the Great Depression. With little to occupy his time, Chester pursued girls, making use of his parents' car. He had never made lasting friends of his own sex, and now he turned to girls for comfort and attention—and more. The nicer girls in the community avoided him, but there was one local girl with a poor reputation who did often go driving into the country with him. Everyone in the community talked about this, and Maud was wild with anxiety.

One of his contemporaries, a young woman of about eighteen who had lived a stone's throw from the manse, told me of a time when she was home alone during the day, and was suddenly surprised to find Chester in the house with her. He tried sweet-talking, without success; then he tried to catch her, and chased her around, telling her he would "never love anyone but her." She was an athletic girl, and she managed to flee the house. After that, she kept the door locked whenever her parents were out.[46]

Finally, Chester started dating Luella Reid, a petite and plain-looking girl in the Norval church. The Reids lived out on a farm, and Luella was not privy to all the village gossip about Chester's behaviour with other girls. Maud and Ewan were relieved because Luella was considered a "nice" girl. They hoped that as soon as Chester went off to the University of Toronto in the fall of 1930, he would buckle down to work, develop more social skills, mature in his interests—and put less focus on girls.

As soon as Chester had departed for university (where he took up residence in Knox College in the University of Toronto), and Stuart was back at St.

Andrew's, Maud started a month-long trip, travelling by train to Prince Albert, Saskatchewan, in Western Canada. She wanted to go out west again for several reasons—to rekindle old friendships, to meet the rest of her father's second family, and to see if she could retrieve some of the money lent to Irving Howatt, Stella Campbell's old beau from Park Corner days.

Everywhere she went she also gave speeches to large audiences: at the Women's Canadian Club and a reception in Saskatoon; at the Canadian Club in Prince Albert; at a school class and at the Press Club in Winnipeg. She visited Irv Howatt—whom she found "shabby as a singed cat"—and she saw it would be impossible to reclaim the $4,000 loan she had given him through Stella. It was enough to educate a son, she grumbled privately.

She travelled to her father's grave and was profoundly moved:

> There separated from me by a few feet of earth was what was left of father—of the outward man I knew. I might call to him but he would not answer. I felt so tenderly, preciously, dreadfully *near* to him. As if, under that sod, his great tired beautiful blue eyes had opened and were looking at me. (October 14, 1930)

Nearby was the grave of Will Pritchard—Laura's brother—who had died very young, and to whose memory she would dedicate her last book, *Anne of Ingleside*, in 1939. He had been a very good comrade when she was sixteen. She assured the future readers of her journals that, "at that time sex meant nothing to my unawakened body," and that she "never felt for him even the passion of sentiment which at that time I thought was love. . . . But I *liked* Will Pritchard better than any boy or man I have ever met in my life." She recounts how she and Will used to "prowl about together" in the hills and bluffs outside Prince Albert (October 10, 1930); a reader may suspect that she is "protesting too much."[47] After Will's death, a thin golden ring he had taken from her was returned to her (October 7, 1897), and she is said to have worn it on her little finger for the rest of her life.

Maud could hardly wait to return home after so many memories were stirred up in the west. Still, she wrote that the emotions had been "a wonderful agony." Her gift of wings brought great highs: "It is wonderful to feel so deeply, even if the feeling be half pain. One lives when one feels like that. Its illumination casts a glow over life backward and forward and transfigures drab days and darkened paths" (October 12, 1930). Her description of this visit continues, showing how her life was affected by living with such a good memory. Every event and place in Maud's childhood was "something that is of eternity, not of time" (October 12, 1930), because she did not—indeed, *could not*—forget it.

When Maud was a girl, the "lure of the west" had been strong. She would have stayed if the new Mrs. Montgomery had not driven her away. Her life, she speculated, would have been a different one: she would have written books, because she *had to* write, but she would have lived a different life and written different books.

Maud returned to new fears at home. When Chester had left for university in the fall of 1930, he had still been courting Luella Reid. Her father, Robert Reid, a successful but rather gruff farmer, was a leading elder in the Presbyterian Church. Maud was very fond of Luella's mother, a refined and charming woman. Nevertheless, she thought Chester was far too young to get serious. The Macdonalds had hoped that the romance would cool off once Chester began university, but in the fall he had instead returned to visit Luella every weekend, neglecting his studies. They saw that Chester was still drifting, with little focus except on girls.

After Christmas, Maud's worst fears materialized. Chester had chosen to study Mining-Engineering at the University of Toronto, something Maud thought very unsuitable for him. He had heard Nora Campbell's husband, Ned, one of Canada's top mining engineers, talk about their travels, and it sounded romantic. It was a difficult course of study, and anyone who worked in it needed to be active and fit. Chester was neither. He was "bone lazy," overweight, and had no self-discipline or self-control. Would he keep up with his studies? The answer soon came.

On February 8, the Varsity Council on Delinquency at the University of Toronto wrote to Ewan and her, recommending that Chester withdraw from the university. Ewan and Maud immediately went into Toronto to talk to Chester's professors, particularly Professor Herbert Haultain (1869–1961).[48] Haultain was a no-nonsense man who gave the distraught Macdonald parents little sympathy. They learned that Chester had been attending his classes only part of the time. Clearly, he had made a very bad impression on several professors in a program where the professors knew all their students by name and kept very close tabs on them.

Maud sensed that there was something else behind the advice to withdraw him. She felt that his professors were somehow prejudiced against him for more than they were willing to say, but she could not fathom it (or would not reveal her suspicions in her journals). Unsatisfied with the professors' explanations, Maud insisted that he stay in school, despite the advice to withdraw him. He remained through the term, promising to mend his ways, but his mother knew too well what his promises were worth.

Maud kept up her own steady pace in public events throughout this dismal February, despite headaches that were increasing in severity. She did readings for the Canadian Authors Association, for the students at the Jarvis Collegiate in Toronto, for a concert in Preston, Ontario, and, for the first time in her life, she performed on the radio. For two weeks, she even took into her home the difficult thirteen-year-old daughter of a parishioner who was in the hospital for an operation.

Chester came home one weekend when the girl was with them. Maud reported later that the girl told a story about something that happened at their house, something too upsetting to confide to her diary. "I can't go into details," Maud wrote, berating the girl for "lying." She added with unconscious irony, "There is not much use in trying to help that class of people. They are incapable of gratitude" (March 14, 1931).

Norval was shrinking rapidly as a result of the mill burning down. The bank closed in April 1931, and its depressed and distraught manager, Mr. Greenwood, died in July. Maud had called him the "best amateur actor" she had ever seen, and she felt his loss personally. He had starred in many of the plays that she had directed for the Presbyterian and Anglican churches. The radial railway also closed in 1931—partly a result of competition from automobiles—leaving her with no easy transportation to Toronto.

Ewan was so eager for Chester *not* to come home in the summer vacation that he himself went in to see Professor Haultain to plead Chester's case in obtaining a summer placement in the Frood mine in Sudbury. Haultain had already told Chester that, given his poor record, there was no place for him, but Ewan could be very persuasive, and the end result was that Chester was given a summer job in the mine. At the end of April, Ewan and Maud drove the three hundred miles to Sudbury to take Chester to his first real job.

A few days later a letter came from Chester saying that he had been fired, but that his peers had intervened and he had been given a second chance to "prove himself." On May 9, the Toronto newspapers published the university "pass lists." Chester's name was not included: he had failed his first year. It was not a question of ability, Maud knew: at St. Andrew's, where he had applied himself at least part of the time, he had graduated with an average of 80 per-cent, with many favourable comments about his ability. On May 19, Chester suddenly arrived home from Sudbury, having made his way back on his own. He said that he had been fired, for good this time.

Chester had wasted a year's worth of university fees, plus room and board, at a time of financial hardship. He would have to repeat the year. The profes-sors already saw him as a slacker. On top of his academic failure—which spoke poorly for his future—Maud worried as always about what others "would think." It would be a public humiliation with parishioners, with people in the other churches, and with family and friends in Toronto and on the Island. For a mother who had such high hopes for her talented sons, she was heartbroken. She had worked so hard to provide them with the kind of ed-ucation that she had wanted for herself, and now Chester did not appreciate the opportunity she had given him.

And worse, Chester would be home all summer—fighting with his father and pursuing Luella, or other girls. Remarkably, Chester managed to convince his mother that he had been treated unfairly at the mine. Someone else might have wondered if Chester had simply taken stock of what would be expected of him—long hours of very hard, dirty work underground—and decided that the best course of action was to get himself fired.

Maud was demoralized, indignant, and feeling increasingly helpless. She felt too paralyzed to work on her next novel, *Pat of Silver Bush*, and turned instead to her journal, her only real confidant. Ewan had always had a prej-udice against manual labour for his children, thinking it beneath those des-tined for the professional classes—except in this case, which connected to Chester's future occupation. Nevertheless, he blamed Maud for Chester's failure (which he had predicted). His repeated line to his wife was a frus-trated, "I told ye so."

Besides suffering from asthma and headaches, Maud was now bothered by a strange eczema on her neck and arms. By June, she complained of feel-ing "nervous unrest all the time." Significantly, she shifted to writing in her diary about Macneill and Montgomery family history. It appears that this restored her self-esteem, her sense of coming from "good stock"—as if that might right Chester's behaviour.

Throughout the fall that year (1931), the Macdonalds continued to watch Chester. He seemed more settled during his repeat year, but Maud knew that he could not be trusted to tell the truth about anything. However, Chester worked harder and got through the year, with a 73 percent, and good standing in his class.

He returned to the University of Toronto and his second year in Mining-Engineering, in September 1932. It was not long before he was slacking again, and visiting Luella too much. Ewan complained to Maud that Chester's behaviour was unwise; the implication was that Maud herself should correct the problem. She grew as angry at Ewan as she was at Chester.

On February 1, 1933, unbeknownst to the Macdonalds, some twenty-three members of the Engineering Faculty Council met to discuss Chester's performance and grades and unanimously voted to have him withdraw for the remainder of the term. The same day, seven members of the Faculty of Applied Science and Engineering's Committee on Delinquents reviewed his case. The council stated that he "had failed in Field Work, Chemical Laboratory and Dynamic and Structural Geology." Further reports of "delinquency" were also received from the departments of Engineering Drawing and Mineralogy, and "two petitions for consideration were read." After prolonged discussion and consultation with Professor Haultain, they recommended to the council that he be directed to withdraw from the faculty, under the provisions of the Calendar, Clause No.1, that "No student will be permitted to remain in the University who persistently neglects academic work, or whose presence is deemed by the Council to be prejudicial to the interests of the University."

On February 3, 1933, Chester received a letter, directing him to withdraw. Ewan immediately made an appointment to speak to Professor Haultain, who told him that Chester had failed four exams and had not been attending classes. Later Chester told his parents that he'd run into two of his professors who had told him that he had *not* failed in their courses. His transcript for that year shows that he received 45 percent in Field Work, 23 percent in Chemistry Laboratory, 13 percent in Mineralogy, and 33 in Dynamic and Structural Geology. He received 65, 53, 60, and 75 in the rest of his courses (Mining Laboratory, Inorganic Chemistry, Theory of Measurements, and Steam Engines, respectively). So it is true that he did not fail in several other courses.

Wanting to think that her son had been badly treated, Maud decided that Haultain had lied to the Committee on Delinquents about Chester's grades. The record, however, does not bear this out. Chester had failed in four courses, and the Engineering Council was clearly fed up with him and wanted him out of the program.

He returned home in February. The entire village could see that he was home, and since the newspapers carried "pass lists," they already knew that he was in trouble again. Maud's humiliation—and her injured pride—can be seen in a letter she wrote to a relative, on February 12, 1933: "Chester is home for the winter. The plain truth is that, as times are, Mr. Macdonald and I decided that we could not afford to keep both boys at college this year." She goes on to explain that they thought at first they would keep Stuart home, but as Chester had been sick for three weeks in the past term, he had fallen behind in his work and was afraid he could not catch up, so she thought he was the one who should stay home. She adds an upbeat conclusion: "We must hope things will brighten up next year."[49]

Maud's upset, her anger over the money wasted on Chester, her worry about his future—these were capped by the receipt of an especially offensive letter from Isabel Anderson on February 6, 1933, announcing that she was coming down, not for a "visit," but for an "interview." She alluded sarcastically to Maud's "overcrowded life" and obviously didn't care whether Maud wanted to see her or not.

The Macdonalds had let Chester choose Engineering himself, but he had made "a mess of it." Maud decided that he would do well in law. Since he had chosen science subjects at St. Andrew's, he now lacked some of the necessary prerequisites for entry into a law course. He would have to go back and take the necessary high school courses: British and Canadian History, and French Grammar and Literature. Unwilling to go back to high school, he decided to study these courses at home.

Distressed as she was over Chester, Maud put on a good face on February 22, and performed in the Old Tyme Concert she organized each year. The next night she entertained all the men in the Church Session for dinner and wrote in her journal that she "gave them a better feed than some of them deserved."

In spring Chester sat for his examinations at Georgetown High School, and passed. But the next step was unclear. To obtain a degree in law at that time, students were required to work in a practising lawyer's office for two

years, and then to attend Osgoode Hall for another three years. All the place-
ments in law offices were already taken up with students who had sought them
earlier. Finally, Maud found Chester a place with a young lawyer in Toronto
named Ernest Bogart. She hoped that this would "take."

In the summer of 1933, there was an unexpected death in Norval—Luella
Reid's mother. She went into the hospital in early July for what was then
called "female surgery." The surgery was routine, and Mrs. Reid came through
the operation well, but soon a mounting fever indicated an infection, a serious hazard before antibiotics. She grew worse and died, but not before begging Maud to look after Luella as if she were her own daughter. Luella, who
was then almost twenty-one, had been a premature baby and a delicate child,
and her mother feared that, left in the care of her insensitive father, Luella
would suffer from a lack of maternal guidance at a crucial time in her life.
Maud liked Luella well enough, and promised, having no choice but to agree
to her dying friend's wish.

This promise was naturally complicated by Maud's reservations about
Luella as a potential wife for Chester, since they were seeing a great deal of
each other. The Reids were a "good family," descended from the same ancestors as Timothy Eaton, the man from the Glen Williams area who had
founded Canada's famous Eaton's department store chain. But with Chester
headed for a career in law, Maud believed he would need a socially adept
wife. Luella did not have her mother's gracious social manner (or her pretty
face), and at any rate, Chester could not support a wife. Maud thought them
both too young and inexperienced to choose a life-partner. Chester would
have many years of study and training ahead. His parents were more worried
about him now than they had ever been before.

Stuart had been completing his high school education at St. Andrew's while
Chester was struggling in the Mining-Engineering course. But as 1932
began, Stuart, who had been getting excellent marks and many prizes, now
started faltering in his academic work. He was putting all his efforts into
competitive gymnastics. When his parents had moved to the seemingly idyllic Norval in 1926, Stuart had been eleven years old and very small and slight
for his age. Some local bullies had beaten him up because he was the
"preacher's son." He'd told no one about this. Instead, he'd undertaken a
rigorous regimen of body-building, and kept a wary eye out to evade the

bullies until he got bigger and stronger and could defend himself. He had continued the regimen at St. Andrew's, which had an excellent program in sports and gymnastics. He was small-boned like his mother, and, proving to be a superb gymnast, he diverted his attention to this sport.

In March 1932, when he was sixteen, Stuart competed for his school in the Junior Gymnastics Championship in Toronto, and he became the Junior Gymnastic Champion of Ontario. He redoubled his efforts to improve his grades, and in the next year they rose again. In autumn 1932 he began his last year at St. Andrew's, and in spring 1933, he again won the province's Junior Gymnastic Championship.

June 1933 brought Stuart's graduation from St. Andrew's. He led his class academically and won the Lieutenant-Governor's Silver Medal. He also won the French Medal and tied for the prize in Latin. Stuart was as adept at language and writing as Chester was poor. In September, Stuart would compete again at the Canadian National Gymnastics Exhibition and win a gold medal, becoming the Junior Champion in Canada.

But by summer 1933, there was a cloud over Maud's pride in Stuart. Like Chester, he had a girlfriend in Norval. Joy Laird was a pretty, bright, and sweet girl, but her parents did not meet Maud's standards. In her journals, Maud called Joy's father, Lewis Laird, the "black sheep of a respectable family," "a drunken sot," a "notorious bootlegger," and a "thief" who "kicked and beat his wife when he was drunk and she did not bear all wrongs in silence but proclaimed them from the housetops. . . . She was a hardworking creature but came of a family in Glen Williams who were simply a bunch of crooks." Maud dismissed Joy herself as "ignorant and shallow," "boy-crazy," and "no companion for my son" (November 30, 1936).

The Laird clan, early settlers in the area, were in fact very capable businessmen and craftsmen. For instance, all the carpentry in the Norval Presbyterian church, started in 1878, had been done by the Laird brothers. Lewis Laird, Joy's thirty-nine-year-old father, was descended from these early Lairds, and his Laird relatives were pillars in the church. In 1933, Joy was sixteen and Stuart was eighteen. Stuart had been in elementary school when they came to Norval, and although he had been away at St. Andrew's for secondary school, he had returned home during holidays and the summers, where he'd spent much time at the Credit River swimming hole. Over the years, Joy had progressed from being Stuart's friend to being his "girl," and he'd corresponded with her regularly while he was at St. Andrew's. Maud had kept a very close watch on Stuart during the summers of his high school years. When he slept in his tent down by the river for all those summers, rather than share a bedroom with Chester, Maud made frequent trips down to the tent in the evenings to make sure Stuart was alone. These visitations, made on various pretexts, irritated him a great deal. At the end of his life, he still spoke of his annoyance at his mother's lack of trust and her intrusiveness over Joy.

Maud expected Stuart to forget about Joy when he went off to university and met other girls. There was no possibility of Joy going to university; although she was very clever, her family did not have enough money to send her, especially during the Depression years. But as time passed, Stuart's relationship with Joy seemed to be deepening rather than diminishing. In August, when Ewan took a much-needed vacation to PEI where he could stay with his sisters, Maud did not accompany him. She was keeping an eye on her boys.

In the autumn of 1933 Stuart began his education at the University of Toronto, intending to study medicine, something his mother had strongly encouraged—she hoped for a lawyer and a doctor. He went into residence at Knox College, as Chester had done before him. (Knox College, being affiliated with the Presbyterian Church, gave special rates to sons of ministers.) Stuart soon noticed that the other students in Knox treated him with watchful wariness. He would eventually learn the reason why: Chester's reputation lingered. He had been known there, and to some extent on the wider campus, as a petty thief. (This reputation had likely reached the Engineering professors like Herbert Haultain.) Students' possessions often disappeared when Chester was around. When he was short of pocket money, he'd remedied this by purloining books, watches, clothes, equipment, and any valuables that could be taken to one of several pawnshops—busy places in the Depression years.[50] Stuart did not want to upset his mother further so he did not tell her this. It is likely that Maud had already observed her own things disappearing, however, and suspected that Chester was the culprit. This could explain part of her earlier comment (July 2, 1932) that there were many problems with Chester.

By October 1933, both boys seemed settled in their respective studies in Toronto. Maud hoped that Chester would stick at law long enough to graduate, but she was rapidly losing hope of him ever using his potential. She wrote in her journals that "Stuart is all I have to live for now and if he fails me I am done" (September 26, 1933).

———

Maud spent much negative energy worrying about her sons' romances during the Norval period. But in a strange twist, she had spent equal amounts of energy trying to *encourage* a match between Marion Webb, Myrtle's daughter, and Murray Laird, who was also descended from the Laird clan, and whose father had also been a pillar in the church. She had promoted this romance when they first moved to Norval in 1926, only to see it fall apart. There were very few choices for Marion on the Island. Ambitious young men who would not inherit a family farm usually left. As a result, and for the same reasons, young women often left the Island too. And Maud, who by now hoped to retire in Norval, wanted family closer. Marion was her particular pet.

Back in 1930, Maud had brought Marion to Norval to promote the romance. Maud would gain a daughter, and be able to count on more visits from Island relatives for the rest of her life. Like so many other Islanders who had moved to the mainland, she tried to persuade friends to follow.

In this same period, there was another change of maids—a major upheaval in Maud's life. The capable Mrs. Mason, who had been their maid since January 1927, announced in March 1931 that she was engaged to a man in Kitchener and was leaving. The search for a new maid started, and through contacts back at Leaskdale, Maud found another woman, Faye Thompson, who needed a position. Like Mrs. Mason, Mrs. Thompson had a small child. She was escaping an unhappy marriage, and she needed somewhere to go where she could take her young daughter, June, with her. Faye Thompson was trim, efficient, alert, and very competent, and Maud was pleased with her. For her part, Mrs. Thompson was delighted to get such a good position.

However, after an expensive engagement ring from her husband disappeared from her room, Mrs. Thompson learned that when Chester was home, she had to watch her possessions. Although she knew that the only person who could have taken it was Chester, Mrs. Thompson did not tell Maud. She did, however, mention this story to friends she made in the community.

The next year, 1932, Maud turned her mind to sorting out a serious family problem on the Island. The fate of the Campbell farm at her beloved Park

Corner had been an ongoing concern since 1919 when the Spanish influenza killed George Campbell, leaving his widow to cope with running the farm and raising their large family alone. Maud had always provided money to cover the shortfalls, but after 1929 she had lost so much on her investments that she felt she could no longer subsidize the family, especially when she was facing the costs of educating two sons in the professions. Fortunately, by 1929 Ella's sons were old enough to assume responsibility for the farm. But things had become a tangled mess at Park Corner, and Maud could not help dealing with the situation since she had so much money and love invested in the farm.

The farm had been in Maud's Aunt Annie Macneill Campbell's name when her son, George Campbell, died. After George's death, Aunt Annie had made over ownership of the farm to George and Ella's oldest son, Dan, stipulating that Dan be responsible for supporting his mother and younger siblings. But as Dan grew up, it was obvious that he had no interest in the farm. Dan was happy-go-lucky, not hard-working, disciplined, and thrifty, like his younger brother, Jim, who was both bright and independent. Since Jim didn't want to work as his older brother's hired man, he was thinking of leaving the farm to take a job in a Charlottetown bank. Dan, living in California with his Aunt Stella, was unwilling to come home, but he didn't want to give up his inheritance, either. If neither son was willing to try to save the farm, Maud felt she was throwing money away trying to keep it in the family.

Heath Montgomery, one of Grandfather Montgomery's sons, had been renting much of the farm, but he refused to do so in 1928 and again in 1931. It was a rundown, marginal farm and Maud knew that it could be saved only if Jim made an all-out commitment to it. He might be persuaded to do so if he was promised that the farm would become his if he succeeded. Ella consulted Maud, and Maud took on the problem of convincing Jim—and Dan—that this was the only way to keep the farm in the Campbell family.

Maud's personal identity was tied up with the family ownership of the Campbell farm. Her Scottish ancestors had come to the new country so that they could own their own land, and to lose their "ancient heritage" after more than a century would have damaged her sense of being a member of the "landed aristocracy"—an old-world concept of great importance to her.

Maud took up her pen. In a letter dated March 7, 1932, she wrote Dan that he was not a farmer—everyone agreed to that. If he would not relinquish his title to the farm, it would have to be sold. If it was sold, she was going to call in her mortgages on it because she needed the money to put her sons through university. This would take most of the proceeds. Then, she continued, Ella and Dan's younger siblings would have to be looked after—that was stipulated in the will that left the farm to him—and this would take the rest of the money. There would be little if anything left for him. He could either sell the farm under these conditions, or he could sign it over to his younger brother Jim, letting Jim, who had been living and working it already, try to make good on it. If Jim failed, then the farm would be sold, and the proceeds would be distributed as above.

Maud's letter made it clear to Dan that he would get no money from the farm, no matter what happened. Maud knew that this would upset the grasping Stella, who had been billeting Dan, but Maud did not care. She had been astute enough to construct her many cash bailouts to the Campbells in the form of loans on the property, even if she expected to forgive the loans in the end. This now gave her leverage in forcing Dan to do the right thing for his mother and siblings. With Maud's rhetorical screws turned tightly on him, Dan capitulated. Maud scraped together $700 in start-up money, and Jim, still in his teens, took over the farm, and did manage to keep it going.

Maud had sound business instincts. She resolved the mess at the Campbell farm brilliantly. However, she could not resolve her own anxieties and her own family's problems. But what she could do was transmute them into fiction.

CHAPTER 18

From 1929 to 1935, Maud's writing life continued to reflect her lived experience—particularly her emotions—refracted through her imagination into stories. She found pleasure, as well as release from her troubles, by creating the more tranquil mental space in which she wrote. In the Norval years, the act of writing moved from being a source of pleasure to a therapeutic activity.

Maud was always happiest when she was writing, living in the imaginary world of her characters, where she controlled everything. She was amused by her characters, with their full range of eccentricities, prejudices, and human limitations. Her sense of humour kept her laughing at the misadventures and comical ironies in their lives. She might temporarily lose her sense of humour about her own life, but she could always laugh over her characters. They always grew out of the human nature she had observed, and her female protagonists were always fashioned out of some elements in their very complex creator.

She had written happily and furiously on *A Tangled Web* all through 1930, finishing her first draft in September. It was a very complex and densely plotted book, aimed at adults. It reconfigured the memories of her own youth, recalled through laughing with Nora over their escapades in Cavendish, and mixed these with the on-again-off-again romance of Marian Webb and Murray Laird.

A Tangled Web (1931)

On one level, *A Tangled Web* is a humorous study of love and romance in a series of intermarried clans like those in PEI or Ontario. The character who precipitates the action of the novel is a manipulative and cantankerous old woman, Aunt Becky. The novel opens with a meeting she has called to discuss the inheritance of a family heirloom (a decorated antique jug), in advance of her imminent death. Aunt Becky says she *may* leave the jug to family members, on certain conditions, or she *may not*: they will have to wait and see. Her instructions will not be revealed for a year. The community is stirred into frenetic agitation, facing the suspense of who will ultimately be the "chosen" one. Everyone attempts to lead an exemplary life for the next year.

Given that greed motivates everyone, the result is a community edginess that precipitates feuds, romances, re-alliances, and general mayhem. All is handled with a comic touch, and the main players are characters whose love affairs keep readers laughing. At the end, just as the contents of the will are to be revealed, it turns out that the will has been lost, accidentally dropped by the person entrusted with it, and most likely eaten by his pigs. And before anyone inherits the jug, it is smashed by the deranged "Moon Man." Maud has had a good poke at folly in human nature; or, in theological language, she has shown that "all is vanity" in this world.

On another level the book shows characters twisting their reality out of shape by obsessing about an unknown future, something Maud knew that she herself often did. On yet another plane, Aunt Becky's will creates a situation that mimics the doctrine of Predestination. Because these characters, all caught up in a "tangled web," do not know what is "written" about their future, they spend all their time trying to keep their credentials intact. Many mess up their lives in the process.

The book was finished right before Maud went on her trip to Prince Albert and the west.

In the years following the publication of A *Tangled Web*, Maud's domestic situation did not grow any easier. The economic depression worsened throughout the 1930s, with Maud losing ever more money. Ewan's salary barely covered basic family expenses. Her sons and their romances kept her on edge. Her asthma grew much worse, and was at times life-threatening. The seemingly endless church events began to wear on her nerves. When she was asked to take on a Sunday School class in the Union church at Glen Williams, she complained in her journal that parishioners expected too much, evidently thinking to themselves, "What do they pay a minister a salary for, if his wife won't work all the time for them?" (January 9, 1931). In July 1931, Maud wrote an article for publication in the October issue of *Chatelaine*. Entitled "An Open Letter from a Minister's Wife," it is revealing as a self-description, and it shows her frayed nerves:

> If at times the minister's wife is a bit absent-minded or preoccupied or "stiff," the congregation should not imagine that she is unfriendly or uninterested or trying to snub them. She has a right to expect that they make a few excuses for her. Perhaps she is so tired that she is not quite sane; perhaps she is one of those people to whom it is torture to show their feelings—dead and gone generations of sternly repressed forefathers may have laid their unyielding fingers of reserve on her lips; perhaps she is wondering if anyone could sell her a little time; perhaps there are many small worries snapping and snarling at her heels; perhaps she has had one of those awful moments when we catch a glimpse of ourselves as we really are; perhaps she has the odd feeling of not belonging to this or any world, that follows an attack of flu; perhaps she is just pitifully shy at heart. Or her own feelings may have been hurt. Because minister's wives have feelings that are remarkably like the feelings of other women, and injustice and misunderstanding hurt us very keenly. (October 1931, *Chatelaine*)[51]

When Maud was asked to judge a speech contest and pleaded that she was feeling unwell, a female parishioner told her: "You'll have to *give up writing*, Mrs. Macdonald." Maud fumed. Her normal diplomacy failed her, as her journal account shows: "Half my worry this winter is that I can't find time to do my own work. I glared at the little fool and permitted myself the luxury of a biting retort. 'No, Mrs. Sinclair, I shall not give up my writing. But I do intend to give up running all over the country doing other people's work for them.'" She added in her journal: "Oh, I can tell you I licked my chops over that" (January 9, 1931).

But in the third week of January 1931, she pulled herself together and gave "a most unusual paper on the well-known and sometimes loved and often hated little animal, the cat," at the Brampton Literary and Travel Club.[52] And she continued to publish, out of financial necessity.

In February 1931, she published a story in the *Canadian Home Journal* called "The Mirror." It is built around a 120-year-old mirror that hung in a home inherited by the heroine, plain, shy Hilary (whose description recalls Maud at a younger age). The mirror, with unique magical powers, reveals the truth to whoever looks into it.

In mid-February she spoke at the Toronto branch of the Canadian Authors Association, reading from her new book. She chose a chapter about the Island clans that, one newspaper reported, "provided rare enjoyment."[53] She explained to the audience that there had been much trouble finding a name for the book, and joked that Donald French was staying up nights reading the Bible to find a title for it, and "even if he doesn't find one," she added, "it will do him good." Three days later, she directed the annual Old Tyme Concert in Norval, said to be the "greatest success ever," filling every seat in the Anglican hall to the back steps.[54] In June, she attended the CAA convention in Toronto as a delegate, attending a full round of luncheons, receptions, dinners, and meetings with other authors. Along with Nellie McClung and the novelist Madge MacBeth ("Gilbert Knox"), she made an address.

In July through September 1931, Maud continued in high-profile activities. She was a judge for a Kodak photography competition held in Toronto, along with other well-known people like Nellie McClung, "Janey Canuck" (Judge Emily Murphy), Wyly Grier (a well-known artist), Canon Cody (prominent clergyman and chairman of the board of governors at the University of Toronto), and Colonel Gagnon (managing director of *Le Soleil*, and vice-president of the Canadian Press). The competition gave Maud a psychological lift. She wrote a high-spirited entry in her diary on the day after she learned she was to help judge, for the other judges were Canada's elite. She was particularly pleased when her arguments decided the winning picture: the silhouette of a Canadian prospector and his pick-axe seen against the darkening sky. She was presented with a moving-picture camera for her services. Her mind was already on the subject of memories: "I hate to think of all the lovely things I remember being forgotten when I'm dead!" (July 11, 1931).

At this time, she was recopying her handwritten journals by typewriter (partly so each son could have a copy), and she had come to the Herman Leard story.[55] Amid all her activities, and her soul-searching in her own journals to understand the intensity of her former attraction to Herman, she fielded the pesky Isabel, eyed Chester for signs of mental instability,

and agonized over Stuart's fondness for Joy. She kept up her speaking engagements through the autumn of 1931. In October she went to Montreal
to make several appearances. On this trip she confided to her journal that
"It is not a disagreeable sensation to be lionized!!" (November 27, 1931).
She took heart in every confirmation that she was still respected in a literary world where styles were changing fast, where critics were attempting
to remould popular taste.

The Canadian novelist Raymond Knister (1899–1932) wrote an article
around this time that demonstrates Maud's disappearance from the literary
screens of young Canadian critics. Entitled "The Canadian Girl," it begins:

> Why is it that though Canadian authors are known and read the
> world over, one cannot think of a single heroine who lingers in the
> memory . . . ? The long line of English romance and fiction reveals
> a prodigious gallery of charming creatures, and American litera-
> ture, though younger, can boast its own types. But why have we no
> such thing as a fictional character who is at once convincingly real,
> convincingly charming, and convincingly Canadian?

Anne, who had enchanted millions of readers worldwide since 1908 and
created a tourist bonanza for the province of Prince Edward Island, had not
impressed Knister.[56]

Still, Maud retained her readership, but she also was under pressure to
continue producing books to avoid a drop in income. In 1930 she had earned
$8,314 from book royalties, reflecting the sales of *Magic for Marigold* (which
were mostly achieved before the effects of the stock market crash were fully
felt). But she brought out no new book in 1930, so in 1931 her book income
was only $1,897. It rose in 1932 to $4,805, thanks to *A Tangled Web*. But *A
Tangled Web* — by far her most ambitious book to date, and one aimed at
adults — did not sell as well as earlier novels. Was this because she was locked
into a children's market, or because of people's obviously diminished buying
power in the Depression, or were her books finally going out of fashion? She
felt nervous.

Political events and allegiances were changing too. Maud alludes in her
journal to "Red Russia" and the "Red menace in Spain and Germany." In
1932, she wrote of her mother's and grandmother's generations:

They lived their lives in a practically unchanged and apparently changeless world. Nothing was questioned—religion—politics—society—all nicely mapped out and arranged and organized. And my generation! . . . Everything we once thought immoveable wrenched from its pedestal and hurled to ruins. All our old standards and beliefs swept away—our whole world turned upside down and stirred up—before us nothing but a welter of doubt and confusion and uncertainty. Such times have to come, I suppose, but woe to us whose kismet it is to live in them. (January 24, 1932)

Like so many others, she felt disoriented by the speed of change.

Maud knew she must get hold of herself before she could begin writing again. She began rereading her old favourite novels—the nineteenth-century Scottish "kailyard" novels, like Ian MacLaren's *Beside the Bonnie Brier Bush* (1894) and *The Days of Auld Lang Syne* (1895). She found in them much the "same flavour" as her childhood in Cavendish, "the memory of which is like a silvery moonlight in my recollection" (January 24, 1932). Around this time, she wrote a whimsical short story that dealt in a way with a parent interfering with a young person's choice of mates—something she was doing herself with both Chester and Stuart.[57]

Following *A Tangled Web*, which had been a massive effort, Maud was distracted over her family; finding a good idea for her next novel was not easy. In the May issue of *Chatelaine*, she published a sentimental story called "The House." The heroine is a lonely, dreamy, plain child—as Maud envisioned her own childhood self—and this child fixes her love on a house. The story grows out of Maud's love for places and homes, like the home of the Campbells in Park Corner, where she had felt so welcome in her Aunt Annie's unconditional love, and where everything always seemed joyously the same. The Campbells might have been on the verge of disaster, but they could always gather round the organ and sing, or entertain each other with funny stories. The more Maud thought about the unhappy state of her own home in Norval, the more she looked back to the homes she had left in Prince Edward Island, even the "old home" with her grandparents. The symbol of a house would become her chief figure in her next book. She started writing *Pat of Silver Bush* at the beginning of April 1932.

Maud had reread her journals until she could fuse the memories of her own childhood with the anxieties of the fifty-nine-year-old woman she was now. From this grew a new heroine, Pat Gardiner.

Maud finished the book at the beginning of December 1932, and typed it up herself in the following twelve days. She dedicated *Pat of Silver Bush* to Alec and May Macneill and the "Secret Field," in memory of a happy walk in October 1932 (November 13, 1932). She was exhausted by the time she finished.

Pat of Silver Bush (1933)

This novel is built on the theme of Pat Gardiner's extreme attachment to her home. The central events in the novel are the threats to her happy and un-changing life in Silver Bush, including a new baby in the family, starting school, the marriage of an aunt, her father's thoughts of selling up and going west, and her older siblings' departures or courtships. Pat's leitmotif from age eight to eighteen, the time span of the novel, is her hatred of change, partic-ularly as it threatens her beloved old-fashioned family home, "Silver Bush."

As has been noted, Maud had two sets of mythologies about her own child-hood. The first was almost factually accurate—that she had a comparatively happy childhood being raised by her grandparents in Cavendish, a settled rural community, where she had plentiful playmates and extended family. The sec-ond, a less true but more compelling myth, is the one recorded in her diaries around 1905—that she was a lonely, solitary, and misunderstood child who was all but orphaned when her mother died and her father left her to be raised by her unsympathetic grandparents. Maud drew on these two mythologies to fash-ion her two primary child characters in this novel, Pat Gardiner and her friend, Hilary Gordon. Pat Gardiner is the child of the first mythology; Hilary Gordon, a boy whose mother has abandoned him, is heir to the second.

Many of Pat's characteristics are similar to those of the young Maud Montgomery. For instance, in Chapter One we are told that Pat is a "queer," emotional child, who loves more deeply than others—and this capacity for deep feeling is accompanied by both intense delight and intense pain. Pat worries unduly over her looks, too, believing that she is ugly. She does not have Maud's youthful exuberance or her creative gifts, but she draws much else from Maud.

Pat's best friend, Hilary ("Jingle") Gordon, is a lonely little boy effectively orphaned when his father died and his mother left him to be raised by rela-tives, so she could go west and remarry. Hilary idealizes his absent mother for his first fifteen years, and is crushed and disillusioned when they meet. This recalls Maud's experience at age fifteen, when she was summoned out west to join her father—only to discover that he wanted her there to help his peevish new wife with her housework and babies.

That a parent may not love its child at all is a devastating recognition for a young person, and it is powerfully portrayed in this novel.

As she continued to recopy her journals in the handwritten volumes, Maud had been thinking a great deal of her own father and stepmother. Unlike Maud's father, Hilary's self-absorbed mother is sufficiently well-off to arrange for his education, but she does this out of a sense of obligation, not love. (Maud's father had sent a modest sum of money for her only when her grandmother strong-armed him to do so.) At least Hilary can fulfill his dream of becoming an architect of beautiful houses for the enjoyment of others. He finally realizes that he must develop his career for his own satisfaction, not to satisfy his shallow mother, who takes no interest in his professional success.

For a time, Pat has another good friend, a girl her age named Bets Wilcox. Bets is perfect, beautiful, and shadowy. Such clues suggest that she is marked for death, just like the too-perfect Beth in *Little Women*. Bets Wilcox dies of flu-pneumonia, like Frede a decade earlier. Pat asks the very same question in the novel that Maud asked when Frede died: "How was one to begin anew when the heart had gone out of life?" . . . "Bets seemed to die afresh every time there was something Pat wanted to share with her and could not" (Chapter 31).

Even with its child protagonists, *Pat of Silver Bush* hardly seems a traditional story for children. Most children *want* to "grow up," and they enjoy the excitement that change brings. Pat's emotional makeup seems highly neurotic, like Barrie's Peter Pan. Maud's sense of being disoriented by the ceaseless post-war change was shared by many adults, but when transplanted into the emotions of a small child who is strikingly articulate about her hatred of change, it seems oddly pathological. However, the novel does catch the *Zeitgeist* of the era, as experienced by many adults.

Although the rather uninteresting Pat lacks Anne's ginger or Emily's spunk, Maud compensates by giving the Gardiner family an Irish servant named Judy Plum, who is full of stories, fairy-lore, and smart answers for everything. Judy gives the house most of its personality, and her stage-Irish brogue may be drawn partly from the descendants of Ewan's "warm" Irish settlers who still attended the Union and Norval churches, and partly from popular plays by Irish writers like Sean O'Casey and W. B. Yeats.

Maud knew how to create atmosphere, and the novel is engaging. The ambience and warmth of the Gardiner home comes through the multiple comforts in Judy's kitchen, the antics of the many cats, the scenes where extended family and friends sit around on winter evenings spinning tales of family and community. Small frictions and spats maintain narrative interest.

Maud would write to a young fan about *Pat* the following year: "My characters are *all* fictitious, as people, but I have met the *types* to which they belong. I gave *Anne* my imagination and Emily Starr my knack of scribbling; but the girl who is more myself than any other is 'Pat of Silver Bush'—my new story which is to be out this fall. Not *externally* but spiritually, she is 'I.'"[58] And Pat *was* her at this point in her life, (as well as Hilary Gordon) just as Anne, the Story Girl, Emily, and Valancy, had been in turn.

Maud had always dreamed of creating a happy home, like that of her merry Campbell cousins of Park Corner, but her dream was failing to materialize. Too many things in her personal life were under threat in the 1930s: her financial security, her professional status, her husband's mental health, and her sons' stability and future. She saw more wars brewing in a world where war had become "a hideous revel of mechanical massacre" (February 25, 1932). She feared more and more for her own state of mind. In *Pat of Silver Bush* she depicted the happy home she wanted for her family, and she mapped the ways that people must adjust and move on when life disappoints them. But she was finding it hard to do this herself.

Still, no matter how she felt, Maud kept up her professional obligations— her writing, her speaking engagements, and her reply to every fan letter. She reacted strongly to a letter that came to her in July 1933, from a bright young reader in Saskatchewan named Roberta Mary Sparks. Roberta wrote Maud that she loved her books, but she thought her characters were unrealistic— they were too idealistic and too faultless as people. Already smarting under certain critics' insinuation that her books were sentimental, Maud wrote sharply to Roberta:

> Do you think *Anne* was happy when her baby died—when her
> sons went to the war—when one was killed? . . . Poor *Valancy* had
> 29 years of starved existence and *Emily* had her bitter years of
> alienation from *Teddy*. . . . You are probably much more cynical

at nineteen than you will be at forty. I am sure there are plenty of
girls and boys just as good and true as any of those in my books. I
have known ever so many. Of course there are plenty of the other
kind, too—always have been and always will be and just now they
are not repressed as they used to be and we hear and see more of
them. But the other sort must have always predominated or the
world wouldn't have gone on at all. (Letter of July 4, 1933)

Roberta felt the sting of Maud's forceful response, and did not answer the
letter, feeling that she had said the wrong thing to an author she loved, and
doubtful that she could explain what she had meant. Roberta had indeed hit
a sore spot: in Chester, Maud had one of the "other kind" of young people
who were not "good and true," and she had no idea how to cope.

On December 2, 1933, Chester and Luella Reid confronted Ewan and Maud
with surprising news: Chester claimed that he and Luella had been secretly
married the previous year, in November 1932. They were twenty-one and
twenty-two, respectively, at the time of the announcement. Chester had
many years of schooling ahead before he would be a lawyer and able to provide for a family. Luella Reid was clever but lacked any education beyond
high school. Maud and Ewan were devastated. To the alleged marriage date,
Ewan's response was to say, over and over, "I don't believe a word of it," and
it was, of course, a lie.

The diminutive Luella was too mortified to speak, for she knew, and her
new in-laws also knew, that such a marriage could mean only one thing—
that a baby was on the way. In that era, pregnancy outside of marriage was the
worst shame a respectable girl could bring on her family. It was almost always
blamed on the woman—women were supposed to be "purer" and better able
to exercise self-control than men. People assumed that a woman who got
pregnant outside of wedlock was either of low morals or was determined to
catch the man by "hook or by crook." She would carry a stigma for life, even
if marriage followed, and the children born in a "forced marriage" also bore
a lingering stigma.

Maud knew the power of sex as a component in the makeup of human
beings. She said that she always tried to answer the boys' questions about sex
as honestly and openly as she could. She recalled how sex had been a taboo

subject in her childhood, something too "vile and shameful to be spoken of" (January 11, 1924). She recalled a doctor's book in the Macneill household that explained sexual functions clearly but was kept hidden from her—with the result, of course, that she dipped into it "by stealth." She gave Chester such a book to read when he reached puberty, and she remarked that the "present generation" had "saner views" on sex than earlier ones. When she was writing the second *Emily* book she could still not bring any hint of physical love into her novels. She was branded as a wholesome writer for the young, and sex was still a taboo subject in fiction for them.

Maud's advice to Luella after their marriage reveals the traditional attitudes towards sexuality in that era. In keeping with her promise to Luella's dying mother to be a "mother" to Luella, Maud took Luella aside to talk about a woman's proper conduct after marriage. According to Luella, she advised her never to let her husband "see her body naked," telling her that she should "always undress behind a screen." Maud explained that this would help keep the "mystery" and "magic" in marriage, and that too much familiarity was a bad thing. Luella, of a different and later generation, found the advice amusing, given that she was married and pregnant.

Luella recalled that Maud herself kept a screen in her own bedroom and dressed and undressed behind it. It was large enough to afford complete privacy. Luella observed that Maud and Ewan were both middle-aged when they married, and she said both were very prudish, Ewan far more so than Maud. Luella said that she could not imagine Ewan "ever trying to get 'peeks'" at his wife's body when she undressed, and she doubted he had ever actually seen Maud naked. Women's nightgowns then were voluminous to protect against the cold in badly insulated and poorly heated houses. Even in summer, nightgowns were roomy enough to undress under if a woman did not have a screen. Describing all this later in her life, after she had read many Victorian novels and histories, Luella smiled over Maud's Victorian views about modesty, but she said they were not unusual for women raised in Maud's generation.[59]

Maud made all the decisions after the 1933 marriage was revealed. Chester had to continue his schooling. He would continue to work in the Bogart law office, and then take his law courses. Maud found and furnished an apartment for Chester and Luella on Shaw Street in Toronto where she hoped they could be a normal, young married couple, with their indiscretion kept secret. Maud agreed to support them financially through Chester's training, but on the condition that there would be no more babies until Chester could provide for them.

Chester's "forced marriage" was particularly hard for Ewan. For the son of a minister of God to get a young woman pregnant was scandal enough, but that the young woman should be the daughter of one of the church's elders put it beyond the pale. Maud and Ewan tried to save face by placing an announcement in the Brampton paper that said the secret marriage had taken place in 1932, the previous year, just as Chester and Luella had presented it to them. The paper, however, printed the accurate marriage date of 1933. The community was abuzz. Ewan and Maud were so humiliated that they could hardly bear to appear in public.

Chester's marriage undoubtedly stirred up Maud's old memories about her own youthful reputation as a high-spirited girl. Maud was a woman who lived in memories, and whose earlier humiliations were never forgotten. She had learned to control her impulsiveness, but she must have worried that she had bequeathed that trait—some "bad blood," so to speak—to Chester. Chester's disgrace opened old wounds, and Maud's fame only intensified her misery. A child's indiscretions *did* reflect on the parents in most people's minds. Slowly, surely, the pernicious idea that everyone she loved deeply was doomed to failure began to deepen its reach in her mind.

From 1933 to 1936 she put her journals aside, too upset by events to face them and write out her humiliation. She had so much trouble sleeping after December 2, 1933, when she learned of Chester's marriage, that she turned again to Veronal, a widely used barbiturate prescribed by doctors as a sleep-aid and sedative. (It was one of the medications that she and Ewan had been given in Leaskdale for anxiety.) When she resumed her journalizing again, three years later, she would reconstruct a long retrospective entry from notes she had made.

Ewan fared even worse: for him, Chester's marriage sparked a major depressive episode. Ewan had been comparatively well for most of the Norval period. He had had some small depressive episodes, but mostly he had been preaching effectively, and was quite fondly regarded by his two congregations, especially after his research into the history of the local Presbyterian churches. His even temper cooled down antagonisms. But after Chester's marriage, Ewan also began to succumb to his old demons, his own *idée fixe*.

His demons again told him that the corruption in his own home proved that he was not one of the "Elect," and that he was doomed to Hell—along with the son who so resembled him. Ewan began to brood once again, telling his already distraught wife that he was not fit to minister to his flock when he himself was an outcast from God. Why else would God let this disaster happen? Ewan knew his Bible well, especially the many Old Testament references to the "iniquities of the fathers" being visited upon the "sons to the third and fourth generation."[60]

Ewan began to change. He had trouble carrying out his regular visitations, and he sat for long, solitary hours in his darkened study, ruminating, and feeling his estrangement from God and everything positive in his life. He would rise in the morning, dress in his heavy, stiff clerical garb, eat his way through a large breakfast, and disappear into his dark study until the midday meal. He would emerge, eat a heavy meal again, and then return to his study for the afternoon. At the evening meal, he re-emerged, looking dishevelled, moody, closed off, and miserable. He would eat a big meal in silence, and return to his study. His sunless study was intrinsically gloomy, with nothing but theological books on the shelves. He became increasingly self-absorbed and spoke little. No doubt Maud's anxiety and discouragement affected him. Perhaps they fed off each other, locked as they were in their own prisons of unhappiness. Maud gritted her teeth, kept up her public face, and suffered terrible headaches in private. Ewan dissembled less well in public, and he increasingly took sedatives prescribed by his doctor to help him cope.

One document written by Ewan during this time remains. It is a set of jottings about the men in his parish. These notes are the work of a man brooding destructively. He names and characterizes many of his parishioners. For example, of Robert Reid (Luella's father) he says: "Explosive and flammable temper—hardly ever under control. Offends people and doesn't see how he does it and when it is pointed out to him says he was only doing his duty. Has a high idea of his own importance, and very intolerant of other people's ideas. . . . The good he does is neutralized by his ill-considered utterances and the impression his whole personality makes . . ." Of George Gollop: "A conceited egotist. Thinks everyone should realize that he is a great man. Selfish and dogmatic. Unforgiving to a great degree." The younger men in the congregation, those born between 1896 and 1905, fared better. Of Murray Laird: "Fine young man—intelligent—not perhaps as aggressive as he might be but in this respect he will grow. Fair-minded, tolerant, popular. Calm in expression and steadfast in purpose."

Luella would later recount a memory of having dinner with her new in-laws during this period. Ewan had been sitting in silence at the table but suddenly erupted to say, apropos of nothing that anyone else had said: "Nobody hates me except Garfield McClure." He repeated it loudly several times in a pressured way, and seemed to be talking only to himself. Garfield was Luella's uncle, so she was particularly surprised and discomfited. She also observed, however, that Ewan was correct in his assessment, and that her Uncle Garfield was a controlling and egotistical person who stirred up trouble, and he did undermine Ewan.

Despite Maud's misery over Chester's marriage, she held her head high, and continued with her public engagements in the community and in Toronto. On January 8, 1934, she was one of several women who spoke on the topic of "Great Books by Canadian Women" at the Canadian Literature Club in Toronto. She had been invited to speak by one of its officials, a gifted young man named Eric Gaskell, who would figure later in her life. She had been asked to speak on *Anne of Green Gables*. Marshall Saunders spoke on her book *Beautiful Joe*, and three other women (not the authors) discussed Mazo de la Roche's *The Whiteoaks of Jalna*, E. Barrington's *The Divine Lady*, and the works of Susanna Moodie. Unlike Ewan, who lost himself in negative brooding, Maud could use language to help manage her frustrations. One poem that expressed her feelings was written in January 1934, after Chester's revelations, and is entitled "Night." The last stanza reads:

> The world of day, its bitterness and cark
> No longer have the power to make me weep,
> I welcome this communion of the dark
> As toilers welcome sleep.

Maud would not begin *Mistress Pat*, the sequel to *Pat of Silver Bush*, until January 15, 1934, some six weeks after the bombshell of Chester's marriage. It, too, would embody her explosive personal emotions.

The end of the Macdonalds' happiness in Norval may have started with the great mill fire that destroyed the village's character and way of life, but it was sealed by Chester's marriage. The baby, also named Luella, was born on May 17, 1934.

By June 9, Luella had left Chester and returned home to her father. She told Maud that the apartment she and Chester lived in on Shaw Street in Toronto was "too hot" for the baby. Eyebrows were raised and members of the community exchanged knowing looks. No one had expected Chester to be a good husband.

A substantial number of the parishioners in Ewan's church were related in one way or another to Luella's parents. Luella was one of their own, even if she had done the unacceptable and become pregnant before marriage. In their eyes, Chester was a "bad egg": he had seduced the naïve and lonely Luella after the death of her mother, when she was left to cope with her short-fused, grief-stricken father. If she'd returned to her father—who was in everyone's view a decent but terribly difficult man—then life with Chester must have been unbearable. People knew that Chester had been thrown out of Engineering, and they wondered how he would fare in his law studies. So did Maud and Ewan, and they were in the uncomfortable position of knowing that everyone else in the community was also watching Chester. Ewan began to feel a chill from his Norval parishioners.

When Luella returned home, she said she was frank with her father about Chester's behaviour towards her. Chester was always explosive. He left her alone, giving no explanations about where he was. She would later say that whatever faults her father had, she would be forever grateful to him for allowing her to return home, and supporting her after she had brought disgrace on her family. (The attitude that equated premarital pregnancy with shame and disgrace continued through much of the twentieth century, only loosening after contraception was developed and the feminist movement began changing views towards sexuality and marriage.)

The week after the baby's birth, in May 1934, Ewan had a nightmare about suicide. This terrified Maud: only a few years earlier, in Butte, Montana, Ewan's brother Alec had gone melancholy, threatened to kill himself, then disappeared. (He was never found.) Ewan was in worse mental health than he had ever been before. He was taking sedatives prescribed by his doctor, and possibly self-medicating with some that were not. He was probably also taking alcoholic spirits for his "constitution," as well. His nighttime sleep was often disturbed, and he sometimes refused to get up during the day. Maud normally wrote in their bedroom, her screen giving her some privacy, but now Ewan lay on their bed groaning with headaches for much of the day.

By now, Maud had a serious cash-flow problem, because of the continuing financial depression and the loss of her investment money. In 1933, her book income was only $1,641, the lowest it had ever been (except for the unusual year 1919, when she got no income from Page, only the settlement). Even in 1908, when *Anne of Green Gables* was first published, she had received $1,732 in book royalties. The drop in 1933 was truly alarming. She attributed it to general poverty arising from the Depression and little disposable income for books, but there always remained that terrible possibility that her books had seen their day.

To add to this, Maud now suffered a professional insult. On May 11, 1934, William Arthur Deacon once again implied that her novels were poor and unsophisticated in *The Mail and Empire*, and compared her unfavourably with Mazo de la Roche:

> Whatever advance, in art or in substance, lies between L. M. Montgomery's *Anne of Green Gables* at the beginning of the period and Morley Callaghan's *Such is My Beloved*, or Alexander Knox's *Bride of Quietness* at the close of it, all that is notable in the Canadian novels falls within this quarter-century. No earlier popular novelist had anything like the skill of Mazo de la Roche.

Maud had long thought that Mazo de la Roche's novels showed little resemblance to any Canadian society she knew. Years ago, she had sent G. B. MacMillan a copy of the first *Jalna* novel, along with the comment that it was "clever" and "modern" (December 2, 1927) but that it didn't reflect life on an ordinary Canadian farm. In a letter to a fan named Jack Lewis she wrote that her own books were true representations of the type of life still lived on the Island. She stated that although her characters were imaginary, they always seemed real when she was writing about them. To her, being judged inferior to Mazo de la Roche was a significant insult.

For his part, Ewan was finding it increasingly difficult to stand in the pulpit and pretend that he was God's chosen representative. He felt himself a fraud. His preaching began to falter. Composing sermons became increasingly difficult, and delivering them even more so. He started reading them instead of delivering them extemporaneously. Then he started having difficulty even reading his own sermons, stumbling over words like a poorly prepared schoolboy. Next he began to balk when it was time to go to church to preach. Maud plied him with drinks of her homemade wine to fortify him enough to get him over to the church. (She, like her grandmother before her, made wine to "help the digestion." It was not served at the table, and she kept it in the cellar, so much out of sight that the Norval maids did not know about it, and declared in interviews with me that there was never any alcohol in the Macdonalds' house. However, there are numerous references to this homemade wine in the journals.)[61]

When Ewan began talking of suicide in May 1934, Maud was already feeling weak with worry. She had presented his ill health everywhere as physical ailments like headaches, dizziness, and vague internal problems. What if people found out that his problems were mental, branding her family with the stigma of mental illness? That would completely destroy her boys' future careers, particularly Stuart's. Nobody wanted a doctor with mental instability in his heritage.

Nora continued to bring consolation and good spirits to the disturbed manse. She had been coming out to visit Maud periodically ever since the Campbell family had come to Toronto in 1928. Like Frede, Nora was Maud's only safe confidante and "kindred spirit." Maud trusted her enough that she could tell Nora about Ewan's mental instability, something she had not even told her relatives in Prince Edward Island.

Nora had been coming out to Norval from time to time, bringing her young son Ebbie, then about ten, with her. Many years later, Ebbie (who became a mining executive, like his father) told a story that is *not* found in Maud's journals. He said that as a child he had instinctively felt some fear of Mr. Macdonald because of what he considered a "crazy look" in his eyes. His instincts were confirmed one time when they were visiting in Norval. His mother and Maud were laughing and joking at the dinner table, telling "in" jokes. Perhaps something in Ewan snapped, or perhaps he thought that he was joining in the fun with a practical joke. He rose from the table where his wife and Nora were talking, stepped out of the room, and returned with a gun. All laughter stopped. He pointed it directly at Nora's head, and acted as if he were going to pull the trigger. Maud was too shocked to move or speak. Ebbie thought his mother was going to be killed by a madman. Then, Ewan lowered the gun and declared it had been a joke.

A few miles west of Norval, in Guelph, Ontario, there was a well-known treatment centre for mental illness and other disorders called the Homewood Sanitarium. Dating from the nineteenth century, this beautifully landscaped private facility treated wealthy and famous patients from all over North America. The grounds were stunning, the buildings baronial, and the doctors as good as could be found when there was no effective treatment for nervous disorders, alcoholism, substance abuse, or mental illness. Homewood was very expensive, and money tight in the 1930s. However, by the middle of June

1934 (after the incident with the gun), Maud decided that she would send Ewan there, telling the parishioners that he needed a full assessment and a rest. If Homewood didn't help Ewan, she knew that it would at least help *her* to have him out of the house for a short period.

Ewan and Maud had both been taking medicines prescribed by various general practitioners: Dr. J. J. Paul of Georgetown, Dr. William Brydon of Brampton, and various other doctors that Ewan had sought out in Toronto. Ewan was making the rounds of doctors, peddling his physical symptoms and collecting medications. But he did not tell the doctors about his underlying depression, or "weakness," as he called it. He was convinced that his heart was weak and he imagined problems with other organs. He was greatly troubled with constipation and he had much difficulty sleeping, as depressed people often do. And he now had periods of losing touch with reality.

Maud administered the various medicines doctors had given him for sleeping: bromides, Veronal, Chloral, Seconal, Medinal, Luminal, Nembutal, tonics with strychnine, and arsenic pills, plus medicines with names such as "Chinese pills," "liver pills," and strong cough remedies, which were all made up in local doctors' offices. Ewan carried one of these cough syrups, which had a strong alcohol base, in his pocket, and took drinks from it all day long to subdue his cough.

Chester and Maud drove Ewan to Guelph, and he was admitted on June 24, 1934. He stayed there until August 17. Maud provided the history of his case.[62] By her account, his melancholic attacks had begun in his early teens, and had existed in mild form throughout his university years. He had suffered a severe attack lasting three months when studying theology in Glasgow. In 1910 he had experienced another one lasting about two months, brought about by worry. After the worry was removed, he'd been perfectly well until 1919, when he'd had a very severe attack at age forty-eight, leaving him unable to work. During the next six years he'd had attacks on and off, lasting anywhere from a few days to a few months. From 1926 until the beginning of May 1934, he had been completely free of attacks, Maud said. Then, he had became worried over his heart and blood pressure, despite being told they were not serious problems. The spells usually started with a nightmare or something distressing, and were followed by "headaches," complaints of "weakness," and fears and phobias that took over his mind. Maud described the fears as ones of "his future destiny." He then obsessed about his physical maladies. He would slump, saying he was unable to preach, and his memory seemed impaired.

It is worth noting that Maud did not tell the Homewood doctor any of their recent family problems, including Chester's forced marriage, the baby's birth, Luella's return to her father, and their public humiliation. She gave Ewan's family history, saying his parents were both of "even temperament," but she did not mention his brother Alec's depression and probable suicide. Maud described Ewan in this record as easygoing and the "jolliest man alive" when completely well. She alluded to unspecified fears and phobias that he would not admit to anyone (which perhaps cover all of the personal matters and events she did not want to mention). She did *not* raise the subject of the medications he had been given, or taken. The admitting physician, Dr. Alex L. Mackinnon, noted that Ewan's wife was an "authoress from PEI who goes by the pen name of L. M. Montgomery." The charge for residence in Homewood was then seven dollars per day. His stay until mid-August would cost Maud more than a year's residence in Knox College for Stuart, at six dollars per week for a minister's son. In 1934, her income from book royalties had risen to $4,403, but she had many expenses ahead, and these included two sons to educate as her husband was nearing the end of his working life.

Maud returned to writing *Mistress Pat* while Ewan was in Homewood, and she made good progress, despite suffering bouts of asthma which sometimes became so severe that she had to call Dr. Paul from the next town to give her a "hypodermic." To other medications she added her homemade wine to help her sleep, and she complained of "a nasty tight feeling" in her head.

Another crisis arose at home. In mid-July, Maud's maid, Mrs. Faye Thompson, suddenly gave notice that she was going to leave. Mrs. Thompson had been a very good maid and this was unexpected. The timing was bad, too, for it occurred right after Luella had left Chester and returned home to her father, and when Chester himself would be spending more of the summer vacation at home, making more work. Mrs. Thompson's departure seemed strange when she did not have another job to go to. She said she expected to get a secretarial job, but this did not make sense, given the lack of employment during the Depression. As well, she had no way of affording childcare. Her daughter June was now a very sweet and pretty little girl, and she could not be left alone. Maud was fond of June, and she was very confused and upset over Mrs. Thompson's curiously inexplicable and sudden departure.

Although Maud hated to lose Mrs. Thompson, she was able to replace her with Ethel Dennis, in August 1934. Ethel was young and naïve, but a respectable, placid young local woman. Ethel was not interested in the hidden inner lives of the Macdonalds, nor intensely watchful of the growing tensions in the family, which was a relief to Maud. Ethel was inexperienced and she require much training, but she was dedicated and loyal.

Ewan was discharged from Homewood on August 17. Maud could not afford to keep him there indefinitely, and she could not see that they were doing anything for him—except teaching him to play Solitaire. He would spend hours and hours on this game for the rest of his life—a big improvement, as far as Maud was concerned, over lying and moaning on the bed next to where she wrote.

Homewood doctors also told him to change his diet: to eat more vegetables, especially salads, to alleviate his ongoing problem with constipation, instead of dosing himself with laxatives. Ewan did not like vegetables or salads, and he did not follow this advice, and the Macdonalds' normal diet at home did not change. It remained heavy in meats, potatoes and gravies, and desserts—a diet designed for active farm people, not sedentary ministers.

On the way home from Guelph and Homewood on the day Ewan was discharged, the Macdonalds stopped to get a prescription for "blue pills" filled in Acton. Pharmacists often made up their own medications at that time. By mistake, the careless young pharmacist filled the pills with bug poison. Maud gave Ewan one of these poisonous pills the next morning, right after a dose of mineral oil for his constipation. He complained of a burning sensation and soon vomited. The doctor was summoned immediately; miraculously, Ewan suffered no permanent effects from the deadly poison, largely thanks to the oil. But to Maud's surprise, even though everyone knew he was now home from Homewood, no Norval parishioners came to welcome Ewan back and wish him well. That tipped the Macdonalds off to the fact that something was quite wrong.

In the next few months, Ewan's mental state worsened. He cycled rapidly between normality and weepy, "sinking," or aggressive spells in which he declared God hated him and he could never preach again. Maud wrote in her journals that he had never been abusive or violent in this way before, and this frightened her (October 10, 1934). It is possible that Maud's reference to Ewan's erratic and threatening behaviour was her way of acknowledging the earlier gun incident without giving the shocking and embarrassing details.

As Ewan's situation deteriorated, she came to rely a great deal on Stuart emotionally. The always upbeat Stuart had become a force of normalcy in her overwrought life. But he would be returning to university in the third week of

September 1934. "Can I continue to endure this hideous life without him?" she asked her journal. Yet, she was glad for him to leave Norval for another reason: his ongoing relationship with Joy Laird.

But, of course, Maud's greater worry was Chester. He had taken smaller lodgings in Toronto after Luella moved out. Maud did not like him living alone, so she urged him to go back to Knox College in the fall when he started to article in law. But even if Chester had been willing, Knox College would not have allowed him back, given his reputation for stealing. He refused to return to dormitory living, and Luella stayed with her father in the fall, even after the weather cooled down. This confirmed to the community that something was seriously wrong with the marriage.

In early October 1934 there was one happy break for Maud. Murray Laird proposed to Marion Webb, and they were married. The wedding was very quiet, given that Murray's father had recently died. The only witnesses were Mrs. Alfred Laird, mother of the groom, and Maud herself. Marion, unattended, wore a gown of blue silk, with a velvet hat, and she carried a bouquet of yellow roses and ferns. But even with this small group, Maud could hardly persuade Ewan to perform the ceremony. His on and off phobias were on again on the day of the wedding. Normally, Ewan was very fond of Marion: he loved to tease her because she blushed so easily. But even so, moments before the ceremony was to start, he declared that he was "under a doom." Luckily he managed to get through the day, and nobody except Maud knew his state of mind.

Ewan was unable to preach in September and October, so Maud arranged for other preachers to come deliver Sunday sermons. Then, on October 12, 1934, Mr. Barraclough told Ewan that the church managers had met and decided to give him sick leave only until the end of December. That meant that he must resign at the end of the year if he was not well enough to resume preaching. With this added pressure, Ewan decided in November to visit his sisters on the Island. Maud was so exhausted by his ups and downs that she willingly acceded. With the disruption, she had been unable to finish *Mistress Pat*. Ewan rarely slept well, and each day he had new symptoms of imagined diseases, took spells of moaning or raving, or sat around in a dull and moody state. She was herself near the breaking point from the strain.

As soon as Ewan left, Maud could write again, putting all of her own emotions into the imaginary framework of a novel. It was completed at the end of 1934.

Mistress Pat (1935)

Mistress Pat continues the tale of Pat Gardiner and her love for her home, "Silver Bush," which has been home to the Gardiners for generations. Maud details the rituals of daily life in the joyous family of Gardiners. Like Maud, Pat believes that when people laugh together, they become friends for life. But Pat's home is under threat—the family is growing up, and the "change" that Pat so dreads threatens from several angles.

The home is given warmth and charm by the presence of rival storytellers: the Gardiners' Irish maid, Judy Plum, and their hired hand, Tillytuck. The hostile elements in the community are embodied in the ever-present Binnie family, who wield considerable power through gossip. "What will the Binnies say?" is a refrain that always hovers in the Gardiners' consciousness (as it had in Maud's), and they must keep assuring themselves they don't care.

Then, the unimaginable happens. Pat's brother, Sid, who will inherit the farm, makes a foolish and precipitous marriage to May Binnie. Silver Bush is invaded by an alien presence, in the form of aggressive, coarse, and gossipy May, who has managed somehow to snag Pat's brother. The Gardiners have always been drawn together by their shared experiences and stories, but May has no appreciation of such ties and sentiment. Silver Bush is just a house to her, and her proprietary presence spoils everyone's happiness.

Mistress Pat is full of Maud's literary mannerisms, and the book dwells, to the point of tedium, on the theme of hating change. But it is still a powerful book, perhaps because of Maud's ability to embody the wrenching change undergone by the western world in the terrible alterations in the Gardiners' private world. The most powerful symbol in the book is that of the Gardiner home catching fire—significantly, this happens while the family is at church. There is nothing they can do but to watch their home burn down. It ignites because May carelessly left a stove burning when they went to church. May, of course, feels no loss whatsoever now that she has destroyed Silver Bush, and she crassly looks forward to getting a new house in its place.

At the conclusion, Pat's old friend, Hilary ("Jingle") Gordon, now an accomplished architect, returns and proposes to Pat. Now that Pat's beloved Silver Bush no longer exists, she is willing to marry and go away to a new home, one he has designed for her—and the book has the trademark happy ending.

This novel was finished in January 1935, about a year after Maud had begun it. It was dedicated to "Mr. and Mrs. Webb and their family," whose own happy home was emptying as their children married and moved away. Maud's life was under threat from many angles: the novel had been written during one of the most unhappy periods in her life. Some readers have found the novel unwholesome, complaining that Pat seems more neurotic than normal and sympathetic.

When Maud shipped *Mistress Pat* off in January 1935 to her American publishers, Stokes, they wrote accepting it within two weeks. But six weeks later, in mid-March, to her dismay, Hodder and Stoughton (her English publishers) refused it. This was a demoralizing and frightening rejection, stirring up the surprise and hurt she had felt when she had been paid a kill-fee for the Marigold stories after being commissioned to write them. Fortunately, by December 1935, she reported that another publisher in Britain, Harraps, had taken *Mistress Pat*.

The old secure world was gone, like Pat's home and Norval's mill. People were now watching with horror as Adolf Hitler became Führer in Germany, and the German Jews were stripped of their rights by the Nuremberg Race Laws. The infamous "Kristallnacht" was still three years away, but the wider world was ready to burn, and Maud's readers quite understood Pat's grief in watching helplessly while her beloved home—the symbol of peace, happiness, and security, burned to the ground.

This would be Maud's last book written in Norval. The burning of Pat's house was also an appropriate symbol for the end of her personal life in this idyllic village, which had initially promised so much joy.

Problems with Chester continued. In January, the Macdonalds learned that Mr. Bogart was fed up with Chester's erratic performance. Chester was good at law when he put his mind to it, but all too often he simply did not show up for work, just as he had not shown up for classes. Ewan and Maud made a quick trip to Toronto to try to salvage the situation, and they managed to persuade Bogart to give Chester another try. Chester pleaded that headaches had kept him from going to work. This was a bad sign to Maud.

Something strange was going on, too, in the Old Tymers' Association. This had always been completely Maud's own production: she called the meetings; she selected and directed the one-act play, which made up half the program; and she guided other people in developing songs, recitations, and skits for the rest. But for some reason, the executive held a secret meeting, one to which Maud was not invited. One of the parishioners—Garfield McClure (now aged fifty)—orchestrated this.

Garfield McClure had always been a problem. Everyone would have conceded that he was an able man, but also an arrogant show-off who always sought the limelight. (This love of show would follow him to the grave: his elaborate tombstone in the Norval cemetery dwarfs all others.) At that time, he was chairman of the board of the church management, and Ewan had included Garfield in his private assessments of parishioners:

> *Garfield McClure:* A conceited clown who would enter into the presence of royalty unabashed and think himself on the same level socially—one who never considers beforehand what his words may produce. One who expects everyone to toady to him—one who has wild ideas and expects everyone to fall in line with them. One who is not above uttering exaggerated flatteries and doing underhanded work. One who could do some good if he had less conceit and more common sense. One who spoils the little good he does by his silly conduct.

Since Garfield was Luella's uncle (and was very fond of her), he was furious at Chester's treatment of her. According to Luella, her Uncle Garfield thought Ewan and Maud should have made Chester treat his wife and child better. Garfield was ready to make trouble for the Macdonalds.

In the Old Tyme Concert, Garfield had always been one of the performing stars (despite a tendency to clown his parts, which irritated many, particularly Maud). He apparently wanted to assume complete control of the organization, taking credit for its success. He called an organizational meeting, telling others he had called it without informing Maud "as a favour to her" because she was so busy with her sick husband. Of course, Maud found out about the secret meeting and learned that she had been deliberately excluded. She was enraged. To her delight, Garfield could not find a suitable play. She graciously provided one. Most of the members saw that he had orchestrated an insult to Maud. The event left a bad taste all around.

But there was far greater trouble brewing. Ewan's salary in Norval had been in arrears throughout 1934. Then suddenly he was paid. The Macdonalds thought that a nice gesture, particularly given that Ewan had been too "sick" to perform his preaching duties. But Maud felt a continuing chill from the Norval parishioners—quite unlike the Union Church people, who were warm and demonstrative and always solicitous about his health. The Macdonalds were even more surprised when no one from Norval said they were happy to have Ewan back when he returned to the pulpit at Christmas. They would learn the reason eventually, but only when it was too late.

On February 14, Ewan went to a Session meeting and was broadsided by an attack. He was told that people "didn't want to come to church because of him." The elders who spoke out—Robert Reid (Luella's father) was one of them—could offer no proof of this, but all of them, even those that the Macdonalds considered their friends, sat in silent concurrence. Ewan was so wounded by their allegations, true or untrue, that he felt he had to resign.

A day later, he went to Robert Reid's home and asked directly for an explanation of the ill will shown at the Session meeting. Mr. Reid told him it was the result of "that letter." Ewan then learned that a letter had been sent out to all parishes from Presbyterian headquarters with directions to keep ministers' salaries from falling in arrears. As chairman of the board, Garfield McClure had felt chastised by the letter, and was sure that Ewan was the source of this complaint. Garfield had not recognized that the letter was a circular sent to every church, not a missive sent to rap specific knuckles at Norval.

Ewan explained the facts of the case, but he discovered that the truth made no difference to the general feeling of his board of management. Garfield McClure was on a personal vendetta to force Ewan's resignation, and he had turned many of the Norval congregation against Ewan. He had whispered that Ewan had been too sick to work, but not too sick to complain about not being paid. People could plainly see that Ewan, sick though he might be, did go out in the car from time to time—to Toronto, to Glen Williams (to visits with the Barracloughs), and to chauffeur Maud to various engagements. Many Norval parishioners were already resentful of the Macdonalds' close friendship with the Barracloughs. Ewan was also criticized for travelling to the Island for a "vacation" when he claimed to be too ill to preach. And since Maud had told everyone that Ewan's troubles were physical, not mental, and they believed her, there was some justification for grumbling that if he could do so much travelling, then he could also preach.

The Norval people were of a mind that it was time for Ewan to move on and let them get a new pastor who would do his job. And, indeed, it was

probably time for him to relocate or retire: church morale was down. Ewan
was sixty-five, and he was finding it too stressful to perform as minister—after
his humiliation over Chester's behaviour. Still, the whole affair had been
badly handled, and Garfield's underhanded scheming had intensified the
bad feeling.[63] Ewan and Maud were profoundly hurt, but they held their
heads high. They rightly suspected that Chester's behaviour had played a big
role in the community's actions against them. Whatever the causes, there was
no turning back.

Ironically, Ewan's indignation at his treatment renewed him, and he
started preaching vigorous sermons again. Righteous anger had dispelled his
demons far better than Homewood's expensive treatment. The word quickly
went through the community that the elders had been wrong about the letter,
and that Ewan had *not* complained about Norval being behind in payments.
This softened people's attitudes; Garfield and the men responsible for the misunderstanding slunk about attempting to clear themselves of blame. But as
Maud noted, with her keen understanding of human nature, the Macdonalds
were now resented by certain Norval parishioners precisely because those
parishioners now knew they had treated their minister and his wife badly.
Resignation was the only possible course of action.

Maud had always hoped that when the time came for Ewan to resign, in
the normal course of events, they would buy a tract of land down by the Credit
River and build their retirement home in Norval. She did not like living in
cities, and she *loved* the beauty of Norval. She had liked almost all of the
parishioners in both parishes before the blow-up. But now the insults she and
Ewan had endured from some of them "stained backward" through her association with everyone. They must pack up and leave as quickly as possible.

Toronto would be their destination. Maud loved to visit relatives in Prince
Edward Island, but it was never a consideration for retirement. Toronto was
where her sons were studying and would start their professions. Maud had
many literary friends in Toronto, as well as Nora. She hoped that in Ewan's
retirement—when she would be free of church work herself—she could employ her formidable organizational and speaking skills for the benefit of
Canadian writers and Canadian literature. Now, with her boys nearly grown,
she could concentrate fully on her own writing, and her own career in the literary world of Toronto. She began looking forward to the future.

William Arthur Deacon, now the influential Literary Editor of *The
Mail and Empire*, had not changed his attitude towards her books. But she

had received an important honour that spring — the invitation to become a member of the Literary and Artistic Institute of France, extremely rare for a foreigner.

The Macdonalds had to find somewhere to live in Toronto, quickly. Maud's investments were still in bad shape, and she did not have enough ready cash to buy a home. She calculated that she could afford fifty dollars a month to rent a home, but the homes she saw at that price were very far below her standard. She hated all the parts of Toronto where the houses were "cheek by jowl" with each other, without space and trees. Then, good fortune intervened. She contacted an innovative realtor named A. E. LePage.

Albert Edward LePage had come into the fledgling real estate industry in 1913. He was a gifted and energetic salesman who catered to the rapidly expanding professional and business classes as Toronto spilled into the suburbs. He was instrumental in establishing the Toronto Real Estate Board and instituting a code of ethics. He was the first Toronto agent to professionalize the business of selling personal homes, devising ingenious ways that people who could not afford to buy a house outright could buy with a mortgage. Maud had found a saviour. Best of all, he was also from Prince Edward Island. Maud felt especial trust in him that was not misplaced.[64]

As it happened, a famous developer and architectural firm was just opening up an area on Toronto's outermost western fringes called "Swansea." On Riverside Drive, the road that Maud and Ewan took to Toronto, she had admired a new development of homes. She fell in love with the property at 210A Riverside Drive (now 210 Riverside Drive). It was listed at $14,000, far more than she could pay all at once.

LePage showed her how she could purchase it with a down payment of a few thousand dollars and a mortgage. She could pay the mortgage off later when some of her stocks rose or when her insurance policies paid dividends. As the agent for that house, LePage negotiated a reduced price of $12,500, and Maud bought the house of her dreams. Her neighbours would all be successful businessmen, entrepreneurs, and professionals. LePage himself lived down the street at 202 Riverside Drive. She could take the streetcar on nearby Bloor Street West and ride downtown on her own. With these negotiations in place, Maud wrote that she "felt like a new creature." "Hope and encouragement flooded warmly over my bleak heart. Everything seemed changed. . . . I felt for the first time in a long while that it might be possible to go on with life graciously after all" (March 8, 1935).

The Toronto papers—no doubt contacted by LePage, who saw a good advertising opportunity—carried a picture of the home that Maud had bought, with a description of it.

> Mrs. L. M. Montgomery, authoress of "Anne of Green Gables" and several other notable books, has just purchased 210A Riverside Drive, an attractive centre hall, old English type of home, designed by Home Smith & Co's architectural department. It is located on a beautifully wooded ravine lot, 52 x 130 feet, overlooking the Humber River and contains seven large rooms and three bathrooms and a two-car heated garage. The sale was negotiated by A. E. LePage, realtor, who was born on Prince Edward Island where most of Mrs. Montgomery's scenes in her books are laid. Morris Small was the builder of the house. It is understood that Mrs. Montgomery, who in private life is the wife of Rev. E. Macdonald, has just completed another book which will be out next fall and that a number of producers are negotiating with her for the screening of her stories.

Wrapping up their last six weeks in Norval was less painful for Maud now, with the prospect of a beautiful new home *of her own*. Luella and her baby would stay on with her father, and Chester and Stuart would live at home again. For all her frustration with Chester, Maud missed him a great deal.

Still, leaving Norval brought sadness. The Macdonalds hated to move away from the Barracloughs, who had been such good friends. Maud really liked many people in Ewan's parishes and resented that everything had been spoiled by a few. More than anything, Maud loved the beautiful and quaint little village on the banks of the Credit River, where she could call her cats and then hear haunting echoes.

There were rounds of farewells in all the different organizations, with speeches and gifts. All brought mixed feelings. Maud, who had been feeling exhausted by her endless obligations, suddenly experienced paroxysms of sorrow whenever she thought this would be the last time she worked with a particular group. When Ewan, who was still fuelled by the injustice he had felt, did so well in his final sermons that Maud felt sad that this was the last time he would be in his own pulpit. If she looked out her windows, she was overcome with "soul-sickness" and would break down in tears. She experienced attacks of claustrophobia, feeling in one moment as if she had to escape the house and the walls around her, but in another afraid of the future outside. Her nights were flooded with bad dreams and then wakefulness. She was engulfed by temporary but terrifying waves of despair, which made her feel "hungry for death." She went to Dr. Paul for a tonic. "He does not however sell peace of mind or relief from a sore heart in bottles," she quipped (April 4, 1935).

When moving day came—April 25, 1935—Maud got up early to take her last leave of the views she loved: "my beautiful river—silver calm with trees reflected in its sunrise water. Little mists were curling along it in the distance." It was "a lovely warm day," and she fought back tears as the rooms were emptied. The vans left for Toronto around 2:00 p.m. She went from room to room in a final check, saying farewell to each. "I have never felt such anguish on leaving any place, not even the old Cavendish home" (retrospective entry, dated April 24, 1935).

As Ewan took their Willys-Knight car out of the garage and they drove away, she puzzled over his absence of sentiment, remarking he "has absolutely no 'feeling' for places, no matter how long he has lived in them. I would not be like this for the world. I 'love' to love places. But at that moment I envied him his incapacity for loving any place" (April 24, 1935).

Maud had become deeply attached to every place they had lived, putting down "deep roots." But she had been a transient sojourner in all her homes. Now she was going to a home of her own. No one could cast her out. She prayed that it would be a permanent and happy home. It would be her *last* "new beginning." She would call the house "Journey's End."

Maud and her Norval Drama Group, around 1927.

Luella Reid Macdonald and children, Cameron and Luella (and right).

Maud in the 1930s.

Stuart, Ewan, and Chester Macdonald, circa 1930.

Chester holding June Thompson in Norval.

Chester Macdonald in kilt.

Maud in cloche hat, probably in the early 1930s.

Joy Laird around age 16.

"ANNE OF GREEN GABLES" TO APPEAR ON SCREEN

Probably no Canadian ever wrote a book nor created a character more famous than "Anne of Green Gables," by L. M. Montgomery, who in private life is Mrs. Ewan MacDonald (CENTRE). Mrs. MacDonald is now living in Norval, Ont., where she is busy on a new novel. Hollywood is picturing "Anne of Green Gables", starring 18-year-old Anne Shirley (UPPER LEFT). For the movie production the author receives nothing, having sold dramatic rights to her book to the publishers in 1919. Mrs. Montgomery, however, pleased with the choice of Anne Shirley to play the leading role and treasures an autographed photo from Miss Shirley. The note written by Miss Shirley is shown above. O. P. Heggie, another actor in the cast (LOWER RIGHT), also sends his regards to the author. Rev. Ewan MacDonald, husband of the author (LOWER CENTRE).

Scrapbook picture of "Anne Shirley," Maud, Ewan, and O. P. Heggie ("Matthew").

Chorley Park in Toronto, where Maud met Stanley Baldwin.

L. M. Montgomery

PART FOUR

———

The Toronto Years

1935–1942

CHAPTER 19

Swansea is "more a nice country village than a city," Maud wrote a fan on March 3, 1936.[1] Located at the western fringe of Toronto, Swansea had many of the features that Maud had loved about Norval: beautiful natural scenery with a small river running through it, and a relaxed village atmosphere. But Swansea also had a good public library, a movie theatre, and a drugstore for ice-cream sodas. Streetcars ran into Toronto proper, with its literary culture and shopping. Just one mile square, Swansea was a tiny, near-perfect community.[2]

In 1935, Riverside Drive was the primary road running down through Swansea to the Lakeshore Boulevard from north of Toronto. When Swansea was opened for development in the mid-1920s, developer Home Smith set aside locations along the cliff on Riverside Drive for the finest houses. These were built to simulate old-world elegance for the growing number of entrepreneurs and professionals with new money. Other areas of Swansea were far more modest, with a cross-section of income levels. Maud's new home was in the expensive enclave, surrounded by mature trees and overlooking the Humber River. The front of her house, built in an impressive English Tudor style, faced east in the direction of Toronto (and ultimately her beloved Prince Edward Island); the back faced the west and the setting sun.

Over cliffs, beyond the Humber River, was countryside. Looking through her bedroom window, Maud could go to sleep watching the waving tops of pine trees, just as in Norval. She loved the sound of the wind rustling through these trees. The meandering Humber was less picturesque than the Credit River, but to compensate, Lake Ontario stretched in the distance until water met sky, like a far-away sea. Ferns, bracken, and wildflowers in the ravine reminded her of the flora of Prince Edward Island, as seen from her bedroom window (or the small second-floor balcony). And just beyond her front door was access to the many advantages of urban life.

The Macdonalds were the first to live in their new "ghostless" home, as Maud called it. She was pleased that she would not displace any previous mistress, and she envisioned introducing her own traditions. A four-level home, built on a square plan with a flagstone entrance, 210A Riverside Drive boasted a spacious basement recreation room, a ground floor with ten windows, and a second floor with three bedrooms. Maud had always loved fireplaces, and had not had one since living with her grandparents. The master bedroom, with pale apricot walls, joined to a bathroom done in turquoise and white tile; this bedroom also included its own bath (a new luxury at that time). Another bedroom, painted blue, would belong to Stuart. Off the main hallway, a second bathroom was decorated in small black and white tile. A third bedroom would be for their live-in maid. Upstairs, on the fourth level, was a private garret bedroom. Chester would claim that. Incredibly, however, Maud still had no "room of her own"—she continued to write in the bedroom that she shared with Ewan, setting off her writing area with her movable screen.

Maud decorated her house with the artwork she had brought from Norval—her own framed and coloured snapshots of favourite locations and her children, plus a few professional paintings depicting Island scenes. She particularly liked her watercolours of the Cavendish shore by Helen Haszard, and an oil of Cavendish Pond by a Mrs. Crownfield. She also hung the original cover art from *Anne's House of Dreams*, and an etching by the 1911 Governor General of Canada, Earl Grey, of himself.

Although artwork made a wall "friendly," nothing made the house "a home" more than her beloved cats. Her captain of cats, "Good Luck" (shortened to "Lucky"), moved to Toronto with them. To Maud's grandparents and most Islanders, her house would have seemed no less than the home of British aristocracy. To any local observer, Maud had achieved the pinnacle of success when she moved to scenic Riverside Drive, dubbed by the poorer villagers "the *rich* street" of Swansea. She had climbed "the Alpine Path" of her youthful dreams. Her disciplined life and hard work had paid off.

Ewan found Swansea a sympathetic place, too. Riverside Drive was exclusive, but not filled with sophisticated "old money" people, with whom he would have felt out of place. Still the country parson, he made regular rounds to the neighbours, knocked on the doors, and was invited in for visits and tea. Dropping in on neighbours was part of the rural tradition Ewan knew from his upbringing (as well as being the pastor's duty), and he continued this in Toronto. The Riverside Drive women were stay-at-home wives, many with maids or other help, and they had leisure time. Dr. Richard Lane, who became the family doctor for Ewan and Maud, lived at 219 Riverside Drive, across from the Macdonalds' home. His daughter, Nora Lane, a university student at the time, remembered Ewan well. He was "a nice old man," she said, "very gentle, friendly, sweet—like a great big teddy bear. . . . a very, very *lovable* person." But, "he was clearly very lonely and, left on his own, he wandered around [the neighbourhood] for companionship." The Lane household tried to make him feel "valued and important." He told them that his wife worked seven hours a day on her writing and he wanted to get out of the house so he wouldn't bother her. "He was friendly and happy at our house, surrounded by people who wanted to make him comfortable," recounted Nora.[3]

The Herbert Cowan family lived next to the Macdonalds on the south, at 208 Riverside Drive. Mr. Cowan was the manager for the new Loblaw grocery stores, which had just introduced the modern concept of "self-serve." Mrs. Cowan took Maud shopping and showed her how this worked. The Cowans had a very pretty unmarried daughter, Margaret, who was four years older than Stuart, and who had just graduated in dentistry. A younger daughter, Elaine, was still in school, as was the only son, Gardiner ("Billy").[4]

Mrs. Cowan frequently gave formal teas and other parties, both in her home and in clubs, and she ensured that her fancy affairs were written up in the "women's pages" of all the major Toronto papers. She welcomed the Macdonalds with pleasure—Maud was "famous" and would add class and distinction to the street. Over the next few years, Mrs. Cowan often asked Maud to recite at her teas, and Maud always obliged. They went for frequent walks together in the first two years. But Maud quickly decided that Mrs. Cowan lacked the discretion and reticence needed in a friend. She was shocked when Mrs. Cowan said she hoped her daughters would "marry money": such an outright admission seemed shockingly "déclassé" to Maud. (Although Maud was equally conscious of social class, she would never have admitted it.)[5]

The realtor A. E. LePage had one of the most expensive homes on the street (in the assessment of 1937, his property was valued at $7,300, compared to the Macdonalds' $4,625). George Mowat, the head of Glidden Paints, and his wife were at 212 Riverside Drive in a house valued at $6,650.

A retired contractor named Mr. Fry lived at 217 Riverside Drive. He had built several upscale homes on the street, including the Lanes', the LePages', and two others. The Macdonalds soon developed casual friendships with neighbours, especially the Frys. The genial Mr. Fry introduced Ewan to the sport of lawn bowling, which Ewan took up with a passion, joining not just one but several lawn-bowling clubs in the area. Maud and Ewan set up regular evenings of card-playing with the retired couples on Riverside Drive. They fit right in as newcomers in the rich part of Riverside Drive and were well liked. Most of the people in the poorer areas, with smaller houses, on other streets had been in Swansea for a long time and all knew each other.

The Macdonalds—particularly Maud—had frequent visitors. Friends from the Women's Missionary Society in Norval and Glen Williams dropped in on visits to Toronto. Many parishioners from Leaskdale also remembered the Macdonalds with great fondness and often stopped by. Ewan and Maud still made trips to Glen Williams to visit with Ernest and Ida Barraclough, who in turn often came to Toronto. In addition, Ephraim Weber and his wife came through in July 1935 for another visit.

Marion Webb Laird, now married and living in Norval, was like a daughter to Maud, and they visited back and forth. Marion's sister, Anita Webb, came up for the birth of Marion's first baby in early October 1935. Marion was very pretty, delicate, and gentle; Anita was sturdy, feisty, and independent, with a hearty laugh. Luella came to visit with little baby Luella from time to time, and Maud termed the baby a "sweet thing" in her journals. Isabel Anderson still tried to intrude on Maud's life, but the distance between them made it easier for Maud to dismiss her by mail.

Toronto-based friends were more accessible now. Nora Lefurgey Campbell lived at 21 Wilberton Road—too far to walk, but Chester was always willing to drive his mother, and Nora herself sometimes took Maud out for drives in the Campbells' car. Maud's earlier friendship with Mary Gould Beal—a very good friend from the Leaskdale period who now lived in Toronto—had been cooling for some time. The talented and gracious Mary, daughter of prosperous and prominent Harvey Gould of Uxbridge, had a sophisticated polish similar to Maud's. She had married a well-to-do

Uxbridge and Toronto businessman, Norman Beal. Beal had once been mayor of Uxbridge, but his inherited leather business had begun to fail after the end of World War I. Mary borrowed substantial sums of money from Maud to maintain their standard of living, which Maud resented, given that she herself was also feeling the pinch. She was frustrated when Mary spent her second loan on a newer car without offering to pay interest on the first. Still, Maud found it hard to say no to a long-standing friend whom she saw as in her own "class." Aside from Nora and casual friendships with neighbours, Maud's main circle of friends now would become those in the literary world. She had wanted all her life to be part of an intellectual community of people who loved books, and now she was on the verge of attaining her wish.

The churches were the social centre of the Swansea community, as they had been in Norval. There were four major churches in Swansea—the Anglican, the Presbyterian, the Baptist, and the United—plus a Salvation Army that was particularly active in the Depression. The Macdonalds joined the Victoria-Royce Presbyterian Church, some distance away, because they liked the minister, Dr. McKerroll. The Young People's Societies in the churches provided one way for young people to meet and socialize, and the Victoria-Royce Presbyterian Church had an especially active program for young adults.

While in many ways Swansea in the 1930s was a strongly ecumenical environment, in other ways it was not. Generally, the ministers of Swansea's four churches knew the names of everyone in their congregations, and of many in other churches, too, and would stop and speak to them on the street. However, it was a strictly Protestant community of people primarily of English and Scottish descent. There was no Roman Catholic church in Swansea, nor would anyone have sold property to Catholics without attracting criticism. Protestant children were told never to talk to Catholics. They were also cautioned not to wander into the poorer districts south of the Swansea Public School, where there were small houses and tarpaper shacks and people might be picking over the dumps to find food. There were no known Jewish families in Swansea, either.

The local schools were the common meeting ground for younger children, and all nationalities and religions mingled there. Elementary students went to Swansea Public School and secondary students to Runnymede Collegiate. The children of the rich might be sent to a private school (as Chester and Stuart had gone to St. Andrew's in Aurora), but generally the public schools were the great social leveller. The public library was in the local school, and everyone used it, including Maud.

Only the wealthy people on Riverside Drive owned cars. Other people walked to their destinations, stopping to chat with neighbours along the way, especially where the more common houses had front verandahs. Women usually shopped daily for food. In the days before refrigerators, iceboxes were used; a forty-pound block of ice would need replacing every two or three days. But for her own new kitchen, Maud bought a real electric refrigerator.

Shopping uptown in Toronto meant an hour's ride on the streetcar or two to three hours of walking, but in those days people were used to walking, and their larger purchases would be delivered to them at home by horse and wagon, or increasingly by motorized vehicles. Horses and deliverymen were a common sight—delivering ice for the icebox, coal for the coal chute, fresh milk, fresh baked goods, groceries, and store purchases. (The Eaton's department store always used distinctive grey or grey-dappled horses.)

The Swansea area was flanked on the south and north by two very different types of public entertainment. To the north, at the corner of Runnymede and Bloor, was the Runnymede Theatre. A grand establishment, the theatre boasted a ceiling painted to look like the sky, with light projecting stars onto it and shadows of airplanes flying across it (until World War II made that too frightening). In the other direction, down by the waterfront, there was a famous beach entertainment area called the Sunnyside Amusement Park. Built in the early 1920s, before the great crash of 1929, it had a massive outdoor public swimming pool and a dance hall called the Palais Royale. In the mid-1930s, at the height of its popularity, famous bands like Duke Ellington's and the Dorsey Brothers played for up to three thousand people at a time. The beaches were public and clean and safe: during serious summer heat waves, before air-conditioning, families would take rugs or blankets down to sleep on the beach through the first part of the night, until the temperature became cooler towards the morning. Maud herself did this during one heat wave in 1935.

Swansea itself was safe. Children wandered without supervision (though they were told not to go near the Humber River or Grenadier Pond, after the three-year-old son of the area's most prominent lawyer drowned in the pond). People knew each other, watched out for others' children, and enjoyed the sense of community.

Maud was delighted that her sons would be living at home again. She wanted her family to rise from the humiliating ashes of Norval and make a new start in Swansea, establishing a different—and better—life in this sophisticated setting. Having the boys at home would save the cost of room and board, and it would bring the Macdonalds together as a family once more. Luella would stay with her widowed father in Norval, keeping house for him, and Chester would take the car and visit her and the baby on weekends. At the time of their move in April 1935, Chester, who would be twenty-three in July, was into his second year of "preliminary articling" in Mr. Bogart's law office; he would be ready to start his three years of the formal study of law in fall 1935, while still working part time at the articling firm. Stuart, who would be nineteen in October, was in his second year of Medicine (out of five years, plus a year to intern) at the University of Toronto.

Maud's dream of a happy home, one filled with laughter, finally seemed attainable. Chester and Stuart would bring home amusing tales from their daily encounters, and the Macdonald household would be filled with stimulating conversation. She prayed that Chester would settle down and study now that he had a family. She also fervently hoped that Stuart would lose interest in Joy Laird, his Norval girlfriend. Now that Ewan was free from the pressure of performing as a minister, Maud expected that his mental health would improve.

Barely three weeks after the move, Maud embarked on her new social life, attending a Canadian Women's Press Club dinner at the Royal York Hotel. Over seventy-five women were there. Maud looked forward to putting her organizational skills and her celebrity to use in a new context. She was public-spirited, and as an ardent Canadian nationalist, she wanted to foster the growing field of Canadian literature.

———

It was not long after the move that Maud received a registered letter from the Prime Minister of Canada, the Honourable R. B. Bennett:

May 20, 1935

Dear Mrs. Macdonald,
No man born, as I was, in the Maritime Provinces can fail to know of the contribution you have made to Canadian literature.

There are few Canadians who have not read at least one of your books.

His Majesty the King is very anxious that in this Silver Jubilee year of His Reign there should be recognition of the work of men and women who have made real contributions to the cultural life of the Empire in Literature, Art, Music, and Science. It will therefore give me very great pleasure if you will permit me to recommend to the Sovereign that on His approaching Jubilee birthday you be appointed an Officer of the Order of the British Empire (O.B.E.) . . .

The notice of this award helped offset a significant failure on the home front. A week after receiving the O.B.E. letter in May, Maud learned that Stuart had failed his second year of Medicine. Stuart had always been an excellent student, and he had passed all his first-year exams, despite his devotion to gymnastics. Perhaps things had come too easily, however, for this young man with such extraordinary intellectual gifts.

According to a classmate, Dr. Richard Braiden, Stuart failed the second year because he'd spent his time playing cards—and *betting* on them (regarded as a sinful form of gambling at that time). This card-playing was done in a hidden area of a men's bathroom where the boys were out of sight of their professors. Stuart was so good at cards—his memory was a great asset here—that other students came to watch him play, a heady encouragement. He began skipping classes and labs. Stuart was accustomed to learning all his texts the night before exams, but the second-year course of study was mostly human anatomy, learned in labs. The final examination consisted of the students being hustled along a table with piles of bones, which they had to identify at lightning speed. Because Stuart hadn't done the lab work, he was unable to identify the bones quickly enough. Classes were small and professors knew the students. The Anatomy professor, the author of a famous text, had noticed that Stuart was merely coasting along, and failed him. Stuart learned a hard and humiliating lesson.

Stuart would have to repeat his year: his tuition money for the previous year had been wasted. Maud was shaken. She had come to expect failing grades from Chester, but never from Stuart. She greatly resented the waste of a thousand dollars for a year's university expenses. Being disappointed in her "one good son" was bad enough, but the public embarrassment was far worse.

Maud was a high-profile celebrity, and everyone who knew her, from the city of Toronto to the province of Prince Edward Island, would hear about Stuart's failure, either from the newspaper "pass lists" or from gossip. In a society where well-to-do women did not work, formal afternoon teas became an agony: boasting about children's success was a staple of conversation and status at these. Unlike Chester, Stuart was genuinely mortified and ashamed of himself. He had never dreamed that this could happen to him, and he made sure it never happened again.

Stuart's failure took the edge off her pleasure over the O.B.E., but conversely the O.B.E. made Stuart's failure easier to bear. Maud's O.B.E. was granted on June 3, 1935, by King George V, but the formal investiture in Ottawa was not held until early September. Neither Stuart, Chester, nor Ewan attended this ceremony. Determined to earn his own tuition money for his repeat year, Stuart had obtained a job in a Campbell Soup factory and worked there until classes started. Chester seemed busy with his law work in Mr. Bogart's office. The trip was too far for Ewan, so Maud arranged for Mrs. Cowan's daughter Margaret to drive her to Ottawa for the ceremony at Rideau Hall. In her journal, Maud wrote of the trip, in which she and Margaret "gabbed away" as if they were both girls (September 8, 1935). Maud saw Margaret as the kind of "nice" young woman she hoped Stuart would start dating.

For the ceremony, which was conducted by the Governor General, Lord Bessborough, Maud was handsomely decked out in a purplish-navy chiffon and cut-velvet dress with a blue felt hat.[6] She received the formal O.B.E. medal, which could be worn only on state occasions, in the presence of a representative of the King. She had a smaller replica of it made to wear with full evening dress. On June 12, 1935, an article in *The Family Herald* entitled "Specially for Women: King's Honours for L. M. Montgomery . . ." described her achievements in great detail. Ewan's reaction to her honour is never described in her journals—only that he was often "dull" and laid around groaning from pain in his head during this period.

Maud's professional life was very busy following the move to Toronto. She was on the executive of the Canadian Authors Association, but the meetings were often tense. William Arthur Deacon was also on the executive, and he put her on edge.

Canadian literature was still a fledgling field in the 1930s. The Canadian Authors Association (CAA) made it a mission to bring attention to Canadian books. Deacon, like Maud, was eager for Canada to develop its own literature. By the mid-1930s, he had become a very powerful force in the Canadian book-reviewing world. As a newspaper critic, he began to consolidate his power in the CAA. He was determined to sweep out all vestiges of Victorian sentiment and style, hoping that Canadian literature would reflect the new trends. As Maud would learn eventually, there was no place for the famous "L. M. Montgomery" in Deacon's vision, either as a writer or even as someone working in the CAA.

On July 21, 1935, when Maud wrote Stuart Kennedy, the national executive secretary of the Canadian Authors Association, thanking him for his letter of congratulation on her O.B.E, she made the subtle point that she, too, was working for Canadian literature:

> Dear Mr. Kennedy,
>   . . . .Thank you so much for your congratulations on the O.B.E.
> I feel the honour is less for me than for Canadian literature, of
> which I am an unworthy representative. . . . It's time something
> was recognized as worthy of honours besides huge fortunes and
> political juggling.
>
> Yours sincerely,
L. M. Montgomery [Macdonald]

When Maud moved to Toronto, she expected to refocus the energy she had spent in church organization towards the promotion of Canadian literature. But she was becoming increasingly aware of the complicated politics in the CAA, and in the Canadian literary scene in general. Deacon was everywhere, involved in everything, and his personal disdain for her was palpable.

The week after she received the O.B.E. award, Maud attended a CAA executive meeting at the home of A. H. Robson. At this meeting, plans were laid to start a new magazine of Canadian poetry to be edited by Professor E. J. Pratt, the noted Canadian poet, of the University of Toronto. Deacon, as always, was present. Maud writes tersely in her journals of Deacon without naming him, "One of the men on it [the CAA executive] is no friend of mine and has gone out of his way many a time to sneer at my books in the nastiest fashion" (September 16, 1935).

Deacon's first public attack on Maud had been in *Poteen* back in 1926 when he had said that "Canadian fiction was to go no lower" than in "sugary" stories like *Anne of Green Gables*. Maud was fully accustomed to negative reviews, but Deacon's ongoing hostility to her and her writing seemed more personal than professional. He sneered at her books, dismissing them, as if any outright discussion of them was beneath his intellect.

Maud used her own celebrity to promote other new writers, and she knew also that the immense sales of her books allowed McClelland and Stewart to take chances on publishing newer Canadian writers. (In fact, McClelland and Stewart eventually became a major twentieth-century publisher of Canadian fiction and poetry.) She feared that Deacon's scorn would make people question their own judgment if they enjoyed reading her books. And if his attacks on her damaged her reputation and her sales, this would hurt not only her own income but also her publisher's.

In her journals, she remarked without naming anyone that some of the CAA members took themselves very seriously, "especially those who did not amount to a row of beans in any department of authorship" (October 13, 1935). Still, the CAA did important work in organizing and lobbying for better copyright protection. It organized many promotional book-centred activities. According to Eric Gaskell, later the national executive director of the CAA, Maud brought many ideas to these CAA meetings. She knew that many of the people in the CAA had only small talent, but that didn't mean the group could not accomplish a great deal working together for a common cause. All her life, she had been an organizer who got others to work together, and she was very skilled at coming up with fundraising ideas.

On September 21, 1935, the *Telegram* reported a press conference at which Mr. Robson, CAA president, formally announced that they had set up a trust fund to support the publication of the poetry magazine by the CAA, one of their early efforts.[7] He also called attention to the CAA's forthcoming Canadian Book Week in November, another big project to get people "reading Canadian." The same issue of the *Telegram* provided a review of Maud's new book, *Mistress Pat*. It described the book as being full of "charming romances" which end in "the orthodox chime of wedding bells so beloved of youthful readers" — just the kind of characterization that was sure to invoke Modernist scorn. "Cosmopolitan" was the new catchword for avant-garde literature in an era when the world had shrunk because of the advances in transportation and communication following World War I. Maud's books had originally been pegged as "regionalism" (once a complimentary term) because they took as their primary subjects unsophisticated people in rural and small towns. In the 1920s, their re-categorization as "children's books"—or as "girls' books"—had frustrated her. She wrote to one of her fans that the Honourable Stanley Baldwin, Prime Minister of Great Britain, had come to Canada, and had come to see her, and had asked to shake her hand, saying he wanted to tell her "what delight" her books had given him![8] Just "tell that" to anyone who taunts you, she advised, for liking "girls' books." Two years later, she wrote him that her newest book, A Tangled Web, was for adults.[9]

Now in the 1930s, her books, even those specifically for adults like A Tangled Web, were being further re-categorized as "provincial"—a highly pejorative catchword that invoked the opposite of all things "cosmopolitan." Critics now looked for "cosmopolitan" literature that had "universal" themes.[10] It didn't matter that all the jealousies, antagonisms, power-grabs, and political manoeuvrings in small rural communities were a microcosm of those same symptoms in the larger world.

As soon as Maud was re-categorized as "a children's writer" and "provincial," most male critics who belittled Maud's books did not actually read them; they just accepted the labels pinned on them. Accepting the prejudices and opinions of others was apparently *almost* the case with Professor Arthur L. Phelps (born 1887), an exceptionally influential critic and personality from the 1920s through to the 1950s. He was part of a group of cultured men who spent their summers in cottages at Bobcaygeon, Ontario, where their families socialized and the men themselves talked over their ideas about the state of Canadian literature, world literature, and politics. This group included other academics, journalists (like Deacon), and writers invited to join them (like Frederick Philip Grove).

Phelps was in the rather ubiquitous category of male critics who judged before they read when dealing with "L. M. Montgomery." Phelps prepared a book called *Canadian Writers*, and he devoted a chapter to Montgomery. He starts by panning her work, lumping her with popular writers like Robert Service, Mazo de la Roche, and Ralph Connor, who as "romantic and sentimental writers," he deems unimportant "by the standards of discriminating literary criticism." He judges Montgomery's work "naïve," and innocent to the point of showing "ignorance of life." He asserts that her readers are only "the nostalgic and sentimental or . . . the uncultured and unsophisticated." Even "modern young girls," he says, can no longer "tolerate" the "soft well-meaning goodness of Miss Montgomery's portrayal." He ends that same paragraph with the rather ironic information that the librarian who lent him the four Montgomery books told him not to keep them too long as they were "out all the time." After he actually reads her books, his essay changes tack. He acknowledges that Montgomery "should not be dismissed too casually just because she has been popular." He continues, "Widespread popularity . . . usually suggests the presence of positive and fundamental qualities," and decides that Maud is somehow better than the other superficial writers of the era because her stories "have qualities of range and subtlety and fine comprehension which make them relatively worthy even today." He does not revise the first part of his essay—he just closes with the advice to get her book and read it. This assessment, however, was not published until 1951, after Maud's death.[11]

Various factors worked against Maud in the 1920s and 1930s. Her narrative style, which reflected her grounding in the oral tradition of Scotland, was one of these. The oral tradition had become unfashionable in the late nineteenth century, along with "fairy tales" and "old wives' tales." The next generation of writers, who saw a fragmented world, wanted new ways of telling stories. And worse, Maud often lapsed into sensuously evocative and lush "purple prose," particularly when writing about nature. The Romantic and Victorian poets had been an important early influence on her, with their belief that Nature should be a primary subject for art. Maud used this style to create atmosphere in her books, and such passages seemed cloying and old-fashioned. The new post-war Modernist critics called for a tough, hard-edged, pared-down style, as well as gritty subject matter, including tortured people, war, criminality, and sex. Maud's writing—humorous, domestic, and localized in a rural region—fell short on all counts.

Maud probably had not fully realized when she moved to Toronto how very small the Toronto literary circle was and how much infighting there would be. She watched as Deacon solidified his position and grew more influential. After his stint as literary editor for *Saturday Night*, he worked for *The Mail and Empire* from 1928 until 1936, and in 1936 began a two-decade position as literary editor for *The Globe and Mail*. According to his biographers, Clara Thomas and John Lennox, he "loved leadership and the feeling of power to influence events; he also loved to be seen to be leading."[12] He saw no place for Maud in the Canadian garden of literature he was cultivating, and he let her know how he felt. She was coldly furious: she knew that her books were sold, read, and enjoyed around the world. It was only her local reputation that seemed under attack—and by men she worked with in the CAA.

To make matters worse, in 1935 Maud's royalty income of $2,770 was the lowest she had seen in years. She was having a hard time covering her new mortgage, the boys' tuition and upkeep, and all their living expenses. Ewan's church pension of $237.60 a year (paying a quarterly $59.40) would not kick in until 1936, and when it did, it would not even cover their food bills.

Canada's National Book Week, held from November 9 to 16, was the biggest fall literary event in Toronto in 1935. To kick it off, the Toronto branch of the Canadian Authors Association arranged and advertised a special fundraising banquet to honour those who had received the O.B.E. that year. Maud's celebrity status with the public made her a huge drawing card for any event. One of its organizers was another prominent male academic critic who scorned her writing: Professor Pelham Edgar, Head of the English and French Departments at the University of Toronto, a man who kept himself in the public eye as much as Deacon.

Maud rarely recorded anything negative said about her or her books in her journals, probably because she intended them for eventual publication; however, she exploded after this particular CAA banquet. She felt that Deacon and Edgar had deliberately snubbed her in front of everyone who attended. It was a large public event that bore witness to the developing rift—a rift that would trivialize her literary reputation and demolish the status she had worked so hard to acquire over her lifetime.

The banquet was advertised as "quite the most outstanding event of the season in the literary circles in this city." The occasion would honour the "three knights and two O.B.E.s" created that year: Sir Ernest MacMillan, Sir Wyly Grier, Sir Charles G. D. Roberts, L. M. Montgomery, O.B.E., and Dr. E. A. Hardy, O.B.E. Everyone who mattered in the literary scene would attend. Nellie McClung came from the west, and, with Marshall Saunders, C.B.E., sat at the head table.

The event began with A. H. Robson, Toronto branch president, reading several messages, including one from the much esteemed Lord Tweedsmuir, Governor General of Canada and honorary president of the CAA. Then Dr. Pelham Edgar, national president of the CAA at that time, proposed a toast to each of the five members.

In her journals, Maud recounts how Pelham Edgar began with long and fulsome toasts describing the individual accomplishments of each of the first three honoured guests: Sir Ernest MacMillan, Sir Wyly Grier, and Sir Charles G. D. Roberts. She continues, rather crossly, that Professor Edgar, "who has a high opinion of Prof. Pelham Edgar's critical acumen," did not consider that *her* books had "*any* literary merit whatever." After finishing off his flowery toasts to the first three men, Professor Edgar merely nodded to Maud and Hardy, dismissing them together in one bald sentence by saying, "The other two who are included in this toast are Dr. Hardy and Mrs. Macdonald."

Maud snaps that Pelham Edgar would have praised Dr. Edwin Austin Hardy, a widely respected educationalist, as much as the others, but he would then have had to praise her. But Edgar "would have died any death you could mention rather than admit *I* represented Canadian literature. So," she steams in her journal, "the good Edgar selected the horn of the dilemma and impaled himself thereon," by slighting both her and Hardy together in this huge public forum.

A lengthy and unsigned piece in the *Globe* of November 11, 1935, describes the situation exactly as Maud did, showing that she reported it accurately. Although it could seem she is over-sensitive (because a knighthood is a higher honour than an O.B.E.), all five being toasted were asked to respond to their toasts. Deacon's piece in *The Mail and Empire* describing the event omits the information that Dr. Hardy and she made replies to their toasts. Maud felt humiliated by this public snub. A special reception at the home of Dr. Herbert A. Bruce, the Lieutenant-Governor of Ontario, on November 26, 1935, fêted her shortly after.[13]

Slowly, over the next two years, Maud would find herself increasingly irritated in the CAA executive by the behind-the-scenes machinations of Deacon. After Deacon was hired as literary editor of the *Globe and Mail* he had enormous influence over who was given favourable review attention and who obtained positions of influence in the CAA. Many in the literary and academic world, wanting favourable press and not wanting to incur his ill will, tended to follow wherever he led.[14]

Deacon continued to subtly disparage Maud's books. It was in May 1934 that he wrote a long column in *The Mail and Empire* tracing the development of Canadian literature. He implied that Canadian literature was initially very poor in quality.

However much Maud was hurt by Deacon's condescension, she also knew that he exerted admirable effort for public causes, like improving Canadian copyright legislation, and he was an indefatigable organizer of literary events that benefited writers, booksellers, and readers. For Maud, the most irritating aspect of feeling sidelined by Deacon's narrow vision of Canadian literature was that she thought him a mean-minded man who was motivated largely by personal ambition. He was trained as a lawyer, not in arts and letters, and lacked the judiciousness of wide, discriminate reading.

Once her critical descent started, Maud's loss of status would continue steadily until her death. Not until near the end of the twentieth century, long after she was dead, would literary critics dismantle and discredit the norms that the entire generation of academic critics had worked so hard to establish in the 1930s, norms that pushed popular fiction—and almost all women's writing—completely out of the canon and off the map of literary culture.

After the move to Toronto, Maud suffered periodically from acute homesickness for the manse and the beautiful Credit River setting of Norval. In retrospect, her Norval life seemed idyllic.

Ethel Dennis, the maid who moved from Norval to Toronto with the Macdonalds, remembered how unhappy Maud sometimes looked after the move. Maud's mental distress caused specific symptoms: she complained variously of a "queer feeling" in her head, of her eyes "pulling," of "old-time headaches" which resulted in vomiting before she had relief. Ironically, Ewan now gave his wife the same futile advice that she had initially given him in his depressive states, telling her to "cast it off" or "don't think of it."

Maud worked at organizing her house after their move, but she suffered periodically from what she called "neurasthenia," a catch-all term for a host of conditions believed to come from "exhaustion of the nervous system." She described the peculiar "waves" that would rush over her, flooding her mind with memories of times past, but selectively choosing and colouring these memories to turn them into painful humiliations. At first, she was afraid to go to church for fear that one of her "waves" of nervous anxiety would wash over her, forcing her to get up and flee in the middle of a service. Ewan often went alone, and she stayed home.

She did not write in her journals about what these flooding memories consisted of—that most likely would have been too revealing—but we can speculate that she was dredging up the ways she had felt unimportant, un-worthy, and unloved as a child and young woman. As an over-sensitive child, Maud had internalized real and imagined slurs that attacked her developing sense of self. When she became a best-selling author at age thirty-three, she believed that she could move beyond this pain. Now, late in life, with her work and celebrity under attack at the precise time she had hoped to begin en-gaging productively in the Canadian cultural scene, she fell into the old, hurt-ful thought patterns. She was sensitive, and any snubs she felt or imagined acted like salt being rubbed in old wounds. New worries over her finances and her sons only added to her emotional instability.

When Ewan had developed mental problems, she remembered her ear-lier fears that she would never be able to attract a desirable mate, a fear that seemed perversely fulfilled after his illnesses surfaced. As her son Stuart later quipped, "My mother wanted an escape [from spinsterhood in PEI], but she did not know that the ship she chose had a faulty boiler." When her sons grew into sexual maturity, she remembered her grandmother's disapproval of her own behaviour, accusing her of "stealing out" to "see some fellow" (December 20, 1904). Having grown up in a culture that taught that sexual urgings must be repressed, she came to her adult life with a great residue of shame over what had been normal feelings for a flirtatious, high-spirited girl. When Chester and Stuart were attracted to the opposite sex, this stirred up feelings from her childhood. Maud was a person given to reliving everything in the past over and over—in her journals, in her writing, and in her imagination.

Maud knew by this time that her mind was its own place, and as John Milton had put it, it could "make a Heaven of Hell, a Hell of Heaven." Her extraordinary memory, her heightened sensitivity to the emotions that washed over her, her clairvoyant vision into the heart of human muddle—these gifts could paralyze her in the process of living, but they could also in-spire and release her into creative work, giving her the "gift of wings." She could see what was happening to herself emotionally, but she was less able to cope with her mood fluctuations as she aged. When her "nerves" were in bad shape, her intellectual understanding of her state and its causes did nothing to reorient her to what *should* have been, and *could* have been—a feeling of having made a remarkable success of her life, despite many trials along the way, trials that would have destroyed a person with less personal discipline. Because she lacked an unshakeable sense of self-worth, her fluc-tuating self-image made her especially sensitive to external slurs and this made her increasingly vulnerable to depression. It could be a self-perpetuating downward spiral.

When "waves" of depression came during those first months in Toronto, Maud would often leave the house for fresh air and a walk in the garden or along the street to infuse her senses with a wholesome present again. She was unable to compose when severely depressed; she could rewrite, revise, adapt, but creative work was not possible. What would happen to her family's income, she worried, if she could not settle her mind enough to write? For years, her happiest moments had always been when she was writing: what if she lost this pleasure? She *lived* when she wrote. Because she always built her writing around her own feelings, it allowed her to gain distance and see things with greater perspective—and to exorcise (or make light of) painful memories.

In Toronto, Maud's symptoms were not all psychological, however. She was writing for much longer stretches than she ever had before, but she was getting far less varied physical exercise without her parish duties and other activities, which had kept her moving. In Toronto, she subjected herself to the strain of long periods at a desk in her urgent need to support her family and a new house.

Oddly, Maud had never purchased a desk that was the proper height for writing. In both Norval and Toronto, she wrote in the bedroom she shared with Ewan, either on a high square table (with an uncomfortable raised decorative braid around the edge) or in a chair with a portfolio on her knees, with her feet propped up on a stool and her back hunched down. She sometimes revised manuscripts by cutting up sections and laying them out on her bed, then bending over as she reassembled them. When Maud typed her book manuscripts, the ergonomics were equally bad. She either put the typewriter on the braided table desk—which was entirely too high for it—or she placed it on a low footstool in front of her and sat, tipped forward with her back rounded, on her rocking chair. Long stints of work in such a position gave her severe muscle strain in her back, shoulders, and neck—something that her aging and overweight body tolerated less well. Muscle spasms caused a vice-like tightness in her head and the pain around her eyes that she complained of in this period. Her headaches sometimes responded to aspirin, but only if she lay down and relaxed directly after taking medication. Chester's wife, Luella, described how in the latter Toronto years something that looked like a "cord" in Maud's neck began to pull out under the skin. Maud would hunch up her shoulders or tip her head to one side, as if this reduced her pain.[15] Maud's increasing fear of this physical pain, without knowing its cause or how to find permanent relief, greatly increased her anxiety. Her old standby to reduce pain and depression—relaxing walks and concentration on the beauty of nature—was more difficult in Swansea because the walking areas were along the street, not on private paths, and the ravine was too steep to really walk in. In varying proportions, Maud was suffering from the tangled effects of real physical pain and from a generalized anxiety over many aspects of her life.

Maud knew that she was too anxious. Her son Stuart later characterized her as someone who worried about every bridge she had to cross long before she reached it. The line her grandmother had drilled into her—*"What will people say?"* made her into a person whose self-evaluation was filtered too much through others' eyes, rather than determined by her own internal moral compass. Then, when she reread her journals, she read a skewed account of her own life, one that gave support to her growing conviction that there was a curse on her and everyone she cared about. That idea lodged itself in her brain as one of the increasingly pernicious fixed ideas that would surface during depressive episodes.[16]

The disconnect between the public record of Maud's busy, productive life and her own distressed inner feelings, as found in her journals in the 1935 to 1936 period, is staggering. Although there is much joy recorded in Maud's early journals (particularly before her boys were teens), the later journals became the primary repository for her thoughtful or morbid moods. In public, she concealed her depressed feelings, even from friends and relatives. Her self-containment was also a function of what might be called pride: she was determined to maintain others' view of her as a successful celebrity. When her journals were first published, revealing so many of her depressions and doubts, older relatives and close friends who had known her were astonished and confused. Most relatives said that this was not the woman they knew. They remembered only a joyous person whose infrequent visits were characterized by joke-telling, high spirits, and good times.

The public record of Maud's activities in 1935 shows that she was a dynamo of activity right after the move to Toronto, giving speeches and readings, attending formal teas and literary functions, tending to her business affairs, writing and adapting stories to send to her New York agent, and continuing to produce longer fiction. As expected by her publisher, she kept up a rigorous speaking schedule, not only in Toronto but also in locations around Ontario. She spoke about her own books, but she also urged people to buy books by other Canadian writers. She begged her audiences to preserve their local culture, as she had in her books, rather than to think a writer had to employ exotic topics and settings. With subtlety and humour, her speeches defended her books against disparagement by the new critical norms of Modernism, which held that regional novels like hers showed only "idyllic life," not real-life hardships.

Maud was caught in the difficult position of being damned if she did and damned if she didn't—she had an audience that expected a certain type of fiction from her, and if she put in any explicit "modern" material describing such things as girls' sexual fantasies, she would be pilloried and her books banned. Yet when she wrote the light, humorous fiction expected by her publisher and audience, the critics like A. L. Phelps condemned her as "ignorant of life." When she introduced a pitiful, dying, unmarried mother into one book (*The Blue Castle*), some libraries banned it and she lost sales. Yet when writers like Morley Callaghan wrote about the underbelly of civilization, and got banned for salacious subject matter, Deacon talked this up in the papers, and it translated into publicity (and presumably increased sales). Maud's speeches began to show her preoccupation and frustration with the prevailing critical attitudes.[17]

Mistress Pat was released in August 1935 (and *Anne of Windy Poplars* was underway), and Maud kept up a rigorous schedule of speeches throughout the autumn. The *Globe* announced on September 24 that she would speak at the annual banquet of the Progressive Business Girls' Club. Two days later, she attended a tea given by Lady Willison (Marjory MacMurchy). In October 1935, she spoke to a capacity audience at the Royal York Hotel for the opening meeting of the English-Speaking Union. At least three newspapers—*The Mail and Empire*, the *Globe*, and the *Telegram*—described this talk in some detail. She began with a light account of how *Anne of Green Gables* was written ("I did not create Anne—she just popped into my mind with her red hair and the 'e' at the end of her name . . ."), and described how it was written on a typewriter which wouldn't print "m" at all and had a crooked "y." Then she described how it was sent to several publishers and was returned each time. She made the point that while writing came easily to her, getting published required persistence—good writing was not always immediately recognized. Her speech also included sketches of Island life, "proving that it is not necessary for the author to seek big cities for material or for 'something to happen.'"[18] (This was a gentle attack on the critics' implicit claims that modern literature should depict a broad canvas of cultural dislocation and loss, treating "universal" themes in "cosmopolitan" localities.) She stuck to her belief that her "local" subject matter was universally relevant.

Maud told her audiences about listening as a child to all the old stories and local folklore. She advised people to write down sketches of their early years, and the stories they had heard from their parents and grandparents, even if they were without literary ability themselves. She insisted that these stories should be preserved to "give colour to our native Canadian history and literature." She tried hard to defend the "regional" and "provincial" — those qualities that modern critics now saw as old-fashioned in a fragmented and increasingly "cosmopolitan" world.

Maud's speaking was always full of humour, but it was also designed to set certain views forth. After the Progressive Business Girls' Club banquet in October, four Toronto newspapers covered her talk: the *Globe*, *The Mail and Empire*, the *Telegram*, and *The Toronto Star*.[19] (Deacon's account was the shortest.) In this era when young women worked only until they could "catch a man," Maud took the contrary position that young businesswomen should not "marry as long as they could help it," but added that "when the right man came along they couldn't help it."[20] She linked this to "writing," saying that you should not try to write unless you couldn't help doing so, for it was a hard way to earn a living. On the current trend in fiction, she told them that "beauty and happiness were 'just as real' as the sordid side of life which was so often stressed in the 'modern insistence on realism.'"[21]

On October 28, she spoke at the Humbercrest United Church. The following day she attended another formal tea given by her neighbour, Mrs. Cowan. A week later, Maud spoke in Owen Sound to the local Business and Professional Women's Club. Although this club had only fifty members, another hundred women appeared to hear her, driving in from locations as far away as Guelph, nearly one hundred miles away. It was a capacity audience. Again, she encouraged her audience to write down their youthful memories because the old ways were passing away. Her speech was shaped to recast "nostalgia" as valuable social history.

The Owen Sound *Daily Times* gave a full account of her talk, which followed a fairly standard format of personal and general, varied only in particulars.

She began with an "intimate picture of the little island of 'ruby, emerald and sapphire.' It is a land, she said, where there are still old maids and grand-mothers, where a family is still proud to claim a minister in its number, a land where the Ten Commandments are still considered reasonably up-to-date." Then she told of clan life on the Island and the result: her father had "157 first cousins, all living on the island at one time within a radius of a few miles." Next came the tale of the three Montgomery brothers emigrating to Canada, and the life of the pioneer women like her great aunt "who had 17 children without medical attention and in one day five of those children died and were buried." She sketched her own career, particularly her earliest writing—"bi-ographies of her cats"—and her early reading, declaring the Bible the most important of books she had access to, and a valuable *literary guide* to any would-be writer. She told about the shortage of paper and her youthful debt to government bills and to "Dr. Pearce's little yellow note-books," which ad-vertised his various remedies. She said that the best reward for being a writer was the pleasure of the actual writing. She amused her listeners with accounts of her fan mail, which, she made very clear, came from all over the world. She concluded by reading three of her poems about ordinary life.[22]

According to newspaper accounts, Maud mesmerized her audiences, and the newspaper reporters strained for the language to describe her. She "skill-fully [blended] homely touches and the heroic." For this speech, she wore her floor-length gown (the purple cut-velvet gown) and she was "a lovely figure, poised, serene, yet engagingly animated, as she stood in the place of honour and her fresh, sweet voice unfolded tales of the romance and unique beauty of her beloved native island . . ."[23] Maud never used notes when she spoke, and she always kept people laughing.

On November 12, Maud addressed the Mission Circles and Auxiliaries and the Canadian Girls in Training of the United Church at Goderich. Once again, she told of her childhood, and of her determination to become a pro-fessional writer. Then she leaped into the critical fray: "To read some books today, one would think there were no good people in the world. I never cater to the prevailing taste for these books. I believe there is a place for sex books, but only a genius should write them." She may have had Morley Callaghan in mind, for she did *not* think him a genius, no matter how much Deacon and the "old-boy network" praised him. But of course she did not mention names.[24] Soon after, Maud spoke in Sudbury at the Women's Canadian Club annual banquet, addressing some 120 people, the largest audience ever gathered by the club, according to the local paper. She warned people that a writer's life was not an easy one. Then she added her oft-cited line that "perseverance, patience, and postage stamps" are necessary for a writer—rejection slips were many and often. She said that *Anne of Green Gables* had been rejected *five* times, and accepted the *sixth*.

At this event, her readings from her "mailbag" were chosen to make a very specific set of points in areas where she felt her reputation was under attack.

First, she cited a letter from a young man, a divinity student, who wrote her that she proved one "could write novels and still be a Christian." Maud laughed over self-righteous people in private, but she knew many in her audience would see it as a compliment, an illustration that her books were morally sound stories, not trashy, sentimental "novels." Unsophisticated listeners would have heard the praise for the morality of her books, but more thoughtful listeners might have felt some of Maud's own bemusement at the young man's priggishness. Another letter she read was from a monk in Tibet thanking her for *Anne of Green Gables*—again, demonstrating the moral seriousness in her novels, and also that her readers were not just women and children, but important and thoughtful *men*.

Next, she told of a "Mohammedan girl in India" who was so inspired by her books that she persuaded her father to allow her to be educated, and she had just matriculated for study at Cambridge University. Another letter was from a Mother Superior in Australia, who wrote, "I do not need to read your books before putting them into the girls' library." And the last letter was from a teacher who asked the names of the wives of Henry the Eighth on a test and found this answer: "Catherine of Aragon, Jane Seymour, and Anne of Green Gables." That always brought a laugh.

Maud knew her small town audiences well. In Sudbury, she won applause for saying: "I have no sympathy for the so-called realists who seem to think that the only things real are sex, obscurity, and filth. I have tried to write books that will bring a little happiness, a little cheer into other lives."[25] She would not have taken this swipe in Toronto, where it would have been reported in the local papers, further sealing her fate among the male critics as a reactionary and a sentimentalist. And she would never have told this rural audience that she railed in her journals about the prudish Mrs. Grundys who would not allow her to write of young girls and their love affairs as they "really were."[26]

On November 26, 1935, the day after finishing the first draft of *Anne of Windy Poplars*, Maud attended a huge reception at Government House (Chorley Park) in honour of the new Governor General of Canada, Lord Tweedsmuir. Tweedsmuir was otherwise known as John Buchan, an immensely prolific and versatile writer, well known for his popular fiction. Over one thousand of Toronto's important society people attended this function, and on November 27, 1935, the *Globe* published most of their names. Maud's name was not included—a surprise, because she would normally have been near the top of any list of important Canadians. She would have read the newspaper account, and she summed the affair up crustily in her journals, saying that she found "a very moderate pleasure" in Buchan's fiction, adding that he was a small "weazened-faced man" and "nothing to look at." It was a far cry from her Earl Grey reception, or even the Stanley Baldwin one. Sadly for her, her years of being lionized in public were starting to pass.[27]

Two days later she was off to Windsor, Ontario, where she gave two addresses. Then she travelled to Leamington. There she had the startling experience of having her mind go blank ten minutes into her talk, but she recovered quickly. This was a frightening event for the woman who spoke so easily. On December 12, she gave a fifteen-minute talk on her books over a radio program in Toronto called "For You, Madame." This talk (apparently no longer extant in the sound archives of Ontario) was part of a remarkable year of advancement for women. At the end of 1935, the *Globe* announced that more programs were produced for women "than ever before in the history of radio," noting that "at one time these offerings always opened with a cup of flour and ended with a spool of thread," but "now they include national and international affairs, music, literature, science and education."[28] Maud was proud of the fact that her novels had an empowering effect on female readers, even though she herself was not a *public* crusader. She encouraged change quietly through the subtle force of the pen.[29]

For Christmas in 1935, Maud put up a small tree. She remained determined and hopeful about her new life. The Macdonald family had a dinner together, a set of nicely wrapped presents, and a warm fire in their fireplace. Ewan was a little melancholy, but not out of touch with reality. Maud spoke of her "tired and anxious heart," but wrote in her journal that things could have been "much worse." After Christmas, she had a small fall and sprained her wrist (while hanging up her O.B.E.), but it was more demoralizing than damaging. At least there had been no real disasters following their move; life was markedly better than it had been the previous Christmas at Norval, when a miasma of misery had settled over the entire house of Macdonald. In many ways she felt optimistic, but she could not ignore ominous rumblings in the distance.

At the end of November 1935, *The Toronto Daily Star* had carried the headline: "JEWS FORCED TO RUN IN CIRCLES TILL DEATH IN REICH." The article stated that "almost three years after the Hitler regime came to power, the Jews of Germany are being hounded to death in a cold pogrom as horrible and cold-blooded as anything history has ever seen." Drawing on information in the London *Times*, the article told of the Jews' loss of citizenship and property, the tortures in concentration camps, and the savage ferocity of the anti-Semitic fanatics.[30] Many people discounted such accounts as unbelievable. Maud's last diary entry in 1935 ended: "I cannot and will not believe that the world will ever repeat the madness of 1914. But it *is* a 'mad world, my masters,' and no one can ever predict what madmen will do." A student of history and a victim of circumstance, Maud knew far too much about "madness"—both personal and collective—to look to the future without justified fear.

Maud was now using a young and able literary agent in New York City named Ann Elmo. Having sold her book rights to Page in 1919, Maud received no royalties for the new 1934 talking movie of *Anne of Green Gables*. However, the enterprising Miss Elmo suggested resuscitating Anne as a heroine for another novel, to piggyback on the popularity of the movie. Maud found a segment of Anne's earlier life that was not yet covered, and this became *Anne of Windy Poplars*. Propelled by the need for money, Maud wrote it in record time, between May and December 1935. In this novel, she makes creative use of her dealings with Isabel Anderson.

Anne of Windy Poplars (1936)

In *Anne of Windy Poplars*, while Gilbert is at medical school, Anne moves to Summerside, PEI, to become the high school principal. Here she faces many challenges. First is the organized hostility from those who had promoted another candidate for her position. Second, she must win the cooperation of a sour vice-principal, who dislikes her before meeting her. Anne has an innate sense of how to win people over and persuade them to co-operate; much of the book's interest is in watching this happen. The rest is episodic, filled with eccentric characters in the community.

Most characters in this book have a chapter devoted to them and then disappear, but one character keeps recurring throughout the novel—the vice-principal, a young woman named Katherine Brooke. She is a strange creature, rude and remote, a puzzle to Anne. Katherine is twenty-eight, but looks as if she were thirty-five. Although she is a very capable teacher, she is sour, sarcastic, and unpopular. She boards in a "gloomy house" and dresses dowdily. Her pupils live in fear of her sarcasm. She has no friends, wants none, and is described as "repellent," a term Maud used for Isabel in her journals.

Anne confesses that she would quit trying to win her over but for her sense that, under all Katherine's rude aloofness, she is starved for friendship. Anne feels sorry for her, even when Katherine insults her openly, telling her: "I can't pretend things. I haven't your notable gift for doing the queen act . . . saying exactly the right thing to every one."[31] She attacks Anne for having more happiness and friends than she can fully appreciate, whereas if she, Katherine, were to die, she says no one would mourn her.

Over time Katherine is softened by Anne's friendship. Katherine admits she's never had a friend, that she has never belonged anywhere, and that she hates teaching. She also dislikes men. She wants nothing more than to be like other people, but she is unable to. Anne helps Katherine become a happier person.

Many of the other characters in this novel also share traits with Maud and her extended family. Young Elizabeth Grayson lives with her undemonstrative great-grandmother; her mother is dead and her father has gone away for business. Elizabeth longs for happiness in her imagined "Tomorrowland." Prompted by Anne, Elizabeth's father comes to claim his daughter at the end of the novel, promising they will never be separated again—the very words Maud had longed to hear from her own father. Another irascible and controlling old man, Cyrus Taylor, torments his family with his sulky silent spells, taking more than a little inspiration from Maud's Grandfather Macneill. Then there is Hazel who keeps a journal into which she pours purple prose and silly, effusive musings, as the young Maud had done. Lugubrious Cousin Ernestine, who sees only dark forebodings and negativity like the Maud of the later journals, shares identical medical problems with Maud (like lying awake nights with a pain that shoots down to her lower limbs). Another character, the nasty old Mrs. Gibson, disabled in body but manipulative in personality, refuses to let her daughters have a life of their own. (The theme of seeking to exert excessive control over adult offspring will appear more strongly in Maud's next book, *Jane of Lantern Hill*.)

The most intriguing character, next to Katherine Brooke, is Miss Minerva Tomgallon; Minerva lives in a decaying Gothic house and romanticizes her dead relatives, making much of the fact that a "curse" is on her family. Despite the fact that Maud had herself become increasingly convinced through the 1930s that there was a "curse" on her own house, she makes old Miss Tomgallon into a comic character. Anne wryly observes that she is a melodramatic old woman who seems to positively *enjoy* the idea of this curse. However, when a bemused and skeptical Anne asks her landlords if there really is a curse on the Tomgallon family, she is told that, yes, it *is* true. Is this Maud's indirect comment on the convictions expressed in her journals? In fiction, Maud examined human faults and eccentricities, including her own, turning all into humour. But in her journals—and in her life—she treated the same issues with deadly seriousness.

During the period Maud was writing *Anne of Windy Poplars*, Isabel Anderson continued to harass her. In July 1935, for example, Isabel insisted that Maud could help her if she "cared." When Isabel told Maud that she wanted to travel to Prince Edward Island with her, Maud wrote a pert *"Fancy that!"* in her journals. Still, in November 1935, Maud allowed Isabel to come to Riverside Drive for a weekend. Isabel surprised Maud by writing her a pleasant letter of thanks after the visit, rather than a complaint. It seemed to Maud that Isabel was finally overcoming her strange infatuation and blossoming into a normal person. In fact, unbeknownst to Maud at the time, Isabel had merely found new victims for her unwelcome attentions. These included at least two unmarried men closer to her age and one older married man. These men found her weird and off-putting, and they scrambled to evade her, nimbly and successfully.

Maud's exasperation at Isabel Anderson has such furious bite in her journals that it is astonishing to see Isabel become the inspiration for a sympathetic character in *Anne of Windy Poplars*. Anne is able to convince Katherine to leave the teaching profession in search of a more enjoyable life. In Maud's journals, Isabel Anderson is presented as a highly disturbed person, a virtual pestilence who ignores all rebuffs. A reader begins to wonder if Isabel is given so much space in the journals because she is a creepy but fascinating character who offsets the surrounding entries, which say, in effect, "Ewan was dull today." But Katherine's transformation during the course of the novel shows what Maud may have hoped for Isabel, and why she put up with her. Maud was able to see a tortured person underneath the hostile exterior, and she genuinely wanted to help this person find a more satisfying life. Isabel, however, did *not* quit teaching.

Maud dedicated *Anne of Windy Poplars* to "Friends of Anne everywhere": an assertion that while her books may not have stood up to modern critics, her fans everywhere still loved them.

The year 1936 began well. Maud continued to be in much demand as a speaker. In the first week of January, she spoke twice: to the Women's Auxiliary of the West YMCA, and to the Canadian Women's Press Club. Both *The Mail and Empire* and the *Telegram* covered these events, announcing them beforehand and describing them afterwards (who poured tea, who sang, who did the "thanks," who came as distinguished guests, and so on). On January 16, she spoke in the Deer Park United Church, and on the 30th, she went to Norval to meet with the Women's Missionary Society. In February, she spoke in Peterborough, and attended a PEN luncheon. In March, she spoke to a large audience at Chalmers Presbyterian Church in Toronto about her background and also about standards in literature,[32] and later that month she spoke to the Lip Reading Circle of deaf people. She recycled some of her speech material, varying the focus and incidents, but her spontaneous and witty delivery kept it fresh.

At a March meeting of the CAA the national secretary, Howard Angus Kennedy, complimented her out of the blue on her "indomitable will." The comment cheered but puzzled Maud: it was not generally known that she had troubles at home. She was cheered by his comment, even if she was curious about what prompted it. Mr. Kennedy did know, of course, about Deacon's attacks on her. Quite likely, he was signalling that he did not share Deacon's pejorative view of her achievement.

On March 26, Maud spoke to the Young People's Society of the Farmer Memorial Baptist Church in Swansea, a church she sometimes attended. (Her Baptist connections harked back to her girlhood days, when the

Presbyterian young people of Cavendish would go to the Baptist church for social events.)

At the annual dinner of the CAA in May, Maud thanked the speaker, Dr. O. J. Stevenson of the Ontario Agricultural College at Guelph, a pioneer in the teaching of Canadian literature at the post-secondary level. Dr. Stevenson spoke about the modernist credo that Canadian poetry should be "more rugged, larger in theme, broader in treatment and more virile in experience." Discussion ensued over how poorly Canadian literature and writers were said to be regarded in England and Europe, with heavyweights such as Dr. Lorne Pierce, Dr. Pelham Edgar, Dr. O. J. Stevenson, and Mr. A. H. Robson pondering the problem. (The Canadian writer whose work was best known in England and Europe, of course, was L. M. Montgomery.)

On the same day, the *Telegram* and the *Star* each announced the release of a book of poetry that typified the kind of sentimental and un-virile poetry that O. J. Stevenson had disparaged in his speech. The *Star* panned the book. Titled *Up Came the Moon*, by Jessie Findlay Brown, it bore a one-page "Foreword" by L. M. Montgomery. Maud's foreword is courteous (and very tepid), but she must have squirmed over the timing of its appearance in the context of Stevenson's lecture attacking this kind of sentimental poetry.[33] On May 26, Maud attended the annual Canadian Women's Press Club dinner. Maud liked the CWPC meetings much better than the CAA; the membership was limited to true professionals who were working or published writers, and women controlled the agenda, giving it a different atmosphere.

Maud, Grove, and Modernism

In Maud's speeches, she often mentioned promising new authors, and she wrote endorsements for Mr. McClelland to use in advertising his new writers.[34] One of her strongest early endorsements had been for Frederick Philip Grove a decade earlier; this evolves into a comic scene in her *Emily* trilogy, which parodies the critical discourses of the 1920–30 period. When his *Over Prairie Trails* had first been published back in 1922, Maud had praised it enthusiastically in her speeches. After that, she wrote Grove a letter encouraging him to write more about western Canada, telling him he had it in him to write *"the great Canadian novel."* Grove and his wife laboriously unscrambled Maud's handwriting, deciphering words and writing them above

her scrawl. Grove took her advice to heart and spent the next summer writing what turned out to be *Settlers in the Marsh*. Maud continued to think
highly of Grove's writing ability. Maud appears to have met Grove sometime
in the mid-1920s, perhaps at a CAA or other literary function. Her reaction
to the man himself was decidedly less enthusiastic than her regard for his
writing. She liked people with a sense of humour, and he took himself *very
seriously*. She also disliked his growing penchant for "tragic endings."

In 1927, Maud had published a spoof on the idea of tragic endings in
Chapter 17 of *Emily's Quest*: Emily drops into a Charlottetown newspaper office at the moment the editor cannot find the last section of a lugubrious pot-
boiler that he is serializing to boost summer circulation. The paper has to go
to press imminently, so she sits down and quickly composes a *happy ending*
for it. Soon after, the book's enraged author—a pompous, self-admiring fool
named Mark Delage Greaves—arrives at her home in a huff and rails against
her for having "murdered" his novel.[35] But he takes one look at Emily and falls
madly in love with her. Calling her a "lyrical creature," he tells her that if she
will marry him he will teach her to write proper *tragic* endings. The only
"artistic" way to end a book is, he opines, with "sorrowful" endings. The scene
is pure slapstick comedy, and it shows Maud's impatience with Modernist critics who made "tragic endings" such an important part of critical discourse on
what constituted a "great novel."[36]

Maud continued to write Grove congratulatory letters on his new novels,
until he went too far in her view with his tragic endings. In 1928, his novel *Our
Daily Bread* concluded rather like Shakespeare's *King Lear*. Maud wrote
Grove, tactfully asking if such unmitigated disaster was not a bit extreme.
Surely at least *one* of the ill-fated hero's children would have come to a better
end, she said. We do not know if he answered.

However, in 1929, Grove gathered some of his essays into a book called *It
Needs to Be Said*. In it, he writes of his scorn for a best-selling female writer
he has met because she writes "happy endings." He attributes this woman's
best-seller status to the fact that her books pander to the uncritical masses.
Maud never mentions reading this essay by Grove; however, she may have,
since she had written Grove congratulatory letters about his other books.
There is no known further correspondence between them following the publication of this book of his essays.[37]

Maud continued to be annoyed by the Modernist focus on cultural dislocation and misery. However, from the 1930s onward, she made a conscious

effort—seen in the "Pat of Silver Bush" novels, and also in her three final novels—to bring some misery and troubled characters into her fiction. These unpleasant elements were always temporary and felt at a narrative distance. Her readers expected happy endings, and these continued.

Through 1936, Maud continued to adjust her sails to an unpredictable market, while still pleasing her regular readers, not to mention attempting to maintain the family's lifestyle. She wrote several magazine contributions, including a piece on Mammoth Cave for a Maritime magazine, named *The Busy East*, and a nostalgic article about change based on her reflections on the diary of the old Cavendish farmer Charles Macneill (father of her special childhood friends Pensie and Alec Macneill). She finished typing up *Anne of Windy Poplars*, and she wrote Charles Gordonsmith, editor of the *Family Herald and Weekly Star* in Montreal, that he could start serializing the "Anne" stories linked to *Anne of Windy Poplars* on May 1, as the book itself would come out in August.

But she could not afford to let the dust settle. In April she started planning her next novel, *Jane of Lantern Hill*, and by mid-August was deep in composition. In a journal entry for September 2, she describes herself as writing as much as five hours per day in an attempt to finish it.

Jane was not the only fiction Maud was writing. Her New York agent, Ann Elmo, had persuaded her to re-enter the market for short stories, recirculating old ones in light of the great demand for cheerful, upbeat "Shirley Temple"-style material, and writing new, sharper-edged stories for an altered time and market. Their 1936 correspondence reveals much activity. Elmo reported that the editor of *Cosmopolitan* liked a story, "Here Comes the Bride," but found the opening confusing. Elmo thanked Maud for another story and hoped to have news soon on yet another story named "The Pot and the Kettle." Maud's attempt to squeeze back into the short fiction market was impressive: on May 29, Elmo reported that she had sold a story called "The Use of Her Legs" to the *Canadian Home Journal*, which would pay $100 for first Canadian rights.

But the literary market demanded a "new" kind of writing which was not Maud's métier. Elmo informed Maud that "The Use of Her Legs" had made the rounds of American journals without success; moreover, while the American editor of *The Country Gentleman* liked "The Pot and the Kettle," he thought it not "robust enough." Maud had experienced plenty of rejections at the beginning of her career, but few after she became famous. This rebuff was a blow, again underlining the change in literary styles, even in popular magazines. On

July 28, Elmo returned "Penelope Struts Her Theories" and "Retribution" with bland hopes they "would find a home" soon.[38]

But there was some success. The editor of *Good Housekeeping* asked Elmo to find more stories like "I Know a Secret," a tale of degraded characters and a thoroughly evil child built on the theme of the terrible damage that can be done to children's lives by gossip. This was a topic that Maud had found congenial after her sons' adolescence and her own experiences as mistress of the manse.

Miss Elmo wrote Maud that she hoped a movie company would pick up *Anne of Windy Poplars*, but the market was becoming increasingly unpredictable. On August 8, Elmo wrote that she had been unable to sell radio dramatization rights for *Anne of Windy Poplars* because Stokes, the American publisher, had offended the radio agent—not a likely excuse if the agent had really wanted the book, and Maud knew this. She had included several maladjusted characters in the book, but apparently that was not enough to suit the temper of the times.

Fortunately, her longer fiction continued to sell to devoted readers. On August 10, her American publisher, Stokes, sent Maud a royalty of $820.40 for the "sales up to today . . . less the US tax of 10%" for *Anne of Windy Poplars*. Maud had signed this contract with Stokes several months earlier, on February 11, so the book's initial sales were reassuring.

Money still being a big concern, when she answered fan letters, she started asking her fans to write RKO in Hollywood saying that they wanted to see more of her books on the screen. Though she received no royalties of any kind from the earlier *Anne* books, she did have the copyright to *Anne's House of Dreams* (1917), the first book published by McClelland and Stewart (and Stokes) after she parted company with Page. Once *Anne of Windy Poplars* was released in late summer 1936, she urged fans to write asking that it be made into a movie, too.

Maud had long chafed at how royalty money had bypassed her completely following the sale of film rights to *Anne of Green Gables* in 1919. Nor did she get any money from the 1934 remake, which she had seen several times in Toronto. She wrote to a correspondent that Anne (played by an actress named Dawn O'Day, who subsequently took the name "Anne Shirley" in her real life) was "good," Diana a "washout," Gilbert only "fair," and Matthew "excellent." She said Marilla (played by Helen Westley) was much more like her idea of Mrs. Lynde than the slim, stern Marilla of the book. But

Maud positively hated the tacked-on *"happy ending"* of romance.[39] Her own ending had focused not on Anne's finding a man to marry, but on the more ambiguous image of the "bend in the road." It pointed a way to interesting ventures in the future, not necessarily to marriage.

CHAPTER 20

Maud had been going at a rapid pace professionally ever since the move to Toronto, and in the early fall of 1936 she desperately needed a break. It had been four years since she had been "down home." She loved the Island for its natural beauty, but she also loved the unqualified admiration she felt there with friends and family.

She travelled by train, arriving at the beginning of October for a month's stay. She noticed changes there: her Uncle John F. Macneill had cut down her beloved old apple tree before he died. "Lovers' Lane" trees had also been cut down, and her friends had aged noticeably. She took her O.B.E. medal to show her friends and family, and all shared her pride in it, except her aging Aunt Emily, who looked at it only long enough to note, dismissively, that it was "pretty" (October 26, 1936). Maud wrote in her journal that Emily should "not grudge me my small morsel of fame and success. God knows I have paid high for it." She did not know that her Aunt Emily told other relatives that she was "ashamed to know" her niece, Maud.[40]

To all other Islanders and relatives, a visit from L. M. Montgomery was, as always, major news on the Island. Lieutenant-Governor DeBlois put on a reception at Government House for her, and over two hundred admiring Islanders trouped to the event. The Charlottetown *Patriot* reported that "Mrs. Macdonald . . . [is] as charming as she is talented . . ." The paper also gave a running account of which people Maud visited each week. The Webbs and Alec and May Macneill in Cavendish and her Campbell relatives in Park Corner were standard, but everyone else honoured with a visit from her felt especially important.

On November 7, 1936, the *Globe* ran a "letter" written while Maud was still in Cavendish. She explained that the farm where *Anne of Green Gables* was set had been purchased by the government for a National Park, ensuring that Anne's haunts would remain forever. Her letter made it clear to the newspaper's readers that even the Government of Canada in Ottawa, as well as the Island's local government, recognized her celebrity and national significance. (Maud had watched the rising influx of tourists to Cavendish since 1908. In the 1920s, Ernest and Myrtle Webb began operating a tearoom and tourist home in "Green Gables." Maud felt pride that her books had made the Island a tourist site, but she also felt terrible sorrow that her old haunts, so private and peaceful, were now overrun with tourists.)

After her return from the Island, she spoke in Goderich, Ontario, at a banquet for two hundred people (a combined group of Mission Circles, Evening Auxiliaries, and CGIT groups). The next night she spoke in Guelph, again at Chalmers Church. Her memory of her Grandfather Macneill was softening after her recent trip home, and she acknowledged that she had learned storytelling techniques and many old tales from him, according to the *Guelph Mercury*.

The Toronto Book Fair started on November 9, 1936, and it ran until the 14th. The Book Fair (which replaced the earlier CAA Book Week) was sponsored by a new organization, the Association of Canadian Bookmen (ACB), founded the previous year by a group of men including William Arthur Deacon. The ACB's ranks were filled with professional men, unlike the CAA, which had many rather undistinguished "scribbling women" among its members. Dr. Pelham Edgar was the president of the ACB, as well as of the CAA. Hugh S. Eayrs, president of the MacMillan Company of Canada, was treasurer and chairman of the Book Fair Committee. Arthur H. Robson, president of the Toronto Branch of the CAA, was in charge of the speakers' program. Major speakers of the official program would include Grey Owl, Margaret Lawrence (not the later writer, Margaret Laurence, but a young critic who had written a much-praised book on women's contributions to literature), novelist Morley Callaghan, activist and novelist Nellie McClung, folklorist Marius Barbeau, Americans Edgar A. Guest and Carl Van Doren, and the Canadian Wilson Macdonald, a flamboyant and self-important poet and performer much touted then but now forgotten.[41] William Arthur Deacon, whose hand was everywhere in this fair, was chair of the opening session. At this evening session, at 8:00 p.m., Sir Charles G. D. Roberts, Sir William Mulock, and Professor Pelham Edgar spoke. At 9:00 p.m., Grey Owl gave the keynote speech. The newspapers, especially *The Mail and Empire* where Deacon was literary editor, carried excited and detailed accounts of the week-long events.

Maud was conspicuous by her absence from the front lineup of speakers, despite her prominence on the CAA executive and her fame as a speaker who drew large crowds. In her journals, she wrote of the 1936 Book Fair as if she were part of it, but in fact she was sidelined into peripheral events, and women's programs, at that. Grey Owl spoke twice during the Book Fair, as the keynote speaker on opening night, and again at the Canadian Women's Press Club luncheon in Eaton's Round Room.

At that luncheon Maud was seated between Grey Owl and William Arthur Deacon. Deacon turned his back on her and spoke only to the woman on his left. Grey Owl turned to his right, and focused only on the woman there, the event's convener. Isolated between them, Maud quietly ate her lunch. Before dessert, Grey Owl turned to Maud and remarked abruptly: "You are a woman after my own heart." Surprised, according to her journals, she responded: "How so?" His reply, to Maud's amusement: "You don't talk."

It was Maud's job to thank him after his speech. She told of hearing an "owl's laughter" in Leaskdale. Grey Owl sprang up, exclaiming dramatically: "You are the first white person I have ever met who has heard owl's laughter. I thought nobody but Indians ever heard it. We hear it often because we are a silent race. My full name is Laughing Grey Owl."[42] This anecdote made the papers the next day, even Deacon's *Mail and Empire*.

Deacon, like most everyone else, was taken in by Grey Owl's fictions about his origins. Grey Owl claimed that he had been born in Mexico, had gone to England with the "Buffalo Bill" show, and had then returned to Canada, where he had lived ever since. At the age of thirteen he could speak "fairly good 'pidgin' English," he said. Deacon's *Mail and Empire* account of Grey Owl's appearance is dramatic:

> Striding, gaunt and tall in fringed elk-skin tunic and leggings, wrapping around him a vividly red Indian blanket, Grey Owl received an ovation from 2,000 gathered at the Book Fair to hear [him]. . . . People stood for an hour to hear his oratory, the peculiarly Indian poetry of his delivery, shot through with humour, as he told of giving up hunting and taking to writing for a livelihood, and his early experiences as an author. There was magnificent pride in the great eagle-feather in his hair, and the scalping knife stuck through the wampum belt, and something almost of challenge as those beaded moccasins trod the dais, to and fro, to and

fro. He dared his audience, as fellow Canadians, to put his people
on a self-respecting basis by making them conservors of wild life,
forests and natural resources. . . . 'I'm almost frantically loyal to
Canada,' he said, declaring '*I speak with a straight tongue; I tell you
only what is true.*' [italics added] (November 11, 1936, p. 7)

The newspaper account builds to a dramatic end: "Well did Chairman
Hugh Eayrs call him 'A great Canadian, a great gentleman, a great friend,
and a great writer.'"

Maud's description of the event in her journals shows her skepticism:
"[Grey Owl] was looking quite the Indian of romance, with his long black
braids of hair, his feather headdress and a genuine scalping knife—at least he
told us it was genuine . . ." (November 10, 1936).

Two years later, Grey Owl would be dead, at age fifty, and his real identity and name discovered.[43] He left an important legacy through his popular
books, including *The Adventures of Sajo and Her Beaver People* (1935), which
showed his great love of the Canadian wilderness. His 1936 speech shows him
to be a man much ahead of his time:

> Canada's greatest asset today is her forest lands. In my latest book I
> have attacked the average Canadian's ignorance of his own coun-
> try. He is prouder of skyscrapers on Yonge Street. . . . He can have
> those any time, but we can't replace the natural resources we are
> destroying as fast as we can. . . . They make us one of the richest
> countries in the world, and I call on you to let my people help in
> preserving these riches for us, as the beaver conserve the water.
> (*Mail and Empire*, November 10, 1936, p. 7)

Maud had liked his speech—she too loved the natural flora and fauna, and
she would remark in 1938, upon hearing of his death, that even though he
had taken people in about his identity, his concern for animals and the natural world was real.

The same day that Deacon described Grey Owl's speech, a fellow journalist gave Deacon a huge puff in the paper. He asserted that Deacon had discovered that Canadians "did not know they had any literature apart from that
produced by a handful of minor poets" and that it was Deacon's "prophetic
eye which saw in the germinating kernel hidden in the earth, the full flower,

the tall tree that was to be. . . . [and] his own assiduous tending, hoeing, weeding and trenching, helped create it and now he can with pride invite anyone to come into the Canadian garden."[44] Maud, addicted to newspaper reading each day, undoubtedly read this mythologizing about Deacon with some annoyance.

A few days later, William Arthur Deacon was officially appointed as literary editor of *The Globe and Mail*, a post he would hold until his retirement in 1961. He would wield enormous influence on Canadian letters, for better or worse, for almost forty years. He could do much to make or break an author, at least temporarily, until time sorted out who deserved to be remembered.

Maud marched through another round of speeches after the Book Fair. On November 12, she spoke to the Civitans' Ladies' Auxiliary in the Eaton's Round Room.[45] The following day, she gave the address at a banquet for the Lampton Mills graduating class, with over 165 in her audience, the largest number recorded there.[46] On November 14, she was the guest of honour at a tea held by the L. M. Montgomery Chapter of the I.O.D.E.[47] That engagement appears to have been her last for 1936, a very demanding year as far as speeches and public appearances were concerned.

A year after moving in, Maud felt that "Journey's End" had started to seem like home. She had hired landscapers to make a small rock garden, a new fashion. But all was not well *inside* her home. Ewan started having his "sinking spells" again. By the second week in January 1936, he was into a "down cycle," lying around and staring vacantly, "pawing at his head," and complaining of "burning sensations."

Maud's novels show a deep understanding of complicated interpersonal relationships. Yet, within her immediate family, contentious or worrying matters were rarely addressed directly. She had grown up in a family where her grandfather's explosive nature was to be avoided rather than confronted. She had learned conflict avoidance rather than discussion and negotiation. In her own family, this pattern was replicated. Instead of discussing contentious issues, the Macdonalds by-passed them, all the while *watching* each other closely. (Maud's ability to "read" people's emotions and character through non-verbal clues was legendary, and she often gives tonal quality to characters' speeches by commenting on something she observes in their demeanour.) There might have been leading questions, but there was little open and

Luella Reid's home outside Norval.

Isabel Anderson, Maud's fan.

Chester, Ewan, Maud, and Stuart Macdonald in Toronto, circa 1935.

Stanley Baldwin, Prime Minister of Britain, made a point of meeting Montgomery when he toured Canada.

"Journey's End," the house Maud bought in Toronto on Riverside Drive.

Maud in Toronto, at the time of *A Tangled Web*'s publication, around 1931.

Maud and Ewan on a boat in Norval, circa 1931.

Toronto street scene, with Eaton's, Maud's favourite store, during the 1930s.

Stuart as member of the
University of Toronto
gymnastics team.

Stuart Macdonald.

Dr. Margaret Cowan, the girlfriend next door.

Maud and Ewan
in Ohio.

Dr. Stuart Mac-
donald and his
mother at his
graduation in
1940.

serious confrontation of issues.[48] Outbursts were rare in this house, which the maids all described as very "civilized," and when tempers did flare, Maud was terribly upset. She certainly could speak her piece on the rare occasion when she reached the point of explosion, but she would suffer for a long time afterwards. Ewan, on the other hand, having grown up in a less intense house, was an excellent negotiator in his public life.

The undercurrent of anxiety in the Macdonald house was spreading. Stuart had applied himself to his studies this year, but by February 1936, Maud described him as being "dull and languid." Typically she did not ask him what was wrong. He became less communicative, not his usual joking self. Stuart knew all too well that his mother was opposed to his continuing relationship with Joy Laird. He did not like to hide his visits to Norval, as he was very uncomfortable deceiving a mother he loved and admired. Also, his mother's disappointment over Chester's marriage was very clear to him, and he did not want to add to her misery. Yet, Stuart believed that he should be able to make his own choice of a girlfriend. He both resented his mother for her attitude and thought himself weak for capitulating to it.

Stuart wanted nothing more than to make his mother happy, but he also felt deep and long-standing affection for Joy, his chum since the Macdonalds moved to Norval when he was eleven. As they grew older, their friendship developed into a romantic relationship. All through his years at St. Andrew's, Stuart and Joy had corresponded. Joy had been offered no opportunity for further education beyond high school, so Stuart had lent her books for self-education. Joy was not only pretty, bright, and witty, but her buoyant personality made her full of laughter and fun, something in increasingly short supply in his own home. According to memories in Norval, the Laird home was always cheerful, a congregating place for young people. Drunk or sober, even her father could be good company. Stuart missed seeing Joy, who was popular in Norval with everyone, it seemed, except his mother.

Strangely, Maud did not contemplate her own role in making Stuart "dull and languid." Even more odd, Maud was just then plotting her new novel, *Jane of Lantern Hill*, in which she depicted a difficult and controlling grandmother interfering in her grown child's love life. The meddling brings grief to everyone concerned in the novel.

But much more immediate problems were at hand. Marriage and fatherhood had not settled Chester. He had solemnly promised his parents that there would be no more babies until he could support them, but he was drifting without focus or discipline, showing minimal interest in his legal studies. Then the stunning news came on April 19, 1936, that Luella had *given birth* to a second child, a baby son. Chester had not even informed his parents that Luella was pregnant again. In 1936, information about contraception was available to married couples, and Maud was furious at Chester's irresponsibility.[49]

Even worse, Luella had not even informed Chester when she was taken to the hospital. It was her father, Robert Reid, who had felt it appropriate, indeed necessary, to inform both Chester and his parents by telephone that a baby boy had arrived. The baby—sadly, wanted and welcomed by no one in the extended family he was born into—was named Cameron Stuart Craig Macdonald. He was the spitting image of his father, from the moment of birth. This event pushed Ewan into another round of deep depression, worse than any he had experienced thus far. He was soon needing medications to sleep. On May 1, 1936, Maud wrote in her journal, "If everything was as it should be how glad and interested I would be in the first little grandson. But as it is I feel only bitterness." On May 3, when Ewan was suffering his worst attack since coming to Toronto, she attributed this to the news of the baby.

Maud felt hopelessly dispirited, grieving over Chester's disinterest in his own children and over his failure to take control of his life. He could speak brilliantly on myriad subjects, but he was impulsive, erratic, arrogant, and dishonest—hardly promising qualities for a lawyer. Maud was beginning to wonder if Chester actually had serious mental problems.

But May 1936 brought Maud one huge relief: in spite of his earlier slump, Stuart passed his second-year Medicine courses with flying colours. Chester would not receive his grades for another month. As she waited to hear the results, Maud needed medications to sleep. When the "pass lists" were finally printed in the paper, Chester had failed two of his law courses: Criminal Procedures and Torts. So soon after the birth of his unwanted baby, this news was overwhelming. Chester would have to write "supplementals" in the coming autumn; this meant a summer of worry for Maud.

July 5, 1936, was Maud and Ewan's twenty-fifth wedding anniversary; no one noticed the date except Maud herself. She wrote in her journal: "The greater part of those 25 years has been a nightmare, owing mainly to Ewan's attacks of melancholia, intensified these past six years by Chester's behaviour" (July 5, 1936).

Another terrible blow came to the Macdonalds on the morning of September 13, 1936: Ewan and Maud opened the *Globe* to read that Ernest

Barraclough was dead, reportedly of a stroke. The death was unexpected, and it hit them hard. The Barracloughs had provided an oasis of discreet friendship in Maud's and Ewan's often beleaguered lives. The Macdonalds rushed out to Glen Williams to give Mrs. Barraclough support. But Ida was prostrate with grief and there was little that they could do. Shortly after Ernest's death, Ewan went across the street to see Dr. Lane to renew his prescription for sedatives.

Ewan and Maud continued to visit Ida, hoping to help her recover emotionally. Unfortunately no on could protect Ida from the blows that were coming, one after another. Immediately, hurtful rumours started circulating—the first was that Ernest had committed suicide.[50] Next, some of Ida's relatives gave her the unwelcome information that Ernest had had ongoing "liaisons" with young women in his factory. This was unbearably hurtful, for Ida had idolized her husband. (Luella, who was also distantly related to Ida, said that everyone knew about Ernest's extramarital dalliances during his lifetime, except, perhaps, his wife and the Macdonalds.) In the 1990s, old-timers still remembered and joked that Ernest had been "very fond of the women." After his death, when the Macdonalds heard about his affairs, they found it very hard to deal with the stories. They had seen him as a pillar of the church and above reproach.

Ida had yet another unpleasant surprise coming—it turned out, when the account books were opened, that the mill was in serious financial trouble. Everyone in the community, including the Macdonalds, had believed the Barracloughs to be quite wealthy. Ernest and Ida had lived very well in a big, finely appointed house, and always drove new cars. Even though Ida was excessively corpulent, she always dressed stylishly, and the small, dapper Ernest dressed impeccably, too. Like most husbands of the era, Ernest had handled all the money, telling Ida nothing.

Ida next discovered that her husband's estate left her only enough money to live on modestly, and that his will specified that she would lose even this if she remarried. It is unlikely that she would have remarried in any case, but this stipulation came on top of the allegations that Ernest had been unfaithful to *her*. Ewan and Maud were very shaken by all the after-death revelations, and their visits to cheer the inconsolable Ida became increasingly difficult "duty visits." (She lived some thirty years after the death of Ernest.) Ernest's death provided one more fallen star in their increasingly unstable firmament.

———

Maud had been worrying all summer over whether Chester would pass his supplemental exams. He had wasted three years in Engineering before he was thrown out. Now he had invested three years in law—two in articling and one in coursework—and he might be thrown out again. But on the morning of September 22, Chester informed his relieved mother that he had passed—with a 92 percent in one and a bare pass in the other. This meant he could continue in law school. If he could pass his second year of courses, there would be only one final year, and he could graduate in 1938. Maud felt relief that he had passed, but she also knew that he would have been at the top of his class had he worked hard.

As Maud ended the ninth volume of her journals in September 29, 1936, she sounded the classic depressive note: "I have lost every hope for things ever being better." She added: "Everything I hoped and dreamed and planned for has gone with the wind. I am broken and defeated."

In actual fact, during 1936 her books were selling well, her readership still adored her, movie rights were in the offing, and Stuart was doing well in medical school and making a name for himself as an exceptionally talented gymnast in the University of Toronto's gymnastic team competitions. The critical reputation of her books might have been under attack, but in 1936 she took in $6,093 in book royalties, and so was able to pay off a large part of her mortgage. Objectively, she had much to be thankful for. But all she could see was that Chester was heading towards failure.

She did not know for sure what was going on with Stuart now, either. Stuart had started a friendship with Margaret Cowan soon after their move to Riverside Drive, and Maud did all she could to foster this, thinking that the pretty, vivacious, and cultured Margaret was just the "right kind of girl" for Stuart. Maud had bought Stuart an expensive membership at the local golf club, thinking it an appropriate place for him to socialize with other nice girls from prominent families. Stuart also had ample opportunity to meet lots of young women at the University of Toronto. Although he was very popular, Maud suspected that he still exchanged letters with Joy and sometimes went to Norval to see her. When she had been on the Island that fall, the Webbs of Cavendish had casually referred to Joy as Stuart's "girl," and had spoken of their relationship as a suitable and serious one. That knowledge had all but ruined Maud's otherwise happy vacation.

Then, a few days before his mother's birthday, Stuart had come in after a date with Margaret Cowan and remarked in a significant way to his mother that it was a "good thing" they had left Norval when they did. Maud took this to mean that he had terminated the relationship with Joy. Nothing could have elevated her spirits more.

On her birthday, November 30, 1936, thinking that the romance with Joy was over, Maud spat out all her objections to Joy and the entire Laird family in her journal. Of Joy, she wrote:

> Joy was common and cheap . . . but I would say with a good deal of the quality detestably called sex appeal. . . . Joy was certainly no companion for my son . . . I warned Stuart not to let himself get tangled up with any such people. . . . All these years [his relationship with Joy] has been . . . spoiling what had always been the beautiful relationship between us. The thought that one day he might ask me to accept that bootlegger's spawn as a daughter was something I could not bear . . . (SJ 5 114–15).

These are strong words—and totally unfair, according to people from Norval. When Maud's comments about Joy were published in 2004 (Joy was by then dead), there was a near-collective howl of indignation at this characterization of Joy and her family. The village asserted that the young Joy had been clever, pretty, poised, and full of personality. She was well liked throughout the community. As for her father being a bootlegger, the older residents of Norval said that every community had one or more, especially during Prohibition, and, in fact, many "respectable people regarded bootlegging as a useful business."[51] The rest of the village took Mr. Laird as he was, and admitted he had a drinking problem; every community had a few characters who imbibed too much, but they were not ostracized unless they were destructive or "mean" drunks. When Lewis did go on a binge, his wife banished him out to "the Blue House," a shack on the corner of their property, a cheerful gathering place for men who dropped in to chat or pick up a bottle and talk. The people of Norval—except for Maud—generally liked Joy's father, despite his faults. No one was rich in Norval, and the other local people did not look down on Josie, Joy's mother, as Maud did, for doing paid work outside her home. But once Maud made up her mind about people and their family status, she did not change her views. Nothing would make Joy acceptable to her.

The belief that Stuart had finally ended his romance with Joy unshackled Maud from the paralysis of worry. She had put her journal aside for three

years, from 1933 to 1936, following Chester's marriage. Now she had such a lift
that she resumed writing up her journal at the beginning of December 1936.
She began filling in retrospective entries from the notes she had kept those
three years. Her creative work flew too: by the time the holidays came, she had
only three chapters of *Jane of Lantern Hill* left to write.

But Christmas 1936 was a gloomy one: both boys escaped, leaving her
home alone with dreary Ewan on an even drearier, rainy day. Stuart went next
door to the Cowans for Christmas dinner, and Chester dutifully went to see
Luella and his children in Norval. When Maud and Ewan tucked into their
own roast goose that night, neither of them felt like talking. On December 31,
1936, Maud closed off her journal with the ominous statement that "a certain
thing is making me very sick at heart." She would not write anything again in
her journal for over a year, until January 1938.

When Maud finally took up her pen on January 9, 1938, to write up all of
the missing periods in her journals, she began by recapitulating her most difficult times. She labelled 1919 a "hideous year" (the year of Ewan's first
breakdown); 1933 and 1934 were "horrible beyond expression" (the year of
Chester's "forced" marriage and Ewan's second breakdown); but nothing,
she wrote, had been equal to 1937.

The story that began to unfold in 1937 about Chester — now twenty-two,
married, and a father of two — is glossed over in her own journals. She felt
that she must censor her journals because others would read them when
she was dead, and "some things it would not be good for anyone but myself
to know . . . [I] can never forget them and cannot tell them — to anyone"
(January 9, 1938).

Nor did she write in her journals another story — that of her growing dependence on sedatives to cope with mounting anxieties. Throughout her journals, Maud mentions from time to time the medications that doctors gave
either her or Ewan to calm them or to help them sleep, but these accounts are
only incidental.

As 1937 opened, Maud, a determined professional, was still trying to write
the ending of *Jane of Lantern Hill*. The book had to end happily, even though
she was so wracked with apprehension over Chester that she could hardly
concentrate. Chester was now taking the second year of his three years of law,
but he was not studying. Nor did he seem to be going into the firm to work

part-time, as required. She suspected the worst—that Chester was seeking female companionship outside his marriage.

Maud partially blamed herself for this turn of events. Understanding the value of social networking, especially for a young law student, she had thought Chester could meet more young people through the church. The Victoria-Royce Presbyterian Church Young People's Society seemed a prime place to meet future community leaders. She had urged Chester to join the YPS, and he'd taken her advice. But instead of the YPS being a place where he could network with the "right kind of friends," it became a venue to recruit new girlfriends.

Her relationship with Chester had become very complicated, and this was another reason why she wanted him to find more friends his own age. Since he had moved back home after his parents took up residence in Toronto, Maud and Chester had each been filling a void in the other's life. They were both lonely, each cut off from the normal intellectual companionship and emotional support one might expect from a spouse. Chester had never been one to establish lasting friendships, and he played no sports, so he had more time to spend with his mother than Stuart did. (Stuart was always out of the house attending classes, practising with the University of Toronto gymnastics team, or socializing with friends, and when he came home, he ate and then went to his room to study.) Chester was always willing to drive his mother around, to accompany her to films, or to escort her to events, instead of studying. He was an insatiable reader—of everything except his law textbooks—and his mother loved discussing books with him. Maud valued his intellectual companionship, at home, walking to movies together, going for sodas at the local drugstore, or taking drives.

Initially a churlish "loner" who lacked social graces, Chester was learning from his mother how to "talk well" on many subjects outside of law. He was developing the ability to sail into a social gathering and make a very good impression with his fluent and informed conversation. Maud undoubtedly saw the "talking time" they spent together as grooming her son for success. He was a quick study.

In adolescence, Chester had smarted because he'd thought that Stuart was his mother's favourite, but finally he had begun to feel like the "number one" son.[52] Perhaps she found in Chester a younger and more intellectual version of Ewan, and she began to dote on her elder son in a way that often made others feel profoundly uncomfortable. Years later, people from Norval remembered how Chester made big public displays of affection to his mother—long after Stuart, three years younger, had quit kissing her in public. In Toronto, Chester bestowed courtly public kisses on his mother, opened doors for her with the flourish of a royal footman, and generally played the role of the adoring and attentive son. In Toronto, Chester kissed Maud often and told her what a "good little mother" she was. To many, Maud appeared quite besotted with him. Some thought Chester's kisses and hugs for his mother seemed more for effect than genuine, but this was probably unfair: like everyone else, he undoubtedly *did* enjoy his mother's company and attention.

Maids remembered how Chester would come into his parents' bedroom when his mother was resting and lie down on the bed beside her to talk, sometimes putting his head on her shoulder. She would pat him or sometimes run her fingers through his hair—in their view, an odd intimacy for a mother and a grown, married son.[53] As Chester became Maud's constant companion and chauffeur, Ewan receded further into the background. Now, in early 1937, with new social skills and confidence under his belt, Chester was ready for a new social life, involving very late hours and the family car. His hyper-excited mood alarmed his watchful mother.

A sense of entitlement had taken hold and flowered in Chester during the final years they lived in Norval. He gloried in his mother's worldwide fame and made sure that everyone knew he was her son. His developing elitist attitude was probably in part the result of his upbringing: his mother's own sense of having come from two superior clans on the Island, and her glorification of all things Scottish. In the Norval and early Toronto days, Luella recalled how Maud, at the dinner table, often launched into romancing Sir Walter Scott and his works, filled as they were with the glamour of the "auld countree" and with noble characters who had a strong "sense of honour."

When Maud talked about the old world and its values and romance, Luella, maids, and other visitors remembered how Ewan would look into the middle-distance, with an unhappy expression on his face. As someone who read very little, Ewan was largely excluded; and also, he knew his own family's life in old Scotland had been very difficult. His tales would have been the stories of peasant Highlander relatives leaving Scotland in order to avoid a miserable life (or death) through near starvation. He had the wrong narrative of the Scottish past, so he kept quiet.

Without a counter-narrative, Chester seems to have bought it all. He had spent much of his life as an unhappy misfit in his own world. It would therefore have been very easy—and appealing—to become drawn into his mother's ide-alized world of chivalric old Scotland. Chester's most-quoted saying from this period was remembered with distaste by many: "There are two kinds of peo-ple in the world—those who are Scots, and those who wish they were." He was not out of sync with many other citizens of Swansea (and other areas): in this era, the Scots did often feel superior to those of other ethnic descent—especially to Poles, Jews, and Chinese, and, to a lesser extent, the Irish and even the English. The social, religious, and ethnic prejudices that held in Swansea, appalling as they may seem today, were typical for that time. However, few would have advertised their perceived sense of superiority as Chester did.

Predictably, the relationship between Ewan and Chester deteriorated even further. The atmosphere between them was heavy and tense, and sometimes the tension sparked sharp words. Ewan had struggled hard for his education and professional standing in the ministry, and he was profoundly upset by Chester's failure to apply himself when given good opportunities. Ewan con-tinued to brood on the public humiliation that Chester had brought on them. People remembered that after Chester and Luella's marriage Maud could cover her upset, but Ewan was openly devastated.

Both Ewan and Maud knew that former parishioners in Norval felt that Luella was being treated shabbily. The facts spoke for themselves: Maud had set the young couple up in an apartment in Toronto, in January 1934. After less than six months of living with Chester, Luella packed up and went back to her father, and she stayed there, even after a second baby came. Both Ewan and Maud cared a great deal about how they were regarded and remembered in Norval. If Chester had shown some remorse for the shame he'd brought on his parents, it would have helped, but instead, Chester's response was to resent his wife and family.

There is no question that Chester had a genuine admiration for his mother. But Chester also knew that she was the one with the car and the money, and that she made all the real decisions. As long as Chester went for one obligatory visit to Luella and his children every month, and drove his mother wherever she wanted to go, he was given unrestricted use of the car. He would claim that he needed it to deliver writs or legal documents for Mr. Bogart's office, and then simply disappear for long and unaccounted-for periods of time.

Ewan was charitable, not judgmental like Maud. But he was no fool, and he saw an irresponsible and self-indulgent son. Both Maud and Ewan began to suspect—rightly—that the family car was being used to troll for women, among other things. Maud thought ruefully of Mr. Bogart's earlier comment that it was a good thing he would be living at home so she could "keep an eye" on him. There was nothing she could do. And more sadness was around the bend.

On January 18, 1937, after only a short illness, Maud's beloved cat "Good Luck" suddenly died, and this temporarily upstaged Chester in his mother's grief index. Little has been said in this biography of Maud's loves for her cats, but her journals are full of accounts of them, with their pictures, and in one of her scrapbooks she even saved their fur. Maud's favourite cat of all time was "Good Luck," or "Lucky," as he was fondly called. He had been a fixture in her life since he was shipped from Alec and May Macneill's Cavendish farm in 1923. He was a connection to the Island, and he had been her most constant companion and comfort over the years.

Maud needed this beloved little pet in her life. He was a loyal and affectionate fellow who sat by his mistress and watched her when she wrote. He purred contentment when she was reading. He curled up with her and slept on her bed. He waited patiently for her when she was out, and greeted her on her return. He was miserable when she went away and remained disconsolate until she returned. When she was distressed, he became even more affectionate. Maud was a woman of many moods, and Lucky responded to all these moods with constant solicitous affection—a trait quite rare for a cat.[54]

Lucky's death was sudden, the result of liver cancer. Bereft, Maud laid him out downstairs on a pile of newspapers inside the front door. For almost a day, she was too distraught to arrange any sort of burial. Ewan, Chester, and Stuart, who always expected Maud to sort out problems, were no help. Finally, Maud called on Mr. Fry, the builder, who brought a shovel and dug a grave. Lucky was wrapped in a shroud and buried in the backyard.

Maud's loving portrait of this affectionate cat in her journals must be a tour de force in the annals of pet obituaries: in her journal entry of January 9, 1938, she writes nearly forty handwritten pages on his endearing qualities. Portions of her description almost eroticize her affection for him:

> He lay there, his tiny flanks heaving up and down under my fingers and his little body vibrating with his rapturous purrs. . . . After Luck

came to me I never cared for another cat. Cats before him I loved
as *cats*. I loved Luck as a human being. And few human beings
have given me the happiness he gave me.

The loss of this beloved cat was devastating. Maud had gone through life
feeling deserted and disappointed. All the men in her life had essentially failed
her, whether through failure to love and value her as a child, to help her get
an education as a young woman, to take her seriously as a writer when she became a best-selling author, to share her joy in accomplishment, or to offer intellectual companionship. Her two grandfathers had failed her, as had her
uncles and father. Deprived of a parent's unconditional love and support, she
had spent her entire life longing for her father's love (since he seemed more
real to her than her mother, whom she could not remember). Her books are
all about young people who want a home and loving parents—and who suffer fear and loneliness until they find them. These were her deepest levels of
longing. She had hoped for real companionship with Ewan, but despite his
well-meaning intent, he could not offer that. She wanted to feel proud of her
sons, but Chester was turning out to be a spectacular disappointment. She
longed for someone responsive to her moods, as well as someone who could
share in the pleasures she felt in her triumphs, her celebrity, success, her enthusiasms. Incredibly, this simple cat had become her most reliable partner in
life, giving her more emotional support than the men in her life ever had.
Losing a loved pet is hard on most people, but Maud's psychological state was
pitifully rendered in her reaction to his death.

Then, on January 19, the day that Lucky was buried, Maud's maid, Ethel
Dennis, gave notice that she would be leaving in March to marry her fiancé,
Gordon Currie. Her youth and naïveté had prevented her from being the intellectual companion that both Mrs. Mason and Mrs. Thompson had been,
but she was reliable, honest, and respectable. Her departure meant that Maud
would have the trouble of finding and training a new maid. This was another
blow.

Maud had heard that her previous maid, Faye Thompson, had not found
another permanent job after leaving them; Maud contacted her to ask if she
would consider returning. Maud had liked Mrs. Thompson—her sense of
humour, her quick wit, her competency in all she did—and she hoped that
she would come back. If she did, Maud would not have to train her. Maud
had been very fond, too, of Mrs. Thompson's sweet and well-behaved little

daughter, June, now seven. The local schools were good, which would be a drawing card. Mrs. Thompson agreed to return.

The next day Maud's worst fears came to pass: on January 20, 1937, she found that Chester had failed one law course (Practice) outright and managed only a bare pass—50 percent—in each of the other three. Her frustration was overwhelming. He seemed to be in a period of unfocused emotional upsurge, heading towards self-destruction.

Numb with frustration and disappointment, Maud again needed medication to sleep. The anniversary of Frede's death, January 25, was always a difficult time for her, but now Maud kept recalling how Frede had adored Chester when he was a baby. When Maud tried to finish the first draft of *Jane of Lantern Hill* on January 27, she found that she simply could not write. How could she write a happy ending to this little waif's search for loving parents and a joyous home? On January 28, she went to a Canadian Authors Association meeting. Her escape, as always, refreshed her. But then she writes a heartbroken entry, notable for its evasiveness.

> There is no entry in my notebook for Friday, January 29. On that day all happiness departed from my life forever. I was sitting at my breakfast, planning out the day's work when the blow fell. It cannot be written or told—that unspeakable horror. Oh God, can I ever forget that day? Not in eternity . . .

The journal gives no further explanation. A little later, she laments that she tried to teach her boys the right values, and she notes that Stuart is a "good boy" (February 8, 1937). We don't know what she learned on January 29, but it seems to have been about Chester.

On January 30, there is another burst of anguish in the journals. She asks God how he could have "let this happen." She fears she is going "mad." She mentions in passing that she takes the drug Medinal to sleep. A few days later she makes a passing reference to taking Veronal to sleep. All these sketchy entries are written from notes and memory much later, hitting only high points of a terrible year. They are not intended as an exact record of events, but should rather be seen as an account of her dominant feelings, thoughts, and emotions at the time.

Maud had begun to feel increasingly anxious over her own mental health. The spectre of mental breakdown sent her to more medications, but there is no indication—in her journals or in other people's memory—that she (or her doctor) had any idea what a dangerous path she was following. On January 31, she wrote that she wished she could only die. "People talk about the bitterness of death. It is not to be compared to the bitterness of life. Bitterness like some gnawing incurable disease . . ."

Then, a few days later, on February 2, Maud learned that Nora's husband, Ned Campbell, had died. Maud, who was only slightly older than Ned, had known him when she taught in the Belmont School. In her distraught state, she went to comfort Nora. Perhaps Nora's loss helped put her own troubles in perspective. She came home, and steeled herself to finish *Jane of Lantern Hill* the next day, managing to do so through sheer grit. She would dedicate this book "To the memory of Lucky."

Jane of Lantern Hill (1937)

This novel depicts Toronto as a miserable place, standing in direct contrast to the magical Prince Edward Island. Jane Stuart is a young girl living with her pretty but weak-willed mother in Toronto; both are under the thumb of a manipulative, controlling, and powerful grandmother, Mrs. Kennedy. The characterization is powerful and the misery palpable.

Jane's young mother had married her father impulsively during a vacation trip to the Island. Although he was a war veteran, Andrew Stuart did not suit his imperious mother-in-law who wanted her daughter to marry into a wealthy, prominent family. Nor did Mrs. Kennedy like the fact that her new son-in-law was a writer. She meddled, and the marriage disintegrated, and baby Jane and her mother returned to Toronto to live with Mrs. Kennedy. The novel opens with Jane living unhappily in the stately but soulless Toronto mansion, the victim of her grandmother's hostility and her ineffectual mother's failure to protect her only child.

One day Jane learns from a mean-spirited schoolmate that the father she had believed to be dead is actually alive, living in Prince Edward Island. Soon a letter arrives from him, demanding that her mother and grandmother send her for a summer with him. Jane does not want to go. But when she is forced to go, she finds that the Island is a magic place full of happiness and soul-healing qualities, in contrast to the soul-pinching Toronto, a place of vicious gossip and empty lives. At the end of the novel, she is instrumental in bringing her parents together again on Island soil.

The parallels with Maud's own life are obvious. Maud herself believed in the Island's remarkable restorative powers, particularly with respect to her own complicated life in Toronto. She also knew that she was herself partly trapped in Toronto by her own ambitions. Furthermore, Jane's grandmother bears uncanny similarities to the woman Maud could sometimes be: a mother who meddled in her children's romantic affairs, who tried to break up relationships she considered unsuitable, and who had fierce ambitions for her offspring. Maud no doubt saw this same behaviour in Mrs. Cowan and countless other aspiring mothers in her social milieu. At the same time, Mrs. Kennedy provides what a psychiatrist might call an extraordinary hate-portrait of Maud written by herself. The novel is resolved with a happy ending when Jane's mother and father are reunited on the Island, to live happily ever after. Jane finds the redemption in life that Maud herself had not. Maud had always wanted her father, but Jane finds both father and mother.

Meanwhile, in the real Toronto home on Riverside Drive, Ethel Dennis had given notice in January of her intention to leave, but she stayed on for several months until her replacement came. Maud's long-time practice was to thoroughly clean one room in the house each month, instead of doing everything in a massive spring cleaning. She always helped her maids with this. Towards the end of Ethel's tenure in the Macdonald house, she and Maud cleaned Chester's room together. Chester's personal diary was lying out, open, where he had left it in his usual sloppy and careless manner. Maud stopped working and read it. Ethel observed that Maud was profoundly upset by what she read.[55]

Ethel Dennis was the least judgmental of all Maud's maids, but she had come to detest Chester. In her view, he was a full-blown problem. "*He* never settled down," she said, "and he *lied*." Ethel was disgusted with the way he treated Luella and his children, and she knew, as Stuart also did, that Chester often claimed to be using the car to go see his family in Norval when he was doing other things. Maud often talked over the problem of Chester with Stuart, and was so preoccupied with Chester that she gave Stuart little positive attention for his own accomplishments—her attention was always on the wayward son.

"She wasn't the type to tell her troubles," Ethel observed, and since Ethel had her own life, she hadn't been interested in what Maud read in Chester's journal, but she remembered Maud's reaction. Ethel disliked Chester's attitude — that since his mother paid her hired help there was no reason for *him* to show consideration to a *servant*. Ethel said she worked hard to wash (with a non-electric hand-paddle washer), starch (by dipping in a solution of cooked-up starch), and iron (heating it on the stove) to keep the Macdonalds' clothes nice — no small feat before permanent-press and wrinkle-resistant fabrics were developed. Chester would throw his clothes on the floor. Ethel would tidy his room, only to find it a dump again. She said that he "didn't talk much" and "wasn't sociable."

Ethel remembered how Chester would lie in the basement recreation room on his back on a sofa, reading novels instead of studying. When he came to the main floor, he upset his father constantly, actively picking fights with him. Stuart simply "ducked out" whenever Chester tried to start arguments with him. Ethel recalled that towards the end of her stay, the Macdonald household was increasingly tense. She said that the Macdonalds read at the table rather than talking to each other — a sign of increasingly unhappy family dynamics. Ethel left, relieved to move on to a new life, in March 1937.[56]

Whatever Maud learned from Chester's diary seems to have forced her to see him in a new light. On that fateful morning when (as she described it later) her world "fell apart," Maud may have confronted Chester with what she had learned from his diary. Or there might have been a call from someone (like the minister at the church), or she simply may have laid a trap for Chester. On February 11, she wrote, without giving specific information, "And to think that the one who has brought me to this was once the little boy I loved so dearly . . ."

But, always able to carry on publicly, on February 12 Maud spoke at the Humber Valley Bird Club. Two days later, she travelled by train to speak at Beaverton, Ontario. The Beaverton newspaper described her as "pleasing and unassuming," giving a talk that was at once "interesting" and "humorous."

The contrast between her public life and private turmoil throughout these years is remarkable. But the strain took its toll. Confrontation with Chester's unacceptable behaviour was often followed by descriptions in Maud's journals of nervous misery, even while her public persona remained witty and gay. On February 21, 1937, she wrote:

I *will not* let this crush me. Chester is not worth suffering so for. Old as I am — broken as I am — I shall rise above it and live my own

life—live it gallantly. I shall have recurrences of agony . . . but I
must and will conquer them. . . . I must live a little longer for
Ewan's and Stuart's sakes. Yet death would be so welcome.

After the speech in Beaverton on February 23, 1937, she recorded in her
journal how she hated to return home; the next night she suffered from one
of her "sick headaches" and vomiting. In fact, she described spending an entire month in "dreadful restlessness."

Regardless of his mother's distress, Chester continued to shirk responsibility. He quit visiting his family at all unless Maud pressured him. Sometimes
she ensured that he actually went to Norval by going with him, visiting
Marion Webb Laird while he went to see Luella.

When Chester did not come to Norval, Luella's father insisted that Luella
take the children to Riverside Drive for visits. Luella liked Maud and Ewan,
but she found these visits humiliating. It was clear that Chester did not want
to see them—he left as soon as they arrived and did not return until after they
had gone (something that Ethel remembered well). Maud and Ewan pretended to be glad to see Chester's family but did a poor job of it. Ewan could
not relate to children—even if he had been well, he was not someone who
would pick up and cuddle a child, or sit down on the floor to play with his
grandchildren. Maud did not enjoy the visits either, given her embarrassment
over Chester's behaviour.

Throughout March 1937 Maud went out at least twice—to speak to the
annual banquet of the Withrow Old Girls Association and to be a guest of honour at the Heliconian Club. Her Withrow speech was vintage Montgomery,
and the *Globe*, the *Star*, and the *Telegram* all carried detailed accounts. She
stated that Australia contributed heavily to her fan mail. On one occasion 87
letters had arrived in one mail following an article in an Antipodean newspaper, and within six months she had 750 letters. The speech was amusing in its
detail, and it packed a strong message to detractors about the international and
varied nature of her readership. She continued to use anecdotes to show that
many of her fans were grown men and women.

At the Heliconian Club luncheon on March 23, Maud learned that the
Montreal *Family Herald* had run a contest among its readers to see who was
their "most read author": she wrote that she was at the top with Charles
Dickens, while Marshall Saunders and Leo Tolstoy were tied for second
place.[57] The featured speaker at the Heliconian Club luncheon was William

Arthur Deacon, and his topic was "the function of a critic." The critic's job, he said, was "to give others a basis for discussion, for a clearer understanding of the author." He asserted that the function of a critic was not to judge whether a book was good, but to answer the question, "Do I like it?" He stated that a critic should address whether a book was capable of "satisfying human wants."[58] No doubt Maud sat in the audience thinking that if she was the most read author in Canada according to *The Family Herald*, then her books must satisfy *some* human wants.

Maud was pleased when Mrs. Thompson returned to work as a maid in March 1937, replacing Ethel. Mrs. Thompson's sense of humour would help lighten the tone in the house, her intelligence made her an engaging companion for Maud, and her daughter June would add sunshine. June, now seven and a pretty and cheerful little girl, would go to school in their district. This eased considerable domestic stress in Maud's life, and in turn Maud reduced her use of sedatives.

On March 27, Maud wrote in her journals that she was "released from one of the most dreadful situations a woman could be placed in." She does not explain further. Perhaps she had one of the several sessions with Chester that culminated with his promise—never kept—to give up his duplicitous life. Around this time, Maud also received some unexpected income: Simpson's paid out $4,000 on her investment. This relieved much financial pressure, but of course it did not solve the problem of Chester. By April, Maud was having serious symptoms of stress again: her eyes and head were bothering her, and she again had a bout of vomiting and dysentery. She was obsessing about Chester and his behaviour: his marks for the year would be coming up in June, and she could see that he was not studying. She could not imagine what the future would hold for him if he failed his year.

Maud distracted herself by turning to thoughts of Frede, and copied out in her journals some "ten-year letters" that she and Frede had written each other in 1907 and 1917. Returning to memories of her Cavendish life always brought happy distraction. But this year was special: it was on April 24, 1937, that the Prince Edward Island National Park was officially opened, with the "Green Gables House" as its centrepiece.

In the first week of May, Maud attended the annual dinner of the Toronto branch of the Canadian Women's Press Club. She sat at the head table with

Lady Willison (Marjory MacMurchy) and others. During the same week, she attended a big banquet held by the CAA.

Not mentioned in Maud's journals is another big social event from the first week in May. The Reverend John Mustard, pastor of the Oakwood Presbyterian Church, retired at age seventy. He was much loved by his congregation, and they gave him a splendid retirement party. He had been every bit as successful and beloved during his eight years at Oakwood as he had been previously at the Dufferin Street Church. At Oakwood, the congregation had risen from 118 to 302, and he'd built a new church seating 350 before he retired. (He was even given a new car by one of his churches.) His service in the Toronto Presbytery over a thirty-year period was so exceptional that the University of Toronto awarded him with an honorary doctorate. He was not one to forget old friends, and he had always maintained contact with Maud and Ewan.[59]

Since March, Maud had been trying to plan her next novel, *Anne of Ingleside,* but it was very hard going. She could not settle her mind enough to concentrate. She took the sedatives prescribed by her doctor to relieve her anxiety. Her symptoms intensified in June: according to her journals, after a vivid "hideous" dream, she thought she could bear the pain in her life no longer and would "break down or go crazy." She forced herself to do preparatory planning on *Anne of Ingleside* but complained of feeling "tired," "queer," "weak," "wobbly," with "shooting pains" in her head behind her eyes. She was frightened: "What on earth is the matter with me?" she asked on June 9, 1937.

Ewan was feeling stress too, and he consulted various doctors, coming away with prescriptions for various compounds to relieve his symptoms. His night-table was loaded with medications, and there was a further supply in the bathroom cupboards. He was dosing himself with multiple prescription drugs, and by early June he was "hearing voices" again, as he had in his breakdowns between 1919 and 1924—symptoms that mimicked schizophrenia but may also have been drug-induced. On June 6, Maud describes his state: he lay on his bed with "staring eyes, his hair standing straight up and he talked unceasingly about himself and his symptoms." Maud says she thought she was "hardened to this" but it got on her nerves unbearably.

Finally, the worst news that Maud could have imagined came—on June 15, 1937, Chester received his grades for his year: he had failed in four separate subjects. His year was lost. He would have to take the entire year all over again. More fees . . . more delay in his obtaining a paid position. But

more frightening, the way things were going, was the possibility that he would
be thrown out of law school, just as he had been thrown out of engineering,
after the investment of a huge amount of time and money.

Ewan was so wrapped up in his own symptoms that he seemed unable to
comprehend or care that Chester had failed his year.

The normally pleasant Ewan became irritable at mealtimes, and he
began tying his handkerchief around his head as he had in his 1919 breakdown. He was growing more anxious: he had promised long ago to deliver a
sermon at ceremonies in Leaskdale and Zephyr in the third week of June. He
no longer felt up to the sermon and wanted to cancel, but Maud would not
let him. She thought that if he forced himself to go ahead, it might help him
focus his mind on something other than his symptoms. Plus they would both
enjoy seeing old friends and remembering their happier years there. She
would soon regret this.

On the advice of various doctors Maud and Ewan had tried different medications to alleviate their ailments, problems ranging from difficulty sleeping to more undefined "nervous disorders." Neither the doctors nor the
patients fully understood the effect of the medications prescribed at that
time—or ones available at drug stores. These sedatives, common at that
time, fell into two general categories: bromides and barbiturates. In periods
of stress after Ewan's breakdown in 1919, he intensified his use of these medications. And so, increasingly, did Maud.

Believed to be relatively safe then, the medications they were given in the
1920s and 1930s are now known to have been both dangerous and habit-
forming. Taken over time and in unregulated and increasing doses, these have
the potential to cause havoc. Barbiturates are addictive, and bromides are
poisonous.

Ewan and Maud's original problems—depression, in Ewan's case, and
anxiety and mood swings with Maud—were greatly worsened by the very sedatives prescribed to help them. These medications could easily have been what
tipped Ewan from his initial "melancholia" (depression) into severe mental
disorder, with psychotic episodes. Likewise, when Maud was distressed by
Ewan's symptoms and driven by her own anxieties, the medications she was
given created dependencies that brought on new and terrifying symptoms;
these symptoms, it now appears, pushed her towards even deeper problems.

Maud and Ewan were not the only victims of these particular medications; for nearly five decades in the twentieth century they were prescribed to millions of people with "nervous" symptoms. We see many descriptions of the mental problems caused by barbiturates and bromides in literature. Earlier in the century, there are many references in novels to "Veronal," a substance taken by both Maud and Ewan. Veronal is believed to have been the drug that Virginia Woolf was using before her suicide. Evelyn Waugh's 1957 novel *The Ordeal of Gordon Pinfold* details his own bromide psychosis.

Bromides and barbiturates are completely different classes of medications, but they are both central nervous system depressants. Both were discovered in the nineteenth century, and by the 1930s and 1940s they were widely used as general sedatives, taken for a host of medical and minor nervous problems ranging from headaches, aching muscles, and insomnia to general anxiety. In fact, in 1938, bromide compounds were outsold only by aspirin in North America.[60] Bromides became a panacea for almost every ailment that could not be treated in other ways (hence the common expression, which could be anything from a joke to a dismissive statement: "Oh, go take a bromide!").

Bromides are not addictive, but they are very dangerous. Substantial doses taken over a period of time build up slowly in the body because the kidneys cannot excrete them fast enough. This results in "bromide poisoning," later called "bromism." The symptoms of bromism can be psychiatric, cognitive, neurological, and even dermatological. Common manifestations are mental dullness, memory impairment, inability to concentrate, irritability, emotional instability, uninhibited behaviour, headaches, decreased visual acuity, slurred speech, lack of muscular control (shaking hands, tremors, unusual gaits), skin rashes, and a transitory state resembling paranoid schizophrenia, with auditory and visual hallucinations, phobias, paranoia, and sometimes violent behaviour, particularly at night. The effect of bromide poisoning on people subject to depressive episodes was to increase and intensify the depression—tragically, the very symptom bromides were often prescribed to alleviate. In large enough doses, bromides could even be fatal.

When Ewan suffered his first sustained depressive episode during the Leaskdale years (1919), he was treated with bromides and Chloral. This was not necessarily the first time he took bromides, but it is the first time Maud records them in her journals. Chloral is a sedative that can create dependency and cause liver damage. Following his treatment, he grew worse and was finally unable to preach. When he became irrational, psychotic, and suicidal, the doctors diagnosed his problem first as a "nervous breakdown" and then as a form of "insanity." Maud accepted this diagnosis; she regarded all his subsequent episodes of mental instability as mental illness.

Ewan actually manifested many of the now-identified symptoms of bromide poisoning in 1919, then again in 1934 and 1937, the three dates of his most severe "mental breakdowns," according to Maud's journals. A tallying of the references to medications he was given (or took) in these years shows that his breakdowns coincided with his heavy use of medications. Although no firm diagnosis is possible at this remove, it does seem likely that Ewan's condition started as simple depression, but that he was medicated into something far worse.

Doctors now believe that many people admitted to psychiatric hospitals between 1930 and 1950 may in fact have been suffering from bromide poisoning rather than real mental illness. Bromide poisoning caused disturbances that mimicked other psychiatric ailments like schizophrenia. And the treatment for these mental problems, unfortunately, was usually more bromides. Tests for bromide poisoning were being devised in the early 1940s, but it took another thirty years for the dangers of bromides to be fully identified and to reach the general medical community and public. Not until the mid-1970s were bromide compounds (like the widely advertised "Bromo-Seltzer" and "Miles Nervine") that could be obtained without prescription taken off the market.[61]

In the days before electronic medical records, people suffering as Ewan did could visit many different doctors in search of an accurate diagnosis and the appropriate treatment. It was not hard to amass, as Ewan did, a collection of these medications, which went by a range of brand names. Patients would combine them, unaware that they were using excessive amounts of the same compound.[62]

Barbiturates were the second class of drugs that Ewan was regularly given for his depression. These medications, also a nineteenth-century discovery, were prescribed freely throughout the early twentieth century as sedatives. Maud had been given her first prescription for barbiturates as early as 1904 when still in Prince Edward Island. The doctor who prescribed it for her prudently warned her against overusing it, but the full dangers were still unknown. Maud and Ewan were given a whole range of barbiturates over their lifetimes, especially following Ewan's 1919 breakdown: Veronal, Barbital, Luminal, Medinal, and Nembutal. They did not realize they were all related, and that combining them was dangerous.[63]

Barbiturates are habit-forming. Users can easily become dependent, both physically and psychologically, requiring increasing doses to achieve the same effect. Growing dependence causes secondary withdrawal problems; severe withdrawal can even lead to death. Withdrawal symptoms can be relieved, of course, by taking more of the drug (or alcohol).

Symptoms of barbiturate withdrawal include irritability, anxiety, rapid mood swings, mental confusion, hallucinations, slurred speech, elevated heart rate, slowed respiration, tremors, and agitation—similar to a response to bromides. All of these were symptoms that Ewan exhibited. Maud often remarked on her inability to comprehend the speed with which he shifted between "crazy" and "normal," but if his problems were drug-enhanced, this would be completely understandable. Dependency on barbiturates often results in sleeping difficulties and increased mood disturbances, especially depression; no surprise that Maud's journals are full of descriptions of these symptoms.

Barbiturates depress normal rapid-eye-movement (REM) sleep, so dependence on them can also produce particularly vivid dreaming, another symptom described by Maud and Ewan. In June 1936, for instance, Maud described an extremely intense dream, almost a hallucination, in which a young girl with red hair walked around the folding screen in their bedroom. Ewan assured her it was only a dream, but the intensity of the image stayed with Maud for some time.

On September 20, 1936, Maud wrote of Ewan's treatment: "Lane, of course, prescribed bromides. There is nothing else for it but they are not good for Ewan in other ways. Medicine will not help an obsessed mind." She seemed to sense on an intuitive level that the treatments might be a problem, but she was not sufficiently convinced to stop them.

Maud's journals chronicle Ewan's mental instability in pathetic and depressing detail. But she had her own problems, too, which undoubtedly originated in her volatile temperament, cycling as it did between flights of imagination and depths of despair. The stress of living with Ewan's mental instability (whatever its cause) took a great toll. Chester's erratic and self-destructive behaviour also caused much greater anxiety in her later years. She was alarmed further by her declining critical reputation in the Toronto book world. She was anxious by nature, but this would have been greatly intensified by the continuing use of barbiturates and bromides.

Maud kept careful note of her symptoms and those of Ewan, but neither she nor Ewan understood that bromides, barbiturates, and alcohol should not be taken together. Sometimes, when Ewan was feeling depressed, Maud would give him a dose of prescribed barbiturates. If it did not take effect, she would give him another dose. If that didn't work, she might try a bromide, or a shot of brandy. Eventually, these multiple doses would tamp him down. Sometimes he would afterwards lie in bed in a stupor for a full day or more. They had no understanding of the toxic relationship between the medication and the perceived disease.

And Ewan also medicated himself when he felt he needed relief; often people who develop a greater and greater tolerance to barbiturates may forget that they have already dosed themselves. They will take another dose, a phenomenon common enough to have its own name ("automatism"). He probably did this without Maud's knowledge.

It appears that the combined effects of increasing amounts of prescribed bromides and barbiturates, in addition to the gulps of the alcohol-laced cough syrup Ewan carried in his pockets, plus the medicinal brandy or homemade wine that Maud sometimes administered, had a cumulative and seriously damaging effect.[64] As early as March 1924, Maud had suspected liver problems in Ewan, and in 1938, he was diagnosed with an "enlarged" liver. The heavy doses of medications he was taking may very plausibly explain the zombie-like demeanour so often described by Maud in her journals. He was neither an athletic nor an energetic man—his temperament was naturally phlegmatic and easygoing until he began his depressive brooding—and the sedating effect of medications and cough syrup would have made him even more lethargic.

In Norval, Maud had sometimes given Ewan a drink of her homemade wine to get him going on a Sunday during an attack of "his malady," and she said that the drink enabled him to stumble over to the church and get through his sermon. This takes on a new meaning in light of what we now know about the properties of barbiturates and bromides. A shot of alcohol could have suppressed the withdrawal symptoms he may have been suffering from, giving him a temporary boost.

Likewise, considering Maud's accounts of Ewan's psychotic episodes and threats of suicide during the Norval period in light of his increasing doses of medications, new interpretations become possible. (See, for instance, the Norval entries of March 25, 1924, and September 4, 1934.) Normally a very peaceable, gentle man, Ewan frightened Maud with occasional shows of violent behaviour in the Norval period (see October 10, 1934). She feared he might go fully insane and kill them all. The episode in which he pointed a

real gun at Nora Lefurgey's head in the Norval manse reflects behaviour totally out of character. In the Toronto period, there were other times in which
his "malady" was entirely consistent with the symptoms of bromide poisoning
and/or barbiturate withdrawal (the symptoms are similar, although the biochemical causes are different).[65]

Ewan did not disclose full details about his "nervous problems," such as
phobias and hallucinations, to the doctors he consulted. To the extent that he
remembered these episodes after the fact, he was terribly ashamed over what
he believed were signs of mental illness. So the doctors did not get the full
story, and they prescribed more of the same medications for him.

Maud did record, however, that one doctor in Georgetown had told Ewan
to moderate his use of barbiturates. But Ewan did not—or could not—follow
this advice. Perhaps he did not understand the reasons for it, and possibly he
had become too dependent on the medications to quit. He was a troubled man,
and clearly he hoped the drugs would make him feel better. People in the community put his memory problems and unusual behaviour down to encroach-
ing senility, when in fact many of his worst symptoms were in fact drug-related.

We know from Maud's journals (as well as from Stuart's account in the
1980s) that Ewan self-medicated extensively in his later years. Stuart called his
father a "hypochondriac." We will never know how many of his problems were
genuine mental illness and how many were caused—or intensified—by the
combination of bromides, barbiturates, and alcohol. Today, experts in forensic pharmacology agree on one thing: that the poorly regulated use of both
barbiturates and bromides caused many problems throughout the early twentieth century. In the 1930s, bromides were the drug of choice for anxious patients, and the Macdonalds certainly qualified in that department.

Maud took a break from her writing in the third week of June to accompany
Ewan on the dreaded trip to Leaskdale. Months before, he had promised to
give the sermons for the seventy-fifth anniversary celebrations of the
Leaskdale and Zephyr congregations. He was still fondly remembered—
almost revered—there, and he had wanted to oblige his old friends. His
worry about this coming engagement intensified his search for new doctors
and drug prescriptions, inevitably leading him into deeper trouble.

He grew more and more agitated the week before, and, according to
Maud, he wanted to back out of the engagement. She stood firm in pressuring

him to go, believing that the trip and the adulation would both be restorative. Two nights before leaving, he was too restless to sleep in his own bed, and the next morning he declared he was "dying." To calm him, Maud dosed him up with "sal volatile."[66] He soon stopped claiming that he was dying, but he continued in a very agitated state. Of course there is every likelihood that he'd taken more medicine on his own during the night, thinking it would steady him.

On the drive up to Leaskdale the next day, he was too befuddled to remember the routes he had driven over scores of times. At dinner, his hands had severe tremors. The next morning he tried to read from the sermon Maud had typed, but he was in too addled a state even for this. After he babbled out disconnected remarks for some ten minutes, he sat down in confusion. People were kind; one parishioner comforted Maud by saying that, "It was enough to hear his voice again, no matter what he said" (June 24, 1937). Many parishioners thought he was simply "showing his age." A second service at the church in Zephyr was a repeat performance and equally agonizing for Maud. At a meal, Ewan could not even lift a cup without his hands shaking so much the contents spilled. Maud felt deeply humiliated both for herself and for Ewan in front of old friends and parishioners.

After dinner, the Macdonalds started on the two-hour drive home, but Ewan was still too confused to remember directions. He became furious at Maud for insisting that they take the correct routes. Worse, he was too disoriented to keep the car on the road, and, like a drunk driver, he kept going too far to the right. Finally, late at night, they landed in a ditch, and they had to wait for help to repair a burst tire and move the car back onto the road again. Following this first mishap, Maud wrote in her journal account, she hauled the sal volatile and brandy out of her case and dosed him up. This brought a temporary improvement. But then, as the immediate effect wore off, Ewan became progressively more irrational and angry. They went over in the right-hand ditch again. Finally, when a fog came up in the very early hours of morning, and they could not see the road at all, Maud insisted that they sit out the night on the roadside.

In her account, Ewan "worked himself up into a fury" (June 24, 1937) whenever she spoke to him. She was terrified, fearing complete insanity. (His memory lapses, bad temper, paranoia, and weird behaviour would all fit the symptoms of either a severe withdrawal reaction from barbiturates or from bromide poisoning, or a mixture of drugs.)[67] After considerable trouble, they finally arrived home early the next day. The trip was a disaster, and Maud was never to forget her fright and her humiliation.

At Maud's urgent request, Dr. Lane examined Ewan after their return and diagnosed his problem as "complete nervous prostration." Following doctor's orders, Maud gave Ewan *more* bromide, thinking sedation the right medicine. Ewan grew very weak. From Maud's description of Ewan's weak pulse, his short breath, and his groaning sleep for long periods through the day, it sounds like a near-fatal overdose.[68]

The inexplicable nature of Ewan's malady was wearing her down; Maud's description of her feelings in her journals is very graphic:

> . . . a man saw a fly fall into a shallow ink bottle on his desk. He fished it out and placed it on a sheet of paper to watch scientifi-cally. The fly went to work to groom itself and soon succeeded in cleaning all the ink away. Then he dropped it in again. Again the fly cleaned itself. And again and again that fiend dropped the poor fly back. Again and again the gallant little fly cleaned itself, albeit a little more slowly every time. And at last, after I forget how many immersions it made no further attempt to rid itself of the ink. It lay inert and spiritless, a mere blot of blackness, resigned to die. It would make no more effort.
>
> I felt I was like that fly. (Dated June 24, 1937, but written in ret-rospect.)

Maud was able to function at a high level publicly, even under this kind of stress. On the very same day they arrived home from the nightmare trip to Leaskdale, she left Ewan in Stuart's care and travelled to the Royal York Hotel to deliver a speech to the Canadian Authors' Association convention. (She had missed the opening night's events on June 28 at the King Edward Hotel, but she probably did not mind: Professor Pelham Edgar had been the opening speaker, with Deacon presiding—two of her least favourites.) A picture of Maud taken on this day with Pelham Edgar, Margaret Lawrence, H. A. Kennedy, Leslie Barnard, and Laurence Brownell shows her looking just as composed as the others.

Ewan continued taking the doctor's prescribed medications (bromides and barbiturates). His mental condition grew worse—irrationality, temper out-bursts, even the inability to construct a complete sentence. He developed a wracking cough that kept him awake. Finally, a week later, he developed a rash—what a doctor thirty years later would likely have identified as the telltale skin rash of bromide poisoning. Even Maud herself began to suspect that he had had too many bromides, and she insisted that Dr. Lane quit giving them to Ewan (July 6, 1937).

In three days, Ewan's blood pressure and pulse returned to normal. But whenever he took the barbiturate called Luminal, he began "talking rather foolishly and forgetting words again." Maud reports that he had vivid dreams of "men cutting themselves to death." He was so addled that he could not dress or shave himself. At one point, Maud describes him as looking like "a fiend from the pit—hair bristling, blue underlip hanging down, eyes glaring, face livid" (July 11, 1937). Yet, he would alternate between periods of delusions and then total lucidity, in which he could read and talk normally (perhaps as the drug wore off). Still, following doctor's orders, Maud gave him sporadic doses of Luminal, but she did fully stop the bromides.

As fewer doses were needed, Ewan predictably improved; by the end of July, he was able to drive again. His cough improved, requiring less medication. His "jolly smile" returned. Maud says that he became "thoughtful and affectionate" again, and on August 4, he told Maud fondly that he could see her "as I saw you on our wedding day." He returned to his lawn bowling clubs and to taking long walks. By the second week of August, he was well enough to go for a visit to the Island for a month. His sisters adored him, and their kindly attentions always made him feel better.

The episode of this illness had taken a great toll on Maud's own nerves, but she was quick to recover. As soon as Ewan had departed on vacation, she perked up, went to a movie, did her work, and enjoyed her freedom. She had time to read, and on August 15, 1937, she writes that she turned to one of her favourite biographies, Clement Shorter's life of Charlotte Brontë, a writer she admired greatly. News reached her, too, that a play by Mildred Barker based on The Blue Castle would be produced in Hollywood. Soon she stated in her journals that she missed Ewan—the cheery Ewan with the jolly smile, the man she had married. Such a statement reminds us that there was another side to the Ewan so often depicted in her journals as a mentally unstable liability.

During all of Maud's disappointment with Chester, Stuart had remained a bright spot in her life. She was pleased that he was still dating Margaret

Cowan next door. However, in the first week of July, Mrs. Cowan broadsided Maud with an astonishing demand—that the two of them should try to break up Stuart's and Margaret's romance. Maud was deeply offended and hurt: she regarded the handsome and witty Stuart as a "good catch" for any young woman. He was by now a very promising medical student and a university athlete of much acclaim. Maud wrote in her journals that Mrs. Cowan said, rather disingenuously, that it was because "Margaret was so fickle," but she believed the request reflected Mrs. Cowan's wish for her daughters to "marry money"; Stuart was not rich enough to suit her.

Quite possibly Mrs. Cowan's real concern was over her daughter marrying into such a troubled family. Out of Maud's hearing, Mrs. Cowan apparently referred to the Macdonalds' home as the "crazy house"—an ungracious term, given that she had often used Maud as a drawing card when she entertained at her formal teas. When Maud experienced Mrs. Cowan's desire to break up the young romance as another attack on her status; she failed to see the irony that Mrs. Cowan's prejudice against the Macdonald family was similar to her own prejudice against Joy Laird's family.

Although Maud continued to socialize with Mrs. Cowan, she was very hurt and angry. She had lived for years with her own lingering baggage from childhood—that although she came from a "good family," she herself did not quite measure up, and perhaps her children would not measure up, either. And worse, the perceived attack was on what she now called her "good" son, not on Chester.

It was in August 1937 that Maud confirmed for herself that Chester was having an affair with a young woman named Ida Birrell. She felt the terrible irony of having encouraged Chester's involvement with the Young People's Society in the first place, for it was under the umbrella of this church organization that he had met Ida. Ida lived at 204 Quebec Avenue, a reasonable walking distance away and easy by car, so it was simple for Chester to slip out to see her.

Maud finally accosted Chester, eliciting from him a promise to break off the romance. On August 25, she describes writing a "certain letter"—perhaps to Ida—and showing it to Chester before mailing it. To her, Chester's behaviour was a dishonour to their family name. Divorce at that time was still a terrible scandal, but conducting an extramarital affair was even worse.

It is hard for our society to understand the anxiety and shame that Maud's era felt over sexual dalliance, adultery, and divorce. These "sins" were scandalous even in Hollywood then, where public disapproval could be felt at the box office. Maud's generation remembered all too well the scandal, for instance, over the 1919 silent movie version of *Anne of Green Gables*, which was well received across North America on its release. But then William Desmond Taylor (1872–1922), the movie's married and middle-aged director, was found murdered, and compromising letters from the actress who played Anne, Mary Miles Minter, as well as her monogrammed underwear, were reportedly found in his room. Mary Miles Minter herself was not suspected of the murder (though her mother, angry at her daughter's "seduction," was under some suspicion). But the public was so shocked at the immorality of a starlet—especially one who was known as "Anne of Green Gables"—having an affair with an older, married man that the film was withdrawn and all copies were said to be destroyed. No known intact copy has survived.[69]

Mary Miles Minter had been a highly paid star with many pictures to her credit when the scandal occurred. Her immense box-office appeal had made her a rival of Mary Pickford, an equally popular silent-film star. But this scandal ended Minter's movie career. Her Hollywood producers dropped her immediately, even though she was still under contract for additional pictures. She was apparently considered too "tainted" even for parts in westerns.

Chester's extramarital affair filled Maud with shame and fear. She knew it could become the talk of the women's afternoon teas in Toronto society, and the gossip would also travel to the Island. Having her own professional status under attack was one thing, but to have her family name besmirched would be more than she could bear. She thought, quite rightly, that it would even affect Stuart's career.

With nerves already frayed, in August 1937 Maud began to increase her doses of barbiturates. She wrote in her journal that she did not like taking them, but claimed they were necessary. An anguished entry about Chester in her journal concludes, "And it is my curse that I can't help loving you . . . my bonny little first born who has changed so much" (August 23, 1937). On September 6, she learned—to no great surprise—that Chester was still seeing Ida, despite his promise to break off the affair.

Hoping a brief change of scene would reorient Chester to respectability, cooling his ardour for Ida, she arranged for him to drive her and Ewan to Cleveland, Ohio, on the third weekend in September. They would visit Ewan's niece, who was married to a medical doctor named Michael Oman. In Cleveland, Chester impressed everyone with his "brilliant" talk. Maud was proud, but despaired because he would not focus on his legal studies.

Little surprise that this trip did not achieve her goal. Chester was in the "grip of one of those infatuations which will make a man do anything," as Maud had put it earlier on August 23, 1937. He was in that over-stimulated emotional high, with its accompanying feeling of well-being, that is unleashed by new sexual affairs, especially where danger and "the forbidden" fan the flames of passion. He was beginning his second year in the study of law *again*, but he suddenly was rushing off in all directions but towards the study of law.

Chester had become involved in the Victoria-Royce Young People's Society's dramatic program back in 1936. According to the church archives, one of the highlights of their 1937 program, performed on October 5, 1937, was a piece in which "Barrister Chester Macdonald argues, far, far into the night with J. Elmo Ewing, as Lionel Marrymore, in a Breech of Promise suit."[70] Chester's verbal pyrotechnics, on dazzling display, must have made him look like one of the most promising young lawyers in the area, and quite likely had an electrifying effect on the young women attending the performance (who did not know he was married). Maud does not mention this performance in her journals. She only says on September 4 that she had encouraged his joining the YPS, and his affair was the result. Chester was indeed riding the wind, and as a biblical proverb has it, he would reap the whirlwind.

Chester's feverish social life was of course affecting his performance at work. Mr. Bogart became enraged with Chester's unreliability and inattention to his work. On October 14, he wrote to the Macdonalds informing them that Chester was fired. This was the second time that Chester had been dismissed by Mr. Bogart. Maud rushed down and humbled herself to plead for another chance, as she had before; Bogart reluctantly granted it. There was no dispute that Chester was exceptionally good at law when he applied himself.

Four days later, Maud complained that Chester was "grim" all the time and his "resentment" hung "like an icy cloud between us." By October 29, Chester was "sulky" and "ugly." The next day, when he drove her to grocery shop at Loblaws, he was silent and glowering. On November 14, in church, Maud saw Chester's new love, Ida Birrell, for the first time. She wept for the rest of the evening at home: "It is so dreadful to find yourself wishing your son had never been born. And I was so happy when he was!" (November 14, 1937).

———

Earlier in the autumn, when Maud was rereading her journals, she became obsessed with a line she had written back in 1897: "Some lives seem to be more essentially tragic than others and I fear mine is one of such" (October 13, 1937). Obsessive negative thoughts are often a feature of depression. Maud knew she was stuck in a mind-set, but still could not shake these "fixed ideas." They became an overwhelming enemy now, not just the annoying "gnats" of earlier years. She continued taking medications to quell her depression, but predictably she only grew more despondent.

In her depressed state, her mind circled like a broken record. She had promoted the courtship of Marion Webb and Murray Laird. Their first little baby, born in 1935, had never looked normal to Maud; now, they confirmed that the child had Down's Syndrome (and in those days would have been called "mongoloid"). This brought back the obsession: "It goes to prove—though I need no further proof—that I am under some curse and always have been. No one I love or am loved by has been fortunate or happy. No matter what I do to help anybody, though from the best and purest motives, it turns out accursed" (June 11, 1937). She knew she was being morbid but could not snap herself out of it.

But while Maud was recording such distress in her journals, once again the public record of her life at this time reveals a very different side. Maud's calendar shows she remained professionally active all throughout the fall: September 22, a CAA executive meeting; October 5, a speech at the Centennial United Church; October 8, an open meeting of the CAA; October 18, another CAA executive meeting (she reports arguments over the forthcoming Book Week program in November); October 19, a tea at Knox College of the University of Toronto (her journal describes the misery of hearing other women brag about their successful sons); it was another tea on October 26. Her journals record that on October 28 she finished planning *Anne of Ingleside*. Back to the outside world: November 6, to Orillia to speak to the Young People's Society; November 8, a PEN luncheon given in honour of Mr. Priestley, the well-known English author imported for Canadian Book Week, then went to the Book Fair to hear Nellie McClung and Katherine Hale speak.

On November 10, Maud did her own turn at the Toronto Book Fair. The November Book Fair was the kind of event that she loved. But the day before her speech, her former PEI fiancé Ed Simpson visited, possibly to show off his new bride, a woman twenty years younger than Ed. An astonished and irritated Maud had to admit that the new wife was surprisingly pretty and charming, in addition to being young. (Maud does not mention in her journals that the new bride was also reputedly wealthy, supposedly attached to the Fisk Tire fortune in the United States.) Maud groused that Ed was as self-obsessed as ever, and he did not once acknowledge her literary success during the visit.

At the Fair, Maud spoke the same afternoon as two other writers, Laura Salverson and Captain Eric Acland. Laura Salverson, whose parents had emigrated from Iceland to Canada when she was ten, had written nine novels and some one hundred short stories. Her best-known novel is *The Viking Heart* (1923), and in 1937 she won the Governor General's Award for *The Dark Weaver*. Mrs. Salverson announced that she would write no more about contemporary Canadian life: Canadians, she said, did not want to read about other Canadians, and American and English folk refused to buy fiction with a Canadian background unless "Mounties" were involved.

In her own speech, Maud took the opposite stand. In a rousing call to promote Canada and its history and culture, she argued that stories were the essence of a culture, embodying the past. She said hearing all the old stories in her grandfather's post office when she was a girl had prompted her to write. She joked that her stories were all set in Prince Edward Island because when she came to Ontario, as a minister's wife, she "thought it not safe to lay the scene in Ontario lest all my husband's congregation think they were in the book."[71] She stressed her belief that Canada and Canadianness were indeed interesting topics, and all it took to make them into literature was a talented writer. Maud's best-selling books should have been ample testimony that even rural areas had characters who were uniquely interesting. Great themes, dramatic events, and larger-than-life characters were not necessarily essentials — all a writer needed was ordinary folk. Her message was the opposite of all the other Book Week speakers; she stood alone in urging pride in Canada and in things Canadian.

In the same Book Week lineup, the thirty-four-year-old Morley Callaghan also asserted that "young writers of talent stood virtually no chance of scoring 'any kind of success' in this country because there was 'no medium for expression in Canada for the authentic writer.'" He continued that the "authentic" Canadian writer "must go some place where his work will be accepted . . . [and] where people will pay him for what he writes." Callaghan, of course, went to Paris.

That Canadians were incapable of appreciating "authentic" and "serious" writing was the same message Frederick Philip Grove had carried across Canada in the late 1920s in a speaking tour. If writers' books did not sell well, it was because Canadians were unable to appreciate serious literature. The implication followed that if an author's books did sell, as Maud's did, then those books were probably of little value.

Another speaker, Bertram Brooker, whose novel *Think of the Earth* had won the 1936 Governor General's Award, continued: "while Canada reaped rewards from a national character of stability and orderliness, this very asset was reflected in a certain 'humdrumness' in her literature, for authors need . . . wide varieties of characters." He argued that it was necessary for authors to make their characters "amusing and intriguing" as well as "interesting." He criticized Canadian men for having adopted a uniform of "grey felt hats and navy blue overcoats" and urged them to be a little more "eccentric."

Arthur Stringer also spoke at the conference. He was identified as a "Canadian born son, now among the most successful authors living in the United States." He argued that "Every country must not only develop itself, but elucidate itself. It must sing its own song," again implying that this had not yet been done. Maud's books seemed to be invisible to these speakers, or perhaps beneath notice as only "children's" or "popular" books. All these fellow writers and critics disparaged Canadian readers as unsophisticated and Canadian subjects as unsuitable for fiction. Maud was beating against the current when she urged Canadian writers to look into their own lives and communities for authentic material.

After a September visit on the Island, Ewan soon slipped back into depression and consequently began taking his medicines again. It was not long before he became much worse. He appealed to his physician brother, Dr. Angus Macdonald, to help him. In November, Angus drove up from Warsaw, Indiana. His unhelpful medical diagnosis was that Ewan was suffering from his "nerves" and that he should merely "forget" about things bothering him. Angus sniffed out other trouble and added to Maud's exasperation by asking: "Is Chester a *good* boy?" The demoralized Ewan must have dosed himself with medication once more that night, because the next day Maud noted that his eyes "look wild and haunted again" (December 1, 1937).

The answer to Angus's question, of course, was that Chester was *not* a good boy at all. Chester was rarely at home, still refusing to explain his whereabouts. On December 29, Chester persuaded Maud to let him hold a Young People's executive meeting in their home. To Maud's surprise, Chester hosted the occasion with an aplomb that she greatly admired; she commented in her journal that he should still be free, not married. But the day after the party, December 30, she wrote that she "just had a terrible scene with Chester. What has happened I am not sure but it seems that Ida Birrell's family have found out he is married!" Apparently those people in the church who knew, like the minister, had not told Ida's parents initially. And although Ida herself knew (according to Maud, indicating that she may have told her in the mysterious letter that Chester already had responsibilities to his family), Ida also had not told her parents. Instead of shame at having deceived Ida's parents, Chester's reaction was rage at being found out. Maud was the one left holding the bag of shame.

Maud had learned extraordinary self-control throughout her often difficult life, and she had determined to hide Ewan's condition as much as she could, not letting it ruin her boys' childhood. Now it seemed that her elder son was intent on spoiling his own life, and she was helpless. Chester, barely passing his law courses, had two babies in the basket and no interest in supporting them. It seemed to her that he regarded her as an endless source of funding. Maud anguished: what could lie ahead for such a man?

Maud and Ewan had been raised in a society where divorce was unacceptable under any condition. The early Island newspapers give ample testimony to the fact that spouses might be beaten, poisoned, or murdered, but divorce itself was not an option. More recently, the smell of the universally reviled divorcée Mrs. Wallis Warfield Simpson was in many people's noses; there was much anger over the belief that she had undermined the British throne when the smitten young King Edward VIII had abdicated to marry her in June 1937. Yet, it is not so much the spectre of divorce that really upset Maud—after all, divorce comes up many times in Maud's journals. It was Chester's failure to accept responsibility for the children he had fathered. Maud was caught between sympathy for Luella, raising her children without a husband's emotional and financial support, and resentment that Luella had allowed herself to get pregnant (since it was always the woman's responsibility to refrain from sexual relations). Maud predictably blamed Luella more than Chester for their growing estrangement, noting that Luella was the one who had left Chester and gone home to her father in the first place—ignoring the reality, which was that Chester's behaviour had driven her to leave.

Even though Maud thought Chester had married too soon and not well, she and Ewan wanted him to make the best of it and support his family. Luella was a fine young woman, and although she lacked social charm, she came from a very respectable family and had many good attributes, including a quick, inquiring mind. Maud was keenly aware of the promise she had given Luella's dying mother to look after Luella. Chester's indifference to his family was simply beyond the comprehension of his parents, who had always worn the yoke of duty even when it became a straitjacket.

Chester's behaviour undermined Maud's self-esteem in a particularly damaging way. She had grown up thinking of the Woolners, the Macneills, and the Montgomerys as elite families in PEI. Only "trash" behaved as Chester was doing. This insult to her pride came from within her own family—from her son, her own flesh and blood. How could he disregard the values of hard work, responsibility, and decency after she had driven herself to earn enough for his education? She had put so many hopes in her sons carrying the family flag into the next generation. Discovering Chester's deceit and corruption was the worst blow imaginable. She had always hoped that he would mature, but it now seemed to her that he was rotten to the core, and her observations of life told her that this kind of person did not change.

She soon discovered that Stuart had known all about Chester's philandering and lying and had not told her. She did not want Ewan to learn of it because he would only interpret this as further proof that God was against him. She put yet another burden on herself—bearing her pain alone.

So, despite all of her composure during public appearances throughout 1937, Maud was finding that her personal anxiety made writing difficult. She had finished the preparatory "spadework" on *Anne of Ingleside* at the end of October 1937, but her mind was jumpy. She was beset by ailments: roving muscle spasms and tension headaches, and other muscular-skeletal symptoms such as leg and foot numbness, neck problems, pain behind her eyes, and shooting sciatic-related discomfort. These intensified her depression, and depression maintained the cycle of misery, serving up obsessive negative images from the past, flavoured with the bitterness of the present. She felt little joy, even in writing. She imagined scenes of future desolation. And that sent her to more medication.

And yet, at Christmas time in 1937, Maud published a charming piece called "My Favourite Bookshelf" in a publication called *The Island Crusader*. It was about the little bookshelf she kept by her desk, the one thing she would "make a desperate effort to save if the house were on fire." The shelves held a few select volumes, including verse, travel books, girls' stories, garden books, historical novels, biography, history, essays, a book about cats, and ghost stories. "These books are my friends . . ." she wrote. "The books in other bookcases are merely agreeable acquaintances. Here is a book for my every mood and the white magic of it never fails. I sink wearily into my 'lazy' chair, open the worn covers, and presto, change! Everything is different as it should be." Maud's writing in this piece about her bookshelf is so light, so cheerful and wistful, that no one could read it and think that she had ever had a trouble in her life.[72]

Yet Maud had written in despair at the beginning of the year: "The present is unbearable. The past is spoiled. There is no future" (February 7, 1937). Mid-year, in August, she would write: "All my old pleasure in my work is gone—I can't *lose myself* in it." At the end of the year, she summed up: "There has never been any happiness in this house—there never will be" (December 31, 1937). Her dream of success—as a writer, as a wife, as a mother—now seemed an empty charade. It would be nearly a year before she would feel like writing in her journal again.

CHAPTER 21

Maud's journals of 1937, written up a year after the fact, are demonstrably not a full and accurate index to her life. They are a reflection of how she recalled her feelings from a distance. Any delay in writing up her journals naturally facilitated a growing compulsion to shape her entries (and her life). She did not feel she had to report all external events, given that she was increasingly treating her journals as the record of her innermost feelings, not as a full account of the facts and events. This emphasis meant that she was fully honest about her upset over Chester, but she edited his story, omitting facts and significant details. Not knowing how Chester's story would end, she did not want to leave a written account that could humiliate him later on.

In other cases, Maud focused on her response to events, rather than on their specifics. Another huge omission in her journals, running concurrently with Chester's story, was her distress over the continuing slippage of her celebrity. She was increasingly annoyed that her books were now being marketed primarily as children's books, although they were written for a general market. But she was silent about her anguish over her books being devalued by modern critics because they were best-selling popular literature. She was too proud to write in journals destined for eventual publication about how upset she was. The full story of events in her professional life, particularly in the CAA, was glossed over so dismissively in her journals that a casual reader would miss the real significance of events between February 1938 and mid-April 1938.

Maud's 1938 social engagements started right after Christmas. On January 4, she spoke to the Victoria-Royce Young People's Society, and she attended another of their meetings two weeks later. In February she addressed an assemblage of women at the Granite Club, "poured" at a CAA tea, and recited for an I.O.D.E. chapter meeting at Mrs. Cowan's house. She joined four others in pouring at a Press Club tea in March for two hundred people held in the Royal York to honour the actress Ethel Barrymore. She also lunched with a relative, Lena McClure, whose father, from Prince Edward Island, was a federal politician (and who always had lots of good Island gossip). Given the tension in the Macdonald house at this time, interacting and laughing with normal, happy people revived her.

The big problem at home was Chester, of course. After her speech at his YPS on January 4, he resumed coming into his mother's bedroom, kissing her, and generally displaying affection. Ever the indulgent mother, Maud commented that he "craves love." It would have been just as apt to observe that she craved her son's love, too—and if she got it, Chester knew he was assured of getting the car.

Chester continued throwing himself into the YPS social and drama activities and neglecting his studies. Still, he managed to pass all his mid-term exams in January 1938, albeit with low marks. He went out every night, but Maud did not know where. She never knew when he would be in a sulky rage and when he would be a loving son. She believed that he was still seeing Ida, and went to another YPS evening with him partly to keep an eye on him. In an entry of February 7, she reports that he has turned sociable again, expressing concern that she looked "tired." He put his head on her shoulders, wanting some petting and sympathy himself, and she stroked his head for a time, but she adds bitterly that "my heart is hard to him." She knew she could never trust him, but she also could not quit loving him. Her memory kept flooding her mind with images of him as a young child. Now that his life was spinning out of control, she could only watch helplessly.

She became obsessed with discovering his whereabouts. She knew that if he went to Norval he would not stay late; and she knew that Ida's parents no longer welcomed him in their house. But she also was quite sure that Chester was up to no good, since he took their car.

In fact, Chester was spending much time cruising around in search of new girlfriends, and his erratic moods likely reflected the vicissitudes of the chase. Eventually Maud found out that Chester was involved with more women than just Ida, but she never mentions this detail in her journals—even though Chester brought at least one of them (who did not know he was married at the time) to meet her. (Some of these other liaisons came to light after Maud's first journal was published, and several women who had dated Chester—without knowing he was married when they were seeing him—inquired what had happened to him.)

She was turning more and more to barbiturates as a sleep aid. In January 1938, a new "much vaunted tonic" was added to their arsenal of palliatives: neo-boronine. This bromide compound, in later decades of the twentieth century was held responsible for much bromide poisoning. The list of medications she records in 1938 is shocking, revealing that she and Ewan were constantly relying on medical palliatives: the barbiturates Luminal and Medinal regularly for Maud, and bromides for Ewan. Ewan had long demonstrated what we would now think of as symptoms of dependency on these sedatives, and Maud now began to follow the same pattern.

Maud's strained nerves showed in other ways, too. Mrs. Cowan may have thought her daughter too good for Stuart, but she still wanted to enliven the social events in her home with Maud's performances. When Maud recited there in February, she closed with a poem she had written years earlier called "To My Enemy." It makes the point that an enemy's sneer can goad one to climb dizzying heights more effectively than friendly encouragement. Maud reported reading the poem with so much "venom" that her "smug audience" was startled. The night after the reading, Maud broke down and wept bitterly. Stuart tried to comfort her, telling her he couldn't see why she still loved Chester so much and felt so "tortured" by his behaviour.

On March 9, 1938, Maud decided she had to take action. Chester was not studying at all. She may have suspected by this time that he was not attending his classes, either. Out all the time, he was churlish at home, making meals tense, and the general atmosphere in the house sour and explosive. She had not told Ewan about Chester's philandering, but Ewan may have suspected it. He too was also exhibiting symptoms of anxiety and distress, constantly searching for new doctors and medications.

Maud's course of action was to rewrite her will. On principle she decided that if Chester abandoned his family, she would ensure that his children were provided for, but Chester himself would be cut out.[73] Despite these tough measures, she agonized over her inability to stop loving this errant son.

Chester, involved in another YPS dramatic production called "Simon the Sorcerer," was off and flying again—and not in the right direction. She makes no mention of this play in her journals, except for a brief allusion to his filling in someone's part in a play. Chester was not a good actor, but he had much force of personality. His bombastic performances seem to have energized the entire cast. This production, competing with the Young People's Societies from many other churches, won the Bible drama championship of the Toronto Presbytery that year.[74]

Through his performance, in the role of "Peter, Christ's Disciple," Chester made other contacts. He met another young woman and courted her steadily throughout the spring, calling and taking her out frequently, giving her the "royal rush." He presented himself as unmarried. (We do not know how much contact he still had with Ida, but her parents' objections to him made it more difficult for them to meet.) With the new woman, a student at Victoria College, he called himself "Jerry Macdonald." She described him as "a courtly, romantic suitor, always arriving with chocolates or flowers." She said that her cousin laughed that "with the 'line' Chester had, *he* should be writing the books." The romance stalled when she went away to work as a waitress in the Muskoka lake district for the summer of 1938.

When she returned in the fall, she was "met with the question, 'How does it feel to be the other woman?'" A friend had found out that Chester was married, and had children. She was shocked. Her family forbade her to talk to him again, and she dropped him abruptly. When he called at her house anyway, her muscular six-foot cousin was enlisted to "strong-arm . . . him off the premises," warning him never to return.[75] By March 22, on the day that Maud went downtown and signed her new will, she wrote: "Tonight I discovered a hideous danger which I cannot write of. Chester *must* be crazy." We can only speculate about this discovery. Maud observed that Luella's picture had disappeared from Chester's bureau. This drove her to further action.

She wrote Chester a bracing letter in the first week of April (April 3, 1938). She told him that he had wrecked both Ewan's and her life by what he had done with Luella, and that Luella was now struggling to bring up his children by herself. Moreover, she wrote, if he thought he would force Luella to divorce him so he could marry another woman, he was in for a surprise: Luella was within her rights to refuse a divorce. In addition, Maud informed him that she had just rewritten her will, stipulating that he would be cut out if he abandoned his wife and children for another woman. If he kept behaving as "a scoundrel," she stated, she "would never look on his face again."

She hoped that the threat of being cut from her will and excommunicated from the family would bring him to his senses. Maud confessed that writing this letter made her unbearably miserable.

Chester likely knew that his mother depended on his companionship too much to enforce her threat, and he knew he could charm his way back into her good graces. He rightly guessed that he would not be thrown out of the house until his law degree was done. Perhaps experience had shown him that he could get his way if he alternated between displaying cold rage and offering shreds of hope that he was reforming. Another possibility is that Chester did not think matters through at all—he was by nature impulsive, not mindful of future consequences. The letter had no immediate effect on his behaviour, aside from making him treat his mother with a stony, angry silence throughout the rest of April.

Maud had also been very impulsive as a child, but her grandmother's training had helped her learn to think out consequences and discipline herself. She could not understand Chester's inability to do the same. Maud sorrowfully admitted that she didn't think Chester was "quite normal" (April 4, 1938). But Chester was only part of her misery in April 1938.

The Canadian Authors Association had been very important to Maud after the move to Toronto. The CAA was a lifeline, in fact, that pulled her out of her personal stress at home. In early 1938, Howard Angus Kennedy, the national executive secretary of the CAA, died suddenly. Kennedy (1861–1938) had been an exceedingly able and much-respected administrator, and the loss left the CAA floundering without leadership. Things began to unravel in February, with no one of his experience and stature to take over. The resulting upheaval in the association would have a profound effect on Maud.

A young man named Eric Gaskell, who had been working in the Toronto and Montreal book worlds in the 1930s and had been assisting Kennedy, was finally given the post, as well as the editorship of *The Canadian Author*, official journal of the CAA. Maud had known and admired Kennedy, and she knew and liked Gaskell. But he was young and had much to learn about internecine politics. In 1937, Maud had been the second vice-president of the Toronto branch of the CAA, and had things progressed normally she might have ascended to the presidency. At the very least, she would have continued working hard behind the scenes on the executive. She liked going to the

meetings. She enjoyed the companionship of the people she knew there—
except for William Arthur Deacon, of course—and she put her ideas and organizational skills to use in the planning sessions. She had always loved using
her gift of "making things go."

Deacon saw this power vacuum after Kennedy's death as a chance to
sweep the "old guard" out of the Toronto CAA executive. Maud was one of his
targets. It was widely known that he was not a fan of Maud's writing. He liked
to be in charge, and he liked even more to be "seen" to be in charge, as his biographers note.[76] The leadership vacuum gave him the opportunity to work
behind the scenes to shake up the executive slate and dump Maud in the
process.

On April 8, 1938, Maud wrote a very short, flat entry in her journals:

> Tonight I went to the Authors. The election of a new executive
> was held and I was elbowed out. It is not worthwhile going into
> details. Deacon had it all planned very astutely and things went
> exactly as he had foreseen. I at once withdrew my name from the
> list of candidates.

We do not know the specifics of what happened, but clearly, in forcing this
issue, Deacon managed to devastate Maud in a way that no one else could
have done. He caught her by total surprise. This happened only a few days
after she had given Chester the "bracing" letter on April 3, and when she
was suffering from his cold rage at home. About Deacon's manoeuvre she
adds—rather disingenuously—that,

> It does not matter in the least to me that I am not on the executive.
> Deacon has always pursued me with malice and I am glad I will
> have no longer to work with him. He is exceedingly petty and vin-
> dictive and seems to be detested by everybody who knows him.

She concludes unconvincingly: "All this would have hurt me once but now
it doesn't matter at all."

Of course, it *did* matter to her—a huge amount. It was the final *coup de
grâce* in the destruction of her courage. It was an attack on her sense of herself as a worldwide celebrity, a beloved Canadian writer, and a valuable con-
tributor to the Toronto literary scene—indeed, on her whole professional

identity. In Maud's depressed periods, she already felt she was a failure as a mother and a wife. Now that she was elbowed out of her position in the literary world she had worked so hard to join, she felt rejected on the public stage, too. (Later she would depict a similar attack on the personal identity of Anne's little daughter in *Anne of Ingleside*.)

She had been frustrated when the 1937 Book Week authors had all bleated about how the outside world was not interested in anything Canadian. She believed that Canada *should* and *could* develop a literature to take a place in the pantheon of world classics. She had devoted much time to privately encouraging younger writers, hoping they would find their own voice. In her many speeches, she urged people to buy Canadian books. Her best-sellerdom helped other new writers get published, but she wanted to help in other, more tangible ways. And now, in April 1938, she was cut off.

Too proud to admit in her journals the impact of this rejection, she retreated in dignified humiliation. She wrote in her journal the next day: "I have been ill all day with nervous collapse. Could not do *anything*. I am sick with dread that I am going to break down altogether. A broken spirit is worse than a broken heart" (April 9, 1938). She had undoubtedly medicated herself more with the same compounds that had been causing various secondary symptoms like vivid dreams, excessive restlessness, and the feeling that her mind was out of control.

She resolved that she would no longer unburden herself to Stuart, and at any rate, was too proud to reveal to him how hurt she was over being ousted from the CAA executive. Had her personal life been in less disarray, she would undoubtedly have bounced back. This final blow left her mired too deeply in her slough of despondency.

For nearly a month after Maud gave Chester the letter telling him that she would cut him out of her will if he kept seeing Ida, he did not speak to her. He continued to drive or accompany her to meetings and to shop, but he did so with a grim silence, as if *he* were punishing *her* for disapproving of his actions. She had increasing problems with headaches, insomnia, and obsessions. She took barbiturates to calm herself, and for weeks she could sleep only with the help of these hypnotics and sedatives. In addition to several barbiturate compounds, she was probably also taking bromides and drinking her homemade wine.

No surprise that a "dreadful restlessness" kept her pacing floors after shutting herself in a room. She had tremors so severe that she could not sit through a church service; she suffered frightening "vivid, symbolic dreams," and periods of uncontrollable weeping. She was unable to find escape either in her "dream world" or in reading. She could not settle her jumpy mind enough to write.

"What is to become of us if I cannot write?" she agonized on April 27, 1938. She felt in the grip of an "icy horror" and was overcome with the fear that she was on the verge of a nervous breakdown, which added to her terror. She did not realize the role that prescribed medications might be playing in her torment, but she did realize the effect of her condition. The medications settled her, but only temporarily: "I *hate* taking such drugs but it seems just now to be the least of two evils," she wrote on April 23, 1938.

For the first time ever, she dreaded social obligations out of fear that she would break down at them. She began turning invitations down. She holed up in her house. She forced herself out of the house towards the end of April, but at the same time she cited one of Frederick Philip Grove's sentences to represent how she felt: "My whole inner consciousness was like the raw flesh of a dreadful wound" (April 26, 1938). She went out again to a Nature Study Club and felt better for the sociability. She had some more outings, and felt better each time she left the house; returning home, however, was hard.

At the end of April, with his mother's nerves still raw, Chester flew into a rage and carried on "like a crazy man" after receiving a letter she believed to be from Ida. It is not clear from Maud's record, or from other women's accounts after 1985, how many women he was seeing at this period, but she *did* know there were others. In her journals, Maud cast Ida as the *only* "other woman," apparently feeling that one affair was preferable to indiscriminate philandering.

A month after the onset of this hostile treatment, Maud wrote that "Chester kissed me again today—for the first time since I gave him that letter. I was weak enough to feel glad" (April 29, 1938). She added, defensively if unconvincingly, that she couldn't take him back into her life when he might have to be ejected again some day. The next day she added "Hell is a place from which hope is excluded."

Determined to carry her own standard proudly, Maud forced herself to go to the annual CAA meeting on May 15. However, attending the meeting upset her profoundly, and she had to take more sedatives afterwards. She continued to feel she was at the mercy of "hideous obsessions" and nervous unrest. On top of this was her concern about Chester passing the year. Grades would be out in June.

Through all of this period, Maud's symptoms alternated with short periods in which she felt passably good—as could be the case if there was interplay between withdrawal symptoms and taking more medicine. Dr. Lane often dropped in to check on her on his way home from his office. She kept taking Dr. Lane's pills, but they did not help her. She focused on the *effects* of her anxiety—her inability to write creatively when under stress (which created stress in itself), her many physical and mental symptoms (which she did not fully understand and thus felt frightened by), and her continuing use of medications. Dr. Lane kept encouraging her, telling her she would recover, but he had little understanding of what was wrong with her. To him, she was merely a highly "neurasthenic" patient, and the standard medical treatments for such people at that time were more barbiturates and bromides.

During these tortured months she began to type up her handwritten journals as a calming task—at this point, she still wanted to be equitable, and to make a copy for Chester—but this process brought its own pain. Maud wrote on June 6, 1938, "I must not think any more of those lost lovely days. The contrast is too terrible between the happy hopeful girl I was then—'always laughing' it was said of me—and the creature, helpless and in torment of today."

Ever the disciplined woman, she was determined to recover. As spring came, she made herself go outside and garden, attend social functions, and walk to the local theatre. This activity, aided by the warmer weather, helped her recover her footing, and she was able to cut down on medications.

She began to accept that she could not change Chester, and with the loss of hope came some peace. She had few hopes that he would enjoy any professional success in his field—he was too lazy and erratic—but she hoped he would at least give up "running around" and reclaim his family. Her anxiety over him was genuine and compelling. All parents would have felt great pain over a gifted child who seemed intent on squandering his future.

For several years, Maud had been reading all the books she could find on psychiatry and mental illness. She hoped to learn something about the abnormal behaviours she had seen in Chester, Ewan, and Isabel Anderson. She ordered books through the local public library, and Stuart brought her books from the University of Toronto, too, where he had been taking a course in psychiatry as part of his medical training. They discussed Chester's behavioural symptoms together, and Stuart told her that Chester had all the classic traits of the "psychopathic personality."[77] Maud wrote in her journals that she had already come to the same conclusion from her own reading (June 7, 1938). She felt that:

> . . . Nothing else can explain certain aspects of Chester's conduct and lack of moral sense. He is not normal and perhaps should be pitied rather than blamed. I am not referring to his infatuation for Ida Birrell, which might happen to any man and especially to one in Chester's unfortunate position, but to certain other things I have not—and cannot—write here.[78]

As mid-June approached, Maud wrote: "Oh, motherhood is awful— motherhood is awful!" as she waited to see if Chester had passed his year (June 15, 1938). Good news came—Chester had passed every single course. In one more year, he could graduate and begin to practise law. With this news, Maud's spirits improved, and with less need for medications, she found herself able to write, and to escape into her "dream lives" again. But her moods were volatile, and depended much on Chester's moods and behaviour. On June 27 she writes in her journal, after sending a letter to Luella, that everything in her life feels "poisoned." However, she adds that she can

> . . . bear my burden again since that terrible obsession and unrest has lifted. Though I am very sad and very weary of life and would be glad if it were over, that terrible craving for death has left me. Nothing is really changed. My problems are still with me in all their ugliness—there is a dreadful year to be lived through. But I can face it again, now that I have subdued that inner conflict.
>
> I feel as if I had shut a crowd of snarling beasts in a cage, the door of which I am holding closed with one hand, while with the other I re-arrange my life. Now and then one of them rakes me with his paw but they cannot mangle me as before—as long as I can keep the door shut.

Maud's journals do not describe a friendship that was very important to her at this time—that of Eric Gaskell, the young man who was the new national executive secretary of the CAA. Eric had worked enough in the CAA to see that Maud's ouster from the executive was a genuine loss to the organization. But Deacon was powerful, and no young man dared cross him if he wanted to advance in the book world. So Gaskell often visited Maud in her home during this period, or talked to her by phone, garnering her ideas for the CAA. His recollections provide another view of Maud.

They had first met in 1931 in Norval, after she had read some of his essays and, impressed by them, had invited him to visit. They had seen each other frequently at CAA meetings since. He said she was:

> unfailingly kind to young and aspiring writers. I had many chances to observe her with many authors of varying reputation, and she was kind to all, even when under personal emotional strain. She was a "gentle" person. She spoke at branch meetings of the CAA, was always interesting, homely, down to earth, unpretentious. She had many good suggestions to make about the management, organization, and fund-raising within the CAA. . . . She told me that her husband was going through acute depression and she steeled herself to cope by getting out to talk to people.

Gaskell saw Ewan only a few times over the years, for very short periods, in their home. Ewan would offer a few perfunctory pleasantries, then disappear. To Eric Gaskell, he seemed "introspective and anti-social, making no effort to identify with his wife's friends." He was "a sad person who was trying to come to grips with situations he did not understand, and with people he was not interested in." His face and posture looked like "he had the weight of the world on his shoulders."[79]

Less than two weeks after Maud was ousted from the CAA executive, Gaskell asked her to write out two of her poems for him. An observant young man, he knew that she was upset by Deacon's manoeuvre. He had visited enough in her home to sense that she was having serious troubles there— troubles she attributed entirely to Ewan's condition. Gaskell thought Ewan a "polite bore," but saw no reason to deduce that there was anything seriously wrong with him mentally. He knew nothing about Chester.

Eric Gaskell described Maud as a "witty and vibrant personality," gracious in her home. He said that there were signs from time to time that she was under personal stress, but she was always full of helpful ideas and jokes, and she laughed a lot. His frequent contact with Maud, by phone or occasional visits, lasted until a few days before her death.

By August 1938, Chester finally appeared to be giving some thought to the future. If he passed his courses over the next academic year, he would graduate in June. The legal profession was greatly overcrowded, however, and only the best young lawyers were taken into firms, while the rest had a hard time making their way. Moreover, his mother's will was still standing, and if he did not reconcile with Luella and his children, he knew that he would be cut out of his inheritance. He started hinting to his mother that he was thinking kindly of Luella again, making little quips like "that's the kind of house Luella likes" (July 25, 1938). Maud's hopes rose.

Four weeks later, she discovered that he was still seeing Ida. Maud started taking more Veronal.

In September 1938, Chester began wiggling his way back into his mother's good graces. He dropped more favourable comments about Luella and his children. With these hopeful hints of reform, Maud's mood improved; this in turn helped her writing. Once she was softened up again, Chester again came into his parents' bedroom, lay down beside his mother, and put his head on her shoulder "in the old way." "I stroked his hair," she writes in her journal, "but the gulf between us seems too wide ever to be crossed" (September 3, 1938). She adds hopefully in the same entry that he seems to be "different in some indefinable way these past two weeks." Three days later, she writes with excitement that Chester has referred to that "youngster of mine" at dinnertime. She notes the change: "He has never referred to either of his children voluntarily for over two years" (September 6, 1938).

Maud watched for other signs that Chester might be thinking of reconciling with Luella. He began inviting his mother to go on drives again. She accompanied him to deliver a writ for Mr. Bogart, and she listened while Chester talked "brilliantly" to her about the origins of languages. Maud opined it was a pity that he didn't "interest himself in his law studies like that" (September 20, 1938). (One of the young women Chester had dated that summer had been studying classical languages at the University of Toronto and was probably the source of his knowledge, but when she learned he was married, she'd immediately dropped him.) When, at the end of October, Chester asked his mother if Luella and the kids might come for Christmas, Maud was beside herself with joy.

Chester became Maud's best friend again. She was inordinately happy at the thought of reclaiming her "old intimacy" with him. Given her estrangement from the CAA, she needed his intellectual companionship even more now. He needed hers, too. Most young people studying for a career establish some lasting friendships, but Chester had not. Friends were transient in his life. His mother noted this and felt sympathy because he was "lonely." She knew all about loneliness.

Through 1938 Stuart continued to see Margaret Cowan, now a practising dentist. Maud did not know that he had maintained his long-standing friendship with Joy Laird. Both boys' personal lives seemed more settled, and in acceptable ways. Stuart was working hard on his course of study in Medicine, and on the University of Toronto gymnastics team he was doing so well that it looked as if he would be one of Canada's entrants in the next set of Olympic Games in Germany.[80] Her anxiety subsided, her need for sedatives again decreased, and she was able to work on *Anne of Ingleside* all through the fall.

Maud had a big psychological boost in September 1938 when Hodder and Stoughton, who had rejected *Mistress Pat*, wrote asking for her next book. Another publisher, Harraps, had taken and published *Mistress Pat*, and it had sold very well. Like so many sensitive people who overreact to insults, Maud carried grudges a long time, and she enjoyed giving Hodder and Stoughton a lofty refusal. Things were again looking up.

Soon a worried Maud contacted the doctor Ewan had seen in the Lockwood Clinic. He had blamed Ewan's problems on general "nervousness." Maud was alarmed because Ewan was amassing so many different medications from different doctors that she feared he might not remember taking one drug before he took another and accidentally overdose. Probably this is what caused the events described in Maud's November 3, 1938, entry.

Ewan experienced chills (but no fever) and hallucinations in the evening. He imagined he was arguing some point before a civic group and broke into sustained oration. Stuart thought perhaps his father was drunk—a telling detail suggesting that Ewan did imbibe, especially if Stuart could smell alcohol on him.

Maud and Stuart finally quieted Evan down by giving him a barbiturate (Medinal). He slept through most of the next day. When he awoke, he remembered nothing of his remarkable impromptu "address." He continued to alternate between irritability (a side-effect of drug withdrawal) and reasonable normalcy (when he may have taken another dose). In his cranky mood, he accused Maud and the boys of being "leagued against him."

Three days after that episode, again in the middle of the night, Ewan got up to go to the bathroom and stumbled into a bookcase, knocking it over. The overwrought Maud lay awake the rest of the night. Even so, during this period she was writing furiously to finish *Anne of Ingleside*.

Maud's state of mind throughout 1938 continued to be dependent on the state of her relationship with Chester. After he reverted to his attentive self, he took her for drives, showed her mystery stories he was writing (and dropped endearing comments, suggesting that they might "amuse the children someday"), and accompanied her to movies. (Some of his writing has survived; it is singularly lacking in any literary quality.) He even visited his family in Norval. A few days before his mother's sixty-fourth birthday on November 30, 1938, he put his arms around her and told her she was "a pretty wise little mother." She called it her happiest birthday in years. "All Chester's old affection for me seems to have come back," she wrote (November 26, 1938). She felt her "tough love" (in changing her will) had worked.

On December 6, 1938, Maud travelled by train to Thornhill to deliver a promised speech on the background of her books, telling her favourite story of the first Montgomery coming to Prince Edward Island. She met a Mrs. Colclough, who filled her in on what had supposedly happened to the other two of the original three Montgomery brothers who came to Canada. One did not like it and returned to Scotland (and was never heard from again), but one (Richard) stayed and figured as the ancestor of the Montgomery who kept Montgomery's Tavern in Toronto. Eglinton Avenue was named for the Montgomery family connection to the earls of Eglinton.

Family had always been an important part of Maud's self-definition. Maud was thrilled to hear about the Montgomery connection to Toronto history. The next day, she wrote that she had not felt so well in years. Chester was behaving, and Stuart loved his obstetrical training (and would be off in January for a short period of training at Queen's University in Kingston). Maud's pen was flying. A day later, she wrote the last chapter of *Anne of Ingleside*. It was, she said proudly, her "twenty-first book" (December 8, 1938). A new book coming would replenish her income.

Chester's redemption as an acceptable son made her less anxious over Ewan. As she hustled through her revision of *Ingleside*, she wrote quite imperturbably that poor Ewan had had a bad day, and that she sometimes found herself wondering "how I ever came to marry this stooped, shambling, blear-eyed man lying round with a hot water bottle *tied* to his forehead. It seems quite impossible that he could ever have been the straight, merry-eyed dimple-cheeked man he was thirty years ago" (December 11, 1938). It was not age, she observed sadly, but his mental condition that had made the change. She mentioned wearily that he was trying every new medicine he could get again (which undoubtedly increased the likelihood of more bad days). With Chester on the right track, however, she could take other frustrations in stride.

Her bruised self-esteem was further restored when, in mid-December 1938, the Canadian Pacific Railway invited her to contribute a piece for *The Spirit of Canada*, an illustrated book that they were preparing to present to King George and Queen Elizabeth during the Royal Tour of Canada the following May. She dashed that essay off easily.

Luella and the children came and enjoyed Christmas 1938 with the Macdonalds—a big contrast to the previous Christmas, when the Birrells had found out that Chester was married. Even Ewan was in good enough spirits that he actually played with his baby grandson, Cameron, now two. Maud described this Christmas 1938 as her happiest ever, fulfilling her dreams of a happy family home. Like the biblical parent with the prodigal son, she rejoiced.

CHAPTER 22

Maud had always been encouraging to younger writers, knowing from her own youth how bleak life was without encouragement. After her ousting from the CAA executive, she continued reaching out to young authors through letters. Most of one set of ongoing correspondence has survived, a series of some nine letters written between April 13, 1936, and March 18, 1939, to a twenty-year-old woman named Violet May King (born 1916), an aspiring young author in Toronto. Violet's mother had died when she was sixteen and the next year, at age seventeen, her best girlfriend died, too. Like Eric Gaskell's recollection of Maud in her final years, these letters show a different side of Maud from her journals.

Violet had been inspired by Maud's books. She took a three-mile walk one evening to hear Maud speak at a local church, followed by "a very dark and scary hike home, but nothing could stop me. Later I wrote to her and she responded. Her letters put a little light in my rather dark world."[81] Maud became a mentor to Violet.

At that time, Violet was writing poems for the "Little of Everything" column on the editorial page of *The Toronto Star*, as well as for the *Globe*. "Montgomery wrote many heart-warming compliments *re* my letters and advised me to write short stories before tackling books."[82] She said that Maud's "kindness to me, expressed in these treasured letters, kept alive a spark that might well have disappeared entirely."[83]

Maud's first letter, written back on April 13, 1936, was warm and encouraging, and gives a glimpse into how poverty affected people in the post-Depression years. After apologizing for the delay in answering her *"very* nice" letter, and explaining that she answers all of her letters in turn, Maud reassures Violet that she completely understands how it is to feel less well-dressed than

others: "when we are shabby we think *everyone* notices it, whereas the majority do *not*." As proof, Maud says that she did not notice any girl dressed
"shabbily"—she only noticed faces, and then only if they were "amazingly
beautiful or ditto ugly." The letters continue in the same friendly tone, talking, among other things, about the loss of their mothers. Maud mentions her
love of cats, and then shifts to the discussion of writing. She advises Violet not
to be disappointed if a novel she has submitted for a prize does not win, for
"*seventeen* is very young" and she may have to be older before being "able to
write books as they should be written." She advises her to learn the craft by
starting with short stories. She comments lightly that she is glad Violet "liked"
her nose, for "I never did!!" She signs off encouragingly, telling Violet: "*You
have real talent. Keep on.*"

Maud's next letter to Violet, on January 25, 1937, was written only six days
after Lucky died. This was the year she was too distressed over Chester to
write anything in her journal—for *the entire year*. Yet, she writes a cheerful
letter to Violet, telling her how she laughed over parts of her last letter. She
continues:

> Yes, you are right to want your own style. Never try to imitate any-
> body. It's well to read good stylists (of which I am *not* one). One
> *soaks* in something by doing that. But never imitate them.

On another point, Maud assures Violet that it is human nature to mistrust
"what puzzles it." Being able to see "beauty" is "a birthright a princess might
envy," Maud says, assuring Violet that she believes that others, including
Violet, can "have the flash" (a reference to "Emily of New Moon," who has
the "flash" and sees "beyond the veil"). Then she comments on the "happy
ending" debate, saying that the "world *must* have something to keep it alive."
Violet seems to have referred to Maud as someone who is always happy, and
Maud gently sets her straight: "As for my being 'supremely happy' nobody is
that for very long in this kind of a world, my dear. . . . But I have *always* been
happy in my work."

About *Mistress Pat*, and Violet's dissatisfaction that Judy died and Silver
Bush burned to the ground (which make the happy ending possible), Maud
writes that books should not be "too fairy-taleish." Then she moves to inci-
dentals: her eye colour is grey-blue, and her cat Lucky died a week ago. After
some loving comments about him, she has to end the letter because she is

crying, a sad way of signing off what has otherwise been a cheerful letter.

Their correspondence continued with advice on writing, publishing, and life. On April 4, 1937, Maud writes to her telling her not to be discouraged that MacMillan's has returned her novel—they had also rejected *Anne of Green Gables*—and, she adds, without a complimentary note like the one the editor sent Violet. Maud suggests that Violet send the novel to her own agent, Miss Elmo, who has offices in New York and London, but warns her that no agent can force publishers to publish a book they don't want. She tells her that getting that first book accepted is hard, and that *Green Gables* was rejected five times. Maud's next letter, on May 17, 1937, is a short response to Violet's news that Miss Elmo is going to try to place one of her stories. She cautions her against getting too excited lest she be disappointed.

Two days after Maud writes in her journal that she doesn't think Chester is "normal" (April 4, 1938), she describes a terrible nervous unrest and anguish which lasts all day, and "a horrible longing for death. It seems to me that everything I have done has been a mistake . . ." (April 6, 1938). Yet, *on that same day*, she writes a fairly long letter to Violet. She apologizes for a slow reply, saying she has less "pep" than she used to have. She agrees with Violet that our dreams of "tomorrow" keep people going, but warns that people can become "too tired to want a tomorrow." Although Maud makes several allusions like this to her depression, her letter is for the most part positive and helpful. Regarding some lines of Maud's in the *Readers' Digest*, Maud tells her that the three dollars they sent her for the six words—"I was moonlighted into loving him"—is the highest payment per word she ever got for anything. She says there will be no more Emily books, then admits that she once said the same about Anne and later produced *Windy Poplars*. And indeed, she says, she now intends to do another Anne book, *Anne of Ingleside*, when she feels better. She reassures Violet that it is fine to write "pot-boilers" and advises her to read magazines for current styles. She expresses surprise that Violet thought the Pat books "sad," because she hadn't seen them that way, but she admits they were written during some very "unhappy" years in her life, adding that "It doesn't do to make books *all* happiness. They aren't true to life then." Then, answering a question, she tells Violet that, yes, she does have some children— two sons at university, but no daughters: "Fate" would have deemed it "too cruel to ask any girl to live up to Anne and Co."

This conjunction of despondent journal entry and cheerful letter demonstrates what a biased view of Maud's complicated emotional life the journals by themselves give. She made huge efforts to pull herself out of despondency, in this case by trying to help others.

In June 1938, Maud again writes, saying that she has wanted to write earlier to thank her for the "dear little handkerchief," but she has not been well. She quotes some favourite lines of poetry from Marjorie Pickthall and Bliss Carman. Violet had not heard from Miss Elmo, and Maud warns her not to bother the agent again, because it takes time to place material.

Maud writes next on November 23, 1938, after Chester has started to repair his relationship with Luella, saying she feels much better than she did in the spring, when she was in the middle of "a very serious nervous breakdown."[84] She adds:

> Don't you think your question, "What on earth could make you nervous?" just a wee bit silly? What is there in being a writer that can fence out the cares and problems that enter into all lives? Nothing, alas! And if a strain is too long continued something must give way. Never judge anyone's life from the outside: Nobody can tell what may be going on under the exterior.

Maud tells Violet that she has finished *Anne of Ingleside* and hopes for its publication the next summer. Maud adds that her own birthday is coming up, on St. Andrew's Day (November 30), and is in the "dourest, dreariest, drabbest month of the whole year." There is chitchat about cats, and explanation of her term "the race of Joseph." (That this began in an old family joke that referred to the biblical phrase "King who knew not Joseph," and it refers to "people who share our taste in loves and jokes and whom we recognize as 'kindred souls' as soon as we meet them.") Finally, Maud comments that Chester is in his last year of law and Stuart in the fifth year of Medicine. Maud adds (presumably to a question Violet has asked in a previous letter) that it is not for her to say if they are "nice" but that she "likes them very much" herself.

The Macdonalds could not sound like a more normal family, and Maud chatters on about a range of incidental topics: making sweet clover silk sachets for their drawers; a letter from an English lady who read *Jane of Lantern Hill* in Jerusalem; a new play by Alice Chadwick (a pseudonym) based on *Anne of Green Gables* that is being put on in Brampton. This full and happy letter was designed to offer Violet encouragement.

Maud's spirits soared at Christmas in 1938 with Chester and Luella back together. The minute January 1939 rolled around, she returned to typing up the revised *Anne of Ingleside*. She and Chester went to movies again, took companionable walks, and discussed books. One day, when he stayed home sick, Chester flattered Maud by telling her he had read all her books that he hadn't read previously. January brought was more good news: Chester had passed his first-term exams, and since two of these were finals, only five remained to pass in the following spring, and then he would graduate in law.

Chester's relationship with Maud improved, but Ewan's situation did not. One evening Ewan came up to their bedroom in the evening while Maud was trying to work. He created a "terrible scene" she says, adding that she was tired of these—*twenty years* of them (January 24, 1959).This comment is a surprise. Everyone who knew him, including his son Stuart, *repeatedly* characterized Ewan as a kind and gentle man. He was someone who smoothed over arguments, not someone who started them. Maud gives no explanation about those "twenty years" of "terrible scenes." She has described Ewan during his so-called mental breakdowns, and perhaps this is what she refers to. She says she cried some after this, but returned to her writing. What was this scene about? Did Ewan want commiseration over his illness, or attention from his wife (such as Chester got, lying on the bed with his mother stroking his hair)? Did Ewan complain about Chester's new-found grace in his mother's eyes and think it insincere? Did Ewan merely want to go to bed, but felt that his own bedroom was not his own space? Or did he have a psychotic episode from the medications he was taking?

Both maids—Ethel Dennis and Anita Webb—said that all real business in the Macdonald household was conducted in the bedroom, behind closed doors. It was Maud who held the purse-strings. When the bedroom became a boardroom, Ewan was not part of these discussions. Since the bedroom was Maud's space, both for writing and for family business, Ewan's entry into his own bedroom could disrupt his wife, and he was of course very conscious of this. Chester, by contrast, regarded Maud's bedroom as his personal roaming territory.

There is a story from Luella describing how Chester barged into the bedroom late in the evening during the Christmas week she was there, looking for Maud. Ewan, sitting naked on the side of the bed, was very embarrassed and quickly grabbed a wad of bedclothes to cover his private parts. Chester went downstairs to the kitchen and laughed about his father's modesty to Maud and Luella, calling his father a "prude." The incident shows Chester's insensitivity—ironic given that Chester's own lack of inhibitions and his "forced marriage" had driven his father into a near-suicidal depression and helped end his career as a minister.

Ewan continued to deteriorate throughout early 1939, with occasional sudden returns to his friendly, normal self. Two doctors told him he needed an "operation" on his "nerves." Others told him more honestly that they could not give him any help. He gathered more medications. In February 1939, when Dr. Lane came to check on Ewan, he commiserated with Maud for having "a heavy problem" on her hands. "Nineteen years of it," Maud writes in her journals. "Ewan will never be well again. And yet most of his trouble is purely psychic . . ." (February 20, 1939). She did not know the full extent to which he was self-medicating, and no one then, including the doctors, *fully* understood the dangers in barbiturates and bromides.

Maud still had remarkable powers of rejuvenation herself. When Chester was agreeable and her writing was going well, she could withstand a great deal. A comment about Ewan's spells of raving, dreadful appearance, and declarations that he "would not last long" is followed by her laconic statement that she "typed all day" (January 26, 1939).

Maud had first started planning *Anne of Ingleside* in 1937, her "terrible" year. Apparently she had been unable to work on it for a long period, with her mind so unsettled by Chester—not to mention addled by the medications she took. But when she started writing again in September 1938, she finished her first draft in three months, and she had it revised and typed up in less than two months. It was finished on January 31, 1939. She signed the contract on February 1, 1939. She dedicated *Anne of Ingleside* to "W.G.P." in memory of Will Pritchard, brother of her best friend Laura Pritchard in Prince Albert. She had been reading over Will's letters and said that she felt the attraction of his "wholesome" personality again.

Anne of Ingleside (1939)

Anne of Ingleside dips back into Anne's married life, filling in the time after Rilla's birth. It is episodic, each chapter built around a self-contained narrative taking place within the Blythe family. Some of the stories are riveting in their depiction of evil and pent-up anger. The narrator tells us that the Blythe household is an idyllic one, in which there is endless laughter and joy, but few of the tales actually demonstrate this. Many chapters show Maud deflecting the misery in her own life into fictional constructs. She lightens her touch with humour and pieces of nostalgic fluff, but it seems likely that frustration over her own family's dysfunction is the main narrative force.

Maud knew that gossip was one key source of female power in a patriarchal culture, and she often used it to instigate action or to move the narrative along. *Ingleside* is built on gossip, reportage, and hearsay—the narrator tells tales, and the people (mostly women) within the narratives relate gossip, sometimes gently, other times maliciously. In the majority of the stories, Maud walks in adult emotional territory even when the primary characters are children. Manipulative, controlling adults (or nasty children) mislead innocent ones; there are also offhand references to tortured marriages (where men are reputed to bully and beat their wives), and even women who have poisoned their husbands. This toxic territory is leavened with sentimentalizing about motherhood, the nurturing power of women's friendship, the cute sayings of children, and love of beauty in the PEI landscape. The fact that many of the stories are told via gossip distances the reader from the pain they reflect.

An example of the intertwining of gossip and narrative appears in Chapter 32, when Anne hosts a quilting party for the Ladies' Aid Society. Anne's son Walter hides under a table and is only later discovered. By that point, he (and the book's readers) have overheard a barrage of salacious gossip not intended for children's ears. In this quilting party, there is reference to "what happened at Peter Kirk's funeral," but the story is not told until Chapter 33.

This chapter describes a disruption at the funeral of Peter Kirk, a pillar in the Presbyterian Church and a rock in the local community. The story is a clear depiction of how long-term suffering in a marriage can grind anyone down. In this case, Peter Kirk's cruelty is deliberate, and we can speculate that Chester's behaviour has helped focus Maud's mind on psychological cruelty.

Peter Kirk was an elder in the church, and a tyrant in his own home. The community assembles at his funeral for the usual eulogizing service. When the sister of his first wife enters, people are astonished and remember that Clara Wilson had vowed at her sister's funeral that she would "never enter" Peter's "house again until she came to his funeral." After the minister finishes the service, Clara Wilson rises and spits out another tale to the assembled mourners saying that she will now speak the truth about him: the maddened diatribe that follows recounts how he made his wife's life a misery by torturing and humiliating her, destroying first her joy, then her soul, then driving her to her death after ten years of marriage.

In the chapter on Peter Kirk, Maud bundles up all the hypocrisy she has witnessed over a lifetime of funerals, takes aim at decorous piety, and delivers herself of an immense amount of anger at men who were tyrants in their own homes—men supposedly like her Grandfather Macneill and Uncle John F. Macneill. And perhaps Maud saw aspects of these men reincarnated in Chester's frightening rages.

Throughout *Anne of Ingleside*, funerals are a constant theme, although they are oddly represented as some of the *happier* events in the community. The narrative catches Maud's core emotions: she knew very well the experience of being imprisoned within a rigid church and patriarchal culture, within social propriety and platitudes that embalm the truth, and within a human community that used cruelty and gossip as social control. She knew the pain of tension in a family home. Though Maud took aim at male tyranny, she also criticized women's gossip.

In Anne's own home, she is described as "surrounded and encompassed by love" (Chapter 3), but this home is invaded by Gilbert's Aunt Mary Maria, a fifty-five-year-old self-pitying spinster who poisons the atmosphere with hurtful barbs and constant complaints. Aunt Mary Maria is also full of ailments— asthma, allergies, and bad headaches—all things from which Maud herself was suffering. It appears that Aunt Mary Maria intends to stay forever. When this aunt is placed beside the depressive Maud of the journals, she begins to sound like a "doppelgänger": she's the shadowy voice behind the cheerful public Maud who wrote happy novels. It almost seems that Maud had developed a spite against her own character, Anne, for having such a happy family, and sharing a space in life alongside Maud's. It seems as though Maud felt some latent urge to inflict on Anne the torments that she, Maud, felt from her "sick" self. Maud's characterization is sharp and funny, and she obviously enjoyed the writing so much that she did not dispense with Aunt Mary Maria until Chapter 16.

In subsequent chapters, Maud moved into very dark territory, depicting how innocent children can be taken in by bad children who lie. In Chapters 28 and 29 we meet Jenny Penny, the first of three evil children who come into the community and mislead Anne's innocent daughters. Jenny Penny is from a trashy family, unsuitable for a Blythe child, and with her "round creamy face," "soot-black hair," and "enormous dusky blue eyes with long tangled black lashes," she bears faint similarity to Stuart's girlfriend, Joy Laird.

Chapters 30 and 31 deal with another malevolent child, Dovie Johnson, who initially seems "nice-mannered," well dressed, and ladylike. This story shows how "secrets" become cruel commodities of trade in child culture: one of Anne's daughters, Nan, trades her new red parasol for the "secret" that evil Dovie then tells her—that Nan is really someone else and that they were exchanged at birth by a malicious nurse who disliked her mother. Nan, devastated at first, thinking she is really the daughter of drunken, six-toed Jimmy, a marginal and very scary fisherman, eventually finds out it is a big lie, but only after terrible grief.

Maud had long been fascinated by the idea of the "changeling" being substituted at birth, a motif from faerie lore that explained how normal parents sometimes found themselves producing children who were truly alien or evil. This novel resonates on many levels. The concept plays with the construction of identity, too, and Maud knew all too well what it was to have others destroy your sense of who you are. As Anne says lightly in Chapter 27, "Life and death are in the power of the tongue."

In the final chapters of *Anne of Ingleside*, marital jealousy threatens the happy Blythe home. The book ends, of course, as do all of Maud's books, with harmony restored to the social order. Maud could not write the ending to her own life so easily, but she had not lost her storytelling ability. Her vision was darkening and her physical energy flagging, but she still maintained her whimsical touch.

No sooner was *Ingleside* finished than Maud went off to a Women's Press Club dinner. In early February 1939, she spoke to a Toronto Ministers' Wives Association, and then gave another talk for the Victoria-Royce Young

People's Society to please Chester. Then, a few days before Valentine's Day in 1939, Chester floated a trial balloon: he told his mother that a prominent local lawyer might take him into his practice if he had sufficient financial backing. On Valentine's Day, he gave his mother a nice box of chocolates. Three days later, she proudly snapped a picture of her son in his 48th Highlander kilt, commenting how well he looked in it—better, she felt, than in his "civilian clothes."

Her energy level soared. She went on a shopping spree downtown and bought, among many other things, the latest Agatha Christie mystery to add to her favourite shelf of other Christie mysteries. She wrote a fat, newsy letter to Myrtle Webb, attended a CAA meeting, played card games with neighbours, and wrote happy entries in her journal, remembering old days. In March she worked for most of the month on an enormous catch-up letter to G. B. MacMillan in Scotland. She travelled to Lucknow, Ontario, to speak at their Book Fair. She got a letter off to Violet King, full of chitchat and advice on Violet's writing. She mentioned she had enjoyed writing *Jane of Lantern Hill* because it was a new heroine and setting, unlike *Ingleside* which was about "old characters." She would not be able to write something "stupendous," as Violet had suggested, she said because that wasn't her style: "The wise writer knows her *métier* and sticks to it." She also informed Violet that she couldn't write a novel about "pioneer days" because it would require too much research, and she didn't have time for that, but she did plan to write some short stories in the spring. "I *love* writing short stories," she concluded in this letter of March 18, 1939.

When Luella and the children next visited, little Cam broke his grandmother's beloved china spotted dog, Gog, to "smithereens"—one of her most prized purchases from her 1911 honeymoon—and even *that* didn't faze her. She merely gathered up the shards of the china dog, trundled downtown with them, and had him professionally restored.

She was even happier in March 1939 when RKO Studios started angling for screen rights to *Anne of Windy Poplars*. They offered $7,500 for the rights and for an option on *Anne's House of Dreams*. This promise coincided with some other good royalty cheques of over $1,500, spurring her to splurge on a new car since Chester would need their old one to visit them once he moved out. On April 4, she was the "guest of honour" at the Toronto Branch of the Canadian Women's Press Club afternoon tea.[85] All seemed to be righting itself in her world.

And, then, on March 29, 1939, Maud suddenly wrote in her journals that something was terribly "wrong in this household" and she could not seem to find her way "to the bottom of it." Everything had changed. She had noticed that Mrs. Thompson's behaviour had seemed strained some months earlier. Her first suspicion was that Chester had in some way behaved offensively towards her. He spent much time reading on the couch in the basement recreation room, an area Mrs. Thompson constantly passed through this area on her way to the laundry room; it was also the place where June's toys were kept and where she played. Chester could be very charming, but Maud knew that he could also be blunt and patronizing, particularly to people he believed beneath him—people like hired help or servants. She suspected a problem with Chester.

A long entry in Maud's journal explains her version of what went wrong on April 5, 1939. It was the last full journal entry, in fact, that she would ever write. There would be only about another fifty entries, all very short, between this entry on April 5 and her final words, written in March 1942.

Maud's entry opens by claiming that the mystery of Mrs. Thompson's strange behaviour of the past *ten days* has been solved. (In a letter to Myrtle Webb, she said the strange behaviour had been going on for *three months*, which would backdate it to the beginning of February.) She writes:

> To find out that a woman whom you have treated with unvarying
> kindness and consideration and who, you were fatuous enough to
> believe liked you, has really been hating you for years and is capa-
> ble of the worst unblushing insolence and falsehood towards you
> is a hard jolt. (April 5, 1939)

Anyone reading the journal expects further explanation. But none is given. Instead, Maud recapitulates Mrs. Thompson's employment history. She started working for Maud in April 1931, and left abruptly in August 1934, with no good explanation. Ethel Dennis replaced her, and after Ethel left in 1937, Mrs. Thompson returned with her seven-year-old daughter, June. And then by early 1939, Mrs. Thompson was again acting strangely. Maud does not explain what makes her think that Mrs. Thompson hates her.

When I interviewed Mrs. Thompson in 1990 about her years with Maud, she was an articulate, insightful, and exceptionally well-spoken elderly woman, dignified but with a humorous twinkle in her eye. She had only good things to say about her former employer, whom she clearly remembered with great respect and genuine affection. She did reiterate, as Luella had said earlier, that Maud was not "naturally affectionate with children in that she would not take a small child on her knees just to be loving." But Maud was always happy to babysit June. She would come back later in the evening to find June tucked in bed with Maud, both sound asleep. Mrs. Thompson found this endearing. She praised the order and organization in Maud's house and commented that "Mrs. Macdonald" always pitched in and helped with the work whenever she could. Mrs. Thompson appreciated that Maud did not treat maids as "servants," as most employers did. She and June sat with the family at the table and were always part of the conversation. During her tenure there, the Macdonald family would sit and talk and joke at the table. The atmosphere in the house was always civilized, she said, even though Chester "liked to argue, and would contradict you and hold his own position."

She thought that Ewan and Maud were "fairly well matched as a good solid couple." She said they were never openly affectionate but you could see that they cared deeply for each other. Mrs. Thompson liked Ewan but saw little of him, because he thought it a man's job to stay out of the women's way in a house. In all the years she worked for Maud, she saw nothing really wrong with Ewan psychologically. She described him as a nice man, just "terribly clumsy," rather "square," and often "very slow in his thought processes," something that puzzled her for she thought him an intelligent man. She made no connection to the medications he might have been taking.

Chester was the only problem in an otherwise entirely pleasant household, she said. Like all the earlier maids, she disliked Chester, who was much "like his father" in "lacking the polish that came naturally to Stuart." But Chester was in fact unlike the gentle Ewan, being outspoken, tactless, and often surly. He did not "mingle well in the community"—a "night and day" contrast with Stuart, who was likeable, sociable, able to "mix well" in a crowd. She observed that Chester "spent a lot of time reading light fiction" at home when he was in law school, and mentioned that he played with June a lot more than Stuart, but added nothing more on this topic. She characterized Stuart as "every inch a gentleman," making an indirect comment about Chester through omission.[86]

When things fell apart so suddenly early in January 1939, Maud wrote in her journal that Mrs. Thompson suddenly refused to join the family, and instead ate with June in the kitchen.

Maud's account leaves the reader waiting for full details of what appears to be far more than a misunderstanding. Instead, we hear about inconsequential matters—that Mrs. Thompson started talking about her mother's health as if she were planning to leave. Then when Chester was bringing his children in for dinner one night, and more leaves would be needed in the table. Mrs. Thompson offered to eat in the breakfast nook with June. But at the last minute Stuart didn't come home, so Mrs. Thompson joined them at the dining table, and they sat talking and drinking tea after the meal. Maud thought Mrs. Thompson might want to finish her day's chores and go out, so she told her that if she would like to clear the table to go ahead. Mrs. Thompson said there was no need to hurry, and she continued sitting with them.

More unilluminating details follow in Maud's account. The next morning Mrs. Thompson stayed down in the laundry room until Chester and Stuart left, and then ate with June and Maud. Maud inquired after her mother, who was supposedly still unwell, and suggested Mrs. Thompson take a few days off to visit her. Mrs. Thompson declined, saying she didn't want June to miss school, even after Maud offered to look after June. Mrs. Thompson did not come to the table again at lunch, or for supper. She ate in the kitchen and kept June with her. More irregularities occurred in the next few days, all of which made it appear that Mrs. Thompson was trying to avoid the Macdonald family. Maud grew alarmed.

Ewan became involved, and here we see a different view of him than the shambling, bumbling personality of the journals. He sat down with the two women, trying to resolve the problem. When he asked Mrs. Thompson why she was not coming to the table any more, she reputedly said, "Mrs. Macdonald knows very well why I am not coming to the table" (April 5, 1939). Ewan responded that Maud had no idea. Mrs. Thompson, flustered, finally said it was because Maud had *ordered* her to get up from the table to clean up the dishes on the Sunday night last. The account of the situation goes on in great detail, suggesting that Ewan conducted the interview quite effectively. Mrs. Thompson, in this account, appears to have been too rattled to talk, or unwilling to explain real reasons.

Incensed that Mrs. Thompson blamed *her*, Maud confronted her again the next day, with Ewan present. Mrs. Thompson kept saying, "I'm not talking about it any more," and fled the interrogation. Mrs. Thompson remained in the household until June's school year was over, but she and June kept to themselves, and the Macdonald household remained very tense until she left.

What *really* happened? The scenario that Maud depicts is so trivial that it could not have caused such a serious blow-up of a mutually beneficial, long-standing working relationship.

Maud's journals usually give the impression that she takes us into her confidence, revealing everything. But there were some stories that she withheld from her journals (such as the episode in which Ewan aimed the gun at Nora's head, and the precise *content* of the gossip about *her* at various points in her life). The story of why Mrs. Thompson left is another lacuna in her narrative. The missing part of this story has come down through oral history. Mrs. Thompson confided the story to her long-time friend in Norval, Josie Laird, and Joy Laird heard it from her mother.[87]

Mrs. Thompson told how she had gone down into the basement one day to attend to laundry, as usual. Chester was there, lying on his back on a couch reading novels, as he often did in the recreation room adjacent to the laundry. When Mrs. Thompson passed by, he suddenly "opened up his pants and began to play with himself in front of her." He did this in an insulting, hostile way. She fled.

She was appalled, but not just for herself. That room was her daughter's playroom. Chester had always spent a great deal of time in the same room with June, lying on the couch reading. Any mother would worry: what might he do in little June's presence?

Paralyzed with shock and embarrassment, Mrs. Thompson did not at first know what to do. Finally, she decided that she must tell Maud about it. Maud's response was shock and then anger. She was not furious at Chester, it appeared, but at Mrs. Thompson for telling her about it. Mrs. Thompson was stunned, confused, and hurt by this reaction. Maud seemed to have turned on *her*. From this point on, Mrs. Thompson did not want June, now a very pretty nine-year-old girl, spending time downstairs alone in Chester's presence. Mrs. Thompson did not know what to do because she liked working for Maud, and June had access to a good school there.

This story recalls Mrs. Thompson's earlier departure from Maud's employment in 1934, when she had no place to go and no real options for self-support as a single mother. June, of course, had been much younger then, and Chester spent much time playing with her. Maud herself commented on this in her journal, thinking it spoke well for him; she even took a picture of Chester holding June.

Back in Norval, by 1934, Chester was already the source of much gossip. Tales about his crude sexual advances towards the young women in the community were rampant. Aware of these stories, Mrs. Thompson would naturally have taken notice when he paid attention to June, and she may have seen something she did not like. Observant and intelligent, but a very gentle woman, and easily intimidated by Maud, Mrs. Thompson may simply have fled the Macdonald house on a flimsy pretext.[88]

Although Maud did confide several times in her journals that there were far more serious problems with Chester than she could bear to commit to the page, it is unlikely that Maud could have imagined him as a sexual menace to a young girl. By the time that Mrs. Thompson told Maud about the incident in the Riverside Drive basement, Chester was back in his mother's good graces, apparently reconciling with Luella. Mrs. Thompson's story would have been very unwelcome: it would have burst her happy bubble and seemed an "insolence." If Mrs. Thompson was rattled by Maud's anger, and tried to buttress her support with details from Norval, any story of Chester's earlier behaviour might explain Maud's baffling statement that she had just learned that Mrs. Thompson had "hated" her all the years she had worked for her.[89]

Maud knew in her heart that Chester had serious problems, and she was worried about them to the point of mortification. But she was a proud woman who could be imperious when threatened. Hearing that her son had committed an indecent act against someone in her employment would have been an unbearable humiliation. She treated her maids with respect, but deep inside she did *not* consider them to be her social equals in any respect, and she would always owe her own son her first loyalty.[90]

Maud's account of her dealings with Mrs. Thompson is told like the story of Herman Leard. It is both true and not true—true in the sense that it represents how Maud felt and how she saw things, but not true in that it is not the *full* story. Maud saw her journals as *her* story, and she described how she felt about things, but she did not feel obliged to roll out and display all the embarrassing facts—especially when she could not fully comprehend them, and in this case, did not actually witness them herself. Chester's behaviour, to her, remained beyond the pale of her understanding.

When she says there are some things about Chester that she simply cannot write in her journals, who can blame her? She intended her journals for eventual publication, and she kept hoping that Chester would eventually dignify his life. She came from a culture in which you kept dirty laundry out of public view at all costs. She makes the occasional statement like "Chester must be crazy" (March 22, 1938), without telling us exactly what he has done. Indeed, how could anyone offer a rational explanation for Chester's exposing himself to his mother's maid when he was trying to get back in his mother's good graces? He set into play factors that would damage everyone.[91]

This story begs another question: why would Mrs. Thompson have consented to return to the Macdonalds' employ in Toronto if she thought Chester might act inappropriately around June? First, she might have expected that marriage would have matured Chester and settled his sexual drives. A law student, with children, was very different from a teenage boy preoccupied with sex. At the Toronto house, little June would be at school much of the time, while Chester would be working in the lawyer's office and going to classes. He would undoubtedly move out of his parents' house when he graduated and went into practice. In addition, Mrs. Thompson had not been able to get another position where she could keep June with her, and in every other way, Maud was a perfect employer. It was a very sad ending to a happy relationship between Maud and Mrs. Thompson and her small daughter, and the subsequent years were much more of a struggle for all of them as a result.

Maud needed to find a new maid. She wrote to Myrtle Webb in Cavendish shortly after the mysterious contretemps with Mrs. Thompson. She asked if Anita, then twenty-seven, would like to come to Toronto and work for her as companion and maid. Maud proposed a trial year and then that if Anita wanted to move on to something else, there would be no hard feelings. Anita had discovered the limited employment opportunities on the Island, and this was an opportunity to go elsewhere. She was, like the other recent maids, to be paid twenty-five dollars a week, with two paid weeks of vacation, and with her evenings and every fourth Sunday off (or every other Sunday afternoon, if preferred). Maud added that if she could completely retire the mortgage on the Riverside house, she would be able to increase Anita's wages (letter of April 6, 1939).

Anita agreed to the terms, and a new chapter in Maud's life began. Not only was Anita "family," she was a big, strong, competent farmgirl, with a jolly sense of humour and a formidable, no-nonsense personality. Chester had never gotten on with any of the Webb children, especially the self-possessed and confident Anita, but would be leaving shortly after Anita arrived, establishing his own home with Luella (assuming he passed his final courses). Maud knew that Anita could well defend herself; she may even have looked forward to the feisty Anita keeping Chester in his place.

Maud wrote Myrtle again on April 29, saying that she still did not know when the "secretive" Mrs. Thompson was leaving. (Maud's inability to discuss this basic question with Mrs. Thompson indicates that she was unnaturally ill at ease over the situation.)[92] She enclosed a snap of Stuart and Margaret with the admission that he wouldn't want it sent to anyone, but since it was so good of him, she was sending it anyway. (Stuart was still writing to Joy Laird, and would in fact give her his 1939 medical pin as a token of a commitment deeper than friendship.)

With her outlook on life improving again, Maud began work on a new book on April 17, 1939, with the provisional title *Jane and Jody*. It was to focus on the maltreated Toronto orphan named young Jody. Maud escaped from the house throughout April on various trips, including one to the Art Gallery of Toronto to look at modern art with the Fireside Study Club. (She quipped that the art looked as though the artists had painted their nightmares.) She spoke at the local I.O.D.E. meeting. Margaret Russell, the talented and attractive daughter of the Russells in Norval, by then a very successful young teacher in Toronto, came for lunch.

When Chester had come to his mother on May 3, 1939, and told her that, "Well, at last you have pushed me through school," she wrote: "He has had his last lecture—after nine years!!" Later she added tersely that he was not worth the worry she had expended on him, but that he had to be "fitted to do something" since he had a family to support. She expected little from him as a lawyer, despite his having "brains that could put him in the front rank if he had worked" (May 18, 1939). She knew there would be other worries with him. "I can never trust Chester, alas," she wrote on June 2, 1939, without further comment.

That month he was called to the bar. He had graduated near the bottom of his class. (In his second year, he had ranked fifth from the bottom—ninety-fourth out of ninety-nine—but the record of his third and final year's grades are now missing.) The legal field was overcrowded. While other young lawyers were attending lectures, working part-time in law firms, and making lifelong friendships with each other that would be useful in networking later on, Chester was out chasing the wind.[93]

One day Chester confirmed that "a friend" of his, the established lawyer Donald F. Downey, wanted to know how much cash Chester could raise to enter Downey's law practice. To Maud, this seemed almost too good to be true. The money from RKO Studios had just come through, and Maud settled on $2,000—a very large sum at that time.[94]

It seemed odd to Maud that Downey did not want Chester in his Toronto office but intended to send him up north to mining country. They discussed one northern location, then another, and finally settled on Aurora, slightly north of Toronto, where Chester had gone to St. Andrew's. Next, Mr. Downey made the rather unusual step of calling Maud—not Ewan—into his office. According to her account, he opened with the statement that he supposed she, like most mothers, thought her son was perfect. Then he told her what she already knew: that Chester was unkempt in his person, cocksure in his opinions, and lazy—all qualities that would militate against success. He did give her one comforting positive: Chester had more "legal brains" than anyone else he knew. That rang true with Maud, of course. Clearly, Downey wanted her to know that he felt he was taking a risk with Chester, and if Chester failed, Downey himself would not be to blame. Her $2,000 was to be a gamble. (As it turned out, Downey dissolved his partnership with Chester within the year.)

After her depressing interview with Mr. Downey on June 26, 1939, Maud wrote: "Will I ever be done hearing people say nasty things to me of Chester? No, I don't think so. He has faults that Mr. Downey does not know of and one of them I fear will wreck him completely yet." However, she admits that she will miss her drives and fellowship with Chester.

There is no picture of Chester and his mother standing proudly on the day of his graduation, only a graduation headshot of him in her journals. Chester found a small house in Aurora, and in July 1939 he moved in with Luella and their two children to start their new life.

In the meantime, Stuart had worked hard to complete his medical degree at the University of Toronto. He finished his fifth year of study in 1939 and began interning at St. Michael's Hospital in Toronto that autumn. He was rarely home. Most of his time was spent in the hospital, sleeping on a cot in the doctors' quarters when on overnight duty. He chose obstetrics and gynaecology as his specialty, having found the happiest event in all medical fields of medicine to be handing a mother her new baby. (His patients laughed about his standard line for announcing little boys: "This one has a handle on him.")

A happy period began when Anita Webb came to live with the Macdonalds on Riverside Drive at the end of June 1939. She quickly learned to
drive the Macdonalds' new car and became Maud's chauffeur. She replaced
Chester and Mrs. Thompson as Maud's companion for movies, for jaunts out
to Norval, or for any other social event. (She recalled how "Aunt Maud" carried a little book every place with her, especially on streetcars. She wrote down
snippets of conversation she overheard that she might use in books.) Steady
and spunky, Anita was a hard worker, and jolly. Maud had a companion to
laugh with again. Best of all, Anita was a clansman who could be trusted.

Anita enjoyed being in Toronto. She had been raised in a plain but homey
Island farmhouse, and the Riverside Drive house seemed a mansion. It was also
a model of organization, run on a set routine. Maud still planned all meals a
week in advance, and each week, promptly at 2:00 p.m. on Thursdays, Anita
and Maud went to the Loblaw store at Jane and Bloor for the next week's groceries. Next they went to Eaton's and bought the week's meat, which came up
fresh from Eaton's farms in the Georgetown area. They had fish once a week,
on Friday. The table was always well set, with clean linens and fine gold-
banded Limoges china. There were two sets of silver, pearl-handled serving
pieces, silver serving bowls, and a silver tea service. Their menu always consisted of meat, potatoes (usually scalloped), and a vegetable, served with rolls
or bread and real butter (which was too expensive for most people in the
Depression era), with canned fruit and tea for dessert. Anita washed up the
dishes, and Maud dried them and put them away. Maud had bought a new
washing machine before Anita came—an electric one—to replace the old
manual, paddle-driven machine, so the laundry work was not hard.[95]

Ewan left pleasant memories for Anita, too. She said that he had been
much liked in Cavendish when he was minister there. About the Toronto
house, Ewan was as punctual as Maud. He came down dressed, ate breakfast,
read for a short while in his study, took a walk, and usually went for a drive.
He continued his lawn bowling. She found it surprising that Ewan never
helped around the house or in the garden, especially since she was used to capable farm husbands. Anita observed that he was not as quick-witted as Maud,
but she certainly did not think of him as a "mental case" in any respect. He
liked a good argument or joke—particularly a practical joke. According to
Anita, Ewan loosened up and became quite sociable after Chester left home.

Anita and Maud went to the movies together about once a week, leaving
the dishes in the sink after supper and doing them when they got home. They

loved *Gone with the Wind,* and Maud went to see it again and again. All this entertainment was new and exciting to Anita. She had grown up in a rural culture where people did not travel out of their area unless they moved to the Canadian mainland or the United States. Her father's first vacation in his life, and his first and only trip off the Island, was in March 1939 when he came to visit his daughter Marion in Norval and the Macdonalds in Toronto.

Anita's recollections show us another side of Maud during these months. Maud received many calls to speak at girls' or women's groups, and Anita drove her everywhere. On the drive, Maud always carried her handiwork, and her fingers never wasted a moment. Maud spoke easily, distinctly, without notes. According to Anita, Maud had a lovely "musical voice," and she kept her audience laughing continuously. Anita said that she never tired of listening to Maud speak, even when the speeches repeated the same basic material. Anita laughed over Maud's first encounter with a "public address system" in a school on the Hamilton mountain. Maud was astonished to find herself seated in the central office, giving her address to a machine. Later she was asked to go through the rooms and talk to students. Afterwards, Maud and Anita drove out to Hamilton's Royal Botanical Gardens to look at the rock garden, which Maud loved.

Anita, a Baptist, attended the Morningside Baptist Church in Swansea, and Maud often accompanied her. To fundraise, the church put on a pageant in which older girls dressed up in wedding dresses once worn by their mothers, aunts, or friends, and paraded across a stage. Maud lent her own wedding dress to Olive Watson, a good friend of Anita's.[96] After the pageant, Maud praised Olive, saying that she had carried herself very well, a compliment that Olive cherished all her life. Olive remembered that although Maud was matronly, she still had "a nice shape," and "always walked like a lady, looking corseted and in control." Anita and Maud continued to enjoy each other's company through the latter part of 1939 and the early part of 1940, despite rising political tensions in Europe. But as 1940 progressed, dark clouds began to appear in the horizon, at home: Chester was in trouble again.

Chester provided one of Anita's most vivid memories from her stay with her Aunt Maud. He could be very personable and charming when he chose, she said, but was brusque, churlish, and anti-social most of the time. She observed that he "always needed cash," and he knew that pawnshops were a quick route to that. She bristled over the memory of Chester's asking to borrow his mother's moving-picture camera—the expensive one she had been given for judging the Kodak contest in 1931. The next day he told his mother it had been stolen from the car. There was nothing his mother could do, and she was very upset. Anita said that they both knew he had pawned it, but of course this was not openly discussed. On matters like this, Maud kept her own counsel.

CHAPTER 23

As soon as Chester was living with Luella and their children in Aurora in July 1939, he began pressuring his mother to revise her will. She did this in August 1939, and she signed it on September 11, 1939, right after war was declared. Chester might have been a lawyer, but his mother did not make him the executor. Instead, she appointed the Toronto General Trusts Corporation her trustee and executor. She made Stuart her literary executor by virtue of specifying that all her literary papers and her ten volumes of handwritten journals would go to him, along with sole right to decide when to publish them. In fairness to both sons—now that Chester was again with Luella—she directed that any income from publication of her writing was to be divided equally between the two of them, and likewise her personal effects. But Chester was cut out of control over any aspect of her estate.[97]

The threat that sons would be called to fight in World War II was a growing source of great concern to many people. Maud had been so intimately involved with comforting mothers of dead sons in Leaskdale that the possibility of another war filled her with horror. She was terrified that her "one good son" Stuart might be sent to war, and she thought he would be killed if he went.

As soon as her will was signed, Maud left for a visit to the Island. The process of dealing with her will had disturbed her, and she was feeling fragile from the previous two years of stress. She travelled with Murray and Marion Laird and family. They arrived on September 16 at Cape Tormentine. Ernest and Myrtle Webb picked them all up. Marion and Murray went to Cavendish, and Maud went to visit Ewan's family on the other end of the Island.

At Ewan's sister Christie's house, the family could not help noticing that Maud's hands trembled uncontrollably from time to time, and she would wring them and move them constantly. Mary Furness, Ewan's niece, recalled Maud's distress over Hitler and the war, but did not think that in itself should have caused the shakiness. She made no mention of Maud taking any medications. In an autographed, presentation copy of the Canadian Pacific Railway's 1939 book *The Spirit of Canada*, Maud's signature is accompanied by the note that she regrets "her hand trembles with illness."

While on the Island, Maud sent cards to George B. MacMillan and Nora Lefurgey Campbell. The handwriting grew markedly steadier. In the card to MacMillan, dated September 23, 1939, she writes in a fine and steady hand that she is on the Island for a month, ending in despair that the world might have to endure another nightmarish war again. Her card to Nora, sent on September 27, says she is having a good time in one sense, but fears the cloud of war. Nora's only remaining living child of four children, her son Ebbie, would go overseas in 1940.

Maud returned home from the Island in a much revived state, and she wrote long and energetic letters in free-flowing handwriting through the remainder of 1939. On November 7, she wrote Violet King that she had suffered from bronchial-pneumonia for most of July and August, and that she had gone to the Island for six weeks. She talked about blocking the sequel to *Jane of Lantern Hill*, to be called *Jane and Jody*. She described her own reading tastes as "catholic" but for "sheer amusement and relaxation I enjoy a good *murder mystery* with at least three corpses." She gave Violet further advice on her writing. She tells her that she was "quite wrong in thinking Stuart 'formidable.' He is very approachable and is a general favourite. Chester is the blunt rather gruff one . . ." She mentions the King's and Queen's visit and is glad they came "before the 'hour of great darkness' fell over the world. . . ." Maud's six-page letter to Violet is written in swinging high spirits. Maud exudes vigour and a clear mind, and there is no shaky handwriting.

On November 28, 1939, she penned a long, friendly note to Jack Lewis, a young correspondent who aspired to become a writer and to whom she had been writing for a number of years. She comments on the war and on her sons. She explains that Chester has graduated and moved out, and she misses him a lot, though he "gets in to see us quite often." Stuart, she says, is living at home while in medical school, and Mr. Macdonald is better than he has been in a long time. She comments on movies being made from her books, on the Webbs' farm being made into a new National Park in Prince Edward Island,

and on the opening of the Green Gables Golf Course in Cavendish (to a crowd of over four thousand people). She tucks in the fact that Ramsay MacDonald, a prime minister of England for many years, told a friend of hers, a member of the local PEI legislature who was visiting in England, that he had "read every Montgomery book he could get his hands on two or three times over." She ends with a comment on the visit of the King and Queen: "She was exquisite—far daintier and more beautiful than any of her photographs. We all loved her. From coast to coast their tour was one long triumph. We realized the 'oneness' of our Empire as never before. . . ."

On November 30, 1939, she wrote a long letter to Ella Campbell at Park Corner to apologize for missing the wedding of Georgie, Ella's youngest daughter. On December 12, she wrote another very long letter to a Mrs. Townsend in PEI, gossiping genially about various joint acquaintances.

Despite this flurry of letters—all of which show Maud full of purpose and power—she wrote no more regular entries in her journals after June 30, 1939, the month of Chester's graduation and departure. She continued keeping notes to write up in her journal, however, when she had time and inclination.

On February 15, 1940, Maud wrote a long and very upbeat letter to her longtime correspondent Ephraim Weber. On March 14, she thanked G. B. MacMillan, her other correspondent, for the "Flower Patch" book he had sent her, as well as for two packets of the British literary magazine "John O'London." She mentioned that Chester was away in a home of his own, and that "Mr. Macdonald" had gone to Florida for the winter, something that was probably responsible for the happy flurry of writing and activity that Anita described. On March 29, she wrote Jim Campbell in Park Corner a cheerful business letter saying she had paid off the loan for the farm that she had taken out for them. On April 24, 1940, she wrote a letter to a fan telling her that *Further Chronicles* was out of print, and had been for fourteen years, and never should have been printed in the first place. This letter was written in a firm handwriting. Anita's presence was steadying her, and her use of sedatives seemed on the wane.

Stuart graduated in Medicine on June 6, 1940. The picture of Stuart at his graduation shows a proud mother; she does, however, look reserved and remote under her hat, like someone who has inner anxiety. And indeed, Chester was once again becoming a very serious concern.

———

Things had not been going well in Aurora with Chester. Many years later, Luella characterized their time there, describing it without rancour but with vivid details. She was home every day, all day, by herself with her two little children. There was never any money, despite Chester's salary. When it got colder, there was no money for coal. Once the weather grew really cold, Luella kept herself and the children warm by going to a derelict barn and taking boards to break up and burn in the kitchen stove. She and the children spent all their time in the kitchen in order to keep warm. Chester was out all day and also in the evenings. She had no idea where he went, and he did not explain.

Luella served all their meals in the kitchen because it was the only heated room in the house. However, she said that Chester—who had long thought of himself as "elite"—snapped that "only peasants eat in the kitchen." He refused to eat any meal there except breakfast. He did not come home for lunch. At dinnertime, he would eat by himself in the frigid dining room, wrapped up in a big coat, hat, and scarf, wearing gloves to keep his hands warm, while Luella and the children ate in the kitchen. Fifty years after the fact, Luella laughed as she gave a bemused account of the difficulty he had holding silverware while wearing thick gloves. She added that at the time she was deeply hurt by his treatment, but she was accustomed to her father being "difficult."

If she tried to talk to him on any given topic, he turned surly, exploded easily, and would go "flouncing out of the house, slam the door, get into the car, and roar away." Once, she said, after an argument he "roared out so fast" that he took off one side of the garage doors. Another time he hit a tree, knocking the bark off. She did not understand his continuous anger, given her belief that he had wanted them to get back together. (She apparently never learned about his mother's will and the stipulation that Chester had to be living with his family to avoid being disinherited.)

Luella became increasingly frightened of his anger. She had no idea what he did with his time, but she was quite sure that he did not spend it in his office. She speculated that he spent time at "the theatre" and at "Marshall Rank's jewellery store." She did not think he ever had a single client during his time in Aurora. She had no one with whom she could discuss her situation—her mother was dead, and her father was not a man with whom you could discuss marital troubles. Luella knew that Chester went to Toronto at least once a month, if not more often, to get more money from his mother, but she had no idea where that money went.

Luella could heat the house with wood she gathered, but food was a different matter. Chester gave her only minimal amounts of money for that. There was no money for clothes for the children; she made them from discarded items Maud gave her. Once she made little Cameron some overalls from Ewan's old clothes, but Ewan became agitated when he saw them, and "carried on" about "overalls" being inappropriate for *his* grandson. Luella thought this outburst strange and out of character, but she decided that he felt working man's garb was not suitable for the grandson of a clergyman and the son of a lawyer. Maud tried to shush him, embarrassed at the odd scene. Luella rarely saw Maud and Ewan, however, for Chester always went to Toronto by himself; he did not offer to take her and the children.

Anita Webb told another version of the story about Chester's visits home to see his mother. "He was *always after money*," she said grimly. She described how he would enter the house abruptly and go straight to his mother's bedroom. The door would be shut firmly. Chester's threatening voice carried outside the room. She said the "pressure sessions" continued until Chester got what he wanted. He would then leave. Maud would not appear for a long time, and when she did she looked very distressed, sometimes as if she had been crying.

Anita was incensed that Chester upset his mother so much, but she was powerless. Maud was far too private to discuss family problems with anyone, no matter how close. She said that Maud's spirit began to break down in 1940 when the troubles with Chester escalated. Maud apparently began to believe that *she* was to blame for how Chester had turned out. As her psychological state deteriorated, Maud suffered what she called "a nervous breakdown." In light of what we now know about the dangers with medications she took, we can deduce that these palliatives, taken to relieve her emotional disarray, only heightened it. Anita saw the symptoms of a disintegrating personality—the very symptoms of severe psychosis that bromide or barbiturate dependency (or excessive usage) can cause.

By Anita's account, her "Aunt Maud" began following her around, weeping like a disturbed and frightened child. She whimpered and hung on to Anita's arm. Anita was hard-pressed to get the housework done. Until now Anita had seen Maud only as a strong woman, and she was bewildered and shocked. Anita blamed Chester. Dr. Lane dropped in often, but Anita had no part in any medication regime Maud may have been following.

Chester's seeming reconciliation with Luella turned sour as soon as he was back in Maud's will. Luella apparently did not understand that Chester was trying to compel *her* to leave *him*. She knew, however, that she was breaking down mentally from his treatment. The death knell to their marriage occurred when she went to a doctor and found that he had given her a venereal disease. She was horrified. She called her father and begged him to let her come back home to recover her mental and physical health.[98]

The next day, both Luella's father and Ewan arrived at the Aurora house and tried to talk her out of leaving Chester. When they saw how determined she was, and had some understanding of why, both fathers returned home. The following day her father came back and moved her out, with the children. She never lived with Chester again, nor did he ever support her or his children. She made her own way and raised her children alone, with heartbreaking difficulty.

Maud was prostrate with grief over the breakup of Chester's marriage. She sank into a deep depression, and her dependency on sedatives apparently increased. War in Europe had broken out, and she was now obsessed by the conviction that Stuart would be killed. There was little doubt that Stuart would be taken into military service as soon as he finished his residency: doctors were badly needed. Maud looked back to *Rilla of Ingleside*, about World War I, in which Anne's beloved and poetic son Walter is killed. Stuart was only a five-year-old child when she wrote that book, but he had already shown the kind of special sensitivity that Walter embodied.

In June 1940, shortly after Stuart's graduation, Maud fell and broke her right arm, tearing the muscles and ligaments. She later typed a letter to Eric Gaskell, still national secretary of the CAA, saying that she was still "laid up" because of her arm and promising to answer him as soon as she could. She explained that she was typing the note with her left hand.

Maud wrote to George MacMillan in Scotland, describing her injury and telling him that she could barely control her right arm enough to write now. She added that this coincided with "a bad nervous breakdown" in which she was plagued by a "fixed idea" that she would never be better. She told him that she can no longer find pleasure in her old joys, but instead feels "turned into another personality (July 23, 1940)." She described being at the mercy of an awful restlessness.

Stuart was then interning in St. Michael's Hospital. As an intern "on call" he usually slept at the hospital, but he telephoned home to his mother every day, according to Anita. At one point he became very alarmed over the deterioration in his mother's health. One day he noticed her weaving and staggering as if she were drunk. He took a blood sample and had it analyzed.[99] It showed a very high concentration of bromides. Doctors at that time did not understand the psychiatric dangers of bromide poisoning, but Stuart begged his mother to cut down on medication because he could see it was affecting her balance. Unfortunately, Maud seems to have been too psychologically dependent on these medications by this time to heed his advice. He was only a young and inexperienced doctor, and she was under Dr. Lane's care. Dr. Lane continued to come in often to check on Maud—he lived across the street— and he also was clearly alarmed at her state.[100]

After Luella's flight and Maud's breakdown, Chester stepped up the pressure for money. Downey had by now dissolved their legal partnership. As Maud's psychological state continued to deteriorate, Chester became increasingly upsetting. Ewan coped no better. Maud grew rapidly worse over the summer of 1940. Again, it seemed that Chester was spinning out of control.

However, apart from these breakdowns, Maud was still mostly lucid, even though she was obviously depressed and on medication. She wrote MacMillan again, telling him that he would never know what his "sane letter" had meant to her. She told him that she had been in "intolerable distress" since her last note to him, but she left out details. She said that Chester had tried to join the Osgoode Hall Contingent of the Canadian Officer Training Corps but was turned down because of short-sightedness. Stuart was interning: the medical council had decreed that interns could not be taken until their intern year was finished. She added that it was *not* the thought of Stuart going to war that had caused her break down. Several things, including the injury to her arm, had happened all at once. This letter of August 27, 1940 is so shaky that it is almost impossible to decipher it. On November 21, 1940, she sent MacMillan a postcard saying she was still not able to write.

Anita was terribly alarmed but unable to turn things around. All Maud's speaking tours had stopped, and they even quit going to movies. Maud lost the sense of humour that had always been the defining feature of her personality. She continued to cry a great deal, and she "couldn't talk to other people—could only talk about herself and her illness in a pitiful way," according to Anita. Unable to eat, Maud rapidly lost a lot of weight.

Anita had never seen anyone in such a condition as Maud, and she didn't understand how Chester's behaviour, odious as she regarded it, could have brought her laughing and gay Aunt Maud to this. Dr. Lane regularly assured Maud that she would eventually improve. There is no record of the medications she took in this period, but it almost certain that her intake increased. No one knows if it was with or without the doctor's knowledge.

And then, on December 6, 1940, Margaret Webb—the wife of Anita's brother Keith Webb—died of a miscarriage, leaving two baby girls and a devastated husband. Myrtle tried to care for her grandchildren, but her health was not good enough to look after them on a full-time basis. Anita was summoned. The loss of Anita was a terrible blow to Maud.

On December 31, 1940, Maud managed a short note to Weber, acknowledging his last letter to her. She told him she had been ill for six months with a terrible breakdown, and she did not expect to recover, although the doctor said she would. She thanked Weber for a "long and true friendship," and she told him that her breakdown had been caused by a serious fall, by the disturbing war news, and by "several private blows." Stuart hired a nurse-companion named Mary A. Powell to replace Anita. By January 18, 1941, Anita was back on the Island.

The news of Maud's troubles now prompted Eric Gaskell, still national secretary of the Canadian Authors Association, to write her an encouraging letter wishing her a restoration of health. He also informed her that at the national executive committee meeting in Montreal, the "following resolution was adopted by unanimous vote of those attending: 'That Mrs. L. M. Macdonald (L. M. Montgomery) be made an Honorary Member of the Canadian Authors Association, in grateful recognition of her rich contribution [to] Canadian literature.'" He added that "an honorary membership is the highest distinction of the CAA, and there may not be more than ten honorary members at any one time. The distinction is held for life, and the member so honoured is not required to pay any further dues (February 8, 1941).

On February 17, 1941, Maud thanked him, saying that her doctor assured her she would improve, but that "so many things combine to keep me down" that she doubted she would ever be her "old self" again.

Eric Gaskell told me that he kept in touch with Maud largely by telephone, drawing on her contacts, ideas, and knowledge behind the scenes to further CAA work.

On February 28, 1941, Maud sent MacMillan another postcard saying her

William Arthur Deacon during the 1930s.

Eric Gaskell in uniform after the war had started and he had resigned as head of the Canadian Authors Association.

CAA officials, June 29, 1937. Back row: Howard Angus Kennedy, Leslie Gordon Barnard, Laurence E. Brownell Front row: Maud, Pelham Edgar, Margaret Lawrence.

Hugh MacLennan, John Morgan Grey, and Violet King at the CAA Convention in June 1946. (Maud corresponded with Violet, encouraging her to write.)

Chester Macdonald and his second wife, Ida Birrell.

E LADY OF THE LAKE.   137

land

and wold,

cks so bright,
s so blue,
less flight,

e beech
ve,
bed,

"Lay on him the curse of the wither'd
    heart,
  The curse of the sleepless eye ;
Till he wish and pray that his life would
    part,
  Nor yet find leave to die."

XIV.

BALLAD CONTINUED.

'Tis merry, 'tis merry, in good greenwood,
  Though the birds have still'd their sing-
    ing ;
The evening blaze doth Alice raise.

From Maud's copy of Sir Walter Scott.

Maud's funeral in Cavendish, PEI, in April 1942.

Toronto *Telegram*

Chester Macdonald at the time of his arrest.

St. Michael's Hospital Archives

Dr. E. Stuart Macdonald of St. Michael's Hospital, Toronto.

University of Guelph Archives

Ruth Steele and Dr. Stuart Macdonald at the time of their marriage.

Most of these pictures are available on the University of Guelph website (www.lmmrc.ca), as well as many others that could not be included for reasons of space.

health had still not improved. On May 10, Mary Powell sent a note to the Webers thanking them for the gift of a plant, saying Mrs. Macdonald was too sick to answer herself, but that she valued their friendship. By June 1941, Maud was despondent.

Maud had some better periods through the spring and summer once she stabilized with the new nurse. She started thinking about the will that she had made in 1939, after Chester had reconciled with Luella. Now that he was no longer with Luella, that will needed attention again. But since Maud blamed both Luella and Chester for the marital troubles and final breakup, she was unsure how to handle it.

On June 24, she attached a codicil to her will that revoked clause c, paragraph III, in her September 11, 1939, will, in which everything had been divided equally between Chester and Stuart (the only exception being her diaries [journals] and papers, which all went to Stuart). This June 24 codicil specified that 180 items on a list she had made on June 21, 1941, were to go to Chester *only if he was living with Luella at the time of her death.*

Maud was thorough: she either documented the importance of each item or explained its provenance. If Chester was *not* living with Luella at the time of her death, these items were all to go to Luella to be held in trust for the children.[101]

Everything else of her goods, furniture, and household effects not on this list was for Stuart, with the exception of her bedroom suite, and the living-room chesterfield and two chairs, which were marked for Ewan. Her sons were to share her books equitably. She specified that if Chester and Stuart wished to make a different distribution of her household goods and effects between themselves, they could do so.

This list of June 21, 1941, was formalized as part of the codicil to her will on June 24, 1941. Did Chester press her to leave him so many specific sentimental items by arguing that Stuart was being left the journals? Maud was apparently trying to force Chester to return to Luella by adding the proviso that he would get these heirlooms and sentimental items only if he was living with Luella at the time of her death. Perhaps she simply thought that she could avoid ill will between her sons after her death by making specific lists. Or perhaps she named all the items to prevent Chester from removing anything before the division took place. She was naturally worried, too, that her journals made enough references to Chester's failings that he might destroy them.

Two weeks after Maud signed the codicil to her will, she wrote in her journal the sole entry for 1941: "July 8, 1941: Oh, God, such an end to life. Such suffering and wretchedness." That was the first entry since June 30, 1939, written just after Chester's graduation from law school, shortly before he moved to Aurora with Luella. There were no more entries until the final entry the following year. Her letters to friends became miserable. On August 20, 1941, she wrote to Ephraim Weber a short note saying that she didn't seem to be getting any better, and that recovery from a nervous breakdown was slow.

Ewan still roamed, collecting prescriptions, some for him and some for Maud. Neither Maud nor Ewan could quit taking the medications that they had become dependent on to make them feel better. On August 26, 1941, Maud wrote MacMillan, that she was "no better" and "never will be." She referred to "the blows" that had fallen on her "for years," which she "tried to hide" from her friends. She added that she thought her mind was "going." On October 3, 1941, Mary Powell was again writing notes on Maud's behalf. To a Miss Small in Manitoba, she wrote, "Mrs. Macdonald appreciated your lovely letter very much. She is too ill to write you. Yours truly, M. A. Powell."

Maud was more forthright about her problems to the Park Corner relatives, and she wrote them directly herself. They were the only people — relatives or friends — to whom she would have felt comfortable admitting that her anxiety was caused more by Chester than by Ewan (whose illness she normally cited to outsiders as the cause of her worries). She wrote them on October 8, 1941, that Chester's wife left him and that

> . . . he has broken our hearts this past 10 years though I have tried
> to hide it and seem bright and happy. . . .
> My heart is broken and it is that has broken me.

In the meantime, Luella was still living with her father while she regained her health. Luella's father insisted that she maintain contact with Maud and Ewan, because the children deserved to know their grandparents. But the Macdonalds were too far gone in illness and mental distress to show interest in the children. Luella found the trips very painful for all.

When Luella visited once in the fall of 1941, she found Maud outside disposing of letters, books, and papers in a bonfire. Luella said Maud was "in the garage in a summer dress. She was having a great deal of trouble keeping on her feet. I don't know how she kept standing. She was so *frail, distraught,* and *wild* looking. I was frightened. I had no experience with anyone looking like that." She described Maud as being all bones and no flesh, a very tiny woman now that her weight was gone. Maud was cordial, but Luella was so disconcerted by her mother-in-law's appearance that she took the children and left as soon as possible.

On December 23, 1941, Maud wrote a last pathetic letter to MacMillan saying the year had been one of "constant blows." She said that Chester had "made a mess" out of his life, and that Luella had "left him." She commented that her husband's nerves were in worse shape than hers. Then she added that she expected conscription would come and take her second son, leaving her without any motive to "recover" and "nothing to live for."

In a December 26, 1941, note to Weber, she said she could write only after "a hypo." She referred again to the many "blows" that had fallen on her during the year. She implied that Ewan's attacks of melancholy were the cause of her misery because people did not want a minister who had such attacks. This, of course, was nonsense: Ewan had been out of the ministry for six years. But an elderly husband who was subject to melancholic attacks was far more socially acceptable than having a young son exhibiting seriously anti-social behaviour.

On January 6, 1942, in a note to Morris Springer, her long-time young correspondent in Chicago, she said she was very ill; she did not think that she would recover. She advised him that the only way to find out if he was any good as a writer was to send his writing out to magazines and newspapers. She said, "Goodbye and God bless you," and ended by telling him she had had so many blows, together with the war, that she was "completely broken."

In her final months, Maud was deeply depressed, and yet she was rational enough that the two people I interviewed who talked to her shortly before her death found her completely lucid. On April 10 (or thereabouts), about two weeks before her death, Eric Gaskell spoke to her. She had been helping him organize a chapter of the Canadian Authors Association in Prince Edward Island. (There had been three famous literary people from the Island: Maud herself, Andrew Macphail [1864–1938], and Cyrus MacMillan [1882–1953]. Maud had agreed to be honorary president. She had given him many important contacts.)

She phoned him again shortly before his trip to ask if there was anything else she could do. He told her everything was covered and thanked her for all the introductions. He remembered her saying almost pathetically, "I do wish people wouldn't think of me only as a writer for children." He talked to her again the following week. She told him that she was not feeling well and she knew she was "depressed," but hoped to correct this by what she called a "period of relaxation."[102]

Eric Gaskell said that Maud was in a happy frame of mind when she last talked to him, and she joked and laughed. He described her as "open and friendly and interested in the project." She spoke of her concern about the CAA—she thought it needed to be a more professional organization, admitting only people who actually were bona fide writers. Mr. Gaskell characterized Maud as a person who was "genuinely kind in a way that came naturally."

Another person who talked to Maud right before she died was Margaret Mustard of Leaskdale. She dropped in to see Maud around April 17, 1942. Margaret was one of several Leaskdale people who had stayed in touch with the Macdonalds. At the end of the visit, Margaret told Maud that she would drop back in a week. Maud responded that she had doubts that she would still be there in a week. Margaret did not understand what she meant, and left puzzled over the comment.

Maud was deeply worried about finances by 1942. Writing had been her joy, but it had also been her income. If no books came out, her income would drop off. In 1940, she had earned substantial book royalties of $6,996. In 1941, without another book out, her book income had dropped to $1,421, the lowest in thirty-four years. She knew that her income would be even lower in 1942 if there was no new book. What would happen to her family without her income? She feared that she couldn't afford to keep help any longer, but she could not do without it. She now felt the terror of possible financial insolvency. She was galled by the knowledge that Lewis Page was still making money from her early books. She had lent others a great deal of money when she had a large income, and now she was facing an old age without adequate resources herself. She had less than $10,000 in her savings account, and although she had stocks and bonds, that money was not readily accessible. She felt desperation about how long her reserves would hold up, especially with Chester demanding money.[103] To a fan named Helen, she wrote a pathetic letter in shaky handwriting telling her that she was "very ill" with a "very bad nervous breakdown" and asking her to write the RKO Studios in Hollywood, California, urging them to make a movie of *Anne of Ingleside*.

Despite all the farewell letters telling all her correspondents about her misery, and despite nothing but the two pathetic entries in her journal in the last years of her life, she somehow produced another manuscript called *The Blythes Are Quoted* in this last year. It is a collection of her stories, many published earlier, linked together through a narrative device. Many of these stories are excellent, written when she was in her prime, and they might have carried the book. Her obituary in the *New York Times* stated that she put this manuscript in her publisher's hands on April 23, 1942, the day before her death, and the manuscript was indeed located there in the 1970's although most of the stories in it had already been published as *The Road to Yesterday* (1974).

Maud found solace in rereading the books from her special bookcase. The writer she loved most, who had most inspired her in childhood, was Sir Walter Scott. His was a world with ideals, she felt. The poem she loved most, and could recite from beginning to end, was *The Lady of the Lake*. There is a four-line passage at the end of Section XIII that describes a curse laid on a character in the poem. It reads:

> Lay on him the curse of the wither'd heart
> The curse of the sleepless eye;
> Till he wish and pray that his life would part,
> Nor yet find leave to die.

In her shaky handwriting, in the pencil she used at the end of her life (rather than the pen used to earlier underline her favourite passages), she wrote:

> *Oh God that is my position.*

Then, on March 23, 1942, she began her final entry on page 479 of her tenth volume of the 500-page journal that had sustained her since she was fourteen years old:

> . . . since then [*referring to the entry of July 8, 1941*] my life has been
> hell, hell, hell. My mind is gone—everything in the world I lived for

has gone—the world has gone mad. I shall be driven to end my life. Oh God, forgive me. Nobody dreams what my awful position is.

The first-born son who had been her pride and joy had been, in the end, her undoing. She had been unable to cope with the anxiety he caused.

Right after Chester's birth, Maud had written some of the most poignant lines ever written about motherhood:

> As I hold little Punch's dear body in my arms I am lost in wonder—and awe—and terror—when I *realize* that *everybody* was once a baby just like this. All the great men, all the good men, all the wicked men of history. Napoleon was once a chubby baby, kicking on his nurse's lap—Caesar once smacked his lips over his mother's milk as does my mannie—Milton once squirmed with colic—Shakespeare cried in the night when he grew hungry. Yes, and—horrible thought—Nero once looked up with just such dear, star-like innocent eyes and Judas cooed to himself with the same sweet noises and vocables—Nay, even that wondrous Person—so grand and wonderful and amazing that it seems almost sacrilege to call him man, even to those of us who can no longer believe him anything but the consummate flower of humanity at its best—even He was once a white, dimple-fisted, waxen-faced little creature like this, cuddled in his mother's arms and drawing his life from her breast. What a terrible thing it is to be a mother—almost as terrible as it is beautiful! Oh, mothers of Caesar and Judas and Jesus, what did you dream of when you held your babies against your beating heart. Of nothing but sweetness and goodness and holiness perhaps. Yet one of the children was a Caesar—and one was a Judas—and one a Messiah! (December 1, 1912)

She had also written about the time when her cat had shrieked, and Chester, a nursing babe at her breast, had "uttered a cry of terror." She had comforted him, and afterwards wrote in her journal: "But ah, little son, some day there may come a Fear into your life such as not even your mother can charm away. The 'twin Eumenides—Fear and Pain'—they cannot be escaped by mortals." Now *she* had come to a point in life where that beloved little son, now a grown man, had brought her more fear and pain than *she* could endure.

—

Stuart knew his mother was very ill, and that she was worried about her finances now that she could not write, but he was caught totally off guard by what happened next. So were many others. On April 24, 1942, Dr. Lane had dropped by to see her before he left to work, as he often did because she was in a fragile state. Later in the day, Dr. Lane called Stuart at the hospital. His mother had been found dead in her bed (by Anita Webb, who was back). Dr. Lane and Stuart each rushed to the house from uptown, arriving at approximately the same time. In the bedroom, Dr. Lane motioned to Maud's bedside table. He told Stuart to "take care" of the things on it and he would "take care of the body." Her bedside table held some bottles and a sheet of paper.

Both doctors took her death as a suicide. Dr. Lane was eager to dispose of evidence that she had taken medicines that might have killed her. The death certificate lists Maud's primary cause of death as "coronary thrombosis," and Dr. Lane attributed it to "arteriosclerosis and a very high degree of neurasthenia." He did not tick the box that listed suicide as a possible cause of death. Dr. Lane knew that Stuart's medical career would be damaged if people thought his famous mother had committed suicide — suicide then brought a terrible stigma to the family — so he would not have ticked this box in any case. Dr. Lane also would not have wanted it spread that his most famous patient might have died of a drug overdose under his watch, whether that overdose had been intentional or inadvertent.

Neither of these two doctors paused in the pressure of the moment to study what the page on the bedside table actually said. Nor did they notice that there was a very specific page number — 176 — at the top of it. The note, which was dated April 22 (two days before her death), was not, as they believed, and as Stuart believed all his life, specifically a suicide note. It was the final page of Maud's journal, her "life-book," her journals, which she had written up in draft form to copy into the formal ledger. This page 176, written in ink, in fairly fluid, confident handwriting, said:

> This copy is unfinished and never will be. It is in a terrible state because I made it when I had begun to suffer my terrible breakdown of 1940. It must end here. If any publishers wish to publish extracts from it under the terms of my will they must stop here. The tenth

volume can never be copied and must not be made public during my lifetime. Parts of it are too terrible and would hurt people. I have lost my mind by spells and I do not dare to think what I may do in those spells. May God forgive me and I hope everyone else will forgive me even if they cannot understand. My position is too awful to endure and nobody realizes it. What an end to a life in which I tried always to do my best in spite of many mistakes.[104]

This page is clearly numbered "176." It is clearly dated April 22, not March 23, the date on the last entry in her journals, or April 24, 1942, the date of her death. The question is: *where did the other 175 pages go?*

Maud's lifelong practice had been to keep rough notes on numbered pages of scrap paper such as this and to write them up in her journal eventually. When she had an involved tale to tell—as was the case with the Herman Leard story—she wrote up one or more rough drafts before transcription. When her trials were particularly upsetting, she waited a long time to see how events would turn out, as in the gap between 1933 and 1936 after Chester's marriage. But she had finally filled that gap in 1936 and after, even though committing the story to paper was painful.

Now she had a gap between 1939 and 1942. This piece of paper—the page 176—appears to have been the final page of an account of those years.[105] These pages would have detailed her terrible heartbreak over Chester, and possibly her fear of his rages. Where did they go?

Chester had had nowhere to go after he failed in his practice in Aurora, Downey having ended his contract, so he had returned to Toronto, in anger and disgrace. When the Toronto General Trust Company began taking their inventory of the house after Maud's death, as part of settling the estate, they recorded that Chester occupied the basement. Chester always had a key, and he had access to everything in the house before and after his mother's death. He certainly could have taken the missing pages and destroyed them. (He would not have dared to touch the ten bound volumes of her formal hand-written journals because they were described in her will, but loose pages that no one knew about would have been a different matter.)

There is no way of determining exactly *when* they disappeared. If some or all of those 175 pages went missing *before* Maud's death, and she discovered this, she would have been devastated. She was a driven and compulsive woman, and she was lucid enough during these last years to have had every intention of finishing her life-book, in spite of all its sadness, so she could leave it for posterity. If the pages went missing before her death, this would explain the very short entries for 1941 and 1942: her data to recopy into the remaining blank pages of Volume 10 of her journal would have been gone. But why would Chester have taken the first 175 pages and not the final one, if they were all stacked together, as presumably they would have been? She had this final page in her possession at the time of her death. Under this possible but unlikely theory, Chester either did not find the final page, or she rewrote page 176 from memory (both implausible scenarios).

It seems more probable that the 175 pages went missing *after* her death, and that the final page was next to her bed, perhaps to signal (as Stuart thought) that it was indeed the end of her story, even though that story was not yet written down in the journals. Or perhaps it was her final message to the world, written two days earlier when she felt her life ebbing (for she was very weak and ill). Perhaps she had felt very weak and fuzzy-headed that morning, and had taken the top page to contemplate, wondering what to do with this manuscript. To her, the life lived on the page was as real as life in the flesh. Her life was in the written manuscript. She had lived to write, and she had written to live.

Chester was out of the house when his mother was found dead. It follows that he would not have known about page 176 having been found on her bedside table; Stuart folded it into his pocket. Stuart would not have known about the other 175 pages being elsewhere. He interpreted this page as a single, stand-alone note written solely to explain her final despondency, and it is easy to see why he did.

Chester had always had free run of his mother's bedroom, and he had every motive to prowl through his mother's business papers after her death, particularly since he knew she was given to making changes in her will that affected his inheritance. He was not living with Luella now, so nothing would or should come to him by the terms of the will—unless she had drawn up another codicil. Ewan was there, but he was so ill that he comprehended only part of the time that Maud had died.

Chester also knew his mother kept a journal, and he had good reason to think it would contain much about him. It is very likely that when he came home later that day, he went rummaging and found the other 175 pages.[106]

Between Maud's last entry in her journals on March 23, 1942, and the dated page 176 of April 22, 1942, Maud had perhaps written her life almost to its conclusion. The statement on March 23 that "I shall be driven to end my life" does suggest that she had at least contemplated suicide, but she did not in fact die until April 24, 1942. Did Maud retire to her room on April 24 to take a modified and private rest cure after bundling her last manuscript (*The Blythes are Quoted*) off to the publisher on April 23, and then accidentally overdose on drugs? It is easy to overdose on barbiturates if one has developed a serious dependency on them. Maud's body weight had dropped so much that a small amount of two central nervous system depressants could easily have killed her. However, Maud's comment to Margaret Mustard the week before her death tips the evidence in the direction of a premeditated death by someone who was in the grip of a major depressive episode, and may or may not have understood that she was dependent on drugs that were killing her. Whatever the case, there is little question that Maud was suffering unbearable psychological pain. Death would have been welcome.[107]

After Maud's death, Chester began removing carloads of materials from the house when Stuart was at the hospital working. He did this before the trust company had taken inventory. Neighbours alerted the trust company and Stuart and the bank immediately changed the locks on the doors so nothing further would be taken until they had made their inventory. Stuart relocated his father to a nursing home as soon as he could. Chester no longer had access to the contents of the house.

Chester was not living with Luella when his mother died, so technically none of the 180 items on the list were to come to him. Many of them were not in the house when the inventory was made, and some were never found. (They may have been pawned.) Chester kept many other items that he valued, including his mother's books, her manuscripts, a large crazy quilt (which he later gave to a relative on the Island), and certain other items such as a china dog figurine and the silver tea service. Stuart offered him what household furnishings he wanted (out of Stuart's share) because Stuart was going to be shipped off to the war. Then a sale was held.

Maud's final journal entries recognize that her mind and creative spirit were damaged. Did she recognize her drug dependency when she wrote: "My position is too awful to endure and nobody realizes it"? Or was she referring to Chester? Or both? In any case, she was still a rational and lucid woman who knew that she had come to a very sad state.

Her final entries in her completed handwritten journal ledgers function to fulfill the tragic trajectory that she had seen emerging for her life back in 1897, as does the final page 176 that was never transcribed into her ledgers. It is a chilling thought indeed that her need for artistic completeness in her journals (her "life-book") might have played a part in making her want to end her own life. We are reminded again of Anne's advice to her daughter in *Anne of Ingleside*, published in 1939:

> An imagination is a wonderful thing to have . . . but like every gift we must possess it and not let it possess us. . . . you must learn to keep on this side of the borderline between the real and the unreal. Then the power to escape at will into a beautiful world of your own will help you amazingly through the hard places of life.

Maud seems once again to have been writing out of her very own experience, and an increasing awareness of the bifurcated nature of her own reality. Her imagination had not deserted her, but the creative spirit that turned the dross and disappointments in life into witty, uplifting laughter in her books was seeping away. Her *gift of wings* — the passionate nature that brought her both depths and glory, and fed her art — began to sink her under the pressure of flight.

Still, Maud had soared gloriously in her lifetime. Her creative spirit produced books that have raised the spirits of millions of readers all over the globe. They are books that changed lives. They inspired innumerable women to greater heights of achievement. They brought comfort and consolation to heads of state yearning for the more tranquil years before the outbreak of World War I. They brought courage and hope to Polish soldiers in the trenches in World War II, inspiring them to fight for home and love.[108] They anchored innumerable grandmothers and mothers and children in shared and joyous spots of time. They brought millions of people from all over the world to see the landscapes she wrote about and loved. They showed women writers that they could write about ordinary women in small towns and have a fascinating subject. Maud knew that what went on in people's minds was the most interesting thing in the world, and that the vagaries of human emotion would almost always trump the intellect. She understood that the grand narratives that direct civilization all begin in the longings and fears of individual human hearts. She understood the complexities of human motivation. Most important of all, her books helped us *laugh* at human foibles, bringing readers into a shared human community. Her best books conveyed a joy in life that has lived long after their creator departed from the "shores of time."

Maud had lived much of her life, like her volatile little heroine Anne, between the soaring of the imagination and the "depths of despair." A fitting epitaph might be found in her own words, written after a period of great distress on January 31, 1920:

> One cannot have imagination and the gift of wings, along with the placidity and contentment of those who creep on the earth's solid surface and never open their eyes on aught but material things. But the gift of wings is better than placidity and contentment after all.

EPILOGUE

Maud's story

Maud wanted to be buried in Prince Edward Island, the isle of her birth, in the Cavendish cemetery where all her kinsmen lay. Her husband and two sons made the thousand-mile train ride with her remains. They crossed the windy Northumberland Strait by ferry, travelled to Hunter River by local train, and were driven the last twelve miles by car.

The burial was in Cavendish on April 29, 1942, in the "cemetery on the hill," next to the schoolyard where she had played, and near her mother's and maternal grandparents' graves. In one direction lay the "Green Gables" house and "The Haunted Wood." In the other direction, towards the sea, lay sand dunes and lingering patches of white ice floating on the Gulf of St. Lawrence. The "reluctant Canadian spring" had not yet come to the Island, and some drifts were still unmelted. Normally, cold winds blew off the sea, but on the day of Maud's funeral a warm, soft wind blew over the land towards the ice. In that gentle breeze, a few songbirds sang, according to accounts at the time.

The little white wooden church was filled to capacity, and many mourners had to stand outside. They had come from all over the Island. The officiating minister was the Reverend John Stirling, who some thirty-one years earlier had married Maud Montgomery and Ewan Macdonald. Recalling the funeral years later, his daughter observed that in 1942 he was close to death himself, facing the most difficult funeral sermon of his life. He fought to control his own emotions as he spoke. His sermon was followed by the comforts of the Twenty-Third Psalm, a prayer by the Reverend J. B. Skinner of Winsloe, and a scripture reading by the Reverend G. W. Tilley, pastor of the Cavendish church.

The official account of this funeral in the *Presbyterian Record* does not record a somewhat unseemly disturbance in the church also recalled by his daughter. Ewan Macdonald kept looking around in confusion and crying out, "*Who* is dead? *Who* is dead?" Each time he was told by his sons who it was, he would ask cheerfully, "Who is she? Too bad! Too bad!" Then the "*Who* is dead?" questioning would begin again.

Ewan's disruptions, which his sons tried desperately to silence, added to John Stirling's distress and, for those who heard them, to the pathos of the service. The church was filled with those who either had known Maud or who felt enormous pride in her achievements. The mourners were stifling the sounds of grief they felt for one of their own, one who had gone away and had now come home in death to the land that had produced her talent. Even people who had never met her basked in the glory she had brought the Island. Those who had read her books instinctively loved anyone who could have written them; they did not have to have known her personally.

There were whispers asking how she had died: it was an open casket, and, wasted to nothing, she did not resemble the woman they had known. She looked "horrible," some whispered, lacking fitting words. Appropriately, the minister's final benediction looked to the future, when visitors would come to visit her grave and "feel their pulses quicken at the thought of their proximity to the dust of one who painted life so joyously, so full of hope, and of sweetness and light."[1]

Adjacent to the schoolyard where Maud played as a child, this Cavendish graveyard was a scene of beauty and tranquillity, with rolling hills surrounding it and the distant sound of the pounding surf. Maud had asked in her journals that her tombstone be inscribed with a line she had adapted from Shakespeare: "After life's fitful fever, she sleeps well." No one had read this request in her journals, and so she sleeps peacefully among her own folk without it, her grave visited regularly by fans from all over the world.

Ewan's story

Ewan gave much wrong information on Maud's death certificate. He said her father's first name was "Ewan" and then he changed that to "Hugh John." He listed Hugh John Montgomery's place of birth as England instead of Prince Edward Island, and her mother's place of birth as Ontario, instead of the Island.

But Ewan was confused only part of the time. He could also be quite lucid. After Maud died, he made a call to Luella, expressing concern for her welfare and distress because Maud's will was being ignored. Luella knew nothing about the will, and the phone connection was poor. She did not know what he was talking about when he said several times, "This isn't what Mother intended, this isn't what Mother intended." The call was cut short by the sound of the phone being slammed down. Luella never heard from Ewan again.

The trust company wound up Maud's affairs and put the house and many of its contents up for sale. Ewan could not live alone, so Stuart arranged for him to go into a private-care nursing facility in Toronto. He was showered with attention there by nurses who loved this gentle, dimpled, smiling old man, and made his final year happy. He died at St. Michael's Hospital on December 18, 1943, at age seventy-two, his cause of death listed as "Arterio-sclerosis Heart Disease and Emphysema." Stuart was in the Canadian Navy by the time his father died, and Chester gave the information on the death certificate, spelling of father's name as the original "Ewen," rather than the "Ewan" that Maud had used.

Ewan's story, as written by his wife in her journals, is that of a man who was a lifelong worry to his family because of his "malady," as Maud termed it. Stuart Macdonald believed that his father suffered from bouts of depression, but he never, *ever* regarded him as mentally unsound. Stuart retained enormous affection for his father's memory, but said that his father became a terrible hypochondriac towards the end of his life, and that the RCMP contacted him about his father's attempts to get drugs like codeine from different doctors as he continued his ongoing search for an elixir to make himself feel better.

In the 1980s, the very bright and observant Luella was adamant, after reading Maud's first nine handwritten journals, that no one would have thought Ewan as psychologically impaired as he seems there. Nora Lane, the daughter of Ewan's doctor, insisted that her family always thought him a sweet, lovable, but lonely old man, with nothing abnormal about him.

Marion Webb Laird lived with Maud and Ewan in Norval for an extended period and said that although they were definitely a "strange couple," they were each clearly very fond of each other. We will never know the extent to which drugs, prescribed by a medical profession that did not yet know their full effects, and continued by Ewan without adequate monitoring, were what damaged this benevolent and unfortunate man's mental and physical health. His side of his story will never be told.

Chester's story

After his mother's death, the bank executors changed the locks on the doors so they could take an inventory of the contents of the house in order to settle the estate, Chester no longer had access to the house. His next recorded address, in December 1943, was 142 Douglas Drive in Toronto. He moved about in Ontario after that, making several attempts to set up a new law practice, always trading on his mother's name. In 1945, his address was Tillsonburg, Ontario. In 1946, it was Fort William, Ontario. An article in the Fort William *Daily Times-Journal* on July 23, 1946, stated that Chester had come to establish a law practice there, and that he was a son of L. M. Montgomery, and he reminisced in the local newspaper about his mother. Next, he turned up in what is now Thunder Bay, where he made another attempt to establish a law practice. Apparently on an impulse, according to someone who lived there then, he "borrowed" a light airplane and flew it successfully, but damaged it when he brought it down. Again, he left town, suddenly this time. His next address appears to have been 18 Skipton Court, Downsview, Ontario, a street whose name appropriately characterized his sad trajectory.

He married Ida Birrell, some two years after Maud died. Chester's first son by his second marriage was born on April 18, 1944; his divorce from Luella became final, according to her records, on May 31, 1944; he married Ida on August 31, 1944. The order of those events would have upset his parents had they still been alive, but then Chester had never walked the straight and narrow path.

At one point, Chester and Ida invited Stuart and his wife, Ruth, for a Sunday dinner in Downsview. Ida had gone to much trouble to cook a meal, and they all sat down to enjoy it. Before Chester carved the turkey, he removed his false teeth and set them down beside Ruth, who was sitting adjacent to him.

They remained there for the entire meal with the casual explanation that they did not fit well.

Stuart, as a gynaecologist, was in charge of the venereal disease clinic at St. Michael's Hospital when Chester needed treatment. There were other such clinics in Toronto, but Chester came to Stuart's clinic and made a point of telling everyone that he was Dr. Stuart Macdonald's brother—a great embarrassment to Stuart in his own professional territory.

By 1954, Chester had obtained a good position working for the Ontario government, in the Office of the Public Trustee. Office staff there remembered how lawyers in Toronto would telephone Chester when they needed to locate a certain case study, particularly about estate or real estate law, which he knew very well. In pre-computer days, Chester's extraordinary memory could recall the book and subsection in which relevant case studies were located.

With a steady income, with a devoted wife and two young children from his second marriage, it appeared that Chester was finally settling down to a respectable life, at age forty-two. But he had many sides—from the "elite" aristocrat who would not eat in the kitchen like a peasant to the host who dumped his dirty false teeth beside his dinner guest's plate.

On September 13, 1954, the Ontario Provincial Police swooped into his office and arrested him. He had put his excellent legal brains to use in the Office of the Public Trustee by devising a scheme of embezzlement. When people died and left an estate, the money was turned over to the Office of the Public Trustee. Chester was in charge of dealing with unclaimed estates. This involved advertising nationally for unknown relatives. If no claimants turned up after a set period of time, the money went into the provincial purse.

Chester almost always managed to turn up relatives in distant places in the very last moment before the waiting period expired. But one day, a bona fide relative turned up at the eleventh hour to claim an estate—and found that it had already been claimed.

Upon investigation, the person who had claimed it did not exist. The trails were easy to follow. In his careless, sloppy way—one that almost invited detection—Chester had left his desk drawers full of incriminating evidence. There were cheque stubs, bank drafts, and copies of letters. Chester had fabricated the identities of the spurious relatives, laying claim himself to the inheritance. He had been squirrelling away money in fictitious accounts, and then emptying these into his own bank account. The embezzling scheme cheated no one but the government, and hurt no one specifically, and it might have gone on until the end of his career but for the fluke of the one man turning up at the last minute, after a ten-year wait, and demanding to know who had claimed his inheritance of $23,045.

When Chester was first arrested, Stuart was called down to the jail by bail officers. Chester assured Stuart that if they could make restitution of the money, the whole thing could be hushed up. In clan tradition, Stuart wanted to avoid the public shame that would be brought on the family name, and put under pressure by the immediacy of the situation, he agreed.

Stuart and Ruth were just negotiating to purchase their first home in an exclusive area of Toronto when Chester was caught. Chester ascertained the amount of Stuart's accumulated down payment for this house, and then he assured Stuart that this money (variously reported as $8,000, $10,000, and $10,500 in the papers, and remembered as $10,000 by Stuart) would cover it exactly. Chester promised Stuart faithfully that he would repay him. It was a weekend, and the affair was not known yet. Stuart laid down the money.

Chester had embezzled not $10,000, but some $35,600, and Chester's picture appeared—with him in handcuffs—in the paper anyway. Stuart and Ruth lost their money, which went back into the public purse as part of what Chester owed. They had been saving for that house since their marriage, and now had to start anew. Chester himself had just bought a new ranch-style house in Etobicoke on Burnhamthorpe Road.

Chester's arrest was big news—it was a major embezzlement scheme, and $35,600 was a lot of money in 1954. The newspapers went after the full story, but, incredibly, they never found out that Chester was L. M. Montgomery's son. Chester had traded on his mother's name from the time he began to study law and especially when he tried to establish new practices after her death, but now, for once, he kept quiet about it.

Reporters descended on his faithful wife, Ida, who had been pleased that her husband was doing so well in his job that he had been able to buy them the house. Chester had handled all their finances, and she was shocked, and bewildered by the devastating news. She lamented to reporters that they would probably lose their house now. They did, of course; Chester not only lost his own house, but orchestrated the loss of the house that Stuart was about to purchase, too. Ida, loyal to her husband, told the reporter: "He must have been born under an unlucky star. Nothing has gone completely right with him, although he did his best to help everyone. Time and time again he went out of his way to help friends in trouble and he got kicked in the face for his pains."[2] Chester did in some ways try to help others, and people were genuinely fond of him. His impulses were always generous, even if his means were not always honourable.

Chester was brought to trial a year later, and sentenced on September 28, 1955, to two years less a day in the Guelph Reformatory for embezzling money from the government. The lawyer representing him was Donald F. Downey, his former partner. While Chester served his term Ida and her children stayed with a brother in Guelph to be near him. He was released on November 24, 1956, before his sentence was up, presumably because of good behaviour.

According to Luella, while Chester was incarcerated, he noticed that there was another inmate named "Macdonald" in the Guelph Reformatory. When Chester inquired who he was, he had the extraordinary experience of discovering that this was his own son by his first marriage, Cameron Macdonald, age twenty. They had not met since Chester and Luella had separated, but young Cameron had inherited some of his father's traits for getting into trouble.

Another person who was shocked by Chester's arrest was his own secretary, and her perspective offers yet another view of Maud's complex son. Like many others, she felt he was a good man, a generous man, and a devoted family man. Chester had always been kind to her. She had first met Chester when he was living up north, attempting to start a law practice. Both were in an amateur theatre production—something he still enjoyed. She was a single parent with a small child to support. Chester, being a lawyer, offered to help her get child support payments from her husband. He did all the paperwork, and she started receiving her payments though Chester.

After Chester and Ida moved to Toronto, and he himself found this job in the Office of the Public Trustee, he urged her to move to Toronto. He told her she would have a better chance of finding work in the city. He helped her get a secretarial position in the office, and she became his secretary. Always paternal and helpful, he continued, along with Ida, to be supportive. She said he was quite "the character," but everyone liked him.

Unfortunately, now that she was in Toronto, her child support payments started faltering. With her secretarial job she was usually able to cover her apartment and food costs. Sometimes, however, she had a shortfall—if she had to purchase clothes for her child, or if she didn't have quite enough for groceries—and then Chester would always produce a little money (usually five or ten dollars) from his own wallet for her. He always told her she did not need to pay him back, given that he knew how she was struggling to make ends meet. She was very touched by his kind consideration.

When the full investigation of Chester's affairs was finished, she was astonished to find out that *her husband had made all his payments on time, and in full.* Chester had taken the money paid in trust for her and kept it for himself, doling out bits when she was herself unable to make ends meet.

After he was caught, Chester promised her that he would return the money to her, and begged her to store his mother's books and other items for him until he got out of jail. He told her he was afraid they would be taken from Ida and sold to make restitution. She felt pity for him and agreed to do so. He had a forlorn and needy quality that softened people, she said, even when he had hurt them. You could not help liking him, for you always felt he meant well, but was weak.

When Chester got out of jail and came to claim his mother's books and manuscripts, he told her she was number thirty-six on the list of people he owed restitution. She kept moving down the list, but never quite made it to number one.

People always wondered why Chester was so short of money. Once, he told this secretary it was because Stuart had defrauded him out of his share of their mother's estate, a bald untruth. In fact, Chester had himself sold his rights to his mother's published books to her publisher (ostensibly to finance his marriage to Ida.) Jack McClelland became the beneficiary of half of Maud's Canadian royalties—a boon that helped him continue in his father's lifelong career of promoting Canadian authors.

Chester's secretary reminisced about Chester's complicated and needy character, and his social life. She said that he always "had other women" and she thought this was one of his expenses. He smoked non-stop, and he never had enough money for this habit, either, so he generally "bummed" his cigarettes off others, to the point where people would duck out when they saw him coming. Always rumpled and untidy, he became a joke at work for his eccentricities. He retained an interest in amateur drama and was known as the person to call if an actor suddenly fell ill. Chester could learn any part—small or large—almost instantly, either by reading the playbook or by watching a single rehearsal. But he was absolutely no good as an actor. He could ham up his parts, but emotions never seemed genuine. "It was as if some part of him was missing," she said, "the part that makes you able to truly empathize with others, and to know how they feel." This is one of the classic traits of the psychopath.

When his secretary asked him, after his jail term was over, if there was anything he would do over, he answered, "Yes. *Not get caught.*"

Released from jail, he eventually found a job at the office of Canadian Law Books as an assistant editor. It is unknown if the company was aware of his past when they hired him. He died suddenly, at age fifty-one, on June 14, 1964, at his apartment at 5785 Yonge Street, in Willowdale. His death certificate gives no cause of death. His last date at work had been in February 1964, three or four months earlier. He was cremated. The obituaries mentioned that Stuart Macdonald was his brother, but not that he was the son of L. M. Montgomery, perhaps the most interesting feature in his short and troubled life.

After the funeral of Chester's wife, Ida, many years later, her sister said sorrowfully to me: "She had a very hard life, filled with many, many disappointments." Ida had pleasure in her children, though; daughter Cathie lived a quiet life with her mother, and son David went on to a very successful career as a teacher and school administrator.

Stuart's story

In March 1943, Stuart Macdonald entered the Canadian Navy, where he became the medical doctor on the *Huron*, a Canadian destroyer that patrolled the English Channel, departing under the cover of darkness to pick up the wounded. On July 10, 1943, he married Ruth Steele, a petite and beautiful nurse he had been courting since before his mother's death. Maud never met Ruth.

Stuart returned safely from the war, but he was disturbed by "survivor guilt" and occasional nightmares about his experiences for the rest of his life. He also suffered a very deep, lifelong sense of guilt that he had not been able to prevent his beloved mother's death—a phenomenon common among those who experience a parent's suicide. He had an understanding of human nature born of deep reflection over his own family. He told others that "you can't save people from themselves." He had been both repelled and fascinated by his brother's lack of conscience, just as Chester had apparently been mystified by his brother's ability to attract loyal and devoted friends without effort.

For many years Dr. E. Stuart Macdonald was considered one of the most skilful obstetricians at St. Michael's Hospital in Toronto, and his obituary in *Maclean's* magazine, in October 1982, described him as a much respected doctor. He had seen his last patient in his office minutes before visiting a neurologist about increasingly severe headaches he suffered a fatal brain aneurysm during the actual examination.

As a young man, Stuart had been embarrassed if people found out that his mother was the famous "L. M. Montgomery" and he kept this a secret during his training. Mid-life, as a very busy doctor who was pestered by people interested in his mother, he sometimes revealed resentment of the burdens that being her son had placed on him. To a few, he expressed an annoyance that she had expected such perfection from her children. When pressed to comment on her shortcomings, he named her "pride" and her tendency to worry, but he clearly admired and loved her. There was a profound bond between him and his mother, and he spoke of the deep affection that she engendered in everyone who knew her. Shortly before his death, he reflected that in a long career practising and teaching medicine he had probably saved only five or six babies that no other doctor could have—a small contribution to the overall "sum of human happiness," he said, compared to his mother's enormous one through her life and her novels.

Stuart and Ruth achieved what his mother had wanted all her life—a home that was always open to friends and guests and young people (some of whom Stuart had delivered). He and Ruth adopted three children, and they cherished their "chosen children" as much as Matthew and Marilla loved their own little "Anne."

At his funeral, the large chapel was filled beyond overflowing with medical colleagues, friends, and patients. Everyone remembered Stuart's storytelling ability and his keen sense of humour, and lamented the passing of a man who, like his mother, was a unique and unforgettable personality.

Luella's story

Luella Macdonald came to the last part of her life—a life filled with unimaginable difficulties and personal tragedy—as a very strong and philosophical woman who had transcended bitterness. She was a woman of much intelligence and intellectual curiosity, and a plucky soul as well. She was well-read and wise, funny and frank. She said what she thought, and she met everything head on. She recovered from two serious strokes in her early retirement years and resumed a full and active life after learning to drive and speak all over again.

Luella had raised her two children by herself, taking a job in an aircraft factory to support them, and her tales of her struggles were heart-rending. At times, she had nobody to watch the children, and no money to hire help. She did her best to "child-proof" the house and left the children locked in it while she worked. Her eyes moistened as she described how the children would cry when she left in the morning. In an era before government social assistance and enforced child support, she said there were many abandoned or widowed women (and fathers who had lost their wives) who had to make choices like hers: leave your children without proper supervision—or go without food.

Luella retained a soft spot in her heart for Chester all her life, despite the way he had treated her. She thought of him as someone to be pitied, and she had come to the opinion that there had been a genetic problem from the beginning. She believed that when he came into life, defeat was already sitting there, just waiting to knock him about. She said there were "signs of compulsive lying from time to time." She picked up many negative feelings from him about his father, but "never about his mother." He "had a brilliant mind but somewhere along the line nothing happened to give him any direction for living. . . . he was a 'mucker,'" she said. When I asked her if the rumours I had heard that Chester had taken his own life were true, she said she didn't know, and then added, sorrowfully but without bitterness, that it would "have been the honourable thing to do—he brought lots of misery into the world, to lots of people." Misfortune pursued some of Chester's first family into the next generation, and Luella's account of the tragedies (accidental death, alcoholism, mental illness, homicide, and suicide) are too terrible to detail. Luella was proud that her daughter, also named Luella, became a nurse, and she spoke of her daughter and grandchildren with great affection.

Joy Laird's story

According to Mr. Justice Douglas Latimer, the Crown Attorney for Halton County from 1968 until his retirement, Joy Laird became the best legal secretary in the entire area. If she had been able to afford the study of law herself, he said that she would have been an excellent lawyer. He described her as very hard-working, reliable, and smart, with a wonderful memory. In her adult years she had a serious no-nonsense demeanour, but she also enjoyed socializing, and had a quick and ready wit. She had an excellent manner with clients, and she mixed regularly and easily on a social basis with the most influential families in the area. She had excellent taste and brought class and natural dignity to the position she occupied.

Joy began her career with the Dale and Bennett law firm in Georgetown, the oldest in the area, as secretary to Sybil Bennett, a very prominent lawyer (the first female Q.C), and a second cousin of Prime Minister R. B. Bennett. Sybil Bennett thought so highly of Joy—who kept the firm running when the partners were otherwise occupied—that she purchased Joy's first car for her as a gift. When the Dale and Bennett law firm was put up for sale, Joy Laird, then a senior secretary in the firm, called Douglas Lattimer and urged him to buy it, which he did the year before he was called to the bar in 1972. She all but ran the firm until he graduated and could take over. The firm then became Dale, Bennett, and Latimer.

Justice Latimer said that Joy, twelve years his senior, knew everyone in the entire surrounding community, from the poorest to the wealthiest. Because everyone knew, respected, and trusted her, people brought their business to the firm. When he became Crown Attorney for Halton County and left the law office, Joy followed him, remaining his loyal secretary until her retirement. He could not praise her enough, and joked about how she had told him that if he ever made a mistake, to blame it on "his secretary," because people would forgive a secretary but not the lawyer himself. Joy, he said, did not make mistakes—she was a perfectionist and a professional in every way.

Joy Laird never married, despite many would-be suitors. She was a very private person, and no one knew that she nursed a memory of her early and only love, Stuart Macdonald. She treasured the scores of letters Stuart had written her over a long period, as well as Stuart's 1939 medical pin. Because she had been unable to afford further education, she borrowed Stuart's advanced math and other textbooks from St. Andrew's, working through them for self-education. She kept every clipping about him or his family, as well as his pictures of him as a gymnast at St. Andrew's and then at the University of Toronto, performing on the high bars. But the memory of their young romance died out in the community, and she never mentioned it to anyone. Only after knowing her for many years did I begin to piece things together. My most unnerving experience was being taken to her beautifully decorated bedroom to be shown something, and to see, in a prominent place, a near life-size, incredibly realistic doll, fully dressed, looking like a real baby. It was introduced as a doll that had belonged to the Brown children, who had been killed in the radial train accident in Norval.

Joy never knew how strongly Maud had opposed her romance with Stuart. She died in 2003, the year before Volume 5 was published, giving the full story of Maud's antagonism to Joy's family.[3]

In a drive through Norval a few weeks before his sudden death in 1982, Stuart pointed out Joy's childhood home and volunteered that his mother had been completely wrong about her—that Joy had been a very nice young woman, no matter what her father did. Stuart remarked with considerable irony that his mother should not have held other families to standards that her own family could not meet. He added bitterly that his mother should have invited Joy into their Norval and Toronto homes to see if she would fit in, and this would have enabled their romance to either go ahead or fall apart naturally. He still felt sadness and shame that he had not had the courage to insist that his mother get to know Joy before condemning her. His mother's health problems, his own busy career, and impending war brought such trauma into their lives that other personal concerns fell aside, and then he met the lovely Ruth, a trained nurse, and married her.

Joy Laird cared for and supported her aging and much-loved mother all her life. She also cared for her father and her feckless, alcoholic brother until their deaths. Mercifully, she never knew that Maud had called her "that bootlegger's spawn" in her journals (October 23, 1936), but those bitter words were seared painfully in Stuart's mind. He knew that his mother wanted him to publish her journals eventually, as a record of her life, but those words were responsible for his keeping his mother's journals under wraps until the end of his life. He felt embarrassment that his mother had said what she did; and he worried that people might believe his mother's assessment of Joy.

The publication of Maud's final journal in 2004 brought shock to the community where Joy lived. No one had imagined that "Mrs. Macdonald" had felt as she did about Joy Laird. Norval people who had been Joy's lifelong friends— Mary Maxwell, the wife of Canon Maxwell of the Anglican church in Norval, and Joan Brown Carter, the postmistress of Norval for many years and an amateur historian—told a very different story about Joy, as did Joan Carter's youngest daughter, Kathy (who grew up as Joy's godchild, and thought of her as a second mother).

Kathy Carter Gastle, who was mayor of the town of Halton Hills from 2000 to 2003, remembered the Laird home as a very happy place where people were always welcome. The house was spotless and well-decorated, and Joy's mother was a kind and cheerful woman, and a splendid cook who liked young people.

Kathy Carter grew up looking through her godmother's scrapbooks. She heard a great deal about Stuart Macdonald from Joy as a fondly remembered childhood chum. Although Kathy never actually met the fabled Stuart Macdonald, he was a fixture in Joy's stories of her own childhood. Joy had always loved children, and took her position as godmother to Kathy Carter very seriously, giving her many advantages, such as special trips that she would not otherwise have had as a youngest child in a large family. They were as close as mother and daughter until Joy's death. At the end of her life, Joy gave Kathy a red silk pouch full of the school crests from Stuart's letters, which she had carefully clipped off each letter before she destroyed the letter itself.

The community did not look down on the Laird family, and after Maud's Norval journals were published, people wondered over the malice directed at them. Perhaps when Maud complained about the fact that she couldn't imagine where Ewan's salary went, she may have suspected that Ewan—like many other respectable men wanting their "nip"—dropped in to pick up the occasional refill for his cough syrup from Lou Laird's little "Blue Room." Maud gave Ewan drinks of her own homemade wine, but she would not have sanctioned his patronizing Lou Laird. Perhaps she worried that her sons were being corrupted by Lou's liquor, too.

In *Jane of Lantern Hill*, Maud disapproves of parents meddling in their children's love matches. But the writer of fiction had an objectivity that the mother of sons did not. As Maud once told Violet King, writers have no special immunity to human frailty and folly.

William Arthur Deacon

When William Arthur Deacon wrote about her books with such lofty contempt, and elbowed her out of the CAA executive, he deprived Maud of doing public service in the world of letters, as well as the celebrity status she had worked hard to achieve.

Deacon lived to a ripe old age, dying in 1977 after long service as literary editor of *The Globe and Mail*, from 1936 until 1961. In an unfinished manuscript about his influential career, he wrote, "Uniquely among Canadians, Miss Montgomery understood the minds and hearts of adolescent girls, about whom she wrote in a manner completely acceptable to them." He observed that her books were popular in Japan, and he couldn't resist remarking that this resulted in Japanese girls writing the literary editor of *The Globe and Mail* (e.g., Deacon himself), asking to put them in touch with Canadian pen-pals. Patronizing to the end, he added: "The P.E.I. Branch of the I.O.D.E. has *shouldered this problem* [italics added]."

Postscript

Readers of Maud's journals and this biography will ponder over what ultimately brought her to such a sad end. Would different choices have enabled this gifted woman—who wrote books that have brought joy to so many adults and young people all around the world—to find more satisfaction in her own life? Maud herself was addicted to asking "what if?" (see her journal entry of November 25, 1933). In her final years, she began to suspect that she was the author of much of her own misfortune, and she combed her journals for clues. But she was equally given to quoting the Persian poet, Omar Khayyam:

> The Moving Finger writes, and, having writ,
> Moves on; nor all thy Piety nor Wit
> Shall lure it back to cancel half a Line
> Nor all thy Tears wash out a Word of it.

ACKNOWLEDGEMENTS

First, I am indebted to Dr. E. Stuart Macdonald for first suggesting that I write a biography of his mother. He died in 1982, and Elizabeth Waterston and I then began editing his mother's journals, bringing them out between 1985 and 2004. The L.M. Montgomery Project, with support from the University of Guelph and the Social Sciences and Humanities Research Council of Canada, continued over a thirty-year period. Elizabeth and I have had many happy years working together on a writer we admire, sharing research with many other international enthusiasts in the process. The early scholars whose research has underpinned Montgomery studies are Gabriella Åhmansson, F.W.P. Bolger, Elizabeth R. Epperly, Carole Gerson, Mollie Gillen, Elizabeth Waterston, and Rea Wilmshurst.

My own research on Montgomery began in the early 1970s. People who generously assisted me are legion, and many credited below are now dead. As my generation knows too well, the early days of the electronic age were fraught with frequent data loss, and I apologize to those whose names have been inadvertently omitted.

In the late 1980s and 1990s, three University of Guelph students helped me with the initial research for this biography, and their exceptional dedication deserves special citation. Evan W. Siddall researched and analyzed Montgomery's publishing history, the legal entanglements, and her financial dealings, setting up timely interviews in the USA with aging parties to these affairs. Kate Wood's invaluable research focused on retrieving the culture of Montgomery's youth and early years from microfilmed Prince Edward Island and Ontario newspapers and books. Morgan Dennis worked on Montgomery's later Ontario years, researching people, places, and transactions. My debt to these three people is incalculable.

Numerous other students did valuable early work on the LMM Project, but special thanks goes to my two daughters, who first began assisting me during their own school years: Jennie Rubio's help included compiling books Montgomery read or quoted from, and Tracy (Rubio) Siddall organized and recorded financial and other data for assessment. Rosemary Waterston also did helpful research in many areas. Others who contributed to the Montgomery project in their student years include Nick Whistler, Marie Campbell, Rebecca and James Conolly, Benjamin Lefebvre, Leanne Wild, Rebecca Olivier, Laura Higgins, Kathy Jia, Stephanie Waterston, and Katie Waterston. Patrick Firth and Angela Lombardi prepared a bibliography for the website: www.lmmrc.ca.

Editorial assistance on this manuscript came from Amy Black at Doubleday Canada, Meg Masters, and Meg Taylor. I am also particularly indebted to Elizabeth Waterston for her advice, responses, and constant encouragement, and to my daughter, Jennie Rubio, for her experienced, vigorous, and sensitive editorial help with the final manuscript.

Relatives and acquaintances of both Montgomery and the other players in her life have been generous with help. For the PEI years, special thanks goes to the following: Ruth, George, and Maureen Campbell of Park Corner; Mrs. Wilfred (Mary) Furness, Gordon, and Sharon Furness of Vernon River; Doris Munsey Haslam of Charlottetown; Doris Stirling Jenkins of Summerside; Georgie and Bruce MacLeod of Kensington; Christine McLeod of Orwell Cove; John and Jennie Macneill of Montgomery's Cavendish home; Dr. Lewis B. Woolner of the Mayo Clinic and Evelyn Woolner of Rustico; and Jean Macphail Weber of the Macphail Homestead Museum in Orwell. I also thank Leta Andrews, Mrs. Ralph Callbeck, Constance Carruthers, Anne Hart, Mrs. Hants B. Hunter, Eileen MacKendrick Leard, Louise Lowther, Helen Macdonald, George MacFarlane, Jean MacFarlane, Nancy MacFarlane, Percy MacGougan, Clayton McLure, Albert Middleton, Mrs. R.C. (Blanche) Montgomery, Helen MacFarlane Nicholls, and Dr. Lemuel Prowse.

For later years in Ontario, in addition to Montgomery's maids, I particularly thank Harold and Wilda Clark, Margaret Mustard, and Isabel Mustard St. John of Uxbridge; Nina Pickering Lunney of Zephyr; Cameron, Fred, and Jessie Leask and Mary Stiver of Leaskdale; Luella Reid Macdonald of Brampton; Joan Carter, Robert and Elaine Laird Crawford, Kathy Carter Gastle, Marion Webb Laird, Mary Maxwell, and Margaret Russell of Norval; Catharine Agnes Hunt, Joy Leard, and Justice Douglas V. Latimer of Georgetown; David and Kay Dills of Acton; Marcella Berger, Dr. Richard Braiden, Nora Lane Braiden, L.E.

"Ted" Jones, Dr. E. Stuart Macdonald, Ruth Macdonald, Lena McClure, Dr. D. McIntosh, Linda Sparks (Olive Watson), Anita Webb, and Robert L. Woolner of Toronto; David Macdonald of Kleinburg; Mike W. Chepesuik of British Columbia; R. W. Macqueen of Waterloo; Ed and Bette Campbell of Haileybury; Violet King Morgan of Guelph; Roberta Mary Sparks Richardson of Hamilton; and Eric Gaskell of Ottawa.

I also thank Emma Andrews, Mrs. Will Bacon, George and Noreen Bell, Merle Collins, J. Austin Cook, Chester Early, Norma Fitzgerald, Ruth Gallant, Evelyn Harrison, Elsie Hunter, Robert Jardine, Ken Leslie, Edna McClure, Margaret McKane, Marjorie McKee, Dorothy Watson McLean, William Steele, Ruth Wade, Winnifred Wake, and Reg Winfield, plus many members of the Leaskdale, Norval, and Guelph church and community organizations.

The scores of archivists and librarians who have assisted me include Linda Armichand, Margaret Beckman, Lorne Bruce, Bev Buckie, Virginia Gillham, Bernard Katz, Ellen Morrison, Nancy Sadek, and Darlene Wiltsie at the University of Guelph; Kevin Rice, David Webber, and Moncrieff Williamson at the Confederation Centre; Merritt Crocket, Frankie Dindial, Mary Beth Harris, and Simon Lloyd of the University of Prince Edward Island Library; Elizabeth DeBlois of the L.M. Montgomery Institute; Marilyn Bell and Charlotte Stewart of the Public Archives in Charlottetown; Peter D. Hingley of the Royal Astronomical Society (U.K.); Alan S. Wakefield and Matthew Lee of the Imperial War Museum (U.K.); Carl Spadoni of McMaster University; Irene Aubrey, Don Carter, Anne Goddard, and Peter Rachon at the National Library of Canada; Kim Arnold at the Presbyterian Church Archives; Judith Colwell of the United Church Archives and the Maritime Conference; Marie Hammond, Anne-Marie Langlois, and Susan Lewthwaite at the Law Society of Upper Canada; Judy Ginsberg of the Osgoode Hall Archives; Ken Ryan of the St. Andrew's College Archives; Carole Lindsay at the Toronto Star; Amanda Valpy at the Globe and Mail; Hazel Robertson at the National Library of Scotland; Ron Rybnikar at the Babson Institute Archives; Orlo Jones and Douglas Fraser at the PEI Heritage Foundation; Paul Sharkey and Karen Teeple of the City of Toronto Archives; Patricia Townsend of the Acadia University Archives; Henry F. Scannell and Aaron Schmidt of the Boston Public Library; Yuka Kajihara and Leslie McGrath of the Osborne Collection of Early Children's Books; Brian Winter of the Whitby Museum; Brenda Dunn, Barbara MacDonald, and Tom Reddin of Parks Canada; Allan McGillivray of the Uxbridge-Scott Historical Society; Michael S. Moss and

Elspeth Reid of the University of Glasgow; Anne Dondertman and Monique Flaccavento of the Thomas Fisher Rare Book Library; Carolyn Cannon and Michael Moore of the York University Library; Steven Whalen of the Uxbridge Library; Marina Englesakis at St. Michael's Hospital in Toronto; Cynthia Murphy of the Connecticut Valley Historical Museum; Katherine Roy of PEN, Margaret Booth and Karen Tinsley of the Imperial Life Insurance Company of Toronto; John Choules, Andrew Cross, and Jim Lewis of the Archives of Ontario; Muriel Lockhart of Springfield, Massachuetts; Garron Wells of the University of Toronto; Lynne Dunlop and Marg Murray of the Tillsonburg United Church; Mary Beth Bagg and Fred Hall of the University of Indianapolis; Laura T. Neil of the Alloa (Scotland) Library; Mary Ann Welch of the University of Western Ontario Law Library; and Ken Puley of the CBC Radio Archives.

Members of the medical community assisted my understanding of forensic pharmacology, psychiatric and mood disorders, and musculoskeletal problems. Special thanks goes to Dr. Angus Beck in Prince Edward Island, and in Ontario to Dr. Michael Howitt of Guelph, and to Professors Harold Kalant, Denis Grant, and Ernest Steib of the University of Toronto. Thanks also to Dr. Alexander Watt, Dr. Ruth Tatham, Danny Lui (B.Sc.Phm), Minette Roy (RMT), Kathy James (RPT) of Guelph; to Dr. Mary McKim MacKenzie of London; to Catherine Munn and Dr. E. Kaminska of Hamilton; and to doctors in Toronto's Clarke Institute, the Centre for Addiction and Mental Health, and Sunnybrook Hospital, including Drs. Anne Bassett, R.A. Cleghorn, Cyril Greenland, Jack Griffin, Steven Hucker, and Zindel V. Segal.

Of the many lawyers contacted, I particularly acknowledge the help of James Innes Stewart, Q.C., president of the 1939 graduating class at Osgoode Hall, and I also appreciate information from Jacie Horwitz, Kenneth Foulds, W.H.C. Boyd, Roy Clement Sharp, W. G. C. Howland, David Ongley, Rupert Parkinson, Mervin Mirsky, Samuel Lerner, Gregory T. Evans, and William Parker. Thanks also to Celia Bobkin of Blake, Cassels, and Graydon.

Others who furnished specific, useful information for this project are Anne Adams, Hans Beck, Michael Bliss, Ruth Compton Brouwer, Donna Campbell, Virginia Careless, Beth Cavert, Carolyn Collins, Peter Coues, Joanne Craig, David Donaldson (Prestwick Golf Club, Scotland), Owen Dudley Edwards (Scotland), Elizabeth Epperly, the Right Honorable Archibald George, Earl of Eglinton and Winton (of London, U.K.), Carole Gerson, Judy Grant, Jack and Linda Jackson Hutton, Bernard Katz, G. Douglas

Killam, Jennifer Litster (Scotland), Klaus Martens (Germany), Kevin McCabe, the Honorable Pauline M. McGibbon, Janice Dickin McGinnis, Lena C. McLure, Heather Murray, Ian Ross Robertson, John Robert Sorfleet, Roger W. Straus, J.R. (Tim) Struthers, Clara Thomas, Barbara Wachowicz (Poland), Gavin White (Scotland), and James W. Wilson, O.B.E. (of Skelmorlie Castle, Ayrshire, Scotland).

I also thank the following people for contributing to my work and research: Yoshiko Akamatsu (Japan), Marian Badgery, Kathy Belicki, Sue Bennett, Jane Waterston Bregha, Keith Brewer (U.S.A.), Susan Brown, Helen Buss, Elspeth Cameron, Lynn Campbell, the Rev. Mary Campbell, Norman and Elaine Campbell, Joan Brown Carter, Ronald Cohen, J.T.H. Connor, Barbara Conolly, Gwendolyn Davies, Marie C. Davis (Zimmerman), Margaret Anne Doody (U.S.A.), Rae Fleming, Carol Gaboury (U.S.A.), Irene Gammel, Virginia Gillham, Billie Godson, Beverley A. Hayden, Marian Hebb, Lynne Hoehamer, Huifeng Hu (China), Yuka Izawa (Japan), Marlene Kadar, Clarence Karr, Phyllis Keeling, Michael Kennedy, Catherine Kerrigan (Scotland), Deirdre Kessler, Don Kuiken, Eleanor Lamont, Marjory Lang, Margaret Laurence, Ruth Law, Jean Little, Ami Lonnroth (Sweden), Margaret MacKay (Scotland), the Rev. Eoin MacKay, Asim Masoud, Mary McDonald-Rissanen (Finland), Ron McKeen, Bill McNeill, John Moldenhauer, Allan L. Montgomery, Kenneth H. Montgomery, Graeme Morton, Heather Murray, Elaine Kalman Naves, Perry Nodelman, Jason Nolan, Mariam Montgomery Perkins (U.S.A.), Ormande Pickard (U.K.), Anna Pisulewska-Zelazny (Poland), David Rehak (Czech Republic), Laura Robinson, Sami Roodi (Iran), Catherine Sheldrick Ross, Malcolm Ross, Paul Salmon, Judi Saltman, Shelley Sanders, Tim Sauer, Ivan Sayers, Carol Shields, Wayne Skinner, Edith Smith, Kay Smith, Glenys Stow, Leon Surette, Clara Thomas, Paul and Hildi Tiessen, William Toye, Fred Turner, Jonathan Vance, Christyl Verduyn, Sandy Wagner, Douglas Waterston, Nick Whistler, Jane E. Wilson, Joanne Wood, Dr. John Woodger, Emily Woods, Christie Wooster (U.S.A.), Lorraine York, and Alan R. Young. I thank Chris Lee of Guelph, my late husband Gerald J. Rubio, and my son-in-law, Tony Collins of McMaster University, for endless and patient computer assistance.

Administrators at Guelph who have greatly facilitated my work over the years are Margaret Beckman, G. Douglas Killam, Wayne Marsh, David Murray, Michael Ridley, and Helen Salmon. Finally, I thank my agents at Westwood Creative Artists (Toronto): first Jan Whitford and then Jackie Kaiser.

ENDNOTES

INTRODUCTION

1. Montgomery's letter to Ephraim Weber, dated November 10, 1907, p. 58.
2. Letter to Mrs. L. O. Ekeberg, from E. S. Macdonald, dated September 24, 1960.
3. Journal entry of November 10, 1908.
4. *Peterborough Examiner*, May 2, 1942.

PART ONE: THE PEI YEARS

1. Maud was named "Lucy" after her grandmother and "Maud" after a daughter of Queen Victoria. In childhood, she was called "Maudie" to prevent confusion with her grandmother's name. As late as 1896, Maud signed her name in her copy of Whittier as "Lucy M. Montgomery," but she used the name "Maud" in adulthood, preferring it to both "Lucy" and "Lucy Maud." The name "Maud" reflected the pleasure in poetry of colonial Prince Edward Island, recalling Tennyson's 1855 poem "Maud" and John Greenleaf Whittier's "Maud Muller" (circa 1856), a ballad about a romance that would have been but for the social disparity between a poor country lass and a prominent judge, and Maud underlined many lines in this poem in her book. (The most prominently underlined was "For of all sad words of tongue or pen, / The saddest are these: 'It might have been.'") She always published under the name "L. M. Montgomery," a publishing convention that obscured a female author's gender since authorship was regarded as more appropriate to men. In popular culture, she has commonly been called "Lucy Maud."
2. "The Gay Days of Old: A Well-known Author's Reminiscences of Her Girlhood on a Canadian Farm," *Farmers' Magazine*, circa 1920, found on p. 176 of *Scrapbook of Reviews*.

)8.

y the villagers in the Cavendish Literary Society programs beth and seventeenth years suggesting the range of interests in this
nclude: "Which is the greater poet, Byron or Burns?" "Should
nt be abolished?" "Which is mightier, the Pen or the Sword?"
er influence on mankind, oratory or music?" "Which is the better
form of government: monarchy or republicanism?" Programs were presented on
"The English Revolution of 1688," "The Life and Writings of Sir Walter Scott,"
"The Works of George Eliot," "The Elizabethan Period," and "The Principal
Events in the Reign of Queen Victoria." Evening programs often began with a formal debate or paper and then the topics were opened to discussion.

5. See "The Flyting Betwixt Montgomery and Polwart," *The Poems of Alexander
Montgomerie*, pp. 99–132, written circa 1629 in Scotland, as an example of traditional Scottish flyting in verse.

6. See Michael Kennedy, *The Island Magazine*, Volume 39 (1996), p. 39. See also the
entry on "Montgomery" in *Malpeque and Its People*. The Montgomerys came
around 1770, but the discovery of the ship register of the *Edinburgh* appears to confirm the date as 1771.

7. See Michael Kennedy, *The Island Magazine*, Volume 39 (1996), p. 42. McShannon
had many other spellings, like O'Senóg, MacShenaig, McShinnocht, etc.

8. See Mark Girouard, p. 110.

9. James W. Wilson, O.B.E., the current owner of the Montgomery castle in
Skelmorlie, Scotland, the ancestral seat of the Montgomerie clan, found a large oil
portrait of the thirteenth Earl of Eglinton in the sheds when he was restoring the
grounds. He believed the portrait was painted circa 1852 by Catterson Smith, one of
Ireland's finest portrait painters, when Lord Eglinton was Lord Lieutenant, i.e., governor, of Ireland. After having the painting restored, Mr. Wilson presented it to the
Prestwick Golf Club, which the thirteenth Earl had founded in 1851. Although
women were not allowed in this all-male club, Mr. Wilson arranged for my daughter, Jennie, and me to view and photograph the picture. We confirmed a distinct resemblance between Donald Montgomery and the thirteenth Earl of Eglinton.

10. This tournament cost an estimated £40,000 (around $10,000,000 in 2007 dollars).
See Ian Anstruther, *The Knight and the Umbrella: An Account of the Eglinton
Tournament, 1839*. See also Mark Girouard, *The Return to Camelot: Chivalry and
the English Gentleman*, Chapter 7, on the Eglinton tournament, pp. 87–110, and
Alan Young, pp. 186–87.

11. Girouard, pp. 108, 110.

12. One, Alexander Montgomerie, had been a court poet in the reign of James VI. Even Maud's father wrote poetry, and one of his poems is preserved in the L. M. Montgomery Collection at the University of Guelph. The Scottish Collection at Guelph contains other Montgomerie clan materials. Several generations of Scottish Montgomerie men were given to excessive romanticism, and ran through their fortunes quickly, but they were also talented and energetic, and repaired their fortunes in the second half of their lives, as described in *The Knight and the Umbrella*. A nineteenth-century Lady Eglinton is credited with starting the Ayrshire cottage lace industry when she brought back a baby's christening robe from France in 1814. Maud mentions that a sixteenth-century Lady Eglinton was responsible for setting up linen and woollen manufactures in Ireland and encouraging the making of tartans there. Maud was herself an exceptionally skilled needlewoman.

13. For an account of the Macneill clan, see Harold H. Simpson's *Cavendish: Its History, Its People*. The name Macneill was spelled variously as McNeill, McNeil, McNeal, and MacNeill.

14. In 1783, when Speaker Macneill was two years old, the Island population was 1,200 people. By 1820, when he was thirty-five and serving in the provincial legislature, there were 15,000 people. By the time of his death, in 1870, four years before Maud's birth, there were almost 100,000 inhabitants. From that time on, the Island exported well-educated young people to Canada and the United States. Not until the middle of the twentieth century would the Island regain the population it had had in Maud's childhood.

15. "Working farmers" were below the "gentry" in the rigid English class system, according to Dr. Ormand Pickard, local historian and curator of the museum in Dunwich, England.

16. The Woolners were a long-lived family whose descendants fanned out across North America, many becoming successful professionals in the twentieth century.

17. In 1913, L. M. Montgomery published *The Golden Road*, using tales that came from her Great-Aunt Mary Macneill Lawson. The first tale is about lovers Ursula Townley and Kenneth MacNair, who eloped to the dismay of their clan. Ursula's father, like Maud's great-grandfather, Speaker Macneill, boasted he "knew every man, woman and child" on the Island. He opposed the marriage because there was bad political blood between the families, as was the case with the Montgomerys and Macneills. Kenneth was a young sea-captain from the next settlement; similarly, Hugh John had spent some time at sea. Ursula, like Clara Macneill, was married in "sea-green silk."

18. See *The Memorials of the Montgomeries*, which describes this typical feature.

19. "The Gay Days of Old," *Farmers' Magazine*, p. 176, in *Scrapbook of Reviews*.

20. See the entry of January 2, 1905.

21. When you were around Lucy Macneill, recalls Jennie Macneill, wife of Lucy's grandson John Macneill, "you stayed on your best behaviour."

22. Luella Reid Macdonald, Maud's first daughter-in-law, described how in the 1930s Maud had frequently talked about her deep affection for her Grandmother Macneill, describing what a wonderful woman she had been. Luella was later shocked to read in the journals Maud's critical comments about her grandmother.

23. *Red Scrapbook*, 1910–12, p. 21.

24. The Scottish position on education was formalized historically in Scotland's Second Education Act of 1696: all children, rich and poor, male and female, were to be given access to free education. In England, public education was only mandated by law in 1870, nearly two hundred years later. See Mary Rubio, "Scottish-Presbyterian Agency . . ." in *L. M. Montgomery and Canadian Culture*.

25. Ian Ross Robertson, *Acadiensis*, Autumn 1990.

26. Marjory MacMurchy, *Scrapbook of Reviews*, p. 50.

27. Maud paid her difficult grandfather few compliments during her lifetime, but when a journalist reported that "She supposes she inherits her love of writing from her father. He and his brothers all wrote poetry . . . ," she changes the word "father" to "grandfather" in her clipping book, following her practice of correcting magazines, newspapers, and books which get things wrong. See Christian Richardson, "A Canadian Novelist," on p. 25 in *Scrapbook of Reviews*. On p. 19 of the same scrapbook, she admits many of the stories in *The Story Girl* were her grandfather's.

28. These Campbell cousins consisted of: Clara, three years younger than Maud; Stella, five years younger; George, seven years her junior; and Frederica, born when Maud was nine. They had the ebullience found in her fictional children, particularly in *The Story Girl*.

29. Maud gives slightly differing accounts of how many books were in her home in her formative years. In the first round of articles about her after *Anne of Green Gables* was published in 1908, she told interviewers that her family had *full sets* of Sir Walter Scott's and Dickens's novels, Bunyan's *Pilgrim's Progress*, the *complete* poetry of Burns, and Milton's *Paradise Lost*, as well as the popular literature of E. P. Roe and the Pansy books. As a new and unknown author, she was probably embellishing her family's library holdings. A later journal entry on January 7, 1910 (recopied after 1919) is more selective: Dickens's *Pickwick Papers*, Scott's *Rob Roy*, Bulwer-Lytton's *Zanoni*, and John A. Clark's *The Memoirs of Anzonetta Peters*. In

another article from this time she talked of reading Talmadge's *Sermons*, *Paradise Lost*, *Pickwick Papers*, Scott's *Ivanhoe* and *Quentin Durward*, and Campbell's poems. By the 1920s, when she was famous, she was more interested in highlighting her achievement by showing early deprivations. She said that her grandparents were too strict to allow "novels" in the house. This differing account may reflect a specialized use of the term "novel" as a derogatory name for "racy" French fictions, while serious historical fiction, like that of Walter Scott, would have been termed "romances," a less derogatory term.

30. Given Maud's many later unflattering references to her Aunt Emily, it is worth noting that Lucy Palmer (Haslam), the young teacher at Malpeque's Fanning school during this period, comments in her diary on what a "nice" woman Mrs. John Montgomery was. (The Lucy Palmer Haslam diary is held by Professor Michael Bliss and his wife.) Ruth Campbell, raised by Maud's Aunt Emily, called Emily "very determined" but "a good person" in an interview in 1980. Ruth Campbell noted that in her childhood she never knew that L. M. Montgomery was Emily's niece; Maud's books were not in the house, nor were they mentioned. Once later Aunt Emily picked up *A Tangled Web*, then slammed it shut with the words, "I'm ashamed I know her." Another time, Ruth mentioned Maud's name and was told, "Never say that name around here." A story lingers in the Campbell family that Aunt Emily said Maud was sent home to Cavendish because the Fanning school was too crowded to admit her. However, the Palmer diaries show that Maud did attend Malpeque school during her stay: in one entry, Miss Haslam says she "signed Maud Montgomery's autograph book" today. After Ruth married Maud's cousin Jim Campbell of Park Corner, she discovered with surprise that he talked of "Aunt Maud" with enormous affection.

31. Maud's character assignations should always be regarded with caution. Her views, distorted by her personal overreaction, are intensified by her command of language. Many people condemned in her journals were remembered kindly by others. However, her Uncle John F. Macneill was not. One relative recounted, "We were all scared of him." Even in old age, he was a man feared by children. His wife, by contrast, was remembered as "a lovely lady." Her good-natured disposition was passed down to many of their children, including Ernest, the son who inherited the farm. Maud hoped Ernest would re-establish the good name of the Macneill clan, sullied, in her opinion, by her uncle. Ernest's son, John Macneill, eventually inherited both the Alexander Macneill and the John F. Macneill property, and still lives there. When he was born, Maud wrote happily: "A letter came today . . . , saying Ern Macneill's wife had a son. So perhaps the old place may remain in the Macneill name yet." (August 7, 1930)

32. This trait is frequently attributed to people with mood disorder, based on the intensity of their feelings of anger and humiliation.

33. See Mollie Gillen, *The Wheel of Things*, p. 29, for a description of Prince Albert.

34. Taken from the letter to Pensie Macneill, dated August 26, 1890, in Bolger, p. 86.

35. See Bolger, letter of October 18, 1890, p. 94.

36. See Bolger, pp. 37–47, for the entire piece.

37. In a typical ad, young girls in long skirts are shown walking towards a school building, and the copy reads: "School days are danger days . . . it takes years to recover lost virility. Sometimes it is never recovered. . . ." The ailments forecast for "school girls" are "headaches, faintness, slight vertigo, pain in the back and loins, irregularity, loss of sleep, tendency to avoid the society of others."

38. They had been whisked away so suddenly that Maud wasn't even given a chance to say "goodbye" to them. Possibly her Grandmother Macneill observed and overreacted to some display of the natural curiosity that children feel about the opposite sex at a certain age.

39. His obituary read, in part: "By the death of Senator Montgomery a strong link between the past and the present has been severed. The Honourable gentleman, has for several years, been one of the most venerable figures in the political arena in Canada. In respect to this Province, he was the most aged and most active politician in active life. His career as a man extended to the time when our community was in its veriest infancy, and as a politician it reached away beyond the time at which the boon of responsible self-government was secured to Prince Edward Island. He was born at Princetown on the 19th day of January 1808, the sixth son of Daniel Montgomery, Esq., a native of Argyleshire [Scotland], and [was] for thirty-five years a member of the House of Assembly for Prince County. When thirty years of age he was elected a member of the Legislature . . . and since that time . . . He continued to hold the office of President of the Legislative council until 1873, when he was called to the Senate of Canada . . ."

40. Senator Montgomery left $100 to each of his daughters: Jane, wife of Charles Crosby; Nancy, wife of Donald Campbell; Elizabeth, wife of A. G. Fogland of Massachusetts; Mary, wife of Duncan McIntyre (Hugh John's former business partner); Margaret, wife of Robert Sutherland; and the same amount to Maud's father, Hugh John, in Prince Albert. This was a fairly typical will: one son would be selected to inherit the farm, and the other children would be given a token amount.

41. Reprinted in Bolger's *The Years Before "Anne,"* pp. 140–42.

42. The legislative record shows that she was paid substantial supplements, but not what these had to cover.

43. Affective mood disorder (often referred to as manic-depression or bipolar disorder) is believed to affect about 10 percent of the world's population, and it may have been responsible for Alexander Macneill's varying and explosive moods.

44. See the article by Margaret Conrad, "The Neglected Majority," p. 41, in Prentice and Trofimenkoff.

45. Girton, a residential college for women established in 1869, was part of the University of Cambridge in England.

46. See Mathilde Blind, *George Eliot*, pp. 1–2.

47. In the 1917 biographical sketches published in *Everywoman's World* (reprinted in *The Alpine Path* in 1975; see p. 60), Maud compresses her successes into a one-week period and adds John Milton to the list of books she bought. She did a long paper on Milton's "Comus" at Dalhousie, and she may have been confusing the contexts in which she read him. She inscribes her copy of Longfellow, "L. M. Montgomery, Feb. 22, 1896"; her heavily underlined Whittier is inscribed "Lucy M. Montgomery, February 22, 1896"; a collection of Wordsworth's poems is dated 1897; apparently her copy of Byron did not survive, for the copy of Byron she left to her son is marked as a gift from G. B. MacMillan on Christmas 1912.

48. This article can be found in the Norton Critical Edition of *Anne of Green Gables*, p. 272, or in Bolger's *The Years Before "Anne,"* p. 161. In it, she says that women were first admitted to Dalhousie in 1881.

49. The year Maud was slogging away at Bedeque in a country school, Murray took a year of maths at the Sorbonne, then a year at Harvard. In 1899 he took a bicycle tour of France; he toured France, Belgium, Switzerland, Holland, and Scotland again in 1910. In 1901 he travelled to Scotland to see the Glasgow Exhibition. In 1907, he brought his young wife to the Island in an elegant touring car, and came again in 1909. All his movements were tracked by the PEI papers even though he was not, technically, an Islander. By 1902, he was lecturing in Mathematics at McGill, and by 1907, he was offered the Chair of Mathematics at Dalhousie, where he had a long and distinguished career. One of his three daughters married Lord Beaverbrook's son.

50. Maud may have picked up her term "kindred spirits" from Schreiner's book, in Chapter 7: "'My dear friend,' said Bonaparte, taking off his hat, 'I came not to sup, not for mere creature comforts, but for an hour of brotherly intercourse with a kindred spirit.'"

51. Lucy Lane Clifford is also the author of a horrifying children's story, oft-anthologized now, called "The New Mother."

52. According to the 1880 Meecham *Atlas* of PEI, Cornelius Leard had one hundred acres to Alexander Macneill's fifty acres.

53. In the 1975 Terry Filgate documentary of Maud's life, Herman is wrongly depicted as a loutish hick.

54. Psychiatric literature details how the heightened sexuality of the manic phase in people with mood disorder can alter behaviour: first and foremost, people become more active sexually, and this may result in promiscuous sex, fed by biochemical changes. But there are numerous other permutations of a manic phase: they may believe that people are in love with them who are in fact often indifferent; or they may become incestuous like Lord Byron. Manic-depression (bipolar disorder) is believed to have affected some of the world's most creative minds: Lord Byron, Charles Dickens, Virginia Woolf, Vincent van Gogh, Sir Isaac Newton, to name just a few. Biographies show that this disorder can powerfully undermine stability in their personal lives. But the manic phase can also help drive the creative process.

55. See Maud's entries of April 8 and July 10, 1898.

56. The Leard family says Herman died of appendicitis.

57. The story of the Herman Leard/Maud Montgomery/Ettie Schurman love-triangle came to me from two independent sources. Shortly after Montgomery's first journal was published in 1985, Mrs. Constance Carruthers, a nurse and local historian on the Island, gave me both an oral and a written account of the story and the social environment in Bedeque. Her mother had been a good friend of Pril Munsey, and had told her of the tragic romance between Herman Leard and Ettie Schurman. In May 1993, I visited Doris Munsey Haslam, the daughter of Ettie Schurman, in a nursing home in Charlottetown, and heard the same story of her mother's engagement to Herman Leard, followed by his death, and then told of her mother's subsequent marriage to Mr. Munsey, followed by her mother's death after giving birth to her (Doris) and Pril. The University of Toronto historian Michael Bliss, whose wife was related to Doris Haslam, also knew the story.

58. For an account of this two-suitor convention, see Helen M. Buss's article "Decoding L. M. Montgomery's Journals."

59. Only because Herman was such a popular young man, and his death was felt as such a tragedy by the community, did memory of him linger longer than Maud would have expected. The local story of Ettie Schurman lays to rest the suggestion that Herman Leard died of a broken heart over Maud, as some readers of the journals have speculated.

60. For the full text of "The Bride Dreams," see the University of Guelph website www.lmmrc.ca.

61. Alexander held the mortgage on his daughter Annie Macneill Campbell's farm.

62. *Scrapbook of Reviews*, p. 195.

63. When Maud's son, Dr. Stuart Macdonald, read these sentiments in the 1980s, he observed quite sharply to me that his mother was simply romanticizing her father, ignoring obvious shortcomings, as abandoned children typically do.

64. See the treatment "the double" in Robert Louis Stevenson's *Dr. Jekyll and Mr. Hyde* (1886).

65. See *Scrapbook of Reviews*, p. 25, in the article by Christian Richardson, dated summer 1911: "Now 'Anne' was not my first [book] at all, but 'Kilmeny of the Orchard,' . . . How did I come to write it [*Anne of Green Gables*]? Well, you see, I was just a little magazine hack, and had to write what the publishers wanted. . . . One order came for a serial of just seven chapters. I tried 'Anne' first, but soon saw I could not make it what he wanted. Then I wrote 'Kilmeny.' Later I took up 'Anne,' and—it just wrote itself. . . . It was only after 'Anne' made a hit that the publisher raked up 'Kilmeny' . . . and got me to pad it out . . . and make a book out of it." See also an article entitled "How I Began," p. 72.

66. We cannot be positive when Maud first started planning *Anne of Green Gables*. There were normally three distinct stages to her writing a novel: planning it (doing the "spadework" in which she blocked out each chapter); writing it in long-hand; revising and typing it. When she says that she "wrote" *Anne* in the "fall and winter" we do not know which stage of writing she refers to. On May 2, 1907, she wrote Ephraim Weber that she had written a book during the previous fall and winter but kept it a secret because she was afraid she would not find a publisher. (She may well be imprecise about timing in this account to Weber.) She says she sent it to the L. C. Page Company in Boston and after a wait of two months heard from them in April 1907, accepting it. In summer 1911, an article by Christian Richardson (p. 25, *Scrapbook of Reviews*) says that she worked on *Anne* all one winter (probably between May 1905 and May 1906). Another account, essentially the same, is on p. 72 of the clipping scrapbook. On p. 40, she writes in the 1912 *Toronto World* that "'Green Gables' was written three years before it was published and 'Avonlea' was written the last of those years. 'Kilmeny' was a serial written a couple of years before 'Green Gables.' . . ." Maud was notoriously careless about dates, and on April 18, 1914, she says in her journals that she had begun *Anne* ten years earlier (which would be 1904, not 1905), right after Ewan moved to Cavendish (which was May 1905). This could be accurate, too, if by that she means she tried blocking it out, but it appears from the small amount of writing in her journals that she wrote *Anne* all through 1905.

67. Maud was well-versed in Scottish literature, with a particular love for Sir Walter Scott's novels and Jane Porter's *Scottish Chiefs* which romanticized the Highlanders.

68. This card is now in the Ryrie-Campbell collection at UPEI.

69. In the 1980s, Professor Gavin White, of Glasgow's Trinity College, said that any student like Ewan who was performing poorly would have been counselled, but there is no record of that, and if he was, it did not help him.

70. This is reported later, in Maud's entry of January 28, 1912.

71. See the entry of January 28, 1912. Maud continued to be angry about her uncle's "selfishness, bad temper, and tyranny."

72. Lucy—who lived until 1974—was well liked by other relatives and neighbours. Maud's damning descriptions are a good example of the way she wrote people off, bitterly and irrevocably.

73. Recounted in her journal entry of August 16, 1907.

74. To Weber, in the letter of May 2, 1907, she implies that she sent it to only one publisher, the Page Company, and they accepted it promptly within two months. This does not square with her many later statements that she sent it variously to five or six publishers, and then left it lying around in a hatbox.

75. For the cover illustration of Anne, he used a glamorous picture of a young woman which had already appeared in *The Delineator*. It does not look like the illustrations of Anne in the book.

76. A comparison of these early editions is available in the Norton Critical Edition of *Anne of Green Gables*.

77. The vacillations of mood disorder are not the same as insanity. In insanity, people lose touch with reality. In mood disorder, they retain the ability to distinguish between what is normal and what is abnormal, but they feel very miserable and out of control, and their rollicking emotions can affect their judgment and willpower.

78. Margaret Ross was a pretty and gracious woman from a "good" Island family. Her sister married Dr. D. C. Harvey, a distinguished professor at Dalhousie University.

79. From 1904 until 1911, Lord Albert Henry George Grey, the fourth Earl Grey, was a very effective Governor General of Canada. He donated the "Grey Cup" to the Canadian Football League, but his greatest interest was in culture. A career diplomat trained in law at Cambridge University, he had been in the British Parliament and had served as Administrator of Rhodesia. His father had been the Private Secretary to Queen Victoria and her husband.

80. Quoted from a letter from Prof. Ian Ross Robertson to me, dated July 12, 1992, from notes he made in 1970, when the Macphail papers were in private hands.

81. Andrew Macphail's father, William McPhail, born in Inverness-shire, Scotland, in 1830, came to Canada with his parents, and to the Island in 1844. His father, a teacher, was School Inspector for Charlottetown and Queen's County until

1882, when he became Supervisor and Steward of Falconwood, the Island's large mental hospital. Andrew changed his spelling to the more fashionable Scottish "Macphail."

82. Macphail's other book titles include *Essays in Puritanism* (1905), which deals with Jonathan Edwards (1703–1758), John Winthrop (1588–1649), Margaret Fuller (1810–1850), Walt Whitman (1819–1892), and John Wesley (1703–1791). *Essays in Politics* (1909) covers politics, tariffs, and government in Canada, Great Britain, and America. *Essays in Fallacy* (1910) deals with women in the United States and women's suffrage in general, as well as with education and theology. Dr. Macphail's interests were broad and his opinions widely sought. When Mark Twain died, *The Daily Examiner* engaged Macphail to write the obituary and ran it on April 26, 1910, under the headline (in caps): "DR. ANDREW MCPHAIL WRITES AN OBITUARY." Twain's name itself only appears in the subheading.

83. *Essays in Fallacy*, p. 99.

84. See *Examiner*, September 10, 1909, p. 1. On March 30, 1909, before the publication of his *Essays in Fallacy*, the Charlottetown *Patriot* carried on page 3 the cryptic note that Dr. Andrew McPhail [*sic*] is "declared to have recently come in to the public eye as a champion of women's rights. He was recently elected President of the Montreal Golf Club."

85. A Boston paper in 1910 quotes Maud as saying what a woman of her era would be expected to say, "I am a quiet, plain sort of person, and while I believe a woman, if intelligent, should be allowed to vote, I would have no use for suffrage myself. I have no aspirations to become a politician." Then she added the cliché: "I believe a woman's place is in the home." See Red Scrapbook #1, p. 13.

86. See "The Movements of the Vice Regal Party," in *The Daily Patriot*, September 14, 1910, p. 1.

87. In *Anne of Green Gables*, Mrs. Lynde warns Marilla that orphans put strychnine in wells. In *Kilmeny of the Orchard*, Maud tags the villain as a "foreigner."

88. In England, the London *Times* ran the story in the midday edition on September 15, 1910.

89. See the article by Christian Richardson, "A Canadian Novelist," in *Scrapbook of Reviews*, p. 25.

90. Neither Canadian nor American literatures had evolved into a university course of study at that time. Literature meant the "Classics." MacNaughton, from Scotland and educated at Aberdeen, Cambridge, Heidelberg, Berlin, and Edinburgh, taught at Queen's College, the University of Toronto, and McGill. In 1919, the *Globe* called him "one of the most prominent figures in the educational life of Canada" (May 16, 1919).

91. Earl Grey's letter, dated September 27, 1910, is in the National Archives. The reference to "young Macphail" is to Jeffrey, Dr. Macphail's son. Andrew Macphail also had a daughter, Dorothy, who was thirteen at the time of this visit. Many years later Dorothy (Mrs. Lindsay) recounted to Professor Ian Ross Robertson that her father had brought Maud into her bedroom to meet her, but they found her asleep with *Anne of Green Gables* open on her bedcovers. She said her father told her that this "pleased Miss Montgomery."

92. He was not a prolific scholar, but he was a legendary teacher and personality, fondly remembered with awe by his students, one of whom called him a "volcano of a man." MacNaughton did manage to write a tribute to Earl Grey after Lord Grey died, probably at Macphail's urging, for it was published in Macphail's *University Magazine* (1917). He describes the trip they took in some detail, adding: " . . . Miss Montgomery, too, another ornament of the Island, whose delicious idyll 'Anne of the Green Gables,' [*sic*] found much favour in his eyes. He took care that we should meet her."

93. One thinks, for example, of Professor Stephen Leacock's humorous sketches which obtained much praise from his McGill and other literary colleagues.

94. She apparently did not know the difference between a wholesale and retail price when she signed her first contract with him, for she had written her pen-pal Ephraim Weber on May 2, 1907, that the book would be published "on the 10% royalty basis." Later she would learn that Page had almost halved her royalties by this trick in phrasing. He also specified that he would not pay *any* royalties on the first 1,000 copies.

95. See "Miss L. M. Montgomery, Author of *Anne of Green Gables*," in *The Republic*, November 19, 1910, p. 5. (in Red Scrapbook #1, p. 15).

96. Towards the end of the nineteenth century, the province had been feeling increasingly isolated from the mainland. By 1904, citizens and politicians lambasted Ottawa for looking after the western provinces while doing little for the Island's isolation in winter (*Examiner*, May 4, 1904); for most of 1904 and 1905, the Island papers put pressure on Ottawa to fund a tunnel to the mainland. In 1909, the government had purchased the icebreaker *Earl Grey* to get through the ice on the Northumberland Strait, which eased the sense of isolation.

97. On August 2, 1931, Maud pasted the 1903 "nymph-of-the-sea" picture into her journals after commentary on Herman Leard. By 1931, she likely did not want to admit that her first glimpse of Ewan—when he was young and full of promise— was really what had prompted the picture. She preferred to link it to Herman, by then constructed as the man she had really loved, but could not marry.

98. Maud developed the negative in her own darkroom, then hid it away for the next twenty-eight years. Then she had it printed to put in her journals, which were themselves locked away for publication long after her death. She selected her audience as the generations yet unborn who would read her journals and ponder the beauty in youthful hope, the evanescence of life, and the permanence of dream—and see the contrast between the young Maud and the aged one where her life had become in Anne's phrase, "a graveyard of buried hopes."

PART TWO: THE LEASKDALE YEARS

1. Ewan Macdonald spelled his name Ewen, but Maud always wrote "Ewan." It appears both ways on their joint tombstone.

2. When Maud was growing up, her grandfather, the family storyteller, would relate how the jug had come to his wife's grandmother from her sister, Harriet Kemp, who had been engaged to a sailor who had had the jug made for her on an 1826 voyage, but drowned on the way home. The jug was brought to his heart-broken fiancée, who could not bear to look at it. She gave it to Maud's Great-Grandmother Woolner, who carried it to Canada. The shards of this jug are now in the L. M. Montgomery Collection at the University of Guelph Archives.

3. In the early 1980s several of these "young people" from her classes commented on how much they had learned from her.

4. Margaret Mustard, *L. M. Montgomery*, p. 9.

5. P.E.N. is a worldwide fellowship of writers (poets, essayists, novelists), established in 1921, working to promote a culture of reading, and to defend free speech.

6. Marjory's father, Alexander MacMurchy, LL.D., an immigrant from Kintyre, Argyleshire, Scotland, in 1840, was a prominent figure in the educational circles of Toronto. He was active in charity work and for twenty-eight years was principal of the Toronto Collegiate Institute (known as the Jarvis Street Collegiate), where Maud often spoke. He also edited the *Canadian Educational Monthly* and was a senator at the University of Toronto. Marjory's brothers, J. Campbell and Angus (solicitor for the C.P.R.), were prominent lawyers. Her sister, Dr. Helen MacMurchy, was a medical doctor who worked successfully in public health in an era when women were still not welcomed in the medical professions. She served as inspector of hospitals and orphanages, and authored *Infant Mortality* (1910), and a series of Federal Department of Health publications, including *The Canadian Mothers'*

Book. Her new theories on child-rearing show up in the Marigold books, and she served in them as a model for the "lady-doctor." In 1949, when she was eighty-seven, Dr. Helen MacMurchy was honoured in the United States as one of the ten leading physicians in the world. Another sister, Bessie, worked in foreign missions.

7.   The first Leask, Peter, had been born in Aberdeenshire, Scotland, in 1822, and emigrated to Canada with his family in 1841. His sons, George and James, moved to Scott Township (Leaskdale's location), and built a sawmill and gristmill. By 1847, George Leask had built the large brick house across from the manse and lived there until he died at age ninety-five. He was postmaster for fifty years, a school trustee for almost thirty years, and such a devout member of the Presbyterian congregation that he had donated the land for the church.

8.   The first of the Mustard clan came from Cromarty, Rosshire, Scotland, to settle in the sparsely settled Markham area in 1801. John's father, Alexander Mustard, emigrated from Scotland to Scott Township about 1832, four years before Maud's family came to Prince Edward Island. Two of John's brothers, Hugh and James, were extremely prominent farmers and mainstays of the Presbyterian congregation of Leaskdale. The contemporary Dr. [James] Fraser Mustard [b. 1927], C.C., M.D., Ph.D., F.R.S.C., LL.D.—medical scientist, educator, innovative thinker, environmentalist, and co-founder of the Canadian Institute for Advanced Research—is the grandson of James Mustard of Leaskdale.

9.   Some of Zephyr's most prominent members were English in origin, unlike the predominantly Scottish-Presbyterian Leaskdale. The English and Scottish immigrants were all from Great Britain, and were all loyal to the "mother country," but there was some traditional antagonism between these two groups. Old newspapers show that in the early period of colonization, the Scots established dominance because they came with better educations than the English working class; this was the source of some resentment.

10. Maud's detested stepmother, Mary Ann McRae Montgomery (1863–1909), also came from this area. She had gone to secondary school in Uxbridge with John Mustard. Her Uncle William Mackenzie still kept his estate in his native Kirkfield nearby. In 1911, the year of Maud's and Ewan's marriage, William Mackenzie had been knighted for his railway entrepreneurship.

11. Locally organized literary societies like the Hypatia Club were a very important feature in nineteenth- and early-twentieth-century Canadian rural communities before radio, television, and movies. Several hundred of them flourished in Ontario alone. Like the men's Mechanics' Institutes, they brought books and culture to citizens wanting self-education. (See Heather Murray, *Come, Bright Improvement*.)

12. Maud had purchased Longfellow's poetry in 1897, and underlined it heavily.

13. See "The Old Minister in *The Story Girl*," by A. Wylie Mahon, where the origins of many stories about ministers are attributed to Maud's Uncle Leander, who told tales about the Reverend John Sprott, born in Scotland, emigrating to Canada in 1818, who was one of the "best loved and most unforgettable of the home-missionary pioneers of the Atlantic provinces."

14. When the second volume of Maud's collected journals were published in 1987, her remarks about the tiresome demands on a minister's wife stirred up consternation among those who remembered the cheerful Mrs. Macdonald. One maid, Elsie, could not believe that Maud had written these journals, and initially suspected they were a fabrication by the editors.

15. Years later Lily remembered her three years in the manse as happy, with amiable banter between Ewan and Maud, whom he called "Pussy." Ewan used to playfully flip Maud's hair as he walked past her.

16. See Red Scrapbook #1, p. 161.

17. Margaret H. Mustard, *L. M. Montgomery*.

18. We will never know if her royalties had really dropped off this much, or if the Page Company had already started "creative bookkeeping" that reduced what they paid her.

19. See Jonathan Vance, *Death So Noble*, p. 35.

20. See Red Scrapbook #2, p. 18.

21. Canon Scott was the father of the famous Canadian jurist and poet Frank R. Scott.

22. Maud's Red Scrapbook #2 shows Ewan's early involvement, including writing an indignant and well-worded letter to the *Globe* refuting a claim that PEI had not sent its fair share of recruits to the war (see p. 57). Ewan also acted as Deputy Registrar in his area, registering citizens for "national purposes" with the Canada Registration Board.

23. Far-fetched as this plot seems, Maud pasted in one of her scrapbooks a story about a man like Dick Moore who was cured by surgery.

24. Lily Reid was the first maid after Maud's cousin, Stella Campbell; the widowed Lily came in December 1912 and stayed until she left to remarry (Rob Shier) at the end of December 1915. Edith Meyers from Zephyr replaced her on January 1916 and stayed until December 1917, and later became Mrs. Lyons. Then Lily Meyers, Edith's sister, replaced her. This second Lily would stay until 1925, a very long time, causing enormous grief to Ewan and Maud with her "tattling" and "perverting" before she left. She eventually became Mrs. Will Cook, and lived into her nineties. She was replaced by Elsie Bushby in 1925; Elsie left in June 1926, and later became Mrs. Cliff Davidson.

25. Goldwin Lapp, the twenty-one-year-old son of the ex-reeve of Scott Township and a pharmacy student in Toronto, was killed January 18, 1917; Robert Brooks, one of the most progressive young farmers in the area and in Colonel Sharpe's battalion, was killed in action on August 8, 1918; Morley R. Shier, age twenty-three, died September 6, 1918, two months and five days before the war ended. Although approximately twenty young men from the area died, she apparently chose these three especially because she knew them and their parents well, and was particularly fond of them.

26. Accounts of Sam Sharpe's death are found in Maud's Red Scrapbook #2, circa p. 60. He had suffered a nervous breakdown before the war, but recovered.

27. *Sunset Canada*, by Archie Bell, about British Columbia, published by Page (1918).

28. For instance, on November 16, 1909, Prince Edward Island's *Daily Patriot* carried a huge front-page article on "The Unpardonable Sin." A prominent divine, a Dr. Elliott, lectured on this sin in Charlottetown. He explained it as "Blasphemy Against the Holy Ghost and Continuing Rejection of [the] Holy Spirit." If Ewan did not actually hear the sermon, he most certainly would have read about it: this was directly after he resigned from his last Prince Edward Island parish when he was preparing to move to Ontario. In the middle of the nineteenth century, Nathaniel Hawthorne had built a story, "Ethan Brand" (1850), on the concept of the "unpardonable sin." In this story he describes the kind of madness that results when a "fixed idea" overtakes a person, something that often happens in a clinical depression.

29. The 113 parishioners in Leaskdale paid him $720 a year, for a total of $1,080. The year 1919 was one of the few times that Ewan's salary and Maud's royalties would be roughly the same: because of the Page lawsuit, she made only $1,006 in royalties. However, in 1918, she had received $45,725 in payments and royalties; in 1920, $21,685. According to the Canadian census of 1921, a woman could expect to earn around $300 a year from gainful employment. By 1921, Maud had made about $97,552.56 from her writing, at mid-career. Over their lifetimes, Ewan's income comprised approximately 5 percent of their total family income.

30. It is worth noting that none of the maids thought was anything seriously mentally wrong with Ewan when they were interviewed prior to the publication of Maud's journals. Stuart insisted that he and Chester did not notice that there was anything amiss with their father when they were younger. As a young boy, Chester used to proudly tell people he was like his father and Stuart was like his mother. What people saw of Ewan was clearly not nearly as dramatic as what Maud wrote in her journals—which indicates either that she was more astutely observant or that she heightened these descriptions for narrative effect.

31. Although the 1911 census showed that there were now 7 divorced men and 8 divorced women on the Island, the comparable Ontario figures were 189 divorced men and 227 women.

32. Maud was too much the Victorian lady to record in her journals the details of the "immorality" and the "shocking stories," but much information about Page came to me from the late Roger W. Straus, who bought the Page firm in 1957, from his chief financial officer, Robert Wohlforth, and from Page's literary executor and cousin, Peter Coues.

33. He would sell silent-film rights to both *Anne of Green Gables* and *Pollyanna*, starring Mary Miles Minter in *Anne* and Mary Pickford in *Pollyanna*. See Montgomery's clipping book, pp. 131–150. See also her scrapbooks.

34. Robert Wohlforth, who negotiated the purchase ($75,000 in 1957) for both the business and the five-storey house at 53 Beacon Street, said that the Page firm was in dreadful disarray by Page's death in 1956. No one wanted it, but Roger W. Straus was interested so they could expand their list with some titles of best-selling books, especially some for young readers, and sell foreign rights to subsidize their firm's growth. They regarded the L. M. Montgomery titles as the firm's greatest asset, with secondary interests in the Eleanor H. Porter titles (including *Pollyanna*, 1913) and two series ("Famous Leaders in Industry" and "Famous American Athletes of Today").

35. Peter Coues's father was a distinguished medical doctor, and his grandfather had been Surgeon-General of the United States Army. Peter grew up with status, but with far less money, and he said that he learned much about the business world from his much older cousin, L. C. Page, during their regular weekly dinners. Peter's wife, Milly, was not invited: it was a man's dinner and a man's world, and they talked business. Dinner was always at 6:30, not a minute before or after. "We had a wonderful time," recalled Mr. Coues. "He was very formal in many ways: we'd have one and one-quarter martinis in a fifteen minute period, then dinner served by an attractive maid, and we would sit at the dinner table until ten, enjoying delicious wines." When they left the room, Page would laugh and turn off the lights, saying "I'm a thrifty man." In the library, Page would reach behind the books for a bottle, saying "It's going to be very cold tonight." They would talk until very late.

36. When Mr. Wohlforth bought the L. C. Page business for Roger Straus, he noted that the first two floors housed the business, but the top three floors, set up for business and social entertainment, also held living quarters for dinner parties and more intimate sleeping situations. They were a convenient location to discuss business matters privately with bright and attractive young female employees. Page could

sleep over if he did not want to return home. Mr. Wohlforth recalled the wife of a retired Boston attorney telling of her brief stint of working for Mr. Page. She had just graduated from an Ivy League university and was very flattered when Page hired her to bring some "new blood" into the firm. One day he told her that he needed another person at a dinner party upstairs that night, and asked her to round out the table. After a sumptuous dinner, with expensive wines and brilliant conversation, Page detained her when the others were leaving, and then tried to seduce her. Finally, Page, a former track letterman and still very fit, chased her around a large desk. She made a grab for her coat and escaped. Later she learned that her experience was not that unusual for those invited to his private chambers. Women succumbing to his charm were well rewarded. He might cheat his authors, but he was very generous with his favourite women. His cousin said he always had "very stylish" young women working in his home and apartments as maids, and he referred to them as "my wenches."

37. His contract with Maud specifies that he is registering the copyright in the name of "L.C. Page & Company (Inc.)." The contract says that he will pay her 10 percent on the *wholesale* price of each hard copy he sells (over and above the first 1,000 copies sold), and 4 percent royalty on any paper-covered or cheap hard-copy reprints. If dramatic rights are sold, he will share the fee with her half and half. If the book goes out of print for lack of sales, he will return the copyright to her.

38. Peter Coues said that L. C. Page had no children, nor are any mentioned in his will, so the paternity of the child "Mildred" is unclear. Maud observed no children when she was there, so the child's paternity could have been a contentious point in the divorce.

39. "If you hear a lurid tale about L. C. Page," Roger Straus quipped in 1991, "I'd say there's at least an 80 percent chance it is true." In the late 1980s, Page's younger cousin, Peter Coues, a retired investment banker in Boston, said sadly and gently, with a sigh, "He was good to me and my wife, but I have heard a *lot* of *other* tales about him, and I expect most are true."

40. See her clipping book, pp. 135–150.

41. The spelling of Page's name is hard to read here, but it looks more like "Louis" than "Lewis." He changed the spelling because he thought "Louis" was more elegant, and his final will and testament in 1956 notes that his name may appear: L. C. Page, Lewis C. Page, or Louis C. Page. The letter to Carman is in the Queen's University Archives.

42. Wanamaker's is credited with being the first modern department store in the United States. It advertised heavily and offered refunds if customers were dissatisfied—all

new business tactics. It also sold a range of merchandise, including books, and lasted as one of the most successful department store enterprises in the United States for over a century. John Wanamaker was a respected philanthropist who also became postmaster-general of the United States.

43. Later he would become the town solicitor for the village of Uxbridge. In 1932, ten years later, Greig's sister, Florrie Greig Gould, would become the mother of Canada's famous pianist, Glenn Gould.

44. A very learned man, Riddell established in 1916 his own archival memorial in the Law Society of Canada at Osgoode Hall, calling it the "Riddell Canadian Library." Beginning with an initial donation of 1,665 volumes, many very rare or priceless, it grew to 9,000 volumes by the time of his death. Of his own personal authorship, Riddell's library held some 14 monographs, 300 book reviews, and 1,258 journal articles (against Montgomery's own lifetime production of 22 books, more than 500 poems, 500 short stories, and approximately 5,000 journal pages). His library held many books by Canadian writers, but he had none of Montgomery's. Riddell had all the volumes of *his own* writing bound and consecutively numbered in gold.

45. Born in 1852, he lived to be ninety-three, sitting on the Ontario Supreme Court bench until his death in 1945.

46. See Hilary Bates Neary, "William Renwick Riddell: Judge, Ontario Publicist and Man of Letters," A *Law Society of Upper Canada Gazette*, Vol. XI, 3 (Sept. 1977), p. 172.

47. Smith was admitted to the Royal Astronomy Society of London on September 10, 1919, three days before he visited the Macdonalds on September 13, and he did not keep up his membership.

48. By April 9, 1907, about three weeks before Maud signed her contract for *Anne of Green Gables*, Ewan was back on the Island, looking for a new position. There were many open positions because ministers were leaving the mainland, but Ewan had a hard time finding a position. This is odd, but perhaps the depression he suffered in Scotland may still have been hanging on him.

49. Although the maple leaf became part of the current Canadian official flag only in 1965, this leaf had a long history of association with Canada, dating back to the 1700s.

50. In her 1911 series on the woods, Maud wrote in "The Woods in Autumn": "Maples are trees that have primeval fire in their souls. . . . maples are the best vehicle for this hidden, immemorial fire of the earth and the woods."

51. The complete ban lasted until 1913, when automobiles were permitted on the roads again, but only on Mondays, Wednesdays, and Thursdays, except in some districts

that were still completely "closed." These anti-automobile laws would not be fully terminated until 1919, at which point automobiles began their noisy assault on the pastoral Island again.

52. As Maud notes, Captain Smith was full of tales from his war experiences. After his graduation from the British Naval Academy, he was appointed to command an armed patrol ship in the North Sea. Here he protected fishing fleets and convoy routes on the east coast of England. In June 1917, he was "transferred to Dover for service on the French and Belgian Coast" where he "took part in . . . the bombardments of Zeebrugge and Ostend until December." In January 1918 he was "appointed to command of [a] flotilla of twelve armed steam trawlers and until October [he] patrolled outside the Dogger Bank, being eight days out and only thirty-six hours in port, each trip," according to his own account. At one point, he was selected to command the Guard of Honour during the visit of the King and Queen to the Naval Base of Grimsby. His fleet was "personally inspected by His Majesty," who complimented him "on their appearance, and also on the appearance of the 144 officers and men" from the ships. It is never quite clear if Captain Smith commanded a genuine "ship of war" or merely "armed trawlers," which were basically little fishing boats with small guns mounted on their sides. Smith, a spellbinding speaker, was quite adept at heightening glamour.

53. Smith had turned to selling insurance after his return from the war.

54. See her entry of September 21, 1919. Maud did not know then that Smith would not rise in the ministry despite his oratorical gifts. Church records show that after three years in Williamsburg, Ontario, (1923–26) Smith interrupted his ministry with another two years in commercial business. In 1928, he returned to the Church, first at Carleton Place, then in 1930 in Warkworth, Ontario; in 1934 he moved again, to Columbus, near Whitby and the lake; in 1936, to Milford, near Pictou, on Lake Ontario again. He retired in 1937, moved into the Toronto area where he and his wife Grace enjoyed their fiftieth wedding anniversary surrounded by their grown, devoted children. At one point late in his life, he spent time selling encyclopedias for money. He lived into his seventy-eighth year, dying in 1948.

55. Smith worked in the commercial world for two stints, and then went back to the ministry in other Ontario parishes near the water, after acquiring a Ph.D. in Indianapolis, Indiana, to bolster his credentials.

56. Over twenty years later, after Edwin Smith died, his wife, Grace, donated this typewriter to Parks Canada for display in the "Anne of Green Gables" house in Cavendish.

57. By 1919, *Anne of Green Gables* had been translated into Swedish (1909), Dutch (1910), Polish (1912), Danish (1918), and Norwegian (1918).

58. For instance, at the time she writes up the 1898 entries after 1919, Maud was buoyed to emotional heights because of the attentions of Captain Smith. She was undoubtedly—at least temporarily—tormented by feelings of attraction to his "wholesome" personality. This would have seemed sinful to her, given that people were taught that God could actually see into people's minds and read their thoughts. In writing up her attraction to Herman, then, it appears that she is able to displace some of her feelings about Smith onto the story of Herman, and get double mileage out of her story by transmuting personal pain into literary art.

59. In 1897, she had been reading Olive Schreiner's *The Story of an African Farm*, which suggested this "tragic" life-myth, given that she was in love with a man she could not marry. In 1920, when recopying her journals, the frustration with depressed Ewan, and the admiration of Edwin Smith, would have made the line even more relevant. If her facts about the Herman affair are tricky, the truth is not in the details, but in the broad sweep of human emotions. Maud was an artist, concerned with truth, not facts.

60. See Rubio, "'A Dusting Off': An Anecdotal Account of Editing the L. M. Montgomery Journals," in *Working in Women's Archives*, pp. 51–78.

61. See *The Blue Castle*, chapter XIV.

62. *Maclean's*, vol. 32, September 1919, no. 9.

63. The following Friday, Captain Smith drove Maud from Leaskdale to Whitby to give readings to the young women at Whitby Ladies' College. On June 11, 1921, Ewan collided with Marshall Pickering.

64. See Red Scrapbook #2, pp. 177 and 192 ff., for Smith's film showings.

65. Significantly, *Emily of New Moon* is dedicated to another man in Maud's life: George Boyd MacMillan, her longtime correspondent in Scotland. Neither Smith nor Ewan would ever have a book dedicated to them, despite their influence in her life.

66. The late Margaret Laurence (1926–1987) remarked to her friend and biographer, Clara Thomas, that Montgomery had everything right in her *Emily* trilogy: Maud had accurately portrayed all the impediments that stood in the way of young women aspiring to become writers in small-town Canada (or America).

67. When I handed Alice Munro a gift copy of the first volume of *The Selected Journals of L. M. Montgomery, Volume 1*, at the Ginger Press Bookstore in Owen Sound, Ontario, in late 1985, she looked at it for only a second to see what it was, and then, without missing a beat or without making any identifying reference to *Emily of New Moon*, she responded by quoting the end of the novel: "I am going to write a diary that it may be published when I die."

68. Carl Berger, *The Writing of Canadian History*, p. 54.

69. Maud would have been very happy if she could have lived to hear Margaret Laurence say in a 1966 CBC television interview with the young Adrienne Clarkson that Canadian women's literature started with L. M. Montgomery, who was read by all the young girls in Canada in the first half of the twentieth century. Later, Clarkson, who would become the Governor General of Canada, wrote in 1999 that in 1942 Montgomery gave her, when she was a young immigrant outsider, a "profound understanding of what Canada is." Clarkson added that Montgomery's fiction shows that "purpose and vision and balancing all aspects of a human life and its obligations to others . . . will bring the richest human rewards." Montgomery "understood emotions and . . . motivation; her people *are* Canada," wrote Clarkson.

70. See "The Author of *Anne*," vol. 32, September 1919, no. 9.

71. It barely seems credible that anyone, especially a child, could memorize this poem. But other people have similar stories about learning all of "The Lady of the Lake." One comes to me through Professor G. Douglas Killam. In the late 1930s and early 1940s, Mr. Canfield, the principal of Lord Lister Junior High School in New Westminster, B.C., would assemble the entire school once a year to listen to him recite this entire Scott poem.

72. In 1991, Jack and Linda Hutton bought Mrs. Pyke's house and turned it into a museum that celebrates the Macdonalds' holiday and Bala's history.

73. Mustard had picked out one of the best spots on the lake, and the place where their cottage was located now holds a multi-million-dollar vacation home.

74. John Mustard's admirable personal qualities had already been clear to his professors when he was an undergraduate at the University of Toronto, where he took an Honours B.A. in Classics. Their letters of reference commented on his "unimpeachable" moral character and his "large share of good common sense which counts for a good deal." One referee even mentioned his "fine physique," noting it was necessary in a schoolteacher. Altogether, his referees praised him as a man of "model character, good parts, and amiable disposition." After teaching in Prince Albert, Mr. Mustard took his theology degree at Knox College in Toronto, finishing in 1894. His niece, Isobel Mustard St. John, characterized him as a scholarly and sincere preacher, not as one who held listeners spellbound. This modesty, earnestness, and kindness inspired enormous devotion and affection in his congregations. In 1946, the Reverend John Mustard was given an honorary Ph.D. for his lifetime accomplishments—fifty years of stellar service to the Presbyterian Church.

75. Isobel Mustard St. John, John Mustard's niece, who knew Maud in the Leaskdale years, commented in the 1990s that she agreed that her uncle would have bored

someone like Maud. But he continued to rise in the Church hierarchy, whereas Captain Smith, whose career in the ministry petered out, moved into smaller churches (partly to be near water).

76. Urea is an ingredient in Veronal.

77. See *Scrapbook of Reviews*, p. 266.

78. See Maud's "An Autobiographical Sketch," *The Ontario Library Review*, March 1929, volume 23, pp. 94–96.

79. At the same time, the Reverend John Mustard, in Toronto, received about $3,000 for a year in one large church.

PART THREE: THE NORVAL YEARS

1. See Red Scrapbook #2, p. 251 ff.

2. Maud's own McShannon ancestors were Scots-Irish, and the Montgomery clan seat in Ayrshire looked over towards Ireland.

3. *The Mail and Empire*, June 23, 1926.

4. Both Chester and Stuart became chain-smokers.

5. Ila May had literary ability and was the Boys' and Girls' Editor at the *Winnipeg Free Press* at the time of her marriage to William D. MacKenzie. Maud did not like her other half-sister, Kate, who was much like her mother.

6. This letter of October 15, 1926, is in the Queen's University Archives.

7. In his 1927 *An Outline of Canadian Literature*, Pierce writes somewhat ambiguously that *Anne of Green Gables* is "deservedly a classic of its kind, not because of its excellence of style or plot, but because of the altogether charming character, Anne" (p. 38).

8. See *The Toronto Telegram*, March 24, 1937.

9. Deacon admired and praised the younger generation of innovative fiction writers like Hemingway and Morley Callaghan, but he did not understand the new Modernist poetry. He characterized these young Canadian poets as "a group of highly mannered writers, who make a cult of obscurity . . ." This statement made him some enemies among the new generation of influential academic critics like A. J. M. Smith. See p. 216, Clara Thomas and John Lennox.

10. Thomas and Lennox, p. 104.

11. "Poteen" is a colloquial term for homebrew, according to Thomas and Lennox.

12. See Thomas and Lennox, p. 214.

13. See Thomas Guthrie Marquis, *English-Canadian Literature*, pp. 564–65.

14. See MacMechan, *Head-waters*, pp. 210–12.

15. See journal entries of November 10, 1936, where she says she has "no love" for him; and April 8, 1938, where she says he has always "pursued me with malice. . . ." See also her letter to G. B. MacMillan about him in June 1930.

16. Thomas and Lennox, p. 42.

17. See Thomas and Lennox, p. 83.

18. In 1922, Maud had written in her journal her own response to this term: "Today I had a nice letter from Sir Ernest Hodder Williams (of Hodder and Stoughton) and some English reviews of *Rilla*. All were kind but one which sneered at my 'sentiment.' The attitude of some English critics towards anything that savors of sentiment amuses me. It is to them as the proverbial red rag to a bull. . . . Can't they see that civilization is founded on and held together by sentiment. Passion is transient and quite as often destructive as not. Sentiment remains and binds. Perhaps what they really mean is sentimentality, which *is* an abominable thing. But my books are not sentimental. I have always tried in them to register normal and ordinary emotions—not merely passionate or unique episodes." (January 27, 1922)

19. Thomas and Lennox, p. 63.

20. See Black Scrapbook #1, p. 165.

21. See Black Scrapbook #1, p. 145.

22. See letter of February 6, 1928, to G. B. MacMillan in *My Dear Mr. M.*, p. 136.

23. See Black Scrapbook #1, p. 145.

24. See letter to G. B. MacMillan, February 6, 1928, p. 136.

25. This letter is in the Queen's University Archives.

26. It was believed by many mental health experts in earlier eras that masturbation could actually lead to mental illness, and the practice of "spilling one's seed," either through masturbation or as a method of birth control, was also condemned in the Bible. See Robert D. Hare's *Without Conscience*, which lists "precocious sexuality" as one of several early indicators of psychopathy on p. 66 and p. 69.

27. Recounting this story in the 1980s, Joy Laird, who had babysat and played with the Brown children, wiped tears from her eyes. The lifelike doll from the Brown children linked her to Stuart, who had experienced the tragedy with the same intensity that she had.

28. When Stuart was in his mid-sixties, he recounted that his mother had kept him home so she would not be lonely herself. He was very fond of his mother, and rarely criticized her, but he still resented this.

29. The Norval contemporaries of Stuart all still had exceptionally fond memories of him in the 1980s. Older people such as Margaret Russell, who had been a teacher

all her life, also remarked that it was "obvious" to her that Maud favoured Stuart, but she added that this was very understandable: he was smart, cheerful, and likeable.

30. As Elizabeth Waterston has noted, Montgomery drew on the many new 1920s ideas about early childhood education that were being studied by Dr. William E. Blatz, an influential professor of early childhood education at the University of Toronto, and the first director of the Institute of Child Study, established in 1926.

31. His obituary is in the Boston *Sunday Herald* of May 29, 1927, p. 4.

32. When L. C. Page died in 1956, his estate had dwindled down to about $300,000, including his firm in Boston and his home in Brookline (worth $34,000). In his will, written a few days before his death, he squared off with some relatives by telling them what he would have left them if they had not displeased him. To his church, St. Aidan's Church in Brookline, Massachusetts (the church where John F. Kennedy's family worshipped and where Kennedy was baptized), Page donated $1,000 for a memorial to *himself*, and $500 towards Mass offerings for the "repose of my soul."

33. I interviewed Nora's son Edward ("Ebbie") Campbell, a mining executive in Haileybury, Ontario, in the 1990s.

34. See Black Scrapbook #1, p. 103.

35. See Black Scrapbook #1, p. 85.

36. This famous recitation poem, "The curfew must not ring tonight," was written by Rose Hartwick Thorpe (1850–1939).

37. See the *Guelph Mercury*, May 11, 1929.

38. Nora's family tragedy is given a passing and sympathetic mention in Maud's journals, but when Maud's favourite cat, Lucky, dies some years later, she spills out nearly forty handwritten pages of grief in her tenth volume.

39. Luella Reid described them as "the oddest teeth ever seen . . . they were like whale's teeth, long and narrow, bunched together, lots piled together, especially on the bottom. They were cruel teeth to have."

40. The severity of the devastating American crash in 1907 led to the establishment of the Federal Reserve system.

41. *CENTENNIAL: Union Presbyterian Church (Esquesing), 1833–1933.*

42. In 1983, the update of Ewan's history stated unequivocally and without factual basis that Mrs. Macdonald had written the 1933 booklet. Luella Reid, later Chester's first wife, remembered vividly how consumed Ewan had been with the project, working on gathering materials, talking about them, and writing them up. She said he positively radiated happiness during this time, and she was indignant over the denial of his authorship.

43. Articles about the possibility of television were written in the late nineteenth century, and in 1927 President Herbert Hoover appeared on an early television, and the papers reported that images could be transmitted up to two hundred miles. Maud first mentions "television" in her journals on December 4, 1927.

44. Maud's "shocking" remark about religion was repeated to me by a Norval resident long before her journals were published. For some of Maud's statements on religion, see October 7, 1897; January 7, 1910; January 31, 1920; October 21, 1921; March 15, 1925 (first entry of two for that date); October 30, 1925; January 24, 1932; August 25, 1932.

45. Isabel Anderson continued teaching elementary school in Acton for forty years. According to some of Isabel's former students in the 1980s and 1990s, parents dreaded the time when their children would advance to her classroom. When she died, at age ninety-nine, she received a fulsome obituary that praised her exemplary life and her great love for her students. I was astonished to find that Isabel, born in 1896, was still alive in the late 1980s, living in my town of Guelph in a nursing home. She was the only hostile person I met in my quarter-century of interviewing people about L. M. Montgomery, who was almost universally remembered with affection and admiration.

46. Interview with Mrs. Dorothy Watson McLean in the 1980s.

47. Maud probably was sexually inexperienced at sixteen, but surely not "unawakened," and it seems likely that she wants to assure her future readers that she "behaved herself," so she glossed and clarified the memory.

48. This legendary civil engineering professor held various patents for new engineering techniques, and after he began teaching at the University of Toronto, he enlisted Rudyard Kipling to write the engineers' creed, which became part of the ceremony that inducts engineers into their professional brotherhood.

49. Letter to Lena McLure, daughter of Chester McLure, Maud's second cousin, sent care of Chester McLure, to Chateau Laurier, Ottawa.

50. Almost everyone I interviewed about Chester talked about his compulsive thieving: maids, Stuart, friends of the family.

51. This article followed, with some irony, on the heels of an earlier one that made her life sound idyllic and her books like didactic Sunday School texts, reinforcing the idea that she was a moral-toting sentimentalist. Following a dinner with her in Norval, author A. V. Brown wrote, "Anyone with the mental equipment of L. M. Montgomery should be happy almost anywhere." He went on to praise her books as "[far more than] just pretty playthings, they are messages, and the pulpit has yet to be built in this country that has any better. There is a moral in them. . . . Every

book she writes is a voice pleading for the rights of childhood, [or] the sterling worth that is disguised by an ungracious exterior, [or] the love which cannot show itself in speech or look, [or] the tenderness which lives beneath an iron creed. . . . If anyone would increase his faith in God, in man, in nature, and in all the finest things of life, let him scan the pages of L. M. Montgomery's books." See *Scrapbook of Clippings* . . . pp. 364–65.

52. Brampton Archives, minutes of the Brampton Literary and Travel Club, Book 5.

53. See Black Scrapbook #2, p. 13.

54. Performers wore pioneer costumes, including high silk hats. The program "consisted of old-time melodies, with a series of tableaux, recalling old-time scenes."

55. The first reference to this love affair is in her "old journal" on December 6, 1906. She rewrote and recopied it into her "handwritten" journals in March 1920. By the time when she was typing the 1931 copy, she left out the Herman affair, writing on June 30, 1897: "The entry in my original diary cannot be written here. I shall present the bare bones of it. I made a terrible mistake and paid the penalty of my folly in intense suffering."

56. Knister's unpublished essay on the Canadian girl was among his papers when he drowned in 1932. Knister had read *Anne of Green Gables,* for he mentioned it in a review he wrote of her *Emily* books. The full article can be read in *The Journal of Canadian Fiction,* vol. iv, no. 2, 1975.

57. Called "The Man Who Forgot," it appeared in the *Family Herald.*

58. Part of letter to Roberta Sparks, Saskatchewan, July 4, 1933, now held in the University of Guelph Archives.

59. When Luella read through Maud's journals at my house in the 1990s, she herself was in her late seventies, and she commented with great personal sadness: "It would have been unimaginably shameful to them," she explained, "I feel very, very sorry for them now."

60. See Exodus 20:5–6; 34–7; Numbers 14:18; Deuteronomy 5:9–10; Jeremiah 32:18; also Greek writers like Euripides speak of the "gods" visiting the sins of the fathers upon the children.

61. For entries referring to Maud's wine see July 11, 1931; July 18, 1934; July 23, 1934; July 24, 1934; August 11, 1934; July 28, 1936. Luella's comment, when asked about it, was to laugh "They were Maritimers!" and she said of course there was "medicinal" alcohol about, and that they used it.

62. In the early 1980s, Dr. Stuart Macdonald and I read through his father's case file at Homewood.

63. Luella Macdonald remembered the night her father came home from the Session

meeting at which they had decided to fire Ewan. As soon as her father came into the house, he kicked a chair across the room. When Luella read through Maud's journals at my house, she said Maud's account of the trouble at the end of Ewan's preaching career in Norval was quite accurate.

64. A. E. LePage was only thirteen years younger than Maud. The LePages, originally from Guernsey in the Channel Islands, were an extended clan on Prince Edward Island. The LePage clan had intermarried into Maud's own family—the Woolners of her grandmother's line, the Macneills of her grandfather's clan, and others. A. E. LePage himself had been raised in Toronto, where his father moved when he was a boy.

PART FOUR: THE TORONTO YEARS

1. Letter to Jack Lewis. March 3, 1936.

2. Swansea's boundaries were Bloor Street to the north, the Humber River to the west, Lakeshore Boulevard to the south, and Grenadier Pond/High Park to the east. Swansea had incorporated as a village with its own reeve, police, and volunteer fire department around 1926, becoming part of Toronto only in the 1960s when Toronto had grown around it and borders had vanished. Today it is merely part of metropolitan Toronto, and the rural area that Maud looked out on from her bedroom window is fully developed, with the ravine behind her house now full of other houses.

3. Personal interview with Richard and Nora Lane Braiden in their home in Toronto. March 20, 1991.

4. Gardiner Cowan was to serve in World War II, was treated for an injury by Stuart, and later become a highly regarded architect in Toronto. He died in 1972.

5. See entry of September 26, 1933.

6. Maud's dress was adorned with two long glass clips at the neck plus two big buckles at the waist. Around her neck she wore a strand of pearls, with an oval-shaped pin in her hat. A little-known secret was that Maud often purchased beads at Woolworth's dime-store, and restrung them herself, quipping that people would think they were real jewels just as they would assume she was wealthy.

7. *Telegram*, p. 2.

8. Letter to Jack Lewis, February 28, 1930.

9. Letter of January 19, 1932.

10. See Black Scrapbook #2, p. 13, where Lorne Pierce calls Canadian literature "objective" rather than "subjective," and says authors must go down "into the very crypt

and abyss of a man's soul and faithfully" report what is there in order to produce "high art."

11. Arthur L. Phelps, *Canadian Writers*.

12. See Thomas and Lennox, p. 202.

13. See Black Scrapbook #2, p. 51.

14. Like many men of his generation, Deacon held a patronizing attitude towards women, despite the immense assistance he received from his own devoted and talented second wife. He had once written to a friend: "Nor about the sex matter can there be any dispute. Females being so tied to physical life are not so imaginative . . . as men who, not so tied, can wander in mental realms . . ." (Letter to Dr. Logan, October 20, 1924). Deacon was a lifelong friend of one powerful woman, Judge Emily Murphy, who had encouraged him early in his career, but strong women who neither admired nor flattered him garnered little respect from him.

15. Luella's description fits that of what is sometimes called a "wry neck," or technically, sternocleidomastoid muscles in spasm. Severe muscle spasms in the neck area can compress the area around the vegus nerve, and this in turn can induce vomiting and a feeling of depression, symptoms reported by Maud.

16. Psychiatric literature says that it is not unusual for "depression" to spread in a family in situations like the Macdonalds's, and her feeling of being doomed was similar to Ewan's. But the difference was that she knew her feelings were abnormal. He did not.

17. See p. 52 of Black Scrapbook #2, where Maud speaks of "the adverse criticism she frequently receives because she portrays the lovelier side of people's natures, and sees so much beauty in the commonplace."

18. *The Globe and Mail*, October 4, 1935.

19. *The Toronto Star* was a huge paper of some thirty to sixty pages, advertising a daily circulation of 255,000, some 90,000 more subscribers than any other paper. It featured some three to five pages devoted exclusively to women's social events, teas, and organizations.

20. Maud was not the first to flaunt social norms here: she had heard Lady Byng speak on the same topic.

21. See Black Scrapbook #2, p. 81. See also the remark about pigstyes in modern literature in the journals on December 30, 1928.

22. These were "Off to the Fishing Grounds," "When the Dark Comes Down," and "The Hill Road."

23. Owen Sound *Daily Times*, November 6, p. 3.

24. See Maud's comments on Callaghan in her journal entry of December 30, 1928. By 1935, the critical debate over how to evaluate literature was gathering steam in

Canada. In a *Mail and Empire* article on September 14, 1935, Deacon had hailed Callaghan's most recent book, *They Shall Inherit the Earth*, as "a great novel, [something] conspicuous in the front rank of Canadian fiction." He stated that it dealt with serious moral issues, even though it had some language that would shock Canadians and showed sympathetic characters "living in sin" before marriage. Deacon noted that such language and issues were allowed in other more *sophisticated* countries, implying that Canada was backward and "provincial." When two of Callaghan's books—*Such is My Beloved* and *They Shall Inherit the Earth*—were banned by the Toronto Public Library system, this stirred up huge controversy in the newspapers. Deacon asked Callaghan if he "thought of himself as a writer of filthy literature," to which Callaghan indignantly swore that he *certainly did not.* Experts were called in to pass judgment on whether they thought Callaghan's novels offended public morality. Deacon ended one of several articles on Callaghan by quoting Hugh Eayrs, managing director of MacMillan (and Callaghan's publisher), who asserted that Callaghan was "most certainly one of the ace-high, first-rank writers of this continent, in fact *of the world*" [my italics].

25. *The Sudbury Star*, December 4, 1935, p. 14.

26. See January 20, 1924, journal entry.

27. See her reference to this in her journal entry of November 27, 1931.

28. See *The Globe and Mail*, December 12, 1935, p. 10.

29. Many women in the second half of the twentieth century have written about the influence of Maud's novels on them at a time women were still fighting for a place in the public sphere.

30. The London *Times*, November 27, 1935, p. 1.

31. *Anne of Windy Poplars*, p. 151.

32. *Toronto Telegram*, March 4, 1936, p. 15.

33. The Canadian literary scene was so small that reviewers and writers invariably knew each other. Maud writes in her journals, for instance, that Marjory MacMurchy asked her to review one of Marjory's new novels. (See the polite but unenthusiastic review on page 46 of Black Scrapbook #2.) She felt obliged to do so, even though she thought the novel very mediocre, because Marjory had given so many teas honouring her. It was particularly hard to refuse reviewing books of friends in the CAA, and most writers were in the CAA. This gave the CAA a not-unjustified image of a booster club.

34. Of Grove's *Over Prairie Trails*, Maud's endorsement read: "This book seems to me one of the few pieces of real and vital literature that Canada has produced. The style is finished and exquisite, the restraint admirable, the atmosphere and close observance of nature wonderful." *Scrapbook of Reviews*, p. 349.

35. The fact that she gives her fictional Greaves a split Scotch-French ancestry points to Grove as a possible model since he had initially claimed split ancestry, with a Scotch mother. He later changed his story, saying he was Swedish, and of noble birth, instead of being of very ordinary birth in Germany.

36. The term "Modernist" seemed to have variable meanings in that time.

37. It had been back in 1926, after she had written the complimentary blurb for *Over Prairie Trails*, that Grove wrote his friend Professor A. L. Phelps, as quoted earlier in the Leaskdale section, that he wondered how a woman who judged other authors so accurately as Montgomery did could stand writing the books she wrote.

38. Maud's correspondence with Miss Elmo is on the back of manuscripts in the Confederation Centre in Prince Edward Island.

39. See the March 3, 1936, letter to Jack Lewis for some of these comments.

40. George Campbell's mother, who had been raised by Maud's Aunt Emily, had no idea what Emily's real objection to Maud was when she said she was "ashamed to know" her—but it was a visceral and strong one, perhaps going back to Maud's childhood stay with her. Perhaps Emily had been influenced by her brother, John F. Macneill, who passed along gossip critical of young Maud's character and behaviour.

41. See Margaret Lawrence (1896–1973), *The School of Femininity, A Book For and About Women as They Are Interpreted Through Feminine Writers of Yesterday and Today* (Stokes, 1936), and *We Write as Women; Bliss Carman's Letters to Margaret Lawrence*.

42. In *Emily Climbs*, published in 1925, there are many references to "owl's laughter" and Emily's first published poem is entitled "Owl's Laughter," which suggests that Grey Owl had not read her books or he would have noticed this.

43. Archie Belaney (Grey Owl) had emigrated to Canada from England at age seventeen, refashioning himself as a native. He married an Indian wife, lived in the wilderness, and became a dedicated conservationist, passing himself off as a native in his lecture tours. Maud wrote in her entry of April 12, 1938, that she had thought he was part Indian, although she did not think him purebred.

44. *Mail and Empire*, November 10, 1936, p. 6.

45. *The Globe and Mail*, November 10, 1936, p. 10, announces it; *The Toronto Daily Star*, November 12, 1936, p. 37, covers it.

46. *Toronto Daily Star*, November 14, 1936, p. 26.

47. *Toronto Daily Star*, November 14, 1936, p. 26.

48. The exception to this was that she and Stuart did discuss both Chester and Ewan, and what was perceived as mental instability in them.

49. It was illegal to advertise or disseminate information about birth control to unmarried people or the public in general, but doctors could discuss methods of contraception with married couples. On February 12, 1937 (p. 3) and March 18, 1937 (p. 3), the *Globe* described a landmark case where a bookstore owner was charged and eventually acquitted on charges brought by the Crown that she distributed a pamphlet containing information about contraceptives. The judgment acquitted her, stating that she was acting for the public good: the argument went that the rich and middle-class people could get contraceptive information from doctors, but the poor were "generally breeding large families" because they couldn't get contraceptive information, and their children, poorly cared for, were "a burden on the taxpayer" and "crowded the juvenile courts."

50. This rumour has been neither confirmed nor disproved.

51. Justice Douglas Latimer (1929–2007) was Crown attorney for this region for many years.

52. All the maids I interviewed, as well as Margaret Russell and Luella, believed that Chester was very jealous of Stuart, thinking him the favoured son and resenting that Stuart attracted friends wherever he went.

53. This grooming intimacy feels almost disturbed psychologically, and it is likely that she was beginning to feel a sense of personal guilt over Chester's aberrant behaviour. Perhaps, like so many of the working mothers today, she felt she had not given him enough physical contact and attention when he was young.

54. Lucky made a lasting impression on the people in Norval, too, for he was remembered as a bit of a clown. In the summer, Lucky would wait at the back of the church until everyone was seated on a Sunday. Then, he would come in and walk up the centre isle majestically, with his tail held high, until he reached Maud's pew. He hopped up beside her, and sat upright and motionless, just like a person, his dignified head showing above the back of the pew (for he was a large cat). He listened with rapt attention while Ewan preached the service. Then he would walk out with the Macdonald family just as if he were a family member. People said that it was worth going to church just to see Lucky's performance.

55. This story comes from an interview with Ethel Dennis Curry in the 1990s.

56. Ethel characterized Ewan as a likeable but shadowy figure. He didn't joke or talk, only said a polite "Good morning." He often played solitaire in the dining room with a strange intensity. He did no gardening, didn't play with the cats, did not even play with his grandchildren beyond speaking to them when they visited. Ethel remembered Maud becoming provoked at him when he would not help with any of the work, either inside or out in the yard. If asked to do some work, he immediately

left and went out visiting around the neighbourhood. She, like the other maids, insisted that she didn't notice anything wrong with him mentally, except for being a
very *sluggish* person, old for his years, and very forgetful.

57. *The Globe and Mail*, March 19, 1937, p. 16. Her journal entry of March 23, 1937,
reports that she and Dickens were tied, but the *Globe* account, presumably by
Deacon, says she ran a close second to Dickens.

58. See *The Globe and Mail*, March 24, 1937, p. 15.

59. See *The Toronto Daily Star*, May 5, 1937, p. 10.

60. Horowitz, 1997.

61. Wacks, Oster, et al., 1990. When I was a teenager, billboards advertising Bromo-
Seltzer lined the American highways.

62. The dangers of barbiturates received much press in the last quarter of the twentieth century, when high-profile entertainers died of overdoses of barbiturates combined with
alcohol. In 2007, the drug chloral hydrate, a central nervous system depressant and sedative that Maud and Ewan record taking (as Chloral) through 1919, 1924, 1925, and 1934,
was said to be part of the toxic drug mix that killed American celebrity "Playboy
Playmate" Anna Nicole Smith. See *The Globe and Mail*, March 27, 2007. It is also suspected of playing a role in Marilyn Monroe's death. Chloral hydrate is illegal without a
prescription now, and is sometimes called the "date-rape drug." References to "chloral"
have appeared in fiction such as Edith Wharton's *The House of Mirth*, Agatha Christie's
And Then There Were None, and Evelyn Waugh's *Vile Bodies*.

63. For instance, on March 25, 1924, when Ewan was having some of his worst attacks,
these were treated with both Chloral and bromides (and maybe Veronal, since this
was prescribed all through this same period for the Macdonalds). Maud notes that
she made Ewan drink water "copiously" because "His kidneys are not acting right,
as is always the case in these attacks. His breath reeks with urea . . . [and she thinks]
his liver is disordered, too, for his skin is such a bad colour." The combination of all
of these medications, taken over a long period in high enough doses, would have
affected his kidneys and his liver. Urea is also a component used in making Veronal.

64. Ewan was very attached to his cough syrup bottle, which he carried in his pocket
all through the Norval and Toronto years, taking gulps from it when he coughed.

65. The symptoms of barbiturate withdrawal may occur some twelve to twenty hours
after the last dose, depending on whether a patient was using a long- or short-acting
barbiturate.

66. Sal volatile (ammonium carbonate) was a drug given as a stimulant, often for hys-
teria, faintness, and lassitude. It was given either as smelling salts, a liniment, or in-
ternally, and overdoses could act as a narcotic and irritant poison.

67. Each of these drug classes, as central nervous system depressants, could mimic the symptoms of being drunk. Ewan's confusion when delivering the sermon, his shaky hands at dinner when he tried to hold the cup, his disorientation and irritability on the trip home, his inability to keep the car on the road—all are symptoms consistent with either too many bromides or barbiturates, or a mixture of the two. His brief sobering up after she gave him alcohol could point to a temporary reprieve from withdrawal symptoms.

68. Because the doctor did not have the full picture of the medications Ewan had taken (or been given), and Maud was giving Ewan doses without knowing what he had already taken, the doctor was diagnosing on incomplete information.

69. There are a number of still shots in Maud's scrapbooks and other periodicals of the early 1920s.

70. The description of this event, still remembered and recounted two years later, actually appears in the Victoria-Royce Young People's Society notes for January 10, 1939.

71. *The Globe and Mail*, November 11, 1937.

72. Luella recounted how her mother-in-law could make her favourite novels and their characters so incredibly vivid that she felt Maud spent more time living in those worlds than in her own, retreating into them when real life became too depressing.

73. See March 9, 1938, in Montgomery's journals.

74. This information came from the Victoria-Royce Church archives.

75. Fifty years later, not knowing what had happened to Chester, this woman wrote the editors of Maud's newly published journals, recounting her dates with Chester, and recalling how Maud had telephoned her mother to say that she and Ewan "now felt that perhaps they had made a mistake when they forced their son to marry his seventeen-year-old pregnant girlfriend. He wanted a divorce." Maud, who was humiliated over Chester's affairs, and undoubtedly trying to save face, had told the mother that "she was the only girl whom 'Jerry' [Chester] had really loved." That did not soften her mother's and father's attitudes towards him, however. Chester's last communication to her was to tell her that he was "posted to Bermuda with the 48th Highlanders." This was a lie, of course—he had been turned down for medical reasons—but the lie gave him a noble exit. Nor was it true that Maud and Ewan had forced Chester to marry Luella; Chester and Luella had married secretly and then informed his parents.

76. See Thomas and Lennox, *William Arthur Deacon*, p. 202.

77. The traits of a psychopath would be laid out three years later in Hervey Cleckley's *The Masks of Sanity* (1941), a book that is still considered the classic and definitive

treatment of the psychopath (or sociopath) and can be read online. Cleckley gives a sixteen-point checklist of the traits of a psychopath, and the definitions do fit the behaviour recounted by Maud, Stuart, and later people who knew Chester in various capacities.

78. We don't know what she had in mind, but maids and many others who knew Chester recounted his compulsive lying and stealing, and some mentioned his impulsive sexual behaviour, which had shown up early and continued after he married. After the journals were published, another woman, also a university student at the time, wondering what had happened to Chester, recounted his driving her to a secluded road in a Toronto ravine, where he made sexual advances. When she vigorously resisted, he took her home.

79. I interviewed Eric Gaskell in Ottawa in the 1990s, and had some phone conversations with him. The courtly Mr. Gaskell was by then a retired parliamentary secretary and government advisor living in Ottawa. He had retained the title of "Commodore" from his wartime service in the Canadian Navy.

80. He was selected to go, but the Olympics were cancelled because of the war.

81. Personal letter from Violet King Morgan, dated October 15, 1992.

82. Violet King's publications included the novel *Better Harvest* (Toronto: J. M. Dent, 1945), numerous poems, and several short stories between this period and 1965. A few of her stories were picked up by international publications.

83. Letter of October 15, 1992, from Violet King Morgan.

84. No doubt largely either caused or intensified by her use of medications.

85. *The Toronto Telegram*, April 4, 1939, p. 89.

86. To my great regret, I did not ask her why she left Maud's employment, and I did not have a chance to get to know her well enough to ask this before she died.

87. Joy only told this to me after I had known her for about ten years and she was in her eighties. Joy died before the fifth and final journal was published, and she never knew that Maud bore her the degree of malice that she did.

88. It is unlikely that Maud herself heard the detailed gossip about Chester back in Norval—telling such tales to the minister's wife would have been like "belling the cat" in the fairy tale—but Maud had already made her own observations about Chester's excessive interest in sex. She also knew that most of the town's young people, including Stuart, congregated in Josie Laird's house, and she would have rightly suspected that Chester was the subject of gossip there. The idea that her family might be talked over in the Laird house would have been a very bitter thought, enough to make her despise Josie and Lewis Laird.

89. In early summer 2004, before Volume 5 of the journals was published, I gave June

Thompson the sections about her mother to read. After seeing what Maud wrote about her mother, June said her mother wouldn't have known how to speak to Maud if she was "put on the mat to answer for herself." She said that her mother was a very non-confrontational person, and would have been unnerved by Mrs. Macdonald's force of personality. There is no *proof* that Chester ever behaved inappropriately towards June, but clearly Mrs. Thompson had taken his measure and was worried about his behaviour.

90. Earlier instances where thefts by sons are covered up by the parents may seem incomprehensible today, but concealing family shame was deeply ingrained in that earlier culture.

91. Did he feel hostility for Mrs. Thompson because she was friendly with Luella, and thought him a cad for many reasons? She had mistrusted him ever since her diamond engagement ring disappeared from her room in Norval, and she had reinforced her bad opinion of him since resuming employment with Maud in Toronto. Or, now that he was back on good terms with his mother, did he act partly out of displaced aggression at his mother for forcing him either to reconcile with Luella or be cut out of his inheritance? He could attack his mother through her maid. Or did his offensive behaviour come from self-loathing? Chester knew that he was not the son his mother wanted him to be. Or did Chester act impulsively on his ill-defined, accumulated resentments, without thinking anything out?

92. As noted earlier, Maud was by nature a non-confrontational person. She would keep silent and watch people, and only when matters had come to a certain point would she explode.

93. His class was full of lawyers who went on to very distinguished careers: the Honourable William Goldwin Carrington Howland, Kenneth Archibald Foulds, His Honour Jacie Charles Horwitz, Mervin Mirsky, Walter Halcro, Calvin Boyd, Rupert Alfred Parkinson, Q.C., and the Honourable Gregory Thomas Evans. In 1991, I contacted all Chester's class members who were still living with a letter asking if they remembered Chester from their class. Most of the lawyers from that class knew each other. But despite the fact that I also enclosed Chester's graduation picture, only two of the lawyers in the group had any memory of ever having seen him. One wrote that he knew almost all of the hundred-odd students in the class, and although he remembered Chester's name, he did not remember his face at all. The second wrote that he could recall no particulars but he was pretty sure he had seen Chester gambling "on the second floor of Osgoode Hall around the rectangular table" where they "rolled the dice." At a time when the other young lawyers were establishing contacts with others in this gifted group, Chester was invisible.

94. In the 1990s, James Innes Stewart, Q.C., the president of Chester's 1939 graduating class, told me that Downey, an established K.C., would have taken Chester into partnership because in 1939 cash was in very short supply. Also, because Maud was so well known, having her son would help advertise the practice.

95. My first interview with Anita was in Toronto, at the Stuart Macdonald residence, in 1982. She was a very forthright, good-humoured woman with a memory for details. I met her later, after Stuart's death, for other talks.

96. Maud's gown fit Olive perfectly; at age eighteen in 1939, Olive was five feet four inches tall, weighing roughly 108 pounds, with a twenty-three-inch waist. Olive later changed her name to Linda, and her married name was Linda Sparks.

97. Maud's real estate was to be converted to cash when she died, and divided between her two sons (or their heirs), except for a fund of $4,000 set aside to care for Ewan during his lifetime. Should neither son survive, nor their issue, the estate was to go to the Prince of Wales College in Charlottetown.

98. This breakup happened while Anita Webb was still with Maud.

99. According to Anita, and Stuart, it was after the fall that Stuart had her blood checked and found she was "over-sedated."

100. At teaching hospitals like St. Michael's, researchers had begun to suspect that too much bromide might cause serious secondary health problems, but its damaging psychiatric effects were not yet understood. Much later medical journals became full of articles on the dangers of bromide poisoning from frequently used medications like Miles-Nervine and Bromo-Seltzer, and around 1975, bromide compounds were withdrawn from the market. Bromide compounds are still used in some medicines and pesticides today, but they are carefully controlled. See Horowitz, 1997.

101. The majority of the 180 items listed held enormous sentimental value for her: several framed paintings and watercolours, including a head view of "Anne of Green Gables" and the original artist's painting for *Anne's House of Dreams*; a large number of framed and unframed photographs of family, friends, relatives, and favourite scenes in PEI; the original manuscripts of *Rilla of Ingleside, Anne of the Island, Rainbow Valley, Emily's Quest, Magic for Marigold, Pat of Silver Bush,* and *Mistress Pat*, plus the typewritten copy of her journal, with no rights of publication, and the manuscript of the story of "Jocelyn's Home," which appeared in *A Tangled Web,* and the manuscript play of *The Blue Castle*; her framed marriage certificate; Frede's bridal nightgown; handiwork that Maud herself had done: a crazy quilt, a bolero of point lace, a tablecloth, plus a handkerchief and lace doily; some things from the "blue chest" at Park Corner; many china, silver, and pottery pieces with

great sentimental value to her; some old coins, candlesticks, jugs; her opera glasses; a gilt parlour mirror; a cherry vase which figures in *The Story Girl*; her silver jewel casket; a silver gazing ball on a stand; a silver tea-set of four pieces which was a wedding gift to Frede from Maud; a pendant of pearls and peridots; a narrow gold bracelet given her by Ewan during their engagement; an old school reader with David Macneill's name written in it, dated 1823; a tea wagon; a tall black vase and a painting given her by Isabel Anderson; Chester's first pair of boots, metallized; a bedroom chair with a cane seat which was one of the six wedding chairs of the Reverend Mr. Geddie, the first missionary of the Presbyterian Church in Canada, given to David Macneill and then to Myrtle Webb; her red-striped glass marble, one of her prized childhood possessions; some specially bound copies of a few of her books; various books and anthologies; her gold thimble; Chester's own baby book and photograph album; a ring with two topazes in it; typewritten script of the talking picture of *Anne of Green Gables*; warrant of her O.B.E. autographed by King George V and Edward, Prince of Wales; her miniature O.B.E. insignia; framed diploma of the Royal Society of Arts and Literature; her pair of small china dogs. Although many of these items had primarily sentimental value, there were some quite valuable.

102. This phrase stuck in his mind over the years because he did not understand it. It could possibly have been a reference to the famous "rest cure" for women advocated by a famous American doctor named Silas Weir Mitchell (1829–1914). This is satirized in a famous short story of 1899 by Charlotte Perkins Gilman (1860–1935) called "The Yellow Wallpaper." This cure of putting "neurasthenic" women into enforced bedrest had grown out of the widespread idea that women were weak creatures who could not handle the stress of life. The term "rest cure" had remained in currency after Dr. Weir Mitchell's death, and bedrest was advocated when women needed to recover from mental distress.

103. When she died, she had stocks and bonds with a face value of about $18,500, but with the war coming on, there was no telling what would happen to them. Her anxiety over money is partly explained by the fact that anyone who had been through the Crash of 1929 never felt secure again.

104. It was written on the back of Frederick A. Stokes Company royalty statement from January 1, 1939, to June 30, 1939, for selling 123 books at $1.44 per copy, with a 10 percent royalty, $17.71, plus balance of $91.77, with a total of $109.48. This was not a recent scrap of paper on which she had scribbled out a suicide note, but part of the advance jottings that she did before copying her entries into a journal ledger later on.

105. She had only twenty free legal-sized pages left in Volume Ten, but the handwritten letter-sized pages could have been greatly condensed into much tighter writing. Or she could have started a Volume Eleven, but I doubt she would have done that because ten was a round number to end off a life, and her life on paper was one that had become as real to her as her lived life.

106. There is, of course, another possibility—that Maud destroyed the first 175 pages herself and kept the last page, 176, and *did* intend it as a final note. The last entry in her journal was dated March 23, and this loose page is dated April 22, so it finished off her life story. Yet, that she could have destroyed the pages herself seems highly unlikely— too much effort had gone into their creation, and they held the key to those final years. Her written life had assumed enormous importance to her, as part of her legacy to the world, an historical document of one woman's journey through time.

It is important to note that page "176" refers to itself as an "unfinished" document of which portions can be published after her death. On it, she makes a reference to a second document, the tenth handwritten journal (which had been finished off on March 23, 1942). She says that this tenth volume must never be made public during her lifetime—an odd thing to say on April 22, 1942, if she was contemplating suicide in the next day or so. In all cases, her will gave Stuart the right to make the decision about what could be published and when after her death. It appears that she expected that he would get the entire 176 pages, which she had not copied into her journals.

107. See Volume 1 of her published journals, page 393, where she discusses suicide in her entry of February 7, 1910. In a later entry on May 10, 1922, she says: "Personally I have never felt the horror in regard to suicide that some feel . . ."

108. See Wachowicz, in *CCL*, and the M.A. thesis by Krystana Sobkowska, describing how the Polish Army during World War II issued Montgomery books to the troops in the field, hoping to inspire them to fight harder for a vision of domestic happiness.

EPILOGUE

1. *Presbyterian Record*, June 1992, p. 45.
2. *The Toronto Telegram*, September 14, 1955.

SELECT BIBLIOGRAPHY

This bibliography is highly selective. With a few exceptions, it cites only items quoted from or referred to in my text. For a more complete listing of books, articles, theses, and clippings that are part of any research into Montgomery's life and worldwide influence, go to the bibliography I prepared for the L. M. Montgomery Research Centre at the University of Guelph <www.lmmrc.ca>. That bibliography is maintained and updated by the University of Guelph library.

I have also excluded from the list below most of the massive body of literature on literary, Church, and Canadian history, as well as material from such contextualizing areas as book publishing, popular literature, feminist studies, and cultural theory. Also excluded are books and articles, both historical and contemporary, on mood disorder, manic-depression, and other psychiatric disorders, which are easily located in libraries or on the Internet. However, some lesser-known references of a general nature which are neither on the Internet nor readily accessible in most libraries but which provided useful background information are cited (e.g., materials relating to Montgomery's Scottish and English ancestors and cultural heritage, her early reading, and recent articles in forensic pharmacology). Some of this material is located in the University of Guelph Scottish Collection of rare books, a partner to the L. M. Montgomery Collection.

The bibliography also excludes scores of documents, booklets, letters, e-mails, and interviews assembled over the years, unless these are specifically cited or referenced in the text. Most of these items relating to Montgomery and her milieu, which have been gathered over a thirty-five-year period, will be donated to the University of Guelph Archives, where they will be catalogued and eventually opened to later researchers.

A longer chronology of Montgomery's life, as well as a list of her published books, can be found online at the University of Guelph website. A bibliography of all of the known editions of *Anne of Green Gables* is in preparation by Bernard Katz and will appear later on the University of Guelph website. An invaluable list of her books and translations, poems, and stories is in the Russell, Russell, and Wilmshurst *Preliminary Bibliography* (1986), which is now being updated by Benjamin Lefebvre and will eventually be available through a link from our website. Scholarly publications on Montgomery's writing (including theses), as well as newspaper and magazine items, are constantly being added to our website at Guelph. Many links to other sources of information about Montgomery are also there.

SELECTED LETTERS FROM L.M. MONTGOMERY TO OTHERS

Published Letters

Montgomery, L. M. *The Green Gables Letters from L. M. Montgomery to Ephraim Weber, 1905–1909.* Ed. Wilfrid Eggleston. Toronto: Ryerson, 1960.

Montgomery, L. M. *After Green Gables: L. M. Montgomery's Letters to Ephraim Weber, 1916–1941.* Eds. Paul Gerard Tiessen and Hildi Froese Tiessen. Toronto: University of Toronto Press, 2006. [A revised version of *L. M. Montgomery's Ephraim Weber: Letters 1916–1941.* Waterloo: mlr editions, 1999. Includes Foreword.]

Montgomery, L. M. *My Dear Mr. M.: Letters to G. B. MacMillan.* Eds. Francis W. P. Bolger and Elizabeth R. Epperly. Toronto: McGraw-Hill Ryerson, 1980. [This selection was republished with a new Preface by Oxford University Press in 1992.]

Unpublished Letters

• Letters to various members of **Aunt Annie Campbell family** 1913–1941. Private Collection of George Campbell, Park Corner. • Letter to **Thane Campbell**. 6 October 1937. Private Collection, Park Corner. [Concerns about family gravestones.] • Letter to **Shirley Ann Colcord**. 22 October 1938. Private Collection. • Letter to "**Evelyn.**" Undated (1927?). Queen's University Archives. • Letters to **Eric Gaskell**. Undated, circa June 1940; 17 February 1941. Source unknown. • Letters to Mr. **Charles Gordonsmith** and **M. O. Hammond** of *The Globe and Mail*. 1909–1936. Provincial Archives of Ontario. • Letters to **Earl Grey**. 26 September 1910; 7 December 1910. Public Archives of Canada. • Letters to **Frederick Philip Grove**.

13 March 1923; 3 April 1930. Grove Collection. University of Manitoba Archives. • Letter to **Katherine Hale** [Mrs. John Garvin]. 9 January 1928. Queen's University Archives. • Letter to **Evelyn Johnston**. Undated. Queen's University Archives. • Letters to **Violet King**. 13 April 1936; 25 January 1937; 14 April 1937; 17 May 1937; 6 April 1938; 2 June 1938; 23 November 1938; 18 March 1939; 7 November 1939. Private Collection of Violet King Morgan. • Postcards to **Nora Lefurgey**. 6 October 1932; 27 September 1939. Private Collection of Ed and Bette Campbell. • Letters to **Jack Lewis**. 3 March 1936; 4 February 1927; 28 February 1930; 19 January 1932; 14 February 1934; 3 March 1926; 28 December 1939. R. S. Lewis Collection. Parks Canada, PEI • Letters to **John David Logan**. 26 July 1912; 12 August 1912. • Letter to **Nellie McClung**. 23 January 1936. McClung Papers. Public Archives of British Columbia. • Letter to **Joan McLennan** (?). 19 March 1930. Private Collection (Davina Curnow). [Letter about a flood of letters from Australia.] • Letter to **Lena McLure** [a cousin]. 12 February 1933. Private Collection. • Letter to **Eva Macneill**. 30 March 1912. Private Collection of **John and Jennie Macneill**. • Letters to **Penzie Macneill**. 1885?–1894?. L. M. Montgomery Collection, University of PEI. • Letters to **Zella Cook Mustard** and **Isabel Mustard**. 1920s–1937. Private Collection, Isabel St. John. • Letter to **Lorne Pierce**. 13 October 1926. United Church Archives. • Letter to **Mrs. Seely**. 17 August 1935. Private Collection of Ron Cohen. [Asking a fan to write to Hollywood about making *Anne's House of Dreams* into a movie.] [A similar letter went to a **"Helen,"** n.d., asking the same thing and mentioning a "nervous breakdown." Source of letter unknown.] • Postcard to **Aileen Small**. 3 October 1941. Private Collection, courtesy Aileen Small Oder. [Handwritten for Montgomery by M. A. Powell who was employed as companion, secretary, and nurse after Anita Webb left in January 1941] • Letter to **Roberta Mary Sparks**. 4 July 1933. L. M. Montgomery Collection. University of Guelph, courtesy Mrs. Roberta Robertson. • Letters to **Morris Springer**, 1936–1942. National Archives of Canada. • Letter to **Mrs. Townsend**. 2 June 1935. Private Collection, Park Corner. • Letters to **Marian Webb** and **Myrtle Webb**. 19 March 1933. Private Collections of Elaine Crawford and Ina Reed. • L. M. Letter to **Ephraim Weber.** 26 December 1941. Transcription by Wilfrid Eggleston. National Archives of Canada. • Letter to **Gladys** [**Mrs. Harold Wilson**, U.K.], n.d., circa 1931. Transcription in private collection of Mollie Gillen. [Published in the Harrap UK edition of *Emily of New Moon*, with a Foreword by Mary Wilson.] • Letter to **"Aunt Margaret** [**Woolner** (MacKenzie)]."** 17 December 1911. Private Collection of Robert Woolner.

SELECTED PERSONAL INTERVIEWS, ETC.
(Excludes a few important "off the record" interviews.)

• **Isabel Anderson**. Personal interview. 29 August 1991. [Isabel was a fan whose persistent attentions caused Montgomery much distress in the Norval years.] • **Edith Bacon**.
Personal interview. 1986. [Daughter of one of Montgomery's earliest maids. Edith often
visited the Macdonalds in the manse.] • **Richard Braiden and Nora Lane Braiden**.
Personal interview. 20 March 1991. Toronto. [Nora's father was Montgomery's doctor and
neighbour; Dr. Richard Braiden was Stuart's classmate in medical school.] • **Ed
Campbell and Bette Campbell**. Personal interviews in Haileybury, Ontario, and cor-
respondence. Circa 1994–96. [Ed, the son of Nora Lefurgey Campbell, and a mining en-
gineer in Haileybury, Ontario, vividly remembered visiting the Macdonalds in Norval.]
• **George Campbell**. Personal interviews and telephone conversations. 1975 ff. Park
Corner, PEI. [George is the grandson of Montgomery's Aunt Annie Macneill Campbell,
and he owns the home at Park Corner, PEI, where Montgomery was married.] •
Constance Carruthers. Personal letter with enclosures, including the manuscript for
"Who was Herman Leard?" dated January 1993. 13 August 1993. [Constance Carruthers
gives many reactions to the Herman Leard love story from relatives and neighbours of
the Leards. Mrs. Carruthers was the Director of Nursing at the Prince County Hospital
in the 1960s and early 1970s.] • **Mike Chepesuik**. Interview. Summer 1985. [His wife
Florence was a Cavendish Simpson, and after their marriage, they visited Montgomery
in Norval.] • **Wilda Clark and Harold Clark**. Letters and interviews. 1975 ff. Uxbridge,
Ontario. [Harold was in Montgomery's Sunday School class, and Wilda, a lifelong fan,
was the initial driving force behind the attempt to save the Leaskdale manse and church
as designated historical sites.] • **Lily Meyers Cook**. Personal interview. April 1986.
Richmond Hill, Ontario. [Lily Meyers was Montgomery's maid from March 1918 to
February 1925. Also, in this same time frame, I interviewed the daughter of Lily's sister,
an earlier maid named Edith Meyers (Lyons), who worked for Montgomery from circa
January 1916 to December 1917.] • **W. Peter Coues**. Interview. 12 September 1991. Boston,
Massachusetts. [Pete Coues was the cousin and literary executor for Lewis C. Page,
Montgomery's publisher between 1908 and 1919. Mr. Coues was a banking executive and
financier in Boston who had close ties to Lewis C. Page all his life.] • **Ethel Dennis
Currie**. Personal interview. 15 February 1999. Milton, Ontario. [Ethel Dennis was
Montgomery's maid from August 1934 to March 1937] • **Elaine Laird Crawford and
Robert Crawford**. Personal interviews. 1975–2008. Norval, Ontario. [Elaine, the daugh-
ter of Marian Webb Laird of Norval, is the granddaughter of Myrtle and Ernest Webb of

Cavendish, and the niece of Anita Webb of Cavendish and Toronto.] • **Elsie Bushby Davidson**. Correspondence and personal interviews. 1980–1993. Uxbridge, Ontario. [Elsie Bushby was Montgomery's part-time maid for six months in early January 1925, and full-time until June 1926.] • **David Dills and Kay Dills**. Interviews and letters. 1992 onward. [As a little boy, David was taught by Isabel Anderson, and his wife Kay edited the Acton newspaper for many years, often publishing Isabel's poetry.] • **Mary Furness**. Personal interviews and visit. Circa 1988. [Mary was Ewan's niece, and she had vivid and fond memories of "Aunt Maud."] • **Eric Gaskell**. Personal interview. April 1997. Ottawa. [Commodore Gaskell was a Canadian Authors Association executive who knew and was in contact with Montgomery for over a decade. Later a parliamentary secretary in Ottawa.] • **Kathy Carter Gastle**. Personal interviews and e-mails. 1990–2008. Norval, Ontario. [Kathy, the daughter of local Norval historian Joan Browne Carter and the god-daughter of Joy Laird, was at one point the mayor of Georgetown. She has worked to get Norval designated as another important Montgomery heritage site. Joan Browne Carter was a classmate of Stuart Macdonald and remembered the Macdonalds well.] • **Doris Munsey Haslam**. Personal interview. Circa 1992. [Daughter of Ettie Schurman Munsey, the fiancée of Herman Leard before he died. Ettie later married Singleton Windham Munsey.] • **Catherine Agnes Mustard Hunt**. Personal interviews. Compiler: *Mustards of North America*, Vol. 1. Georgetown, Ontario: Catherine Agnes Mustard Hunt, 1980. [Family historian, related to John A. Mustard.] • **Mrs. Hants B. Hunter**. Interview. 17 July 1983. [Memories of the Bedeque school in Montgomery's time.] • **Doris Stirling Jenkins**. Personal interview. 1 July 1996. Summerside, PEI. [Daughter of the minister, John Stirling, who officiated at L. M. Montgomery's marriage and funeral; Doris's mother was a long-time friend of Montgomery.] • **L. E. (Ted) Jones**. Personal interviews. Summer 1997–98. [Taught in the Mining-Engineering field at the University of Toronto, and remembered Chester Macdonald.] • **Joy Laird**. Many personal interviews, with correspondence. 1991–2001. Norval, Ontario. [Friend and contemporary classmate of Stuart Macdonald in Norval.] • **(Justice) Douglas Latimer**. Interviews and correspondence. 1995 onward. [He employed Joy Laird in his law firm and later when he became a Justice in the Ontario Court of Justice. He was an invaluable source of information on both the Glen Williams and Norval communities.] • **Cameron Leask and Jessie Leask**. Personal interviews. 12 May 1986. [Cameron was a classmate and playmate of Chester and Stuart Macdonald. Leaskdale was named for his and Jessie's forebears.] • **Nora Lefurgey**. Personal diary. Private collection of Ed and Bette Campbell. [Nora was a life-long friend of Montgomery. Nora's only surviving child was Ed ("Ebbie").] • **Nina Pickering Lunney**. Personal Interview. Circa 1985. [Granddaughter of Marshall Pickering.] • **Cameron Macdonald**. Personal interview. Circa 1996. [L. M. Montgomery's first grandson.] • **David Macdonald**. Personal interview. 31 August 1983. Ontario. [Grandson of Montgomery and a school principal.] • **Ewan Stuart Macdonald**. Personal interviews, with correspondence 1975–82. Toronto. [L. M. Montgomery's son; medical doctor and professor at St. Michael's Hospital in Toronto.] • **Luella Reid Macdonald**. Personal interviews, with correspondence 1988 ff. Ontario. [Montgomery's first daughter-in-law, and mother of her first two grandchildren; longtime Norval resident.] • **Ruth Steele Macdonald**. Personal discussions. 1980 ff. [Wife of Dr. E. Stuart Macdonald.] • **Pauline McGibbon**. Personal letter. 16 November 1992. [Montgomery's books as a part of her "growing up," and information about Montgomery's books in the West Indies. The Honourable Pauline McGibbon was a Chancellor of the University of Guelph from 1977 to 1983.] • **Marjorie McKee**. Phone conversation. 16 June 1992. [Vivid memories of Robert Reid, Luella's father, and met Montgomery at church functions.] • **Dorothy Watson McLean**. Personal Interview. 6 July 1992. Norval, Ontario. [Contemporary of Montgomery's sons in Norval.] • **John Macneill and Jennie Macneill**. Interviews, visits, and correspondence. 1985 ff. [John inherited the farm of his grandfather, Montgomery's Uncle John F. Macneill, and he and his wife, Jennie, have developed the site of L. M. Montgomery's "old home." Montgomery expresses joy in her 1930 journal entry when John is born and the family will continue.] • **Helen Mason (Mrs. Ed Shafer)**. Personal interview. Circa 1995. [Helen's mother, Mrs. Mason, was Montgomery's maid from circa January 1927 to March 1931.] • **Mary Maxwell**. Personal interviews. 1997–2002. Norval, Ontario. [Norval schoolmate of Stuart Macdonald; later wife of Anglican minister in Norval.] • **John Mustard**. Telephone conversation. 11 December 1998. [Information about the Reverand John A. Mustard, his grandfather.] • **Margaret Mustard**. Interview. Circa 1980. Uxbridge, Ontario. [Good friend of Montgomery and one of the last people to visit her in Toronto.] • **Ormand Pickard**. Personal interview. Letter. 13 October 1991. Dunwich (Suffolk), England, UK. [Local historian and expert on the Woolners of Dunwich, Montgomery's Grandmother Lucy Woolner Macneill's family.] • **Lem Prowse and Pauly Prowse**. Personal interviews. Circa 1982. Charlottetown. [Dr. Prowse, from PEI, was Stuart's classmate in medical school in Toronto and remained a lifelong friend.] • **Margaret Russell**. Interview. Circa 1990. Norval, Ontario. [Margaret had helped Montgomery with the church choir and knew her well; after a career teaching in Toronto, she retired to Norval, and lived in the family home on the "hill o' pines."] • **Linda Sparks [Olive Watson]**. Personal interview. 4 February 1998. [Through her friend, Anita Webb, Olive wore Montgomery's wedding dress in a pageant.] • **Isabel Mustard St. John**. Personal interviews and correspondence. 1990s ff. Uxbridge, Ontario. [Daughter of Zella Cook Mustard, who knew L. M. Montgomery; the several related

Mustard families in Leaskdale were pillars in the community and church.] • **Roger W. Straus**. Interview (telephone). Summer 1991. [After Lewis Page's death in 1956, Straus bought out the Page Company to get the copyright to Montgomery's titles, and he and his CFO, Robert Wohlforth, gave me information about Page and his firm.] • **Mrs. Faye Thompson and June Thompson**. Personal interview. 26 March 1991. [Mrs. Thompson was Montgomery's maid from April 1931 to August 1934, and then again from March 1937 until June 1939. I interviewed June again in 2004.] • **Barbara Wachowicz**. Letters, documents, playbills, etc. 1982 onward. [A radio and television personality, writer, and librettist (*The Blue Castle* musical in Poland), Wachowicz provided much historical information about Montgomery's reception in Poland.] • **Anita Webb**. Personal interviews. 1982–83. Toronto and Norval, Ontario. [Anita Webb, daughter of Myrtle and Ernest Webb of Cavendish, was Montgomery's maid from circa July 1939 until early January 1941.] • **Reg Winfield**. Personal Interviews. December 1987. [Associated with the Barracloughs in Montgomery's era.] • **Robert Wohlforth**. Personal interview. 11 September 1991. [Wohlforth was the Chief Financial Officer of Farrar Straus (later Farrar, Straus, and Giroux) from 1952 to 1990 who orchestrated the purchase of the L. C. Page Company at 53 Beacon Street by Roger Straus after Page's death in 1956.] • **Robert L. Woolner**. Personal letter, with enclosures. 1 May 1995. [An attorney in Toronto who is descended from the PEI Woolners.]

ARCHIVAL MATERIALS COMPILED BY MONTGOMERY

Black Scrapbook #1, ca. 1923–27. L. M. Montgomery Collection, University of Guelph Library Archives, Guelph, Ontario. [In *Scrapbooks of clippings, programs & other memorabilia / compiled by L. M. Montgomery, ca. 1910–1936.*]

Black Scrapbook #2, 1931–1935. L. M. Montgomery Collection, University of Guelph Library Archives, Guelph, Ontario. [See *Scrapbooks of clippings, programs & other memorabilia / compiled by L. M. Montgomery, ca. 1910–1936. XZ5 MS A002.*]

Red Scrapbook #1, ca. 1910–1914. L. M. Montgomery Collection, University of Guelph Library Archives, Guelph, Ontario. [In *Scrapbooks of clippings, programs & other memorabilia / compiled by L. M. Montgomery, ca. 1910–1936.*]

Red Scrapbook #2, ca. 1913–1926. L. M. Montgomery Collection, University of Guelph Library Archives, Guelph, Ontario. [In *Scrapbooks of clippings, programs & other memorabilia / compiled by L. M. Montgomery, ca. 1910–1936.*]

Scrapbook of Reviews from around the world which L. M. Montgomery's clipping service sent to her, 1910–1935. L. M. Montgomery Collection, University of Guelph Library Archives, Guelph, Ontario. XZ5 MS A003. [See pages 131–50 for clippings on the Mary Miles Minter firm.]

Scrapbooks of clippings, programs & other memorabilia / compiled by L. M. Montgomery, ca. 1910–1936. L. M. Montgomery Collection, University of Guelph Library Archives, Guelph, Ontario. XZ5 MS A002.

OTHER CITED SELECTED WRITINGS BY MONTGOMERY

Autobiographical writing

Montgomery, L. M. *The Alpine Path.* Markham, Ontario: Fitzhenry and Whiteside [1975]. [Reprint of Montgomery's 1917 biographical sketches published in *Everywoman's World.*]

———. "An Autobiographical Sketch." *The Ontario Library Review.* March 1929 (Vol. 23): 94–6.

———. "The Gay Days of Old: A Well-known Author's Reminiscences of Her Girlhood on a Canadian Farm," *Farmers Magazine* (circa 1920: p. 176). In *Scrapbook of Reviews from around the world which L. M. Montgomery's clipping service sent to her, 1910–1935.* L. M. Montgomery Collection, University of Guelph.

———. "I Dwell among My Own People." *Towards A Canadian Literature: Essays, Editorials and Manifestos. Vol 1. 1752–1940.* Ottawa: Tecumseh Press, 1984. [Also in *Scrapbook of Reviews.* University of Guelph.]

———. *The Selected Journals of L. M. Montgomery.* Eds. Mary Rubio and Elizabeth Waterston. Toronto: Oxford University Press, 1985–2004. [*Vol. 1, 1889–1910:* 1985; *Vol. 2, 1920–1921:* 1987; *Vol. 3, 1921–1929:* 1992; *Vol. 4, 1929–1935:* 1998; *Vol. 5, 1935–1942:* 2004. See introductory essays and notes.]

———. Unpublished Sections of the Holograph Journals, 1889–1942. L. M. Montgomery Collection, University of Guelph.

Other Montgomery references

Montgomery, L. M. "The Blue Castle." *Canadian Countryman.* 1927. [Serialized installments of this novel.]

———. "The Blythes are Quoted." L. M. Montgomery Collection. University of Guelph. [Her April 25, 1942, obituary in *The New York Times* states that she had been in ill health for two years, but that a collection she compiled "last winter" was turned over to her publishing house "today." That manuscript is in the University of Guelph Archives, and many of the stories were published earlier in *The Road to Yesterday*. McGraw-Hill, 1974; Seal Books, 1993.]

——. "The Bride Dreams." *The Canadian Bookman*. March 1922: 101.

——. "Each in His Own Tongue." *Chronicles of Avonlea*. Boston: L. C. Page, 1912.

——. "The Man Who Forgot." *Family Herald* January 1932: 23–24, 41, 44.

——. "Spring in the Woods." *The Canadian Magazine*. May 1911: 59–62. Followed by "The Woods in Summer." September 1911: 399–402; "The Woods in Autumn." October 1911: 574–77; "The Woods in Winter." November 1911: 62–64. [This four-part series provides another link to the travel and nature writing and speaking of Edwin Smith, John Burroughs, and the imaginary "John Foster" in *The Blue Castle*.]

TEXTUAL REFERENCES AND SOURCES

[Anon.] *A Bad Boy's Diry, By the Author of Blunders of a Bashful Man, etc.* New York: J. S. Ogilvie Publishing Company, 1880.

[Anon.]. *CENTENNIAL: Union Presbyterian Church (Esquesing), 1833–1933.* Glen Williams, Ontario: Union Presbyterian Church. Reprinted and updated in 1983 as *1833–1933 / Union Presbyterian Church / 1933–1983* [The 1933 booklet was researched and written by the Reverend Ewan Macdonald.]

[Anon.] "Latest Gossip of Book World . . . Miss Montgomery's Visit to Boston." In *Red Scrapbook #1, ca. 1910–1914*, p. 13. L. M. Montgomery Collection, University of Guelph.

[Anon.] "Miss L. M. Montgomery, Author of *Anne of Green Gables*." *The Republic*. November 19, 1910, p. 5. In *Red Scrapbook #1, ca. 1910–1914*, p. 15. L. M. Montgomery Collection, University of Guelph.

[Anon.] *One Hundred Years to the Glory of God: Norval Presbyterian Church, 1878–1978*. Norval, Ontario: Norval Presbyterian Church.

[Anon.] "Says Woman's Place is Home: Authoress Gives Views on Suffrage," *The Republic*, November 19, 1910, p. 5. In *Red Scrapbook #1, ca. 1910–1914*, p. 15. L. M. Montgomery Collection, University of Guelph.

[Anon.] *Toronto Telegram*, March 24, 1937. [W. A. Deacon on the function of a critic.]

Åhmansson, Gabriella. *A Life and Its Mirrors: A Feminist Reading of L. M. Montgomery's Fiction*. Vol. 1. Uppsala [Sweden]: Almqvist and Wiksell International, 1991.

[Excellent study of Montgomery's writing from a feminist perspective.]

Allen, David. *Virtue, Learning and the Scottish Enlightenment: Ideas of Scholarship in Early Modern History*. Edinburgh: Edinburgh University Press, 1993.

Anderson, Robert David. *Education and Opportunity in Victorian Scotland*. London: Oxford University Press, 1983.

Anstruther, Ian. *The Knight and the Umbrella: An Account of the Eglinton Tournament, 1839*. London: Geoffrey Bles, 1963.

Auld, Walter C. *Voices of the Island: History of the Telephone on Prince Edward Island*. Halifax, NS: Nimbus Publishing Co., 1985.

Bacon, Jean, & Stuart Bacon. *The Suffolk Shoreline and the Sea*. Colchester, Essex: Segment Publications, 1984.

Baglole, Harry, ed. *Exploring Island History: A Guide to the Historical Resources of Prince Edward Island*. Belfast, PEI: Ragweed, 1977.

Betts, E. Arthur. *Pine Hill Divinity Hall: 1820–1970, A History*. Halifax, NS: Pine Hill Divinity Board of Governors, 1970. [Where Ewan Macdonald studied.]

Blind, Mathilde. *George Eliot*. London: W. H. Allen, 1883. [Influential as a model for young L. M. Montgomery.]

Bolger, F. W. P. *The Years Before "Anne."* Charlottetown: Prince Edward Island Heritage Foundation, 1974. [An invaluable resource containing the Penzie MacNeill letters and early publications of Montgomery.]

Bone, T. R. *Studies in the History of Scottish Education, 1872–1939*. London: University of London Press, 1967.

Bruce, Marian. *A Century of Excellence: Prince of Wales College, 1860–1969*. Charlottetown: Island Studies Press, 2005.

Bulwer-Lytton, Baron Edward. *Zanoni*. New York: Harper, 1847. [A very influential book on the young Montgomery.]

Bumsted. J. M. "Scottish Emigration to the Maritimes, 1770–1815: A New Look at an Old Theme." *Acadiensis*. Spring 1981 (vol. 10, no 2): 65–85.

Buss, Helen M. "Decoding L. M. Montgomery's Journals / Encoding a Critical Practice for Women's Private Literature." *Essays on Canadian Writing* 54 (Winter 1994): 80–100.

Carter, Joan (Browne). *Norval History: 1820–1950*. Norval, Ontario: Privately printed, 1996. [School contemporaries of Stuart Macdonald.]

Cavendish Literary Society Notes. Prince Edward Island Public Archives and Records Office, Charlottetown. [Complete minutes and other records of the Cavendish Literary Society from its organization, February 19, 1886, until it discontinued meeting, January 7, 1924.]

Chapman, Ethel M. "The Author of 'Anne.'" *Maclean's Magazine*. October 1919 (vol.

32): 103–104, 106. [Maclean's Magazine Series: Women and Their Work.] Also located in *Scrapbook of Reviews:* 170–71.

Clark, (Rev.) John A. *The Young Disciple; or, A Memoir of Anzonetta Peters.* New York: The American Tract Society, 1854(?).

Clarke, Edward Hammond. *Sex in Education, or a Fair Chance for Girls.* 1873. [Available through Project Gutenberg texts.]

Clarkson, Adrienne. Interview with Margaret Laurence. CBC TV. Toronto. 1966.

———. Foreword. *L. M. Montgomery and Canadian Culture.* Eds. Irene Gammel and Elizabeth Epperly. Toronto: University of Toronto Press, 1999. ix–xii.

Cleckley, Hervey. *The Mask of Sanity.* St. Louis: C. V. Mosby Co., 1941. [This book is still considered the classic book on the psychopath (or sociopath) and is available online.]

Clifford, Lucy Lane (Mrs. W. K. Clifford). *Love Letters of a Worldly Woman.* Chicago: Donohue, Henneberry & Co, 1891.

Colley, Linda. *Britons: Forging the Nation, 1707–1837.* New Haven: Yale University Press, 1992.

Conrad, Marjory. "Recording Angels: The Private Chronicles of Women from the Maritime Provinces of Canada, 1750–1950." *The Neglected Majority: Essays in Canadian Women's History. Vol. 2.* Eds. Alison L. Prentice and Susan Mann Trofimenkoff. Toronto: McClelland and Stewart, 1977. 41–60.

Corr, Helen. "An Exploration into Scottish Education." *People and Society in Scotland. Vol. 2.* Eds. W. Hamish Fraser and R. J. Morris. Edinburgh: John Donald Publishers in association with the Economic and Social Society of Scotland, 1990. 290–309.

Corse, Sarah M. *Nationalism and Literature: The Politics of Culture in Canada and the United States.* Cambridge: Cambridge University Press, 1997.

Corston, John B. *Twenty Years at Pine Hill Divinity Hall.* Halifax, NS: Maritime Conference Archives Committee, United Church of Canada, 1982.

Cousins, Elizabeth M. B. L. *Montgomeries of Eglinton.* Strathclyde Department of Education, Ayr Division (Scotland). n.d. [circa 1980–90?]

Daly, Whitman Cecil. *Prince Edward Island, the Way It Was: A Glimpse into the Past.* PEI: Privately printed, 1978; reprinted 1984.

Davie, George. *The Democratic Intellect: Scotland and Her Universities in the Nineteenth Century.* Edinburgh: University of Edinburgh Press, 1961. See also by Davie: *A Passion for Ideas: Essay on the Scottish Enlightenment.* Vol 2. Edinburgh: Polygon, 1994, and *The Scottish Enlightenment and Other Essays.* Edinburgh: Polygon, 1991.

Davies, Robertson. "The Creator of 'Anne.'" *Peterborough Examiner.* 2 May 1942: 4.

[Obituary for Montgomery by a young newspaperman who became a major Canadian novelist.]

De la Motte Fouqué, Baron Friedrich Heinrich Karl. *Undine: A Tale*. (1811). Translated from the German by Edmund Gosse. Connecticut: Hyperion Press, 1978. [Important influence on Montgomery.]

Deacon, William Arthur. Letter to Dr. Logan. 20 October 1924. Deacon Collection. Robarts Library, Toronto.

——. *Poteen: A Pot-Pourri of Canadian Essays*. Ottawa: Graphic Publishers, 1926. [The book leading the attack on Montgomery's celebrity.]

Dwight, Phoebe, "Want to Know How to Write Book? Well Here's a Real Recipe / Author of 'Anne of Green Gables' tells the Right Time to Mount Pegasus and Give Him the Rein." In *Red Scrapbook #1, ca. 1910–1914*, pp. 13–14. L. M. Montgomery Collection, University of Guelph Library Archives, Guelph, Ontario.

Egoff, Sheila. *The Republic of Childhood: A Critical Guide to Canadian Children's Literature in English*. Toronto: Oxford University Press, 1967. Rev. 1975. Rev. and expanded, with Judith Saltman, as *The New Republic of Childhood*, in 1990.

Ehrenrich, Barbara, and Deirdre English. *For Her Own Good: 150 Years of the Experts' Advice to Women*. Garden City, NY: Doubleday, 1978.

Epperly, Elizabeth R. "Approaching the Montgomery Manuscripts." *Harvesting Thistles: The Textual Garden of L. M. Montgomery*. Ed. Mary Henley Rubio. Guelph: Canadian Children's Press, 1994. 74–83.

——. *The Fragrance of Sweet-Grass: L. M. Montgomery's Heroines and the Pursuit of Romance*. Toronto: University of Toronto Press, 1992.

Franklyn, Charles Aubrey Hamilton. *A Genealogical History of the Families of Montgomerie of Garboldisham, Hunter of Knap and Montgomerie of Fittleworth*. UK: Ditchling Press, 1967.

Fraser, Sir William [1816–98]. *Memorials of the Montgomeries, Earls of Eglinton*. Volumes 1 and 2. Edinburgh: 1859.

Fullarton, John. *Historical Memoir of the Family of Eglinton and Winton: Together with Relative Notes and Illustrations*. [1864]. ·

——. *Records of the Burgh of Prestwick in the Sheriffdom of Ayr, MCCCCLXX–MDCCLXXXII*. (1834).

Fussell, Paul. *The Great War and Modern Memory*. London: Oxford University Press, 1975.

Galbraith, John Kenneth. *The Scotch*. Toronto: MacMillan Company of Canada, 1964.

Gammel, Irene, ed. *Making Avonlea: L. M. Montgomery and Popular Culture*. Toronto:

University of Toronto Press, 2002.

Gerson, Carole. "Canadian Women Writers and American Markets, 1880–1940." *Context of North America: Canadian / US Literary Relations.* Ed. Camille La Bossière. Ottawa: University of Ottawa Press, 1994. 106–18.

——. "'Dragged at Anne's Chariot Wheels': The Triangle of Author, Publisher, and Fictional Character." *L. M. Montgomery and Canadian Culture.* Eds. Irene Gammel and Elizabeth R. Epperly. Toronto: University of Toronto Press, 1999.

——. "'Fitted to Earn her own Living': Figures of the New Woman in the Writing of L. M. Montgomery." *Children's Voices in Atlantic Literature and Culture: Essays on Childhood.* Ed. Hilary Thompson. Guelph: Canadian Children's Press, 1995. 24–35.

Gillen, Mollie. *The Wheel of Things: A Biography of L. M. Montgomery.* Don Mills: Fitzhenry and Whiteside, 1975. [An excellent early biography.]

Girouard, Mark. *The Return to Camelot: Chivalry and the English Gentleman.* New Haven: Yale University Press, 1981. [See Chapter 7 for the account of the Eglinton Tournament.]

Golomb, Beatrice Alexandra. *Vol. 2. A Review of the Scientific Literature as it Pertains to Gulf War Illnesses: Pyridostigmine Bromide.* National Defense Research Institute: RAND, 1999. [Recent research on bromide poisoning. See also Horowitz, 1997, and Wacks, Oster, *et al.*, 1990.]

Grant, Nigel, and Walter Humes. "Scottish Education." *Scotland: A Concise Cultural History.* Ed. Paul H. Scott. Edinburgh: Mainstream, 1993. 357–72.

Graves, Dianne. *A Crown of Life: The World of John McCrae.* St. Catharines, Ontario: Vanwell Publishing, 1997. [McCrae, who met Montgomery in 1910, links to Anne's son, Walter, who dies in World War I.]

Grey, Earl. Letters to L. M. Montgomery. 20 September 1910; 30 September 1910; 3 October 1910; 1 December 1910. Letter to Prof. John Macnaughton. 27 September 1910 (reply from Macnaughton: 29 September 1910). Earl Grey Fonds. National Archives of Canada.

Grimble, Ian. *Highland Man.* Edinburgh: Highlands and Islands Development Board, 1980. See also by Grimble: *Scottish Clans and Tartans.* London: Hamlyn, 1973.

Halliday, James. *Scotland: A Concise History,* B.C., *to 1990.* Edinburgh: Gordon Wright Publishing, 1990.

Hare, Robert D. *Without Conscience: The Disturbing World of the Psychopaths among Us.* (1993). New York and London: Guilford Press, 1999.

Harrington, Lyn. *Syllables of Recorded Time: The Story of the Canadian Authors Association, 1921–1981.* Toronto: Simon and Pierre, 1981.

Haslam, Lucy Palmer. Personal diaries. Private collection of Michael Bliss family. [Lucy

Palmer Haslam taught Montgomery briefly.]

Henderson, Hamish. "The Oral Tradition." *Scotland: A Concise Cultural History*. Ed. Paul H. Scott. Edinburgh: Mainstream, 1993. 159–71.

Humes, Walter M., and Hamish Paterson. *Scottish Culture and Scottish Education, 1800–1980*. Edinburgh: John Donald, 1983.

Hutton, Jack, and Linda Jackson-Hutton. *Lucy Maud Montgomery and Bala: A Love Story of the North Woods*. Gravenhurst: Watts Printing, 1998. [Creators of the "Bala Museum with memories of L. M. Montgomery."]

Insch, George Pratt. *School Life in Old Scotland: From Contemporary Sources*. Edinburgh: Educational Institute of Scotland, 1925.

Kalant, Harold. Numerous e-mails (1990s to 2007). [University of Toronto specialist in pharmacology.]

Karr, Clarence. *Authors and Audiences: Popular Canadian Fiction in the Early Twentieth Century*. Montreal: McGill-Queen's University Press, 2000.

Kennedy, Michael. "'The People are Leaving': Highland Emigration to Prince Edward Island." *The Island Magazine*. Spring/Summer 2003. 31ff.

——. "Emigrants on the Edinburgh, 1771: A New Passenger List for Prince Edward Island." *The Island Magazine*, vol. 39 (Spring-Summer 1996), pp. 39–42. See also by Kennedy: *Is leis an Tighearna an talamh agus an lan: [The earth and all that it contains belongs to God: The Scottish Gaelic Settlement History of Prince Edward Island]*. Ph.D. thesis, University of Edinburgh, 1995. See also: The P.E.I. Ships Database http://www.islandregister.com/ship_data.html and http://www.ralstongenealogy.com/ edbrglst.htm for "Two lists of Intending Passengers to the New World, 1770 and 1771" which lists Hugh and Neill Montgomery on the *Edinburgh*, going to "St. Johns." See also: Passenger list to the brigantine "Isle of Skye" in 1806 which includes Macdonalds.

King [Morgan], Violet. Letter to Mary Rubio. October 15, 1992. Private collection.

Knister, Raymond. [Unpublished article.] *The Journal of Canadian Fiction*, vol. IV, no. 2, 1975. [This apparently unpublished essay on the Canadian girl was among Knister's papers when he drowned in 1932. Knister had read *Anne of Green Gables*, for he mentioned it in a review he wrote of the *Emily* books.]

Ladies' Indispensable Assistant, Being a Companion for the Sister, Mother, and Wife, containing more information for the price than any other work upon the subject. Here are the very best directions for the behaviour and etiquette of Ladies and Gentlemen . . . New York: Published at 128 Nassau Street, 1852. [A well-circulated North American "manners" book with samples of proposals like those in Montgomery's journals.]

Logan, John Daniel, and Donald G. French. *Highways of Canadian Literature: A*

Synoptic Introduction to the Literary History of Canada (English) from 1760 to 1924. Toronto: McClelland and Stewart, 1924.

Lynch, Michael. *Scotland: A New History.* London: Pimlico, 1991. See also: Lynch, "Scottish Culture in Its Historical Perspective." *Scotland: A Concise Cultural History.* Ed. Paul H. Scott. Edinburgh: Mainstream, 1993. 15–45.

Macdonald, E[wan] Stuart. Letter to Mrs. L. O. Ekeberg of Sweden. 24 September 1960. Private collection.

Macdonald, Rev. E[wan]. "P. E. I. Recruiting Record." Letter to the *Globe.* Undated. In *Red Scrapbook #2, ca 1913–1926,* p. 57. L. M. Montgomery Collection, University of Guelph Library Archives, Guelph, Ontario.

MacGillivray, Allan. *Decades of Harvest: A History of the Township of Scott, 1807–1973.* Uxbridge, Ontario: Scott History Committee, 1986. [Invaluable source of information on the Leaskdale area by local historian and museum curator.]

Macgregor, Forbes. *Greyfriars Bobby: The Real Story at Last.* Edinburgh: Gordon Wright Publishing, 1990. [Cf. "Dog Monday" in *Rilla of Ingleside.*]

MacMechan, Archibald. *Head-Waters of Canadian Literature.* Toronto: McClelland and Stewart, 1924.

MacMurchy, Marjory. "L. M. Montgomery: Island Writer," p. 50. *Scrapbook of Reviews from around the world which L. M. Montgomery's clipping service sent to her, 1910–1935.* L. M. Montgomery Collection, University of Guelph.

Macnaughton, John. *Some Personal Impressions of the Late Earl Grey.* Montreal: McGill University Publications #9, 1926. [This article was reprinted from *The University Magazine,* October 1917.]

Macphail, Andrew. *Essays in Fallacy.* New York: Longmans, Green and Co., 1910. [Other Macphail material came from PEI newspapers, from the Macphail Homestead Museum in Orwell, PEI, and from Ian Ross Robertson, Macphail's biographer.]

Mahon, A. Wylie. "The Old Minister in *The Story Girl.*" In *Scrapbook of Reviews from Around the World Which L. M. Montgomery's Clipping Service Sent to her, 1910–1935.* L. M. Montgomery Collection, University of Guelph Library Archives, Guelph, Ontario. [Attributes many tales about ministers to Leander Macneill's stories of the Reverend John Sprott.]

Malpeque Historical Society (compiled by). *Malpeque and Its People.* PEI: Malpeque Historical Society, 1982. [See entry on "Montgomery."]

Marquis, Thomas Guthrie. *English-Canadian Literature.* Toronto: Glasgow, Brook, & Company, 1913. [An early and positive assessment of Montgomery.]

McKillop, A. B. *The Spinster and the Prophet: Florence Deeks, H. G. Wells, and the*

Mystery of the Purloined Past. Toronto: Macfarlane Walter & Ross, 2000.

Mechie, Stewart, with James Mackintosh. *Trinity College Glasgow, 1856–1956*. Glasgow: Collins Clear-type Press, 1956. [The Presbyterian Seminary where Ewan Macdonald did advanced study.]

Memorables of the Montgomeries: a Narrative in Rhyme, composed before the present century, printed from the only copy known to remain, which has been preserved above sixty years by the care of Hugh Montgomerie senior at Eaglesham, long one of the factors of the family of Eglintoun. Glasgow: Foulis, 1770. [Foulis Collection at Guelph, #511.]

Montgomerie, Alexander [1545?–1611?]. *The Poems of Alexander Montgomerie: with biographical notices*. Edinburgh: James Ballantyne & Co, 1821. [See "The Flyting Betwixt Montgomerie and Polwart," written circa 1629, pp. 99–132, as an example of Scottish flyting in verse.] [Scottish Collection at Guelph]

Montgomery, Hugh John. "When Cast Away on the Magdalen Islands, For his Sister M. Montgomery, January 20, 1865." L. M. Montgomery Collection. University of Guelph. [This is an unpublished poem by Montgomery's father.]

Murray, Heather. *Come, Bright Improvement: The Literary Societies of Ontario*. Toronto: University of Toronto Press, 2002.

Mustard, Margaret H. *L. M. Montgomery as Mrs. Ewan Macdonald of the Leaskdale Manse, 1911–1926*. Leaskdale, Ontario: St. Paul's Presbyterian Women's Association, 1965. [Commentary by people who knew Montgomery in Leaskdale years.]

Neary, Hilary Bates. "William Renwick Riddell: Judge, Ontario Publicist and Man of Letters." *A Law Society of Upper Canada Gazette*. September 1977 (vol. XI, 3): 172. [For a fuller look at the range of Riddell's publications, see Neary's 1977 M.A. thesis, Department of History, University of Western Ontario.]

Page, L. C. Letter to Bliss Carman. 10 April 1919. Queen's University Archives. [A small slice of fascinating literary history.]

Parker, Rowland. *Men of Dunwich: The Story of a Vanished Town*. London: Collins-Paladin Grafton Books, 1980.

Petlock, Bert. "Trustee Lawyer Held on $35,600 Counts." *Toronto Telegram*. 14 September 1955. Front page. [Story of Chester's arrest.]

Pierce, Lorne. *An Outline of Canadian Literature (French and English)*. Toronto: Ryerson Press, 1927.

Prebble, John. *The Highland Clearances*. London: Penguin Books, 1969. [First published in 1963 by Martin Secker & Warburgh.]

Reimer, Mavis, ed. *Such a Simple Little Tale: Critical Responses to L. M. Montgomery's*

Anne of Green Gables. Metuchen, NJ: The Children's Literature Association and Scarecrow Press, 1992.

Rendall, Jane. *The Origins of the Scottish Enlightenment (1707–1776)*. London: MacMillan, 1972.

Richardson, Christian Richardson, "A Canadian Novelist." In *Scrapbook of Reviews from around the World Which L. M. Montgomery's Clipping Service Sent to Her, 1910–1935*, p. 25. L. M. Montgomery Collection, University of Guelph Library Archives, Guelph, Ontario.

Robertson, Ian Ross. Letters to M. H. Rubio. 12 July 1992–2008.

——. "Reform, Literacy, and the Lease: The Prince Edward Island Free Education Act of 1852," *Acadiensis*, Autumn 1990 (Vol. XX, No. 1): 52–71.

——. *Sir Andrew Macphail: Life and Legacy of a Canadian Man of Letters*. McGill-Queen's University Press, 2008. [Forthcoming biography.]

Rubio, Mary, and Elizabeth Waterston. *Writing a Life: L. M. Montgomery*. Toronto: ECW Press, 1995. [A compact biography of Montgomery online at <www.lmmrc.ca>.]

——. "L. M. Montgomery: Scottish-Presbyterian Agency in Canadian Culture." *L. M. Montgomery and Canadian Culture*. Eds. Irene Gammel and Elizabeth R. Epperly. Toronto: University of Toronto Press, 1999. 89–105.

——. "'A Dusting Off': An Anecdotal Account of Editing the L. M. Montgomery Journals." *Working in Women's Archives: Researching Women's Private Literature and Archival Documents*. Eds. Helen M. Buss and Marlene Kadar. Waterloo, Ontario: Wilfrid Laurier University Press, 2001.

Ruggle, Richard. *Norval on the Credit River*. Erin, Ontario: Press Porcépic, 1973. [Vol. 1 Credit Valley History Series] [Useful history by local historian and pastor.]

Russell, Ruth Weber, D. W. Russell, and Rea Wilmshurst. *Lucy Maud Montgomery: A Preliminary Bibliography*. Waterloo: University of Waterloo Library, 1986. [An essential reference book. Currently being updated and put online.]

Sangster, Margaret E. *Good Manners for All Occasions*. New York: The Christian Herald, 1904. [A manners book.]

Schreiner, Olive. *The Story of an African Farm*. Introduction by Doris Lessing. London: Century Hutchinson Ltd., 1987. [First published in Great Britain by Chapman & Hall, 1883, under the author's name Ralph Iron, and an influential book with Montgomery.]

Sher, Richard B. *Church and University in the Scottish Enlightenment: The Moderate Literati of Edinburgh*. Princeton: Princeton University Press, 1985.

Simpson, Harold H. *Cavendish: Its History, Its People*. Amherst, NS: Harold H. Simpson and Associates Limited, 1973. [Invaluable collection of materials about Cavendish, PEI, history.]

Smith, Donald. "Culture and Religion." *Scotland: A Concise Cultural History.* Ed. Paul H. Scott. Edinburgh: Mainstream, 1993. 47–60.

Smith, Edwin. M.A. thesis. 1903. University of Manitoba. [Subject: Heredity.]

Smith, W. O. Lester. *Education in Great Britain.* London: Oxford University Press, 1964.

Smout, T. C. *A History of the Scottish People, 1560–1830.* London: William Collins and Sons, 1969.

Sobkowska, Krystana. "The Reception of the *Anne of Green Gables* Series by Lucy Maud Montgomery in Poland." Dissertation, University of Lodz [Poland], 1983.

Sorfleet, John Robert, ed. *L. M. Montgomery: An Assessment.* Guelph, Ontario: Canadian Children's Press, 1976. [Early attempt to establish Montgomery's position in Canadian literary history.]

Stevenson, Lionel. *Appraisals of Canadian Literature.* Toronto: MacMillan, 1926.

Stewart, James Innes ("Hud"), Q.C. Letters to Mary Rubio. 22 October 1991–92. Private Collection. [Class president of Chester's graduating class in law school.]

Stobie, Margaret. *Frederick Philip Grove.* New York: Twayne, 1973.

The Delineator. LXV, No. 1. January 1905. [Cover picture on this issue was used for the L. C. Page 1908 edition of *Anne of Green Gables.* Page later displayed the original of this picture in his library in his home in Brookline, Massachusetts.]

Thomas, Clara, and John Lennox. *William Arthur Deacon: A Canadian Literary Life.* Toronto: University of Toronto Press, 1982. [Invaluable study of the Toronto literary culture in the mid-twentieth century and Deacon's role in it.]

Vance, Jonathan F. *Death So Noble: Memory, Meaning, and the First World War.* Vancouver: University of British Columbia Press, 1999. [Fills in social history surrounding the war.]

Vipond, Mary. "The Image of Women in Mass Circulation Magazines in the 1920s." *The Neglected Majority: Essays in Canadian Women's History.* Vol. 1. Eds. Susan Mann Trofimenkoff and Alison Prentice. Toronto: McClelland and Stewart, 1977.

Wachowicz, Barbara. "L. M. Montgomery: At Home in Poland." *CCL: Canadian Children's Literature* 46 (1987): 7–36. [Wachowicz, a journalist and writer in Poland, wrote the libretto for the Polish musical *The Blue Castle*, and organized a trip for Rubio, Waterston, and Ruth Macdonald to see this musical and a production of *Anne of Green Gables* in Poland in 1984.]

Wade, Ruth. *The Hypatia Club: The First Hundred Years, 1907–2007: A History for the 100th Anniversary of the Hypatia Club.* Uxbridge: Ruth Wade / Hypatia Club, 2007. [Montgomery contributed generously to this literary club.]

Wardle, David. *English Popular Education, 1780–1970.* London: Cambridge University Press, 1970.

Waterston, Elizabeth. *Kindling Spirit: L. M. Montgomery's "Anne of Green Gables."* Toronto: ECW Press, 1993. [A study of the novel.]

——. "Lucy Maud Montgomery 1874–1942." *The Clear Spirit: Twenty Canadian Women and Their Times.* Ed. Mary Quayle Innis. Toronto: University of Toronto Press, 1966. 198–220. [Also in *L. M. Montgomery: An Assessment.* Ed. John Sorfleet. Guelph: Canadian Children's Press, 1975. 9–26 / *CCL: Canadian Children's Literature* 3 (1975): 9–26. Waterston's 1966 essay was the first in-depth scholarly article that attempted to recover Montgomery as an important early Canadian woman writer.]

——. *The Magic Island: The Fictions of L. M. Montgomery.* Don Mills, Ontario: Oxford University Press, 2008. [An academic study of Montgomery's writing intended as a companion to this biography.]

——. "Marigold and the Magic of Memory." *Harvesting Thistles: The Textual Garden of L. M. Montgomery.* Ed. Mary Henley Rubio. Guelph: Canadian Children's Press, 1994. 155–66.

——. *Rapt in Plaid: Canadian Literature and the Scottish Tradition.* Toronto: University of Toronto Press, 2001. [See Chapter on "Barrie, Montgomery and the Mists of Sentiment," pp. 175–191.]

Weale, David. *Them Times.* Charlottetown, PEI: Institute of Island Studies, 1992.

Wood, Kate. "In the News: Anne of Green Gables and PEI's Turn-of-the-Century Press." *CCL: Canadian Children's Literature* 99 (2000): 23–42.

——. "Patriotic Discourse: Historicizing *Anne of Green Gables* and PEI's Turn-of-the-Century Newspapers." M.A. dissertation, University of Guelph, 1999.

Young, Alan R. "L. M. Montgomery's *Rilla of Ingleside*: Romance and the Experience of War." *Myth and Milieu: Atlantic Literature and Culture, 1918–1939.* Ed. Gwendolyn Davies. Fredericton: Acadiensis, 1993. 95–122.

——. *Tudor and Jacobean Tournaments.* London: George Philip, 1987. [See pages 186–87 for the earl of Eglinton's legendary 1839 tournament.]

RECENT CRITICAL EDITIONS OF ANNE OF GREEN GABLES

Montgomery, L. M. *Anne of Green Gables* [1908]. Ed. Cecily Devereux. Peterborough, Ontario: Broadview, 2004. [A Broadview Critical Edition with useful critical essays on many aspects of the novel and the literary culture it evolved from.]

——. *Anne of Green Gables* [1908]. Eds. Mary Henley Rubio and Elizabeth Waterston. New York: Norton, 2007. [A Norton Critical Edition which contains essays on the publishing history, the surrounding context, and the reception of the novel.]

——. *The Annotated Anne of Green Gables* [1908]. Eds. Wendy E. Barry, Margaret Anne Doody, and Mary E. Doody Jones. New York: Oxford University Press, 1997. [An edition rich with supplementary material and pictures.]

INDEX